7072

*Endsheets: (left to right, top) H. L. Mencken, Cleanth Brooks, Waldo Frank, R. P. Blackmur; (left to right, bottom) Lionel Trilling, T. S. Eliot, Van Wyck Brooks, Ezra Pound.*

Dictionary of Literary Biography • Volume Sixty-three

# Modern American Critics, 1920-1955

# Dictionary of Literary Biography

## Documentary Series

## Yearbooks

## Concise Series

Dictionary of Literary Biography • Volume Sixty-three

# Modern American Critics, 1920-1955

Edited by
**Gregory S. Jay**
*University of Wisconsin-Milwaukee*

A Bruccoli Clark Layman Book
Gale Research Company • Book Tower • Detroit, Michigan 48226

Manufactured by Edwards Brothers, Inc.
Ann Arbor, Michigan
Printed in the United States of America

**Library of Congress Cataloging-in-Publication Data**

Modern American critics, 1920-1955

(Dictionary of literary biography; v. 63)
"A Bruccoli Clark Layman book."
Includes index.
1. Criticism—United States—History—20th century. 2.
Criticism—United States—Bio-bibliography. 3. Critics—
United States—Biography—Dictionaries. 4. American liter-
ature—History and criticism—Theory, etc. I. Jay, Gregory
S. II. Series.
PS78.M58    1987    801'.95'0922         87-25138
ISBN 0-8103-1741-9

# Contents

# Plan of the Series

*. . . Almost the most prodigious asset of a country, and perhaps its most precious possession, is its native literary product—when that product is fine and noble and enduring.*

Mark Twain*

The advisory board, the editors, and the publisher of the *Dictionary of Literary Biography* are joined in endorsing Mark Twain's declaration. The literature of a nation provides an inexhaustible resource of permanent worth. We intend to make literature and its creators better understood and more accessible to students and the reading public, while satisfying the standards of teachers and scholars.

To meet these requirements, *literary biography* has been construed in terms of the author's achievement. The most important thing about a writer is his writing. Accordingly, the entries in *DLB* are career biographies, tracing the development of the author's canon and the evolution of his reputation.

The purpose of *DLB* is not only to provide reliable information in a convenient format but also to place the figures in the larger perspective of literary history and to offer appraisals of their accomplishments by qualified scholars.

The publication plan for *DLB* resulted from two years of preparation. The project was proposed to Bruccoli Clark by Frederick G. Ruffner, president of the Gale Research Company in November 1975. After specimen entries were prepared and typeset, an advisory board was formed to refine the entry format and develop the series rationale. In meetings held during 1976, the publisher, series editors, and advisory board approved the scheme for a comprehensive biographical dictionary of persons who contributed to North American literature. Editorial work on the first volume began in January 1977, and it was published in 1978. In order to make *DLB* more than a reference tool and to compile volumes that individually have claim to status as literary history, it was decided to organize volumes by topic, period, or genre. Each of these freestanding volumes provides a biographical-bibliographical guide and overview for a particular area of literature. We are convinced that this organization—as opposed to a single alphabet method—constitutes a valuable innovation in the presentation of reference material. The volume plan necessarily requires many decisions for the placement and treatment of authors who might properly be included in two or three volumes. In some instances a major figure will be included in separate volumes, but with different entries emphasizing the aspect of his career appropriate to each volume. Ernest Hemingway, for example, is represented in *American Writers in Paris, 1920-1939* by an entry focusing on his expatriate apprenticeship; he is also in *American Novelists, 1910-1945* with an entry surveying his entire career. Each volume includes a cumulative index of subject authors and articles. Comprehensive indexes to the entire series are planned.

With volume ten in 1982 it was decided to enlarge the scope of *DLB*. By the end of 1986 twenty-one volumes treating British literature had been published, and volumes for Commonwealth and Modern European literature were in progress. The series has been further augmented by the *DLB Yearbooks* (since 1981) which update published entries and add new entries to keep the *DLB* current with contemporary activity. There have also been *DLB Documentary Series* volumes which provide biographical and critical source materials for figures whose work is judged to have particular interest for students. One of these companion volumes is entirely devoted to Tennessee Williams.

We define literature as the *intellectual commerce of a nation:* not merely as belles lettres but as that ample and complex process by which ideas are generated, shaped, and transmitted. *DLB* entries are not limited to "creative writers" but extend to other figures who in their time and in their way influenced the mind of a people. Thus the series encompasses historians, journalists, publishers, and screenwriters. By this means readers of *DLB* may be aided to perceive litera-

*From an unpublished section of Mark Twain's autobiography, copyright © by the Mark Twain Company.

ture not as cult scripture in the keeping of intellectual high priests but firmly positioned at the center of a nation's life.

*DLB* includes the major writers appropriate to each volume and those standing in the ranks immediately behind them. Scholarly and critical counsel has been sought in deciding which minor figures to include and how full their entries should be. Wherever possible, useful references are made to figures who do not warrant separate entries.

Each *DLB* volume has a volume editor responsible for planning the volume, selecting the figures for inclusion, and assigning the entries. Volume editors are also responsible for preparing, where appropriate, appendices surveying the major periodicals and literary and intellectual movements for their volumes, as well as lists of further readings. Work on the series as a whole is coordinated at the Bruccoli Clark Layman editorial center in Columbia, South Carolina, where the editorial staff is responsible for accuracy of the published volumes.

One feature that distinguishes *DLB* is the illustration policy—its concern with the iconography of literature. Just as an author is influenced by his surroundings, so is the reader's understanding of the author enhanced by a knowledge of his environment. Therefore *DLB* volumes include not only drawings, paintings, and photographs of authors, often depicting them at various stages in their careers, but also illustrations of their families and places where they lived. Title pages are regularly reproduced in facsimile along with dust jackets for modern authors. The dust jackets are a special feature of *DLB* because they often document better than anything else the way in which an author's work was perceived in its own time. Specimens of the writers' manuscripts are included when feasible.

Samuel Johnson rightly decreed that "The chief glory of every people arises from its authors." The purpose of the *Dictionary of Literary Biography* is to compile literary history in the surest way available to us—by accurate and comprehensive treatment of the lives and work of those who contributed to it.

The *DLB* Advisory Board

# Foreword

The last two decades have witnessed a rapid growth in the field of literary criticism, and many readers feel the need for a better understanding of its origin and recent history. The two volumes of *Modern American Critics* aim to meet this need by providing introductory discussions of the lives and ideas of over fifty critics who have played important roles in the development of this changing field. The first volume begins with the rise of modern criticism after World War I and extends through the culmination of New Criticism. The second volume covers contemporary figures who have built upon, revised, or in some cases rejected the tradition established by their predecessors. These volumes should be of use to students, teachers, researchers, and general readers across a broad spectrum, since the men and women discussed here worked in a variety of areas and often addressed vital cultural issues beyond the confines of literature itself. Indeed, I have chosen deliberately not to brand them under the title of "literary" critics, since so often their study of literature ranged into the arenas of society, politics, history, language, philosophy, and the arts and humanities in general.

The figures included in the first volume were largely responsible for the invention of modern American criticism, and particularly for its transition from a largely independent enterprise to a discipline chiefly housed in college and university literature departments. The modernist revolt against the major forms of nineteenth-century criticism—chiefly historical philology and personal impressionism—informs the work of diverse critics in this period. Irving Babbitt, from within the college setting, challenged historicism; his student T. S. Eliot, a poet as well as critic, used the review essay to call for a rigorous technical emphasis to replace romantic impressionism. A new generation—including Van Wyck Brooks, Vernon L. Parrington, Perry Miller, and F. O. Matthiessen—rediscovered in American literature a powerful cultural tradition that speaks to the issues of the present age. During the 1920s and 1930s, periods of acute social upheaval, literary criticism and cultural commentary converge in

the nonacademic and often iconoclastic work of Kenneth Burke, H. L. Mencken, Lewis Mumford, and Edmund Wilson. The complex poems, novels, and plays of literary Modernism in this period had a tremendous effect on criticism, for they required the development of methods for "close reading" and of theories that could define the nature of literature itself. Inspired in part by Eliot, the New Criticism arose to become the dominant school during the 1940s and 1950s, and to offer the most sophisticated approaches to literature as literature. Literary studies also felt the competition from the sciences. There appeared a strong desire to fashion a systematic approach to literature that would place it on the level of science and so justify literary criticism's claims for space and funding within the growing institutions of higher education. Close reading, especially as popularized by the textbooks of Cleanth Brooks and Robert Penn Warren, also made the teaching of literature a practical enterprise as the expansion of higher education brought hundreds of thousands of new students into the classroom, often from immigrant or lower- and middle-class backgrounds. Heir to both the traditions of cultural commentary and the New Criticism, Lionel Trilling emerged as the leading figure of the early 1950s as he explored the social, psychological, aesthetic, and cultural functions of literature. Much criticism, of course, went on outside these mainstreams, most importantly the work of black American critics, beginning during the Harlem Renaissance and continuing largely unrecognized until decades later. The new social, literary, and educational realities of the 1960s began that recognition, marked the advent of contemporary feminist criticism, and saw the work of Trilling and the New Critics attacked or ignored by the critics who came after them.

Contemporary American criticism, the period of the second volume, may be conveniently described as issuing from two events: the turn away from New Criticism and the turn toward European critical theories. Northrop Frye's *Anatomy of Criticism* (1957) marked a shift from close reading to interpreting larger structural and cultural forms, even as Frye maintained the project of defining a scientific criticism which could exactly describe the qualities of literature rather than reflect the aesthetic sensibility of the reader. The bias against Romanticism that informed much of Modernism and New Criticism was reversed by a new generation of critics—including M. H. Abrams, Geoffrey Hartman, Harold Bloom, and Paul de Man—who put close reading to work on the texts of William Wordsworth, John Keats, and Percy Bysshe Shelley. This attention to the philosophical dimensions of figurative language would, in turn, prepare the way for the importation of deconstruction from France. While New Criticism, archetypal studies, and other brands of American formalism had developed theories of literary structure, the models they used were not primarily based on the structures of language. European structuralism, on the other hand, grew out of the linguistics of Ferdinand de Saussure and offered an attractive model for reading literature and culture as discourses or texts. The formalist and even aesthetic tendencies of early structuralist and deconstructive criticism were contested by figures such as Fredric Jameson and Edward Said, who advocated historical study and political concern and drew on different strands of European thought (such as Marxism) for their inspiration. The political struggles of the 1960s brought many students and faculty into conflict with the institution of the university, which occasioned a growing self-criticism on the part of the profession. Meanwhile the humanism which had long dominated American academic thought had its defenders in the work of E. D. Hirsch, M. H. Abrams, George Steiner, Wayne Booth, Lionel Trilling, and others. Another challenge to this humanism came from feminist criticism, for women had long been excluded from the canon of "great writers" as well as from positions of power in the academy itself. Similarly Afro-American criticism proposed altering the content and method of literary studies and, like feminist criticism, drew from a variety of theoretical schools in developing its lines of inquiry and argument. In sum the period after 1955 brought a much-heightened emphasis on theoretical criticism and a real debate about the function of literary studies within the institutions of education and society. While the business of providing interpretations of individual works continued, many critics sought a place "beyond interpretation" or "beyond formalism" where the study of lit-

erature and the criticism of culture could be systematically joined.

Controversy is inevitable whenever one sets out to select a group of major figures from a wealth of achievement. This is particularly true in the case of *Modern American Critics,* and I anticipate that every reader will find what he or she regards as significant omissions or puzzling inclusions. Since today there is renewed debate over the very nature of literature and criticism, it is not surprising that immediate difficulties arose in defining the scope of figures considered and in establishing the principles for selection and exclusion. How was one to distinguish among critics, scholars, biographers, or literary researchers? What about cultural critics who commented only marginally on literary texts, or whose work in some other area became influential among literary critics themselves? At what point did a poet or novelist merit inclusion as a critic? Did a person's stature in the past earn coverage here even if now unread or forgotten? The job was further complicated by the sometimes conflicting goals of the project: to describe the careers of major individual voices *and* to represent fairly the various schools, movements, and critical ideas of the modern period. In cases such as the New Criticism, myth criticism, or deconstructionism one could cover the movement adequately through entries on individual participants. In other cases, such as feminist and Afro-American criticism, the biographical format appeared ill-suited to a just account of the movement's ideas and achievements. Retaining the format, I have nonetheless endeavored through selected representative figures to give some indications of these schools, which I am confident will in the years ahead produce many major figures as women and minorities take their rightful place in institutions which have excluded them for too long.

Initially I circulated lists of well over a hundred names to scholars around the country. Their responses quickly showed a surprising consensus on a core group of about forty names, mostly of figures whose careers peaked before 1965. Much dispute arose over which other figures to include, what genres of literary commentary to represent, and which contemporary critics had earned inclusion. The final decisions were my own, and I accept full responsibility for them. In general I chose to exclude persons whose vital achievements were principally in biography, empirical research, or bibliography. While such work is essential to the life of criticism, it falls outside the volumes' focus upon individuals whose concepts of literature and methods for interpretation have been decisively influential in charting the course of modern American criticism. I have also chosen to offer longer entries on major figures rather than shorter entries on minor ones because the exposition of careers, theories, ideas, and methods was in many cases too complex for brief treatment. Often the essay offered here is one of the few, if not the only, systematic treatments of the critic's life work now available. Contributors were also encouraged to evaluate the critic's career from the standpoint of contemporary developments; thus these volumes may serve as a kind of revisionary history of American criticism, and they will doubtless betray the concerns of our age. This perspective will, I hope, increase their interest for the reader and provide the stimulus for future debate.

One major difficulty with modern American criticism is its vocabulary. As criticism evolved from a conversational commentary of an appreciative or evaluative kind for the general public into a specialty area with technical and philosophical aspects, its language became increasingly complex. As with any discipline, literary criticism developed a vocabulary of terms required by the need for exact analysis and expression. At the same time, critics drew methodologically on other fields—psychoanalysis, philosophy, linguistics, history, anthropology, sociology—and so imported an assortment of terms and concepts unfamiliar to the general reader. In an effort to address this problem, the publishers requested the development of a glossary, which appears at the conclu-

sion of the second volume. Rather than duplicate the kind of dictionary already widely available in a number of paperbacks on literary terms, I chose to commission the writing of short expository discussions of some major concepts and movements that have influenced the development of modern criticism. Particular attention was paid to schools of European thought that have recently had an enormous impact on American critics but which are largely unfamiliar to many students of literature. These glossary discussions are cross-referenced to the entries on particular critics, thus allowing the reader to follow a topic from the glossary through the relevant critics working on—or against—the idea or movement. At the back of the second volume readers will also find a list of "Suggestions for Further Reading." This is not a comprehensive bibliography but a selective set of sources on the history of American criticism, including introductions to major figures, schools, and ideas. More specialized bibliographies are presented in each of the individual entries.

Many people contributed to the guidance of these volumes during the three years of their production. I particularly want to thank those who advised on the initial selection of critics and contributors, especially Geoffrey Hartman, William Cain, Gerald Graff, John Paul Russo, Houston Baker, Henry Louis Gates, Jr., Walton Litz, Elizabeth Meese, Annette Kolodny, Jonathan Culler, Ralph Rader, and Vincent Leitch.

*—Gregory S. Jay*

# Acknowledgments

This book was produced by Bruccoli Clark Layman, Inc. Karen L. Rood is senior editor for the *Dictionary of Literary Biography* series. Ellen Rosenberg Kovner was the in-house editor.

Copyediting supervisor is Patricia Coate. Production coordinator is Kimberly Casey. Typesetting supervisor is Kathleen M. Flanagan. Laura Ingram and Michael D. Senecal are editorial associates. The production staff includes Rowena Betts, Charles Brower, Cheryl Crombie, Mary S. Dye, Charles Egleston, Gabrielle Elliott, Sarah A. Estes, Judith K. Ingle, Maria Ling, Warren McInnis, Kathy S. Merlette, Sheri Neal, Joycelyn R. Smith, and Elizabeth York. Jean W. Ross is permissions editor. Joseph Caldwell, photography editor, and Joseph Matthew Bruccoli did photographic copy work for the volume.

Walter W. Ross and Rhonda Marshall did the library research with the assistance of the staff at the Thomas Cooper Library of the University of South Carolina: Lynn Barron, Daniel Boice, Kathy Eckman, Gary Geer, Cathie Gottlieb, David L. Haggard, Jens Holley, Dennis Isbell, Marcia Martin, Jean Rhyne, Beverley Steele, Ellen Tillett, and Virginia Weathers.

Dictionary of Literary Biography • Volume Sixty-three

# Modern American Critics, 1920-1955

# Dictionary of Literary Biography

# Irving Babbitt

*(2 August 1865-15 July 1933)*

Andrew Ross
*Princeton University*

BOOKS: *Literature and the American College: Essays in Defense of the Humanities* (Boston & New York: Houghton Mifflin, 1908);

*The New Laokoon: An Essay on the Confusion of the Arts* (Boston & New York: Houghton Mifflin, 1910; London: Constable, 1910);

*The Masters of Modern French Criticism* (Boston & New York: Houghton Mifflin, 1912; London: Constable, 1913);

*Rousseau and Romanticism* (Boston & New York: Houghton Mifflin, 1919);

*Democracy and Leadership* (Boston & New York: Houghton Mifflin, 1924; London: Constable, 1924);

*On Being Creative and Other Essays* (Boston & New York: Houghton Mifflin, 1932; London: Constable, 1932);

*Spanish Character and Other Essays,* edited by Frederick Manchester, Rachel Giese, and William F. Giese (Boston & New York: Houghton Mifflin, 1940).

OTHER: "Humanism: An Essay at Definition," in *Humanism and America: Essays on the Outlook of Modern Civilisation,* edited by Norman Foerster (New York: Farrar & Rinehart, 1930), pp. 25-51;

*The Dhammapada, translated from the Pāli, with an Essay on Buddha and the Occident, by Irving Bab-* bitt (New York & London: Oxford University Press, 1936).

Although he followed upon other critics who had pursued their work with an eye to its professional academic context, Irving Babbitt was the first American critic to turn the academy itself into a polemical arena. If Babbitt viewed his work as a battle of light against darkness, then it was because he espoused a set of ideas about culture and learning which differed "on first principles" from what he took to be the prevailing philosophy of his age, a philosophy which celebrated intuition and naturalism over the reasoned discipline which had traditionally shaped the classical ethos of Western learning. While he claimed his criticism ran against the grain of society in the largest possible sense, Babbitt scrupulously avoided the tendency which Julien Benda, the French thinker he admired, had characterized as "the treason of the intellectuals"–the inclination of writers, critics, and artists to indulge their ideas in the active realm of politics, rather than to hold themselves aloof from the partisan choices of political patronage. Even in 1920, at the height of popular interest in the New Humanism, a neopolitical movement of intellectuals inspired by Babbitt's teachings, he was still adamant about the limited sphere of influence available for his ideas, affirming "that the battle that is to determine the fate of American civilization will be fought out first of all in the field of education." Babbitt refused to see that his ideas were the result of political choices even before they became curricular issues for educators. In the retrospective light of the ideological ink-slinging which was to characterize the critical scene of the 1930s, Babbitt's refusal has come to be seen as a symptom of an earlier age in which Anglo-American thinkers had not yet had to respond to their political vocation as "intellectuals" in the tradition of the Russian intelligentsia or the French "Dreyfusards."

A more fundamental problem, however, haunted his philosophical crusade from beginning to end: his willful detachment not only from the cultural values of contemporary America but also from the powerful historical effects of these values. Babbitt addressed himself to the "saving remnant" (to describe the ideal audience for his first book. He invoked the famous Virgilian image of a few shipwrecked survivors struggling to swim against a whirlpool—*rari nantes in gurgite vasto),* and thus his ideas appealed directly to an aristocratic ideal that could never expect to have more than a small and anomalous constituency in a country which even he viewed as having made a religion of democracy.

Irving Babbitt was born in Dayton, Ohio, on 2 August 1865 to Edwin Dwight and Augusta Darling Babbitt. He was the third son and fourth child in a family of five. His socialist father was a businessman, physician, and philanthropical inventor who, among other eccentric schemes, founded the New York College of Magnetics. After a largely midwestern upbringing in the course of which he worked as a reporter on a Cincinnati newspaper and as a cowboy on an uncle's ranch in Wyoming, Babbitt entered Harvard College in 1885 with financial aid from his uncles. He graduated with final honors in classics four years later. With his earnings from a two-year teaching stint as professor of classics at the College of Montana in Deer Lodge, he went to Paris in 1893 to study Sanskrit and Pali under Sylvain Lévi, returning to the Harvard graduate school where he took the A.M. degree in 1893. His appointment as an instructor in Romance languages at Williams College was followed by his second return to Harvard in 1894, this time to stay for the rest of his life. Unable to pursue a career in the Department of Classics, he taught French and comparative literature for almost forty years in the belief that he was teaching, as he privately admit-

ted, "a cheap and nasty substitute for Latin." As an untenured assistant professor, Babbitt was outspoken, both in conversation and print, in his offensive against the established critical spirit of philology espoused by many of his departmental colleagues. He was nonetheless made a full professor in 1912, and his classes and courses became a popular and celebrated fixture in the Harvard curriculum, dwarfing in their range of influence and effect the small body of truly devoted disciples to which he actually laid claim. Among the students enrolled in Babbitt's course on literary criticism in France was T. S. Eliot. Babbitt's influence on the antiromantic direction of Eliot's thinking was profound, and the two men corresponded until Babbitt's death (on occasion Eliot addressed his letters "Dear Master").

In London, on 12 June 1900, he married Dora May Drew, his former Radcliffe student. A daughter and a son, Esther and Edward Sturges, were born to the couple within the next three years. In 1926 Babbitt became a corresponding member of the Institute of France, and in 1930 he was elected to the American Academy of Arts and Letters. He was also a fellow of the American Academy of Arts and Sciences. In 1932 he received an honorary degree from Bowdoin College. Irving Babbitt died in Cambridge, Massachusetts, on 15 July 1933.

Babbitt's criticism is characterized by an unyielding consistency. While the object and context of his criticism are different in each instance, his attack on Romanticism and all its effects is essentially the same in his first book as in his last. Indeed, Paul Elmer More, the contemporary thinker closest to him, remarked that "he seems to have sprung up, like Minerva, fully grown and fully armed." The polemical result is often tiresomely repetitious, but the final impression is one of a formidable adversary. Babbitt never intended to be a cutting-edge thinker, and it is with some degree of irony that he argued, in *Rousseau and Romanticism* (1919), for what he saw as "a point of view so modern that compared with it, that of our smart young radicals will seem antediluvian." Since he viewed the world in essentially adversarial terms, he instinctively presented himself as a one-man opposition, and it was the studied isolation of this position which, on the one hand, distinguished him from the reactionary who comfortably represents a conservative body of opinion and, on the other hand, characterized him, in Arthur Lovejoy's famous ironical retort, as a romantic, militantly quixotic enough to want

*Irving Babbitt at thirty-four (Notman Photo Co.)*

tutionalized effects of the romantic cult of self-expression compounded by the worst effects of modern relativity: professionalism, the service ethic, and training for power. Against the decadent effects of this "educational impressionism" Babbitt posits the classical virtues of restraint, discipline, and above all, selection. An extensive curricular training in the broad, classical spirit of the humanities would serve to reinstate standards of good taste and judgment in an age of "cheap contemporaneousness" which had seen generations of young minds "eroded" by "the American newspaper" and the "modern erotic novel," and which had thus led to the same "dangerous and excessive mobility of mind" that had been the late, fateful product of Greek skepticism. To distinguish this selective spirit from the expansive temper of a democratic education, Babbitt employs the "Socratic method," a "process of right defining," to trace the properly aristocratic origins of *humanitas* both in the social philosophy of the ancient world and in the cultivated manner of the Renaissance gentleman and scholar. It is fatal, Babbitt points out, to confuse this *humanist* concern for the perfection of the individual with the *humanitarian* sympathy for mankind "in the lump" and the allied philanthropic desire to serve the democratic cause of enlightened progress.

Babbitt goes on to distinguish two strains of humanitarian influence on education in the ideas of Francis Bacon and Rousseau, the respective fathers of *scientific* naturalism—dedicated to the positivism of progress, power, and results—and *sentimental* naturalism—devoted to pursuing the fruits of intellectual liberty and self-assertion. It is Rousseau's influence in particular that Babbitt is opposed to, describing his thought as "the most powerful insurrection the world has ever seen against every kind of authority." Both types of naturalism defy Ralph Waldo Emerson's ruling that there should be a "law for man" separate from a "law for thing." For Babbitt the individual man is subject to the first of these laws and thereby constitutes a "measure" of the world in the classical sense of a humanist model of universal standards, as opposed to the Romantic model of an original and expressive creator in deep communion with the patterns and laws of the natural world.

Babbitt recognized that he was engaged in yet another round of the time-honored battle of the books between ancients and moderns. What was immediately at stake for him, however, was a

to charge at will, even without an army to back him up.

The essays collected in his first volume, *Literature and the American College: Essays in Defense of the Humanities* (1908), have both a local and a general context, and many of them had been previously published in topical magazines such as the *Atlantic Monthly* and the *Nation*. Essays with titles like "The College and the Democratic Spirit" and "Literature and the Doctor's Degree" explicitly contained attacks against what Babbitt saw as the excesses of the elective system of undergraduate education developed by President Charles William Eliot at Harvard, where students freely elected to plan their own courses of specialized study. In this elective system Babbitt saw the insti-

literary curriculum guided by a critical taste that could decide "what is essence and what is accident in human nature." In calling for such a curriculum, Babbitt invokes the critical ideals of neoclassicism–universality and timelessness–and reaffirms the canonical privilege of classical literary criticism to contemplate a "golden chain of masterpieces" which, if taught in the right manner to a select body of students, will heal the spiritual illness of modern thinking and restore the "manly" virtues of restraint, discipline, and right reason to a "society that hopes to be saved by what it does for its negroes and its newsboys." In the context of such a crusade, Babbitt saw that the "permanent human values" enshrined in the literary classics were being threatened by the critical orthodoxy of his time, the school of historical philology by the then-dominant ideas in graduate education. Philology, a disciplinary child of Germanic positivism, saw literature as a structure of historical and textual facts and distanced itself from any critical treatment of ideas. Babbitt wanted to replace the existing Ph.D., perceived as a program of discipline in historical facts, with a program of discipline in universal ideas. Such a program would be devoted to fashioning the kind of critical judgment that could discriminate on the basis of moral virtues and evaluate an author's place in the history of literary merit accordingly. The philological emphasis on pedantry would be dissolved, and the sane, tranquil, and mature spirit of disinterested criticism would prevail once more in the minds of young graduate scholars pursuing a professional career.

Babbitt's commitment to ideas and not facts was intended to be a clarion call for conservative humanists, a call, moreover, that would draw attention to the dangers of falling back upon the "happy stupidity" of the English Tory tradition. What was needed was an "imaginative conservatism" that could meet the radical on equal intellectual terms. The call became all the more urgent when coupled with the images of barbarianism which Babbitt often drew upon to depict the modern critics "even now battering at the gates of Oxford." But it was his studied ignorance of what the "moderns" were really doing at this time that flaws his own practical criticism of the arts. This neglect of contemporary art practices is nowhere more conspicuous than in his second book, *The New Laokoon: An Essay on the Confusion of the Arts* (1910), an assessment of the Romantic era.

Babbitt cites one of the founding texts of the German Enlightenment, Lessing's *Laökoon*

(1776), as spiritual precursor for his own attempt to evaluate what he saw as the confusion of arts and genres that had flourished during the Romantic period. Lessing's book had appeared toward the end of a neoclassical movement which had taken the theory of imitation to heart, so much so that the Horatian maxim *ut pictura poesis* had been interpreted too literally to allow for the maintenance of what Lessing saw as the *proper* boundaries of the arts. On the one hand, word-painting and descriptive writing had flourished, while the mechanical homage paid to rules led to the empty and "changeless formulae" so characteristic of what Babbitt saw as the neoclassical confusion of form with formalism. Like Lessing, Babbitt looked unfavorably upon both of these developments, neither of which reached the heights of delinquency scaled by the wave of impressionistic art that accompanied the Romantic worship of spontaneity. Consequently Babbitt devotes most of *The New Laokoon* to describing the symptoms of what he calls "the greatest debauch of descriptive writing the world has ever known."

The symptoms of this debauch are variously manifest as forms of heightened sensation, or hyperaesthesia, and more classically, the outright mix of the senses, or synesthesia, inducing an "attenuated hypnosis" in which genres and arts intermingle. Word-Painting, Programme-Music, and Color-Audition are Babbitt's terms for the ways in which literature suggests painting, music suggests the poetic or the pictorial, and light or color suggests sound or tone. As examples of extremes of these sense mixtures Babbitt cites Schlegel, who claims that architecture is frozen music, Wagner, who imagines a *Gesamtkunstwerk* of the future in which "all the separate arts are to melt together voluptuously," and Rimbaud, who announces that the vowel *a* is black, *i* is red, *u* is green, and *o* is blue. This last observation, Babbitt suggests, is of more interest to the "nerve-specialist" than to the literary critic. Expression triumphed over form in its capacity to suggest powerful feeling, the only common bond between the arts and genres which does not depend upon some formal base. While Babbitt saw this practice still alive in his day, one of his examples being the "sheer lawlessness" of modern partisans of vers libre in their attempts to write neither verse nor prose, he is most comfortable in ascribing it to a general tendency he terms "eleutheromania"–the instinct to throw off all limitations whatsoever. The counterimpulse to this tendency is presented as the famous "inner check," or the power to refrain from acting, a phrase which Emerson had learned from Eastern philosophy and which was eventually to become the polemical touchstone by which Babbitt's thought was popularly known. Toward the end of *The New Laokoon,* the outlines of an alternative humanistic aesthetic begin to emerge as Babbitt tries to mediate between the mechanical formalism of the eighteenth century and the naturalistic excess of the nineteenth. While the essence of a truly humanist method was to be found in "creative imitation," a temper that could mediate between the extremes of inspiration and formal control, the impulse to balance that temper, for Babbitt at least, would always come from the "inner check." Only the latter could offer a Platonic *frein vital* to rein in the Rousseauistic urges of Henri Bergson's élan vital, which, at the time Babbitt was writing, had come to enjoy a huge popularity.

In *The Masters of Modern French Criticism* (1912), Babbitt extended his review of the nineteenth century into the realm of criticism proper, characterizing the work of each of the most important French critics of the age: Madame de Stäel, Joseph Joubert, François-René de Chateaubriand, Charles-Augustin Saint-Beuve, Hyppolite Taine, Ernest Renan, Ferdinand Brunetière, and others. The result is more than just scholarly scrutiny; Babbitt was writing a genealogy which would historically explain his own point of view, and so these were writers toward whom he expressed a certain intimacy even if he disagreed on first principles with many of them. Unlike Joubert, who was prepared to overlook Chateaubriand's Rousseauism—"When my friends have only one eye, I look at them in profile"—Babbitt commits himself to exposing the dialectic of the century as it runs through each of his chosen critics: on the one hand, the Rousseauistic worship of enthusiasm, updated in the pragmatist and Bergsonian emphasis on spontaneity and intuition, and on the other, a more Socratic definition of intuition as spiritual, based, ultimately, on principles of judgment.

In effect Babbitt exercises his own judgment by giving with one hand and taking with the other. He is prepared, for example, to credit Madame de Stäel for having spent years of exile "in the panorama of the Alps . . . without receiving from it the suggestion of a single image," but she is all too soon revealed as a disciple of Rousseau and thus guilty of relativism, expressionism, historicism, and all "the usual sophistries of the primitivist." Worst of all, she errs, as Babbitt sees it, like all women and all male disciples of Rousseau, "in the excess of the feminine virtues." So too, Chateaubriand is presented as an interested classicist with a genuine perception of form, but in the final analysis "he betrays on every page his passion for the primitive."

Babbitt is most absorbing when, as in the case of Chateaubriand, he diagnoses the confused interplay between classical, pseudoclassical, and romantic elements in terms of a dialectic between naturalism and humanism. The high point, however, is his treatment of Saint-Beuve, the critic whose portrait hung alone in his study. For Babbitt, Saint-Beuve was a writer whose allegiance shifted from an early acquiescence to the "naturalistic temper" toward a later acceptance of the need for classical judgment. As a closet libertine, Saint-Beuve first "penetrated philosophy through pleasure" and soon reached the point of intellectual indulgence: "The flood is driving me on and my ship has no anchor," he wrote to Abbé Eustache Barbe. Babbitt argues that this romantic strain is balanced by Saint-Beuve's later criticism which reveals a taste for universal pronouncements about an author or work's place in the roll call of historical judgment. If local and personal or historical details continue to color his criticism, it is because he lived in a desperate time, when, as Babbitt put it, "the world wishes to be deceived" (*Vult mundus decipi*).

While Renan is characterized as the perfect embodiment of modern romantic criticism—a philologist, a historian, a curiosity-monger, and an intellectual voluptuary—both Joubert and Brunetière are presented as Babbitt's own kindred spirits for their advocacy of consistent and judicial standards in criticism. Joubert, for example, had perceived that Rousseau and his followers upset classical morality by "conceiving of virtue not as a bridle but as a spur" and thus below reason rather than above it. His own taste was for that Platonic type of enthusiasm which Babbitt associates with "light and serenity" rather than "heat and movement." Like Joubert, Brunetière belongs to the class of critics which Babbitt unites by virtue of their solid agreement on essentials and their tribute to what is unchanging in art. Brunetière is further praised for his "stern," "ascetic," and "eminently masculine qualities" in an age in which Babbitt felt that "literature had fallen to a great extent under the influence of women." Brunetière's attack on the imperviousness of Romanticism to ideas *tout court* stands as a protest against the absorption of man into nature and the threat offered to aesthetics by a critical impressionism that is ultimately little more than "a form of gossip."

By contrast, Taine's critical determinism is entirely devoid of any humanistic counterpoise, and it is presented as the most advanced expression of what Babbitt called scientific naturalism. Babbitt describes how Taine took from Hegel a philosophy of history based around the idea of a development according to fixed laws. As a result, a writer's work was seen as the determined product of race, environment, and historical moment. Babbitt likens this kind of criticism to botany because it seeks to subordinate value to the kind of inexorable laws that are assumed to govern the natural world. Taine, for example, proposed to study the 1870 revolution like a naturalist observing "the metamorphosis of an insect." Of course Babbitt held the opinion that a writer's significance was not at all dependent on environmental factors but upon his unique capacity to express universal values for all time. He concedes, however, that, after Taine and Saint-Beuve, it was no longer possible to treat a book as though it had "fallen like a meteorite from the sky." Babbitt himself displays little of this concrete historical sense in his own assessments of the Romantic movement, limiting himself to the most general observations about social and historical ruptures; he proposes, for example, that Saint-Beuve's developing taste for the humanistic is an anticipation of the general disillusion with Romanticism that followed the failure of the 1848 revolution. Above all Babbitt was interested in history only inasmuch as it could provide, for those who wished to invoke it, a tradition of established values, resistant to all forms of change, social and intellectual alike. His call, at the end of *The Masters of Modern French Criticism,* for a true critic of tradition was to be fully answered by his own student, T. S. Eliot: "What we are seeking is a critic who rests his discipline and selection upon the past without being a mere traditionalist; whose holding of tradition involves a constant process of hard and clear thinking, a constant adjustment, in other words, of the experience of the past to the changing needs of the present."

There is no doubt that Rousseau stands at the antagonistic center of all of Babbitt's thinking. Indeed, a Harvard undergraduate joke of his day was that Babbitt looked under his bed each night to see if Rousseau was there. Babbitt did not need a scapegoat (even though he felt that Rousseauism in itself encouraged the making of scapegoats); he needed an adversary whom he could represent as consistently worthy of his own attention as a critical watchdog and moral vigilante. Rousseau, after all, had "moved the world," and Babbitt's mission, as much as anything, had been to expose zealously the Frenchman's heretical influence wherever he saw it hold sway. When it came to confronting Rousseau head on, however, the result was an anticlimax, and so *Rousseau and Romanticism* (1919), although the most well known of his books, is the least interesting. It contains little that is new in the way of ideas, and it lacks the critical edge of his previous, and less direct, critical encounters with those symptoms of Romanticism that Babbitt thought it dangerous not to suppress. Although it proposes to give a more descriptive and evenhanded account of the central features of the Romantic movement and life-style, *Rousseau and Romanticism* is eclectic, sweeping, and finally just as prescriptive as his other books. So, too, its ethical stakes are high, for if Babbitt is right about the unsoundness of Rousseau's philosophy, then "the total tendency of the Occident at present is moving away from rather than towards civilisation." The East presents a more progressive model, not in the indulgent, heady Orientalism espoused by the Romantics, but in the ethical solidity of the teachings of Confucius and Buddha. This view influenced Eliot in "The Waste Land" (1922), where the poet turns to the ascetic precepts of Buddhism as an alternative to the failed romanticism that pervades modern culture in the West.

Confucianism, challenged by the naturalism of Taoism, affirmed its commitment to those principles of decorum and measure which Babbitt praised as fundamental to classical or Aristotelian humanism. Buddhism placed ultimate value on the authority or self-control of the individual will— "Self is the lord of Self "—and thereby raises the "higher" will of the ethical self above the ordinary and imperfect will of the natural self. "Buddha and the Occident," an essay that accompanied his translation of *The Dhammapada* (1936), is Babbitt's most direct tribute to the virtues of Eastern philosophy, but he wrote frequently and urgently about the need to reconstruct the decadent Western life-style in accordance with the ascetic disciplines of the Buddhist "path of virtue." Babbitt's Asia was intended to be much more than an antitoxin to the romantic concept of the East as an exotic continent filled with turbaned warriors, harems, odalisques, eunuchs, flashing scimitars, and opium.

The central complaint of *Rousseau and Romanticism* is that Rousseau's influence discredited the "analytical intellect" and disabled the faculty of *definition.* To define is to recognize the commonality of things and therefore to distinguish what is absolute or universal about general terms or categories. Rousseau and his followers acted in accordance with what they thought words should mean rather than what they had meant in the past. Consequently much of the Romantic movement was borne along by the energy created by attributing new values and new meanings to words like "romantic," "enthusiasm," "Gothic," "sentimental," "picturesque," and "spontaneity." Babbitt's aim is to counter this neologistic impulse by Socratically examining the original, classical meanings associated with many of the key terms of Romanticism. The notion of *genius,* for example, valued now for its associations with originality, change, and imaginative liberty, was, for the Greeks, a quality indissociable from the creative perception of universals or elements of irreducible difference. Like the concept of *irony,* it was once cognate with the idea of a firm "ethical centre," whereas Babbitt claims it has become predicated upon the "repudiation of the very idea of an ethical centre." Babbitt presents similar arguments in favor of recovering for classical humanism such terms as "love," "virtue," "nature," "imagination," and "individualism."

Finally Babbitt's philippic against the Romantic cult of novelty and its taste for the primitivistic comes to rest upon the vagabond moral center of Rousseau himself, the "votary of the god Whirl," whose own "undoubted genius" seems less open to question by Babbitt than does his flight from the classical norms of intellectual virility. For as Babbitt scurrilously remarks, "there is indeed much in his make-up that reminds one less of a man than of a high-strung impressionable woman." To cast a difference of the intellect in the metaphorical terms of a difference of gender was, perhaps, the most compact solution available in the misogyny-ridden milieu of Babbitt's academy for expressing the utter heterogeneity of his position to that of another man. This same discourse demands, however, that he recognize Rousseau's "feminine charm," and in doing so, he inadvertently exposes some of his deeply ambivalent feelings about him.

Babbitt was not born into the patrician class, and he belonged to the generation that suc-

ceeded the "genteel" rule of the Boston Brahmins at Harvard. The Brahmin spirit of aristocratic aloofness and social inconsequence lingered on, however, in a quasi-monastic environment where a strenuous effort had to be made if one wanted to promote one's views outside of the limited academic channels of intellectual exchange. Early on, Babbitt made the decision to publish in national journals like the *Nation* and *Atlantic Monthly* to ensure a large audience, and by the early 1920s a group of humanist sympathizers around the country were publishing in the same public manner. The sense of a political moment was growing, and in response to the social confusion that followed World War I, Babbitt's work increasingly addressed itself to what he regarded as the decadent state of American democracy, gorged on the dreams generated by the previous half-century of expansion and material progress. The country was drifting unchecked toward a radical and "unlimited" democracy which was aimed at equality, but which for Babbitt could only result in anarchy and class warfare.

In *Democracy and Leadership* (1924), Babbitt ranges over the history of Western political philosophy, characterizing the "view of life that prevails at any particular time" as either naturalistic, humanistic, or religious, and then describing the corresponding political forms as either imperialist, limited democratic (with a "natural aristocracy"), or theocratic. He expresses the belief that the kind of humanitarianism that accompanies the naturalistic or libertarian imagination leads directly to an imperialist politics. To support this view Babbitt cites Edmund Burke's famous prophecies about the despotism and anarchy that would follow the French republicanism of the 1789 revolution. He argues that if America is to avoid further extending its internationalist largesse in the form of foreign intervention, it will have to exercise its own "veto power," or will to refrain, and recognize, at the same time, that it has been betrayed by its leaders.

Babbitt believed that the American ideal was "external freedom and inner control." In other words, the individual should look after his own conduct and interests, while the government's job is merely to protect the liberty of each individual. The result of Jefferson's Rousseauistic "declamation of liberty" had been to promote too much social control by government in the way of direct democracy, but Babbitt believed that this "natural impulse" had been curbed by the Constitution with its system of vital checks upon the will of the people. A truly humanist form of limited democracy should always provide for a ruling elite, but because of the extension of universal suffrage to the new immigrant population, Babbitt was concerned that "the stocks to which the past has looked for its leaders is dying out and the inferior or even degenerate breeds are multiplying." Even worse were the humanitarian experiments of other countries, especially the Soviet commitment to scientific socialism, a project which Babbitt saw as only one more of history's attempts to subordinate the individual will to a political fate outside of itself, the prototype for which lay in Stoic utilitarianism and its appeal to service in the community.

When Babbitt looked to the near future he feared that the time was propitious for the rise of an "imperialist leader" who would appeal to the mass demand for "direct action." In such an event, he felt that "the American equivalent of a Mussolini" would be the lesser of two evils: "he may be needed to save us from the American equivalent of a Lenin." Perhaps less embarrassing, in retrospect, was Babbitt's attempt to resurrect the "imaginative conservatism" of Edmund Burke, the English thinker whose realistic allegiance to traditional values could be offered as a counterpoise to Rousseau's humanitarian sympathies. Burke's interpretation of the social contract as the "permanent ethical self" of the community and his recognition of a "natural aristocracy" of leaders were fundamental principles of political thought which Babbitt instinctively shared and steadfastly promoted.

By the end of the 1920s the ideas associated with this "imaginative conservatism" had gone public. Babbitt had talked before 3,000 people at Carnegie Hall in New York. His sympathizers had been loosely congregated into a movement known as the New Humanism, and the issues they promoted had drawn fire from a host of young, liberal critics. Even the daily newspapers had reported the resulting hue and cry among the East Coast literati, accustomed to changing fashions in criticism but still taken aback by the news that "humanism" had become a fighting word. The movement itself brought together former students, colleagues, and correspondents of Babbitt: Stuart Sherman, Frank Jewett Mather, Jr., P. H. Frye, W. C. Brownell, Sherlock Bronson Gass, Norman Foerster, W. F. Giese, Robert Shafer, P. H. Houston, and others. Babbitt and More, between whom More carefully claimed there was "a fundamental sympathy of

mind not incompatible with clashing differences," were regarded as the leaders of the movement, even though more independent thinkers like Sherman had long since doubted and challenged their capacity or willingness to shape the movement into a platform for educational and social reform. The New Humanists had established a forum for the expression of their ideas in the *Bookman* and the *Forum,* and in England in T. S. Eliot's *Criterion,* while their critics published their attacks in the *New Republic, Scribner's,* and the *Hound and Horn.* The *Forum* did publish Eliot's negative response to *Democracy and Leadership* in its issue of July 1928. Having recently converted to the Anglican Church, Eliot judges humanism as an insufficient substitute for religion. His tone toward Babbitt is respectful but severe. Babbitt believed himself misrepresented by Eliot, who qualified and restated his views in "Second Thoughts on Humanism" (1922), where he switches targets to Norman Foerster's "impure" humanism of ethics without religion.

The debate reached its high point in 1930 with the publication of two books, *Humanism and America: Essays on the Outlook of Modern Civilization,* edited by Norman Foerster, and *The Critique of Humanism: A Symposium,* edited by C. Hartley Grattan. *Humanism and America,* luridly advertised on its dust jacket as "the challenge of culture to the anarchy of our times," was grandly dedicated by its editor to "the fundamental needs of America as the dominant world power and inadequate model of civilization in the twentieth century." Babbitt's contribution, "Humanism: An Essay at Definition," recapitulated his central ideas and then addressed the relation of humanism to religion, noting that humanism brought together the best of each religion while dispensing with the ecclesiastical dogmas which make up their respective differences. The issue of religion was already a point of disagreement for at least two of the other contributors; More, who had begun his exploration of Platonism and Christian mysticism, and Eliot, who was shortly to assume a polemical voice within the Anglican Church. Eliot had come to disagree with his former teacher's faith in the "inner check," and against humanism Eliot argued for the necessity of a guiding supernatural authority.

In the absence of any ultimate appeal to external authority, the New Humanism was seen by its critics to be based upon the assertion that the free will of each individual to choose his own mechanism of self-control is sufficient to provide a code of ethical action distinct from and superior to that of naturalism. For Christian converts like Eliot, the suggestion that humanism could not only provide an alternative but also act as a substitute for religious dogma was unacceptable, and he came to characterize Babbitt's emphasis on the "inner check" as "self-control for control's sake." So too, in his contribution to *The Critique of Humanism*, Allen Tate argued that the Humanists' values were worthless without "a definite and living religious background" and added that their idea of self-imposed restraint actually courted the kind of "external control" which he equated with "moral Fascism." One of the most prevalent secular responses to Babbitt's fellow travelers was that they had succeeded in shaking off Puritan theology but were still, as Edmund Wilson put it, in the dogmatic thrall of a "bigoted Puritan heritage . . . which they persist in mistaking for eternal and universal laws."

For those young liberals who contributed to *The Critique of Humanism*, critics like Malcolm Cowley, Kenneth Burke, R. P. Blackmur, Yvor Winters, and Lewis Mumford, and for others like Wilson who added their dissenting voices elsewhere, a more immediate point of contention was the assumption that literature was the exclusive repository of value in a democratic culture. Moreover, the New Humanists championed a traditional canon of literature at the cost of neglecting and derogating virtually all modern writing and art, especially the kind of novelistic literature which the liberals increasingly saw as a possible agent of social redemption. Indeed, the impatient polemical mood of the anti-Humanists was symptomatic of the burgeoning demand among American critics for social relevance. Wilson, for example, thought it absurd that Babbitt could imagine that "our clerks, our factory workers and our respectable professional and business classes were all in danger of falling victims to the rhapsodical enthusiasm and lawless individualism of romanticism." In a similar vein, Cowley pointed out that it is "almost impossible to be either human or Humanist on ten or twelve dollars a week" and went on to pose the celebrated question that, for better or worse, became the vulgar obituary for the New Humanist movement: what possible validity could a "communion" of "angry professors" have for "the mill hands of New Bedford and Gastonia, for the beet-toppers of Colorado, for the men who tighten a single screw in the automobiles that march along Mr. Ford's assembly belt?"

From the evidence of his last two collections of essays, Babbitt emerged from the so-called "battle of the books" with his polemical reserves largely intact. Against those who had argued for the virtues of Christian authority, he reaffirmed, in the introduction to *On Being Creative and Other Essays* (1932), that he was offering a viable critical option to those "many men of good will for whom dogmatic and revealed religion has become impossible." So, too, in the matter of cultural values, he suggested that the Humanist debate had proved only that "our critical standards have suffered even more severely than had been expected." It seems that in the responses of the anti-Humanists Babbitt had found particular justification for his claims about imminent "cultural collapse," especially when critics like Edmund Wilson had been heard to assert that "the characters of Sophocles have no more ethical substance than those of Mr. Eugene O'Neill." Otherwise, the bulk of the essays in this collection raise familiar themes for Babbitt's reader, concentrating on the shortcomings of the Romantic ideology of expressionist creativity associated with writers like Schiller, William Wordsworth, and Samuel Taylor Coleridge and arguing instead for a more humanistic definition of *creativity*.

The last collection of Babbitt's essays, *Spanish Character and Other Essays*, was published posthumously in 1940 by some of his friends and fellow Humanists. Composed largely of articles which had appeared in the *Nation* and other journals, the essays in this volume cover the extraordinarily wide range of Babbitt's interests in politics, literature, philosophy, education, and Eastern religion. Especially useful is the chronological bibliography of Babbitt's published writings and a 100-page index to the seven major collections of his essays. A year later, Frederick Manchester and Odell Shepard edited and published a collection of short memoirs of Babbitt called *Irving Babbitt: Man and Teacher* (1941), written by students, friends, teachers, colleagues and intellectual acquaintances and arranged in chronological order as if to suggest a biographical narrative. While no major biographical study has appeared, Thomas R. Nevin's *Irving Babbitt: An Intellectual Study* (1984) is a remarkably cogent and sympathetic assessment of Babbitt's career as a thinker, critic, and teacher. In *Irving Babbitt: Representative Writings* (1981), George Panichas provides a useful selection of Babbitt's essays alongside a reasoned introduction and a short biographical index of names which appear frequently in Babbitt's work. Panichas, along with Claes Ryn, has also edited a collection of essays by various hands, *Irving Babbitt in Our Time* (1986), which ranges widely over many aspects of his work while placing it within the tradition of American conservative thought.

For the generations of critics that succeeded first the Humanists and then, in turn, the anti-Humanists, Babbitt continues to appeal to conservatives who advocate the traditional virtues of teaching and studying a canon of classical authors. Walter Jackson Bate, for example, in his widely used textbook *Criticism: The Major Texts* (1952), describes Babbitt as "one of the most important English and American critics of the past half century" precisely because he had made "traditional critical issues a vivid and living concern, applicable to almost every aspect of modern life." So, too, in the subsequent reaction to critical attacks in the 1960s upon the institutionalized sexism and racism of the "canon," Babbitt's humanism has been readily invoked as a significant source of support for defenders of literary traditions. In a long introduction to a new edition of *Literature and the American College* (1986, National Humanities Institute) the eminent conservative thinker Russell Kirk argues that Babbitt's defense of a humanist education has never been more pertinent to those who seek to "reclaim" (to use the words of William Bennett, President Reagan's Secretary of Education) the "legacy" of classical education.

Finally, of course, Babbitt's conscientiously conservative voice is best seen in the context of its historical moment. The New Humanists were not at all the latest practitioners of the genteel tradition, as George Santayana had characterized the intellectual aloofness of the Boston Brahmins. Indeed, it was precisely because they sacrificed the academic privilege of disinterestedness for a responsible, if virulent, defense of conservative ideas that they drew so much fire from a younger, and arguably more brilliant, generation of critics. There was nothing new about a debate between defenders of conservative and proponents of liberal values, or, as Babbitt liked to dramatize it, the battle between ancients and moderns. For the first time, however, the object of that debate was literature itself—how to recognize it, how to study it, how to teach it, how to put it to use, and how to sanctify it. Although Babbitt was unable to recognize that literature was itself a way of ideologically legitimizing moral and political values, he was one of the first modern critics to approach literature as if it were a legitimate way of talking about those same values.

**Bibliography:**

Frederick Manchester, Rachel Giese, and William F. Giese, eds., bibliography in *Spanish Character and Other Essays* (Boston & New York: Houghton Mifflin, 1940), pp. 249-259.

**References:**

Daniel Aaron, "Statement and Counterstatement: Literary Wars in the Early Thirties," in his *Writers on the Left* (New York: Harcourt, Brace & World, 1961);

R. P. Blackmur, "Humanism and Symbolic Imagination: Notes on Rereading Irving Babbitt," in his *The Lion and the Honeycomb: Essays in Solicitude and Critique* (New York: Harcourt, Brace, 1955);

Hsin-Hai Chang, "Irving Babbitt and Oriental Thought," *Michigan Quarterly Review*, 4 (Fall 1965): 234-244;

T. S. Eliot, "The Humanism of Irving Babbitt" and "Second Thoughts about Humanism," in his *Selected Essays* (New York: Harcourt, Brace & World, 1960);

Hugh L'Anson Fausset, "The New Humanism Refuted," in his *The Proving of Psyche* (London: Cape, 1929);

C. Hartley Grattan, ed., *The Critique of Humanism: A Symposium* (New York: Farrar & Rinehart, 1930);

J. David Hoeveler, Jr., *The New Humanism: A Critique of Modern America 1900-1940* (Charlottesville: University Press of Virginia, 1977);

Henry S. Kariel, "Democracy Limited: Irving Babbitt's Classicism," *Review of Politics*, 13 (October 1951): 430-440;

Alfred Kazin, "Liberals and New Humanists," in his *On Native Grounds: An Interpretation of Modern American Prose Literature* (New York: Harcourt, Brace, 1942);

Folke Leander, *Humanism and Naturalism: A Comparative Study of Ernest Sellière, Irving Babbitt and Paul Elmer More* (Göteberg, Sweden: Wettergern & Kerber, 1937);

Harry Levin, "Irving Babbitt and the Teaching of Literature," in his *Refractions* (New York & London: Oxford University Press, 1966);

Ronald Lora, "The New Humanism of Irving Babbitt and Paul Elmer More," in his *Conservative Minds in America* (Chicago: University of Chicago Press, 1972);

Arthur Lovejoy, Review of *Rousseau and Romanticism* in *Modern Language Notes,* 35 (May 1920): 302-307;

Frederick Manchester and Odell Shepard, eds., *Irving Babbitt: Man and Teacher* (New York & London: Putnam's, 1941);

F. O. Matthiessen, "Irving Babbitt," in *The Responsibilities of the Critic* (New York & London: Oxford University Press, 1952);

Louis J. A. Mercier, *The Challenge of Humanism: An Essay in Comparative Criticism* (New York & London: Oxford University Press, 1933);

Paul Elmer More, "Irving Babbitt," in his *On Being Human,* New Shelburne Essays, third series (Princeton: Princeton University Press, 1936), pp. 25-42;

Gorham Munson, "An Introduction to Irving Babbitt," in his *Destinations: A Canvass of American Literature Since 1900* (New York: Sears, 1928);

Thomas R. Nevin, *Irving Babbitt: An Intellectual Study* (Chapel Hill & London: University of North Carolina Press, 1984);

George Panichas, Introduction to *Irving Babbitt: Representative Writings,* edited by Panichas (Lincoln: University of Nebraska Press, 1981);

Panichas and Claes Ryn, eds., *Irving Babbitt in Our Time* (Washington, D.C.: Catholic University of America Press, 1986);

David Spitz, "The Undesirability of Democracy," *Patterns of Antidemocratic Thought* (New York: Macmillan, 1949; revised, New York: Free Press, 1965);

Allen Tate, "Humanism and Naturalism," in *Reactionary Essays on Poetry and Ideas* (New York: Scribners, 1936);

Rebecca West, "Regretfully," in her *Ending in Earnest: A Literary Log* (Garden City: Doubleday, Doran, 1931);

Edmund Wilson, "Notes on Babbitt and More," in his *The Shores of Light: A Literary Chronicle of the Twenties and Thirties* (New York: Noonday Press, 1967).

**Papers:**

Nine boxes of Babbitt's lecture and reading notes are in the Harvard University Archives, Cambridge, Massachusetts.

# R. P. Blackmur

*(21 January 1904-2 February 1965)*

## William E. Cain
*Wellesley College*

BOOKS: *For Any Book* (Cambridge, Mass.: Privately printed by F. W. Murray & P. E. Rowe, 1924);

*A Funeral for a Few Sticks* (Lynn, Mass.: Lone Gull Press, 1927);

*T. S. Eliot* (Cambridge, Mass.: Hound & Horn, 1928);

*Dirty Hands; or, The True-born Censor,* as Perry Hobbs (Cambridge, U.K.: Minority Press, 1930);

*Psyche in the South* (Tryon, N.C.: Tryon Pamphlets, 1934);

*The Double Agent: Essays in Craft and Elucidation* (New York: Arrow Editions, 1935);

*From Jordan's Delight* (New York: Arrow Editions, 1937);

*The Expense of Greatness* (New York: Arrow Editions, 1940);

*The Second World* (Cummington, Mass.: Cummington Press, 1942);

*The Good European and Other Poems* (Cummington, Mass.: Cummington Press, 1947);

*Language as Gesture: Essays in Poetry* (New York: Harcourt, Brace, 1952; London: Allen & Unwin, 1954); abridged as *Form and Value in Modern Poetry* (New York: Doubleday, 1957);

*The Lion and the Honeycomb: Essays in Solicitude and Critique* (New York: Harcourt, Brace, 1955; London: Methuen, 1956);

*Anni Mirabiles 1921-1926: Reason in the Madness of Letters* (Washington, D.C.: Library of Congress, 1956);

*New Criticism in the United States* (Tokyo: Kenkyusha Press, 1959; Folcroft, Pa.: Folcroft Library Editions, 1971);

*Eleven Essays in the European Novel* (New York: Harcourt, Brace & World, 1964);

*A Primer of Ignorance,* edited by Joseph Frank (New York: Harcourt, Brace & World, 1967);

*Poems of R. P. Blackmur* (Princeton: Princeton University Press, 1977);

*Henry Adams,* edited by Veronica Makowsky (New York: Harcourt Brace Jovanovich, 1980; London: Secker & Warburg, 1980);

*Studies in Henry James,* edited by Makowsky (New York: New Directions, 1983).

OTHER: Henry James, *The Art of the Novel,* introduction by Blackmur (New York & London: Scribners, 1934);

John Wheelwright, *Selected Poems,* introduction by Blackmur (Norfolk, Conn.: New Directions, 1941);

Conrad Aiken, *Collected Novels of Conrad Aiken,* introduction by Blackmur (New York: Holt, Rinehart & Winston, 1964).

The standard account of R. P. Blackmur's career that few readers have questioned has him beginning as a New Critic producing his best essays, including those on Wallace Stevens, Marianne Moore, D. H. Lawrence, and other poets, in the 1920s and 1930s. It is this period of Blackmur's career, when he was most purely a "close reader" of texts, that the majority of his readers admire and on which they base their classification of him as a New Critic. Laurence B. Holland states that Blackmur is "the most brilliant and durable of the New Critics"; A. Walton Litz concludes that he "was in many ways the most satisfactory literary critic of his generation"; and Russell Fraser, most boldly of all, asserts that *The Double Agent: Essays in Craft and Elucidation* (1935) and *The Expense of Greatness* (1940) constitute "the best literary criticism produced in our time."

To characterize Blackmur as the exemplary New Critic is inaccurate, however, for he transcends this category as much as he belongs in it. John Crowe Ransom, to be sure, did point to Blackmur as the typical "new critic" in his preface to *The New Criticism,* a book that appeared in 1941 and assigned a label to the movement as a whole, and like many of the New Critics, Blackmur is an intensive close reader. But unlike the others, he rarely engages in lengthy explications. His analyses often concentrate only on parts of texts, or they strategically develop a general argument about a poet's techniques. Cleanth Brooks's "readings" of poems by John Donne, Alexander Pope, Thomas Gray, William Wordsworth, John Keats, and others in *The Well-Wrought Urn* (1947), which proceed through the text image by image, are more representative of New Critical procedure. This is not the kind of analysis that Blackmur prefers to engage in; his commentary generally involves more speculative problems: "authority" in Thomas Hardy's poetry, the relation between literature and belief in T. S. Eliot's writing, or the nature of artistic "consciousness" and dramatic "form" in Herman Melville's novels. Blackmur "elucidates" rather than "explicates," aiming to discover how words sound and feel as well as how they mean. He strives for depth and difficulty, and his arguments seem dauntingly intricate when set alongside those of the other New Critics. In further contrast to Brooks, Blackmur does not gear his criticism toward pedagogy, which the New Critics generally emphasize and see as the testing ground for their interpretive tools. Blackmur's goals sometimes cost him clarity, but he generally avoids descending into the banal and formulaic—which is the price Brooks and his New Critical brethren sometimes pay for their lucid, teacherly methodology.

Blackmur once wryly noted that "whenever any of my own work is attacked I am attacked as a New Critic. Usually when people wish to make more pleasant remarks about me they say how it is that I have departed from the New Criticism." As "the outsider" (his favorite name for himself), Blackmur felt uneasy about being portrayed as a member of a movement and did not wish to be designated as one of the leading executives in the business that Ransom described as "Criticism, Inc." In two essays in *The Lion and the Honeycomb* (1955), Blackmur treats the New Criticism harshly, condemning its narrow canon, its adherence to methods that are "useless" when applied to Chaucer, Goethe, Racine, and Dante, and its bad effect on creative writing. He is not a spokesman for New Critical doctrines in his theoretical writings, and when he does refer to the New Criticism and its proponents, he calls attention to defects and misplaced emphases.

Many contemporary critics nevertheless persist in identifying Blackmur as the best of the New Critical close readers, largely because his concern in his early essays for the language of the texts themselves seems so different from the later trends of the 1970s and 1980s toward "theory"

and methodological inquiry. In his later work, however, Blackmur himself became increasingly theoretical, and he sought to refine a lyrical, "creative" style for critical discourse that was as much an object of verbal complexity and dazzle as any literary text. Those who praise Blackmur's early work usually dismiss what followed it, judging the later pieces to be queerly distant from literature and grotesquely mannered in presentation. Fraser, for example, laments the transformation of Blackmur from "absolute critic" into an "inferior metaphysician"; the savvy explorer of texts turned, Fraser contends, into a "magnificent crank." "Blackmur came to believe," concurs Robert Boyers, "that he too had better things to do than to write the best essays on poets and poetry that anyone had ever written. He bought the notion that an ambitious critic was well advised to move away from texts, to discover Ideas, to talk about things instead of allowing his discourse to be penetrated by the voice and thought rhythms of poets and their verses. . . . He ceased effectively to write about poetry by the late forties, and much that he wrote in the period between 1950 and his death in 1965 is simply unreadable."

Yet it is precisely these later writings that have earned Blackmur the acclaim of those contemporary critics who stress the importance of theory and advocate innovative kinds of style and argument in critical practice. Geoffrey Hartman, for example, describing Blackmur as "perhaps the first of our witch critics," says his "involuted style betrays an extreme awareness of how the mind is textured by texts and how the critic's, if not the poet's, authority is always under the shadow of imposture." Even more extravagantly, Edward W. Said has proclaimed that Blackmur—dense, difficult, and abstract though he may be—is "the greatest genius American criticism has produced." For Hartman and Said, Blackmur is a great critic because in his later writings he travels beyond the boundaries set by the New Criticism. He treats social and political issues, connects literature and criticism with economics, philosophy, and other disciplines, and admirably chooses to write in a style that is sophisticated and allusive.

What makes Blackmur so absorbing, then, is not only the intrinsic interest of his career but also the compelling way in which his writings help to focus debates about the definition and authority of the critic's role. Critics of Blackmur reveal as much, if not more, about their own conception of the critic's job of work as they do about Blackmur himself.

Richard Palmer Blackmur was born in Springfield, Massachusetts, in 1904 to Helen Palmer and George Edward Blackmur. His mother, the daughter and granddaughter of well-known ministers, was a physical therapist. His father tried his hand at a number of business-related endeavors without really succeeding at any. In 1905 the family moved to New York City where the senior Blackmur was employed as a stockbroker. By 1910 they returned to Massachusetts, and Helen Blackmur supported the family by running a boardinghouse in Cambridge. Blackmur was tutored at home by his mother until he was nine, when he was enrolled in the fourth grade at Peabody Grammar School. In 1916 he began attending Cambridge High and Latin school. He was expelled in 1918 after a dispute with the headmaster, and he never completed a formal education. He worked in bookstores, frequented the local libraries, and managed in the process to teach himself literature and criticism in a passionate, if uneven and unstructured, fashion. In his biography of Blackmur, Russell Fraser notes the young Blackmur's high seriousness and dedicated attention to literature, but he adds that Blackmur always felt uneasy about his homemade education and did his anxious best to conceal its shortcomings.

Blackmur's first real distinction came in 1928 when his friends Lincoln Kirstein and Bernard Bandler asked him to serve as editor of *Hound and Horn*. He began to publish elegant essays, written with a rare kind of penetrating intelligence, on modern poetry and other subjects. His acute two-part essay on T. S. Eliot, which first appeared in the little magazine in 1928 and was reprinted the same year as a pamphlet, established his reputation in America and also brought him to the attention of readers in England. *Hound and Horn* moved to New York in 1930, the same year Blackmur married painter Helen Dickson. Although he ceased editing the magazine, he contributed articles to it until it closed down in 1934. He was, in Fraser's words, "supremely the writer as opportunist," and by 1932 he had written more than seventy essays and reviews. His first essay collection, *The Double Agent,* appeared in 1935, the same year in which he started his labors on a critical biography of Henry Adams. As a free-lance writer, Blackmur found it extremely difficult during these years to earn a living, but he did receive both intellectual and financial support from friends and institutions. The Guggenheim Foundation awarded him a fellowship in

*R. P. Blackmur, circa 1930-1931 (photograph by R. D. Darrell)*

1937 and renewed it for the following year. Through the good offices of Allen Tate, he began an association with Princeton University in 1940 that led to his organizing the Princeton Seminars in Literary Criticism (later the Christian Gauss Seminars) in 1949. That association eventually culminated—after a good deal of bureaucratic strain and departmental infighting—in a tenured full professorship in 1951. He was an elliptical and riveting teacher, and he won the affection and awestruck respect of a generation of Princeton students, many of whom have said that Blackmur was the only worthwhile intellectual presence on the entire campus. His famous course on the European novelists (including Gustave Flaubert, Leo Tolstoy, Fyodor Dostoyevski, James Joyce, and Thomas Mann), which he gave during the 1950s, still lives in academic legend as a startlingly original display of pedagogical brilliance and improvisation.

By the 1940s Blackmur was generally acknowledged as one of the most adept and influential modern critics. His honors and awards were many and included his election to the National Institute of Arts and Letters in 1956, an invitation to present a series of lectures at the Library of Congress in the same year, and worldwide travel as cultural critic and American ambassador of the intellect during the 1950s under the auspices of the Rockefeller Foundation. He also served as honorary consultant in American letters at the Library of Congress from 1961 to 1964, and from 1961 to 1962 he taught and lectured as the Pitt Professor of American History and Institutions at Cambridge University. He died in Princeton in 1965 and was buried in Pittsfield, Massachusetts.

One of the many peculiar things about Blackmur is that he never wrote an integrated book. He aspired toward the wholly rounded book-length triumph of craftsmanship but lacked the discipline and patience to produce it. He could not complete his planned books on Henry James and Henry Adams and never quite managed to muster the energy and resolve required for other projects to which he sometimes alluded—a full statement, for example, of his "poetics" and also monographs on Joyce and Dostoyevski. There are also plays, short stories, and two novels among his unpublished papers, which testify to the balked creative temperament of this writer and which give a sense of Blackmur as a marvelously gifted figure whose finest work somehow fell short of what he hoped for himself. But though he did not shape a book on a particular author or topic, his critical as well as creative output is still very impressive and substantial. He published three books of interesting, if often overwrought lyrics that draw upon and, in their best moments, bear comparison with Blackmur's fellow modernists Hart Crane and Allen Tate: *From Jordan's Delight* (1937), *The Second World* (1942), and *The Good European and Other Poems* (1947). More significantly, his gatherings of essays and reviews are imposing in their range and adventurousness. Following *The Double Agent,* he published *The Expense of Greatness* (1940), *Language as Gesture: Essays in Poetry* (1952), *The Lion and the Honeycomb: Essays in Solicitude and Critique* (1955), and *Form and Value in Modern Poetry* (1957). In all of these collections there is some overlapping of material from one volume to the next. *New Criticism in the United States* (1959) is a fairly superficial group of lectures that Blackmur delivered in Japan in 1956, and *Eleven Essays in the European Novel* (1964) traffics too often in self-serving obscurity and verbal charlatanry (Louise Bogan opined

that Blackmur wrote "academic Swahili"), but there are nevertheless good things in both books, particularly the chapters on Dostoyevski in the second book. Blackmur also left much material uncollected and unpublished, and several additional books have appeared since his death: *A Primer of Ignorance* (1967), the complete *Poems of R. P. Blackmur* (1977), and books devoted to Henry Adams (1980) and Henry James (1983).

Blackmur's books are either collections of essays, or patchwork affairs combining new work with material from earlier books, or assemblages of material—some of it previously published in a different form, some of it not—stitched together by an editor after Blackmur's death, and they are, therefore, difficult to summarize. On the whole Blackmur's "books" count for less than do his individual pieces on particular writers; he is basically an essayist. Readers, consequently, go to a book in order to find out what Blackmur has to say in a specific essay about a given writer or text. Blackmur provides many rewards, but the effectively conducted book-length argument about a single writer or literary problem or period is not one of them.

If one were, nevertheless, inclined to select Blackmur's best books, one would clearly choose, along with Russell Fraser, *The Double Agent* and *The Expense of Greatness. The Double Agent* mostly concentrates on modern poetry and addresses questions of method and form. The first six essays treat E. E. Cummings, Ezra Pound, Wallace Stevens, D. H. Lawrence, Hart Crane, and Marianne Moore. The next two essays focus on T. S. Eliot both as a poetic craftsman and as a Christian who seeks to voice and integrate his religious views in complex literary texts such as "Ash Wednesday" and *Murder in the Cathedral.* Blackmur then supplies briefer chapters on the Marxist critic Granville Hicks and the Victorian satirist of the Church of England, Samuel Butler. Both chapters, which are reprints of book reviews, show him again dealing with the relationships between literature, politics, and religion.

The final two essays in *The Double Agent* are among Blackmur's most famous: "The Critical Prefaces of Henry James" and "A Critic's Job of Work." "Critical Prefaces" pays elaborate tribute to James's artistry in his prefaces to the New York edition of his writings. "What we have here," Blackmur declares, "is the most sustained and I think the most eloquent and original piece of literary criticism in existence." After his overview of James's achievement, Blackmur furnishes a statement of the "major themes," including "art and the artist," "art and life," and "art and morals," that "inhabit all the Prefaces." Some critics–notably F. R. Leavis in *The Great Tradition*–have complained that Blackmur is so immersed in James and so celebratory about the Master's art that he is not really helpful in a critical sense about the prefaces themselves. But while it is true that Blackmur does not demonstrate much skepticism toward the excesses of the prefaces and, thus, perhaps fails actually to address them in an evaluative spirit, he does supply readers with a valuable summary of James's aims and preoccupations in them. Blackmur's systematic labor was extremely important for heightening response to James as an artist and critic, and it did much to spur the James revival that began in the 1930s and has flourished since.

"A Critic's Job of Work" is Blackmur's formalist credo. In it he carefully discriminates between his own favored approach to texts and those approaches evident in the criticism of George Santayana, Van Wyck Brooks, Granville Hicks, I. A. Richards, Kenneth Burke, and the Blake scholar S. Foster Damon. Blackmur admires these critics, but he continually rejects signs in them of a failure to honor, above all, the art and technique of poetry. Literary criticism cannot be, as Richards hopes, a method akin to the sciences, nor should it measure literary texts, as Hicks's approach does, against the imperatives of the class struggle. What the critic must do is achieve "intimate contact" with the poem itself. He must feel his way into it, hear and weigh its words, absorb and ponder its inner structure. This is the critic's fundamental "job," the real "work" he ought to perform but which most critics regularly fail to accomplish in their misapplied efforts to align literature with some nonliterary doctrine or dogma.

The chapters on poetry in *The Expense of Greatness* are equally impressive. There are subtle analyses of Thomas Hardy, Emily Dickinson, and William Butler Yeats that rank with the best pieces in the earlier book. Blackmur also devotes chapters to T. E. Lawrence and Herman Melville. These are uneven in merit, doubtless reflecting Blackmur's difficulty in coming to terms with prose texts whose massive scale poses problems for his close-reading approach. But they are also sometimes quite illuminating, as Blackmur seeks to articulate the ways in which Lawrence's and Melville's private obsessions both enriched and skewed their attempt to create literary form.

*The Expense of Greatness* also includes re-prints of several substantial review articles on modern poets and novelists. These, too, are uneven in quality, in part simply because some of the writers Blackmur examines have badly failed the test of time and are of no interest today. The book concludes with a short piece on Marian Adams, a longer assessment of Henry Adams, and an intriguing, if occasionally exasperating, study of "the profession of writing" titled "A Featherbed for Critics." This final essay, an exercise in theory and methodology, demonstrates Blackmur's reverence for "inward mastery," the great writer's ability to give fully controlled expression of his subject through the deftly managed "form" of his art. One senses here the influence of Eliot and James upon Blackmur's thinking; he admired both of these writers' fidelity to art and abiding concern for well-executed forms. But one can also see the limits to Blackmur's perspective in some of his brief and rather curt references to writers who displease him, as when he narrowmindedly remarks that Richard Wright's *Native Son* (1940) "is one of those books in which everything is undertaken with seriousness except the writing."

Critics have often debated the extent to which Blackmur, especially in his early work, reveals an interest in theory as opposed to practical tasks of elucidation and adheres to a specific "method" as opposed to allowing the text at hand to dictate the method required. Blackmur was never averse to theory altogether, as his descriptions of the critic's role and authority in "A Critic's Job of Work," "A Featherbed for Critics," and other essays and reviews published in the 1930s and early 1940s make clear. But Denis Donoghue offers the right discrimination when he states that Blackmur "wanted from theory only a hint, a nudge, a gesture, pointing to possibility." Blackmur responds to and pursues suggestions from a variety of sources, including Aristotle, Coleridge, Henry James, Benedetto Croce, George Santayana, Eliot, I. A. Richards, and Yvor Winters. Theory did attract him powerfully at moments in his later career, as an essay like "Between the Numen and the Moha: Notes Toward a Theory of Literature" (included in *The Lion and the Honeycomb*) reveals. But for the most part, Blackmur emphasized the operations of the practical critic rather than the theorist. "I wouldn't suppose," he conjectured in an essay on his "critical perspective" in *New Criticism in the United States,* "that a frog cares too much about the systematic organization of the way by which he jumps; neither do I. And I assume that perhaps no more so than in other activities one's mind has to do a great deal of jumping."

While Blackmur may not have held to a theory, in the best of his early essays he did show signs of a consistent method, which one might define as a tactfully managed probing of the rational organization of words. Blackmur treats words with reverential deliberation, and he loves to unfold the ways in which writers connect and interanimate them. He is concerned, as he indicates in *The Double Agent*, to attune himself to the verbal structure and texture of poetic form:

> The sense of continuous relationship, of sustained contact, with the works nominally in hand is rare and when found uncommonly exhilarating; it is the fine object of criticism: as it seems to put us in direct possession of the principles whereby the works move without injuring or disintegrating the body of the works themselves. The sense of intimacy by inner contact cannot arise from methods of approach which hinge on seized separable content. We have constantly—if our interest is really in literature—to prod ourselves back, to remind ourselves that there was a poem, a play, or a novel of some initial and we hope terminal concern, or we have to falsify facts and set up fictions to the effect that no matter what we are saying we are really talking about art after all.

Blackmur does not want to interpret works as much as to place himself and his reader "intimately" in contact with the central principles, movements, and patterns that fortify the writer's art. In this respect one might even risk saying that Blackmur wants above all to inform and prepare the mind of the reader, to exhibit for the reader what internally motivates a body of poems, and to convert him or her to the attitudes that these poems insist readers bring to them. For example, in *The Double Agent*, he offers a limiting judgment on the poetic practice of Hart Crane. He first quotes a passage from "Lachrymae Christi": "Let sphinxes from the ripe/Borage of death have cleared my tongue/Once and again. . . ." He then inquires into, and tries to sort out, the meanings of Crane's language, in order to express how this language shuns rational organization and evades understanding:

It is syntax rather than grammar that is obscure. I take it that "let" is here a somewhat homemade adjective and that Crane is making a direct statement, so that the problem is to construe the right meanings of the right words in the right references; which will be an admirable exercise in exegesis, but an exercise only. The applicable senses of "let" are these: neglected or weary, permitted or prevented, hired, and let in the sense that blood is let. Sphinxes are inscrutable, have secrets, propound riddles to travellers and strangle those who cannot answer. "Borage" has at least three senses: something rough (sonally suggestive of barrage and barrier), a blue-flowered, hairy-leaved plant, and a cordial made from the plant. *The Shorter Oxford Dictionary* quotes this jingle from Hooker: "I Borage always bring courage."

Blackmur's sense of the dictionary as a treasure and resource may be similar to William Empson's approach in *Seven Types of Ambiguity* (1930), but Blackmur has a persuasive generalizing power that his English contemporary lacks: his verbal inspections are more controlled and directed toward larger impersonal kinds of statements and evaluations. Continuing his discussion of Crane, Blackmur says that by "borage" one can guess

> that Crane meant something to the effect that if you meditate enough on death it has the same bracing and warming effect as drinking a cordial, so that the riddles of life (or death) are answered. But something very near the contrary may have been intended; or both. In any case a guess is ultimately worthless because, with the defective syntax, the words do not verify it. Crane had a profound feeling for the hearts of words, and how they beat and cohabited, but here they overtopped him; the meanings in the words themselves are superior to the use to which he put them. The operation of selective cross-pollination not only failed but was not even rightly attempted.

This analytical concern for rational control and order is essential to Blackmur, and it is evident throughout the essays in *The Double Agent* and *The Expense of Greatness*, particularly in his critique of the private musings of the poet in "Notes on E. E. Cummings' Language" and in his account of flawed craftsmanship in "Masks of Ezra Pound." "What I want to evangelize in the arts," he insists in a later essay in *The Lion and the Honeycomb*, "A Burden for Critics" (1948), "is rational intent, rational statement, and rational technique; and I want to do it through technical judgment, clarifying judgment, and the judgment of discovery, which together I call rational judgment." Blackmur seems to be implying that the writer should be respectfully devoted to words without wholly capitulating to them. This posture entails an appreciation for words while one exercises a measure of control over them. It is different from a "surrender" to words, which suggests abandonment, "intoxication" (a word Blackmur invokes often), and disorder. Such a discrimination stresses the distance and detachment that Blackmur advocates in both literature and criticism, even as he appeals for an intimate, "inner contact" with texts.

If sustained "inner contact" gets at one key aspect of Blackmur's performance as a critic, then "irony" gets at another—one that is even more privileged in his vocabulary. In "The Dangers of Authorship," an essay in *The Double Agent*, he observes that "the writer . . . is . . . an independent mirror of the processes of life which happen to absorb him; he creates by showing, by representing; and his only weapons for change are the irony of the intelligence that can be brought to bear on the contemptible and the stupid, and the second irony of a second point of view, implicit in his work, but alien to that of his subject-matter." Still more eloquently—especially when we recall the ideological turbulence of the 1930s—Blackmur describes, in "A Critic's Job of Work," from *The Double Agent*, the "imaginative skepticism and dramatic irony" that are so invigorating in Plato and Montaigne:

> Is it not that the early Plato always holds conflicting ideas in shifting balance, presenting them in contest and evolution, with victory only the last shift? Is it not that Montaigne is always making room for another idea, and implying always a third for provisional, adjudicating irony? Are not the forms of both men themselves ironic, betraying in its most intimate recesses the duplicity of every thought, pointing it out, so to speak, in the act of self-incrimination, and showing it not paled on a pin but in the buff life? Such an approach, such an attempt at vivid questing, borrowed and no doubt adulterated by our own needs, is the only ra-

tional approach to the multiplication of doctrine and arrogant technologies which fills out the body of critical thinking. Anything else is a succumbing, not an approach.

The approach that Blackmur recommends here equips him to scrutinize other dogmas and doctrines very shrewdly, as in "Humanism and Symbolic Imagination: Notes on Re-reading Irving Babbitt," in *The Lion and the Honeycomb*. But there are limits to what Blackmur counsels, and these emerge, to cite a notable example, in his strictures on the Marxist critic Granville Hicks. "The process of becoming a communist is not the deep obliterating dye of religious conversion; it is the adoption of an additional view which modifies but which ought rather to vitalize than to destroy the existing structure of the mind. Thus the best communists—those whose ideas have most value for society—will be those who claim least for their doctrines." This angled shot at Hicks makes a certain sense, particularly when one remembers the evaluative oddities of Hicks's *The Great Tradition: An Interpretation of American Literature Since the Civil War*. But Blackmur's plea for reasonableness and his ironic restraint led him, in effect, to rebuke Hicks for failing to act like a good liberal. Blackmur cannot really understand someone passionately absorbed in a cause, for his skepticism promotes not only a stringent self-criticism but also an ingrained dubiousness about any form of radical politics. Blackmur is a person interested in politics, but unlike Hicks, he is not a political person. The revolutionary temper is alien to him—which may explain why he seems never to have written about Milton or Blake.

Blackmur learned the scrupulous power of irony, as he indicates, from Plato and Montaigne, but even more from Henry Adams. It is the action of irony that makes the early Blackmur so memorable, and it is its disappearance in much of his later writing—above all in the final installments of his book on Adams—that registers his decline or, at the least, exposes his journeying into territory where irony is not adequately expressed.

Adams, one might say, was Blackmur's intellectual and imaginative patron, and he is richly present in the critic's career from beginning to end. His book on Adams, assembled into an almost-coherent form by Veronica Makowsky and published in 1980, shows Blackmur at his best and his worst and enables us to see striking examples of him as both formalist interpreter and cultural commentator and theoretician. Blackmur labored on this project for most of his professional life; it was to be his masterpiece, but he failed to finish it. So doubtful, in fact, did the book's publication finally come to seem that Blackmur's colleagues and acquaintances began to regard the enterprise as a kind of farce, joking about the advances that he had received from his publisher and the deadlines he missed. It is apparent, however, that this was no ordinary scholarly work. In examining and meditating upon Adams, Blackmur saw reflections of himself, and he used his subject as an opportunity to locate terms for his own life and brood upon their meanings. He felt a kinship with Adams's sense of failure, loss, and painful awareness of being "outside" society's institutions. He was also drawn to Adams's vivid, eccentric irony and notions of "distance" between the truly intelligent observer and the events that occur around him.

In her introduction, Makowsky helps us to grasp the scale of Blackmur's enterprise. According to the revised outline that Blackmur assembled in the late 1940s, his study would divide into two sections. The first would begin with Adams's education at Harvard and would survey his life and career until the turn of the century, just before the major books, *Mont-Saint-Michel and Chartres* (1904) and the *Education of Henry Adams* (1907), were composed. The second section would consist of a detailed analysis of both texts, with additional commentary on Adams's other writings and theory of history, and it would conclude with a biographical review of Adams's final years.

As Makowsky has organized it, the book basically focuses on the second section of Blackmur's projected work. It opens with "The Expense of Greatness: Three Emphases on Henry Adams," a brief general account that first appeared in the *Virginia Quarterly Review* in 1936 and that Blackmur included in *The Expense of Greatness* and *The Lion and the Honeycomb*. The next part of the book is titled "The Virgin and the Dynamo" and is more than 250 pages in length. Most of this material appears here for the first time and provides us with Blackmur's interpretation of Adams's masterpieces. Blackmur's manuscript for this section breaks off in mid sentence, however, and at several points in the text, he refers to chapters that either he did not complete or that his editor has omitted. Part three, "King Richard's Prison Song" (the title is taken from a medieval lyric that Adams loved), is also mostly new, though a section of it appeared in the *Kenyon Review* in 1940

and was reprinted in *A Primer of Ignorance*. The book's fourth and final part, never published before, is titled "At Rock Creek: Adams: Images: Eidolon." It is six pages long and represents Blackmur's attempt to imagine Adams's meditations at his wife's grave side, next to the monument sculpted by Augustus Saint-Gaudens.

*Henry Adams* is clearly something of a patchwork affair: it supplies, to borrow a phrase Blackmur used about his *Eleven Essays in the European Novel,* grand "fragments of an unfinished ruin." It is also yet another—and perhaps the greatest—example of that odd modern critical genre, the "great book" that the critic never wrote or left incomplete. One thinks of T. S. Eliot's study of seventeenth-century poetry, F. R. Leavis's systematic account of "the elements of practical criticism," Kenneth Burke's monograph on Samuel Taylor Coleridge, and John Crowe Ransom's rendering of "aesthetic theory," "The Third Moment." Our sense of Blackmur's grappling with his "great book" and his obsessive inquiries into Adams's life and work grow all the more keen when we realize that even at 350 pages, *Henry Adams* leaves out much that Blackmur wrote about his subject over the span of many years. He left among his unpublished papers essays that deal with Adams's nine-volume *History of the United States of America During the Administrations of Jefferson and Madison* (1889-1891), the journalistic writings, and the biographies of Albert Gallatin and John Randolph. Also omitted are three essays on "Foreign Affairs, 1895-1908," one of which appeared in the *Hudson Review* in 1952. Nor does the book include Blackmur's essay on Adams's novels, *Democracy* (1880) and *Esther* (1884); his review of Marian Adams's letters; his comparative study of Henry and Brooks Adams; and his treatment of Adams's letters to his niece, Louisa Hooper. The amount of material on Adams that Blackmur produced is quite astonishing, and the extent of his absorption in this single writer seems unparalleled in modern criticism.

Much of Blackmur's commentary in *Henry Adams* is shrewd, as he traces the patterns, imagery, and formal systems of the texts. No one has exhibited more distinctly the complex symbolic structures that Adams created in *Mont-Saint-Michel and Chartres* and *The Education of Henry Adams.* Denis Donoghue has referred to Blackmur's criticism as a "supplication of texts," and this seems especially true of the writing on Adams. Indeed, Blackmur might even be seen as engaged in his own act of re-creation, as he strives to reshape and illuminate the great symbols of the Virgin and the Dynamo in his own prose. Even when Blackmur is merely repeating commonplaces, he states them with just the right feeling for tone and nuance, as when he observes that Adams "had not the faith, only the apprehension of its need which made him struggle toward it all his life." Blackmur also astutely notes Adams's "doubts" about his audience but his ultimate "faith" in his symbols.

Blackmur has often been celebrated for his ability to demonstrate how words are used in literary texts, but he is also alert to the power generated in texts by what a writer leaves unspoken. For example, though Blackmur never managed to deal at length with Adams's response to his wife's suicide in 1885, he does comment in detail on the "gap" in the *Education of Henry Adams* between the twentieth and twenty-first chapters. This gap excludes from Adams's life story the years of his marriage, his wife's death, and his attempt to recover from the shock of the blow. "In leaving out twenty years," Blackmur observes, Adams

> is not only making an enormous understatement; he is bringing to bear on all his later chapters the force of the unaccountable—the sum of all that has happened which is not recounted—by means of deliberately inexplicit or only partly explicit symbols. The feeling is thus thicker than the prose: the meaning continues after the words have stopped because it was active before the words began. We have thus a recapitulation, here and there in these chapters, of material that was never given in the book and yet refers both the reader and Adams to it with all the more strength because of its deliberate disguise as the shared unaccountable.

Adams himself had characterized his early writing as showing "a feeling for form; an instinct of exclusion." That is, his texts receive their major intensities from the facts and feelings not expressed in words. Among the critics of the *Education of Henry Adams*, Blackmur is exceptional in perceiving that Adams's exclusions inform what is explicitly "said." Blackmur teaches the reader to see that the form of the book is permeated by Adams's sense of the formless, chaotic, and inexplicable. His deepest feelings are expressed not in words but through conspicuous omissions and silences that exist precisely at what

might have been, in a different book, its most verbally active and fluent part.

Blackmur's kinship with Adams exacts penalties, however. As often happens when F. R. Leavis deals with D. H. Lawrence or Lionel Trilling with Matthew Arnold, Blackmur is not always able to separate himself from his valorized subject and preserve a critical detachment from the texts he is analyzing. *Henry Adams* manifests countless instances of profound critical intelligence and skill, yet it also lapses frequently into excessive paraphrase and summary, dwells self-satisfyingly in solemn cadences, and, most seriously of all, shows a disturbing lack of judgment and balance. In the best of Blackmur's early essays on modern poetry, he aims to distinguish the good from the bad and strives to highlight and evaluate basic techniques, ideas, and structures. "What we really ask of our criticism," he once remarked, "is that it be critical, that it should seize the central point of any subject, and discuss that with all the learning, logic, and insight it can command." In *Henry Adams,* unfortunately, Blackmur appears so unironically enmeshed in his subject that he can propose critical judgments only if he is certain he can then diminish or explain away their impact.

At one point, for instance, Blackmur concedes that "there is a little plain nonsense" in Adams's symbols, "a little hoc est corpus turned hocus pocus." But instead of taking hold of this issue, Blackmur sidesteps it by maintaining, in his next sentence, "Yet nonsense has a right in one's symbols; for there is nonsense at the center of the major as well as the minor contradictions in man's mind." How much "nonsense" is contained in *Mont-Saint-Michel and Chartres* and the *Education of Henry Adams*? How much does it damage the books? Does its presence reveal something about the tragic self-imprisonment of Adams's mind in his later years? These are the questions that Blackmur would seem obligated to answer, but he settles instead for wordplay ("sense" and "non-sense") and universalizes the problem in such a way that he is not required to confront it.

Even more disquieting is Blackmur's adaptation of Adams's terms as a means to interpret the modern world. When he does this, his attitudes take on a peculiar tone, and his observations are hard to follow, let alone fathom. "To preserve the absolute values in the new relation" was Adams's "true problem," Blackmur states:

and he was right to insist on it even if his view of the new relations was prejudiced and erroneous. It would have altered only his exaggerations and nothing of his judgments, had he seen how the population problem of India and Southeast Asia under the impetus of a mild injection of artificial energy in the absence of western resources suggests the need of a mechanization of sex there. Even war, in itself, no longer cuts population much in areas dominated by new forces, and its effect on race in Russia is doubtful. Further, inertia of race among the decimated Jews seems to have intensified. Thus Adams was righter than he might have thought.

Here and elsewhere in *Henry Adams,* Blackmur criticizes or corrects Adams only to progress to new reasons for admiration—"Adams was righter than he might have thought." As Makowsky observes, much of Blackmur's work on Adams was done in the 1940s and 1950s, during the period when the war raged in Europe and the horrifying truth of the Holocaust became public knowledge. These facts of history make Blackmur's generalizations all the more insensitive. To refer to the "decimated Jews" in such a shallow fashion and to leave unexamined the question of Adams's notorious anti-Semitism, are failures of critical judgment and responsibility. They exemplify ironic mannerisms that lack the self-awareness and sense of others that true irony furnishes.

It is because *Henry Adams* is both powerfully insightful and terribly blind that final assessments about it prove difficult to make. Depending upon one's point of view (Adams once said that "one sees what one brings"), Blackmur's book will seem an achievement of the highest order or a disheartening illustration of the ways in which a critic's ambition and self-dramatizing sympathy for his subject interfere with and forestall good criticism. Possibly Blackmur might have eliminated the failings in *Henry Adams* if he had been able to revise and restructure it. But the problems in this book tell us something important about Blackmur's criticism taken as a whole. His critical writing combines an extraordinary responsiveness to formal structures with an inability or unwillingness to really absorb and understand what they contain.

As many sections of *Henry Adams* demonstrate and as his later work generally testifies, Blackmur is interested in ideology, politics, inter-

national affairs, and related matters. He is, in this respect, much more than a mere formalist. His efforts to get beyond formalism are not often successful, however, both because they are filtered through Adams's terms and because they are themselves "formalist" in their orientation. Though Blackmur does address issues and ideas, and not just technique and style, his analyses invariably take a "formal" direction. As his vexing remark about the "decimated Jews" indicates, his commentaries on real-world events are often highly abstract, as though these events are formal patterns or pieces of an intricate design that the critic may fondly contemplate. Blackmur is generally concerned not to explain what values, beliefs, and attitudes *are,* but how they *function in texts*—how, that is, they serve to undermine textual structures or make them more coherent.

John Crowe Ransom, interestingly enough, made exactly this point, with unsettled fascination, in his 1953 review of *Language as Gesture.* He found Blackmur's work unduly technical and removed from connection with the world. Blackmur invariably examines poetry, says Ransom, "along linguistic lines, procedural lines, strategical lines; whatever may be the gravity of the content. There is no ideological emphasis; the social or religious ideals are looked at shrewdly, but they are appraised for their function within the work; even though they may be ideas from which, at the very moment, out in the world of action, the issues of life and death are hung."

No sooner does one assent to this judgment, however, than one feels obliged to qualify it. In several essays in *The Lion and the Honeycomb* and *A Primer of Ignorance*—essays that both impressed and baffled Blackmur's sponsors at the Rockefeller Foundation—Blackmur deals with "the economy of the American writer," the "American literary expatriate," and other social and cultural topics. He discusses them in a thoughtful manner that his formalist predilections do not distort. Blackmur is a complicated, even an enigmatic figure, and in summarizing his achievement and career, one has to be prepared to qualify even those judgments of him that seem most fundamentally correct. Like his hero, Adams, Blackmur appears anxious to avoid settling into a single role or position, and he likes to parry his readers' attempts to place him as one type of critic or other.

There is also a good deal of uncertainty and contradiction in Blackmur's work. Indeed one sometimes feels a spirit of anarchy (or maybe

*R. P. Blackmur in Egypt, 1953 (photograph by Daniel Seltzer)*

one should say, evangelical fervor) in the body of his writings that unnerves the apparent order. Blackmur recognizes that formalist studies of a writer's craftsmanship suit his talents, and he keeps returning to what he calls in *New Criticism in the United States* the primacy of "formal and technical" criticism. Yet he also feels constrained by a criticism that binds him to the words on the page, perceiving that such a procedure misses art's eruptive energy and social impact. Sometimes, slighting the social himself, he seeks to devise a more elaborate style and casts himself as devotee of the religion of art. When Blackmur acts as a high priest of criticism, indulging his tendency to pontificate, his essays flaunt an "eddying standstill" (to borrow a phrase from his poem "The Dead Ride Fast") of aestheticism that badly imitates Walter Pater and Oscar Wilde. But this is only part of the story, for Blackmur's sacramental essays sit in his collections alongside sensible probings of politics, culture, and intellectual life. In the latter work, Blackmur is a valuable commentator on society, not an obsessively stylized escapist from it. Here, his writing is marked by a finely restrained and deftly modulated passion that is evident, for instance, in his definition of "the intellectual" in *A Primer of Ignorance*:

> He is committed for the purposes of reaching understanding of the grounds of action and of finding a frame for decision, or alter-

native decisions. It is his obligation to see what is likely to happen and to be prepared to deal with–to respond to–what does actually happen. He will therefore keep himself a little outside the avowed interests of the society–or the institution–which he serves. His true allegiance will be to the contentious, speculative, imaginative nature of the mind itself and to the dark, problematical, reversible nature of the experience with which the mind deals. That is to say, his allegiance is to the whole enterprise of the mind, and far from being remote from it, it will move him from both without and within. That is why he will be skeptical of any particular commitment and will be rebellious to any attempt to make conformity a simple or narrow thing. Like Dante, he will be rebellious to merely social or political authority. Like John of Salisbury, he will know that rebellion to tyranny is obedience to God. Like the young Jefferson, he will say that if he has to go to heaven in a party he would rather not go at all.

Perhaps it is most accurate to conclude by saying that Blackmur sought to be a European intellectual rather than an American literary critic. He wished to enlarge the lucid irony and reasoned detachment of the critic's performance into the intellectual's skeptical relation–involved but unaffiliated–to history. Such an intellectual–

one thinks, for instance, of Walter Benjamin and Roland Barthes–writes essays on whatever subject grips him at the moment: for the intellectual, the accidental as well as the momentous thing is meaningful and merits investigation. The goal of the intellectual is to speak for the mind of a continent, culture, and tradition, and the hazard is to speak for the solipsistic preoccupations of one's own mind only. Another way to formulate (and extend) this point is to remark that Blackmur, like even more lofty precursors such as Emerson, Carlyle, Ruskin, and Nietzsche, was drawn not only to social and political diagnostics but also to the exhortatory mode of cultural seer and sibyl. Like these writers, he cultivated a style both oracular and aphoristic. In *A Primer of Ignorance*, for example, he makes the pronouncement that "Whitman wrote *Leaves of Grass*, Melville *Moby Dick; or The Whale*. One is the rush, the other the mighty effort to organize the rush." In another comparison of authors, he says: "In Auden it is the rugged mass that just escapes the habit of form. In Tennyson, the habit of verse keeps warm the inner form." And he finds that "Byron is a kind of sensorium of attitude, Williams a kind of omnibus of sensation." Blackmur's severely foreshortened contrasts will seem splendid or foolish depending upon how much you sympathize with his mannered acts of fervent compression and how much labor you are willing to expend to unpack them.

Witnessing Blackmur in this style–gnomic, meditative, theatrical–enables us to perceive why his early criticism, wonderful though it is, was too limited to express what haunted and allured him. His later writings strain toward challenges he could not consistently meet, succeeding sometimes but more often failing, Adams-like, in a cryptic mixture of fantasy and wisdom, whimsy and prophecy.

**Bibliographies:**

Carlos Baker, "R. P. Blackmur: A Checklist," *Princeton University Library Chronicle*, 3 (April 1942): 99-106;

Allen Tate, *Sixty American Poets, 1896-1944*, revised edition (Washington, D.C.: Library of Congress, 1954), pp. 15-16;

Gerald Pannick, "R. P. Blackmur: A Bibliography," *Bulletin of Bibliography and Magazine Notes*, 31 (October-December 1974): 165-169.

**Biography:**

Russell Fraser, *A Mingled Yarn: The Life of R. P. Blackmur* (New York: Harcourt Brace Jovanovich, 1981).

**References:**

Robert Boyers, *R. P. Blackmur: Poet-Critic, Toward a View of Poetic Objects* (Columbia: University of Missouri Press, 1980);

Cleanth Brooks, *The Well-Wrought Urn: Studies in the Structure of Poetry* (New York: Reynal & Hitchcock, 1947);

Denis Donoghue, "R. P. Blackmur and *The Double Agent*," *Sewanee Review*, 91 (Fall 1983): 634-643;

Robert Fitzgerald, *Enlarging the Change: The Princeton Seminars in Literary Criticism, 1949-1951* (Boston: Northeastern University Press, 1985);

Richard Foster, *The New Romantics: A Reappraisal of the New Criticism* (Bloomington: Indiana University Press, 1962), pp. 83-106;

Joseph Frank, "R. P. Blackmur: The Later Phase," in *The Widening Gyre: Crisis and Mastery in Modern Literature* (New Brunswick, N.J.: Rutgers University Press, 1963), pp. 229-251;

Russell Fraser, "My Two Masters," *Sewanee Review*, 91 (Fall 1983): 614-633;

Fraser, "R. P. Blackmur: America's Best Critic," *Virginia Quarterly Review*, 57 (Autumn 1981): 569-593;

Fraser, "R. P. Blackmur: The Politics of a New Critic," *Sewanee Review*, 87 (Fall 1979): 557-572;

Geoffrey Hartman, *Criticism in the Wilderness: The Study of Literature Today* (New Haven: Yale University Press, 1980);

Granville Hicks, *The Great Tradition: An Interpretation of American Literature Since the Civil War*, revised edition (Chicago: Quadrangle Books, 1969);

Laurence B. Holland, "A Grammar of Assent," *Sewanee Review*, 88 (Spring 1980): 260-266;

Stanley Edgar Hyman, *The Armed Vision: A Study in the Methods of Modern Literary Criticism*, revised edition (New York: Vintage Books, 1955), pp. 197-236;

Interview with Edward Said, *Diacritics*, 6 (Fall 1976): 30-47;

Alfred Kazin, *On Native Grounds: An Interpretation of Modern American Prose Literature* (New York: Harcourt, Brace & World, 1942);

F. R. Leavis, *The Great Tradition* (London: Chatto & Windus, 1948);

A. Walton Litz, "Literary Criticism," in *The Har-*

*vard Guide to Contemporary Writing,* edited by Daniel Hoffman (Cambridge: Harvard University Press, 1979), pp. 51-83;

Litz and Lawrence L. Lipking, eds., *Modern Literary Criticism, 1900-1970* (New York: Atheneum, 1972);

John Crowe Ransom, *The New Criticism* (Norfolk: New Directions, 1941);

Ransom, "The Shores of Criticism," *Partisan Review,* 20 (1953): 108-111;

Delmore Schwartz, "The Critical Method of R. P. Blackmur," in *Selected Essays of Delmore Schwartz,* edited by D. A. Dike and D. H. Zucker (Chicago: University of Chicago Press, 1970), pp. 351-359;

Walter Sutton, *Modern American Criticism* (Englewood Cliffs, N.J.: Prentice-Hall, 1963), pp. 135-147;

Grant Webster, *The Republic of Letters: A History of American Postwar Literary Opinion* (Baltimore: Johns Hopkins University Press, 1979), pp. 149-161;

René Wellek, "R. P. Blackmur Re-Examined," *Southern Review,* 7 (Summer 1971): 825-845.

**Papers:**
The most important collection of material by and pertaining to Blackmur is located in Princeton University Library. There are many other relevant collections, the largest of which include the holdings at the American Academy of Arts and Letters, New York; the Beinecke Rare Book and Manuscript Library, Yale University; the University of Delaware; the Houghton Library, Harvard University; and the University of Illinois Archives.

# Randolph Bourne

*(30 May 1886-23 December 1918)*

Casey Blake
*Indiana University*

BOOKS: *Arbitration and International Politics,* International Conciliation, no. 70 (New York: American Association for International Conciliation, 1913);

*Youth and Life* (Boston & New York: Houghton Mifflin / London: Constable, 1913);

*The Tradition of War,* International Conciliation, no. 79 (New York: American Association for International Conciliation, 1914);

*The Gary Schools* (Boston & New York: Houghton Mifflin, 1916);

*Education and Living* (New York: Century, 1917);

*Untimely Papers,* edited by James Oppenheim (New York: Huebsch, 1919);

*History of a Literary Radical, and Other Essays,* edited by Van Wyck Brooks (New York: Huebsch, 1920);

*The State* (New York: Resistance Press, 1942);

*War and the Intellectuals: Collected Essays, 1915-1919,* edited by Carl Resek (New York: Harper & Row, 1964);

*The World of Randolph Bourne; An Anthology,* edited by Lillian Schlissel (New York: Dutton, 1965);

*The Radical Will: Randolph Bourne, Selected Writings 1911-1918,* edited by Olaf Hansen (New York: Urizen, 1977).

OTHER: *Towards an Enduring Peace; A Symposium of Peace Proposals and Programs, 1914-1916,* compiled by Bourne (New York: American Association for International Conciliation, 1916);

Maurice Larrouy, as René Milon, *Vagabonds of the Sea,* translated by Bourne (New York: Dutton, 1919).

Randolph Bourne was a spokesperson for the Greenwich Village "Little Renaissance" of the mid 1910s and the foremost intellectual opponent of American intervention in World War I. Writing in a self-consciously prophetic style, Bourne gave voice to other young intellectuals who saw in progressive education, cosmopolitanism, and artistic modernism the means to a radically democratic society. In his critical writings Bourne insisted on the interdependence of culture and politics and sought in both the enrichment of "the good life of personality lived in the environment of the Beloved Community." His hopes for a "Beloved Community" were dashed when liberals and other progressives endorsed President Wilson's war effort, and Bourne turned his fury on John Dewey, the editors of the *New Republic*, and other prowar intellectuals for betraying their roles as social critics and creators of values. Bourne's antiwar essays of 1917-1918 were his greatest achievement; they still stand as a searing indictment of the theory and practice of pragmatic liberalism. Bourne's unrivaled gifts as a cultural critic and polemicist, his steadfast moral opposition to the war, and his early death at age thirty-two in the influenza epidemic of 1918 have subsequently made him an icon of intellectual radicalism. John Dos Passos immortalized Bourne in *1919* as "a tiny twisted unscared ghost in a black cloak" haunting New York with the refrain, "War is the health of the State."

Randolph Silliman Bourne was born on 30 May 1886 in Bloomfield, New Jersey, the first child of Charles and Sarah Barrett Bourne. Deformed at birth by a forceps delivery that wrenched and scarred his face, Bourne suffered spinal tuberculosis four years later which left him a hunchback and a dwarf. Bourne wrote eloquently of his disability in an anonymous essay on "The Handicapped" for the *Atlantic*, lamenting that he lived a precarious life between health and helplessness. "I was truly in the world, but not of the world," he explained; and his early sense of difference undoubtedly informed his mature stance as an intellectual determined to effect changes through an uncompromising criticism rather than direct political activism. His father's drinking problems and business failures left Bourne in the care of his mother, who seems to have been bewildered by her intellectually precocious but physically disabled son. At an early age Bourne chafed at the genteel social life of middle-class Bloomfield and sought other outlets in literature, music, and the radicalism of Henry George. When Bourne graduated from high school in 1903 his uncle, who supported Sarah Bourne and her four children, refused to pay for Randolph to attend Princeton University. As a result, he spent six years working at odd jobs, including one at a small shop for the manufacture of player-

piano rolls that he later described in an essay on economic exploitation. Finally in 1909 Bourne received a full tuition scholarship at Columbia University, which permitted him to explore his growing interests in social science and literary criticism.

"College furnishes an ideal environment," Bourne wrote, "where the things at which a man handicapped like myself can succeed really count. One's self-respect can begin to grow like a weed." Bourne flourished at Columbia, attracting a circle of friends who looked up to him as a prophet of a modern youth culture and encouraged his literary talents. Meanwhile the new developments in philosophy and social thought championed by such Columbia scholars as John Dewey, Franz Boas, Charles Beard, and James Harvey Robinson confirmed Bourne's radicalism, which now tended less to George's agrarianism than to a quasi-Marxist socialism. The intellectual and social milieu of Columbia provided the impetus for Bourne's first essays in cultural criticism for the *Columbia Monthly* and the *Atlantic*, some of which were later collected and published in 1913 as Bourne's book, *Youth and Life*. When Bourne graduated from Columbia in the spring of 1913 with a travel fellowship that would take him to Europe the following year, he was already recognized as a leader of those young intellectuals impatient with the relics of Victorian moralism.

Like Walter Lippmann's *A Preface to Politics* (1914), *Youth and Life* combined political radicalism with insights from Nietzsche and Freud to argue for an American cultural revolution and a regenerated American democracy. Bourne's position in *Youth and Life* anticipated by over a half century the claim that "the personal is political." Bourne drew on his own predicament—as a disabled person, a marginal intellectual, and a youthful rebel against political and cultural conventions—to express that of other young intellectuals and professionals in search of a fulfilling career and a meaningful personal identity. Unlike H. L. Mencken and other debunkers of "Puritanism," Bourne did not deride the Victorian cults of family, region, and religion as confining ideologies that stifled individual freedom. Rather he attacked these staples of the genteel tradition for their failure to sustain an alternative moral and artistic standard to the values of a commercial civilization. The doctrine of "self-reliance" had become a travesty in an age of corporate bureaucracies, Bourne claimed, at the same time that liberal Protestantism capitulated to the demands of

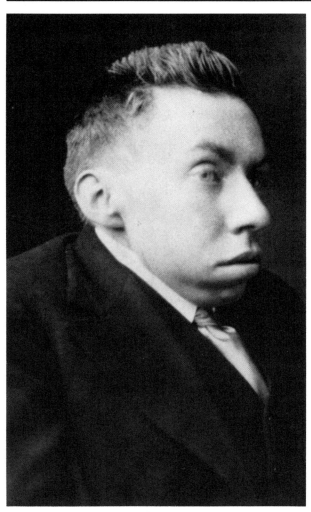

*Randolph Bourne*

*Nineteen-sixteen photograph (courtesy of the Rare Book and
Manuscript Library, Columbia University)*

the powerful. It was not enough, for Bourne, to
condemn the sentimental culture of late-
Victorian America as anachronistic. Young intellectuals had to formulate an ethos of their own,
one hardy enough to nourish egalitarian values
in an industrial capitalist society.

Bourne believed that the democratization of
public life first required a new orientation to personal life. He expresses this idea in *Youth and Life*
in a variety of guises: "the experimental life,"
"the excitement of friendship," "the life of
irony," and in the concept of "personality." In all

of these concepts Bourne returned again and
again to the paradox of living "in the world, but
not of the world" that he had confronted in his
essay on "The Handicapped." Bourne delighted
in the spontaneous give-and-take of his college
friendships and looked to the mutual interests
and shared affection of such relationships to enable "personality" to achieve full expression. Yet,
at the same time, Bourne's essays and letters reveal an ambivalence about such ties, as he found
himself torn between his longings for community
and his fears that group membership would stifle
his critical independence. Against the appeal of
friendship Bourne balanced "the life of irony."
Ironic intellectuals would achieve "perpetual
youth" by maintaining an antagonism between
the utopian possibilities of unfettered "personality" and the realities of social life. "Things as
they are," Bourne wrote, "thrown against the background of things as they ought to be–this is the ironist's vision."

*Youth and Life* established Bourne's reputation as a cultural critic and herald of the emerging young intelligentsia. It also introduced the
major elements of Bourne's life work. In these
early essays Bourne developed the prophetic
voice that would become his stylistic trademark.
Viewing the upheavals in modern culture
through the filter of his own personal experience, Bourne gave his search for purpose and fulfillment a meaning for a generation of contemporaries. Bourne's fascination with "personality" both paralleled the rise of a therapeutic
conception of the self as a successor to competitive individualism and rejected such an alternative for a far more radical notion of personal
growth and self-expression. For Bourne the free
development of personality required participation in a fully democratic society, in which citizenship flourished within a community of friends.
*Youth and Life*'s uneasy pairing of friendship and
irony–of loving communion and critical distance–
was Bourne's first step toward the "Beloved Community" that would prove the central vision of
his critical career.

The Columbia fellowship that took Bourne
to Europe in 1913-1914 allowed him to explore
sympathetic currents in European politics, culture, and social thought. Like Henry Adams and
other turn-of-the-century American intellectuals,
Bourne admired the "organicism" of French culture which he attributed to the tenacity of Catholic, preindustrial values in the modern age. But
Bourne was also drawn to Germany's experi-

ments in municipal socialism and urban planning which confirmed his progressive inclinations toward social efficiency and public administration. The trip ended on a dark note, however, as Bourne witnessed the beginnings of Europe's rush to a war that would eventually overwhelm both the organic community he treasured in France and the progressive politics he witnessed in German cities.

Bourne returned to New York in the fall of 1914 and joined the staff of a newly formed magazine, the *New Republic,* as a contributor on educational and cultural issues. Although Bourne always felt estranged from the magazine's inner circle, his writing for the *New Republic* placed him at the center of intellectual progressivism in the United States. In effect Bourne became a disciple and popularizer of John Dewey's philosophy of pragmatism and theory of educational reform. The books that grew out of his writing for the magazine, *The Gary Schools* (1916) and *Education and Living* (1917), drew heavily on Dewey's ideas, as Bourne promoted progressive education as a means to self-expression and democratic renewal.

Readers of Bourne's lyrical essays from *Youth and Life* must have found *The Gary Schools* a surprisingly dull book. Despite his enthusiasm for the progressive school system in Gary, Indiana, and his obvious admiration for William Wirt, the city's Deweyite school superintendent who had written the introduction to the book, Bourne's writing remained dry and plodding. The book quickly became a primer for progressive educational reformers, but Bourne's talents as a polemicist and ironist were wasted on its outlines of Wirt's "platoon system" of rotating classes and activities.

*Education and Living,* a collection of some of Bourne's *New Republic* articles, was a more representative guide to Bourne's newfound faith in pragmatism and progressive education. Yet the book also revealed fundamental ambiguities in Bourne's thinking about cultural change which would only be resolved under the pressure of World War I. Like Dewey, the author of *Education and Living* was uncertain about the appropriate relationship between the school and its surrounding environment. Bourne sought to foster in students an attitude of critical inquiry and independent thought that would guide them in the democratic renovation of American society. Along with his friend Van Wyck Brooks, Bourne railed against the Arnoldian "cult of the best" in genteel culture and urged educators to promote the creation and appreciation of a native American art. As in Brooks's *America's Coming-of-Age* (1915), Bourne's contempt for "highbrow" parochialism reflected his belief that genteel pieties only reinforced artificial conventions while leaving everyday realities unchanged. The alternative was not to celebrate "lowbrow" practicality, Brooks and Bourne agreed, but to encourage an indigenous, democratic culture that would equip Americans with the intellectual and artistic resources to control their own lives. "Indigenous style is the only art that really means anything," Bourne wrote. "Out of an education in taste will grow creative art as a flower from rich soil."

At the same time, however, Bourne often agreed with Dewey that schools had to reflect the changes in culture and social organization resulting from the industrial revolution. In embracing this aspect of Dewey's progressivism, Bourne's educational essays promised a culture as efficiently managed and administered as the new corporations of industrial America. The most ambitious statement of this technocratic tendency in Bourne's thought was his essay "A Moral Equivalent for Universal Military Service," collected in *War and the Intellectuals: Collected Essays, 1915-1919* (1964), where he called for a two-year period of compulsory education for young people in "flying squadrons" dedicated to cultural improvement. Under the command of "that new type of teacher-engineer-community worker that our best schools are already producing," Bourne's cultural army would remake the United States in the image of the progressive school—which would itself adopt the specialization of labor introduced with the factory system. "I have a picture of a host of eager young missionaries swarming over the land," he wrote, "spreading the health knowledge, the knowledge of domestic science, of gardening, of tastefulness, that they have learned in school."

Ironically it was in Bourne's least political essays from this period that the ideas he would later elaborate in his antiwar essays first found expression. While many of his articles on education and social thought for the *New Republic* were in keeping with that magazine's commitment to a politics of professional administration, Bourne's writings on literature and national community pointed the way to the communitarian radicalism that lay behind his attacks on prowar liberalism in 1917-1918. In these essays and reviews Bourne charged that the Anglophilic tastes of American literary critics had obscured the native intellectual tradition of Emerson, Thoreau, Whitman, Twain, and William James. The failure of critics to cultivate that tradition had meant that official American culture was essentially British, marginalizing not only the achievements of the New England renaissance and its heirs but the contributions of immigrant cultures as well.

In "Trans-national America," published in the *Atlantic* in July 1916, Bourne made his case for a truly American cultural community, one that would free his fellow white Protestants from their dependence on British standards while integrating immigrants and racial minorities into the mainstream of national life. This classic statement of Bourne's ideal of a "Beloved Community" followed up on his early treatment of irony and friendship in *Youth and Life,* but now he grounded his heterogeneous community of interdependent personalities in a more durable terrain than that of Columbia's student bohemianism. Bourne called for a cosmopolitan federation of cultural traditions as a democratic alternative to the nationalistic militarism invoked by conservatives and the "centrifugal, anarchical" tendencies released by a commercialized mass culture. "America is coming to be, not a nationality," he wrote, "but a trans-nationality, a weaving back and forth, with the other lands, of many threads of all sizes and colors."

Bourne was neither a simple cultural pluralist nor a romantic enthusiast of folk cultures. He placed great emphasis on the need for a new intelligentsia, including young people from immigrant and working-class backgrounds, to articulate the common values of the country's many subcultures. Such an intelligentsia would strive to create democratically the "impelling integrating force" that the Victorian bourgeoisie had tried to impose on American society as a whole. An organic culture would flourish in the United States not by harking back to a collective memory of the past—as Bourne believed was the case in France—nor by the expert leadership of cultural administrators, but by dedication to a cooperative enterprise. "All our idealisms must be those of future social goals in which all can participate, the good life of personality lived in the environment of the Beloved Community."

Bourne's "trans-nationalism" marked a significant step beyond the Deweyite enthusiasms of *Education and Living*. While still sharing Dewey's theory of mind and knowledge as simultaneously shaped by and acting upon their environment, Bourne gave a highly subjectivist reading to Dewey's principle that a democratic culture must derive from lived experience. Far more than Dewey, Bourne stressed the importance of aesthetic and intuitive consciousness, of moral values and utopian ideals, as elements of a critical mind capable of apprehending and transforming industrial society. He also returned to the underlying assumption of *Youth and Life* that a revolution in culture was necessary to insure that institutional reforms made fundamental changes in everyday life. This renewed attention to art, morality, and culture meant that Bourne sharply differentiated the prospects for communitarian democracy from the centralizing tendencies at work in industry and politics. The organization of men and women in the state and factory, Bourne was coming to understand, had nothing in common with his own project of creating a "Beloved Community." An oppositional culture would have to challenge the dominant trends in industrial life, emphasizing the capacities for reflection, criticism, and independent action endangered by the new authority of technical expertise. Such a culture needed intellectuals to articulate "a restless, controversial criticism of current ideas," not adopt the stance of experts or of a romanticized proletariat. "The only way by which middle-class radicalism can serve," Bourne argued, "is by being fiercely and concentratedly intellectual."

These new currents in Bourne's thought came to a head in the polemical antiwar essays of 1917 that he wrote for the *Seven Arts*, the little magazine of culture and politics edited by his friends Brooks, Waldo Frank, and James Oppenheim. Increasingly at odds with the prowar progressivism of the *New Republic*, which he accused of subordinating art and literature to public policy, Bourne found the *Seven Arts* the appropriate forum for his most sophisticated critical writings. In "The War and the Intellectuals," "A War Diary," and "Twilight of Idols," collected in *The Radical Will: Randolph Bourne, Selected Writings, 1911-1918* (1977), Bourne challenged not only the assumptions of Wilsonian foreign policy but the political stance of the liberal intelligentsia as well. The war was not simply a case of mistaken means (total war) for a given end (a world safe for democracy), in Bourne's mind. It represented the culmination of developments in the histories of the state, popular culture, and modern intellectuals that now threatened to destroy all the achievements of the "Little Renaissance" and its revolt against Victorianism. "The whole era has been spiritually wasted," he raged.

Bourne's distinction between a "Beloved Community" arrived at through democratic association and the coercive cohesion of the nation-state echoed throughout his antiwar essays. The intellectuals' refusal to encourage a popular cosmopolitanism had left ordinary people helpless in the face of wartime mobilization and "Red scares." The debunking of Victorianism had discredited values, thereby encouraging resignation and acquiescence in the sham patriotism of the state. What was new about total war, Bourne observed, was that the state's capacities for mass mobilization rendered obsolete the need for any popular outcry for war. "The government of a modern organized plutocracy does not have to ask whether the people want to fight or understand what they are fighting for," he wrote in "A War Diary," "only whether they will tolerate fighting."

Intellectuals were especially to blame for this state of affairs, Bourne held, in which the absence of popular alternatives in culture and politics complemented the organized onslaught of official opinion. In their fascination with technical achievements, progressive intellectuals had rushed to the aid of the war effort, choosing action over critical thinking. "The American intellectual class, having failed to make the higher syntheses, regresses to ideas that can issue in quick, simplified action," he wrote in "The War and the Intellectuals." The progressives' concern with reuniting theory and practice, ideas and experience, meant in reality the abdication of the intellectual's vocation. "Thought becomes an easy rationalization of what is actually going on or what is to happen tomorrow.... The thinker dances with reality."

Bourne attributed the intellectuals' default to three interrelated causes: their training in the new research universities that had replaced the classical curriculum of the New England college with specialized studies in the social sciences; the coming to power of intellectuals as an elite class of administrators and experts; and the widespread influence of Dewey's pragmatism among members of that class. It was this last charge that marked the distance Bourne had traveled from the progressivism of his educational writings. He now condemned the pragmatic notion of adjusting knowledge to experience for failing to explain how such an approach might generate creative values critical of their social environment. Dewey's educational methods still appealed to Bourne, but outside the classroom he found

Dewey's vagueness about the relationship between scientific means and ethical ends increasingly disturbing. "Vision must constantly outshoot technique," he countered in "Twilight of Idols," his most explicit indictment of Dewey's philosophy. Intellectuals had to uphold the primacy of vision and act as "value-creators," even if that meant inviting the charge of acting irresponsibly in a time of national danger.

To fulfill their responsibility as intellectuals, Bourne insisted, critics would have to act in socially irresponsible ways, becoming "thorough malcontents" guided by a "skeptical, malicious, desperate, ironical mood." Above all else they had to sustain the tension between their ideals and social reality, refusing to allow the "premature crystallization" of thought as an apology for the existing order. "If the American intellectual class rivets itself to a 'liberal' philosophy that perpetuates the old errors, there will then be need for 'democrats' whose task will be to divide, confuse, disturb, keep the intellectual waters constantly in motion to prevent any such ice from ever forming."

Bourne's wartime essays suggest that he was about to undertake a project to formulate exactly that body of oppositional values he condemned liberals for ignoring. His death on 23 December 1918 of influenza cut short that project and ended the career of a thinker who would undoubtedly have played a leading role in the intellectual debates of the 1920s, 1930s, and after. Van Wyck Brooks speculated that, at the time of his death, Bourne was already turning back from political to cultural issues. Bourne's interest in Brooks's work on Twain and on the need for a "usable past" and his enthusiasm for the "unanisme" of French novelist Jules Romains and his followers may confirm Brooks's suspicions. But it is unlikely that Bourne would have given up political and social considerations altogether. On the contrary many of his posthumously published essays, a number of them collected in Olaf Hansen's *The Radical Will,* show him still grappling with the complex relationship between culture and power in the modern age. A fragmentary essay on "The State" traced the ascendancy of the centralized American state, borrowing heavily from Charles Beard's interpretation of American history. Another such fragment, "Old Tyrannies," indicates the depth of Bourne's bitterness over the collapse of his hopes for community in a period of total war. "We live almost entirely a social life, that is, a life as a constituted unit in society," he complained, "rather than a free and personal one." Yet Bourne had not completely lost faith in his "Beloved Community" in the last days of his life. The autobiographical "History of a Literary Radical" pointed to "little pools" of workers and intellectuals and to "intensely self-conscious groups" that might yet renew the promise of a "transnational" culture.

After his death Bourne's legacy was claimed by an array of different critical movements, from the cultural nationalism of Brooks, Frank, and Lewis Mumford to the proletarian literary criticism of Mike Gold and the *New Masses*. Both Mumford and Dwight Macdonald cited Bourne as a precedent for their different positions on American involvement in World War II, and both men echoed him after that war, when they agreed that the war against Nazism had made the United States more totalitarian. The anarchist communalism of Dorothy Day's Catholic Workers and the participatory democracy of the early New Left also claimed Bourne's inheritance, and Bourne's indictment of the liberal intelligentsia later inspired similar critiques of "cold war liberals" by C. Wright Mills, Noam Chomsky, Christopher Lasch, and others. Still, Bourne's influence, like his work, is fragmentary: there is no coherent "Bournean" tradition in American cultural or political criticism. At best, he has been discovered anew by each emerging generation of "malcontents," who have found compelling his vision of democratic community and defense of the critical intellect and have drawn strength from his polemical fire.

**Letters:**
*The Letters of Randolph Bourne: A Comprehensive Edition*, edited by Eric J. Sandeen (Troy, N.Y.: Whitson, 1981).

**Biographies:**
Louis Filler, *Randolph Bourne* (Washington, D.C.: American Council on Public Affairs, 1943);

Sherman Paul, *Randolph Bourne* (Minneapolis: University of Minnesota Press, 1966);

John Adams Moreau, *Randolph Bourne: Legend and Reality* (Washington, D.C.: Public Affairs Press, 1966);

Bruce Clayton, *Forgotten Prophet: The Life of Randolph Bourne* (Baton Rouge: Louisiana State University Press, 1984).

**References:**
Edward Abrahams, *The Lyrical Left: Randolph Bourne, Alfred Stieglitz, and the Origins of Cultural Radicalism in America* (Charlottesville: University Press of Virginia, 1986);

Casey Blake, "Beloved Community: The Cultural Criticism of Randolph Bourne, Van Wyck Brooks, Waldo Frank, and Lewis Mumford," Ph.D. dissertation, University of Rochester, 1987;

Paul F. Bourke, "The Status of Politics 1909-1919: *The New Republic*, Randolph Bourne and Van Wyck Brooks," *American Studies*, 8 (August 1974): 171-202;

Christopher Lasch, *The New Radicalism in America 1889-1963: The Intellectual as a Social Type* (New York: Norton, 1965);

Henry F. May, *The End of American Innocence* (New York: Knopf, 1959);

James R. Vitelli, *Randolph Bourne* (New York: Twayne, 1981).

**Papers:**
Randolph Bourne's papers are collected at the Rare Book and Manuscript Library, Columbia University, New York, and in the Alyse Gregory Papers, Beinecke Rare Book and Manuscript Library, Yale University. Other documents may be found at Princeton University and the Charles Patterson Van Pelt Library at the University of Pennsylvania, Philadelphia.

# Cleanth Brooks

*(16 October 1906-    )*

James J. Sosnoski
*Miami University of Ohio*

SELECTED BOOKS: *The Relation of the Alabama-Georgia Dialect to the Provincial Dialects of Great Britain* (Baton Rouge: Louisiana State University Press, 1935);

*Modern Poetry and the Tradition* (Chapel Hill: University of North Carolina Press, 1939; London: Editions Poetry, 1948);

*The Well Wrought Urn: Studies in the Structure of Poetry* (New York: Reynal & Hitchcock, 1947; London: Dobson, 1949; revised edition, London: Dobson, 1968);

*Modern Rhetoric*, by Brooks and Robert Penn Warren (New York: Harcourt, Brace, 1949);

*Fundamentals of Good Writing: A Handbook of Modern Rhetoric* (New York: Harcourt, Brace, 1950; London: Dobson, 1952);

*Literary Criticism: A Short History*, by Brooks and William K. Wimsatt (New York: Knopf, 1957); part 4, published as *Modern Criticism: A Short History* (London: Routledge & Kegan Paul, 1970);

*The Hidden God; Studies in Hemingway, Faulkner, Yeats, Eliot, and Warren* (New Haven & London: Yale University Press, 1963);

*William Faulkner: The Yoknapatawpha Country* (New Haven: Yale University Press, 1963);

*A Shaping Joy: Studies in the Writer's Craft* (London: Methuen, 1971; New York: Harcourt Brace Jovanovich, 1972);

*William Faulkner: Toward Yoknapatawpha and Beyond* (New Haven & London: Yale University Press, 1978);

*William Faulkner: First Encounters* (New Haven & London: Yale University Press, 1983);

*The Language of the American South*, Mercer University Lamar Memorial Lectures, no. 28 (Athens: University of Georgia Press, 1985).

OTHER: *An Approach to Literature; A Collection of Prose and Verse with Analyses and Discussions*, edited by Brooks, John Thibaut Purser, and Robert Penn Warren (Baton Rouge: Louisiana State University Press, 1936; revised edition, New York: Crofts, 1939);

*Understanding Poetry: An Anthology for College Students*, edited by Brooks and Warren (New York: Holt, 1938; revised and enlarged, 1950);

"The Poem as Organism," in *English Institute Annual 1940*, edited by Rudolf Kirk (New York: Columbia University Press, 1941);

*Understanding Fiction*, edited by Brooks and Warren (New York: Crofts, 1943); abridged as *The Scope of Fiction* (New York: Appleton-Century-Crofts, 1960);

*The Percy Letters*, edited by Brooks and David Nichol Smith, 6 volumes (Baton Rouge: Louisiana State University Press, 1944-1961);

*Understanding Drama*, edited by Brooks and Robert B. Heilman (New York: Holt, 1945; London: Herrap, 1947; enlarged edition, New York: Holt, 1948);

"The New Criticism and Scholarship," in *Twentieth-Century English*, edited by W. S. Knickerbocker (New York: Philosophical Library, 1946), pp. 371-383;

"Literary Criticism," in *English Institute Essays 1946*, edited by James L. Clifford, Kirk, and David Allan Robertson, Jr. (New York: Columbia University Press, 1947), pp. 127-158;

"The Quick and the Dead: A Comment on Humanistic Studies," in *The Humanities: An Appraisal*, edited by Julian Harris (Madison: University of Wisconsin Press, 1950), pp. 1-21;

"Irony as a Principle of Structure," in *Literary Opinion in America: Essays Illustrating the States, Methods, and Problems of Criticism in the United States in the Twentieth Century*, volume 3, edited by Morton D. Zabel (New York: Harper, 1951);

*Poems of John Milton: The 1645 Edition with Essays in Analysis*, edited by Brooks and John Edward Hardy (New York: Harcourt, Brace, 1951; London: Dobson, 1957);

"Metaphor and the Function of Criticism," in *Spiritual Problems in Contemporary Literature*, edited by S. R. Hopper (New York: Harper, 1952), pp. 127-137;

*An Anthology of Stories from the Southern Review,* edited by Brooks and Robert Penn Warren (Baton Rouge: Louisiana State University Press, 1953);

*Tragic Themes in Western Literature,* edited, with an introduction, by Brooks (New Haven & London: Yale University Press, 1955);

"Implications of an Organic Theory of Poetry," in *Literature and Belief,* edited by M. H. Abrams (New York: Columbia University Press, 1958), pp. 53-79;

"Literary Criticism: Poet, Poem, Reader," in *Varieties of Literary Experience: Eighteen Essays in World Literature,* edited by Stanley Burnshaw (New York: Columbia University Press, 1962), pp. 95-114;

*American Literature: The Makers and the Making,* edited by Brooks, Warren, and R. W. B. Lewis, 2 volumes (New York: St. Martin's Press, 1973);

"T. S. Eliot as 'Modernist' Poet," in *Literary Theory and Structure: Essays Presented to William K. Wimsatt,* edited by Frank Brady, John Palmer, and Martin Price (New Haven & London: Yale University Press, 1973), pp. 353-377;

"William Faulkner and William Butler Yeats: Parallels and Affinities," in *Faulkner: Fifty Years After The Marble Faun,* edited by George H. Wolf (Tuscaloosa: University of Alabama Press, 1976), pp. 139-158;

*The Correspondence of Thomas Percy and William Shenstone,* edited by Brooks (New Haven: Yale University Press, 1977);

"Eudora Welty and the Southern Idiom," in *Eudora Welty: A Form of Thanks,* edited by Ann J. Abadie and Louis Dollarhide (Jackson: University Press of Mississippi, 1979), pp. 3-24;

"Thomas Percy, Don Quixote, and Don Bowle," in *Evidence in Literary Scholarship: Essays in Memory of James Marshall Osborn,* edited by René Wellek and Alvaro Ribeiro (Oxford: Clarendon, 1979), pp. 247-261;

"The Crisis in Culture as Reflected in Southern Literature," in *The American South: Portrait of a Culture,* edited by Louis D. Rubin, Jr. (Baton Rouge: Louisiana State University Press, 1980), pp. 171-189;

"Southern Literature: The Past, History, and the Timeless," in *Southern Literature in Transition: Heritage and Promise,* edited by Philip Castille and William Osborne (Memphis: Memphis State University Press, 1983), pp. 3-16.

PERIODICAL PUBLICATIONS: "A Note on the Limits of 'History' and the Limits of 'Criticism,' " *Sewanee Review,* 61 (Winter 1953): 129-135;

"Metaphor, Paradox, and Stereotype," *British Journal of Aesthetics,* 5 (October 1965): 315-328;

"Allen Tate and the Nature of Modernism," *Southern Review,* 12 (October 1976): 685-697;

"Faulkner's Mosquitoes," *Georgia Review,* 31 (Spring 1977): 213-234;

"Walker Percy and Modern Gnosticism," *Southern Review,* 13 (October 1977): 677-687;

"The Sense of Community in Yoknapatawpha Fiction," *University of Mississippi Studies in English,* 15 (1978): 3-18;

"The New Criticism," *Sewanee Review,* 87 (Fall 1979): 592-607;

"For Allen Tate," by Brooks, Malcolm Cowley, Louis Coxe, William Meredith, William Jay Smith, and Eudora Welty, *Library of Congress Quarterly,* 36 (1979): 349-355;

"Episode and Anecdote in the Poetry of Robert Penn Warren," *Yale Review,* 70 (Summer 1981): 551-567;

"The Critics Who Made Us: I. A. Richards and Practical Criticism," *Sewanee Review,* 89 (Fall 1981): 586-595.

No less a historian of criticism than René Wellek has called Cleanth Brooks "the critic of critics." Both senses of the phrase are appropriate descriptions of Brooks. Not only was he considered to be *the* critic of his generation of critics but also, as Wellek reminds us in an essay collected in *The Possibilities of Order: Cleanth Brooks and His Work* (1976), he was critical of other critics. During the 1940s and 1950s he was widely regarded as the most lucid and instructive close reader of literary texts. The readings he published in *Modern Poetry and the Tradition* (1939) and *The Well Wrought Urn: Studies in the Structure of Poetry* (1947) were considered to be outstanding instances of New Critical practice. He further carried the tenets of New Criticism to countless university students through *An Approach to Literature* (1936), which he edited with John Thibaut Purser and Robert Penn Warren, and his widely used anthology *Understanding Poetry* (1938), edited with Warren. This text revolutionized literary pedagogy by employing the criterion of shared aesthetic properties, rather than subject, author, or chronology, to organize poems. *Under-*

*standing Fiction* (1943), which Brooks edited with Warren, and *Understanding Drama* (1945), edited with Robert B. Heilman, were among other textbooks through which Brooks reached college students with his new formalist perspective.

Lest we place too much emphasis on Brooks as a New Critic, Wellek cautions us to remember that he is also "an antiquarian-eighteenth-century scholar" and "a historian of criticism," as such works as his editing of the Thomas Percy correspondence with David Nichol Smith (1944-1961) and his collaboration with William K. Wimsatt on *Literary Criticism: A Short History* (1957) respectively demonstrate. In Brooks's many essays and reviews, continues Wellek, he has also assessed most of the "prominent figures in the history of English and American criticism." In Brooks's work there are several recurrent concerns, some of which—paradox, tension, irony—can easily be associated with the internalist, New Critical view of literature, and others of which—dehumanization, moral dignity, time, and history—might also seem to contradict that formalist view; but these concerns are also central to his thought. Thus readers should be careful not to frame his work in too narrow a New Critical mold. Following the work of I. A. Richards, Brooks called literature, in Robert Penn Warren's "A Conversation with Cleanth Brooks" in *The Possibilities of Order* (1976), a form of knowledge different from science that can be described "as a kind of dramatic knowledge, a knowledge of 'what it is like' to go through a process, to fight a battle against foemen, or to fight an internal battle with oneself, to mourn, to be happy, to test one's courage, and so on." He believes this sort of knowledge is extremely valuable to our culture because it can "diagnose" problems. It cannot give us remedies, but it tells us about the nature of the problems. The study of literature is not political or theological or philosophical but specifically literary. The historical, social, moral, and religious contexts of the literary work are crucial but subordinate to its intrinsic, organic life. Therefore the proper focus of critical work is always the literary work itself. Anything else moves us away from it. In his later writings Brooks is concerned that his emphasis on the text has been misread as a disregard for its various historical contexts. He likes to point out that a substantial portion of his scholarly work is devoted to understanding the social, political, moral, religious, and biographical contexts of the writings of William Faulkner, John Milton, and Thomas Percy.

Brooks's criticism is always preoccupied with specific uses of language, particular techniques that surface in the work as a consequence of the writer's concrete immersion in his world. Thus Faulkner's evocation of "the South" has been a special and longstanding subject of Brooks's study. He was very much influenced by contemporaneous literary theory but his enemy was reductiveness. He agreed with his longtime friend Warren that critics need "a double vision" "to keep a sense of the immediacy and the concreteness—in John Crowe Ransom's phrase, 'the world's body'—in contrast to the abstract formulations which deny experience as experience."

Cleanth Brooks was born 16 October 1906 in Murray, Kentucky, to Bessie Lee Witherspoon and Cleanth Brooks, Sr., an Episcopalian minister. Because of his father's pastoral duties, Brooks spent most of his boyhood in little towns near Memphis, Tennessee. When Brooks was five, his father, who loved reading and valued education, gave him a volume of tales from the *Iliad*. He later attended the McTyeire School, a small classical academy in Tennessee, which acquainted him further with Greek and Roman literature.

In 1924 Brooks entered Vanderbilt University, the bastion of the 1920s literary group known as the Fugitives. Pro-agrarian and anti-industrial, these critics and writers laid the theoretical groundwork for the New Critical movement. From 1920 to 1925 they published a journal, the *Fugitive,* that articulated their concerns. Of the original group associated with the Fugitives, John Crowe Ransom and Donald Davidson were still at Vanderbilt when Brooks arrived. Though Allen Tate, also associated with the original group, had already left, there was still a great deal of ferment in literary studies, and Brooks abandoned his intention to become a lawyer in favor of pursuing the study of literature. As a freshman Brooks met Robert Penn Warren, who was at the time a senior and a protégé of Ransom's. Brooks did not know Ransom well at this time nor was he involved in the group centered around him; he was more influenced by conversations with other students and course work with Davidson. "My Vanderbilt years were—as far as having John's tutelage was concerned—largely wasted," Brooks has said. "A melancholy reflection. I have only myself, in my ignorance and innocence, and my confused romanticism, to blame." He was invited sporadically to meetings of the Fugitive group after they had already ceased publishing the *Fug-*

*tive.* Nonetheless, he reported later, "the thing that I got most out of Vanderbilt was to discover suddenly that literature was not a dead thing to be looked at through the glass of a museum case, but was very much alive. Walking around on the campus were people who were actually writing poems, who were talking about the making of poems, who were getting them published."

He received his B.A. in 1928, and from Vanderbilt Brooks went to Tulane University, where he pursued graduate studies. He describes himself, after his experience of literature at Vanderbilt, as "appalled at the fact that so much of the conventional graduate study seemed to have nothing to do with the interior life of the poem.... Graduate training at that time didn't pay much attention to it. It was all purely historical and biographical." Soon after he arrived, he met Edith Amy Blanchard, whom he wanted to marry. However, their marriage had to be postponed because Brooks did not hold an academic position and because the Depression limited his job possibilities. After he received his M.A. in 1929, Tulane nominated him for a Rhodes Scholarship. He studied at Exeter College, Oxford, where he was reunited with Warren, who was the Rhodes Scholar from Kentucky. In his first year abroad, he met Allen Tate and Charles Pipkin (a former Rhodes Scholar and then dean of the graduate school at Louisiana State University) in Paris in December 1929. While at Exeter, he elected to do the honor's program in English with Nevill Coghill as his tutor. There he read I. A. Richards's *Principles of Literary Criticism* (1924) and *Practical Criticism: A Study of Literary Judgement* (1929). Though he objected to Richards's scientific approach, Brooks was "fascinated with the way he was opening up poems and talking about them." Ransom was at this time in England as a Guggenheim fellow, and Brooks visited him. Despite such contacts, Brooks began a historical project which was to occupy him off and on for thirty years—to edit the letters of Bishop Percy in cooperation with David Nichol Smith. He received a B.A. with honors from Exeter College in 1931 and another honorary degree in 1932.

In fall 1932 Brooks was brought by Pipkin to Louisiana State University, which at that time was enjoying a period of expansion under the governorship of Huey Long. Shortly afterward, Warren was also hired by Louisiana State University. After Warren's arrival, Brooks reports, they "talked incessantly." In 1934 he was finally able to marry Blanchard. A year later Brooks published a philological study entitled *The Relation of the Alabama-Georgia Dialect to the Provincial Dialects of Great Britain* (1935), a project he would return to in his retirement.

During his years at Louisiana State University, Brooks participated in an intellectual circle that included political scientists, musicians, painters, and his friends Warren, Robert Heilman, and Charles Hyneman, one of the group's leaders, later to be the president of the Political Science Association. The group was not in any sense officially organized or named but operated loosely as a social network bound by common cultural and political interests. It was, according to Brooks, "a wonderfully electrifying environment." In "Cleanth Brooks: Some Snapshots, mostly from an Old Album," collected in *Possibilities of Order,* Heilman recalls the diversity of the individuals who, as a group, created "unexpected repercussions." Heilman continues:

> "Liberals" and "conservatives," anti-Francoists as well as sympathizers with the New Germany and with Trotskyism and perhaps the New Russia generally, we had in common mainly a feeling that LSU was capable of improvement, and we got out a statement on this subject, naming a few things that could be done. To our astonishment, its appearance filled the air with the noise of denial and denunciation. Nineteen of us had signed the statement, and "the 19" became the day's strongest term of opprobrium; some 160 faculty members signed a counterstatement ... asserting that LSU was a treasury of academic excellences; and there was some vague talk of "haircutting," i.e., nonreappointment, nonpromotion, etc., for the 19....
>
> Cleanth Brooks was very active in [the affair of the nineteen]; we often held meetings at his house. He had a high degree of institutional concern and, if I may use an almost defunct word, loyalty; unlike many members of the profession, he did not use the pressure of other concerns (teaching, editing, an extensive program of criticism and scholarship) to justify indifference to the university.

While at Louisiana State, Brooks was a vital member of this intellectual circle, often entertaining visiting lecturers in his home—John Crowe Ransom, David Nichol Smith, Katherine Anne Porter, Andrew Lytle, I. A. Richards, and Marshall McLuhan. With Pipkin's encouragement and the administration's interest in establishing a national quarterly, Brooks began working as managing editor of the *Southern Review* with Robert Penn Warren in 1939. Under their direction it soon became, in Ransom's words, "the organ of the most powerful critical discussion in the language," publishing the work of many well-known critics, including Ransom and Kenneth Burke. The *Southern Review* was suspended in 1942, during the war, about the time Warren left for the University of Minnesota. Ransom offered to merge it with the *Kenyon Review,* and though a complete merger did not take place, Brooks and Warren were listed as advisory editors of the latter journal for several years.

During their early years at Louisiana State University, Brooks and Warren were confronted with the problem of teaching a sophomore introduction to literature without adequate textbooks, and so they determined to develop their own. With John Thibaut Purser, they edited *An Approach to Literature; A Collection of Prose and Verse with Analyses and Discussions,* which was published in 1936. In 1938 Brooks and Warren produced *Understanding Poetry: An Anthology for College Students.* They omitted biographical material, not as a polemical gesture but because they felt most of the teachers who would use the textbook were already well primed through their graduate training to present it to their students. They tried to deal with what they considered a widespread problem, namely to get students to do a close analyses of the literary works. Therefore, they provided model analyses as well as questions that might provoke students to do their own analyses. This approach was quite controversial. As Brooks said, "it raised the backs of a good many old line scholars who felt we were doing all sorts of wicked things such as taking the poem away from the author, imposing our own interpretation on it, or neglecting the author's background, or neglecting the cultural history of its time, or the history of ideas out of which the poem comes." At the time, both authors were well "aware of the importance of biography." Nonetheless the emphasis on close reading, generated by Richards's *Practical Criticism,* shaped the structure of their textbook. They saw themselves diverging significantly from his "subjective" orientation, however, toward a more text-oriented criticism.

In 1939 *Modern Poetry and the Tradition* was published by the University of North Carolina Press. This was the first collection of critical essays by Brooks to reach print; together with *Under-*

*standing Poetry,* it established his reputation as an outstanding practical critic. Brooks explained how the book came about. His "conception of poetry as alive" had led him "to an interest in contemporary poetry." Among his friends and colleagues, especially at Oxford, he was always "arguing . . . defending the new poetry, trying to win them to an interest in it." Brooks found that as he tried to explain his ideas he was, he says, "partly talking out loud to myself, because I was secretly having my own difficulties in relating this startlingly new poetry to the poetry that I had always been taught was 'good' poetry. Anyway, I conceived that book initially for one of these Oxford friends."

As the book developed Brooks incorporated ideas that resulted from his reading I. A. Richards, Ransom and Allen Tate and the Fugitives, and also T. S. Eliot. Brooks says he was struck by something Eliot had written in his work on the metaphysical poets. That is, Eliot had "suggested that the metaphysical poets were not to be regarded as a rather peculiar offshoot of the main course of English poetry, but that they had a deep, hidden connection with its central line of development." Brooks tried to incorporate this "new way of looking at the tradition of English poetry" into *Modern Poetry and the Tradition.* In some sense Brooks was attempting to "find a common ground" between Eliot and Richards.

The effect of the book, however, was to illuminate poems whose verbal texture was dense with difficulties for the average reader. When Ransom reviewed *Modern Poetry and the Tradition* in the *Kenyon Review* in 1940, he wrote that Brooks was "very likely, the most expert living 'reader' or interpreter of difficult verse." First published in 1937 in the *Southern Review,* his classic essay, "The Waste Land: An Analysis" (also known as "The Waste Land: Critique of the Myth"), is a perfect example of Brooks's achievement. Eliot's poem was often regarded at the time as impenetrable, but Brooks's lucid explanation of the poem's symbolism, background, and thematic unity made it accessible to readers. His treatment of William Butler Yeats's volume of poems *The Vision* (1925) was similarly instructive. Though the book, as its title declares, is an attempt to link modern poets with a long-standing poetic tradition, Brooks's emphasis on their formal similarities gives it more the character of an apology for modern poetry than a discussion of the historical development of a particular poetic tradition. As in much of his later work, Brooks tried to describe

*Cleanth Brooks in the 1940s (courtesy of the author)*

the formal properties of complex poems. In the chapter "Frost, MacLeish, and Auden," for instance, he argued that Robert Frost's poetry is not merely, as many other critics would have it, "homely, salty, direct" but shares with the poetry of Ransom, Tate, and other modern poets a formal structure that belies its surface simplicity. As Brooks remarked in his preface, the "thesis frankly maintained in this study is that we are witnessing (or perhaps have just witnessed) a critical revolution of the order of the Romantic Revolt."

During the next six years, Brooks's reputation grew steadily. An important essay, "The Poem as Organism: Modern Critical Procedure," appeared in *English Institute Annual 1940*. That same year, to his surprise, Yale adopted *Understanding Poetry*. He was visiting professor of English during the summer of 1941 at the University of Texas, visiting professor of English during the summer of 1942 at the University of Michigan, and a participant at the Bread Loaf Writers' conference in 1945. All the while Brooks continued, with Smith, to edit *The Percy Letters*, a project that, as Brooks enjoys pointing out, involved considerable historical research. At the invitation of Neo-Aristotelian Ronald Salmon Crane,

Brooks taught as a visiting professor of English at the University of Chicago in 1946. Crane was highly critical of Brooks's work, as is apparent in his well-known essay, "The Critical Monism of Cleanth Brooks," and the two frequently discussed the differences between their critical points of view. Though such disagreements never affected their personal relationship, Brooks did not feel comfortable teaching the Chicago curriculum and left the university after the second quarter. Later that same year at the Modern Language Association convention, he met René Wellek, with whom he found himself far more in agreement and of whom he would soon be a colleague.

Brooks left Louisiana State University and moved on to Yale University in 1946. At Yale the younger faculty was interested in *Understanding Poetry* and the approach to literature it exemplified. There he became involved in another intellectual circle, including Wellek, Louis Martz, William K. Wimsatt, and Maynard Mack. Over the years Wimsatt and Wellek were to become, together with Richards, the shaping influences on Brooks's conception of literature.

Brooks gave consummate expression to his theory of poetry in *The Well Wrought Urn: Studies in the Structure of Poetry* (1947), which collected much of his best work since 1940. No volume better represents the New Criticism or gives clearer statements of its aesthetic principles and interpretive methods. In the preface Brooks describes the book as an attempt "to examine, in terms of a common approach, a number of celebrated poems, taken in chronological order, from the Elizabethan period to the present" in order to determine whether or not they reveal "some common structural properties." Answering the advocates of biographical or historical interpretation, Brooks warns against turning literary study into "cultural anthropology" or a tool of partisan political, religious, or moral disputes. "We had better begin . . . by making the closest examination of what the poem says as a poem."

The scope of Brooks's volume indicates his continued concern with the connection between modern poetry and the tradition. Specifically, Brooks intends to argue that the kind of difficult literary language characteristic of modernist poetry had not only been a principal feature of the metaphysical poets, as Eliot had argued; instead poetry itself will be defined as the self-conscious and often paradoxical use of language. While Eliot argued that a "dissociation of sensibility" had set in after the Jacobeans, robbing the Romantics and Victorians of the linguistic sophistication evident in John Donne or Andrew Marvell, Brooks finds the qualities of ambiguity, metaphorical complexity, and unified aesthetic tension in such works as Gray's "Elegy," the odes of Wordsworth and Keats, Tennyson's "Tears, Idle Tears," and Yeats's "Among School Children." These readings are preceded by chapters which analyze in detail Donne's "The Canonization," Shakespeare's "Macbeth," John Milton's "L'Allegro" and "Il Penseroso," Robert Herrick's "Corinna's going a-Maying," and Alexander Pope's "The Rape of the Lock." This list includes a variety of poetic forms, from tragedy and satire to lyric and meditative verse, and spans a wide spectrum of historically different periods. Yet in each case Brooks discerns many of the same aesthetic and verbal qualities; together these characterize not only a tradition of English poetry but the essence of poetry itself.

In the widely reprinted opening essay, "The Language of Paradox," Brooks defends his thesis that "the language of poetry is the language of paradox." Brooks bases his definition on an axiomatic distinction between scientific and poetic language. "It is the scientist whose truth requires a language purged of every trace of paradox; apparently the truth which the poet utters can be approached only in terms of paradox." This distinction implies a basic difference between referential and literary uses of language that will be a constant and controversial feature of literary theory from Brooks to the deconstructionist theories of Paul de Man and J. Hillis Miller. Brooks first illustrates his point with a brief discussion of Wordsworth's sonnet "Composed upon Westminster Bridge," where he finds that "paradox informs the poem, though, since this is Wordsworth, rather timidly." Closely reading the sonnet, Brooks demonstrates that its "revivified" use of "old metaphor" is an instance of "the revelation which puts the tarnished familiar world in a new light." This resurrection of language through poetry occurs, writes Brooks, through freeing the connotational powers of language. "The tendency of science is necessarily to stabilize terms, to freeze them into stricter denotations; the poet's tendency is by contrast disruptive. The terms are continually modifying each other, and thus violating their dictionary meanings." Brooks justifies this linguistic instability and violence as the only means adequate to the expression of emotional experience: "All of

the subtler states of emotion, as I. A. Richards has pointed out, necessarily demand metaphor for their expression." This argument makes sense in light of Brooks's earlier effort with Eliot's *The Waste Land,* for Eliot's poetry and criticism explicitly concerned the expression of complex and often contradictory, even terrifying, emotions. Brooks's theory that poetry is essentially the innovative use of old words is also analogous to the Russian Formalist doctrine of "defamiliarization" developed just before and after World War I and in response to the experimentation of modern literature.

What, however, prevents poetic language from breaking down into sheer incoherence or following the liberties of connotation into free play and nonsense? The answer is implied by the bulk of the remainder of "The Language of Paradox," which is dedicated to a close reading of Donne's "The Canonization." Again like Eliot, Brooks will find in theology—specifically in the Christian dogmas of the Incarnation and Resurrection—the formal principles to support the authority of his aesthetic and poetic ideas. The paradoxes of time and eternity, God and man, body and soul, and life and death which are resolved by the images of the Incarnation and Resurrection are the fundamental tensions informing the language and emotions of Donne's poem. Aesthetic and cosmic unity coalesce in a divinely inspired and authorized harmony, thus rendering problematic Brooks's claim to reading the poetry as poetry without recourse to external frameworks—such as religion—to make his interpretation cohere. The contradiction between carnal and spiritual love, for example, is resolved in orthodox fashion: "The lovers in rejecting life actually win to the most intense life." Agony, desire, and paradox find their sublimation and harmony through faith in an eternal unity, and so the dangers faced by poetry are countered by a theological imperative. What keeps poetry from incoherence, chaos, or sacrilege turns out to be the same authority that saves the soul. One is left wondering whether or not the unity Brooks finds in the poem is aesthetic, or whether the aesthetic of unity is imposed upon the poem by the religious structures of Christian philosophy.

Brooks's brilliant readings, here and throughout the volume, are modernist in an important respect. "The poem," he writes, "is an instance of the doctrine which it asserts; it is both the assertion and the realization of the assertion." This self-reflexive quality is one commonly found in modern works of literature, and here Brooks extends it to the tradition of poetry back to Shakespeare. This considerably enhances the complexity of his reading, since each poem in the book turns out to be about itself–to be a work of literary or poetic theory. Donne's poem is only superficially about two lovers; in essence it is about the poetic issues Brooks's book addresses. The chapter on Gray similarly ends by arguing that "it is the whole 'Elegy' that is *his* storied urn–it is the poem itself, the 'lines' in which he relates the 'artless tale' of the villagers–all the lines of the poem, taken as a poetic structure." Similarly, "Wordsworth and the Paradox of the Imagination" states that the ode on immortality "is about the synthesizing imagination" that resolves ambiguities and paradoxes (though Brooks remains dissatisfied with Wordsworth's solutions, these being more Protestant than Episcopal). And of course Keats's "Ode on a Grecian Urn" demands reading as a discourse on art and poetry, and Brooks underscores how in his interpretation the urn itself speaks in the poem "to make a commentary on its own nature," much as every poem for Brooks speaks to the close reader about its own nature as a poem.

In combining aesthetic formalism with linguistic self-reflexivity, Brooks's readings mark a real turning point in the development of poetic theory, one that (to Brooks's chagrin) leads eventually to deconstructionist practices. On the other hand, Brooks also thus moves even further from the kind of political or social or cultural criticism so many called for in the troubled decades of the 1930s and 1940s. Brooks's chapter on "Keats's Sylvan Historian" firmly rejects a sociological view of poetry, and in his final chapter on "The Heresy of Paraphrase" Brooks reiterates his thesis that the poems he discusses share a common structure, but not a common paraphrasable content: "The structure meant is a structure of meanings, evaluations, and interpretations; and the principle of unity which informs it seems to be one of balancing and harmonizing connotations, attitudes, and meanings." Poetic structure "unites the like with the unlike," not by negating or subordinating one to the other but by holding "contradictory attitudes" in an "achieved harmony." To comprehend and describe such structures, critics need such terms as " 'ambiguity,' 'paradox,' 'complex of attitudes,' and–most frequent of all . . . 'irony.' " After Brooks, irony becomes the key term in most accounts of New Critical poetic theory and will be taken up by critics such as Paul

de Man when attempts are made to disrupt the "achieved harmony" Brooks defines as the essence of poetic language. Cultural critics, eager to have literature and theory stake out effective positions on nonliterary issues, will argue that the legacy of Brooks and New Criticism is that of an aestheticism that becomes paralyzed by its perception of complexities and ironies. Brooks's irony, in fact, bears a resemblance to the tragic moral and literary psychology advanced by Lionel Trilling at about the same time and in response to similar debates over aesthetics and politics.

Brooks spent the summer of 1948 as a visiting professor of English at Kenyon College, where he had an opportunity to engage Ransom, whose view of literature he remembers as "very different." During this period Warren and Brooks were invited to develop a textbook on composition and developed *Modern Rhetoric* (1949) and *Fundamentals of Good Writing: A Handbook of Modern Rhetoric* (1950). Warren accepted a position at Yale as professor of play writing in 1950, putting him in closer contact with Brooks. In 1953 Brooks received the first of two Guggenheim fellowships, worked as a visiting professor at the University of Southern California, and started a ten-year period as a Library of Congress Fellow.

About this time, an editor at Alfred Knopf publishers asked Brooks if he would write a history of literary criticism. "I was sensible enough," he reports, to say, "I'm not a theorist nor an historian . . . but I know somebody who I think is an ideal man; I'll see whether he's interested–maybe we can do it together." He then approached Wimsatt, who already had such a book in mind and became the guiding spirit of *Literary Criticism: A Short History* (1957). Brooks contributed "Part IV," the final section of the history, on contemporary critics, focusing on Eliot, William Empson, Pound, Ransom, Richards, and Yvor Winters and the influence of Nietzsche, Freud, and Carl G. Jung on literary critics. The volume is a collaborative attempt to show "the continuity and intelligibility in the history of literary argument," but in an admittedly "argumentative" way. In retrospect the continuity and intelligibility of their history now seems a justification of the sort of formal argumentation their critical work exemplifies. In the first chapter written by Brooks, "Tragedy and Comedy: The Internal Focus," he distinguishes several views of tragedy and comedy, emphasizing, with respect to the latter, the work of Freud. The next chapter, "Symbolism," traces the symbolist movement from Coleridge, Ralph Waldo Emerson, and Edgar Allan Poe to Baudelaire, through Verlaine and Valéry to Yeats. The middle chapters, "I. A. Richards: A Poetics of Tension," "The Semantic Principle," and "Eliot and Pound: An Impersonal Art," trace the development of the formalist theory of literature Brooks and Wimsatt advocate in their work. Thus they focus entirely upon the relationships among the forms intrinsic to the work. This section begins with a contrast between Richards's, Ransom's and Winters's theories of art, turns to a delineation of Richards's and Empson's theories of meaning, and ends with an account of Eliot's and Pound's view of poetry, with Yvor Winters's critique of modern poetry as a counterpoint.

The last section of Brooks's contribution is made up of two chapters, "Fiction and Drama: The Gross Structure" and "Myth and Archetype." In the first, he presents Henry James's, Joseph Conrad's and Ford Madox Ford's views of the novel, and Francis Fergusson's and Elder Olson's views of drama. In the second, he focuses mostly upon Ernst Cassirer and Susanne Langer's theory of symbolic forms and Jung's theory of archetypes, briefly describing Northrop Frye, Richard Chase, Leslie Fiedler, Maud Bodkin, and W. H. Auden as critics whose work concerns the relationship of myth and literature. Brooks's treatment of the history of contemporary criticism largely dovetails with his own critical concerns. This is probably easiest to see in the remarkable emphasis he gives to the work of Yeats, a frequent subject of his practical criticism, and Winters, a staunch opponent of his view of literature.

Brooks was now well established as a leading practitioner of New Criticism, and he began to be honored for his achievements. He received an L.H.D. from the University of St. Louis in 1958, was appointed Gray Professor of Rhetoric at Yale, and received his second Guggenheim fellowship in 1960 and the D.Litt. from both Upsala College and the University of Kentucky in 1963.

In 1963 Yale University Press published *William Faulkner: The Yoknapatawpha Country*, the first of Brooks's three books on Faulkner and a departure from his earlier work. In this study Brooks showed how Faulkner developed out of a particular milieu and how this manifested itself in terms of ethical and religious themes in his work. The opening chapters connect Faulkner with other regional writers and delineate the social strata upon which his work depends. After briefly considering the relationship between Faulkner's na-

ture poetry and his later fiction, Brooks then turned to a consideration of the Yoknapatawpha novels. In the remaining chapters of the book Brooks explored themes central to Faulkner's work such as the role of the community, isolation and alienation, puritanism, and the contrast between the old order and the new.

In the same year Brooks's *The Hidden God; Studies in Hemingway, Faulkner, Yeats, Eliot, and Warren* was published. This volume brings together five lectures he delivered in June 1955 at a conference on theology at Trinity College in Hartford, Connecticut. In the book he argued that of such significant modern writers as Hemingway, Faulkner, Yeats, Eliot, and Warren, none except Eliot associated with Christianity, exploring issues that preoccupy theologians. Thus he defended modern writers against the view that they have nothing to say to Christians.

In 1964 Brooks was appointed cultural attaché at the American Embassy in London. During the next two years he lectured all over England, representing America at a memorial service for T. S. Eliot at Westminster Abbey and at a ceremony at which the Society of Authors made an award to the laureate John Masefield. By the end of the decade Brooks's reputation was secure: he had received honorary degrees from the University of Exeter in 1966, from Washington and Lee University in 1968, and from Tulane University in 1969.

*A Shaping Joy: Studies in the Writer's Craft*, published in 1971, is a collection of the papers Brooks had read at various places during the previous ten years, including those he delivered while cultural attaché. They range widely across a spectrum of concerns: some are instances of his familiar practice of close reading; others are rearticulations of his theoretical position. Brooks's work had been the subject of so much commentary that he felt it necessary to remark: "The pigeonhole assigned to me carries the label 'The New Criticism.' Now, it is bad enough to live under any label, but one so nearly meaningless as 'The New Criticism'–it is certainly not *new*– has peculiar disadvantages. For most people it vaguely signifies an anti-historical bias and a fixation on 'close reading.'" Brooks hoped in this volume to "mitigate the effects of an overshadowing generalization."

In 1975 Brooks became Professor Emeritus at Yale. In his retirement, he continued to write and lecture. His second book on Faulkner, *William Faulkner: Toward Yoknapatawpha and Beyond*

(1978), is a study of Faulkner's development as a writer. It takes up aspects of his work not included in the earlier study. The first six chapters deal with Faulkner's early work up to the inception of Yoknapatawpha County. The next three chapters deal with *Pylon, The Wild Palms,* and *A Fable,* novels not set in Yoknapatawpha County. The book ends with an essay in which Brooks addressed two of Faulkner's most common themes: time and history. In 1983 Brooks published *William Faulkner: First Encounters,* an introduction to Faulkner's work intended for general readers and beginning students of Faulkner. More recently Brooks returned to his very first scholarly project, publishing in 1985 *The Language of the American South,* a series of lectures he had given at Mercer University in October 1984.

Brooks's accomplishments are considerable. He has been in every respect an exemplary literary scholar. Despite his and Wellek's disclaimers, he is important in the history of criticism as a "close reader" of complex modern literary texts. His two greatest achievements are that he made difficult modern writers accessible to a generation of scholars for whom it was inconceivable that a great writer could exist in the twentieth century, and he taught the next generation of critics how to read closely. He has never regarded him-

self as a theorist, but he has been a sensitive reader of contemporary literary theory and has articulated an approach to literature that made excellent sense to students of literature in the 1950s and 1960s.

**References:**

R. S. Crane, "The Critical Monism of Cleanth Brooks," in *Critics and Criticism: Ancient and Modern,* edited by Crane, et al. (Chicago: University of Chicago Press, 1952), pp. 83-107;

Thomas W. Cutrer, *Parnassus on the Mississippi: The Southern Review and the Baton Rouge Literary Community, 1935-1942* (Baton Rouge: Louisiana State University Press, 1984);

Lewis P. Simpson, ed., *The Possibilities of Order: Cleanth Brooks and His Work* (Baton Rouge: Louisiana State University Press, 1976);

Kermit Vanderbilt, *American Literature and the Academy: The Roots, Growth, and Maturity of a Profession* (Philadelphia: University of Pennsylvania Press, 1986).

**Papers:**

Brooks's papers are collected at the University of Kentucky; the Beinecke Rare Book and Manuscript Library, Yale University; the Newberry Library, Chicago; and the Joint University Libraries at the University of Tennessee.

# Van Wyck Brooks

*(16 February 1886-2 May 1963)*

Brook Thomas
*University of Massachusetts-Amherst*

See also the Brooks entry in *DLB 45, American Poets, 1880-1945,* First Series.

BOOKS: *Verses by Two Undergraduates,* by Brooks and John Hall Wheelock (Cambridge, Mass.: Privately printed, 1905);

*The Wine of the Puritans: A Study of Present-Day America* (London: Sisley's, 1908; New York: Kennerley, 1909);

*The Soul: An Essay Towards a Point of View* (San Francisco: Privately printed, 1910);

*The Malady of the Ideal: Obermann, Maurice de Guérin, and Amiel* (London: Fifield, 1913; Philadelphia: University of Pennsylvania Press, 1947);

*John Addington Symonds: A Biographical Study* (New York: Kennerley, 1914; London: Richards, 1914);

*The World of H. G. Wells* (New York: Kennedy, 1915; London: T. Unwin Fisher, 1915);

*America's Coming-of-Age* (New York: Huebsch, 1915);

*Letters and Leadership* (New York: Huebsch, 1918);

*The Ordeal of Mark Twain* (New York: Dutton, 1920; London: Heinemann, 1922; revised edition, New York: Dutton, 1933; London: Dent, 1934);

*The Pilgrimage of Henry James* (New York: Dutton, 1925; London: Cape, 1938);

*Emerson and Others* (New York: Dutton, 1927; London: Cape, 1927);

*The Life of Emerson* (New York: Dutton, 1932; London: Dent, 1934);

*Sketches in Criticism* (New York: Dutton, 1932; London: Dent, 1934);

*Three Essays on America* (New York: Dutton, 1934); revised as *America's Coming-of-Age* (Garden City: Doubleday, 1958);

*The Flowering of New England, 1815-1865,* volume 1 of *Makers and Finders* (New York: Dutton, 1936; London: Dent, 1936; revised edition, Cleveland: World, 1946);

*New England; Indian Summer, 1865-1915,* volume 2 of *Makers and Finders* (New York: Dutton,

*Van Wyck Brooks at Martha's Vineyard, 1950*

1940; London: Dent, 1941);

*On Literature Today* (New York: Dutton, 1941);

*Opinions of Oliver Allston* (New York: Dutton, 1941; London: Dent, 1942);

*The World of Washington Irving,* volume 3 of *Makers and Finders* (New York: Dutton, 1944; London: Dent, 1946);

*The Times of Melville and Whitman,* volume 4 of *Makers and Finders* (New York: Dutton, 1947; London: Dent, 1948);

*A Chilmark Miscellany* (New York: Dutton, 1948);

*The Confident Years; 1885-1915,* volume 5 of *Makers and Finders* (New York: Dutton, 1952; London: Dent, 1952);

*The Writer in America* (New York: Dutton, 1953);

*Writers and the Future* (New York: Spiral Press, 1953);

*Scenes and Portraits: Memories of Childhood and Youth* (New York: Dutton, 1954; London: Dent, 1954);

*John Sloan: A Painter's Life* (New York: Dutton, 1955; London: Dent, 1955);

*From a Writer's Notebook* (Worcester, Mass.: A. J. St. Onge, 1955; enlarged edition, New York: Dutton, 1958; London: Dent, 1958);

*Helen Keller: Sketch for a Portrait* (New York: Dutton, 1956; London: Dent, 1956);

*Days of the Phoenix: The Nineteen-Twenties I Remember* (New York: Dutton, 1957; London: Dent, 1957);

*The Dream of Arcadia: American Writers and Artists in Italy, 1760-1915* (New York: Dutton, 1958; London: Dent, 1959);

*Howells, His Life and World* (New York: Dutton, 1959; London: Dent, 1959);

*From the Shadow of the Mountain: My Post-Meridian Years* (New York: Dutton, 1961; London: Dent, 1962);

*Fenollosa and His Circle, With Other Essays in Biography* (New York: Dutton, 1962);

*An Autobiography* (New York: Dutton, 1965)—includes *Scenes and Portraits, Days of the Phoenix,* and *From the Shadow of the Mountain;*

*Van Wyck Brooks: The Early Years, A Selection from his Works, 1908-1921,* edited by Claire Sprague (New York: Harper & Row, 1968).

For over half a century Van Wyck Brooks devoted himself to understanding and shaping American culture. His career is divided in two. In the first part he was one of the most important cultural critics of the progressive era, looked to by American writers as their spokesman in articulating the condition the artist faced in America. In the second part, after a long nervous breakdown, he turned from criticizing American culture to defending it, as he set out to record the history of the writer in America. The change in his career has resulted in a debate over his skill as a literary critic. Yet almost all agree that he played one of the most important roles in starting serious study of American writers.

Brooks was born in 1886 in Plainfield, New Jersey. Growing up in this New York City suburb, the young Van Wyck saw people's lives made and broken by the American commercial system. The second son of Sarah Bailey Ames, a social favorite in Plainfield, and Charles Edward Brooks, a lover of art and music soon to become a business failure, Van Wyck experienced both the social status of the leisured upper class and the economic insecurities of the middle class. Convinced that America's emphasis on commerce destroyed artistic sensibility, Brooks blamed the life of a businessman for his father's numerous illnesses and lack of success. Later Van Wyck attributed the suicide of his brother, Charles Ames Brooks, a lawyer who commuted from Plainfield to New York, to the harshness of the business world. As children both brothers had shared their father's interest in the arts; Van Wyck felt that the poet in his brother had not been able to survive exposure to the Wall Street inferno.

Unlike his brother, Van Wyck chose to stay true to the poet in himself, although after a youthful attempt at writing poetry he turned his talents to criticism rather than verse. Considering Harvard the best university to prepare him for a career as a writer, he headed to Cambridge in the fall of 1904, a year behind his boyhood friend, Maxwell Perkins. Active in the literary life at Harvard, Brooks and his fellow student John Hall Wheelock had a volume of poems printed in 1905. Although he studied with such notables as George Santayana and Irving Babbitt, even hearing a lecture from Henry James, who visited Cambridge in 1905, Brooks found that Harvard never lived up to his expectations. He hurried to finish a year early, in 1907, although his A.B. was awarded in 1908.

Leaving Harvard in pursuit of a literary career, Brooks went to New York City. Brief, mostly unsuccessful interviews with leading editors Paul Elmer Moore and William Dean Howells confirmed his sense of the bareness of the literary scene in America, and he jumped at an opportunity to go to London. Immediate prospects there were no better than in New York, however, and Brooks supported himself by producing mostly hack journalism. Feeling the need to write, Brooks escaped London in February 1908 for a farmhouse in Sussex. There he worked on a manuscript he first called "What Is America?" and later published as *The Wine of the Puritans: A Study of Present-Day America* (1908). Brooks paid half the publishing costs of this book, and while it brought him neither fame nor fortune, it does introduce some of the themes that would help to make him famous.

A dialogue between two young men contemplating America from Italy, the book attributes the sterility of American culture to the fact that unlike "the founders of all the great original races," the founders of the American race were "full-grown, intelligent, modern men, with a self-conscious purpose." Already shaped to maturity by the cultures of their European homelands, the character of these settlers was not primarily molded by the special traits of the New World. As a result Americans never achieved a culture in harmony with their environment. In short the American culture was not organic. Instead the Puritans' settlement of America is likened to putting old wine into new bottles. When the explosion results "the aroma passes into the air and the wine spills on the floor. The aroma, or the ideal, turns into transcendentalism, and the wine, or the real, becomes commercialism." The two extremes of transcendentalism and commercialism render American culture barren and make full artistic development impossible. This pessimistic scenario was countered by the suggestion that a tradition could be consciously created. Ending prophetically Brooks imagines a day "when the names of Denver and Sioux City will have a traditional and antique dignity like Damascus and Perugia—and when it will not seem to us grotesque that they have."

The logic of such a vision demanded Brooks's return to America, even though he had no better prospects than before. The journalistic work he found in New York took too much energy and paid too little, so he wrote dictionary entries thirty hours a week to support himself and allow time to devote to his criticism. His impatience was increased because he wanted to accumulate enough money to marry Eleanor Stimson, a friend from his Plainfield days to whom he had been secretly engaged since 1906. The daughter of Eleanor Manson Stimson and John Ward Stimson, the founder of the art school of the Metropolitan Museum, Eleanor suffered from her parents' unhappy, broken marriage. An intellectual, she was afraid that marriage might, as it had for her mother, mean the end of her career in art. Finally, however, she consented to marry, and in February 1911 Van Wyck took the train to California where she was living with her mother in Carmel. They were married on 1 June and eventually had two sons: Charles Van Wyck and Oliver Kenyon.

Brooks landed a job at Stanford University where he taught surveys of American and English literature. Teaching for Brooks was merely a job allowing him to afford marriage, and he resented the time it took from writing. During his two years in California, however, he managed to work on three books. They can be seen as a trilogy, displaying the dialectical bent of Brooks's

mind already at work in *The Wine of the Puritans*.

The first two books, *The Malady of the Ideal: Obermann, Maurice de Guérin, and Amiel* (1913) and *John Addington Symonds: A Biographical Study* (1914), point to opposite causes of artistic failure. The third, *The World of H. G. Wells* (1915), seeks a successful synthesis. In the first, Brooks treats three aesthetes, Etienne Pivert de Sénancour's fictional Obermann, the French poet Maurice de Guérin, and Swiss critic Henri Fredéric Amiel, who in Amiel's phrase have succumbed to "the malady of the ideal." Locked in the realm of the ideal, these three had failed fully to express their vision in coherent works of literature. Refusing to submit to the compromise necessary to embody the ideal in rhetoric, they produced only fragments in letters and journals.

Symonds's failure was just the opposite. Unlike the aesthetes, Symonds was capable of compromising the ideal—too much. Symonds produced, not fragments, but twenty volumes of criticism. Nonetheless those twenty volumes did not express a unified personality because they were written to satisfy a "sheer pathological necessity of turning out words." That need to turn out words was itself a sign of Symonds's failure, like the aesthetes, to achieve a full personality. Symonds's failure resulted not from the malady of the ideal but the pressure of the real. Symonds's poetic spirit had been crushed by a Calvinistic heritage, a father's false ideal of manhood, and an Oxford education that emphasized the practical.

Avoiding both the extremes of the aesthetes and those of Symonds, H. G. Wells achieved the full realization of personality that allowed him to become an artist of society. Wells maintained a detachment while staying actively involved in the world. One reason was that his visionary ideal—socialism—was itself socially based. Wells, Brooks argued, showed that socialism is itself a natural outgrowth of those best things that have been thought and said in the world. Wells, in other words, was a modern-day Matthew Arnold, superior to Arnold because he did not distrust science. Significantly Brooks envisioned America as the most likely place for the synthesis Wells embodied to manifest itself. America, he argued, would be the country in which ideal and real would achieve a balance.

Very likely Brooks wrote the sections on America in the Wells book while in England. Offered a teaching position with the Workers' Educational Association, Brooks returned to England in the summer of 1913. Impressed by his working-class students' desire to understand the essence of literature, not just facts about it, Brooks was more satisfied with teaching than he had been at Stanford. Other experiences reconfirmed a belief he had held since childhood that his American birth had put him at an intellectual disadvantage that was unrecoverable. As a youth he had traveled to Europe a number of times and marveled at its culture. His 1907-1908 stay in England had been disappointing and had somewhat altered his jealous admiration of European culture, but now he envied the way in which an intellectual elite had practical effect on political life. What England had that America lacked was centralization. "Centralization is the secret of all thought and art here," he wrote his wife. "Every act and thought has its place and affects every other act and thought–like the solar system." The need for centralization in America was the theme of the book he wrote in the winter of 1913-1914.

Written under the working title "A Fable for Yankees," *America's Coming-of-Age* (1915) clearly marked Brooks's coming of age as an important critic. In many ways the essay merely repeated points Brooks made in his earlier works, but it made them in a more confident and economical voice. The famous opposition between "highbrow" and "lowbrow," established in the first chapter, corresponded to the split between transcendentalism and commercialism in *The Wine of the Puritans*. These undesirable extremes divided American life between them and caused the failure of American culture. Brooks defined the difference in American highbrows and lowbrows by comparing Benjamin Franklin to Jonathan Edwards. Franklin was the lowbrow man of commerce and practicality, Edwards the religious philosopher of spiritual ideals. Crudely generalized, one could say that the highbrows were the idealists and artists who isolated themselves from the mundane worlds of business and society, while the lowbrows were vulgar materialists and moralists who lacked both imagination and taste. Brooks's dialectical approach, however, saw that these extremes often coexisted in particular works or individual authors. Walt Whitman would represent to Brooks the possibility of a middle way that drew profitably from both tendencies.

Culture, he argued, should express ideal visions while remaining actively engaged in social reality. American culture had failed because of its unattached idealism. At the same time the failure of American culture could be blamed on the social conditions in America, where the emphasis on practicality and commercialism provided infertile soil for artists to develop the full personalities necessary to produce coherent visions. "You cannot have personality, you cannot have the expressions of personality so long as the end of society is an impersonal end like the accumulation of money."

The split between highbrow and lowbrow had affected the country's artists and found expression in their thought. William Cullen Bryant and Henry Wadsworth Longfellow were concerned about social reality and understood the country's need for moral values, but they lacked the artistry to turn their poetry into anything more than moral promptings. In contrast Edgar Allan Poe and Nathaniel Hawthorne were skilled artists who lacked the social instinct to give their work substance. "No European can exist without a thousand subterranean relationships; but Americans can so exist, Americans do so exist," Brooks wrote. "Edison, for example, resembles Poe as a purely inventive mathematical intellect and with Edison, as with Poe, you feel that some electric fluid takes the place of blood; you feel that the greatest of inventors cannot be called a scientist at all, that his amazing powers over nature are not based in any philosophical grasp of the laws of nature, that he is in temperament a mechanic rather than a philosopher." Hawthorne and Poe, however, are not to blame for their lack of social substance, Brooks believed. The lack was within society itself. "They had to do what they could in society as it was–and what happened? Outwardly accepting it, but having nothing in common with it, they neither enriched society nor were enriched by it; they were driven to create and inhabit worlds of their own,–diaphanous private worlds of mist and twilight."

The division between highbrow and lowbrow was best exemplified by the Transcendentalists because they embodied both extremes within themselves. They had no sense of the relationship between theory and practice. "The world they lived in was an excessively concrete world–a world of isolated facts. . . . There was no fusion, no operative background of social forces, no unwritten laws." Their transcendental philosophy provided exactly what this world lacked. "German philosophy when it was released over the world inevitably came to port in this society, for above everything else it appeared to let one into the secret of universal experience." Transcendentalism justified Emerson's prose style, the sentences which he called "infinitely repellant particles," which, Brooks said, corresponded with fragmented New England life and its "white wooden houses, the farms, the patches of wood, the self-contained villages, each with its town-meeting." It was faith in a transcendental unity that held those sentences and that life together.

Without any sense of history, Emerson looked at the world as a transcendental text. Noting Emerson's habit of referring to "Plato and Paul and Plutarch, Augustine, Spinoza, Chapman, Beaumont and Fletcher," Brooks remarks, "There would be something quite ludicrous in this glimpse of St. Paul, Fletcher, Phidias and Spinoza arm in arm if you felt Emerson had ever realistically pictured to himself these men as they individually were. To him they were all thrice-purified ghosts, ghosts of the printed page." The disjunction between philosophy and the world of historical reality allowed both to coexist without disturbing one another. Emerson "perfectly combined the temperaments of Jonathan Edwards and Benjamin Franklin;–the upper and lower levels of the American mind are fused in him and each becomes the sanction of the other." This fusion had important social consequences. "For if the logical result of a thorough-going, self-reliant individualism in the world of spirit is to become a saint, it is no less true that the logical result of a thorough-going self-reliant individualism in the world of the flesh is to become a millionaire."

The one American poet who Brooks believed offered hope was Walt Whitman. "The Precipitant," as Brooks called Whitman, had given substance to the national character by opening up the possibility of "a middle tradition, a tradition which effectively combines theory and action, a tradition which is just as fundamentally American as either flag-waving or money-grabbing, one which is visibly growing but which has already been grossly abused." The abuse of Whitman was the topic of Brooks's fourth chapter, "The Apotheosis of the 'Lowbrow,'" and the object of his attack was Gerald Stanley Lee, the author of *Inspired Millionaires: A Forecast* (1908). Believing that the choice for America lay between the socialized millionaire and socialism, Lee argued that making a fortune was itself a creative act. Therefore, Lee continued, the country should place its faith in the visionary control of its successful capitalists. Brooks countered by exposing the lack of vision in Lee's view of society. Rather than offering a real alternative to the present system, Lee gives "a transcendental *cachet* to the established fact." Such idealism was "the most

dangerous thing in the world," for it was infused with "everything that makes honest thinking in America so nearly impossible." Bitterly dismissing the idealistic justification Lee gives to commercialism, Brooks proclaimed, "To be a prophet in America it is not enough to be totally uninformed; one must also have a bland smile." Nonetheless Brooks did not completely condemn Lee. He agreed "that most of the really first-rate forces in America have been and still are absorbed in business." Idealism, however, should not legitimate that situation but combat it.

In the tradition of the American jeremiad, Brooks turned in his last chapter from criticism to prophecy. Guided by cultural thinkers, the energy lying under "the glassy, brassy surface of American jocosity and business" could be transformed into an organic unity. If our thinkers could "create a resisting background," Americans could "leave behind the old Yankee self-assertion and self-sufficiency" and create a socialist state in which they would "work together, think together, feel together."

The combination of criticism and prophecy in *America's Coming-of-Age* made Brooks a spokesman for a generation of writers and critics. Especially important was his faith that intellectuals could lead the way in transforming American society. In the next few years Brooks would play an active role as a member of a newly established group of cultural critics. Satisfied with his life in England, he had agreed to teach at least another year. Then the war broke out, and Brooks hurried back to New York where *America's Coming-of-Age* was about to be published. By 1916 he was on the advisory board of a newly founded magazine called the *Seven Arts*. Run by James Oppenheim and Waldo Frank, the *Seven Arts* drew heavily on the work and advice of Randolph Bourne, Louis Untermeyer, Sherwood Anderson, and Paul Rosenfeld. Forcing Brooks to test his ideas against the immediate pressures of the time, the *Seven Arts* became a forum for some of his best work, republished under the title *Letters and Leadership* (1918). In these essays, especially "Young America," "Toward a National Culture," and "Culture of Industrialism," Brooks elaborated his criticism of American culture for lacking organic centrality. In "The Awakeners" he made a pointed attack on the pragmatists William James and John Dewey for being merely "students of the existing fact" and failing to provide the imaginative vision necessary to alter the facts of American life. The *Seven Arts*, however, was shortlived, a victim of an editorial dispute over America's war policy. Brooks turned instead to the *Dial* to publish his cultural criticism.

His *Dial* essays include his famous "On Creating a Usable Past," a piece that displays the strength Brooks drew from his immersion in Western culture. Like much of his early work, it depends on a comparativist perspective. "So far as our literature is concerned, the slightest acquaintance with other national points of view than our own is enough to show how many conceptions of it are not only possible but already exist as commonplaces in the mind of the world. . . . The history of France that survives in the mind of Italy is totally different from the history of France that survives in the mind of England, and from this point of view there are just as many histories of America as there are nations to possess them." It may be no accident that Brooks's early books on European subjects were mostly written in America, while his books on America were written in Europe. But as Brooks set about to create the centered culture he felt America lacked, he increasingly wrote books about his country from within an American perspective. As a result he started to lose the dialectical tension that gave his earlier works their critical edge.

Brooks's dialectical turn of thought still organized the work he produced immediately following the publication of *Letters and Leadership*. But these subsequent volumes also display his increasing concern with exclusively American topics. Forming a trilogy similar to the one he wrote before *America's Coming-of-Age,* his next three studies focused on American artists. In *The Ordeal of Mark Twain* (1920) Brooks analyzed the cost Twain paid for staying within the confines of American society, while in *The Pilgrimage of Henry James* (1925) he tallied the cost James paid for trying to escape those confines by living in Europe. In *The Life of Emerson* (1932) he portrayed Emerson as a positive synthesis of the two, clearly marking a change in his attitude from *America's Coming-of-Age.* How Brooks arrived at that changed attitude tells much about the cost *he* paid to create a usable past in America.

Brooks was happy with *The Ordeal of Mark Twain.* He wrote Waldo Frank, "I've written the book I dreamed of, a book more tragic than I had dreamed of: and for the first time I have put away a piece of work feeling that it is finished. . . ." The thesis is by now familiar: Twain's submission to the commercialism of the Gilded Age deprived him of developing the full personal-

ity necessary for a first-rate writer. A psychological study of arrested development as well as a work of literary criticism, *The Ordeal of Mark Twain* draws on Bernard Hart's *The Psychology of Insanity,* a handbook on Freud published in England in 1912. Brooks had already used Hart in his book on Symonds. His analysis of Twain is similar but more fully worked out. Brooks started by insisting that Twain's comments on the meanness of the human race resulted from a deeply felt despair rather than the public pose of a witty humorist. Indeed humor and despair operate in *The Ordeal of Mark Twain* much as highbrow and lowbrow had in *America's Coming-of-Age.* They coexisted in Twain, supporting one another, and they signaled his failure to reach the full vision that he was naturally equipped to develop: that of a satirist.

A satirist, Brooks wrote, "is one who holds up to the measure of some more or less permanently admirable ideal the inadequacies and the deformities of the society in which he lives." In short he has the complete social vision Twain lacked. "Mark Twain satirizes the facts, or some of the facts of our social life, he satirizes them vehemently. But when it comes to the spirit of our social life, that is quite another matter." Producing "all the gestures of the great unfulfilled satirist he was meant to be," Twain remained a mere humorist. His gestures were "empty gestures" informed by "an impotent anger." His "preoccupations are those merely of a bitter and disillusioned child." The risks he took with his humor were not real risks. "If the real prophet is he who attacks the stultifying illusions of mankind, nothing, on the other hand, makes one so popular as to be the moral denouncer of what everybody else denounces." Rather than countering the spirit of the age, Twain succumbed to it. Never knowing what civilization was, he mistakenly assumed "that all civilization is inevitably a hateful error, something that stands in the way of life and thwarts it as the civilization of the Gilded Age had thwarted Mark Twain." Ending in despair, Twain could not write satire because "it requires a measure, an ideal norm." No matter how futile the satirist makes life seem, he never truly despairs because he instinctively senses that "what makes things petty is an everpresent sense of their latent grandeur." Lacking an ideal norm to measure against reality, Twain and his humor were inevitably accompanied by despair.

If Twain was "the victim of an arrested development, the victim of a social order which had given him no general sense of the facts of life and no sense whatever of its possibilities," Henry James, in trying to escape the confines of that social order by fleeing America, developed an aesthetic that negated life. As early as *The Wine of the Puritans* Brooks had defined a dilettante as "an artist without a country, an artist who feels no vital connection with some one spot of soil and the myriad forms of life that have grown out of it. He is unduly concerned with perfection of technique, ignoring the ruder elements of life that come to him." *The Pilgrimage of Henry James* set out to prove that James became such a dilettante. It was also Brooks's indirect attack on the modernist movement that James's emphasis on form had helped to launch and that began to dominate the literary scene after World War I. Thus Brooks tried to counter the prevailing critical climate and argued that the early James, not the late James, was superior. He lost that battle, and another—with himself.

Brooks struggled with the James book as he had not with the study of Twain. Part of his struggle was for money and time. After the failure of the *Seven Arts* he had supported himself by writing essays and working in publishing. He had also switched publishers to E. P. Dutton, which gave him advances and time to work. Nonetheless after *The Ordeal of Mark Twain*, Brooks became an associate editor for the *Freeman,* traveling to Manhattan several times a week from his home in Westport, Connecticut, to work on "A Reviewer's Notebook," his column for the journal. At the offices of the *Freeman* and the *Dial*, which was nearby, Brooks met a number of promising and prominent literary figures, including Malcolm Cowley, Lewis Mumford, John Dos Passos, and Edmund Wilson. With some of these people he became involved in a number of worthwhile literary projects which consumed much of Brooks's time. In 1924 he received the *Dial* award in recognition of his achievements. The $2,000 stipend freed him to complete his Henry James manuscript. But Brooks needed more than time. Finishing a version of the James book, he felt dissatisfied and planned to let it sit for a year before rewriting it. In the meantime he sought a subject for a book of synthesis, not analysis, about success, not failure. Considering and rejecting Herman Melville, Whitman, Hawthorne, and Poe, he finally decided on Emerson after a careful reading of his journals. To get on with the Emerson project he published the James book

without the major revisions he had planned. Seven years would pass before he would publish *The Life of Emerson,* for in 1925, shortly after the publication of *The Pilgrimage of Henry James,* he began to undergo a process of emotional deterioration which culminated in a full-blown nervous breakdown by 1927. He actually completed the bulk of the Emerson manuscript during this period and tried to destroy it. It was saved and sorted out by Brooks's wife, who saw to it that sections of the manuscript were published along with other essays in *Emerson and Others* (1927).

In *Days of the Phoenix: The Nineteen-Twenties I Remember* (1957), Brooks described the period of his breakdown, from 1925 to 1931, as "a season in hell." He sought care, he said, "in the houses of the dead, or . . . the wounded, or the about-to-be-reborn, at Stockbridge, at Katonah, at White Plains and in England." Brooks received treatment from several therapists, including Carl G. Jung, who diagnosed him as suffering from "chronic melancholia," for from his high school days Brooks had suffered from depressions, which increased in severity.

Very likely Brooks's depressions had physiological roots. It is interesting, however, to examine the issues upon which his breakdown seemed to focus. Searching for a subject to follow James, Brooks had told Eleanor he needed to write a book that would make him sane again. Most likely the James book had disturbed Brooks's composure because he so strongly identified with a subject he declared a failure. Brooks's emphasis on the national roots of great literature ruled out a life of literary exile for himself. Yet he, as much as the James he criticized, felt a powerful attraction to Europe and its cultural heritage. The only fate for a writer who stayed in America seemed to be that of Twain: arrested development. Yet to justify his own return to America from Europe, Brooks had to prove that James's development stopped when he abandoned his American roots. But to make that proof was itself a sign of failure, because as Brooks himself admitted it was to distort James's life by imposing a thesis upon it. During his breakdown Brooks was haunted by nightmares in which James "turned great luminous menacing eyes upon me," as if the internationalist James had his revenge on Brooks's nationalist project.

According to the logic Brooks had created, American artists needed to find a middle ground, yet for Brooks no middle way seemed possible. To leave America for Europe, as James had done, was to admit failure. To stay in America was to invite failure. No doubt this analysis of the plight of the American writer caused Brooks great anxiety about his own career. And when that anxiety contributed to Brooks's breakdown, the breakdown itself became a sign that like those he had written about, Brooks had succumbed to arrested development. Thus an important part of Brooks's cure was to get him to write again. If Brooks could regain the ability to write, he might convince himself that he had escaped the plight he had written about. But he could not write just anything. In his autobiography he recalls that "One could scarcely maintain any longer the negative view of the twenties." With the editorial help of Lewis Mumford, *The Life of Emerson* finally saw print in 1932, and Howard Mumford Jones heralded it as a "prose poem." Jones saw the Emerson book as marking a decisive turn away from the dark contradictions that had obsessed Brooks in his work on James and Twain. A resurgent nationalism lay within Brooks's account of Emerson and hinted at Brooks's new view of himself and of his task. He had to write something that would prove his own development in the spirit of Emerson's "American Scholar." This meant not only calling for the creation of a usable past but the active construction of it. Brooks's choice to remain in America and concentrate on a national literature could be justified only if America proved to possess the tradition that artists needed to develop a full personality. To discover such a tradition would make Brooks feel less alienated in his native land.

The function of criticism for Brooks, as for Arnold, was to make creation possible. His analytical criticism behind him, Brooks now needed to synthesize. He also needed the discipline demanded by a life's work. In a letter he urged his friend Lewis Mumford, who had supported him throughout his crisis, to read Gibbon's autobiography "and see what a wonderful thing it is to have a life occupied for years with an immense work like this that possesses all your thoughts. . . ." Brooks's five-volume *Makers and Finders: A History of the Writer in America, 1800-1915* (1936-1952) became that immense work for Brooks.

Brooks took his title for *Makers and Finders* from the poem "Mediums" in Whitman's *Leaves of Grass*: "poems and materials of/poems shall come from their lives, and they shall be makers/ and finders." His purpose was to create the living tradition for American artists that in his earlier years he felt was lacking. His method was to dem-

onstrate the existence of a community of writers. He would start with a setting–Gilbert Stuart's Boston, Oliver Wendell Holmes's Boston, Washington Irving's New York–and populate it with literary figures, major and minor, showing how they responded to places and events, to each other, and to each other's writings. His task required devoted discipline and an enormous expenditure of energy. He had to read endlessly, not only the primary works of writers but also their letters and memoirs and all he could about their lives and the worlds they inhabited. When Edmund Wilson praised Brooks for *The Flowering of New England* (1936), the first volume of the series, Brooks responded, "They've none of 'em read the books." The books he read and the connections they allowed him to make caused Brooks to assert that his youthful judgment of America's lack of tradition had been too hasty. There was an organic community of artists in America's past, and in making and finding that tradition Brooks joined their ranks.

In *Makers and Finders* Brooks identified the American tradition as Jeffersonian, that is, a belief that an agrarian economy would best develop the personal and civic virtues essential to America's unique destiny. Jefferson offered his democratic agrarian vision as an alternative to the commercial system of Alexander Hamilton. But Brooks's view seems more Emersonian than Jeffersonian. Emerson saw virtue as emerging from a spiritual life in union with the natural world, rather than from the mere adoption of an agrarian occupation. Farming could be just as commercialized and materialistic as banking. Whereas Jefferson dreamed of an actual, agrarian utopia, Emerson prophesized a transcendental community in which the soul of man and the soul of nature existed in organic harmony. *The Life of Emerson* had started a process of personal healing for Brooks, but it was in *The Flowering of New England*, the single most important work of the series, that Brooks's dependence on Emerson for a unified point of view became most apparent. The book won Brooks the 1936 Pulitzer Prize for history and, most important, attracted the "middlebrow" audience for which he had hoped. In a little over a year the book went through forty-one printings and was on the best-seller list, an amazing feat for a book of criticism. Bringing in about $40,000 for Brooks, it helped to ease his financial insecurity. Displaying Brooks's later strengths at their fullest, it also most clearly reveals the costs he paid for his unified vision.

Drawing on the technique with which he had begun his first book, *The Wine of the Puritans*—a set-piece description of a scene—Brooks begins *The Flowering of New England* with a sketch of "The Boston of Gilbert Stuart." By evoking the name of a portrait painter at the start of his monumental history, he sets the style for the series, which, throughout, offers interrelated portraits of artists and places. This device reflects his lifetime interest in the visual arts which had begun when he was a boy traveling in Europe, and he had been most impressed by Renaissance paintings. Above all the opening chapter sets up the theme of unity with which Brooks tries to comprehend the New England experience.

*The Flowering of New England*, abundant with descriptions of Boston, Cambridge, Concord, and Salem, focuses on the communities which allowed artists to establish a vital relationship with their society. New England, as Brooks explains it, had a cultural and commercial center in Boston, which "favored the growth of the region in all its parts. For while Boston attracted the masterminds and took them away from the smaller towns, it rendered them more active and efficient; and, precisely because of this concentration of powers, it was able to send forth influences that were beneficial to the rural districts." Born into a centered, homogeneous world, New England artists were provided the conditions for growth that Brooks had found lacking in his early career. Artistic growth, Brooks found, was not confined to a few isolated figures but pervaded the entire population. Certainly some of the power of *The Flowering of New England* is its ability to bring to life minor figures as well as major ones, showing them all interacting to create a unified "New England mind."

In a chapter entitled "The Younger Generation of 1840," Brooks showed how Boston's faith in education affected an entire generation. For him, "this was the age of 'internal development,' mental as well as commercial." He points out that starting in 1826 with the Lyceum system, lecture series spread throughout New England. "There were constant courses in every town and village,—where Rollo and Lucy sat at the feet of Jonas,—on chemistry, botany, history, on literature and philosophy; and almost every eminent man in New England joined in the general effort to propagate knowledge." In one paragraph he touches on the linguistic accomplishments of Thomas Wentworth Higginson, Theodore Parker, and Elihu Burrett of Worcester, a blacksmith, who,

"as an apprentice, had kept a Greek grammar in the crown of his hat to study while he was casting brass cow-bells, who made a version of Longfellow in Sanskrit and mastered more than forty other tongues, toiling at the forge or in the evening, after a full day's work. . . ." Not only was learning widespread, it changed in character as well. Members of the younger generation "refused to talk about railroads, banks, and cotton. They had no use for Blackstone and Justice Story. They were unwilling to be 'mere' lawyers,—heaven save the codfish in the State House!" In short the flowering of New England was a moment in American history when the artistic mind overshadowed the commercial, when a middlebrow culture was achieved.

Not far from Boston, Concord was an ideal spot for the younger generation to develop. Emerson's Concord in *The Flowering of New England* is quite different from the fragmented world of isolated facts that spawned the Emerson of *America's Coming-of-Age*. The Concord that Emerson moved to in 1834 was idyllic. "Having a little income, he had bought a house on the Boston turnpike, surrounded with pine and fir-trees. There was a garden by the brook filled with roses and tulips. In the western window of his study he placed an Æolian harp. It sang in the spring and summer breezes, mingling with the voices of the birds, fitfully bringing to mind the ballads that he loved, the wild, melodious notes of the old bards and minstrels." It was this idyllic setting that cultivated the Transcendentalist movement.

Not all New England outposts from Boston were forward-moving like Concord, however. In the chapter on Hawthorne, Brooks describes Salem as having been "stricken by the War of 1812" and having "lapsed into quietude and decay." While Salem's faded grandeurs gave it an immemorial air, it "had much in common with . . . the ancient ports of northern Europe, where the Gothic fancies of the Middle Ages have not been dispelled by modern trade." In gothic Salem the "mediæval mind had lingered" and the town had become the center for "old wives' tales and old men's legends." In such a town where "history is ever-present, lying in visible depths under the unstirred waters," there were "odd corners and shadowy households where symbols and realities seemed much the same." Brooks argued that Salem had both shaped Hawthorne's artistic sensibility and provided the legends for his fictions.

Brooks's account of Salem attracted the criticism that his description was not objective but filtered through the lens of Hawthorne's fiction. Specific passages from "Hawthorne in Salem" would seem to substantiate the objection. In trying to convey the town's sleepy silence, for example, he writes: "One caught the tinkling of the bell at the door of some little cent-shop, even the quiver of the humming-birds darting about the syringa bushes. The rattling of the butcher's cart was the only event of the day for many a household, unless perhaps one of the family hens cackled and laid an egg." Clearly this description draws on *The House of the Seven Gables* for some of its details, as does Brooks's claim that in Salem's "moss-grown, many-gabled houses, panelled with worm-eaten wood, and hung with half-obliterated portraits, dwelt at least the remnants of a race that retained the mental traits of a far-away past." Brooks would argue that the details of Hawthorne's fiction entered his account of Salem because Salem's life had constituted Hawthorne's artistic imagination. Hawthorne's fiction and Salem life were intricately interwoven. Even though his own book might have "an air of fiction," Brooks in his preface assures "the sceptical reader that I have not indulged in fiction." Every phrase that appears in the book, he argues, can be documented "in some trustworthy source of the time, some diary, memoir, letter or whatever." Brooks's claim that his book is factual, however, is as questionable as Hawthorne's claim in the preface to *The House of the Seven Gables* that his book is a romance, having more to do with castles in the air than the actual soil of Essex County. Just as Hawthorne writes a work that draws on the historical world of Salem, Brooks writes a work that is in part a fictional construct.

Brooks's oversight, in this regard, was that he did not question why an artist like Hawthorne felt it necessary to make a radical distinction between fiction and history and to declare his works purely fictional. The reason for this omission is that Brooks's account of how a work of art is related to history was a narrow one. Art, he felt, must have an organic relationship to the society that produced it. Having once found an organic relation between artist and society lacking, Brooks in *Makers and Finders* feels it necessary to construct one. What Brooks would not admit was that his need to construct such a relationship grew out of the same conditions that made Hawthorne deny one. The history of the American artist that Brooks brings to life in *The Flowering of New England* is largely the product of Brooks's powerful rhetorical skills.

In *The Malady of the Ideal* Brooks had defined rhetoric as "a form of infidelity by which the writer conveys the impression that he has not felt, in order to give his expression the form and consistency demanded by art." The malady of the ideal is to refuse to make the compromise signified by rhetoric, to realize that the truly free spirit stays true by remaining silent. For Brooks to remain silent, however, was to fail and to admit that the conditions of American society that made fully developed artistic expression impossible had triumphed. Instead of remaining silent, during his period of recovery from his breakdown after 1931, he mastered a rhetoric that allowed him to produce a massive number of pages, pages with an internal form and consistency but pages that naggingly convey the impression that Brooks has tried to feel what he has not felt.

One of the most noticeable aspects of Brooks's later rhetoric is the almost seamless merger of his prose with the prose of the writer he is treating. Although Brooks argues that he can "quote chapter and verse" for any material he uses, he refuses to supply documentary footnotes. This practice has caused critics to accuse him of indulging in an uncritical merger between biographer and subject. To a certain extent this criticism is accurate, but it ignores the possibility that Brooks consciously worked to create the effect criticized. Through his prose he quite literally merged with the tradition he wrote about. Rooted in a usable past, his prose brought that past alive. When a writer's subject is the very tradition that allows him to write, a merger between writer and subject is not a fault.

A more telling criticism of Brooks's later style is not only that it uncritically merged biographer and subject but that in trying to do so it distorted both by creating a unity that did not exist. Brooks's first extended use of this style had appeared in *The Pilgrimage of Henry James*. He used it because he was obsessed with a very Jamesian desire: to capture the inner drama of James's mind in conflict with the world. This technique, however, did not lead to a successful merger. Instead, Brooks sensed that he had written a fictional account of James, and he went so far as to ask his brother, the lawyer, if he could be sued for libeling a dead man. Paradoxically, then, when Brooks first used the style that was to dominate his later work, instead of finding a unity with his subject he was forced to face what he called "a division within myself." Recognition of that division coincided with his breakdown. His cure coincided with an ability to use the same style without feeling an internal division. Covering up divisions in himself, Brooks denied divisions within American culture. The rhetoric of *Makers and Finders* was accommodated to that task.

"There were," Brooks noted, "many strains in the Boston mind, a warm and chivalrous Tory strain, a passionate strain of rebelliousness, a strain of religious fervour, a marked and even general disposition." Nonetheless, he argued, these many strains together created a unified New England mind and a unified culture. In "The Boston of Gilbert Stuart," Brooks repeatedly generalized about the New England mind to create the sense of this unity. Note his use of "every" and "all" in the following excerpts. He reported that Stuart liked to begin his anecdotes by saying, " 'When I lived in the Athens of America.' " Brooks explains that "Everyone knew what he meant by the phrase: he was referring to Philadelphia. And every Bostonian knew that he was mistaken." To depict Boston's cultural habits, Brooks wrote, "In every house one found the standard authors, Hume, Gibbon, Shakespeare, Milton, Dryden, Addison, the *Arabian Nights, Don Quixote,* Sir William Temple's works in folio, a set of Hogarth's original plates, perhaps, or two or three first editions of Pope, books that were worthy of their calf bindings, on shelves that have been carved by Grinling Gibbons, surmounted by marble busts." Later he writes that, "in Boston, all the boys and girls went to the Lowell lectures. . . . The boys invited the girls, and after the lecture they walked home together, ending the evening with an oyster-supper."

This lovely portrait of the homogeneous cultural life that allowed Boston to become the center of New England's flowering clearly leaves out many people living other sorts of lives in the region at that time. Brooks's subsequent portrait of Emerson's idyllic Concord also neglected the transient life of many of its residents who, searching for hard-to-find jobs, did not live in houses with gardens by a brook filled with roses and tulips. Needing to show that New England's literature grew organically out of its centered culture, Brooks found no tension between Emerson's and Thoreau's idealization of nature and a region in which "factory-towns were rising on every hand." Needing to establish the people of Boston as a homogeneous race, Brooks found no room to elaborate on conflicts between classes. "The slum," we

hear in the first chapters, "was a thing of the future, and most of the rich men acquired their wealth by the superior exercise of traits that almost every Yankee shared and applauded." Only in a note do we learn that there was one region in Boston "that is said to have been extremely squalid and vicious. It was filled with crowded, tumble-down tenements where crime ran riot. The population was largely black, with a worse white intermixture."

These slums do not reappear until over four hundred pages later. It is significant that this occurs during a discussion of Maria Cummins's *The Lamplighter,* a book parodied by James Joyce in the "Nausicaa" chapter of *Ulysses* (1922) and one of the few texts written by a woman that qualifies for inclusion in *The Flowering of New England* (Brooks does give extended positive treatment to Harriet Beecher Stowe). Commenting on the popular fiction of the era, Brooks writes that "*The Wide, Wide World* of Susan Warner was a swamp of lachrymosity. It was a malarial book. So was *The Lamplighter,* by Maria Cummins, the story of another Cinderella, which had, however, something vigorous in it that *The Wide, Wide World* totally lacked. One felt and saw the Boston slums,—for slums had appeared in Boston with a vengeance,—the streetlamps and the snow, suggesting Dickens's London." This sudden, brief appearance of slums reminds us to what extent Brooks's marvelous account of a coherent New England culture depended upon repressing the conflicts that the existence of slums would raise. Neither Brooks nor his American middlebrow readers cared to review at length the possibility that New England's literate classes enjoyed their flowering at the expense of others who suffered the effects of the factories and the slave trade. In *Makers and Finders* Brooks had little use for such conflicts in America's past.

In addition to *The Flowering of New England,* the *Makers and Finders* series included *New England; Indian Summer, 1865-1915* (1940), *The World of Washington Irving* (1944), *The Times of Melville and Whitman* (1947), and *The Confident Years; 1885-1915* (1952). *New England; Indian Summer* starts with a sketch of "Dr. Holmes's Boston," which depicts the New England mind as having lost its antebellum vigor and retreated into itself. American society was undergoing rapid industrialization, but the cultured set of Boston, Brooks shows, turned to an adoration of the past. Entering this world from the west was William Dean Howells. Howells's broad democratic appreciation of life allowed him to preserve and extend the native American tradition and keep alive a living community of writers. Howells's task was a difficult one, however, because the social conditions of the Gilded Age that had arrested Twain's development served to cause divisions in the greatest New England minds of the period, such as those of Henry James, Henry Adams, and Emily Dickinson. These divided minds made the establishment of a truly cohesive artistic community impossible, just as the lack of that community contributed to the divided minds of the period's artists. Nonetheless the book ends positively.

The last chapter, "Second March," starts with Robert Frost returning from England in 1915 and picking up a copy of the newly established journal, the *New Republic*. The founding of such journals and the publication of the poetry of figures like Frost, Ezra Pound, and Amy Lowell signaled that "a new literature was coming to birth, a poetry more vigorous than had been seen for fifty years, a vital American theatre, a flowering of the novel." After a sleepy Indian summer, the dry old Yankee stalk was flowering again, which is exactly what Brooks in 1915 had predicted in *America's Coming-of-Age*. Indeed *New England; Indian Summer* leads into the revival of American culture that Brooks himself had helped to get in motion. "America was undergoing a transformation. It was rousing itself like a strong man after sleep; and it was casting off its sloth of literary dullness,—eager, impressionable, receptive, it was vocal also. It had suddenly received a gift of tongues. The signs of a maturing life, self-scrutiny and discontent, that had characterized the confusion of the pre-war years, foreshadowed the revelations of the years that followed. It was generally felt that America was coming of age."

The difference between Brooks's sense of American history in *America's Coming-of-Age* and *Makers and Finders* is that in the early work Brooks felt America's organic culture still needed to be created, while in the later work he believed that it had once existed, dissolved, and needed to be reformed. In the new work Brooks abandoned his dialectical model for a cyclical theory of history, a theory that included his own impressionable and vocal call for America to come of age as part of that cycle.

The passions and contradictions evident in Brooks's vision of America in the first two volumes of *Makers and Finders* also informed his public activities during the 1930s. Thus his involvement in the radical politics of the decade was limited. His autobiography states that he "had always been a socialist on the understanding that the levelling was to be not down but up." He joined the League of American Writers, which grew out of the 1935 American Writers' Congress and in which Brooks's old friend Waldo Frank played a key role. During the next years he rose through the official ranks of the league to one of seven vice presidencies. He took a brief fling at politics when he ran as a socialist candidate for the Connecticut legislature, but turned, with many American leftists, against the Marxist cause after the revelation of the Moscow Trials and the announcement of the Stalin-Hitler pact of August 1939. Shortly thereafter he resigned from the league, which he felt was being used by the Marxists.

Brooks's ambivalent relation to America's literary leftism during the 1930s expressed divisions inherent in his critical approach. The kind of cultural criticism that Brooks pursued emphasized the conflict between society and the artist. Underlying that emphasis, however, was a deeply rooted desire to transcend conflict. Both Brooks's aesthetic and social visions were informed by that desire. As early as his 1910 essay "The Soul" he describes literature as a refuge. His quest for a refuge helps explain his attraction to socialism, since he saw socialism as the system that would resolve the conflict between society and the artist by freeing the artist from economic pressures impinging upon full artistic expression, which in turn would shape the proper society. Brooks's social vision reveals that as a cultural critic he was, from the start, an aesthete. It also explains why, despite his desire to transcend conflict, he found himself in direct conflict with American Marxists.

Brooks resisted the Marxist emphasis on materialism and class conflict, and in this remained an Emersonian idealist. Drawing on William Carlos Williams's phrase, Brooks argued that "there is an American grain, and I wish to live with it, and I will not live against it knowingly. . . . this country can only be socialized in the American grain." Brooks saw Marxism as a reductive materialism that ran against the idealism of the American grain. The function of the artist and the critic was to express the moral ideals of its culture. "Democratic in economics, aristocratic in thought," Brooks fondly quoted George Russell. Brooks's portrait of antebellum New England in *Makers and Finders* projects this mixture of democratic and aristocratic thought but does so at a time when both Brooks and his country sought to overcome depression and historical crisis with new deals and ideal visions. Brooks's personal vision of an organic cultural tradition coincided with the needs of an American middle class that wanted a version of the natural past stressing harmony, not conflict.

The publication of *New England; Indian Summer* in 1940 confirmed Brooks as an important and controversial spokesman for what was being called "Nationalism in American Literature." The social and political upheavals of the 1930s had intensified American debates over the role and function of artists and intellectuals, especially as concerned the realization of America's special destiny in the world. In May 1940 Archibald MacLeish, Librarian of Congress, published a polemic in the *Nation* entitled "The Irresponsibles," chiding the disengaged, ivory-tower writers and the coterie authors who ignored their duty to oppose totalitarian oppression in Germany, Spain, and Russia. Brooks sided with MacLeish in the debate that followed and became an early advocate of a declaration of war. In 1941 Brooks became a contributing editor of the *New Republic* and continued expressing his views on politics, philosophy, and American life through the mask of a series called "Opinions of Oliver Allston." He dropped the artifice, however, in a pamphlet, "On Literature Today" (1941), in which he attacked the fatalism of literary modernists such as T. S. Eliot, Ezra Pound, James Joyce, H. L. Mencken, and Ernest Hemingway. This and other diatribes of that year were collected in *Opinions of Oliver Allston* (1941). This book also included Brooks's charges against the emergent New Critics (particularly John Crowe Ransom, R. P. Blackmur, and Cleanth Brooks), whose attention to literary language rather than cultural history Brooks saw as a theorizing "*in vacuo*. It was not only that they wrote exclusively in relation to pupils, but that they wrote of literature without reference to feeling; and this was because they did not possess feeling, however they explained the matter otherwise." One of the feelings the "coterie-writers" and "coterie-critics" lacked, suggested Brooks, was for the value of the American tradition; too many were expatriates or espousers of European literature and English poetry.

Brooks's salvos prompted a counterattack by Dwight Macdonald in the November/December 1941 issue of *Partisan Review*. Macdonald saw Brooks's prescription for an affirmative American literature as itself a kind of totalitarianism

designed to support "the swing behind the government in the war crisis." The following issue of *Partisan Review* (January/February 1942) contained responses from various hands. William Carlos Williams, Henry Miller, and Louise Bogan weighed in against Brooks, while Allen Tate bridled at Macdonald's pronouncements on "the decomposition of the bourgeois synthesis in all fields." James T. Farrell shared some of Macdonald's criticisms of Brooks but agreed with Brooks's negative judgment on T. S. Eliot, who himself responded with a brief letter in defense in the next issue. Brooks's involvement in these arguments reflected his lifelong career as an advocate of the public function of the "man of letters" and sheds some light on the tendencies and results of the final volumes in *Makers and Finders*.

The nationalism Brooks espoused encompassed, as in the case of New England, an appreciation for the cultural resources of the nation's various regions, and so Brooks developed a regional theory of American culture in these ensuing books. Regional allegiance, he felt, would unite artists and allow each region to develop its own tradition. While at first the various regions established their independence by reacting against New England, eventually they could complement one another to achieve a grand synthesis of American culture. Thus after two books on New England, Brooks turned his attention to other regions, although he did not devote an entire book to each region. Instead within a book on a specified period he had such chapter headings as "The South," "The Middle West," and "The West."

More than any other book in the series *The World of Washington Irving* reveals Brooks's conviction, one he shared with Vernon L. Parrington, that the true grain of American thought was the democratic agrarianism articulated by Thomas Jefferson. Although Brooks places Irving's name in the title, he does not confine himself to describing the particular locales that Irving inhabited. Instead, "the world" in the title refers to the cultural climate outside of New England that created a figure like Irving. The cultural cycle occurring in the rest of the country between 1800 and 1840 was not as dramatic and cohesive as the flowering of New England. Nonetheless, it had its own centers in New York, Philadelphia, and Charleston. The major figures Brooks wove together with his Jeffersonian thread are Irving, James Fenimore Cooper, William Cullen Bryant, and Edgar Allan Poe. Poe's antidemocratic pretensions would seem to disqualify him for inclusion with this group, but he became the exception that proved the rule. Outside the American tradition Poe was a supreme artist, but he was not an artist of society. A "sick" man, he could not be a voice for the American people. Ending by referring to two writers of genius coming of age in and about New York in the 1840s, Brooks prepared the way of his next work.

*The Times of Melville and Whitman* moved from the 1840s to the 1880s. The title indicates a possible return to Brooks's dialectical method. Indeed he argued that *Moby-Dick* (and *Leaves of Grass*) are complementary books. "One gave the dark side of the planet, the other the bright." But Brooks, as he had as early as *America's Coming-of-Age,* felt that the true American tradition was represented by Whitman; the original working title of the volume had been "Whitman and His Contemporaries." Whitman remained central, and Mark Twain joined Melville as a figure contrasted with Whitman. The Twain of the new work is essentially the same as in *The Ordeal of Mark Twain,* but Brooks was now careful to emphasize how Twain's democratic vision shone through his despair just as it did through Melville's darkness.

In *The Confident Years; 1885-1915* Brooks brought his literary history outside of New England to a conclusion similar to that of *New England; Indian Summer.* The thirty years of the title constitute a cycle leading to the rise of the cultural critics of his generation. The book concentrated on the tension between the country's prewar confidence and the criticism of writers such as Stephen Crane, Frank Norris, and Theodore Dreiser. Considered pessimistic by many, these writers were firmly lodged in the democratic cultural tradition that Brooks had defined throughout *Makers and Finders. The Confident Years* was Brooks's most explicit definition of the humanistic Jeffersonian tradition, and in the last four chapters he used that standard to measure the course of American literature from 1915 to 1950. He especially railed against the exiled writers who forsook their native tradition to worship the abstract religion of art, who sharpened their technique rather than used their art to speak for the people. T. S. Eliot was Brooks's favorite target. Eliot was commended for affirming the importance of tradition but condemned for failing to recognize a truly American tradition. Turning his back on the American past, Eliot, Brooks found, had no faith in the American future and thus dislodged himself from a position within the American tradition. The last paragraph of *The Confident Years* affirms Brooks's own place within that tradition by declaring his faith, with Thomas Wolfe, that "the true fulfillment of our spirit . . . is yet to come."

Taken as a whole, *Makers and Finders* embodied Brooks's conviction that literature's social value lay in its capacity to express the wholeness too often compromised by life within society. Through this expression the writer embodied certain fundamental human values and fulfilled the highly moral task of heralding the possibility of full human expression. If as a cultural critic Brooks demanded that the artist engage society, it was because the artistic vision was necessary to bring about the ideal society. The ideal society was a socialist one in which the artist in each individual could flourish. In turn the artist was the vehicle through which that society could find its expression. The aesthete in Brooks saw art offering a refuge from societal pressures. The social critic in him saw socialism offering the artist that refuge.

Because America was not socialist and because Brooks was not a member of the aristocracy, he had to find some way to afford the leisure needed to produce his aristocratic thoughts. That leisure was provided in a large measure through the labors and sacrifices of his wife. In addition to sacrificing her own career for his, Eleanor created the orderly environment her husband needed to create his massive work of synthesis. Much of her labor was to shield Brooks from the forces that he felt had destroyed other American writers. According to her, Brooks refused to look at bills. His aversion to them lay deeper than a mere irritation over the disruption they caused to his routine. Bills were a reminder of the material pressures he feared. Even Eleanor's labors on his behalf served to remind him of the pressures. The harder she worked to provide him the space he needed to work, the more he was aware of his failure to provide financial security for his family. It is no accident, for instance, that Brooks's cure from his breakdown was hastened when Eleanor's cousin, the Secretary of State under Hoover, created a trust fund to guarantee Eleanor's support.

Eleanor did not accept her role as supportive wife without complaints. The marriage experienced bitterness, tension, and unhappiness. Nonetheless both Eleanor and Van Wyck stayed true to their commitments. When Eleanor died in August 1946 Brooks felt "cast adrift without a rudder" and wondered if he could go on without her. He did, marrying again within a year. His new wife, Gladys Rice Billings, had an independent income from a previous marriage. She provided Brooks with some of his happiest years. More social than Eleanor, she entertained graciously in the style Brooks felt suited a respected man of letters. She also protected him from the quotidian concerns of life, allowing him to continue his literary career. In short, by the end of his life, Brooks achieved success and was recognized for it.

But Brooks was never allowed to rest securely in his success. A number of writers who had admired his early cultural criticism questioned the value of the works that brought Brooks widespread recognition. In a sense when he became an established man of letters Brooks stopped serving as a leader for previous literary allies. For them the later Brooks too easily fit into a pattern the early Brooks had so eloquently criticized. Although he had rejected the Wall Street commercialism that surrounded him in his Plainfield youth, he retained the drive for success that Gerald Stanley Lee claimed had inspired America's millionaires. Before his first marriage he had written Eleanor, "It seems to me so infinitely important, this *getting somewhere*." Given the way he analyzed American society, getting somewhere for Brooks meant appealing to a middlebrow audience. It is a wonderful tribute to his rhetorical powers that *The Flowering of New England* was a best-seller; historical studies of America's literary culture rarely achieve such status. And yet one of the paradoxes of American culture is that the status of a best-seller is itself suspect. To reach a wide audience Brooks had to compromise the point of view that had enabled his poignant criticism of American culture. Brooks's later success may be read as a sign that he had succumbed to the contradictions he exposed in American life rather than as a sign that he had escaped them. For many critics, Brooks's success became a sure sign of his failure.

This view was especially widespread in the universities where New Criticism increasingly influenced the standards by which literature was read. For those adhering to New Critical doctrine, Brooks's merger of his own language with his subjects' and his refusal to focus on close textual analysis made *Makers and Finders* amateurish. In a significant review of *The World of Washington Irving*, F. O. Matthiessen criticized Brooks's study

for its paucity of literary analysis, its anecdotal method, and confused chronology. Matthiessen called Brooks a "lyric poet manqué" and also took exception to Brooks's nationalistic self-confidence. Writing in 1944, Matthiessen said that while Brooks "may be right . . . it could be argued that we will emerge from this war the most confident of all countries in the superiority of our ways, and that what we need more is an astringent antidote to shake us out of any complacent and fatuous dream of 'the American century.' " Matthiessen's own *The American Renaissance: Art and Expression in the Age of Emerson and Whitman* (1941) had already usurped Brooks's territory, for Matthiessen subsumed the previous generation's interest in cultural history and political criticism under his New Critical emphasis on style and symbol. This was a foreshadowing of things to come, as Brooks's work would be elbowed aside by studies such as R. W. B. Lewis's *The American Adam* (1955), Richard Chase's *The American Novel and Its Tradition* (1957), Harry Levin's *The Power of Blackness: Hawthorne, Poe, Melville* (1958), and Charles Feidelson's *Symbolism and American Literature* (1959), all of which emphasized the literary in literary history and deemphasized sociopolitical criticism in their analyses of cultural myths and symbols. These studies were further supported by the new brand of cultural criticism promulgated by Lionel Trilling, whose skeptical view of the "liberal imagination" and negative commentary on the American tradition won out over the nationalism Brooks had promoted. Soon Brooks would be a quaint or mostly forgotten figure in university and college discussions of American literature.

Nonetheless Brooks continued to write and publish after completing his monumental *Makers and Finders*. This later work, which has not earned much attention or appreciation for Brooks, includes portraits of the painter John Sloan (1955) and of Helen Keller (1956). His earlier interest in American writers and their relation to Europe was rekindled in *The Dream of Arcadia: American Writers and Artists in Italy, 1760-1915* (1958). Turning his attention once more to the native brand of realism, he published *Howells, His Life and World* in 1959. Beginning with *Scenes and Portraits: Memories of Childhood and Youth* (1954), Brooks began a series of autobiographical memoirs that would eventually run to three volumes in the collected edition of 1965, which also included *Days of the Phoenix: The Nineteen-Twenties I Remember* (1957) and *From the Shadow of the Mountain: My Post-Meridian Years* (1961).

Of some real interest is his 1962 collection, *Fenollosa and His Circle, With Other Essays in Biography.* Ernest Fenollosa had been an avid disciple of Emerson and had sought in the Far East for a culture that could provide a dialectical complement to America's increasingly materialist character. Fenollosa's writings on Asian art and especially his *The Chinese Written Character as a Medium for Poetry* were major influences on Ezra Pound, who revised and edited the latter work from Fenollosa's manuscripts and published it in 1920. In writing on Fenollosa, Brooks showed the persistence of his concern with the cultural identity crisis of American artists and writers who look to far-off times or places for visions that may be applied to the crises of the present epoch.

The style of Brooks's last books persisted in the middlebrow manner that had lost him favor among academic reviewers. Yet Brooks, while not a professional academic, was certainly no amateur. He was a masterful prose stylist. And he did his homework. He rarely wrote on an author until he had read everything the author had written. Although Brooks created his own canon of literary greats, he gave careful attention and credit to other writers, since for him a literary tradition consisted of more than great works. Brooks always conceived of the critic's task more widely than did the New Critics. His goal was to be a critic of culture, not one confined to the narrow definition of literature espoused by the New Critics. Brooks's limitation was not that his literary criticism was too broad but that his cultural criticism was too narrow.

In *America's Coming-of-Age* Brooks had acutely suggested that America's Emersonian tradition of cultural criticism was a mirror image of its tradition of commercial materialism. Despite this critical insight Brooks could not escape the Emersonian tradition. In "The Transcendentalists" Emerson acknowledged that commercial times breed idealism. Similarly Brooks's aversion to commercial materialism made him insist that idealism was the only alternative to it. Rather than pursue the possibility that to define culture as idealism was too narrow, Brooks felt that the problem with the American cultural tradition was that a truly idealized culture had not been realized. In Emersonian fashion Brooks argued that such a culture had to be imagined by the country's artists. Thus, as is the case with so many artists in America, Brooks found himself identifying with America's mission. What the country needed to fulfill a potential that seemed so tantalizingly close to realization was the proper imaginative vision. In such a tradition the artist's coming-of-age merges with the country's. Few have been able to sustain such a burden.

The effect on Brooks is concisely expressed in a series of images from his writings first juxtaposed by William Wasserstrom. In his early essay, "The Soul," Brooks compared men's lives to ships "sailing, tacking, drifting across the ocean," an ocean with no shore. Occasionally someone would drop a line into the ocean to take his bearings. But the bottom he thought he touched was in fact "only the wreckage of other ships floating near the surface." Brooks ends the passage by declaring, "I will be this ocean: and if I have to be a ship I will be only a raft for the first wave to capsize and sink." Five years later, in *America's Coming-of-Age*, he likens America to "a vast Sargasso sea," whose restless energy will come to fruition when an imaginative mind gives it shape and form. Instead, in the midst of his breakdown, Brooks had seen himself as "a capsized ship with the passengers drowned underneath and the keel in the air."

Taking on the burden of charting the course for the American people across its Sargasso Sea was too much for Brooks. His images of shipwreck could provide material for an American chapter to a book written by the German philosopher Hans Blumenberg. *Shipwreck Looked Upon* traces the image of the title from Lucretius through European literature up to the Vienna Circle's Otto Neurath, who compared the modern epistemological dilemma with the task seafarers faced in rebuilding their ship at sea. Over the years the distance between gazer and wreckage has narrowed, so that by the twentieth century the spectator has no secure point from which to contemplate the disaster. Thrust onto the wreckage at open sea with no haven to retreat to, the gazer senses the urgency to rebuild the ship but has to wonder where the material can be found for a successful reconstruction. Blumenberg's answer was a question: Probably from earlier shipwrecks? Locating the foundation for this reconstructive act within his own imagination, Brooks found himself temporarily shipwrecked. His recovery, if it can be called that, was achieved when he claimed that in the American cultural tradition he had found a bottom to the bottomless sea upon which he floated, while in effect he was producing one more wreck from which other sailors can get their bearings. At least they may be used as markers to get critical bearings. As with so many American writers, then, it is in his failure that Brooks becomes an important part of our usable past.

**Letters:**

*The Van Wyck Brooks-Lewis Mumford Letters: The Record of a Literary Friendship,* edited by Robert E. Spiller (New York: Dutton, 1970).

**Biographies:**

James Hoopes, *Van Wyck Brooks: In Search of American Culture* (Amherst: University of Massachusetts Press, 1977);

Raymond Nelson, *Van Wyck Brooks: A Writer's Life* (New York: Dutton, 1981).

**References:**

Alfred Kazin, *On Native Grounds* (New York: Harcourt, Brace, 1942);

Kermit Vanderbilt, *American Literature and the Acad-* *emy: The Roots, Growth, and Maturity of a Profession* (Philadelphia: University of Pennsylvania Press, 1986);

James R. Vitelli, *Van Wyck Brooks* (New York: Twayne, 1969);

William Wasserstrom, *The Legacy of Van Wyck Brooks: A Study of Maladies and Motives* (Carbondale: Southern Illinois University Press, 1971);

Wasserstrom, *Van Wyck Brooks: The Critic and His Critics* (Port Washington, N.Y.: Kennikat Press, 1979).

**Papers:**

Brooks's papers may be found among over seventy collections at libraries across the country. Among the largest collections are those at the Museum of the American Academy of Arts and Letters in New York and the Charles Patterson Van Pelt Library at the University of Pennsylvania, Philadelphia.

# Sterling A. Brown

*(1 May 1901-    )*

R. V. Burnette
*Old Dominion University*

See also the Brown entries in *DLB 48, American Poets, 1880-1945;* and *DLB 51, Afro-American Writers from the Harlem Renaissance to 1940.*

BOOKS: *Outline for the Study of the Poetry of American Negroes* (New York: Harcourt, Brace, 1931);
*Southern Road* (New York: Harcourt, Brace, 1932);
*The Negro in American Fiction* (Washington, D.C.: Associates in Negro Folk Education, 1937);
*Negro Poetry and Drama* (Washington, D.C.: Associates in Negro Folk Education,1937);
*The Last Ride of Wild Bill and Eleven Narrative Poems* (Detroit: Broadside Press, 1975);
*The Collected Poems of Sterling A. Brown,* edited by Michael S. Harper (New York: Harper & Row, 1980).

OTHER: "The Blues as Folk Poetry," in *Folk-Say: A Regional Miscellany,* volume 1, edited by Benjamin A. Botkin (Norman: University of Oklahoma Press, 1930);
*American Stuff; an Anthology of Prose and Verse by Members of the Federal Writers' Project* (New York: Viking, 1937);
"The Negro in Washington," in *Washington City and Capital,* Federal Writers' Project (Washington, D.C.: U.S. Government Printing Office, 1937);
"Blues, Ballads, and Social Songs," in *Seventy-five Years of Music* (Washington, D.C.: U.S. Government Printing Office, 1940), pp. 17-25;
*The Negro in Virginia,* edited by Brown, The Writers' Program (New York: Hastings House, 1940);
"Lone Gone," "Slim in Hell," "Southern Road," "Old Lem," "Break of Day," and "Strong Men," in *The Negro Caravan, Writings by American Negroes,* edited by Brown, Arthur P. Davis, and Ulysses Lee (New York: Dryden Press, 1941);
"Athletics and the Arts," in *The Integration of the Negro into American Society,* Papers of the Fourteenth Annual Conference, Division of

*Sterling Brown (courtesy of the Prints and Photographs Collection, Moorland-Spingarn Research Center, Howard University)*

Social Sciences, Howard University, edited by E. Franklin Frazier (Washington, D.C.: Howard University Press, 1951), pp. 117-147;
"Negro in the American Theatre," in *Oxford Companion to the Theatre,* edited by Phyllis Hartnoll (London & New York: Oxford University Press, 1951), pp. 565-572;
"The New Negro in Literature (1925-1955)," in *The New Negro Thirty Years Afterward,* edited by Rayford Logan, Eugene C. Holmes, and G. Franklin Edwards (Washington, D.C.: Howard University Press, 1955);

Entries on Matthew Arnold, Charles Baudelaire, Emily Brontë, Robert Burns, Emily Dickinson, Ralph Waldo Emerson, Benjamin Franklin, Robert Frost, Heinrich Heine, A. E. Housman, Thomas Jefferson, Abraham Lincoln, Henry Wadsworth Longfellow, Herman Melville, *Moby-Dick,* Edgar Allan Poe, Henry David Thoreau, Mark Twain, and Walt Whitman, in *The Reader's Companion to World Literature,* edited by Lillian D. Hornstein, G. D. Percy, and others (New York: New American Library, 1956);

Langston Hughes and Arna Bontemps, eds., *The Book of Negro Folklore,* includes poetry by Brown (New York: Dodd, Mead, 1958);

"And/Or," in *American Negro Short Stories,* edited by John Henrik Clarke (New York: Hill & Wang, 1966).

PERIODICAL PUBLICATIONS: "Our Literary Audience," *Opportunity,* 8 (February 1930): 42-46, 61;

"Unhistoric History," *Journal of Negro History,* 15 (April 1930): 134-161;

"Negro Character as Seen by White Authors," *Journal of Negro Education,* 2 (April 1933): 179-203;

"The Negro in Fiction and Drama," *Christian Register,* 114 (14 February 1935): 111-112;

"The American Race Problem as Reflected in American Literature," *Journal of Negro Education,* 8 ( July 1939): 275-290;

"The Negro Writer and His Publisher," *Quarterly Review of Higher Education Among Negroes,* 9 ( July 1941): 7-20;

"The Approach of the Creative Artist to Studies in Folklore," *Journal of American Folklore,* 59 ( January-March 1945): 506-507;

"Spirituals, Blues and Jazz–The Negro in the Lively Arts," *Tricolor,* 3 (April 1945): 62-70;

"Negro Folk Expression," *Phylon,* 11 (Autumn 1950): 318-327;

"The Blues," *Phylon,* 13 (Autumn 1952): 286-292;

"Negro Folk Expression: Spirituals, Seculars, Ballads, and Worksongs," *Phylon,* 14 (Winter 1953): 45-61;

"Seventy-Five Years of the Negro in Literature," *Jackson College Bulletin,* 2 (September 1953): 26-30;

"A Century of Negro Portraiture in American Literature," *Massachusetts Review,* 7 (Winter 1966): 63-96.

Since his retirement in 1969 from Howard University's English department, Sterling Allen Brown has become known among colleagues and associates as "the dean" of black American critics, an epithet first used by Darwin Turner. "No other black critic," comments Turner, "has inspired as much admiration and respect from his students and his successors in the field. In every stream of creative black literature, Sterling Brown is the source to which critics return." As poet, scholar, teacher, and critic, Brown profoundly influenced American black literary theory and practice.

Born in Washington, D.C., on 1 May 1901, Brown was the only son and youngest child of Adelaide Allen and the Reverend Sterling Nelson Brown. His father taught in the department of religion at Howard University and was pastor of Washington's historic Lincoln Temple Congregational Church. Among the minister's associates were black leaders Frederick Douglass and Booker T. Washington, senators B. K. Bruce and John R. Lynch, sociologist W. E. B. Du Bois, and cultural critic Alain Locke. From these men, whom Brown met as a youth on Howard's campus, and especially from his father (himself a former slave), Brown acquired a knowledge of black history and a commitment to the importance of black life in America.

Educated in Washington's public school system, Brown attended Dunbar High School. "I think there were more Phi Beta Kappa Black teachers at Dunbar and Armstrong and Cardoza [segregated high schools] than there would be in the white schools," Brown recalls. Among Brown's teachers at Dunbar were the authors Angelina Weld Grimké and Jessie Redmon Fauset, and Frederick Douglass's grandson Haley Douglass. After graduating from Dunbar in 1918, Brown attended Williams College in Williamstown, Massachusetts, on an academic scholarship. Although blacks were segregated from whites at the school, Brown excelled, earning the Phi Beta Kappa key in 1921, during his junior year. Upon graduating from Williams with a B.A. in 1922, he entered Harvard University where he studied with critics Bliss Perry and F. O. Matthiessen. After receiving his master's degree in 1923, he taught at Virginia Seminary and College in Lynchburg (1923-1926), Lincoln University in Missouri (1926-1928), and Fisk University in Tennessee (1928-1929). In 1929 he joined the faculty at Howard University where he remained until his retirement.

While teaching in the South, Brown steeped himself in the folk cultures of rural blacks. A buoyant and unpretentious personality, he actively sought out folk communities and became an appreciative member of the audience for the songs, sayings, and folkways of rural and semirural blacks. In the black vernacular he found qualities urged by the modernists: a concreteness and a vivid compression of imagery. Out of this language he attempted to forge an authentic art that was capable of portraying black life and black people while it avoided the simplistic and inadequate stereotypes that had come to dominate American letters.

His first volume of poetry, *Southern Road* (1932), is a synthesis of contemporary poetic practice, traditional forms, and Brown's firsthand experience with folk idioms. The results were best summarized by Brown writing about himself in *Negro Poetry and Drama* (1937):

> He has made a fairly close study of folkways and folksongs, and has used this in interpreting folk-experience and character which he considers one of the important tasks of Negro poetry. He is not afraid of using folk-speech, refusing to believe dialect to be "an instrument of only two stops—pathos and humor."

Later critics John Blassingame and Henry Louis Gates, Jr., have claimed that the publication of *Southern Road* "truly ended the 'Harlem Renaissance,' primarily because it contained a new and distinctly Black poetic diction, and not merely the vapid claim for one." In the late 1930s he completed a second volume of poetry, "No Hiding Place," which was accepted but never published by Harcourt, Brace. It did not appear until its inclusion in *The Collected Poems of Sterling A. Brown* (1980). Preceding *The Collected Poems* was another volume of poetry, *The Last Ride of Wild Bill and Eleven Narrative Poems* (1975).

As a poet Brown brought to bear upon his craft an appreciation and mastery of the dominant tendencies of American literature—realism and a new poetic vernacular—while consciously adopting the imagery, idioms, and structures of black folk expression. His involvement with the black oral tradition had important consequences for his critical undertakings as well. As commentator Joanne Gabbin puts it, "For Brown, folk expression constitutes a very adept self-portraiture of a people and serves as an important source, model, and measure for literary interpretation." Appear-

ing primarily in black publications, his critical statements called attention to black folk art. He insisted on his audience showing an appreciation of the "wit and beauty possible to folk speech, the folk-shrewdness, the humanity, the stoicism of these people."

At the same time folk expression was an index to social realities that were frequently distorted or obscured by American writers who exploited black life. In articles that were at times tendentious and frankly polemical, Brown took issue with what he considered dangerously romantic works, particularly those by southern writers. "Today the tradition of glorifying the South gains momentum," he wrote in his 1930 *Journal of Negro History* essay "Unhistoric History": "Certain evils of modern life furnish the impulse to an easy romantic escape in dreams to a pleasanter past. Young men of the South, keen of mind, having set themselves up as 'liberals,' after having learned the most advanced technique, now use that technique for the buttressing of ancient prejudices." While he wrote appreciative and generous appraisals of works by such writers as Harriet Beecher Stowe, George Washington Cable, Herman Melville, William Faulkner, and Erskine Caldwell, Brown nevertheless insisted that a full and realistic assessment of the black experience could come only from Afro-Americans themselves—a conclusion that followed logically from his adherence to a realism grounded in "observation and understanding" (*The Negro in American Fiction*, 1937). Too frequently, however, the consciously literary effort of many black writers revealed a dearth of originality that sprang from a slavish imitation of white models. In *Negro Poetry and Drama* Brown wrote:

> Dialect, or the speech of the people, is capable of expressing whatever the people are. And the folk Negro is a great deal more than a buffoon or a plaintive minstrel. Poets more intent upon learning the ways of the folk, their speech, and their character, that is to say better poets, could have smashed the mold. But first they would have had to believe in what they were doing. And this was difficult in a period of conciliation and middle-class striving for recognition and respectability.

Brown undertook the task of dismantling what was false in American literature concerning blacks, while promoting a black literary movement grounded in the kind of social realism and creative originality found in black folk expression. His approach was essentially unacademic, and he attempted to create a body of criticism serviceable to ordinary readers.

In 1931 "The Literary Scene: Chronicle and Comment" began appearing in *Opportunity*, where it ran until the late 1930s. Ostensibly a review column intended to "bring before the reader . . . a list of . . . books and articles . . . that bear directly or indirectly upon our concerns," the column served as a forum for Brown's critical ideas. Assuming a posture reminiscent of William Dean Howells as editor of the *Atlantic Monthly*, Brown argued for realism as a mode in literature and against such romantic interpretations of the South as the ones presented in *I'll Take My Stand* (1930), the manifesto of southern agrarianism produced by contributors to the *Fugitive*, including John Crowe Ransom, Allen Tate, and Robert Penn Warren. "At their worst," he wrote of the twelve essays included in the volume, "they are all fairly old stuff; at their infrequent best they are Emerson (a 'damyank'), and diluted Matthew Arnold." Although he praised the efforts of white writers like Howard Odum ("he is a poetic craftsman as well as a social observer"), he was relentless in his criticism of popular works that distorted black life and character. His March 1935 review of the film based on Fannie Hurst's *Imitation of Life* initiated a long debate in the columns of *Opportunity*. Brown had said of the movie that "It requires no searching analysis to see in [it] the old stereotype of the contented Mammy, and the tragic mulatto; and the ancient ideas about mixture of the races." Hurst wrote a letter, complaining that Brown's attitude was "ungrateful, but what is much more important, it is also unintelligent."

One of the critical positions that inform "The Literary Scene" is Brown's belief in the need of black writers for an ethnic audience, a need whose urgency was most apparent in the theater. In "A Literary Parallel" he cites the Irish theater as an example of the accomplishments that might result from a consciously black literary movement: "Differences between the histories of these two submerged peoples, the Irish and the Negro, are of course manifold and obvious. But one of their problems ran parallel to one of our own, and their solution deserves our deep attention." The problem was the tendency of dominant groups to stereotype minorities—a problem addressed by Irish poets and playwrights, particularly William Butler Yeats and John Millington

Synge. Brown thought that their pioneering efforts to reinterpret Irish life and character were worthy of emulation by black Americans: "All of our philistines to the contrary, the reinterpretation of the Negro character in literature is not one of our least concerns."

In any such reinterpretation the role of black writers was crucial, but Brown did not underestimate the difficulties involved. Reviewing Edwin R. Embree's *Brown America* in *Opportunity*'s June 1932 issue, Brown acknowledged Embree's list of "Odds Against the Niggers"—disease, poverty, illiteracy, crime, and white indifference—but added to this list the odds against black artists:

> The difficulties confronting the Negro artist are not those, thrice-told, of caged genius, ineffectual and sensitive, beating its wings against the bars of a cruel world. The Negro artist, like the artist of many minority groups, is betrayed often by what is false within. The hardship he faces is an alienation from Negro life, largely self-directed, although helped along by miseducation and social pressure. The danger he risks for this alienation is artistic aridity.

What was needed, concluded Brown, was a *reeducation* of black Americans to "a consciousness of the common past of all Negroes, and our common destiny," a consciousness largely rooted in a black folk tradition. During a career that spanned four decades, his pioneering criticism of blacks in American literature and of expressive black traditions that redress misrepresentations and misconceptions helped lay the foundations for a renewed interest in black culture and black studies.

While an associate professor at Howard University, Brown completed *The Negro in American Fiction* and *Negro Poetry and Drama*. Published in 1937 by the Associates in Negro Folk Education, both works were concerned with an analysis and evaluation of Afro-Americans as subjects and authors in American literature. Robert Bone comments that in these surveys Brown "undertook the necessary labor of destruction" by discrediting false or distorted representations of black life. According to Alain Locke, *The Negro in American Fiction* differed "from the usual academic survey by giving a penetrating analysis of the social factors and attitudes behind the various schools and periods considered." In his introduction Brown makes the same point by way of a fable:

> The blind men gathered about the elephant. Each one felt the part of the ele-

phant's anatomy closest to him, the trunk, tusk, eyes, ear, hoof, hide and tail. Then each became an authority on the elephant. The elephant was all trunk, or all hoof or all hide, or all tail. So ran their separate truths. The single truth was that all were blind. This fable, pertinent to our study, might be continued to tell how some of the blind men returned to their kingdoms of the blind where it was advantageous to believe that the elephant was all trunk or tusk.

This myopic perspective, usually in the service of social policy, led to stereotypes whose identification has been one of Brown's most enduring contributions to American criticism: the contented slave, the wretched freeman, the comic Negro, the brute Negro, the tragic mulatto, the local-color Negro, and the exotic primitive. (Brown had already provided a survey of American literature employing these types in "Negro Character as Seen by White Authors," published in the *Journal of Negro Education* in 1933.) Admitting that "there is no stereotype without some basis in actuality," Brown nevertheless argued against generalizations about the race drawn from these types.

In *Negro Poetry and Drama* he argued for a recognition of the complex reality expressed in the blues, in folklore, in the idioms of black folk. Surveying the works of black poets prior to the twentieth century, he wrote that "the so-called 'conscious' poets were frequently self-conscious. While they were 'poetizing,' folk-Negroes were creating poetry of depth and originality. For the genuine poetry of the Negro of this period . . . one must go to the sly and sardonic folk-rhymes and the profoundly revealing spirituals." In the same volume Brown surveyed the images of blacks in American drama, giving particular attention to the developments after the minstrel tradition: "The Negro entered American drama in a walk-on role, as self-effacing as he was supposed to be in real-life," he says. "Today, instead of coming downstage to deliver or be a joke and then retiring to upstage, or hovering in the wings with a letter or a glass, he is often found center-stage full in the lime-light." Despite this encouraging development, much remained to be done. Pointing to the absence of convincing portrayals of the black middle class or working class, Brown argued that fulfillment of the latent dramatic possibilities in black life could probably be achieved only by black dramatists who possessed the requisite intimacy. Aspiring black playwrights, however, lacked sufficient opportunities for theater apprenticeship and, more significantly, lacked an appreciative black audience. In addition to these already foreboding limitations, America's legitimate theater, Brown wrote, "for all of its growing liberal attitude, is still entranced with the stereotypes of the exotic primitive, the comic stooge and the tragic mulatto." While the persistence of little theater groups like Cleveland's Gilpin Players and the Howard Players, for which Brown had served as director, constituted a hopeful sign, black playwrights were needed who were sufficiently honest to portray black life, and a black audience was needed to give sufficiently sophisticated support to an ethnic theater.

Brown's concern for the necessary and vital relationship between artist and audience was evident in his attempt to familiarize his readership with traditional black music. In numerous essays on the blues, spirituals, and ballads Brown brought attention to and appreciation for black music and black singers. In "The Blues as Folk Poetry," published in the 1930 volume *Folk-Say: A Regional Miscellany,* Brown approached the blues as an art form whose structural elements and language deserved close attention. "The Blues," published in the Autumn 1952 issue of *Phylon,* examined the social reality expressed in the blues tradition. Brown praised the "frankness of revelation" and the "bitter honesty" of blues lyrics. "Because of their elemental honesty, depth of insight, and strong, original phrasing," he wrote, "the blues at their best belong with the best folk poetry." At the same time he argued that the blues tradition alone is not completely revelatory of black folk. While the blues represents the secular and the profane, the religious side of the folk experience is found in the spirituals and the gospel songs.

In "Negro Folk Expression: Spirituals, Seculars, Ballads, and Worksongs" (1953) Brown attempted to define what is uniquely "Negro," and therefore original, about black music. As in the blues, the imagery in the spirituals is stark and terse, while the lyrics themselves reveal a social reality quite unlike such popular notions as "the slave did not contemplate his low condition." In secular music Brown found such qualities as satire, irony, and a bitterly robust humor: "Unlike Stephen Foster's sweet and sad songs such as 'Massa's in the Cold, Cold Ground,' the folk secular looked at slavery ironically. And where Foster saw comic nonsense, they added satiric point." Prison songs "make stark drama out of the pain, and hopelessness, and shame" of the singers, while other work songs are vehicles for sharp social protest.

The implications of Brown's interest in black folk culture are manifold. Not only could a knowledge of folk traditions serve as a common milieu between artist and audience, but folk expressions themselves possessed qualities that Brown believed would invigorate American literature generally. Speaking at the Conference on the Character and State of Studies in Folklore (April 1942), he defined his approach to black folklore as a "social-historical" one, concluding with his own sense of the importance of folklore to an American literary tradition:

> American literature will be enriched by a deeper understanding, a greater knowledge, of the folk literature. I think that American literature stands in need of some of the vigorous qualities that such knowledge can bring.

In 1941 appeared what many believe to be the most comprehensive anthology of black literature, *The Negro Caravan, Writings by American Negroes,* edited by Brown, in collaboration with Ulysses Lee and Arthur P. Davis. This collection, while providing ample space for more consciously literary efforts, devoted considerable space to the folk traditions Brown championed. Noteworthy, too, are the fine critical introductions which Brown provided for the anthology as a whole and for the section on folk literature. The volume's introductory essay provided a succinct reiteration of Brown's ideas concerning the relationship between literature and social policy, as well as his belief that black writers "must be allowed the privilege and must assume the responsibility of being the ultimate portrayers of their own." Here, too, was Brown's attempt to situate black literature in an American literary context:

> In spite of such unifying bonds as a common rejection of the popular stereotypes and a common "racial" cause, writings by Negroes do not seem to the editors to fall into a unique cultural pattern. Negro writers have adopted the literary traditions that seemed useful for their purposes. . . . The bonds of literary tradition seem to be stronger than race.

Brown objected to the term "Negro literature" because he believed it to be ambiguous. " 'Negro literature,' " he complains, "has no application if it

means structural peculiarity, or a Negro school of writing. The Negro writes in the forms evolved in English and American literature." A more important objection he made was against a double standard of judgment. Black writers face certain hardships as artists, and those hardships are reflected in their works, Brown says. Nevertheless, "in their own defense they must demand a single standard of criticism." However, there was some justification for including in the anthology works that were clearly not examples of literary excellence, because "Literature by Negro authors about Negro experience is a literature in process and like all such literature (including American literature) must be considered as significant, not only because of a body of established masterpieces, but also because of the illumination it sheds upon a social reality." Nowhere was that social reality more vividly and cogently expressed than in folk literature, as Brown's introductory essay to that section demonstrates. Spirituals, which Brown believed to be among the most important and original contributions of blacks to American culture, revealed a complex and multilayered awareness. Agreeing with Zora Neale Hurston in her refusal to accept the inclusive title "Sorrow Songs," Brown commented that they were robust and vital. Spirituals also demonstrated freshness, originality, and the importance of black folk contributions: "Neither European nor African, but partaking of elements of both, the result is a new kind of music, certainly not mere imitation, but more creative and original than any other American music." Despite the inevitable effects of modern technology, migration to the North, and the commercialism of black folk culture, Brown believed that the spiritual would continue to be the creative source for black art and an important factor in American culture.

As editor of Negro affairs for the Federal Writers' Project, a position he assumed in 1936, Brown strove to ensure the integrity and authenticity of slave narratives that were being recorded under the auspices of the Federal Writers' Project: "I should like to recommend," he wrote to the state directors, "that the stories be told in the language of the ex-slave, without excessive editorializing and 'artistic' introduction on the part of the interviewer. The contrast between the directness of the ex-slave speech and the roundabout and, at times, pompous comments of the interviewer is frequently glaring." Into this undertaking he hoped to introduce the same principle that governed his own use of black dialect: that "truth to idiom be paramount, and exact truth to pronunciation secondary." While serving as editor, Brown urged a more extensive investigation of black history, a concern reflected in his own historical essays, such as "The Negro in Washington" (1937) and "Saving the Cargo: Sidelights on the Underground Railroad" (1941). In *Washington City and Capital* (1937) and *The Negro in Virginia* (1940), Brown also made important contributions to the study of blacks in American society.

Throughout his career Brown sponsored young writers whose efforts he thought commendable. Poets Claude McKay and Langston Hughes and novelists Jean Toomer and Wallace Thurman were among the Harlem Renaissance writers whose works received favorable comment from Brown. He wrote enthusiastic reviews of Richard Wright's *Native Son* and Zora Neale Hurston's *Their Eyes Were Watching God* and was among the first critics to recognize the importance of Hurston's folklore collections. In 1966, near the end of his career, Brown included in his retrospective survey, "A Century of Negro Portraiture in American Literature," more recent black writers whose achievements were noteworthy. About Chester Himes he commented: "No one can stay long near Himes's characters and feel at all easy with such 'racialistic characteristic' abstractions as humility, forgiveness, cheerfulness and contentment." Ralph Ellison's triumph was "that it will be hard for cardboard heroes and villains to occupy the fictional stage any longer." James Baldwin was recognized as an important and innovative playwright and "the most powerful and prophetic voice of the young militants in SNCC and CORE." These writers provided evidence that "stereotyping is on the way out," while works like Norman Mailer's *Advertisements for Myself* (Brown called the work "a Greenwich Village refurbishing of old stereotypes") served as reminders that "stereotyping is not altogether out."

While Brown continued publishing critical essays during the 1950s and 1960s, most of his efforts went into teaching. He is reported to have said that his legacy is his students and, indeed, he has exerted an inestimable influence on succeeding generations. Amiri Baraka and Albert Murray have acknowledged their indebtedness to Brown's studies of black music. His analysis of black drama and the need for a black theater anticipated many of the ideas later expounded by cultural critic Harold Cruse. His belief that in addressing black literature "one must deal somewhat with the folksong, folktales, folk sayings and

folk speech" anticipated Houston Baker's anthropological approach to criticism as well as Stephen Henderson's important study, *Understanding the New Black Poetry*. What Gabbin has called his "dual aesthetic approach"—"a thorough knowledge of literary traditions [and] a profound understanding of Black folk culture"—bears a striking resemblance to efforts by Addison Gayle, Jr., and Henry Louis Gates, Jr., to define a black aesthetic philosophy. Brown himself, however, has never suggested that black literature required a distinct critical apparatus and has been wary of any attempt to treat black literature separately, as something apart from American literature. In his last essay, "A Century of Negro Portraiture in American Literature," he quoted a passage from his article "Negro Character as Seen by White Authors" as a summary of his own critical philosophy:

> One manifest truth, however, is this: the sincere, sensitive artist, willing to go beneath the cliches of popular belief to get at an underlying reality, will be wary of confining a race's entire character to a half-dozen narrow grooves. He will hardly have the temerity to say that his necessarily limited observation of a few Negroes in a restricted environment can be taken as the last word about some mythical *the Negro*. He will hesitate to do this, even though he had a Negro mammy, or spent a night in Harlem, or has been a Negro all his life. The writer submits that such an artist is the only one worth listening to, although the rest are legion.

**Bibliography:**

Robert G. O'Meally, "An Annotated Bibliography of the Works of Sterling A. Brown," in *The Collected Poems of Sterling A. Brown*, edited by Michael S. Harper (New York: Harper & Row, 1980), pp. 243-255.

**References:**

Richard K. Barksdale and Keneth Kinnamon, eds., *Black Writers of America: A Comprehensive Anthology* (New York: Macmillan, 1972);

Black History Museum Committee, *Sterling A. Brown: A UMUM Tribute* (Philadelphia: Black History Museum, 1976);

Joanne Gabbin, *Sterling A. Brown: Building the Black Aesthetic Tradition* (Westport, Conn.: Greenwood Press, 1985);

Addison Gayle, Jr., ed., *The Black Aesthetic* (New York: Doubleday, 1971);

Eugene Clay Holmes, "Sterling Brown: American Peoples' Poet," *International Literature,* 8 (June 1934): 117-122;

Nathan Irvin Huggins, *Harlem Renaissance* (New York: Oxford University Press, 1971);

Blyden Jackson and Louis D. Rubin, Jr., *Black Poetry in America* (Baton Rouge: Louisiana State University Press, 1974), pp. 58-62;

James Weldon Johnson, ed., *The Book of American Negro Poetry* (New York: Harcourt, Brace, 1922);

Ulysses Lee, "Criticism at Mid-Century," *Phylon,* 11 (Winter 1950): 328-337;

J. Saunders Redding, *To Make a Poet Black* (Chapel Hill: University of North Carolina Press, 1959);

Charles H. Rowell, "Sterling A. Brown and the Afro-American Folk Tradition," *Studies in the Literary Imagination,* 7 (Fall 1974): 131-152;

Jean Wagner, *Black Poets of the United States: From Paul Laurence Dunbar to Langston Hughes,* translated by Kenneth Douglas (Urbana: University of Illinois Press, 1973).

---

# Kenneth Burke
### (5 May 1897-    )

### Paul Jay
*Loyola University of Chicago*

See also the Burke entry in *DLB 45, American Poets, 1880-1945,* First Series.

BOOKS: *The White Oxen and Other Stories* (New York: A. & C. Boni, 1924);

*Counter-Statement* (New York: Harcourt, Brace, 1931);

*Towards a Better Life, Being a Series of Epistles, or Declamations* (New York: Harcourt, Brace, 1932);

*Permanence and Change: An Anatomy of Purpose* (New York: New Republic, 1935; revised edition, Los Altos: Hermes Publications, 1954);

*Attitudes Toward History,* 2 volumes (New York: New Republic, 1937; revised edition, Los Altos, Cal.: Hermes Publications, 1959);

*The Philosophy of Literary Form: Studies in Symbolic Action* (Baton Rouge: Louisiana State University Press, 1941; revised and abridged edition, New York: Vintage, 1957);

*A Grammar of Motives* (New York: Prentice-Hall, 1945; London: Dobson, 1947);

*A Rhetoric of Motives* (New York: Prentice-Hall, 1950; London: Bailey Bros. & Swinfen, 1955);

*Books of Moments: Poems 1915-1954* (Los Altos, Cal.: Hermes Publications, 1955);

*The Rhetoric of Religion: Studies in Logology* (Boston: Beacon Press, 1961);

*Perspective by Incongruity* [and] *Terms for Order,* ed. Stanley Edgar Hyman with Barbara Karmiller (Bloomington: Indiana University Press, 1964);

*Language as Symbolic Action: Essays on Life, Literature, and Method* (Berkeley & Los Angeles: University of California Press, 1966);

*Collected Poems 1915-1967* (Berkeley & Los Angeles: University of California Press, 1968);

*The Complete White Oxen: Collected Short Fiction* (Berkeley & Los Angeles: University of California Press, 1968);

*Dramatism and Development* (Worcester, Mass.: Clark University Press, 1972).

OTHER: Thomas Mann, *Death in Venice,* translated by Burke (New York: Knopf, 1925);

"Fact, Inference, and Proof in the Analysis of Literary Symbolism," in *Symbols and Values: An Initial Study,* edited by Lyman Bryson (New York: Harper, 1954), pp. 283-306;

"Dramatism," in *International Encyclopedia of the Social Sciences,* volume 7 (New York: Macmillan & Free Press, 1968), pp. 445-452.

PERIODICAL PUBLICATIONS: "William Carlos Williams, The Methods of," *Dial,* 22 (February 1927): 94-98;

"Counterblasts on 'Counter-Statement,'" *New Republic,* 69 (9 December 1931): 101;

"A Sour Note on Literary Criticism," review of *A
Note on Literary Criticism* by James T. Farrell,
*New Republic,* 87 (24 June 1936): 211;

"Is Mr. Hook a Socialist?," answer to Hook's review of *Attitudes Toward History, Partisan Review,* 4 ( January 1938): 40-44;

"On Poetry and Poetics," review of *The World's
Body* by John Crowe Ransom, *Poetry,* 55 (October 1939): 51-54;

"Key Words for Critics," review of *Intent of the
Critic* ed. Donald Stauffer, *The New Criticism*
by Ransom, and *Reason in Madness* by Allen
Tate, *Kenyon Review,* 4 (1942): 126-132;

"Kinds of Criticism," *Poetry,* 68 (August 1946):
272-282;

"American Scholar Forum: The New Criticism,"
*American Scholar,* 22 (Winter 1950-1951):
86-104; (Spring 1951): 218-231;

"*Othello:* An Essay to Illustrate a Method," *Hudson Review,* 4 (Summer 1951): 165-203;

"Three Definitions," *Kenyon Review,* 13 (Spring
1951): 173-192;

"The Criticism of Criticism," review of *The Lion
and the Honeycomb* by R. P. Blackmur, *Accent,*
15 (Autumn 1955): 279-292;

"The Encyclopaedic, Two Kinds of " review of *Literary Criticism: A Short History* by W. K.
Wimsatt, Jr., and Cleanth Brooks, and *Anatomy of Criticism: Four Essays* by Northrop
Frye, *Poetry,* 91 (February 1958): 320-328;

"On Catharsis, or Resolution," *Kenyon Review,* 21
(Summer 1959): 337-375;

"Myth, Poetry and Philosophy," *Journal of American Folklore,* 72 (October-December 1960):
283-306;

"Catharsis—Second View," *Centennial Review,* 5
(Spring 1961); 107-132;

"As I was Saying," *Michigan Quarterly Review,* 11
(Winter 1972): 9-27;

"Dancing with Tears in My Eyes, A Response to
Wayne Booth," *Critical Inquiry,* 1 (September
1974): 23-31;

"(Nonsymbolic) Motion/(Symbolic) Action," *Critical Inquiry,* 4 (Summer 1978): 809-838;

"Methodological Repression and/or Strategies of
Containment," *Critical Inquiry* (Winter 1978):
401-416;

"In Haste," *Pretext* 6 (Fall/Winter 1985): 329-377.

It would be misleading to label the work of
Kenneth Burke "literary criticism," for his concerns extend far beyond the confines of that discipline. Burke is the most theoretically challenging,
unorthodox, and sophisticated of twentieth-
century speculators on literature and culture, a

*Kenneth Burke*

surprising feat in light of his irregular career.
Without a college degree, with minimal formal
training in literature, philosophy, psychology, or
political science, with no permanent full-time academic appointment, and with no conventional
area of specialization, Burke has worked for over
sixty-four years in rural New Jersey producing a
body of work whose breadth, rigor, and theoretical grounding is unmatched by the work of any
other American critic. Novelist, poet, translator,
and philosopher, Burke is first and foremost a
critic in the broadest sense of the word. Indeed
his work starts from the recognition that "all living things are critics." Humans have a
metacritical capacity that separates them from
other organisms, for, as Burke wrote in *Permanence and Change* (1935), "though all organisms
are critics in the sense that they interpret the
signs about them, the experimental, speculative
technique made available by speech would seem
to single out the human species as the only one
possessing an equipment for going beyond the criticism of experience to a criticism of criticism. We
not only interpret the character of events . . . we
may also interpret our interpretations." Here
Burke locates his own broadest interest, for all

his theoretical and practical criticism (though he would question such a distinction) is aimed precisely at the "criticism of criticism."

Another way to approach Burke's work is to see it as a fundamental and relentless analysis of interpretive behavior. In one way or another all of his work focuses on the language, and the underlying assumptions, of interpretive systems, be they historical or sociological modes of literary interpretation, philosophical ones worked out by philosophers like Immanuel Kant, Georg W. F. Hegel, or George Santayana, or the more elaborate and central explanatory systems of Karl Marx or Sigmund Freud. Each has come under Burke's critical eye in his attempt to "interpret our interpretations." In this respect Burke's work is double-edged: he wants to identify what it is that motivates interpretive behavior of any kind and to work out a system for analyzing it. For this reason the body of his work is relentlessly interdisciplinary (a quality that has brought it much criticism). His writing broadens out from early work that is clearly literary criticism until, book by book, his focus shifts from an examination of the nature of literary communication to the nature of communicative behavior per se. Burke's project ranges over a sometimes dizzying number of disciplines, but always with its eye on two things: structure and power; structure because of his conviction that the aims of any text are embedded in its formal principles, and power because in the end it is both literature's effect on the writer and the reader and its relation to cultural and political power that interests Burke. Part formalist and part rhetorician, Burke is fundamentally a cultural critic, but one whose particular interest is in the workings of language, and whose first love is literature.

Kenneth Duva Burke was born in Pittsburgh, Pennsylvania, on 5 May 1897 to James Leslie and Lillyan Duva Burke. He attended Peabody High School where, along with his good friend Malcolm Cowley, he began to develop an avid interest in language and literature. His circle of friends was decidedly intellectual, and from an early age Burke was reading widely and writing stories and plays. Recalling those days in *Exile's Return* (1934), Cowley wrote that "we felt that we were different from other boys . . . At seventeen we were disillusioned and weary . . . we contributed artificial little pieces to the high-school newspaper, in which vice triumphed over virtue, but discreetly, so as not to be censored by the faculty adviser. We were launching or drifting into

the sea of letters with no fixed destination and without a pilot." The group at Peabody High, which also included James Light, who would later become a director for the Provincetown Players, was avidly modern in its orientation. The degree of paradox in a writer was, for them, a measure of his modernity: "If they were paradoxical–if they turned platitudes upside down, showed the damage wrought by virtue, made heroes of their villains–then they were 'moderns.' "

Cowley records that they all read tirelessly, from Rudyard Kipling, Robert Louis Stevenson, George Meredith, Thomas Hardy, George Gissing, H. L. Mencken, Joseph Conrad, Oscar Wilde, and George Bernard Shaw, to Jules Laforgue, Fyodor Dostoyevski, and Gustave Flaubert. In the fall of 1915 Cowley went off to Harvard, while early in 1916 Burke went to Ohio State with James Light. Together they started a literary magazine, *Sansculotte*, and Burke took up his studies in French, German, Greek, and Latin. After his parents moved to Weehawken, New Jersey, he dropped out of Ohio State and returned home to be nearer New York City. Later in 1917 Burke enrolled at Columbia University and began to study philosophy. It is clear from his letters to Cowley that this period was an enormously productive one. But by the end of the year, Burke grew uncomfortable with the restrictions and limitations of a formal education whose scope and direction were determined by others. In January of 1918 he wrote Cowley: "I am quitting Columbia. A long story . . . but the essential fact is that I am going in a new direction. Suddenly becoming horrified at the realization of what college can do to a man of promise. . . . I shall get a room in New York and begin my existence as a Flaubert." Burke's withdrawal from Columbia marked the end of his formal education and the beginning of his self-education. Freed from the restrictions of a college curriculum, he began a systematic study of classical and European literature, focusing at the outset on Homer, Virgil, John Milton, John Keats, Percy Bysshe Shelley, Robert Browning, Thomas Mann, Dostoyevski, and Flaubert. He continued the wide-ranging reading of philosophy he had begun at Columbia, wrote plays, poetry, and short stories, and translated works from the German. Once, when a publisher lamented to Burke that there was no English translation of Thomas Mann's *Death in Venice*, Burke casually informed him that he had one at home in his desk. He had translated the entire novel as practice. It was published in 1925 as the first translation of Mann's novel. In 1919 Burke married Lillian Mary Batterham; they eventually had three daughters.

An important part of Burke's "new direction" announced in the letter to Cowley involved moving to Greenwich Village. It was here that Burke began the hard work of becoming a writer, working long hours on the short stories that would comprise his first published book, *The White Oxen and Other Stories* (1924). It was while laboring over these tales that Burke's early ideas about aesthetics and literary form began to develop, ideas that would come to form the substance of his first book on literature and criticism, *Counter-Statement* (1931). The more carefully he worked on revising and restructuring his stories, especially during the years 1921-1923, the more interested he became in formulating the structural principles of narrative that he had discovered for himself. The longer he worked on his stories, the more interested he became in the nature and function of form in fiction. Although he continued to write fiction for another ten years, so strong was this interest in form that by February 1922 his real vocation seemed clear to him. In that month he wrote to Cowley that "I shall surely become a writer on aesthetics."

When *Counter-Statement* appeared in 1931 it was, in fact, the culmination of ten years' work in the area of aesthetics. This work led Burke into an often uneasy alliance with the 1920s avant-garde movement. He had reservations about Dadaism and surrealism, but he felt that it would be out of such radical impulses that a revitalized American literature would emerge. Burke's interest in Dada was spurred by the fact that in the early 1920s Cowley was in France, writing to him often about his involvement with the Dadaists. Burke was fascinated by Cowley's reports, but wary. His letters to Cowley are full of warnings about the dangers of remaining abroad when there was so much work to be done on American soil in the name of American literature. Thus, Burke remained in New York. He did, however, become active in a number of avant-garde publications, contributing stories and reviews, and helping to edit modernist magazines like *Broom* and *Secession* in 1920-1923.

During this period Burke also became friends with a number of writers and critics in New York City, including E. E. Cummings, William Carlos Williams, Hart Crane, Van Wyck Brooks, Waldo Frank, and Paul Rosenfeld. When Burke and his wife moved to the New Jersey countryside and began commuting to New York City, Williams and other writers would congregate on weekends at Burke's place in Andover, where animated discussions of fiction, poetry, and criticism would be mixed with tennis playing, long walks, drinking, and dancing. At the *Dial,* where he had obtained work as an editorial assistant, and where from 1927 to 1929 he was the music critic, Burke was able to meet a wide range of writers, including Marianne Moore. His practical experience at the *Dial* ran from writing book reviews to helping prepare T. S. Eliot's *The Waste Land* for the printer. Almost miraculously Burke was beginning to make it as a writer on his terms, supporting his family as an editor, translator, writer, and reviewer. The family lived frugally, in a small home, sustaining themselves with an elaborate vegetable garden, many fruit trees, and a highly organized canning operation each fall.

By 1932, after the publication of *Counter-Statement* and his novel, *Towards a Better Life* (1932), the direction of his work turned decidedly toward criticism. His novel had done poorly, and writing it had taken a tremendous toll on him, as had the financial pressures brought on by the Depression. Burke divorced his wife and in 1933 married her sister Elizabeth, by whom he had two sons. After the cool critical reception and low sales of *Towards a Better Life,* he began to build on the work he had started in *Counter-Statement.* By 1941 he had published three more books, one on literature and literary criticism, *The Philosophy of Literary Form* (1941), and two with a more general focus on communication, interpretation, and meaning. These two books, *Permanence and Change* (1935) and *Attitudes Toward History* (1937), marked the beginning of Burke's massive interdisciplinary project, which he would come to call "dramatism."

Although published in 1931, *Counter-Statement* had been mostly written in the early 1920s and had been published in essay form. While the early essays elaborate a theory of literary form, the later essays focus on the relationship between art and ideology and elaborate an oppositional program for both creative writers and literary critics. There is, then, something of a split in the book that reflects Burke's changing orientation as he moves, under the influence of Marxism, away from conceptualizing art in aesthetic terms as self-expression and toward viewing it as a socially symbolic act.

As an embodiment of his work on literary form in the 1920s, *Counter-Statement* seeks both to define what constitutes form and to elaborate a critical method for analyzing it. Burke begins with the key supposition that *"form* in literature is an arousing and fulfillment of desires. A work has form in so far as one part of it leads a reader to anticipate another part, to be gratified by the sequence." Form is determined by the *effect* the writer seeks. Its relationship to psychology has to do with the fact that, for Burke, form is determined by the author's effort to move the audience, or reader, through a sometimes complex series of expectations and fulfillments. Form, in this respect, is tied to the mental and emotional state of the audience/reader, and "psychology," as Burke uses it here, is "the psychology of the audience" because it denotes "the creation of an appetite in the mind of the auditor, and the adequate satisfying of that appetite."

Forms in literature, Burke argues, come from the forms of our own experience and therefore have an a priori existence. Moreover these forms are transhistorical, universal. This kind of formulation represents a Kantian tendency in Burke's work that persists through most of his books, though in a continually diluted form. As Burke describes it in *Counter-Statement*, "a form is a way of experiencing," and there are formal patterns which distinguish our experience, such as "the accelerated motion of a falling body, the cycle of a storm, the gradations of a sunrise, the stages of a cholera epidemic, the ripening of crops." These forms, along with more abstract ones such as the gradual rise to a crisis or crescendo, are for Burke, recurrent, universal forms of experience: "We 'think' in a crescendo, because it parallels certain psychic and physical processes which are at the roots of our experience." Burke's method of formal analysis involves categorizing such forms and examining how they function in any given work, but the theory upon which it is based views these forms as reflections of forms in experience which "seem to be inherent in the very germ-plasm of man," as "innate forms of the mind"–which is precisely why they work on the psychology of the audience.

This theory of form would seem to suggest that literary works are essentially ahistorical, that they partake of, and continually perpetuate, universal, transcendent forms of experience that are beautiful and moving *because* they stand outside time, history, and particular cultural moments. However, Burke anticipates this critique and incorporates his response to it in his theory of form. This response is important to recognize, since if

it is missed we will mistake Burke as simply a protoformalist or protostructuralist. He is both, but he is more.

"Art," Burke writes in *Counter-Statement*, "is 'eternal' in so far as it deals with the constants of humanity . . . the recurrent emotions, the fundamental attitudes, the typical experiences. . . . But art is also historical–a particular mode of adjustment to a particular cluster of conditions." This view is incorporated into his approach to form by his postulating the principle of "individuation." This principle insists that while art takes the form of a priori structures, innate arrangements of experience, each particular work of art is an "individuation" of such structures. The specific individuations of a form of experience "change greatly with changes in the environment and the ethical systems out of which they arise."

Burke's discussion of "individuation" and its sources in changing environmental and ethical systems leads him to a discussion of the relationship between form and ideology. This discussion grows out of his recognition that "the artist's manipulations of the reader's desires involve his use of what the reader considers desirable." The writer's form will engage the psychology of the audience to the extent to which he or she draws on what Burke calls the "vocabulary of belief" in any given culture. The correctness and the efficacy of the form will depend, then, upon the shared ideology of the writer and the audience/reader. Simply put, "if people believe something, the poet can use this belief to get an effect."

"Ideology" is a concept that recurs again and again in all of Burke's books; its workings are one of his central preoccupations. In later books the concept surfaces under the heading of a number of different terms–orientation, attitude, frame–and is defined in an ever-expanding way. What Burke means in *Counter-Statement* "by an ideology is . . . the nodus of beliefs and judgments which the artist can exploit for his effects." He does not so much see ideology as a unified, monolithic structure but as an "aggregate of beliefs sufficiently at odds with one another to justify opposite kinds of conduct." For Burke form is generated in a literary work by the stressing of a particular aspect of ideology as a pattern of experience. He sees the writer's use of ideology in terms of his or her exploiting or discrediting certain assumptions and beliefs in order to contribute "to the formation of attitudes, and thus to the determining of conduct." Burke's early discussion of ideology clearly has limitations which, for the most part, are dealt with in later books as the concept is refined. Due to Burke's emphasis in *Counter-Statement* on the author's manipulation of shared ideas and beliefs, his concept of ideology does not explore how those ideas and beliefs come to be thought of as "natural," "self-evident," or derived from "common sense."

In the chapter called "The Status of Art," Burke wants both to acknowledge the importance of understanding a literary work in terms of its specific historical context and to argue that the historical moment can never be simply thought of as the *cause* of the work. What he rejects here is any view of art which sees the literary work as simply a by-product of material or social forces, "the result," as he puts it, "of more vital and important forces." On the one hand, Burke holds "irrefutable" the idea "that to appreciate a work we must understand the environmental conditions out of which it arose," that "insofar as a social context changes, the work of art erected upon it is likely to change in evaluation." On the other hand, he belies the notion that because a literary work arises out of a specific social or economic context (how could it not?) that context *causes* the work, or that the work is a mere *reflection* of its social or economic context. For Burke art reflects a particular social situation in the way it deals with that situation, not in the way it mirrors or reproduces it. In this sense, as Burke explains in one of his more fundamental axioms, "art is not *experience*, but *something added* to experience."

Such a formulation marks off Burke's work from the formalism of the New Critics, or from structuralist approaches to literature that follow it. The political "Program" announced in a *Counter-Statement* chapter by that title does more than anything in the book to belie the notion that the early Burke was simply interested in aesthetics, literary form, and art for art's sake.

Burke's program builds on his insistence that his aesthetic orientation as a critic constitutes a political attitude which is meant to be part of an intervention in history:

> The "Program" proposes to trace the possible political and economic implications of an attitude which–so far as our primary concerns go–is not political or economic at all . . . the "Program" seeks to consider, in a general way, what this social structure would have to become if our principles were to prevail.

Burke's program makes it clear that his interest in aesthetics is not just an elaborate response to his own attachment to literary beauty, but an interested and willful attempt to act on prevailing social and political attitudes. Whether any literary critic, especially one as highly theoretical as Burke, can have this kind of impact is, of course, questionable, but the important thing is that Burke is working out of such a conviction, that he sees his work in these terms.

In the program he outlines, Burke juxtaposes his aesthetic attitude against what he calls the "practical" attitude that has accompanied rapid industrialization, mechanization, and the rise of science. In so doing he makes it clear that something like a social vision drives his formalist bent, and that the attitude underlying it is decidedly oppositional. The aesthetic attitude Burke seeks to foster is called a "means of reclamation," for the aesthetic must serve as antimechanization, the corrective of the "practical." By "practical," Burke means "efficiency," "material acquisitions," "increased consumption," "power," "energy," "sales drives," and "ubiquitous optimism." By "aesthetic," he means "distrust," "non-conformity," "bad sportsmanship," "experimentalism," "risk," "dislike of propaganda" and "certainty," and "the redistribution of wealth by some means." The program here insists that the aesthetic nature of Burke's critical orientation is a response to the historical moment and a practical act of resistance. For the aim of both writer and critic, as he sums it up at the end of his program, is to institute a "process of disintegration," to make "propaganda difficult" by "fostering intellectual mistrust," in the end, gravely interfering "with the cultural code behind our contemporary economic ambitiousness."

Burke's program in *Counter-Statement*, though based on what he calls an aesthetic attitude, actually represents his move away from an analysis of literature as aesthetic self-expression toward an interest in communication per se. This shift, this widening of his interests beyond an analysis of the forms of literary discourse to an examination of language as symbolic action in a much broader social and political context, was due in large measure to two things: the Depression and his reading of Marx. Burke had come to realize in the late 1920s that what he has recently called "those run-down movements," like Dadaism and surrealism, left "no place else to go." Moreover having invested during this period in a theory of art as self-expression, he was at first "forlorn" when he saw Marxist-influenced criticism taking hold among friends of his like Malcolm Cowley.

However in the early 1930s Burke began a careful reading of Marx, something he had not done before completing *Counter-Statement*. Marx's influence on him can be seen in *Permanence and Change* (1935), which Burke described in a letter to Cowley as "concerned with Marxian criticism," but "independently—in neither total agreement nor total disagreement." What interested Burke about Marx's writings was not his social vision (which he thought to be idealistic and utopian) but the dramatic and rhetorical features of his work. *Permanence and Change* is Marxian in that Burke translates some of those features into his own terms. Marx's critique of ideology, for example, Burke saw as an exemplary rhetorical analysis, and it clearly informs his discussion of the relationship between a person's ideological "orientation" and how that person interprets the world around him.

Of all Burke's books, *Permanence and Change* and the one that quickly followed it, *Attitudes Toward History* (1937), are the least concerned in an explicit way with literary criticism. However they are both crucial to understanding the course his literary-critical investigations took in the ensuing years, since in these two books Burke begins to formulate the theoretical principles upon which his later literary criticism and theory are based.

In *Permanence and Change* Burke, in effect, attempts to work out a philosophical grounding for the program he elaborated in *Counter-Statement*. He extends the analysis of motive begun there, but this time within a more general analysis of human, rather than strictly literary, motivation. The first part of the book focuses on the role of ideology ("orientation") in the interpretation of "reality," the second contains a more sophisticated reprise of his call in *Counter-Statement* for a new, aesthetic orientation (here called "poetic"), and the third continues that reprise in conjunction with a discussion and critique of important nineteenth-century philosophical systems.

In his long opening section, "On Interpretation," Burke insists that experience does not have *absolute* meanings, but that "any given situation derives its character from the entire framework of interpretation by which we judge it." There are, therefore, no self-evident meanings, only interpreted ones. Moreover interpretations are crucially determined by what Burke calls "orientations," the term he uses in place of ideology. By "orientation" he means "a bundle of judgments

as to how things were, how they are, and how they may be." Thus meanings are not self-evident precisely because people produce them as they interpret events in terms of their presuppositions about them. For Burke an "orientation" works like a vocabulary, providing a serviceable schema for making sense of the world. Furthermore if people are motivated to make certain kinds of interpretations in light of their orientations, they are simply using the only vocabulary they have to explain experience to themselves. For this reason Burke sees explanations and interpretations as essentially human utilization (whatever the nature of those interpretations might be) of the only social codes people know. Thus his analysis of the relationship between reality, orientation, and interpretation leads Burke to his first important insight about motive, a term that forms the focus of the two books he was to write in the 1940s, *A Grammar of Motives* (1945) and *A Rhetoric of Motives* (1950). "A motive," he writes, "is not some fixed thing, like a table, which one can go and look at. It is a term of interpretation." One's motives, in other words, are not natural, but are motivated by the interpretive framework through which one views experience. Burke goes on to examine how interpretive vocabularies both authorize and delimit one's views of reality and how explanatory accounts of human motivation are motivated by interpretive frameworks.

As the title of Burke's book indicates, he is centrally interested here in the *tension* between states of permanence and states of change. A particular orientation or interpretive framework, to the extent that it remains unquestioned, creates a kind of static view of things in which reality seems fixed (a specific interpretation of reality being mistaken for the permanent, natural state of things). In Burke's view, in order for there to be change—social, political, economic—one's orientations must change. Here is an aspect, of course, of Burke's neo-Marxism. Base and superstructure are reversed, in Burke's formulation, as he argues that changes in consciousness must necessarily precede material and economic ones. The argument in *Permanence and Change*, which sometimes seems overwhelmed by Burke's theoretical formulations, is an extension of that presented in *Counter-Statement*'s program. Again he is insisting on the necessity of what is here called a "reorientation" away from a practical and toward an aesthetic attitude. What was described as an aesthetic orientation in his earlier book is here called a poetic one. The aim, in *Permanence and*

*Change,* is to elaborate a "corrective philosophy with poetic standards" so that society can begin "to revise the productive and the distributive patterns of our economy to suit our soundest desires, rather than attempting to revise our desires until they suit the productive and distributive patterns." The "center of authority" for such a change, he insists, "must be situated in a philosophy, or psychology, of poetry."

Burke's "corrective philosophy" has a poetic orientation that sets it in explicit opposition to a mechanistic one, and out of it he elaborates a "dramatic" method of critical analysis. This method uses a language which is based on a poetic operation and an essentially dramatistic system of analysis. Burke proposes the use of a particular kind of terminology, one that will yield what he calls a "perspective by incongruity." He derives this kind of terminology, which involves "extending the use of a term by taking it from the context in which it was habitually used and applying it to another," from Nietzsche and Spengler. His description of such terms or phrases as constituting a "methodology of the pun" is itself a good example of what he means by a perspective by incongruity, since the word "methodology" provides an incongruous perspective when juxtaposed with the word "pun."

Underlying Burke's claims for the productivity of poetic language in analysis is his insistence that all truth claims are made by the substitution of a metaphor for a fact. He denies any essential difference between abstract and metaphorical language in this regard: "when we describe in abstract terms we are not sticking to the facts at all, we are substituting something else for them just as much as if we were using an out and out metaphor." As far as Burke is concerned, the poet's metaphors and the scientist's abstractions are both examples of substitution, the discussing of one thing in terms of another. So when he utilizes the methodology of the pun by coining perspectives by incongruity, Burke is not seeking to get beyond the workings of ordinary language, but simply to exploit to the maximum its inherent resources. Such phrases, which constitute much of Burke's critical terminology ("bureaucratization of the imaginative," "socialization of losses," etc.) are readings or interpretations in miniature, and they are meant to have a radical and disruptive, as well as an enlightening effect: "planned incongruity should be deliberately cultivated for the purpose of experimentally wrenching apart all those molecular combinations of

adjective and noun, substantive and verb, which still remain with us. It should subject language to the same 'cracking' process that chemists now use in their refining of oil."

Dramatism thus grows out of Burke's insistence that forms of experience exist prior to their material embodiment (a position he works out in *Permanence and Change* in the context of a critique of Marx's materialism). As it is elaborated in his later book, *A Grammar of Motives,* this method will be developed as a way to analyze the ways in which these forms emerge, and the nature of their interaction. At the end of *Permanence and Change,* such a method is loosely sketched in. Here Burke notes that the vocabulary of tropes as formulated by rhetoricians is ready-made to "describe the specific patterns of human behavior," since like art, social life is a *"problem of appeal."* A dramatistic analysis, informed by rhetoric, will examine what he calls the informal art of living by measuring motivation less in terms of utility than "with reference to the communicative, sympathetic, propitiatory factors clearly present in the procedures of formal art." With his choice of a dramatic metaphor for his analytical system, and his glimpse of the importance of rhetoric, Burke charts the central emphases of his work for the next fifteen years, culminating with *A Rhetoric of Motives* in 1950.

Burke's first sustained attempt to apply the dramatic method outlined in *Permanence and Change* came in his next book, *Attitudes Toward History,* which he began to write immediately after finishing the former book. *Attitudes Toward History* uses what Burke calls "poetic categories" to examine historical change. These categories correspond to a set of conventional literary-critical terms: the epic, tragedy, comedy, the elegy, the satiric burlesque, the grotesque, the didactic, and the comic. Burke employs these categories convinced that they illustrate "major psychological devices" by which the human mind "equips itself to name and confront its situations." In what amounts to a dramatistic analysis of the relationship between ideology and change, he describes these categories collectively as frames and attitudes: "Each of the great poetic forms stresses its own peculiar way of building the mental equipment (meanings, attitudes, character) by which one handles the significant factors of his time."

These poetic categories are used to characterize the general orientation of each of the five eras of Western history Burke goes on to analyze in the next part of the book: "The Curve of History": "Christian Evangelism," "Medieval Synthesis," "Protestant Transition," "Native Capitalism," and "Emergent Collectivism." This section of the book extends Burke's analysis of the dynamic relationship between permanence and change, employing a dramatic metaphor to chart historical change by explaining history in terms of its unfolding as a five-part drama. What emerges is a long analysis of historical change as a series of ideological transitions and syntheses.

The curve of history is characterized, in general terms, by what Burke calls shifting "frames" of acceptance and rejection. By "frame," he means "the more or less organized system of meanings by which a thinking man gauges the historical situation and adopts a role with relation to it." A variant of what in *Counter-Statement* he called "ideology," and in *Permanence and Change* he called "orientation," frames of acceptance and rejection are organized systems of meaning that regulate individuals and communities. Burke's discussion of historical change is preceded by an analysis of the personal "frames" of rejection and acceptance he detects in William James, Walt Whitman, and Ralph Waldo Emerson. In his much longer discussion of historical change, the transitions Burke charts from era to era are collective changes in organized social systems, such as what he calls the "shift from the classical emphasis upon resignation to the liberal ('Faustian') emphasis upon freedom." Thus a thinker like Marx, who, according to Burke, was "born into the great century of rejection philosophies," laid the "foundations for a vast public enterprise out of which a new frame of acceptance could be constructed."

Together, *Permanence and Change* and *Attitudes Toward History* represent a turn in Burke's work away from the literary and critical concerns of *Counter-Statement* toward a much broader and more ambitious attempt to work out a critical theory of historical change, human motivation, and the role of language in collective behavior. This cross-disciplinary orientation characterizes the rest of the Burkean project as it unfolds in the 1940s. However literary criticism, and the theory behind its practice, will remain a central part of that project. Indeed while Burke was busy writing his second and third theoretical books, he was also producing a number of essays on literature and criticism, which were collected and published as *The Philosophy of Literary Form: Studies in Symbolic Action* in 1941. During this time he also began to accept what would over the years become a number of part-time teaching positions,

first at the New School for Social Research (1937), then at the University of Chicago (1938), and for eighteen years (1943-1961) at Bennington College in Vermont.

In the essays comprising *The Philosophy of Literary Form*, Burke extends in a more sophisticated and refined way the discussion of the nature and function of literary form he began in *Counter-Statement*, linking this discussion to his evolving method for the dramatistic analysis of discursive forms. Where his earlier interest was in the *psychology* of form, and in *what* form was, his interest now had become the *philosophy* of form, elaborating, that is, a theory and method for its analysis. Form in these essays is treated as internal structure, and the aim of Burke's analytical method is to examine how internal structure produces meaning in literary works. This method grows out of Burke's desire to know "what is going on" in a literary work, to chart its action as a verbal construct, and to examine the interaction of internal structures, symbols, metaphor, binary oppositions, and key words.

Such an analysis relies particularly on the identification and interpretation of symbols. In *The Philosophy of Literary Form* the emphasis is on interpreting symbols by paying attention to how their significance or meaning in a text is generated by *internal* associations. He insists on distinguishing between his use of the term "symbol" and "Symbolism" as it is associated with the late nineteenth-century movement in poetry. He does so because he feels "symbol" in this context implies "the unreality" of the world, suggesting nothing can simply be what it is but "must always be something else." Since for Burke all discursive action is symbolic action he wants to avoid the connotations of unreality and irrationality he feels traditional conceptions of symbolism have.

With his interest in the way symbols are generated within literary works by a network of internal associations, Burke proposes an analysis of symbolism which is keyed to internal organization, rather than to an external "pool" of symbols: "To know what 'hoe, or house, or bridge' " symbolizes in a work, he writes, "you don't begin with a 'symbolist dictionary' already written in advance. You must, by inductive inspection of a given work, discover the particular contexts in which" these words appear in order to understand what they symbolize. In this way the critic interpreting symbols in a literary work is faced with "a problem in bookkeeping." Burke explains this conception in "Freud and the Analysis of Poetry." He points out that in the early years of psychoanalysis Freud did not work with a preconceived set of ideas about the absolute meaning of symbols, but interpreted them in the context of a patient's dreams and free associations. Burke's approach, with its stress on examining a work's internal structure of references and associations, is meant to be true to Freud's early method.

Such a blend of symbolism and formalism, as critics like Frank Lentricchia have begun to point out, also anticipates aspects of structuralist-oriented literary criticism as it developed in the mid 1960s. Burke's structural analysis of a Clifford Odets play in *The Philosophy of Literary Form,* for example, looks forward to the transformational structuralism of Claude Lévi-Strauss, and the semiological analyses of narrative of Roland Barthes. Burke's reading of Odets's *Golden Boy* shows how its verbal action is determined by the associations clustered around two opposing principles, the one symbolized by a violin, the other by a prizefight. Each stands as one term in a binary opposition, the violin being the "symbol" of the protagonist and signifying "cooperative social unity, disdain of money, staying home, not needing the girl," while the prizefight stands as the "symbol" of the antagonist, signifying "competition, cult of money, leaving home, getting the girl." Burke's theoretical point here is that neither a violin nor a prizefight are symbols drawn from a symbolist dictionary: they do not, in and of themselves, have any symbolic meaning. Rather that meaning is generated within a network of signification; it is generated by a network of associations *internal* to the play itself.

With its focus on form in literature as internal structure, and with its insistence that "meaning" is generated in and by those structures, Burke's critical method here seems to recall the essential formalism of *Counter-Statement* and to look forward to the New Criticism. However, as he did in his earlier book, Burke pushes his critical system well beyond the bounds of a simple cataloguing function. Formal analysis again becomes incorporated into a more ambitious explanatory project, one which seeks to identify a cathartic function in writing and reading and to propose a "sociological" literary criticism.

Form remains an embodiment of the psychology of the audience in *The Philosophy of Literary Form,* but it also is seen to embody the psychology of the author. Burke begins to draw together a number of disparate observations he had been making since *Counter-Statement* about language,

form, symbolism, and catharsis into a theory of literature as *symbolic action,* action, that is, which embodies a symbolic presentation of real personal and social contradictions. It is based on the crucial idea that the writer's subject is first and foremost his own maladjustments, and that in the act of writing those maladjustments are treated (in both senses of the word) in terms of social issues that correspond to them. Thus Burke wants to understand "the psychology of the poetic act" because "if we try to discover what the poem is doing for the poet, we may discover a set of generalizations as to what poems do for everybody. With these in mind, we have cues for analyzing the sort of *eventfulness* the poem contains. And in analyzing this eventfulness, we shall make basic discoveries about the *structure* of the work itself," and about how it mediates between the personal and the social.

Burke's focus on the psychology of the poetic act grows out of the conviction expressed in *Counter-Statement* that writing is an "efficient" business to the extent to which the writer can perform "a ceaseless indwelling, a patient process of becoming expert in himself." He argues that art's "spontaneous subject" is the artist's own "maladjustments." Burke does not simply mean that artists write *about* their own problems, but that their own problems are *expressed* symbolically in their art, that there is always an attempt to use art to represent and resolve contradictions. In *Permanence and Change* this process is given the name "hypochondriac incentive" (another of Burke's perspectives by incongruity), and it is inspired by Thomas Mann. Burke writes that Mann understood that the "hypochondriac's preoccupation need not by any means be confined to his own personal symptoms, but may merely serve to *force* integrity of outlook upon a man." Such an incentive, he continues, "will transcend its beginnings in that the thinker attempts to socialize his position, and in doing so must include areas of symbolization not at all local to himself." What is particularly valuable about the thinker's "disease" is that it can lead to larger insights "precisely from the fact that the diseased man's burden sharpens him to some corresponding issue involving society at large."

It is the artist's use of symbols to "socialize his position" that leads Burke to view literature and, indeed, language itself as symbolic *action.* Outlining a method in *The Philosophy of Literary Form* that seeks to analyze "tactics of expression" and the "situations behind them," he argues that readers "will find tactics that organize a work technically" because they "organize it emotionally." His formalist readings of individual works, in this book and others, invariably focus on analyzing this dynamic; some examples include his reading of "The Rime of The Ancient Mariner" in *The Philosophy of Literary Form*, his discussion of Keats's "Ode on a Grecian Urn" in *A Grammar of Motives*, and his analysis of Milton's "Samson Agonistes" in *A Rhetoric of Motives*. The form of symbolic action in each of these works, according to Burke, is ritual catharsis, a kind of poetic unburdening in which tactics of expression are formulated by the writer to organize emotion *and* socialize a position. Burke's central point about literary form in *Counter-Statement*—that "form is the psychology of the audience"—acknowledges his debt to Aristotle's idea that drama is always structured to create a cathartic or purifying experience in the audience. He does not abandon that point in the essays included in *The Philosophy of Literary Form*, but he does shift his emphasis by insisting that literary works are also structured to achieve a catharsis or purgation for the author. This shift involves his reading such works as Coleridge's "Rime of the Ancient Mariner" or Milton's "Samson Agonistes" from a kind of autobiographical perspective, on the assumption that their action is symbolic of the writer's inner, private drama, and that the action represents an attempt to purge or resolve contradictions that are very real to the author. Burke thus changes the emphasis of Aristotle's theory of catharsis from the psychology of the audience to the psychology of the writer. Essentially he blends Thomas Mann's hypochrondriac method with Aristotle's ideas about ritual catharsis to produce a theory of form that takes account of the fact that writing usually is meant to do something for the writer as well as for his audience. Whether manifested in poetry, fiction, or on the stage, Burke argues that "ritual drama" is the "Ur-form" of human action. Creating a foreground to drama in this way may seem purely strategic on Burke's part, since it too exquisitely fits his critical method, dramatism. But the method itself grew out of Burke's analysis of drama, and out of his conviction that it was the most effective metaphor for talking about human relations.

Burke's focus on catharsis and symbolic action, then, tends to separate his critical method from a formalism which concentrates wholly on the workings of internal structure, to the exclusion of whatever we might deem to be "outside"

the text. The other aspect of the method, as presented in *The Philosophy of Literary Form*, that separates it from formalism is Burke's attempt to define its aim as ultimately sociological. Such an objective is the result of his assimilating analyses of internal structure into an essentially *rhetorical* investigation of literary meaning, an investigation that is based on the assumption that literary works always constitute "*strategies* for dealing with *situations*" that are "typical and recurrent in a given social structure." There is no "pure" literature, Burke writes, because literary works can always be seen to be designed in strategic ways to a particular purpose, developing *names* for situations in order to dramatize strategies or *attitudes* for handling them. From this point of view, literary art is always socially purposeful.

Formal analysis in this mode has the further aim to identify and examine strategy and purpose. Linguistic, symbolic, and dramatic elements in any given literary work should be classified, according to Burke, in terms that suggest their "active nature," or which are based on "some strategic element common to the items grasped." Acknowledging that the formal aspects of a literary work can be classified in any number of ways, Burke proposes doing so with reference to a work's strategies in the social sphere out of his conviction that literature is first and foremost a form of *action* with purpose and power. It also has the virtue, he notes, of satisfying both the requirements of "technical criticism" (by "discovering important facts about literary organization") and "sociological" criticism (by viewing such facts in terms of their cultural and social function). "It automatically breaks down the barriers," he writes, "erected about literature as a specialized pursuit." Indeed it "would derive its relevance from the fact that it should apply both to works of art and to social situations outside of art." Burke points out, in conclusion, that such sociological categorizing as he proposes would "lie on the bias across the categories of modern specialization," implying the need for a "new alignment" among traditional disciplines and faculties. Such an alignment might "outrage good taste," he admits. But "good taste" has become "inert": "The classifications I am proposing would be *active*. I think that what we need is active categories."

"Literature as Equipment for Living," in *The Philosophy of Literary Form*, provides a brief sketch of the kind of rhetorical criticism Burke elaborated in detail a few years later in *A Rhetoric of Motives*. As such it exemplifies how in each of his books Burke tends to build on a previous insight or proposal, evolving a sophisticated method or theoretical statement from a line of thought in one of his earlier books. What seems to be repetition is often in fact refinement and systematization. Such is the case with Burke's next book, *A Grammar of Motives* (1945), where his earlier ideas about a dramatic or poetic metaphor for the formal analysis of discourse becomes fully and systematically realized as dramatism.

The *Grammar of Motives* was begun as part of a trilogy, to be rounded out by *A Rhetoric of Motives* and by a "Symbolic of Motives," which was never completed for publication. Nonetheless the *Grammar of Motives* is something of a watershed in Burke's work, for it is here that he draws together and "methodizes" his earlier theoretical work on the psychology of form, his speculations about essential categories of human thought, and his definition of language as verbal or symbolic action. The book was conceived most explicitly as an attempt to give his sometimes diffuse critical project on motive and behavior a grounding in formal considerations that are *prior* to both rhetorical and symbolical considerations.

Burke states at the outset that "the book is concerned with the basic forms of thought which, in accordance with the nature of the world as all men necessarily experience it, are exemplified in the attributing of motives." It seeks in general to answer the question "What is involved, when we say what people are doing and why they are doing it?" The word "say" is the operative one here; Burke's focus, as it was throughout the essay on interpretation in *Permanence and Change*, is metacritical. He insists that he is not trying to isolate "forms of experience," but to elaborate a method for analyzing "forms of *talk about* experience." Dramatism posits five terms necessary for any complete analysis of motive. Burke calls these terms, collectively, his Pentad: a term for what was done (act); a term for when or where it was done (scene); a term for who did it (agent); a term for how he or she did it (agency); and a term for why (purpose). Recalling the Kantian treatment of form in *Counter-Statement*, *A Grammar of Motives* insists that these terms are " 'transcendental' rather than formal," since they are "categories which human thought necessarily exemplifies." Again, however, it is important to remember the metacritical orientation of Burke's project, for the terms, as forms of *talk* about experience, are derived from an "analysis of *language* rather than" from an "analysis of 'reality.' "

Dramatism does not equip us to analyze the reality of our experience, it equips us to analyze and criticize our experience of reality, and the ways in which we talk about that experience. What "transcends" the particular in Burke's formulation are the forms for representing experience it has isolated.

At the beginning of the book Burke explains that *as a grammar of motives* his method for analyzing motivation is going to be concerned with the "terms alone," his Pentad, rather than with "actual statements about motives." Thus in practice, the terms serve as a critical vocabulary for isolating motivation in discourse, that is, for measuring the extent to which, say, in a given narrative an *act* is motivated by some aspect of the scene, the agent, an agency, a purpose, or some combination of one or more of them. Moreover, to stress one particular term (or combination of terms) is to produce a different interpretation of motive. That is, an explanation of an act that focuses on the "agent" might interpret motivation in terms of the power of an *individual* to act, one that focuses on the "scene" might interpret motivation as having a social origin, and one that focuses on "agency" or "purpose" might produce a religious or theological interpretation of motive. Burke's analysis of philosophic schools (including sections on Aristotle, Aquinas, Hegel, Marx, Santayana, and others), which takes up some two hundred pages of *A Grammar of Motives*, proceeds along such dramatistic lines.

Burke views philosophical explanations of motive as modes of action, and dramatism begins by analyzing them in terms of their internal structural relationships. With his focus on their active nature and their purposefulness, Burke's method looks forward to the rhetorical emphasis of his next book, as well as back toward the kind of "sociological" criticism outlined in "Literature as Equipment for Living." In fact Burke's entire project since the essay on interpretation in *Permanence and Change* focuses on the reality of rhetorical tactics rather than the (illusory) notion that statements about experience contain some immanent reality or truth. In *A Grammar of Motives*, Burke notes that as statements about "observable realities" all "theology, metaphysics, philosophy, criticism, poetry, drama, fiction, political exhortation, [and] historical interpretation" could simply be construed as "nonsense." But what *would* be real, would make nonsense words "real words, involving real tactics," are their strategies.

While the attitude motivating dramatism is "linguistic skepticism," Burke writes, such skepticism is synonymous with "linguistic appreciation." Thus while his focus throughout is on an analysis of language rather than reality—since he is convinced that language does not reflect so much as it interprets experience and motivates us to deal with it in certain ways—that analysis focuses on the *resourcefulness,* rather than on the *undecidable* nature, of discourse. The linguistic skeptic in Burke knows that competing statements about the truth are in fact competing interpretations, various metaphors which, as Nietzsche insisted, individuals have forgotten *are* metaphors. But the rhetorician in Burke, insisting that language is the " 'critical moment' at which human motives take form," insists on the reality of words and the tactics they reflect. He insists, then, that dramatism's central orientation be rhetorical rather than epistemological, and that his criticism be productively engaged in a discussion of social forces. This is why his critical categories must be active.

With this kind of emphasis running through *A Grammar of Motives,* it is not surprising that Burke's next book would be *A Rhetoric of Motives* (1950). This volume represents another moment when a long-standing, but diffuse, interest is treated in a sustained, systematic, and methodical way. *A Grammar of Motives* performed the function for Burke of "methodizing" his ideas about form, its relationship to transcendent categories, and the semantically productive nature of its internal relationships. *A Rhetoric of Motives,* on the other hand, performed that same function for Burke in terms of his longstanding interest in form as the psychology of the audience, the strategies and tactics of symbolic action, and the relationship between language and ideology.

Burke's aim is one of "reclamation." He wants to show "how a rhetorical motive is often present where it is not usually recognized, or thought to belong. . . . We would but rediscover rhetorical elements that had become obscured when rhetoric as a term fell into disuse." More than simply reclaim rhetoric (which became overshadowed, he argues, by the rise of specialized academic disciplines), Burke wants to develop a method for the analysis of discourse beyond the traditional bounds of rhetoric, to "contemplate" the basic principles of rhetoric "for their bearing both on literary criticism in particular and on human relations in general."

Burke divides this contemplation into two parts, the first focusing on "The Range of Rheto-

ric" within discourse and as a tool for its analysis, the second on "Traditional Principles of Rhetoric." (A third section of the book, "Order," contains a more disparate group of essays.) Burke subscribes to the Aristotelian definition of rhetoric as "speech designed to persuade," but he insists that it would be more accurate to speak of rhetoric as "persuasion 'to attitude,' rather than persuasion to out-and-out action. . . . Insofar as a choice of *action* is restricted, rhetoric seeks rather to have a formative effect upon *attitude.*" This refinement of Aristotle is important for Burke's desire to use rhetoric as a tool in literary criticism, since "the notion of persuasion to *attitude* would permit the application of rhetorical terms to purely *poetic* structures; the study of lyrical devices might be classed under the head of rhetoric, when these devices are considered for their power to induce or communicate states of mind to readers, even though the kinds of assent evoked have no overt, practical outcome."

In trying to "systematically extend the term 'rhetoric' " for the kind of wider application he envisions, Burke refines the term by pointing out the role of *identification* in the workings of rhetoric. "Here is perhaps the simplest case of persuasion," he writes: "You persuade a man only insofar as you can talk his language by speech, gesture, tonality, order, image, attitude, idea, *identifying* your ways with his." For example, in *Othello,* Iago is what Burke calls a "demon of Rhetoric," systematically building up by the sheer power of his words and actions a set of false identifications in the mind of Othello that creates, first, the *attitude* of jealousy, and later, induces him to the *act* of murder.

Since Burke sees all active forms of identification as embodying a rhetorical purpose aimed at changing attitudes and inducing action, he argues that the principle of identification is at work not only in literary discourse, but in the discourse of religion, magic, witchcraft, politics, psychoanalysis, philosophy, economics, and science. Thus *A Rhetoric of Motives* ultimately proposes rhetorical analysis as a kind of cross-disciplinary critical tool for examining the relationship between language and motivation *per se.* Burke wants to extend rhetoric as a critical term into these discourses because, in effect, it is already there. "Identification" lies, for Burke, at the very heart of socialization itself. "*Belonging,*" Burke writes, "is rhetorical" in the sense in which it is based on *identification,* the process by which a "specialized activity makes one a participant in some social or economic class." Rhetoric as identification shades into ideology, for Burke insists that we must think of rhetoric not just as "one particular address, but as a general *body of identifications* that owe their convincingness much more to trivial repetition and dull daily reinforcement than to exceptional rhetorical skill."

For Burke there is an element of mystification at work in the way a rhetoric of identification socializes individual attitudes and behavior, since what is repeated and reinforced is an explanatory vocabulary that necessarily interprets or frames reality in a certain way. Burke sees Marx's critique of capitalism as essentially "a critique of Capitalist rhetoric," for example, one designed to "unmask" the " '*factional*' interests concealed in the bourgeois terms for benign *universal* interests." This is the element of mystification Burke sees working in ideology (or in a body of identifications). A state of things having its roots in material, historical, or economic forces is approached *rhetorically* (by a ruling class) as an expression of some other, "higher" immaterial force, such as "spirit," "consciousness," "the absolute." The mystification here–for Marx and Burke–is the translating (or identifying) of material relations into "products" of a "Universal Spirit." Such mystifications have the effect "of imputing . . . universal or generic motives" to particular material ones, which Burke sees as the "concealment" of a "specific motive." The Marxist analysis of such mystification, Burke argues, is a contribution to rhetoric because it "admonishes us to look for 'mystification' at any point where the social divisiveness caused by property and division of labor is obscured by unitary terms."

All told, Burke argues, such rhetorical mystifications reverse the actual relationship between matter and spirit, "treating ideas as *primary* where they should have been treated as derivative." Burke refers to the words for these ideas as "god-terms," since they sum up a whole cluster of ideas and associations in the expression of what is essentially a metaphor for something not present to consciousness at all. Such terms stand at the top of a kind of terminological hierarchy in Burke's view, with a word like "spirit" seeming absolute and unconditional when in fact it is a summarizing term or "*title for all the conditions*" it is used to comprehend. Such summarizing terms make clear, Burke points out, that language is essentially "a means of transcending brute objects," and that in this process there is a built-in " 'temptation' to come upon an idea of 'God' as the *ulti-*

*mate* transcendence." He calls this "the dialectical transcending of reality through symbols."

This process becomes the focus of Burke's next book, *The Rhetoric of Religion* (1961). Picking up on his discussion of "god-terms," he is concerned in this book not with religion per se, but with the language of religion and theology, "not directly with man's relationship to God, but rather with his relationship to the *word* 'God.' " Religion is treated rhetorically because Burke views it as a language designed to persuade, to work by a complex series of identifications to motivate individual and collective behavior, grounding or authorizing attitudes in and by a language based on a hierarchy of terms.

Burke's approach in this book bears some relationship to structuralism, for he examines both motivation and meaning as they are generated within a formal, grammatical system of differences, where the "truth" is not immanent but based on conventions. "God" is treated here as "a *formal* principle," with any "thorough statements about 'God' . . . expected to reveal the formality underlying their genius as statements." From this point of view, Burke can analyze theological statements about the nature of God in "their sheer formality," *as* "observations about the nature of language." The premise of the study, then, is that an examination of the forms of theological language will present the best possible understanding of "the nature of language itself as motive."

Two of the more important aspects of Burke's investigation of the rhetoric of religion are: his stress on the dialectical borrowing that goes on between secular and religious terms, and his description of how logical or moral principles get transposed into the form of narrative. Consistent with his focus on the nature of language rather than the nature of reality, Burke points out that whether or not there are transcendent, supernatural states of being, there are words for them. Obviously these words are borrowed from the realm of everyday experience, borrowed, that is, from secular terminology and raised up to the level of a religious vocabulary. This borrowing ultimately works, Burke writes, because it can be reversed. That is, once a secular word has been "borrowed" or "developed for special theological purposes," it is inevitably borrowed back, but transformed in its transit from the secular to the theological and back again, carrying now "supernatural connotations." Thus the meaning of religious words is not immanent in the words themselves; it is generated by a system of borrowings. He points out here that terms for the supernatural are "derived by analogy from the empirical realm," and when they are borrowed back their meaning is based on the analogy they suggest between the supernatural and the empirical realms. For example, Burke points to the transformations undergone by words like "grace," "create," and "spirit." "Create," he notes, originally came from the Indo-European root meaning "to make." Borrowed by theology, it came to have the meaning of production ex nihilo. Borrowed back again into the secular world, but infused with supernatural connotations, it gives rise to something like Coleridge's view of poetic creation as a "dim analogue of Creation."

When Burke goes on to discuss the way logical or moral principles become transposed in the rhetoric of religion into temporal, and ultimately into narrative forms, he focuses on the first three chapters of Genesis. Here he examines how one theological idea implies another, and how, out of such a web of implications, an explanatory and didactic narrative can evolve. Briefly put, the idea of a covenant implies the possibility of a fall; a fall implies the possibility of the creation of a second realm, which in turn implies the existence of a set of conditions and the likelihood of a punishment or banishment if they are not kept, which in turn implies the need for some kind of grace or redemption. Such an account of the story of the Creation is an interpretation of it in terms of its dealing primarily with *principles.* "That is," Burke writes, "the account of the Creation should be interpreted as saying in effect: This is, in principle, a statement of what the natural order must be like if it is to be a perfect fit with . . . conditions that come to a focus in the idea of a basic Covenant backed by a perfect authority." We should note that this Covenant, embodied in the principle standing behind the story of the creation, is analyzed dramatistically, with Burke focusing on the way in which a purpose implies an agency, a scene, an agent, and an act.

*The Rhetoric of Religion* is important both as a theoretical study of the nature of language and for its exemplary readings of the first three chapters of Genesis and of "Verbal Action in St. Augustine's *Confessions*" (a dazzling essay that takes up nearly 130 pages of the book). Burke's next—and to this date his last—book of criticism borrows its title from a course on literary criticism Burke taught for many years at Bennington. *Language as Symbolic Action: Essays on Life, Literature, and Method* (1966), has as its centerpiece a dozen es-

says on particular literary works and writers. These essays demonstrate the kinds of readings produced by analyses of literary works in terms of the "symbolic action(s)" they seem to be enacting. The book has two major aims: "to define and track down the implications of the term symbolic action," and to reveal such action at work in a number of specific literary works. To this end, the book is divided into two sections on the *theory* of symbolic action, and one long section where Burke analyzes particular works and authors in one of the largest single collections of his analyses of specific literary texts: three essays on Shakespeare (*Coriolanus, Antony and Cleopatra,* and *Timon of Athens*), two on Goethe's *Faust,* one on the *Oresteia,* another on Emerson, one each on the poetry of Coleridge, Theodore Roethke, and William Carlos Williams, and discussions of E. M. Forster's *A Passage to India* and Djuna Barnes's *Nightwood.* With its sustained discussions of dramatism and symbolic action, and its essays demonstrating his theories in practice, Burke's final book of criticism stands as a kind of summarizing text for the literary/critical aspects of his project.

The book begins, in fact, with a group of what are called "Summarizing Essays." This section contains one of Burke's fullest and most important statements about the activity of literary criticism. Built around a careful discussion of Edgar Allan Poe's essay, "The Philosophy of Composition" (which purports to describe how he wrote his poem, "The Raven"), Burke's essay argues that the critic's fundamental role should be to "formulate the critical precepts implicit in [a] poet's practices." What interests Burke about Poe's essay is not that it may be an accurate narrative account of how Poe wrote his poem (Burke acknowledges that as a *story* it may be a lie), but that it exemplifies the essential nature of a formalist critical procedure. Poe's attempt in the essay, as Poe himself put it, was to show that " 'The Raven' proceeded, step by step, to its completion with the precision and rigid consequences of a mathematical problem." Burke's analysis of Poe's explanation is based on the assumption that the principles of the poem's composition, formulated after the poem's completion as the story of how it was written were, in fact, logically *prior* to that explanation. That is, what Poe did, in Burke's view, was to inspect his poem, formulate the principles by which it appeared to have been composed, then translate those principles into a narrative history of its composition.

Poe's procedure (which Burke also sees exemplified in Wordsworth's "Preface" to the *Lyrical Ballads*) is invoked here as the "ideal procedure for *critics* to follow": "In sum, the poet as poet makes a poem; and his ways of making the poem are practices which implicitly involve principles, or precepts. The critic, in matching the poetry with a poetics, seeks to make these implicit principles explicit." Thus a criticism based on poetics would follow Poe's example in that from inspection of the poem as an aesthetic object the critic would formulate the principles by which it was composed. Then, reversing the process, he or she would test the reading it produced "by 'deducing' or 'deriving' the poem from its principles." Tongue in cheek, Burke calls this kind of critical theory "prophesying after the event."

How can this critical method be reconciled with the kind of sociological criticism Burke proposed in the "Literature as Equipment for Living" essay, or with the kind of structural analysis of symbols exemplified in his discussion of the Odets play? Part of the seeming differences between these approaches can be accounted for by noting that the critical procedure outlined in the essay on Poe is based explicitly on *poetics*, whereas the other two are based on rhetoric and symbolism. It is derived from a discussion of poetic principles by a poet and treated by Burke, in the main, as the basis for an analysis of poetry. Even so the difference between what Burke proposes in this essay and what he has proposed in the earlier ones is not as great as it seems. For his proposal for an exacting study of a poem *qua* poem is meant to illustrate the beginning of a thoroughgoing criticism, not the end of one. As such it is consistent with the fundamental axiom in *A Rhetoric of Motives* that "the ability to treat of form is always the major test of a critical method." Burke conceives of this ability or procedure as a necessary preliminary step to other modes of literary analysis: "The very thoroughness of the critic's attempt to discuss the poem exclusively in terms of Poetics should help us realize the points at which the poem requires analysis not just in terms of Poetics . . . [but] as the product of a citizen and taxpayer"; that is, the very severity of the analytical procedure he outlines should make clear that it is not enough. At the very end of his essay on Poe, Burke insists that such a method is one step in "inquiring *humanistically* into the poem's full nature as a symbolic act." Such an inquiry is only possible, he continues, if the critic follows two steps and integrates them. The first is to say "*only* what

could be said about a work, considered in itself," and the second is "saying all that might be said about the work in terms of its relation to the author, his times, etc." Formalism, in and of itself, Burke calls an "error," an error which has its sources in "an attempt to get a kind of criticism as different as possible from Marxism." Marxism "has many faults," he writes, "but it also has many virtues. And it can be wholly rejected only at a great sacrifice of intelligence." Conventional formalism—the New Criticism—"sets up antithetical demands" to Marxism's overriding interest in the relationship between a literary work "and the non-literary context from which it arose." The value Burke sees in a Marxian perspective is thus integral to his critique of the New Criticism. Whenever he elaborates what seems to be a formalist or structuralist approach to criticism it is inevitably presented as preliminary to a critic's accounting of a work in rhetorical, "sociological," and historical terms.

Since the publication of *Language as Symbolic Action*, Burke has continued to publish a number of these "summarizing essays." A book-length manuscript, "Poetics," conceived as a "Symbolic of Motives" to complement the *Grammar* and *Rhetoric*, remains unpublished. In the essays, he continues to refine both dramatism and logology. His 1969 essay on *King Lear* demonstrates the analytical usefulness of dramatism in the linked examination of internal literary structures and the social realities they mediate. "Theology and Logology" (1979) emphasizes how the logological scheme he developed in *The Rhetoric of Religion* can be extended to analyze the general role that language plays in the constitution and perpetuation of what any given culture takes to be its "reality." As he does in his earlier essay, "(Nonsymbolic) Motion/(Symbolic) Action" (1978), Burke here uses the distinction between nonsymbolic motion (body, matter) and symbolic action (mind, spirit) to chart the "verbal transformations by which we extend the world of symbolic action" from birth to adulthood. Many of these essays also contain a thoroughgoing critique of technology (which Burke calls "counter-nature") and its impact on contemporary life.

Burke argues that dramatism—a critical vocabulary that focuses specifically on the complex of motives animating any symbolic act—uniquely possesses "the philosophic character adapted to the discussion of man in general." Burke claims what he calls "special favors" for dramatism because he believes it is specifically equipped to analyze and explain symbolic action, or more specifically, to analyze language and thought as modes of action rather than simply as the means for conveying information. This claim is worked out through what Burke sees as a series of implications. If *action* is to be the key term for analyzing human behavior and the motives behind it, then that implies the presence of *drama,* since it is "the culminative form of action." Drama, in turn, implies *conflict,* which for Burke leads to the idea of *victimage* and the necessity of *scapegoating.* In this series of logical implications Burke is essentially reiterating the assertion he made in *The Philosophy of Literary Form* that "*ritual drama*" is the "hub" or "Ur-form" of action, with "all other aspects of *human* action treated as spokes radiating from" it. Since Burke views such ritual drama as the Ur-form of human action, dramatism—which analyzes symbolic action as a kind of poetic unburdening where tactics of expression organize emotion and socialize a particular position—emerges with special claims as an explanatory system.

The special favors Burke wants to claim here for dramatism are clearly linked to his strategic assertions about the primacy of ritual drama and the way in which it authorizes the kind of critical procedure he has developed to deal with it. There is, of course, something unavoidably circular about this argument, and it has to stand, finally, *as* an assertion. That is, Burke's definition of what is essential about human behavior has to be accepted in order to grant his method of analysis "special favors." Yet that primacy cannot, by Burke's own conception, be anything other than an interpretation of action and what is essential about it. Dramatism directs our attention, as Burke says all terministic screens do, toward one phenomenon rather than another, and it does not seem able, finally, to avoid his further point about how explanatory observations are inevitably a product of the terminology by which they are made. If we think of the reading that a dramatistic analysis produces as a *narrative* about a text, we can see that that narrative is produced in a way analogous to how Burke argued the first three chapters of Genesis were created: by taking a logically prior set of "special" principles (in the case of Genesis, action, drama, conflict, victimage, and scapegoating) as the essential "hub" of human action, and then finding them operative in the narratives and plays being analyzed. The principles seem to direct the inquiry toward certain *kinds* of texts, and the results of

the inquiry end up reinforcing the usefulness of the principles *for* those texts. But in looking at dramatism critically, it is difficult to tell which came first, the principles, the explanations it produces, or the things that are being explained. Saying that dramatism can demand special favors as a critical system because it is especially equipped to analyze the symbolic action the system *itself* posits as the Ur-form of human action comes close to the kind of "prophesying after the event" Burke refers to in his essay on Poe.

In part it has been Burke's insistence on dramatism's "special favors" as a form of analysis, and the seemingly circular relationship between the claims of his theory and what it discovers in practice, that have contributed to the mixed reaction his work has always elicited. Reviewing *A Rhetoric of Motives* in 1951, for example, Kermit Lansner worried that "we are never quite certain whether Burke's literary criticism is determined by his general theories or these theories by his practice of criticism." In an earlier review of *Permanence and Change,* Austin Warren questioned the theoretical grounds upon which Burke argued for the primacy of the dramatic metaphor, suggesting that Burke falls into "the universal trap" of first making his reader "conscious of how inevitably *we* look through our own professional *pincenez,*" then looking through his own as if they were less distorting than any others.

Burke's place in twentieth-century literary criticism, and his place in American intellectual life in general, has been an enigmatic one for a number of reasons. He has no formal training in the conventional disciplines his work engages, and until he began teaching at Bennington in the early 1940s, he had no ongoing academic affiliation. More and more his marginal status has come to seem an advantage rather than a disadvantage, but for many years it contributed to a studied disinterest or hostility on the part of many critics—or a tendency to incorporate his insights without ever referring to him. One of the central ironies of Burke's career, it seems, is that remaining outside of the mainstream of American academic publishing has allowed him to produce wide-ranging work, but it has severely limited the reception of that work by academic critics.

The critical reception of Burke's work has, in general, focused on its interdisciplinary range and Burke's unconventional critical style. Beyond the repeated criticism that Burke focuses too exclusively on language and rhetoric at the expense of "reality," the bulk of what has been said against him has concerned the style of his writing, the method of his inquiries, and the ways in which his books are organized. The complaint that most frequently recurs in the critics who have written on Burke is that his style of writing is too abstract, technical, and opaque, full of proliferating sets of terms. Often, critics have pointed out that this tendency is a result of two of Burke's real virtues: his philosophical grounding and his skepticism. Charles Glicksberg made the observation in 1937, for example, that Burke's work "suffers—and was bound to suffer—from the defects of its primary virtues. It is too technical and abstract in its operations to reach a wide audience. Every sentence posits a problem, forms a link in a closely-knit logical chain, intrudes a doubt, shatters a privileged truth."

Other critics have complained that Burke's abstract, technical language conflicts with the essentially poetic and dramatic orientation of his method, or that his style is too *literary* for the treatment of a grammar or a rhetoric of motives. Still others have complained that Burke's books have organizational problems, that they are digressive or weak in structure. The cross-disciplinary nature of Burke's work, of course, and his ultimate aim of generating a broadly applicable system of analysis, make some of his books seem disorganized, though this may in part be because they try to achieve an unconventional kind of synthesis.

An important part of that synthesis involves the willful combining of philosophical analysis and poetry. The alternating complaints that Burke's work is either too technical and abstract, or too literary and creative, stems from Burke's attempt to create this synthesis at the level of critical *style*. His method of generating "perspectives by incongruity," for example, is a stylistic one, and so his insights often move by way of association rather than logic (a trait he sometimes shares with the French philosopher and critic Jacques Derrida), or are based on etymological research and an ensuing series of observations grounded in the methodology of the pun. This aspect is another element of the language-oriented nature of Burke's work that has annoyed more empirically oriented critics. Burke's style, of course, is founded in his fundamental insistence that there is no essential difference between abstract and metaphorical language.

For all of these reasons Burke has remained an enigmatic and much-criticized writer. But he has not been without his admirers. Reviewing *A Grammar of Motives* in 1948, Bernard Duffey

wrote that while it must be admitted that "Burke has produced a very impure philosophy" it must also be said that "he has formed something like the fullest and most independent theory of literature in existence, and that he has done this in an age which has witnessed almost a plethora of brilliant literary theory." Since the publication of his first book, Burke's work has received much praise and positive attention, especially for its reassertion of the role of rhetoric in literary studies, its approach to poetry and narrative as an *act*, and for the value of its creator's skeptical attitude. Since the mid 1930s, he has also received a good deal of attention beyond the field of literary studies. The value of his insights for work in rhetoric, history, sociology, philosophy, psychology, and, more recently, the teaching of composition are recorded in the impressive number of articles on Burke by writers in these fields.

Nevertheless, unable to place or explain Burke with much ease, historians of twentieth-century literary criticism have tended until very recently to either ignore or dismiss him. W. K. Wimsatt and Cleanth Brooks, for example, in their *Literary Criticism: A Short History* (1957), leave Burke virtually unmentioned, save for one short quote reproduced without comment. René Wellek's chapter on Burke in volume 6 of his *A History of Modern Criticism: 1750-1950* (1986), on the other hand, is a disparaging and unsystematic dismissal of Burke as an eccentric skeptic, indifferent to aesthetic values, who moves in a "self-created verbal universe where everything may mean everything else." It is difficult for someone who has actually read Burke with any care and understanding to decide which is more lamentable, Brooks and Wimsatt's complete omission of Burke, or Wellek's mean-spirited skewering of him. Brooks and Wimsatt's approach to Burke has the virtue, by not saying anything at all about him, of not caricaturing him. Wellek, on the other hand, in a strategy that becomes apparent not far into his chapter, threads together many of Burke's more outrageous asides and treats them as if they formed the core of Burke's method, all the while failing to give any sense of what his various books are about.

The kind of criticism Burke's work has elicited since the mid 1930s, with its mixture of praise, puzzlement, bemusement, and dismissal, has recently begun to give way to decidedly more positive and appreciative assessments of his contributions to literary and critical theory. Indeed in the wake of recent developments in the theory and practice of literary criticism, principally, the impact of structuralism, deconstruction, reader-response, psychoanalytic, and Marxian criticism on American critical theory, Burke has emerged as something of a model and a pioneer.

The great paradox in Burke's shifting fortunes is that he is now embraced for the very qualities in his work which for nearly forty years brought him the kind of scorn Wellek's chapter epitomizes. Criticized for decades for his relentless focus on the relationship between language, reality, knowledge, and power, for the cross-disciplinary nature of his work, the eclectic dialogue he has always created between Marx, Freud, rhetorical theory, and literary criticism, and for the creative, associative style of his writing, Burke is now being praised by contemporary theorists for just these qualities in his work.

The first sign of this interest in Burke might be dated by the publication in 1982 of *Representing Kenneth Burke: Selected Papers from the English Institute*, edited by Hayden White and Margaret Brose. The essays in this volume, covering a range of topics which include Burke's theory of catharsis, his discussions of ideology and history, and his work on St. Augustine, are incisive and appreciative. Since the publication of *Representing Kenneth Burke*, both Geoffrey Hartman and Fredric Jameson have written on Burke, Hartman praising the creative critical style of his writing in *Criticism in the Wilderness* (1980), Jameson using Burke's theory of symbolic action in *The Political Unconscious* (1981). More recently Frank Lentricchia's *Criticism and Social Change*, (1983) has become the first in what will no doubt be a growing number of books tracing the congruity between Burke's work and contemporary literary and critical theory. Lentricchia contrasts the social and political dimensions of Burke's rhetorical theory with that of Paul de Man, whose work as a rhetorician and critic was profoundly influenced by deconstruction.

Burke's importance for many contemporary critics has its source in the fact that his work pays close and systematic attention to language as a purposeful and powerful act. The rhetorical orientation of Burke's critical theory provides a starting point for rethinking the relationship not only between literature and other related disciplines but between literature and culture. Lentricchia is one among a number of critics, including Terry Eagleton and Gerald Graff, who want to move literary criticism away from its traditionally narrow (and some argue, benign) focus on the apprecia-

tive reading of canonical "great books," toward its broad reformation along the lines of what is usually called "cultural criticism" or "cultural studies." When, at the end of *Literary Theory: An Introduction* (1983), Eagleton describes what he means by cultural studies (a form of criticism which would focus less on literature as a specialized, expressive kind of writing, than on the various discourses that cultures produce), it turns out to be just the kind of rhetorically oriented criticism Burke has been practicing for sixty years. Eagleton wants to return to "Rhetoric" because it "examined the way discourses are constructed in order to achieve certain effects. It was not worried about whether its objects or enquiry were speaking or writing, poetry or philosophy, fiction or historiography: its horizon was nothing less than the field of discursive practices in society as a whole, and its particular interest lay in grasping such practices as forms of power and performance." Eagleton's proposal provides a succinct example of why Kenneth Burke is receiving so much attention among contemporary theorists, for Burke's project is precisely the one Eagleton describes. Eagleton's proposal also serves as a reminder of how European critics are continuing to neglect Burke; his name goes unmentioned in Eagleton's book.

Twenty years ago, Alvin Kibel, in a review of an edition of some of Burke's essays, perceptively observed that "Burke's intention . . . is to provide a philosophical basis for the practice of 'cultural studies.'" Kibel's insight is proving to be prophetic. He understands, along with more recent critics, that to criticize Burke, as R. P. Blackmur did in 1935, because "his method could be applied with equal fruitfulness either to Shakespeare, Dashiell Hammett, or Marie Corelli," is to miss one of the central *strengths* of that method. What Wellek says in damning Burke—that "art with Burke cannot be distinguished from persuasion, from rhetoric"—Lentricchia would say in praising him. Wellek says that because Burke's work lacks this distinction literature, as Burke defines it, "has really no relation to reality." What Wellek does not see in Burke is that in not dismissing the elements of rhetoric and persuasion in literary language and form in the interest of practicing an idealized aesthetic formalism Burke defines literature's relationship to what can be called reality perhaps more acutely than any other twentieth-century American critic. For this reason Burke's work will no doubt continue to gain the kind of positive attention it has so long deserved. If criticism until lately has missed Burke, it is perhaps simply because it has taken so long for it to catch up with him.

**Letters:**

*The Selected Correspondence of Kenneth Burke and Malcolm Cowley,* edited by Paul Jay (New York: Viking Press, forthcoming in 1988).

**Interviews:**

"A Conversation with Kenneth Burke: On Literature in a Scientific Age," *Riata* (Winter 1963): 45-50;

"Counter-Gridlock: An Interview with Kenneth Burke," *All Area,* No. 2 (Spring 1983): 4-33.

**References:**

W. H. Auden, "A Grammar of Assent," *New Republic,* 105 (14 July 1941): 59;

Marius Bewley, "Kenneth Burke as Literary Critic," in his *The Complex Fate* (London: Chatto & Windus, 1952), pp. 211-243;

Malcolm Cowley, "Prolegomena to Kenneth Burke," *New Republic,* 122 (5 June 1950): 18-19;

Bernard Duffey, "Reality as Language: Kenneth Burke's Theory of Poetry," *Western Review,* 12 (Winter 1948): 132-145;

Francis Ferguson, "Kenneth Burke's Grammar of Motives," in his *The Human Image in Dramatic Literature* (Garden City: Doubleday/Anchor Books, 1957), pp. 193-204;

Armin Paul Frank, *Kenneth Burke* (New York: Twayne, 1969);

Charles I. Glicksberg, "Kenneth Burke: The Critic's Critic," *South Atlantic Quarterly,* 36 (January 1937): 74-84;

Robert L. Heath, *Realism and Relativism: A Perspective on Kenneth Burke* (Macon, Ga.: Mercer University Press, 1986);

Laura Virginia Holland, *Counterpoint: Kenneth Burke and Aristotle's Theories of Rhetoric* (New York: Philosophical Library, 1959);

Stanley Edgar Hyman, "Kenneth Burke and the Criticism of Symbolic Action," in his *The Armed Vision* (New York: Knopf, 1948), pp. 347-394;

Fredric Jameson, "The Symbolic Inference; or, Kenneth Burke and Ideological Analysis," *Critical Inquiry* (Spring 1978): 507-523;

Ronald C. Kimberling, *Kenneth Burke's Dramatism and Popular Arts* (Bowling Green, Ohio: Popular, 1982);

William Knickerbocker, "Wam for Maw, Dogma versus Discursiveness in Criticism," reviews of *The New Criticism* by John Crowe Ransom, and *The Philosophy of Literary Form, Sewanee Review,* 49 (October-December 1941): 520-536;

George Knox, *Critical Moments: Kenneth Burke's Categories and Critiques* (Seattle: University of Washington Press, 1957);

Kermit Lansner, "Burke, Burke, the Lurk," review of *A Rhetoric of Motives, Kenyon Review,* 13 (Spring 1951): 324-335;

Frank Lentricchia, *Criticism and Social Change* (Chicago: University of Chicago Press, 1983);

Gorham B. Munson, "In and About the Workshop of Kenneth Burke," *Destinations* (New York: Sears, 1928), pp. 136-159;

*Pretext,* special Burke issue, 6 (Fall/Winter 1985);

William H. Rueckert, *Critical Responses to Kenneth Burke: 1924-1966* (Minneapolis: University of Minnesota Press, 1969);

Rueckert, *Kenneth Burke and the Drama of Human Relations* (Berkeley: University of California Press, 1963);

Rueckert, review of *The Rhetoric of Religion, Nation,* 194 (17 February 1961): 150;

Austin Warren, "Kenneth Burke: His Mind and Art," *Sewanee Review,* 41 (April-June 1933): 225-236; (July-September 1933): 344-364;

Warren, "Skeptic's Progress," *American Review,* 6 (December 1935): 193-213;

René Wellek, *American Criticism, 1900-1950,* volume 6 of his *A History of Modern Criticism* (New Haven: Yale University Press, 1986);

Hayden White and Margaret Brose, eds., *Representing Kenneth Burke: Selected Papers from the English Institute* (Baltimore & London: Johns Hopkins University Press, 1982).

**Papers:**

Burke's papers are dispersed through some twenty-eight publicly held collections. Among the largest of these are at the Newberry Library, Chicago; the Beinecke Library, Yale University; the Morris Library, Southern Illinois University, Carbondale; Washington University, St. Louis; the Fred Lewis Patee Library at Pennsylvania State University; and the Suzallo Library, University of Washington, Seattle.

# R. S. Crane

## (5 January 1886-12 July 1967)

David Richter

*Queens College, City University of New York*

BOOKS: *The Vogue of Medieval Chivalric Romance during the English Renaissance* (Menasha, Wis.: George Banta Publishing Company, the Collegiate Press, 1919);

*The English of Business,* by Crane and Franklin B. Snyder (New York: Harcourt, Brace, 1921);

*The Languages of Criticism and the Structure of Poetry* (Toronto: University of Toronto Press, 1953);

*The Idea of the Humanities and Other Essays Critical and Historical,* 2 volumes (Chicago & London: University of Chicago Press, 1967)— includes "History versus Criticism in the Study of Literature" (1935), "Shifting Definitions and Evaluations of the Humanities from the Renaissance to the Present" (1943), "Critical and Historical Principles of Literary History" (1967), "Questions and Answers in the Teaching of Literary Texts" (1953), "Every Man His Own Critic" (1956), "Criticism as Inquiry, or, The Perils of the 'High Priori Road' " (1957), "On Hypotheses in 'Historical Criticism': Apropos of Certain Contemporary Medievalists" (1961), and "The Houyhnhnms, the Yahoos, and the History of Ideas" (1962);

*Critical and Historical Principles of Literary History* (Chicago & London: University of Chicago Press, 1971).

OTHER: *New Essays by Oliver Goldsmith,* edited, with an introduction and notes, by Crane (Chicago: University of Chicago Press, 1927);

*A Census of British Newspapers and Periodicals, 1620-1800,* edited by Crane and Frederick B. Kaye, with the assistance of Moody E. Prior (Chapel Hill: University of North Carolina Press, 1927; London: Holland Press, 1966);

*A Collection of English Poems, 1660-1800,* edited, with a preface, by Crane (New York & London: Harper, 1932);

"English Criticism: Neo-Classical Criticism," in *Dictionary of World Literature: Criticism, Forms, Techniques,* edited by Joseph T. Shipley (New York: Philosophical Library, 1943), pp. 193-203;

*English Literature 1660-1800: A Bibliography of Modern Studies Compiled for Philological Quarterly,* edited by Crane, Louis I. Bredvold, Richmond P. Bond, Arthur Friedman, and Louis A. Landa, 2 volumes: 1926-1938, 1939-1950 (Princeton: Princeton University Press, 1950, 1952);

Introduction, "English Neoclassical Criticism: An Outline Sketch," "The Critical Monism of Cleanth Brooks," "I. A. Richards on the Art of Interpretation," "The Concept of Plot and the Plot of *Tom Jones,*" in *Critics and Criticism Ancient and Modern,* edited by Crane, W. R. Keast, Richard McKeon, Norman Maclean, Elder Olson, and Bernard Weinberg (Chicago: University of Chicago Press, 1952); abridged as *Critics and Criticism: Essays in Method* (Chicago & London: University of Chicago Press, 1957);

"The Rationale of the Fourth Voyage," in *Gulliver's Travels,* by Jonathan Swift, edited by Robert A. Greenberg (New York: Norton, 1961), pp. 300-307;

"The Chicago Critics," in *Princeton Encyclopedia of Poetry and Poetics,* edited by Alex Preminger, Frank J. Warnke, and O. B. Hardison, Jr. (Princeton: Princeton University Press, 1965), pp. 116-117.

PERIODICAL PUBLICATIONS: "Imitation of Spenser and Milton in the Early Eighteenth Century: A New Document," *Studies in Philology,* 15 (April 1918): 195-206;

"An Early Eighteenth-Century Enthusiast for Primitive Poetry: John Husbands," *Modern Language Notes,* 37 ( January 1922): 27-36;

"The Diffusion of Voltaire's Writings in England, 1750-1800," *Modern Philology,* 20 (February 1923): 261-274;

"Gray's *Elegy* and *Lycidas,*" *Modern Language Notes,* 38 (March 1923): 138-184;

"Anglican Apologetics and the Idea of Progress,

1699-1745," *Modern Philology,* 31 (February 1934): 273-306, 349-382;

"Suggestions toward a Genealogy of the Man of Feeling," *ELH,* 1 (December 1934): 205-230;

"Interpretation of Texts and the History of Ideas," *College English,* 2 (May 1941): 755-765;

"Literature, Philosophy, and the History of Ideas," *Modern Philology,* 52 (November 1954): 77-83.

Ronald Salmon Crane was the leader and moving spirit of the Chicago School of Neo-Aristotelian criticism, the formalist movement which–together with its rival formalism, the New Criticism–shifted the center of the American literary scholar's vocation away from the historical and biographical penumbra of literature to the direct exegesis of the text itself. The outpouring, over the last fifty years, of books about theory, of books about other books, thus owes a great deal to the force of Crane's arguments about humanistic education. But it owes very little to his example. For R. S. Crane himself was, paradoxically enough, a parsimonious publisher, fond of telling his students that most books could be recast as articles, most articles as footnotes. Crane was true to his own laconic principles: he wrote only one treatise, *The Languages of Criticism and the Structure of Poetry* (1953), as a standard theoretical book. The principal part of his prodigious output appeared as sixty academic articles, many of them deep with learning and dense with thought.

In general Crane's labors were devoted more to the needs of the profession than to the erection of a personal monument. For nearly twenty-five years he expended much of his energy writing review articles of legendary erudition and producing annual annotated bibliographies of Restoration and eighteenth-century studies for the journal *Philological Quarterly.* As a director of doctoral dissertations, he was an intellectual father to several generations of critics, scholars, and historians of ideas. It was only at the insistence of some of these former students and friends that eighteen of his ripest essays were revised and collected, not long before his death, into the two-volume set, *The Idea of the Humanities and Other Essays Critical and Historical* (1967). Quite apart from his ideas, Crane was, even in his own time, a paragon of intellectual and personal integrity and an unrivaled exemplar of those virtues today.

Ronald Salmon Crane was born in Tecum-seh, Michigan, on 5 January 1886, the eldest of three children of Theodore H. Crane and Bricena Chadwick Crane. Crane's father was a house carpenter noted both for his sturdy and elegant stairways and for having read through Thomas Babington Macaulay's *The History of England* (1849) at the age of four. Both his male children seem to have picked up his erudition and his taste for tidy construction. Crane's younger brother was the historian Verner Winslow Crane, professor at Brown University, author of monographs on Benjamin Franklin. His younger sister Judith died unmarried relatively young. Crane was educated at local schools in Tecumseh and went to college at the University of Michigan at Ann Arbor, working summers on a celery farm. He received his A.B. in 1908 and took his doctorate at the University of Pennsylvania in 1911. His doctoral dissertation was "The Vogue of Medieval Chivalric Romance during the English Renaissance." For over twenty years after taking his doctorate, Crane pursued a highly productive but completely conventional academic career, beginning as an instructor at Northwestern University in 1911 and rising through the ranks to associate professor. In 1917 he married one of his former students, Julia Fuller, by whom he had two children and who survived him until 1980. The children were Ronald Fuller Crane, professor of English at the University of Wisconsin at Oshkosh, and Barbara Chadwick Crane, who until his death in 1987 was married to noted Mark Twain scholar William M. Gibson, professor of English at the University of Wisconsin at Madison.

In 1924 he took a post at the University of Chicago, where he became a full professor of English in 1925 and chairman of the department in 1935. During this period Crane published historical scholarship, including monographs derived from his dissertation, essays on Samuel Richardson, Voltaire, and Thomas Gray, and an edition of Oliver Goldsmith's fugitive essays, and produced such scholarly tools as a bibliography of journalism from 1620 to 1800 and the exemplary annual survey of current scholarship in eighteenth-century studies for *Philological Quarterly.*

It is possible, however, that nothing in Crane's career would have qualified him for inclusion in the history of American criticism had it not been for the revolutionary reorganization of the college of the University of Chicago under Robert Maynard Hutchins in the early 1930s. Undergraduate education was then restructured into a series of interdisciplinary studies—with emphasis on the reading and comprehension of primary texts (especially Mortimer Adler's "Great Books of the Western Tradition")—which were given final shape by the philosophical semantics of Richard P. McKeon in his course "Organizations, Methods and Principles." The direct influence of Adler and McKeon in informal faculty seminars, along with the general intellectual ferment of the period, seems to have subverted Crane's commitment to historical scholarship as the exclusive or even primary task of humane learning. The place of historical scholarship was becoming a significant issue in academe, partly as a result of the introduction of the New Criticism. In his 1935 essay, "History versus Criticism in the Study of Literature," first published in *English Journal: College Edition* (October 1935), Crane came out against teaching undergraduates literature purely through its historical origins and in favor of a new approach using textual explication and aesthetics. As chairman of the department, Crane was able to hire over the next decade a number of humanists who assisted him in developing a critical theory and practice that has become known as Neo-Aristotelianism or Chicago Criticism; this group included Elder Olson, Norman Maclean, and W. R. Keast in addition to McKeon and Crane himself.

Though Crane had placed himself on the side of the New Critics on the issue of history versus criticism, he and his group were scornful of New Critical theories of literature, which they considered reductive, simplistic, and a serious distortion of the nature of literature and language. As a result, in the 1940s and 1950s, there was an acrimonious debate in the pages of scholarly journals and little magazines, intemperate on both sides, between Crane's group and such New Critics as Cleanth Brooks, William K. Wimsatt, Robert Penn Warren, and Robert B. Heilman.

When by 1960 the dust had settled, the New Critics were left in possession of the field, primarily because their critical methods, propagated by successful textbooks like *Understanding Poetry* (1957), had revolutionized undergraduate and even secondary school training in literature across America. The textual explications of the Chicago School, on the other hand, were primarily confined to scholarly books and learned journals. And the Neo-Aristotelian method of analyzing literature was also a multi-dimensional affair which did not lend itself easily to popularization. Crane's failure to win this battle may also

have had something to do with his writing style, which can be ponderous, almost Johnsonian, though its difficulty comes from the effort to express a complex meaning without distorting it. Cleanth Brooks, by contrast, had a graceful, effortless style, one whose limits were never tested, the Neo-Aristotelians might argue, by having to explicate a rigorous critical methodology.

From the longer vantage point of the 1980s the winners and losers are less obvious. The New Criticism was successful in its day, and its techniques of explication are still being widely taught—in versions that owe little to their theories of literature and language—but it found, for all its many students, few disciples who could advance and develop its ideas (though many have seen the work of American structuralism and deconstructionism as indebted to the New Criticism). Neo-Aristotelianism, on the other hand, had developed a second generation of critics: Wayne Booth, Sheldon Sacks, Ralph Rader, Robert Marsh, Norman Friedman, Mary Doyle Springer, and Austin Wright. They were interested in revising and extending Crane's notions and in adapting these ideas to new projects. A third generation, now just beginning to flower and including among many others Don Bialostoski, Walter A. Davis, Barbara Foley, Elizabeth Langland, James Phelan, Peter Rabinowitz, and Adena Rosmarin, has continued this work of revision and adaptation, treating Crane's work not as a dead text to be analyzed but as a living voice with the power to inspire, chasten, and subdue.

One reason for Crane's continuing legacy was his legendary power as a teacher and as a midwife to the work of his students and colleagues, historical scholars, and editors, as well as literary theorists and critics. Rather than a Mr. Chips dispensing advice and encouragement, Crane was, as his students have testified, a mind with which they wrestled. More important, he had a conscience dedicated to truth, so that his students could count on him to be their toughest critic, to ask the difficult and embarrassing questions they had hoped to evade. As a result he became and has remained, twenty years after his death on 12 July 1967, a ghostly presence—like a detached superego—still influential at Chicago and wherever his students have gone.

Unlike his colleague McKeon, Crane distrusted theory as such, and though he was often attacked as a literary taxonomist, Crane in fact resisted the temptation to systematize and to cre-

*Caricature of Crane from the February 1937 issue of* Phoenix, *the University of Chicago campus humor magazine (courtesy of the University of Chicago Library)*

ate empty structural categories. It is not particularly useful to present his thought as developing and evolving between the late 1930s and his death some thirty years later. Though it is tempting, because of the late publication of *Critical and Historical Principles of Literary History* (1971), to see Crane as having left history for criticism and then returned to his first love, the fact is that the notes on which that monograph was based were written around 1950, concurrent with the development of his system of textual interpretation in

*The Languages of Criticism and the Structure of Poetry.* In practice Crane moved from one pragmatic project to another, always developing and expanding upon theoretical ideas as they were needed for each essay or monograph from within a system of thought that in its broad outlines remained essentially static.

The most abstract feature of Crane's contribution to literary theory, and perhaps its least controversial, was his commitment to instrumental pluralism. This metatheoretical feature of

Crane's thought derives ultimately from Immanuel Kant's categories, but it is most immediately indebted to McKeon's philosophical semantics, which suggest how the various systems of philosophers throughout history were generated by their prior choice of organizations, methods, principles, and modes of thought.

Spelled out most forcefully in *The Languages of Criticism and the Structure of Poetry*, Crane's pluralism begins with the premise that criticism is not a field like biochemistry which slowly advances along a single front, based upon a common set of factual and methodological assumptions–what Thomas Kuhn was later to call a paradigm. Criticism is instead "a collection of distinct and more or less incommensurable 'frameworks' or 'languages'" differing widely in "matters of assumed principle, definition and method." Each of these "languages" has its own intrinsic powers and limitations, has certain areas of insight–questions it can pose and answer–while remaining blind to other, equally significant issues. Each separate mode of criticism should therefore be considered an instrument, a useful tool for one or more specific purposes and ill-adapted to a great many others.

Crane's pluralism was a way of coping with the Babel of critical languages which had begun, even by midcentury, to generate terminological squabbles and to make it difficult for literary scholars to understand one another. One reason is the fact that incommensurable frameworks of thought are nonetheless forced to use the limited terms of natural languages in a variety of discrepant or ambiguous ways. The "content" of a poem, for example, would be a very different thing to a Marxist than to a Freudian. The word "form" has been used in nearly as many ways as there have been critics.

Crane rejected any form of syncretism–some eclectic combination of the satisfactory elements from a variety of critical systems into a single "rounded" view, such as was proposed decades ago by Stanley Edgar Hyman in *The Armed Vision: A Study in the Methods of Modern Literary Criticism* (1948) and more recently by Paul Hernadi in *Beyond Genre: New Directions in Literary Classification* (1972). Crane argued that any such "rounded" view was a chimera, because critical systems have an integral structure that precludes their being mixed at will. Even if one could unambiguously use controversial terms (like "symbol"), the significance of such terms reflects assumptions and emphases that vary from system to sys-

tem. As a result eclectic complications of terms and methods, such as we find in Northrop Frye's *Anatomy of Criticism: Four Essays* (1957), tend to deprive each critical mode of its intellectual underpinnings and hence of its genuine, though limited and partial, validity. Similarly Crane attacked historians of ideas like A. O. Lovejoy for unfairly extracting "unit ideas" from the integral systems in which they are embedded.

Crane's pluralism must be distinguished, too, from the passive, live-and-let-live toleration we practice with critics whose ideas we disagree with or do not understand. For Crane demands that critics carefully examine any critical theory so as to be aware, not only of its conclusions but of its tacit definitions, methods, and ways of organizing data, and how these features differ from their own. Analyzing another critical system is not easy, but, in a way, turning the glass on oneself is even harder, partly because one's own theoretical assumptions are seldom to the forefront of awareness. One might say they are transparent to thought, because an individual thinks *with* them, not *about* them.

Crane's sense of the qualified validity, each within its own sphere, of incommensurate critical systems, is not hard to accept when the discrepancies are great enough. Few would feel that the Freudian critic who finds evidence, in a certain work, of the neurotic conflicts of its author is in radical disagreement with the Marxist who, in the same work, finds expression instead of the author's class concerns. Such readings are readily felt to be complementary, not contradictory. Pluralism can be harder to maintain when the controversy turns on the nature of literature–as in L. C. Knight's attack on A. C. Bradley in "How Many Children Had Lady Macbeth?" In this case Crane was able to show that the title question of Knight's essay–which Knight successfully ridiculed as meaningless within his own formalist New-Critical system, in which poetry is a purely symbolic structure–nevertheless makes perfectly good sense within Bradley's mimetic criticism, in which dramatic characters are seen as imaginative analogues of real persons.

What is hardest, of course, is to maintain this pluralistic stance, not merely at the metacritical level, in neutrally officiating quarrels between rival critics, but in the defense of one's own ideas in scholarly controversy. By this ideal of pluralism Crane must himself be found wanting. For every page he wrote recommending the necessity of instrumental pluralism, he wrote two denouncing the validity of rival schools of criticism, most notably Cleanth Brooks and the New Critics (in "Cleanth Brooks, or, The Bankruptcy of Critical Monism," first published in *Modern Philology*, May 1948). He also denounced A. O. Lovejoy's "unit idea" methodology in the history of ideas (in "Literature, Philosophy, and the History of Ideas" from *Modern Philology*, November 1954), anthropological myth-criticism ("Criticism as Inquiry; or, The Perils of the 'High Priori Road' " [first delivered as a lecture in 1957] and elsewhere). He attacked as well the medievalists of the school of D. W. Robertson ("On Hypotheses in 'Historical Criticism': Apropos of Certain Contemporary Medievalists," first delivered as an oral paper in 1961). In his analytic mode Crane was capable of neutrally differentiating between his own "literal" method of interpretation and those of other critics which consider literature through its analogues with other human activities. A few pages later Crane might sneer at the "mere" analogies which rival critics were content to explore, ignoring the fact that his own method too was "merely" literal.

Before denouncing Crane as a hypocrite, a dogmatist in pluralist's clothing, one should point out three things. (1) At its extreme limits, a pure relativism of the sort Crane seems to endorse is probably not only humanly impossible but philosophically vacuous. There are always going to be reductive theoretical positions we are going to wish to exclude (e.g., poetry judged by its suitability for landfill), but Crane did not explicitly develop the grounds for exclusion. Furthermore one must distinguish between accepting the general utility of a critical methodology and endorsing good, bad, and indifferent enactments of that method. (2) There was an ineluctable rhetorical conflict between Crane's *critical* position, as the chief advocate for the Neo-Aristotelian mode of interpretation, and his *meta-critical* position as pluralist; and while any critic needs some version of pluralism to be able to learn from his colleagues, arguing for his own system requires putting relativism aside to argue against conflicting interpretations. (3) Even in his polemics, Crane was generally much better at reading his rivals' work, and assessing their virtues as well as their defects, than they were at reading him. For example, the distortions perpetrated by William K. Wimsatt in "The Chicago Critics: The Fallacy of the Neoclassic Species" and John Crowe Ransom in "Humanism at Chicago" are palpably cruder and more mean-spirited than Crane's own attacks on

Brooks and I. A. Richards. Crane could also be candid about the inherent limitations of Neo-Aristotelianism, as when he wrote in *The Languages of Criticism and the Structure of Poetry*:

> It is a method not at all suited, as is criticism in the grand line of Longinus, Coleridge, and Matthew Arnold, to the definition and appreciation of those general qualities of writing–mirroring the souls of writers–for the sake of which most of us read or at any rate return to what we have read. It is a method that necessarily abstracts from history.... It is a method, above all, that completely fails, because of its essentially differentiating character, to give us insights into the larger moral and political values of literature or into any of the other organic relations with human nature and human experience in which literature is involved.

The patient reader may glean the outlines of Crane's Neo-Aristotelian critical theory from the introduction to *Critics and Criticism*. But Crane presents his case in a more synoptic form in his lectures on *The Languages of Criticism and the Structure of Poetry*, particularly the last lecture, "Toward a More Adequate Criticism of Poetic Structure," and develops many of its consequences in "The Concept of Plot and the Plot of *Tom Jones*."

Aristotle is claimed as a forebear by so many major critics, from Horace and Longinus to Frye, that one should start with a sense of the uses to which Crane puts Aristotle. First, Aristotle's concept of *mimesis*, or imitation, is not as central to Crane as it is to other self-styled Aristotelians; Crane points out that Aristotle may in fact be implying, at one point in the *Poetics*, that not all art is mimetic. For Crane the central Aristotelian passages are those in the *Metaphysics* and some of the scientific texts, which discuss the concept of the *synolon*, or a "concrete whole" of formed matter, found in nature or manufactured by art, and the ways such *synola* may be analyzed, via their formal, material, efficient, and final causes.

The concept of the *synolon* is central to Crane's thought and to the other Neo-Aristotelians of his generation. The "concrete whole" was matter shaped by form, and shaped so as to be coherent, comprehensible, and meaningful in itself. Meaning comes from the inferred sense of the whole, not from the parts; in fact our sense of the whole *as a pattern* is what for Crane governs the perceived meaning of the parts. Bits of language, symbols or metaphors, once abstracted from the whole, lose their sense and meaning. Not even plot, which was so crucial for Crane's notions of form, is wholly decisive. As proof Crane gives a deadpan recital of the plot of J. H. Moore's "The Duke of Benevento," which by itself suggests "a vaguely tragicomic romance . . . of a kind common enough in the 1770s," but which actually belongs to an "anti-Romantic comedy." Though our sense of the whole takes shape through our experience of the parts (especially language), we revise our sense of the parts through our growing sense of the whole to which they contribute. And while the powers of some literary works may require temporary or permanent ambiguities, many merely *potential* ambiguities within a text are cleared up by this shaping process. This is a gestaltist idea, and indeed that psychological movement may underline Crane's thought almost as much as Aristotle does.

Crane viewed Aristotle primarily as the founder of a positivistic and "differential" method (one opposed to Plato's idealistic and synthesizing method). The method was positivistic in the sense that Aristotle sought scientific knowledge of things in their real-life contingency, rather than through a dialectical approach to an ideal world; and it was differential in that Aristotle saw various *synola* as existing for a variety of purposes, and that they could be judged by no ground higher than their capacity to fulfill their final cause.

For Crane the *Poetics* was an instance of this general methodology, applying this mode of analysis to tragedy and tragic epic. Poetic works of art are *synola* in which plot, character, and thought (the formal cause) give shape to language (the material cause) using various techniques or devices of disclosure (the efficient cause) to create an object with the power to affect us in various ways (the final cause). In tragedy the final cause, the *dynamis*, is the catharsis of pity and fear, and Aristotle judges various Attic tragedies by how well their various elements are designed–the ultimate criterion being their capacity to effect the tragic *dynamis*. Crane viewed the proper application of Aristotle as the extension of the systematic approach of the *Poetics* to other genres, which other structures of plot, character, thought, language, and technique had been designed to serve. In his critical practice Crane's genres were based primarily upon the formal and the final causes, with the efficient and material causes unofficially relegated to relatively subordinate roles.

Genre was central to the criticism of Crane and the other Neo-Aristotelians in that their way of analyzing a difficult text would involve an attempt to locate it within a system of genres, or at least to place it in relation to texts that were already better understood. Thus Crane's analysis of *Macbeth* in *The Languages of Criticism and the Structure of Poetry* proceeds by noting that the power of that tragedy is not that of classical tragedies (the ones praised by Aristotle in *Poetics*, 13) involving the downfall of a good man, such as the *Oedipus* or, later, *Hamlet;* nor that of another sort of serious drama popular in the Renaissance (but characterized as inferior by Aristotle) involving the downfall of a villain, such as *The Jew of Malta. Macbeth* was for Crane related to both these genres but a member of neither; it was instead a masterwork of a new kind, in which the destruction of the protagonist is desired by the reader/audience, not only for the sake of those whom he has injured, but also as an end to his own torments. Macbeth, Crane tells the reader, "is one who commits monstrous deeds without becoming wholly a monster, since his knowledge of the right . . . is never altogether obscured. . . . The catharsis is effected not merely by the man's deserved overthrow but by his discovery, before it is too late, of what he had not known before he began to act. If we are normal human beings we must abhor his crimes; yet we cannot completely abhor but must rather pity the man himself and . . . wish for such an outcome as will be best, under the circumstances, not merely for Scotland but for him."

It was no accident that Crane preferred to demonstrate his theory on masterpieces like *Macbeth* and *Tom Jones*, where a complex plot and a great variety of characters have been marshaled with efficiency to the service of a single end. Crane's genres have an ideal quality to them, and like many other theories with a component of idealism, Crane's was less compelling on mixed forms like *The Vicar of Wakefield* or *Moby-Dick*, or partial failures like Henry Fielding's *Amelia*, where the author had failed to coherently integrate didactic materials into a mimetic plot, or where extraformal intentions were realized at the expense of the reader's emotional affect. A later generation of Neo-Aristotelians, including Wayne Booth and Ralph Rader, was to explore more adequately how architectonic notions of form could be reconciled with the multifarious intentions of authors and with the institutional shapes that culture bequeaths to literature.

Crane was a nominalist who spoke of his genres as heuristic categories, mere aids to understanding, by-products of analysis rather than reified concepts with independent significance. To characterize a text as belonging to a genre was to make a hypothesis about its nature, a hypothesis with teeth in it, entailing logical consequences that reach beyond the data used in forming the hypothesis. The hypothesis can then be tested against that data and either confirmed or refuted by it. (One could test Crane's theory of *Macbeth*, for example, by asking how it accounts for the presence of certain minor characters, or for the heavy use of the soliloquy as a device of disclosure.)

Furthermore the hypothesis must be tested against alternative hypotheses to see whether there is a better explanation of the text. At any point, however well supported, the hypothesis is a conjecture that may be corrected or refuted by a better one. The virtue of an open system of genres is that a set of alternative hypotheses is always readily present to the mind of the critic. Crane considered this method intrinsically superior to that of the Robertsonian medievalists, for example, who know in advance of reading a particular text that they will find in it displaced versions of patristic allegory. Crane's attack on the "monism" of Cleanth Brooks was essentially of the same kind—that Brooks knew in advance of analyzing a particular poem that, if it was any good, it would contain paradox and irony aplenty. This was the "high priori road" Crane wished to avoid, and he claimed that his own hypotheses were formed a posteriori using the inductive, positivistic method of the natural sciences.

In this Crane undoubtedly went too far. Crane's genres are not generated in any pure a posteriori fashion; they result from the articulation of a sizable, but nonetheless limited and foreknown, number of structural predicates, many of which Crane outlined in "The Concept of Plot and the Plot of *Tom Jones*." For example, the protagonist may be either better, worse, or of the same moral quality as ourselves, and this moral nature may be either static or capable of moving from one to another of these levels; the protagonist's fate may be either fortunate or unfortunate, in greater or less degree, in the short run or the long run; the protagonist may be responsible for this fate, or it may be the result of chance, destiny, fortune, providence, or historical necessity;

the plot as a whole may turn on a change in the protagonist's circumstances, moral character, or way of thinking; the text as a whole may be an imitation of human action (mimetic) or of an argument (didactic); and so on. The intercalation of these predicates would generate hundreds, perhaps thousands of distinct genres; certainly neither Crane nor his followers (whom Eliseo Vivas accused in "Literary Classes: Some Problems," *Genre*, 1968, of "pedantic microtaxonomy") ever enumerated them. But even a *million* possible hypotheses derived from these distinctions would not make the generic system truly a posteriori or inductive.

It is likely that Crane wished to describe his system as inductive because that was how the scientific method was then described. It was not until shortly after Crane had developed his system that Karl Popper in *The Logic of Scientific Discovery* (1955) was to suggest that the vaunted inductive method of science was an illusion, and that the true logic of discovery in the natural sciences involved hypothetical conjectures whose source was immaterial, so long as these conjectures lent themselves to testing—confirmation and refutation—and so long as the researcher always held his hypotheses open to further revision. Crane's methodology was in fact closer to real scientific method than he knew, but for somewhat different reasons. The hypotheses generated by Crane's heuristic genres make relatively strong predictions which the text itself (or features of its creation and reception) can falsify. Theories which cannot be falsified by the facts (usually because they permit ad hoc modifications that allow them to flex so as to accommodate any data whatever) can never fail, but to the scientific mind they cannot explain very much either. This is the real essence of Crane's attack on the Robertsonians and the New Critics.

Such a scientific stance suggests that Crane's motivations as a critic included the attainment of power through the successful search for some objective truth. This attitude, that of a displaced scientist, stands in marked contrast with that of most of the New Critics, whose motivations, by their own accounts, were more like spoiled priests searching in literature for a new Word to replace the one the world had lost. This contrast may also suggest why so many erstwhile New Critics have succumbed to the negations of the deconstructive angel, with its diabolically messianic overtones, while most of the Neo-Aristotelians have remained entirely immune.

*R. S. Crane in the early 1940s (courtesy of Mrs. William M. Gibson)*

Despite Crane's attacks upon the New Critics, he adopted one major feature of their program, the autonomy of the literary text, which was seen as interpretable independent of authorial intention, audience affect, and other extrinsic factors. Crane did not (like Wimsatt and Beardsley) erect a series of fallacies and heresies to defend the various flanks of textual autonomy. But like them he tended to exclude these aspects. "What is held constant," Crane wrote in the introduction to *Critics and Criticism,* "is the whole complex of accidental causes of variation in poetry that depend on the talents, characters, educations, and intentions of individual authors, the opinions and tastes of the audiences they address, the state of the language in their time, and all the other external factors which affect their choice of materials and conventions in particular works. The provisional exclusion of these factors is necessary if the analysis is to concentrate upon the internal causes which account for the peculiar construction and effect of any poem qua artistic whole."

any poem qua artistic whole."

Crane presents the exclusion of the extrinsic as a tactical gesture more than as a statement of the nature of literature, but it nevertheless may have seriously distorted his readings of poetry. In particular the notion of autonomy blinded Crane (and most of his contemporary followers) to fundamental differences between many forms of lyric poetry and other literary modes, such as drama and fiction. With the author excluded, the lyric "I" had to be viewed as an externalized speaker, the principle character in a tiny agon that could be analyzed by the same terms Crane had used for prose fiction and theatrical drama. This externalized speaker is seen as either "moved in a certain way by his situation" or "acting in a certain manner in relation to it" or as "deliberating morally in a certain frame of mind." Lyric poems thus have, like plays and novels, something analogous to a plot; in fact they have plots of thought, action, or character, respectively. This sort of analysis works best for poems where the "I" is indeed a dramatic character, felt as "other" to the poet, as in Robert Browning's "My Last Duchess." But in the majority of poems in the Western tradition the poet is immanent within the poem; a condition of reading them is that we recognize the speaker's voice as a projection, displaced or immediate, of the poet's. It is not a mere "accidental cause of variation" but integral to the nature of lyric poetry that readers for the last two hundred years have viewed the words of "Elegy in a Country Churchyard" as the expression of one Thomas Gray, rather than that of a nameless, fully externalized "virtuous, sensitive and ambitious young man of undistinguished birth," as Crane was forced to see him. The New Critics had made the same mistake of banishing the author and positing an autonomous speaker within the poem, but for their mode of thematic analysis, it made little practical difference whether the thematic focus was ascribed to the author or his creation. Given Crane's emphasis on character and action, the separation of speaker/actor from poet seemed considerably more artificial. In fact there is no reason within Crane's system to insist upon such a rigid textual autonomy, and the poet/character relation in all its variations can be compassed under the aegis of Aristotle's efficient cause.

Although critics had by the time of Crane's death ceased to fear the intentional fallacy, and although disciples of Crane's like Booth and Sheldon Sacks had begun to move toward the internal handling of "extrinsic" questions like authorial motives, Crane never adapted his critical system to bring such issues within its direct purview. Consistent with his pluralistic stance, he was content that Neo-Aristotelianism continue as a method to "abstract from history." Instead Crane saw historical issues as part of a larger schematization. In "Questions and Answers in the Teaching of Literary Texts," Crane presented his sense of the relations of different critical tasks as a series of concentric circles ranging ever outward from the text itself. At the center came the most basic problems of textual explication and hermeneutics. Next came critical questions evaluating the text as an artistic whole (Crane's Neo-Aristotelian criticism would be situated here). Third came "the criticism of qualities or of literary personality." This concept moves beyond the individual work or genre; it would include the Longinian criticism of the sublime, for example, as that quality appears in various texts by various authors, or the realm of biographical criticism, where the critic tries to define the artistic essence of a Henry James or an Ernest Hemingway. Fourth were issues of "literary history, or criticism of circumstances." Fifth and last came "the criticism of moral, social, political, and religious values" that give the texts of the past their significance for the present.

Crane never himself attempted to provide a set of principles for hermeneutics, for biographical or qualitative criticism, or for the various ideological approaches, but he did go beyond Neo-Aristotelianism to discuss his fourth category, the criticism of circumstances, about which he wrote *Critical and Historical Principles of Literary History*. This densely written monograph, published with *The Idea of the Humanities* in 1967 and separately in 1971, begins with the notion that any literary history will be naturally limited by the comprehensiveness of its critical theories about literature.

First of all, Crane tells us, there is the "preconstructional" aspect of a text, the work's origins, sources, and analogues. For a writer working within a given genre, the preexisting tradition offers a storehouse of literary conventions—plot devices, character types, verbal strategies, narrative techniques—to which the author looks in composing his original work. Second, there is the "postconstructional" aspect, comprised of the effects works have upon audiences, in terms of the central themes of human discourse, such as language, the mind, society, history. Third and last, there is the "constructional"

approach to the text, essentially the Neo-Aristotelian approach that Crane had elaborated in *The Languages of Criticism and the Structures of Poetry*. Ideally the literary historian must take all three of these factors into account in historical analysis of the genesis of the text.

After the literary historian has taken account of these critical principles, he or she is faced with two major issues: mode of organization and principles of explanation. In terms of organization Crane recognized that most literary histories in his time were what he called *atomistic;* these are the familiar traditional surveys offering coverage (description with or without qualitative judgments) of works produced in the same country around the same period. Here, typically, each chapter would be devoted to an author—or a group of related authors—and his works, presented in a simple chronological order, and each chapter would necessitate, more or less, a new beginning for the narrative. Crane did not attack the life-and-works approach as such, but he pointed out the limitations of that sort of "scissors and paste history," as R. G. Collingwood called it, particularly its lack of continuity, to say nothing of "the dynamic quality which the best histories of political . . . affairs have had."

The alternative mode of organization is *dialectical* and leads to what Crane calls *organic* literary history by applying to a succession of authors some integrating dialectic which derives the history of literature from a historical process outside literature. Here is where we find social thinkers like Hippolyte Taine, Louis Cazamian, and the Marxists on the one hand, and the historians of ideas on the other. Crane finds that approaches of this sort tend both to exalt a single cause beyond what it is capable of effecting, and to reduce and distort the individual qualities of works, each of which must be made somehow to reflect its age. Instead of atomistic or dialectical organizations, Crane recommends seeking within history for "narrative-causal sequences" with definite beginnings and ends, a continuous matter that changes, and then seeking for a cause or a converging sequence of causes, formal and extraformal, that can account for the change defined.

The last half of the monograph is devoted to a rich and complex analysis of the three types of cause-and-effect which literary historians need to take into account in investigating such narrative-causal sequences: (1) formal motives "depending primarily on the nature of the specific art form . . . being attempted"; (2) "extraformal motives

. . . in the writer himself "; and (3) "the material circumstances of his productive acts." The division and order are typical of Crane, who was always wary of using biography or psychology–to say nothing of economics–to explain aspects of the text that were already adequately determined by reasons of art. But Crane insists that the historian cannot afford to neglect factors like critical theory, literary reception, biography, the history of ideas and of culture in general, and the economic factors in literary production. Characteristically each time Crane presents an aspect of literary causality he spends as much space exposing the abuses of its devotees as recommending its proper use.

One major problem with this monograph is the leakiness of Crane's pluralism. That is, at the beginning, Crane asserts that any complete history of a genre must take all three aspects of the text into account–constructional, preconstructional, and postconstructional. But by the end Crane has abandoned this position to concentrate on the constructional aspect, which he felt could alone supply both the necessary and sufficient causes of a text's character. Crane develops in detail the principles of causal explanation relevant to constructional literary history. But instead of doing the same for preconstructional and postconstructional histories, he subjects well-known histories written on these principles to intense scrutiny, faulting them mainly for genuine flaws of logic and common sense, but also for failing to be constructional literary history.

Thus Crane evaluates the achievement of *The Road to Xanadu* in these terms:

> Thanks to one of the triumphs of modern philology, we can trace a great proportion of the words in *Kubla Khan* to certain miscellaneous books of travel; but the delicate method by which these facts are established does not enable J. L. Lowes to make clear, except in terms of a myth about the creative imagination, why it was that only these few words, out of the hundreds of thousands which Coleridge must have read in the same sources, became part of the poem.

Crane's point is that, no matter how diligently and successfully we may seek out the sources that influenced the creation of a text, the sources are not the text and are never sufficient in themselves to explain its form. What feels unworthy of Crane is his sneer at Lowes for wasting his time

with a merely preconstructional problem.

It is equally unfortunate that, owing to Crane's commitment to constructional literary history, he never accords serious treatment to the principles of explanation of histories of the other types. Even committed Neo-Aristotelians might like to know what makes Lowes's influence-study a masterpiece of its kind while so many other influence-studies fell short. And given Crane's focus on the form of the individual work as a concrete whole, he was, if anything, relatively sympathetic to preconstructional modes of history which place the creative process of the individual artist at the center. Postconstructional historians–like Taine and Cazamian, "to say nothing of the Marxists"–those who have succumbed to the lure of "organic" history–get not a sneer but rather the broad swipe of his paw, usually for the sin of "causal monism":

> Authors of such histories rarely introduce any mediating causal steps between the integrating principle and the peculiarities of content and form exhibited by the works it purports to explain. The result is that we are never given the sufficient causes of literary works considered as concrete objects or events (if we are given causes at all) but only the conditions *sine qua non* of the presence in some works and the absence from others of certain combinations of general traits.

For all its omissions and its faults of temperament, *Critical and Historical Principles of Literary History* is a savvy and judicious theoretical document that, like much of Crane's criticism, is most annoying when it is most perceptive. It blandly and cogently argues for an ideal methodology that most scholars would have a hard time living up to. Furthermore to take these arguments seriously is to admit that most literary histories in print are unworthy of the name, and that writing one that would meet Crane's standards would be a massive and difficult achievement. This monograph was Crane's last legacy to his students and to the profession as a whole; it bequeathed a task that, if it is shouldered, will last for generations.

**Bibliography:**
John C. Sherwood, *R. S. Crane: An Annotated Bibliography* (New York & London: Garland, 1984).

**References:**

Bruce W. Bashford, "The Humanistic Criticism of R. S. Crane," Ph.D. dissertation, Northwestern University, 1970;

Wayne C. Booth, "Ronald Crane and the Pluralism of Discrete Modes," in his *Critical Understanding: The Powers and Limits of Pluralism* (Chicago & London: University of Chicago Press, 1979), pp. 37-97;

Kenneth Burke, "The Problem of the Intrinsic (as Reflected in the Neo-Aristotelian School)," *Accent,* 3 (Winter 1943): 86-94;

Walter A. Davis, *The Act of Interpretation: A Critique of Literary Reason* (Chicago: University of Chicago Press, 1978), pp. 1-61;

Robert D. Denham, "R. S. Crane's Critical Method and Theory of Poetic Form," *Connecticut Review,* 5 (April 1972): 46-56;

John Crowe Ransom, "Humanism at Chicago," *Kenyon Review,* 14 (Summer 1952): 647-659;

David H. Richter, "The Second Flight of the Phoenix: Neo-Aristotelianism Since Crane," *Eighteenth Century,* 23 (Winter 1982): 27-48;

Sheldon Sacks, "Golden Birds and Dying Generations," *Comparative Literature Studies,* 6 (September 1969): 274-291;

Eliseo Vivas, "The Neo-Aristotelians of Chicago," *Sewanee Review,* 61 (Winter 1953): 136-149;

William K. Wimsatt, Jr., "The Chicago Critics: The Fallacy of the Neoclassic Species," in *The Verbal Icon: Studies in the Meaning of Poetry,* by Wimsatt and Monroe C. Beardsley (Lexington: University of Kentucky Press, 1954), pp. 41-65.

# T. S. Eliot

## *(26 September 1888-4 January 1965)*

### Michael Beehler
*Montana State University*

See also the Eliot entries in *DLB 7, Twentieth-Century American Dramatists, DLB 10, Modern British Dramatists, 1900-1945,* and *DLB 45, American Poets, 1880-1945,* First Series.

BOOKS: *Prufrock and Other Observations* (London: The Egoist, 1917);

*Ezra Pound: His Metric and Poetry* (New York: Knopf, 1918);

*Poems* (Richmond: Leonard & Virginia Woolf at The Hogarth Press, 1919);

*Ara Vos Prec* (London: Ovid Press, 1920); republished with one substitution and one title change as *Poems* (New York: Knopf, 1920);

*The Sacred Wood: Essays on Poetry and Criticism* (London: Methuen, 1920; New York: Knopf, 1921);

*The Waste Land* (New York: Boni & Liveright, 1922; Richmond: Leonard & Virginia Woolf at The Hogarth Press, 1923);

*Homage to John Dryden: Three Essays on Poetry of the Seventeenth Century* (London: Leonard & Virginia Woolf at The Hogarth Press, 1924);

*Poems 1909-1925* (London: Faber & Gwyer, 1925; New York & Chicago: Harcourt, Brace, 1932);

*Journey of the Magi* (London: Faber & Gwyer, 1927; New York: Rudge, 1927);

*Shakespeare and the Stoicism of Seneca* (London: Oxford University Press, 1927);

*A Song for Simeon* (London: Faber & Gwyer, 1928);

*For Lancelot Andrewes: Essays on Style and Order* (London: Faber & Gwyer, 1928; Garden City: Doubleday, Doran, 1929);

*Dante* (London: Faber & Faber, 1929);

*Animula* (London: Faber & Faber, 1929);

*Ash-Wednesday* (London: Faber & Faber, 1930; New York & London: Putnam's, 1930);

*Marina* (London: Faber & Faber, 1930);

*Thoughts After Lambeth* (London: Faber & Faber, 1931);

*Triumphal March* (London: Faber & Faber, 1931);

*Charles Whibley: A Memoir* (London: Oxford University Press, 1931);

*Selected Essays 1917-1932* (London: Faber & Faber, 1932; New York: Harcourt, Brace, 1932);

*John Dryden: The Poet, The Dramatist, The Critic* (New York: Terence & Elsa Holliday, 1932);

*Sweeney Agonistes: Fragments of an Aristophanic Melodrama* (London: Faber & Faber, 1932);

*The Use of Poetry and The Use of Criticism: Studies in the Relation of Criticism to Poetry in England* (London: Faber & Faber, 1933; Cambridge, Mass.: Harvard University Press, 1933);

*After Strange Gods: A Primer of Modern Heresy* (London: Faber & Faber, 1934; New York: Harcourt, Brace, 1934);

*The Rock: A Pageant Play* (London: Faber & Faber, 1934; New York: Harcourt, Brace, 1934);

*Elizabethan Essays* (London: Faber & Faber, 1934); republished, with omission of three essays and addition of one, as *Essays on Elizabethan Drama* (New York: Harcourt, Brace, 1956); republished as *Elizabethan Dramatists* (London: Faber & Faber, 1963);

*Words for Music* (Bryn Mawr, Pa., 1934);

*Murder in the Cathedral*, acting edition (Canterbury: H. J. Goulden, 1935); complete edition (London: Faber & Faber, 1935; New York: Harcourt, Brace, 1935);

*Two Poems* (Cambridge: Cambridge University Press, 1935);

*Essays Ancient & Modern* (London: Faber & Faber, 1936; New York: Harcourt, Brace, 1936);

*Collected Poems 1909-1935* (London: Faber & Faber, 1936; New York: Harcourt, Brace, 1936);

*The Family Reunion* (London: Faber & Faber, 1939; New York: Harcourt, Brace, 1939);

*Old Possum's Book of Practical Cats* (London: Faber & Faber, 1939; New York: Harcourt, Brace, 1939);

*The Idea of a Christian Society* (London: Faber & Faber, 1939; New York: Harcourt, Brace, 1940);

*The Waste Land and Other Poems* (London: Faber & Faber, 1940; New York: Harcourt, Brace, 1955);

*East Coker* (London: Faber & Faber, 1940);

*Burnt Norton* (London: Faber & Faber, 1941);

*Points of View* (London: Faber & Faber, 1941);

*The Dry Salvages* (London: Faber & Faber, 1941);

*The Classics and the Man of Letters* (London, New York & Toronto: Oxford University Press, 1942);

*The Music of Poetry* (Glasgow: Jackson, Son & Company, Publishers to the University, 1942);

*Little Gidding* (London: Faber & Faber, 1942);

*Four Quartets* (New York: Harcourt, Brace, 1943; London: Faber & Faber, 1944);

*What Is a Classic?* (London: Faber & Faber, 1945);

*Die Einheit der Europäischen Kultur* ["The Unity of European Culture"–bilingual] (Berlin: Carl Habel, 1946);

*A Practical Possum* (Cambridge, Mass.: Harvard Printing Office & Department of Graphic Arts, 1947);

*On Poetry* (Concord, Mass.: Concord Academy, 1947);

*Milton* (London: Geoffrey Cumberlege, 1947);

*A Sermon* (Cambridge, U.K.: Cambridge University Press, 1948);

*Selected Poems* (Harmondsworth: Penguin/Faber & Faber, 1948; New York: Harcourt, Brace & World, 1967);

*Notes Towards the Definition of Culture* (London: Faber & Faber, 1948; New York: Harcourt, Brace, 1949);

*From Poe to Valéry* (New York: Harcourt, Brace, 1948);

*The Undergraduate Poems of T. S. Eliot published while he was in college in The Harvard Advocate*, unauthorized publication (Cambridge, Mass., 1949);

*The Aims of Poetic Drama* (London: Poets' Theatre Guild, 1949);

*The Cocktail Party* (London: Faber & Faber, 1950; New York: Harcourt, Brace, 1950; revised edition, London: Faber & Faber, 1950);

*Poems Written in Early Youth* (Stockholm: Privately printed, 1950; London: Faber & Faber, 1967; New York: Farrar, Straus & Giroux, 1967);

*Poetry and Drama* (Cambridge, Mass.: Harvard University Press, 1951; London: Faber & Faber, 1951);

*The Film of Murder in the Cathedral*, by Eliot and George Hoellering (London: Faber & Faber, 1952; New York: Harcourt, Brace, 1952);

*The Value and Use of Cathedrals in England Today* (Chichester: Friends of Chichester Cathedral, 1952);

*An Address to Members of the London Library* (London: London Library, 1952; Providence, R.I.: Providence Athenaeum, 1953);

*The Complete Poems and Plays* (New York: Harcourt, Brace, 1952);

*Selected Prose*, edited by John Hayward (Melbourne, London & Baltimore: Penguin, 1953);

*American Literature and the American Language* (St. Louis: Department of English, Washington University, 1953);

*The Three Voices of Poetry* (London: Cambridge University Press, 1953; New York: Cambridge University Press, 1954);

*The Confidential Clerk* (London: Faber & Faber, 1954; New York: Harcourt, Brace, 1954);

*Religious Drama: Mediaeval and Modern* (New York: House of Books, 1954);

*The Cultivation of Christmas Trees* (London: Faber & Faber, 1954; New York: Farrar, Straus & Cudahy, 1956);

*The Literature of Politics* (London: Conservative Political Centre, 1955);

*The Frontiers of Criticism* (Minneapolis: University of Minnesota Press, 1956);

*On Poetry and Poets* (London: Faber & Faber, 1957; New York: Farrar, Straus & Cudahy, 1957);

*The Elder Statesman* (London: Faber & Faber, 1959; New York: Farrar, Straus & Cudahy, 1959);

*Geoffrey Faber 1889-1961* (London: Faber & Faber, 1961);

*Collected Plays* (London: Faber & Faber, 1962);

*George Herbert* (London: Longmans, Green, 1962);

*Collected Poems 1909-1962* (London: Faber & Faber, 1963; New York: Harcourt, Brace & World, 1963);

*Knowledge and Experience in the Philosophy of F. H. Bradley* (London: Faber & Faber, 1964; New York: Farrar, Straus, 1964);

*To Criticize the Critic and Other Writings* (London: Faber & Faber, 1965; New York: Farrar, Straus & Giroux, 1965);

*Complete Poems and Plays* (London: Faber & Faber, 1969);

*The Waste Land: A Facsimile and Transcript of the Original Drafts Including the Annotations of Ezra Pound*, edited by Valerie Eliot (London: Faber & Faber, 1971; New York: Harcourt Brace Jovanovich, 1971);

*Selected Prose of T. S. Eliot*, edited by Frank Kermode (New York: Harcourt Brace Jovanovich/Farrar, Straus & Giroux, 1975);

*The Composition of "Four Quartets,"* edited, with commentary, by Helen Gardner (New York: Oxford University Press, 1978).

PLAY PRODUCTIONS: *The Rock*, London, Sadler's Wells Theatre, 28 May 1934;

*Murder in the Cathedral*, Canterbury, Chapter House of Canterbury Cathedral, 19 June 1935;

*The Family Reunion*, London, Westminster Theatre, 21 March 1939;

*The Cocktail Party*, Edinburgh, Scotland, Edinburgh Festival, 22 August 1949;

*The Confidential Clerk*, London, Lyric Theatre, 16 September 1953;

*The Elder Statesman*, Edinburgh, Scotland, Edinburgh Festival, 25 August 1958.

OTHER: Paul Valéry, *Le Serpent*, introduction by Eliot (London: Cobden-Sanderson, 1924);

Charlotte Eliot, *Savonarola: A Dramatic Poem*, introduction by Eliot (London: Cobden-Sanderson, 1926);

Edgar Ansel Mowrer, *This American World*, preface by Eliot (London: Faber & Gwyer, 1928);

Ezra Pound, *Selected Poems*, edited, with an introduction, by Eliot (London: Faber & Gwyer, 1928);

"Experiment in Criticism," in *Tradition and Experiment in Present-Day Literature* (London: Humphrey Milford, 1929);

Charles Baudelaire, *Intimate Journals*, translated by Christopher Isherwood, introduction by Eliot (London: Blackamore Press/New York: Random House, 1930);

St.-J. Perse, *Anabasis a Poem*, translated, with an introduction, by Eliot (London: Faber & Faber, 1930; New York: Harcourt, Brace, 1938; revised edition, New York: Harcourt, Brace, 1949; London: Faber & Faber, 1959);

*Pascal's Pensées*, translated by W. F. Trotter, introduction by Eliot (London & Toronto: Dent/New York: Dutton, 1931);

"Donne in Our Time," in *A Garland for John Donne, 1631-1931*, edited by Theodore Spencer (Cambridge: Harvard University Press, 1931), pp. 1-19;

Charles-Louis Philippe, *Bubu of Montparnasse*, preface by Eliot (Paris: Crosby, 1932);

"Address by T. S. Eliot, '06, to the Class of '33, June 17, 1933," *Milton Graduates Bulletin*, 3 (November 1933): 5-9;

*Harvard College Class of 1910. Seventh Report,* includes an autobiographical note by Eliot (June 1935), pp. 219-221;

Marianne Moore, *Selected Poems,* edited, with an introduction, by Eliot (New York: Macmillan, 1935; London: Faber & Faber, 1935);

Alfred Tennyson, *Poems of Tennyson,* introduction by Eliot (London, Edinburgh, Paris, Melbourne, Toronto & New York: Nelson, 1936);

Djuna Barnes, *Nightwood,* introduction by Eliot (New York: Harcourt, Brace, 1937); introduction and preface by Eliot (London: Faber & Faber, 1950);

Rudyard Kipling, *A Choice of Kipling's Verse,* edited, with an introduction, by Eliot (London: Faber & Faber, 1941; New York: Scribners, 1943);

"The Christian Conception of Education," in *Malvern, 1941, The Life of the Church and the Order of Society, Being the Proceedings of the Archbishop of York's Conference* (London: Longman's, 1942);

Samuel L. Clemens (Mark Twain), *The Adventures of Huckleberry Finn,* introduction by Eliot (London: Cresset Press, 1950);

"Ezra Pound," in *Ezra Pound: A Collection of Essays,* edited by Peter Russell (London & New York: Peter Nevill, 1950), pp. 25-36;

Joseph Chiari, *Contemporary French Poetry,* foreword by Eliot (Manchester: Manchester University Press, 1952);

Josef Pieper, *Leisure: The Basis of Culture,* introduction by Eliot (London: Faber & Faber, 1952);

Simone Weil, *The Need for Roots,* preface by Eliot (London: Routledge, 1952);

Pound, *Literary Essays,* edited, with an introduction, by Eliot (London: Faber & Faber, 1954; Norfolk, Conn.: New Directions, 1954);

Chiari, *Symbolisme from Poe to Mallarmé,* foreword by Eliot (London: Rockliff, 1956);

Paul Valéry, *The Art of Poetry,* translated by Denise Folliot, introduction by Eliot (New York: Pantheon, 1958);

*From Mary to You,* includes an address by Eliot (St. Louis: Mary Institute, 1959), pp. 133-136;

*The Criterion 1922-1939,* 18 volumes, edited by Eliot (London: Faber & Faber, 1967).

PERIODICAL PUBLICATIONS: "The Noh and the Image," *Egoist,* 4 (August 1917): 102-110;

"Reflections on Contemporary Poetry [III]," *Egoist,* 4 (November 1917): 151;

"In Memory of Henry James," *Egoist,* 5 (January 1918): 1-2;

"The Hawthorne Aspect [of Henry James]," *Little Review,* 4 (August 1918): 47-53;

"Studies in Contemporary Criticism [I]," *Egoist,* 9 (October 1918): 113-114;

"Studies in Contemporary Criticism [II]," *Egoist,* 10 (November/December 1918): 131-133;

"American Literature," *Athenaeum,* 4643 (25 April 1919): 236-237;

"A Sceptical Patrician [Henry Adams]," *Athenaeum,* 4647 (23 May 1919): 361-362;

"Reflections on Contemporary Poetry [IV]," *Egoist,* 6 (July 1919): 39-40;

"The Romantic Generation, If It Existed," *Athenaeum,* 4655 (18 July 1919): 616-617;

"London Letter," *Dial,* 70 (April 1921): 448-453;

"Marianne Moore," *Dial,* 75 (December 1923): 594-597;

"Whitman and Tennyson," *Nation and Athenaeum,* 40 (18 December 1926): 426;

"A Note on Poetry and Belief," *Enemy,* 1 (January 1927): 15-17;

"Literature, Science, and Dogma," *Dial,* 82 (March 1927): 239-243;

"The Idealism of Julien Benda," *Cambridge Review,* 49 (6 June 1928): 485-488;

"Freud's Illusions," *Criterion,* 8 (December 1928): 350-353;

"American Critics," *Times Literary Supplement,* 1406 (10 January 1929): 420-422;

"Poetry and Propaganda," *Bookman,* 70 (February 1930): 595-602;

"The Problem of Education," *Harvard Advocate,* 121 (Freshman Number 1934): 11-12;

"Literature and the Modern World," *American Prefaces,* 1 (November 1935): 19-22;

"The Responsibility of the Man of Letters in the Cultural Restoration of Europe," *Norseman,* 2 (July/August 1944): 243-248;

"The Influence of Landscape upon the Poet," *Daedalus,* 89 (Spring 1960): 420-422.

No name is more closely associated with the course of modern poetry and literary criticism than that of T. S. Eliot, for no writer has had a greater hand in shaping the sensibilities, expectations, and projects of modern critical and creative letters. His formidable contributions to modern poetry and drama are the subjects of other volumes, but it is in his role as theorist, critic, reviewer, editor, and public man of letters that Eliot's influence has most profoundly and enduringly affected modern thinking about literature. This influence had a particularly direct impact upon New Criticism, the most important American literary theory of the first half of the twentieth century, and upon its most visible practitioners: John Crowe Ransom, William K. Wimsatt, Cleanth Brooks, and Allen Tate, among others. Eliot's critical work provided the theoretical foundations for New Criticism, and his poetry supplied the New Critics with texts ideally suited to their methodology.

The linkages between Eliot's criticism and the theories of New Criticism can be seen in three areas: 1) models of what a poetic text is; 2) models of what true literary criticism is and what it should seek to accomplish; and 3) models of the relationship between the aesthetic world of the poetic text and the world at large. With respect to the nature of a poetic text, Eliot in his early essays envisions texts as autotelic, self-sufficient objects whose meanings inhere in their own internal structures and organizations. His focus is always on what happens in a literary work rather than upon either an author's intentions (or other aspects of a text's production) or a reader's response. His impersonal theory of poetry and his stress upon the material objectivity of the text are codified as central tenets of New Criticism by Wimsatt and Beardsley's discussions of the pathetic and intentional fallacies, and Eliot's own attention to textual details serves as a model of New Critical close reading.

In a similar vein Eliot derides the impressionistic criticism of the late nineteenth century and seeks instead an objective criticism whose tools are comparison and analysis. With these tools the critic can probe the literary object in the same way that a scientist probes a natural object, and it is this objective model of criticism that is strongly endorsed by such New Critics as Brooks and Ransom. Indeed, it is Eliot's project, shared by the New Critics, to make literary criticism an autonomous, rigorous field of knowledge distinct from biography, psychology, philosophy, and the other humanistic disciplines. Against the chaotic relativism of impressionistic criticism, Eliot asserts the standards and authority of a literary tradition within which a work must be set in order to be evaluated. Thus the act of criticism, like the work itself, is de-subjectivized and de-historicized, and poetic meaning becomes impersonal, public, and objective.

Such a model of objective criticism is especially well tuned to a particular type of poetry, one which is intellectually complex and filled

*T. S. Eliot in 1926, outside the offices of Faber & Gwyer (photograph by the poet's brother, Henry Eliot)*

with paradoxes, tensions, and ironies for the critic to explore and explain. Thus Eliot's rewriting of the Western literary tradition, his devaluing of eighteenth- and nineteenth-century Romanticism, and his promoting of the metaphysical poetry of the sixteenth and seventeenth centuries moved to the center of the tradition the very texts New Criticism was able to deal with most effectively, thereby validating its theories and methodologies. In this validation process, Eliot's own poetry played a crucial role. Cleanth Brooks's essay on *The Waste Land* ("The Waste Land: Critique of the Myth," in *Modern Poetry and the Tradition,* 1939) is itself a model of New Critical work, deriving many of its assumptions from Eliot's critical essays and applying them to his poetry. Through a close, detailed reading of this difficult and complex poem, Brooks, in what became a typical New Critical gesture, shows that the poem develops through a series of complicated paradoxes and tensions and demonstrates that its fragmented and confused surface is in fact integrated by a coherent form and theme that is "right and inevitable." Thus Brooks, acting as the objective analyst of a poetic object, saves *The Waste Land* from the charge of a chaotic nihilism through a New Critical appeal to formal unity and a modeling of poetry as a special kind of language distinct from its prose explication, one that harmonizes the paradoxes and tensions of a secularized modern age into a higher, unified coherence.

This theological model of poetry and poetic language links itself strongly to Eliot's own criticism which, after his 1927 conversion to Anglo-Catholicism, blends the aesthetic with the overtly ethical and theological. Indeed the New Critics share with Eliot a political and theological conservatism that ties their aesthetics to the politics of the world at large. For both Eliot and the New Critics, the modern secular age is a time of discontinuity, alienation, and meaningless chaos, a time Eliot's critical term, the "dissociation of sensibility," neatly characterizes. In such a time, the special language and aesthetics of poetry, their formal order and paradox-resolving integrations, and the knowledge they presumably convey to us about ourselves and our world can restore to the poet and critic the unity missing from the rest of the contemporary scene. In this fashion, then, poetry becomes for the New Critics the modern equivalent of religion (more so than for Eliot himself, who turns directly to orthodox religion), with poetic language being a special, sacred language in which differences are integrated into a unified whole. The poem itself becomes a fetishized object cut off from the entanglements of social and political history. The desire for secure order and authority in the face of the paradoxes of modern life inscribes itself in the work of Eliot and the New Critics, taking the form, for Eliot at least, of a certain aesthetic classicism, a politically conservative monarchism, and a theological orthodoxy. This desire forms the common background that links Eliot's literary criticism to his social and political essays and connects his work to the New Criticism he directly and indirectly helped to legitimate.

Because there is as yet no authorized Eliot biography and many of his papers and letters are either unpublished or sealed, discussions of Eliot's life remain provisional. There is, however, a considerable amount of public data from which to construct a tentative biography.

Thomas Stearns Eliot was born on 26 September 1888, the second son and last and late child in a family of seven children. On both sides the family tree included an imposing, if not intimidating, assortment of prominent New Englanders, dating back to the settlement of the colonies by the Puritans. The influence of Eliot's family upon his development appears to have been considerable. Eliot's grandfather, William Greenleaf Eliot, combined the moral leadership of a Unitarian minister with the public spirit of a nineteenth-century humanitarian, creating the model of self-denial, ethical propriety, and community service that would continue to influence his grandson throughout his career. So strong was this influence that, as a child, Eliot could not buy sweets because "it had been impressed upon him that to do so was an example of needless self-gratification." Eliot's early life was also molded by his mother, Charlotte Champe, who wrote poems and directed Eliot toward literary matters and self-improvement. His father, Henry Ware Eliot, the wealthy president of the Hydraulic-Press Brick Company, embodied the refinement and taste of a distinguished turn-of-the-century businessman. Eliot himself was born with a congenital double hernia and grew up a relatively frail and bookish child. His family, although wealthy, lived in what had become an unfashionable and rundown section of St. Louis, but summered in New England, where they retained their historical roots. But in neither industrial St. Louis nor in staid New England could the young Eliot find a viable society with a living tradition; and Unitarianism, the embodiment of nineteenth-century liberalism, similarly offered him no appealing model of order or belief. Rejecting these early influences, Eliot was later to describe himself as a "resident alien" in America and sought a tradition of order and discipline stronger than the one offered him by his immediate background.

Eliot completed his early education in 1905 at the Smith Academy in St. Louis and at the Milton Academy, Massachusetts, in 1905-1906, which prepared him for his entrance into Harvard University in 1906. During the three years he took to complete his A.B. Eliot studied a broad range of topics but particularly emphasized French literature and ancient and modern philosophy. One of his peers described the student Eliot as "so widely read by the time he came to Harvard that he could correct one's misquotations and tell you what you meant to say," while another observed that he was "never the gutsy talker and seemed even then to cultivate a scholarly detachment." He joined several of the influential Harvard clubs and served on the board of the *Harvard Advocate*. Also on the board was the poet Conrad Aiken. He and Eliot struck up a friendship that, while at times uneasy, lasted a lifetime. His teachers included George Santayana and Irving Babbitt, whose insistence upon the classical virtues of reason, order, proportion, and objective standards encouraged Eliot's developing search for an authority and order that transcended the limitations of personal sentimentality and emotionalism. Babbitt's brand of humanism remained a touchstone for much of Eliot's later work on literary, social, and educational matters. It was also through Babbitt's courses and his own reading of Arthur Symons's *The Symbolist Movement in Literature* (1899) that Eliot first encountered the poems of Jules Laforgue and the other French poets of the late nineteenth century in which he discovered the use of the ironic commentator, a persona that came to characterize the voice of his early great poetry, written between 1910 and 1911: "Portrait of a Lady," "Preludes," "Rhapsody on a Windy Night," and "The Love Song of J. Alfred Prufrock."

After completing his M.A. at Harvard in 1910, Eliot traveled to Paris in search of the intellectual and cultural stimulation he could not find in either Boston or St. Louis. He studied at the University of Paris (Sorbonne) in 1910-1911. As he later recalled, "I had at that time the idea of giving up English and trying to settle down and scrape along in Paris, and gradually write in French." He abandoned his plan within a year, but while in Paris he came in contact with several figures who were to influence his later work, especially Henri Bergson. Bergsonianism had captured the Parisian intellectual world in 1911, and although Eliot attended the French philosopher's lectures at the Sorbonne, he found little in them consonant with his desire for a well-ordered philosophical discipline. Eliot's friends in Paris included novelist Henri Alain-Fournier, who gave him French lessons, and a medical student named Jean Verdenal, who shared Eliot's literary tastes and knew Jacques Rivière, editor of the *Nouvelle Revue Française*. Rivière became a lasting influence on Eliot, and the *Nouvelle Revue Française* later provided a model for Eliot's own *Criterion*. Verdenal also shared Eliot's interest in Charles Maurras, leader of the monarchist politi-

cal group Action Française. With its emphasis upon nationalism and antidemocratic principles of political order and its distrust of romanticism, Maurras's political theories fit well with Eliot's own sensibilities, and the Frenchman's thinking informs much of Eliot's social criticism of the 1930s and 1940s.

Eliot's dismay over the modern world and his search for a systematic order to replace its flaccid subjectivism returned him to Harvard in 1911 as a graduate student in philosophy. He took a course in symbolic logic from Bertrand Russell and a course called "A Comparative Study of Various Types of Scientific Method" from Josiah Royce, for which he wrote an essay on "The Interpretation of Primitive Ritual," emphasizing the relativism of conceptual systems and exhibiting his skepticism about such systems' claims to objective truth. In an address to the Philosophical Society he complained of the twentieth century's lack of moral standards and defined the ideas of progress and relativism as the two principle vices of modern thought. His skepticism and his keen awareness of the limitations of human knowledge led him to study Sanskrit, Indian philosophy, and Christian mystical literature, and also influenced his decision to write his dissertation on F. H. Bradley, a philosopher whose skepticism, like Eliot's, was modified by idealism.

Eliot wrote his dissertation between 1915 and 1916, years that brought significant changes to his way of life. In 1914, using the Sheldon Traveling Fellowship offered by Harvard, he began a year of study at Merton College, Oxford University, with Bradleyian Harold Joachim. While in England he first met Ezra Pound, the American expatriate, poet, and promoter of various modernist movements, and they began a personal and intellectual relationship that lasted throughout both writers' lives. Eliot also became acquainted with the works of T. E. Hulme, who shared Eliot's attitudes toward classical authority and order and whose ideas would play an important role in Eliot's criticism.

Sometime early in 1915 Eliot met Vivien Haigh-Wood, a vivacious, sharp-witted, and sensitive woman whose adventurous personality was in marked contrast to Eliot's shy formality. They were married on 26 June 1915, and the wedding shocked Eliot's family when they were apprised of it. Eliot's father went so far as to add a provision to his will excluding Vivien from inheritance should her husband die (though he did not cut off Eliot's own allowance). The marriage soon revealed itself a disaster for both parties. The incompatibility of their personalities, including Vivien's nervous illnesses and Eliot's sexual anxieties, resulted in great emotional suffering for each before their eventual separation in 1933. Biographical speculation has often seen the marriage as the source for much of the disillusioned treatment of sex and romance in Eliot's poetry, and for the concern with good, evil, and sublimation in the essays on Dante (1929) and Baudelaire (1930).

In July of 1915 Eliot returned briefly to the United States to face his parents. He rejected their plea that he return to Harvard with his wife and pursue a life as a philosophy professor, though he accepted the argument that he ought at least to finish the dissertation. Returning to England, he and Vivien sojourned at the coast in Sussex before accepting, in September, an offer from the philosopher Bertrand Russell to temporarily share his small two-bedroom flat. Russell's involvement with the Eliots and his relation to Vivien have occasioned much curiosity, though Russell maintained his interest was paternalistic, as the young couple was obviously having problems—emotional and financial. Eliot took a teaching post at High Wycombe Grammar School in fall 1915 and at the closer Highgate Junior School through 1916. After Christmas the couple moved from Russell's flat for a stay with Vivien's parents, and by early summer they had their first apartment. Eliot also wrote reviews at the time for such journals as the *New Statesman* and the *International Journal of Ethics*. Somehow he did complete the dissertation, which the Harvard philosophy department accepted, although World War I travel restrictions prevented Eliot (perhaps to his relief ) from returning for his defense.

Eliot's doctoral thesis, finally published in 1964 under the title *Knowledge and Experience in the Philosophy of F. H. Bradley*, is his first and only piece of sustained philosophical prose. In the book's preface he looks back at his dissertation with puzzlement: "Forty-six years after my academic philosophizing came to an end, I find myself unable to think in the terminology of this essay. Indeed, I do not pretend to understand it." Since it was not published until long after Eliot had done his major critical work, the dissertation itself had no impact upon the eventual influence and reputation of that work. And yet it is an important if stylistically complicated document that raises in a philosophical rhetoric some of the issues and themes that are central to Eliot's mature criticism.

The dissertation both explains and modifies Bradley's English brand of German idealism and focuses on the philosopher's two-tiered scheme of reality, in which he distinguishes thoughts, distrusted as distortions of the way things really are, from "immediate experience," a wholeness unaffected by thought and known only as "feeling." Articulated by this binary scheme are such oppositions as appearance/reality, thought/feeling, and difference/identity, each of which postulates an undivided reality anterior to and more fundamental than our diverse and fragmentary experiences of it. Given Eliot's skepticism of human systems of knowledge and his desire to believe in a higher, unified reality that transcends them, it is not surprising that he was drawn to Bradley. And yet Eliot modifies Bradley's dualistic scheme in an interesting fashion. Where Bradley asserts that by thought we know only mere appearances while by feeling we know the underlying wholeness of reality and that therefore thoughts and feelings can be separated from each other, Eliot states that our thoughts can never be separated from our feelings, and that therefore immediate experience is known only along with the thoughts that distort it. This skepticism suggests that perhaps Eliot could not bring himself to believe in Bradley's figure of undivided wholeness. It also de-idealizes immediate experience and describes the problematic relationship in which thought and feeling, difference and identity, interpretation and truth are found in Eliot's later critical work. Eliot concludes the dissertation with the observation that "A philosophy can and must be worked out with the greatest rigour and discipline in the details, but can ultimately be founded on nothing but faith," a statement that foreshadows his later conversion to Anglo-Catholicism.

Another key aspect of the dissertation can be found in its discussions of language. Bradley had said that our ideas of objects are separate from objects themselves and thus function only as their signs. He thereby maintained a representational understanding of language. But Eliot, opposing Bradley on this point, derives his theory of language from the semiology of Charles Sanders Peirce. In asserting that "we have no objects without language," Eliot grants privilege to language in a way Bradley does not. For Eliot words are not simply representatives of a separate object from which they derive their significance;

rather, they are "woven into our reality" as essential components of its makeup. Thus Bradley's distinction between word and object is one that for Eliot makes no sense, since, just as there is no feeling without thought, there are also no objects without words. We use words to construct our reality, the organized systems that are our own private worlds. Hence the apparent solipsism of Eliot's quotation from Bradley in one of his notes to *The Waste Land* (1922): "My external sensations are no less private to myself than are my thoughts or my feelings. . . . Regarded as an existence which appears in a soul, the whole world for each is peculiar and private to that soul." Eliot's emphasis upon language's productive power denies the existence of a common, solid, external world of shared objects; this idea is the error of the epistemologist's theory of knowledge that he spends two chapters of *Knowledge and Experience* discussing. But it also suggests that our worlds, our "finite centers" or "points of view," do interfere with and make a difference to each other—we can "partially put ourselves . . . at each other's point of view"—and it is through these interferences that what we take to be an object world is built up. Thus Eliot reverses Bradley's theory of language; in his view, we begin with words and, in a somewhat unconscious and public way, construct the reality that Bradley understands words to represent simply.

Peirce's influence on Eliot's dissertation can be seen in the fact that, for Peirce, signs produce and refer to other signs, and, for Eliot, words function the same way. Readable in the dissertation, however, is Eliot's will to believe in something beyond words, and the conflict between this will and his skepticism concerning such a nonverbal transcendence. Peirce's influence can also be seen in the dissertation's conclusions about truth and interpretation. For Eliot truths are always "partial and fragmentary" interpretations, and thus "every interpretation, along perhaps with some utterly contradictory interpretation, has to be taken up and reinterpreted by every thinking mind and by every civilization." This passage points to the dynamic sense of tradition Eliot wrote of several years later in "Tradition and the Individual Talent." It also suggests the open-ended hermeneutics prevalent in Eliot's work but often suppressed by his early emphasis on classicism and objective standards and his later, highly Christianized rhetoric. In Eliot's criticism there is a tension between idealism and skepticism, a centripetal will to believe in an impersonal, uninterpreted

truth—an undivided Word—countered by the centrifugal pull of endless interpretation and proliferating words. *Knowledge and Experience* is an early trace of that tension.

In 1916 Eliot resigned his teaching post at Highgate Junior School and in March 1917 joined the Colonial and Foreign Department of Lloyds Bank, where he continued to work until 1925. Nineteen seventeen was also the year of publication of *Prufrock and Other Observations*, Eliot's first collection of poems, and the beginning of his most important work in literary criticism in essays written for the *Egoist*, where he became assistant editor in June. By 1919 he was writing reviews for the *Times Literary Supplement* and articles for John Middleton Murry's *Athenaeum*. The *Egoist* pieces, primarily reviews and reflections on contemporary poetry, sharply criticize the vapid rhetoric Eliot finds to be characteristic of most contemporary verse. Such rhetoric is not, however, simply a stylistic problem for Eliot; rather, it is symptomatic of the decadence of contemporary thought in general, a vice shared, according to Eliot, by the Elizabethans. Having no coherent, received system to organize his thoughts and feelings, the contemporary poet simply lapses into the insincere vagaries of empty rhetoric. Thus Eliot describes, in "Reflections on Contemporary Poetry [III]" (*Egoist*, 1917), the need of modern poetry to "wring the neck" of rhetoric and to escape the betrayals of human feeling such rhetoric causes. In the last of his "Reflections on Contemporary Poetry" (*Egoist*, July 1919) he suggests, in an idea that will be fully articulated elsewhere, that writers require a "profound kinship" with earlier writers and that such personal intimacy is more important than lived experience, since it forces the writer outside of himself and places him in contact with a tradition of which he can then become the intelligent bearer and not simply the rhetorical borrower. It is this learned aspect of Pound's poetry that he extols in *Ezra Pound: His Metric and Poetry* (1918), an anonymous pamphlet written partly to help promote Pound at the same time Pound was helping Eliot's poetry into print. For Eliot, Pound's poetry has the tension between freedom and restraint, personality and learned tradition missing in other contemporary poetry.

Like the poet, the critic, according to Eliot, must work by intelligence and not by emotions. In a series of articles for the *Egoist* entitled "Studies in Contemporary Criticism," Eliot describes the critic's job as comparison and analysis and suggests that this methodology is the only way criticism can isolate the merits of individual works and assert the literary standards against which such works must be judged. He attacks the intellectually lazy criticism that replaces comparison with judgment and analysis with appreciation and argues against a criticism of personality that seeks to study the man through the work or the work through the man. His early call is for a study of literature that would be a field of inquiry distinct from other disciplines, such as biography, history, or psychology, with which it is often confused and diluted. The distinction was the foundation for much of the formalist literary criticism of the first half of the twentieth century.

By 1920 Eliot's reputation as a literary journalist had grown larger than his reputation as a poet. It was through his poetry, however–and particularly through his 1920 collection, *Ara Vos Prec*–that he met I. A. Richards, whose enthusiasm for Eliot's poetry led him to become one of Eliot's earliest critics and commentators in academia. Richards and Eliot became friends, and although Eliot often used Richards's works as examples of a literary criticism too influenced by what Eliot considered to be the pseudoscience of psychology, their friendship bridged the distance between the worlds of journalistic and academic literary studies and solidified Eliot's reputation in and effect upon the academy.

Early in 1920 Eliot contracted with Methuen for a book of essays. By July he had completed the manuscript–revisions of earlier articles and reviews, plus a few new pieces, all of which appeared in periodical form before the book's publication at year's end. *The Sacred Wood: Essays on Poetry and Criticism* received mixed reviews but firmly established Eliot as a leading new voice in British letters. F. W. Bateson, an Oxford undergraduate at the time, recalls the volume as "our sacred book," an opinion not shared by Amy Lowell, who mocked its "grave erudition." Although Eliot, characteristically, felt it needed significant revision, it nevertheless contains some of his most influential statements on literature and tradition and the connections between literary order and cultural and personal order. In essays the logical, learned tone of which reflects his earlier philosophical writings, Eliot analyzes the works of such authors as Algernon Swinburne, William Blake, Dante, Philip Massinger, Ben Jonson, and Shakespeare, while introducing into the language of English criticism his specialized concepts of "objective correlative," "tradition," "im-

personality," and "dissociation of sensibility," which later shaped his vision of literary history. In contrast to the disorderly, unscientific, and subjectively impressionistic criticism he attacks, Eliot offers to literary studies a critical rhetoric characterized by reason, certainty, discipline, and objective order. Although, as Eliot admitted, there is an "element of subtle bluff" behind the certainty of many of the essays' pronouncements, *The Sacred Wood* remains a crucial text in the history of modern criticism.

The book opens with a series of reviews and commentaries in which Eliot distinguishes between various "Imperfect Critics" and sketches out what the real job of "The Perfect Critic" should be. In the introduction he acknowledges the almost irresistible temptation, to which he believes Matthew Arnold regrettably succumbed, "to put literature into the corner until he cleaned up the whole country first." Thus Arnold the literary critic became Arnold the propagandist, who moved "outside of criticism" and "wasted his strength." According to Eliot contemporary writers like H. G. Wells and G. K. Chesterton abandoned the literary tradition and instead wrote a social criticism that betrays a "poverty of ideas" and an atrophied sensibility. Eliot asserts that "it is part of the business of the critic to preserve tradition–where a good tradition exists. It is part of his business to see literature steadily and to see it whole . . . to see it beyond time." Though Eliot lauds Swinburne for his interest in and knowledge of the works he discusses (rare virtues in English criticism, according to Eliot), he nevertheless describes him as one of the imperfect critics who judges literature by his transient emotions rather than as a perfect critic who analyzes it with ideas.

In a discussion of George Wyndham's essays, Eliot equates this kind of impressionistic criticism, this "verbal disease," with a romantic psychologism that "leads its disciples only back upon themselves" and has its antecedents in Elizabethan rhetoric and Victorian sentiment. He argues that appreciation and "intellectual" criticism are not two different responses to literature–one natural and the other contrived–but rather that the critic's perceptions of literature "do not, in a really appreciative mind, accumulate as a mass, but form themselves as a structure; and criticism is the statement in language of this structure." It is the structure, the intellectual "development of sensibility," that is important for Eliot and not the disorganized impressions of the critic, which produce a "bad criticism" that is "nothing but an expression of emotion." He concludes his critique of psychologism and impressionism in criticism with the assertion that "the end of the enjoyment of poetry is a pure contemplation from which all the accidents of personal emotion are removed; thus we aim to see the object as it really is."

This theme of the depersonalization of art and the elimination of subjective emotions from criticism is repeated by Eliot's discussions of poetry and particularly by his most famous and influential essay, "Tradition and the Individual Talent." In this essay Eliot argues for the importance to poetry of a literary "tradition" that transcends the limited personalities of individual poets. What exactly Eliot means by "tradition" has been the subject of much critical debate, but in this essay he explicitly rejects the genealogical understanding of tradition as a passive handing down or "timid adherence" of one generation of writers to the successes of an earlier one. Rather, tradition suggests a dynamic process by which a writer does not inherit a body of texts but obtains, "by great labour," the "historical sense," the "perception, not only of the pastness of the past, but of its presence." According to Eliot, "the whole of the literature of Europe from Homer and within it the whole of the literature of [a poet's] own country has a simultaneous existence and composes a simultaneous order." The poet perceives this order as a timelessness transcending his temporality. And yet this ideal textual order is not simply static and fixed, for it is "modified by the introduction of the new (the really new) work": when the new text supervenes upon the old, "the *whole* existing order must be, if ever so slightly altered; and so the relations, proportions, values of each work of art toward the whole are readjusted." Thus tradition is not simply the influence of the past upon the present but also, in a very dynamic sense, the influence of the present upon the past, the way in which each text reinterprets and reshapes its own literary ancestors. Although "Tradition and the Individual Talent" has been most widely read for its affirmations of the authority of an ordered literary tradition, Eliot's dialectic of literary history both asserts such ideal order and questions its apparent stability.

He explains his "impersonal theory of poetry," derived partially from Remy de Gourmont's discussions of Laforgue, by the analogy of the catalyst, in which he compares the mind of the poet to a filament of platinum that, when introduced "into a chamber containing oxygen and sulphur dioxide," effects the transmutation of these gases into sulphurous acid. In the analogy the poet's emotions and feelings are the gases, the mind of the poet the shred of platinum that remains "inert, neutral, and unchanged," and the poem the sulphurous acid. In this way Eliot seeks to distinguish completely between "the man who suffers and the mind which creates" and to see poetry not as the expression of a personality but rather of a "particular medium, which is only a medium and not a personality, in which impressions and experiences combine in peculiar and unexpected ways." The poem is thus a "new object which is no longer purely personal, because it is a work of art itself," and the poetic process is a "continual self-sacrifice, a continual extinction of personality." Eliot writes that he is struggling to attack the "metaphysical theory of the substantial unity of the soul," and his impersonal theory does make the medium itself the active agent in the production of poetry, again seeming to subordinate the accidents of personality to an order—in this case, language itself—that transcends them. But he admits that "this is not quite the whole story," since "there is a great deal, in the writing of poetry, which must be conscious and deliberate," thereby suggesting the skepticism with which he must finally treat this idealistic theory. Thus although both "tradition" and "impersonality" find their way from Eliot's essay into New Criticism as the names for a certain ideality, Eliot's own use of the terms suggests their provisional and uncertain nature.

Eliot criticizes the present age for its formlessness, for its lack of a tradition or intellectual framework that restrains and organizes the poet's impressions into an ordered whole and provides him with a precise way of thinking and feeling. An example of such formlessness is the poetry of William Blake, whom Eliot extols as a poet "endowed with a capacity for considerable understanding of human nature, with a remarkable and original sense of language and the music of language, and a gift of hallucinated vision." What Blake lacked, however, was a "framework of accepted and traditional ideas which would have prevented him from indulging in a philosophy of his own." Again it is the presence of such an orderly framework that, for Eliot, resists the centrifugal pull toward disorderly or idiosyncratic impressionism. This is what, in Eliot's view, makes Dante superior to Blake: the presence in the Italian's work of an "eternal scheme" in which the individual emotions are not lost but are "modified" by their position in a unified "emotional structure." Eliot's emphasis upon formal structures and emotional wholes influences the theory of organic unity central to such New Critics as Cleanth Brooks.

In "Hamlet and His Problems" Eliot critiques Shakespeare's play for its lack of such a clarifying framework and notes that "the only way of expressing emotion in the form of art is by finding an 'objective correlative'; in other words, a set of objects, a situation, a chain of events which shall be the formula of that *particular* emotion." In Shakespeare's play, however, there is an "absence of objective equivalent" to Hamlet's feelings, which are "in *excess* of the facts as they appear." Lacking an adequacy between the external presentation and the internal emotion, *Hamlet* loses "artistic 'inevitability,' " and the emotion itself remains "by hypothesis unknowable." Eliot writes elsewhere in *The Sacred Wood* that "permanent literature is always . . . either a presentation of thought, or a presentation of feeling by a statement of events in human action or objects in the external world." For Eliot, the absence of an "objective correlative" for Hamlet's emotions spoils the presentation, and thus damages the intelligibility, of the play.

Ideally, an objective correlative is a literary device uniting the presentation of emotions and ideas. The modern dissociation of thought from feeling and word from sensation becomes the major thesis in Eliot's theory of literary history as it develops in the early and middle 1920s. This theory, first explicitly discussed in his 1921 essay "The Metaphysical Poets" (later published in the 1924 collection, *Homage to John Dryden: Three Essays on Poetry of the Seventeenth Century*) and fully articulated in the 1926 Clark Lectures at Trinity College, Cambridge, postulates the "dissociation of sensibility" as a key turning point in Western literary history. In this essay Eliot compares seventeenth-century poetry (including the work of John Donne, George Herbert, Henry Vaughan, Richard Crashaw) to nineteenth-century poetry (the work of Alfred Tennyson and Robert Browning) and discerns a difference of sensibility between the two. According to Eliot this difference is "something which had happened to the mind of England between the time of Donne or Lord Herbert of Cherbury and the time of Tennyson and Browning: it is the difference between the intellectual poet and the reflective poet." Whereas Donne could feel a thought as an experi-

ence modifying his sensibility, poets like Tennyson and Browning could not "feel their thought as immediately as [they could sense] the odour of a rose." For Eliot the dramatists of the sixteenth century and their heirs, the metaphysical poets of the seventeenth century, "possessed a mechanism of sensibility which could devour any kind of experience" and amalgamate disparate, chaotic, fragmentary, and irregular experience into new wholes. They, like the French poets of the nineteenth century (Laforgue, Edouard Joachim [Tristan] Corbière), had the "essential quality of transmuting ideas into sensations, of transforming an observation into a state of mind." The transformation by the late seventeenth century of this amalgamating sensibility into a dissociated one was, according to Eliot, aggravated by John Milton and John Dryden, who refined language while making feeling more crude by failing to "look into the cerebral cortex, the nervous system, and the digestive tracts." This sterile refinement precipitated the sentimental poetry of the eighteenth century, which revolted against its ratiocinative ancestors and became reflective and unbalanced, thinking and feeling by "fits." Thus the story of literary history Eliot begins to develop in "The Metaphysical Poets" is the story of literature's fall from a unified sensibility into a fragmented one, a history of misfortune and loss in which Eliot revalues the major figures of the English literary tradition.

*The Sacred Wood* appeared at a time of increasing personal pain and confusion in Eliot's life. The general catastrophe of the war had also brought the death in 1915 of Jean Verdenal, to whom Eliot had dedicated *Prufrock and Other Observations* (1917). Eliot's strained relations with his family were compounded by grief for his father's death in 1919 and his mother's continued antipathy toward Vivien, who was moved to the country during Charlotte Eliot's London visit in 1921. Vivien was showing increasing symptoms of mental illness, and her sicknesses became a financial as well as emotional burden for the couple. Her disturbed state combined with Eliot's divided life as a banker by day and man of letters by night to precipitate a breakdown of his own in the fall of 1921. He took a leave from the bank, spent October at a Margate resort with Vivien, and then traveled to Europe, where he sought a cure at the Swiss sanitorium of Roger Vittoz in Lausanne. He left Vivien in Paris, where she stayed with Ezra Pound and his wife and at another sanitorium outside the city.

It was in 1921 and 1922 that Eliot wrote most of *The Waste Land*, his most famous and influential poem, which he completed at Lausanne. The poem put into practice the doctrines of *The Sacred Wood*, as here Eliot passed his own emotional chaos through the imposing orders of the mythic and literary traditions of the West. "These fragments I have shored against my ruins," says the speaker near the end, striking a personal note within an impersonal cacophony of allusions, quotes, and echoes that left many readers stunned and baffled. The disorder of modern civilization and the shattered subjectivity of the individual soul constitute a waste land through which the speaker seeks for a redeeming word. Everywhere his quest encounters the dissociation of sensibility, most bitterly in the many failures of romance that it recalls. One couple talks restlessly in their flat of the woman's bad nerves and the man's haunted distraction. Most poignant is the loveless and mechanical intercourse of the "young man carbuncular" and the typist. Eliot renders the scene in a parodically formal meter and rhyme scheme which imitates the want of life and passion within the forms of modern experience, and so his own language becomes an ironic objective correlative of the world it depicts. Renouncing the temptations of desire, the speaker seeks a supernatural or religous revelation in the final section, "What the Thunder Said," but the poem ends ambiguously between despair and faith.

Concerned for Eliot's physical and emotional health, Pound and others devised schemes of monetary support for him in order to get him away from the bank and give him time to write. For various reasons—not the least of which was Eliot's own interest in his bank work and the sense of personal value he derived from it—each of these schemes was ultimately abandoned. An important development in Eliot's career occurred in 1922, when he took on the editorship of the *Criterion*, a new literary review established with the financial backing of Lady Rothermere, wife of the owner of London's *Daily Mail*. *The Waste Land* was published simultaneously in October 1922 in the *Criterion*'s first issue and in the *Dial*. After lengthy financial negotiations between Eliot and *Dial* editor Scofield Thayer, the magazine had agreed to award Eliot its $2,000 annual prize for the poem. Published after 1926 by Faber and Gwyer (later Faber and Faber), the firm Eliot had joined one year earlier, the *Criterion* ran until 1939 and became a major vehicle of expression for Eliot, both as an outlet for his own essays, com-

mentaries, and reviews and as a forum for the writers whose works he selected and commissioned. From the beginning Eliot sought through the *Criterion* to bring together an international fraternity of thinkers and writers conducive to his own developing sense of classicism and literary and cultural order. Important to the wide-ranging yet focused sensibility behind the *Criterion* were such writers as Julien Benda, T. E. Hulme, John Middleton Murry, Charles Maurras, and Wyndham Lewis. Although he never allowed it to lose its character as a literary journal, Eliot opened the *Criterion* to essays on an eclectic variety of topics ranging from politics and economics to religion, philosophy, history, and science and used the journal to explore the implications that principles of literary and critical order suggested for larger social contexts. Often combative in its aggressive assertion of its critical principles, the *Criterion* was a reflection of its editor's interests and attitudes.

Two of Eliot's essays, both appearing in the first two years of the *Criterion*, deserve particular attention for their articulations of his critical position in the mid 1920s. In "The Function of Criticism," published in 1923, Eliot expands upon the figure of tradition he had sketched out in "Tradition and the Individual Talent" and discusses the "problem of order" in both creative and critical writing. Order is also the subject of Eliot's 1923 *Dial* review of James Joyce's *Ulysses* (1922). In this essay Eliot praises Joyce for his use of myth (his "manipulating a continuous parallel between contemporaneity and antiquity") as a way of "controlling, of ordering of giving a shape and a significance to the immense panorama of futility and anarchy which is contemporary history." The description obviously suits Eliot's own use of myth in *The Waste Land*—not surprisingly, since Eliot had been reading fragments from Joyce's novel during the period of his poem's composition. In "Tradition and the Individual Talent" he had emphasized the importance of "something outside the artist to which he owes allegiance, a devotion to which he must surrender and sacrifice himself in order to earn and to obtain his unique position." In "The Function of Criticism" he similarly criticizes the idea of a privileged, individualistic "inner voice," which he notes "breathes the eternal message of vanity, fear, and lust" and to which he describes himself as an "Inner Deaf Mute." Against the perversions of the inner voice, or romanticism, Eliot asserts the need for "Outside Authority," or classicism, and refutes the equation of the two in Murry's understand-

*T. S. Eliot in Sweden during the spring of 1942 (courtesy of the Houghton Library, Harvard University)*

ing of Catholicism as a pursuit of self-knowledge leading to knowledge of God. To Eliot's way of thinking, "the Catholic did not believe that God and himself were identical." The terms of the Eliot/Murry debate join literary criticism to social and theological issues in a way that became even more prominent in the years after Eliot's conversion to Anglo-Catholicism.

"The Function of Criticism" also argues that literary interpretation depends on outside authority. Interpretation is "only legitimate when it is not interpretation at all, but merely putting the reader in possession of facts which he would otherwise have missed." Interpretations are suspect because they rely on the inner voice of the critic and not on the verifiable literary facts of the text itself. Eliot closes the essay by suggesting that critical work may be seen as a "cooperative activity, with the further possibility of arriving at something outside ourselves, which may provisionally be called truth." The essay's final sentence, however, makes problematic this provisional truth and the literary facts to which the rest of the essay seems to have granted authority: "But if anyone complains that I have not defined truth, or

fact, or reality, I can only say apologetically that it was no part of my purpose to do so, but only to find a scheme into which, whatever they are, they will fit, if they exist."

In 1925 Eliot left the bank to take a position on the board of directors of Faber and Gwyer. It was through his role as editor for this major publishing firm, which specialized through the 1960s in poetry, that Eliot shaped in a very practical way the literary tastes and expectations of writers and readers of his time. While his journalistic and poetic reputation continued to grow in the 1920s, his expanding academic reputation led, in 1926, to his being invited to deliver the Clark Lectures at Trinity College, Cambridge. These lectures, as yet unpublished, provide the most complete account of Eliot's vision of literary history and of the "dissociation of sensibility" that shapes that history. In these eight talks, titled "Lectures on the Metaphysical Poetry of the Seventeenth Century" and conceived as the groundwork for three books (to be called "The School of Donne," "Elizabethan Drama," and "The Sons of Ben"), Eliot seeks to articulate his interpretation of metaphysical poetry by focusing on seventeenth-century works, especially those of Donne and Crashaw, comparing them to the poems of Dante and other writers of the thirteenth century and suggesting the ways in which the mental habits they reflect are similar to and different from those characteristic of English and French poetry of the nineteenth century. Expanding on his earlier discussion of metaphysical poetry, Eliot asserts that it is the function of poetry to integrate thought into feeling and feeling into thought by either incarnating or clothing the abstract in the sensual or elevating the sensual into abstract thought. This unity of thought and feeling is, for Eliot, the real achievement of Dante and his thirteenth-century peers and constitutes a key characteristic of his definition of metaphysical poetry.

The history Eliot writes, however, is one of the dissociation of thought from feeling and feeling from thought, a story of the shifting economies between thought and feeling in the thirteenth, seventeenth, and nineteenth centuries. According to Eliot, in Dante one finds an architectonic ability and a system of thought and feeling so complete that the distinction between the intellectual and the emotional cannot be made, because both thought and emotion appear as the reverse sides of each other. By the seventeenth century, however, this integration had deteriorated, and Donne's poetry is Eliot's central example of the disintegration. In Donne, Eliot finds not a Dantean unity of thought and feeling but rather a sequence or flow of thoughts that are made to appear roughly equivalent to a sequence or flow of feelings. And in Crashaw he finds a reversal of Donne's equivalency: a sequence of feelings roughly equivalent to a sequence of thoughts. In neither Donne nor Crashaw is there the perfect balance of thought and feeling he found in Dante. Eliot expands on this balance in a long 1929 essay on Dante, in which he calls the Italian "the most *universal* of poets in the modern languages."

Dante's universality hinges on his thought as well as his artistry, and so for Eliot more is at stake in this scheme than just literature. Dante's universe comes to seem a kind of paradise lost. He embodies a real historical moment of cultural unity and orthodoxy. Eliot describes the course of European thought and belief since Dante as a dissolution of an ordered ontology, the decline of a European *sensus communis* or a system of common belief into the modern disorder of subjectivism, psychologism, and democracy. Contributing

to this dissolution were, according to Eliot, the Jesuit movement, the Spanish mystics, and the Protestant churches, which helped to demote Rome from its position as disinterested, impersonal arbiter of ideas to simply the supporter of one system of ideas in a field of competing systems that increasingly relied for their success upon the whims of an expanding semiliterate public. The groundwork for Eliot's later critiques of democracy can be found here, as can his sense of the radical disjunction between classic scholastic philosophy and the psychologically oriented philosophies of the modern age. According to Eliot most English and French literature of the nineteenth century lacked a belief in the difference between "good" and "evil." With no definite system of belief behind it, this literature does no more than simply entertain and mechanically play with combinations of ideas. But the real metaphysical poetry of the nineteenth and twentieth centuries stems from a background of belief in the reality of good and evil and a conscious craving for an order in which the moral and intellectual are integrated with the nonmoral and unintellectual. This is the poetry, in Eliot's central example, of Jules Laforgue, who craves an order in which every feeling has its intellectual equivalent and every idea its emotional justification. It is only in poets like Laforgue, Corbière, and (he says in a 1930 essay) Baudelaire that the sensibility of metaphysical poetry, running from the thirteenth to the seventeenth centuries, is continued into the modern age.

The literary history traced by the Clark Lectures is thus one of inevitable disintegration and rupture. The lectures also suggest that, for Eliot, all literature is the sign of such discontinuities, for in the first essay he describes literature as the belated trace of an always already-vanished unity of feeling. Thus although these lectures seem to suggest a nostalgia for the lost unity of an idealized thirteenth century, they nevertheless express a certain skepticism about that nostalgia and recognize a clearly provisional and pragmatic element in the pattern of history they draw. In the final lecture Eliot admits that he has as much imposed his pattern on his materials as he has derived it from them, and that he has had to cut and compromise those materials to make them fit. He also muses about the practice of literary criticism as an unresolvable dilemma, a discipline without determinate frontiers that cannot isolate itself from other subjects of study but that also cannot hope to embrace all the points of view these other subjects suggest. Although he asserts that he has tried to focus on literary values and to criticize poetry as poetry, he also confesses to having trespassed on other disciplinary territories and therefore to having written a criticism that is seriously flawed. In the connections they make between literary and theological and moral values, however, the Clark Lectures point clearly in the direction of Eliot's subsequent criticism.

On 29 June 1927 Eliot's growing emphasis on the need for a public and systematic source of belief, authority, and value resulted in his baptism into the Anglican Church, an event that can be interpreted as a rejection of his family's liberal humanitarianism and an adoption of British tradition and history. In Anglo-Catholicism Eliot found both that background of good and evil lacking in modern humanistic philosophies and a tradition of belief that he asserted to be central to the development of the European mind. In November he became a British citizen, legally confirming what had been true of his life for some time. Although his adoption of British culture was willful and wholehearted, there nevertheless remained in it an artificial element, leading one of his friends to describe Eliot as not "a bit like an Englishman."

In 1928 Eliot published *For Lancelot Andrewes*, a collection of essays written in the previous two years. In its preface he makes explicit the revised tenor of his thinking by declaring himself to be "classicist in literature, royalist in politics, and anglo-catholic in religion." In this volume Eliot expands literary criticism into the broader moral, social, and theological areas suggested by the Clark Lectures. His focus is on Lancelot Andrewes, and he contrasts the precision, intensity, and ordonnance of that seventeenth-century cleric's sermons with those of Andrewes's fellow churchman, John Donne. For Eliot, where Andrewes speaks with the authority of the visible Church behind him and an emotion that is not personal and self-expressive, Donne speaks with a voice that is simply personal and self-expressive. For this reason Eliot assigns to Andrewes a higher place in the spiritual hierarchy than the romantic Donne. In an essay on John Bramhall, he criticizes Thomas Hobbes for producing a philosophy in which standards of good and evil are simply relative, and in a discussion of F. H. Bradley he attacks Matthew Arnold's notion of the "best self," which looks to Eliot like Irving Babbitt's "inner check" and Romanticism's "inner voice." Opposing Arnold, Eliot asserts that

the principle distinction in man is not between his private and public self, but "between the individual as himself and no more, a mere numbered atom, and the individual in communion with God." He therefore points out the danger of Babbitt's humanism, which he finds to be a substitute for religion that suppresses "the divine, and is left with a human element which may quickly descend again to the animal from which [the humanist] has sought to raise it." For Eliot the "inner check" of humanism must ultimately rest on religious grounds that transcend and discipline limited human intellect and personality. Thus he lauds the wisdom of Bradley which is based on the skepticism and uncynical disillusion that are "useful equipment for religious understanding." The aggressively moralistic tone of *For Lancelot Andrewes* and its overtly religious perspective on literary criticism alienated many of Eliot's friends, including Pound, Wyndham Lewis, and Virginia Woolf, and led Conrad Aiken to comment that the book exhibits the "presence of a spirit which is inimical to everything new or bold or generous."

Other essays of the late 1920s reflect Eliot's growing concern for the social function of literature, and throughout the 1930s he opened the *Criterion* more and more to discussions of politics and economics. In "The Literature of Fascism," for example, he attacks the muddle produced by the attempt of both fascism and communism to substitute political beliefs for religion. At the same time, however, he asserts the value of social order and authority and suggests that democracy has gone wrong because of its unrestricted lack of discipline. And in "Mr. Barnes and Mr. Rowse," a response to *Criterion* articles by these two writers on fascism and communism, Eliot derides both political theories as "the natural idea for the thoughtless person" and a mingling of science and feeling that lacks the coherence of a rigorous theology. In general Eliot's commentaries throughout the late 1920s and 1930s on social, economic, and political questions approach these issues by moving them to the more generalized and abstract grounds of religion and morality, and by analyzing them on the basis of Christian standards and values. He spells out his abstractly Christian perspective on contemporary political forms in *Thoughts After Lambeth* (1931), a small pamphlet in which he describes the world's recent experiments in forming a civilized world with a non-Christian mentality and concludes that such experiments must always fail, since humanitarianism, which considers humanity apart from its relation to God, can lead only to the excessive love of created things and the oppression of humans. As he writes in a 1933 essay, "Catholicism and International Order," worldly wisdom is incomplete without otherworldly wisdom. He therefore encourages Christians to take an active part in renewing and rebuilding civilization to, in the words of *Ash-Wednesday,* redeem the present time. In a *Criterion* commentary from 1933 he asserts that modern thinkers must both maintain the ideal of a perfectable earth and at the same time recognize the inadequacy of this ideal. Thus the idealism and skepticism that marked the philosophy of his dissertation continued in his social criticism.

In 1932 Faber and Faber published Eliot's *Selected Essays 1917-1932,* which brought together the most important essays from his earlier collections and other introductions and reviews. This volume, expanded in the 1950 edition, remains the most important collection of Eliot's literary criticism, covering a time when he was doing his most significant and influential work. Eliot also published *John Dryden: The Poet, The Dramatist, The Critic* (1932), a reprint of three BBC broadcasts in which he considers Dryden's influence on thought and feeling. According to Eliot, Anglo-American society owes its civilization to Dryden, whom Eliot describes as the first master of English criticism and whom he praises for his common sense and his sense of order. The talks reflect Eliot's continuing interest in drama and his own growing role as a public figure and spokesman for British culture. He gave such radio broadcasts and other public lectures fairly regularly throughout the rest of his career.

The quantity of Eliot's prose writing during the 1920s greatly exceeded that of his poetry. Indeed in these years Eliot often despaired of his talent for verse and managed only fitful attempts. "The Hollow Men" (1925), *Ash-Wednesday* (1930), and the Ariel poems (1927-1930) are each composed of fragments arranged, or rearranged, in expressions of spiritual longing and loss of hope. The religious turn of Eliot's social criticism is matched in *Ash-Wednesday* by the poet's adoption of Christian liturgy and the figure of Mary as the traditional elements for ordering his chaotic emotions. Gone are the satiric wit and prophetic power evident in *The Waste Land,* as Eliot's speaker prays to the Holy Mother for salvation from temporal life. The more Eliot sees the structures of religion and politics as the orders that can save modernity from itself, the less he seems to trust or explore the traditions or inventions of poetry. By the late 1920s Eliot had become in practice the editor of a quarterly and a journalist of ideas rather than the leading poet of modernism.

Eliot had not been to the United States since 1915, but in 1932-1933 he returned to accept Harvard's appointment to the Charles Eliot Norton professorship of poetry. The long trip abroad conveniently allowed Eliot to initiate a physical and formal separation from his wife. Through seventeen troubled years of marriage Eliot had felt duty-bound to Vivien. Now he came to realize that neither of them could but suffer from continuing a relation that threatened the sanity of both. The failure of romanticism which Eliot so documented in his criticism was evidently a feature of his own marriage and psychology. In *Ash-Wednesday* and *Marina* (1930), Eliot still figured the image of salvation in a female form and did so in a surprisingly lyric voice. The criticism he produced during his American sojourn would exhibit the traces of his marital woes, his strained nerves, his flights into dogmatism, and his increased recognition of the truth he spoke in "Tradition and the Individual Talent," that "only those who have personality and emotions know what it means to want to escape from those things."

At Harvard Eliot delivered a series of eight lectures, published in 1933 as *The Use of Poetry and The Use of Criticism.* Thirty years later, in an introduction to the book's 1964 reprint, he calls "Tradition and the Individual Talent" one of his most juvenile essays (although he refuses to repudiate it) and hopes that future anthologies will contain a selection from this present group of more mature works. And yet these lectures have not had the impact of Eliot's earlier criticism. They include a discussion of Elizabethan poetry and drama, a consideration of Dryden, critiques of William Wordsworth, Samuel Taylor Coleridge, Percy Bysshe Shelley, John Keats, and Matthew Arnold, and an analysis of the modern mind. As in the Clark Lectures, Eliot again traces out a tradition of English literature, but his emphasis here is somewhat different from that of those earlier lectures. He begins with the assumption that we do not know what poetry is and examines the relations between poetry and criticism in an effort to ascertain "what the use of both of them is." His concern is primarily for the social utility of poetry, and it is around this theme that the lectures revolve. But they also stress the assertion that criticism is never distinct from the personality of the critic: that "one's taste in poetry cannot be isolated from one's other interests and passions; it affects them and is affected by them, and must be limited as one's self is limited." Though this recognition of the provisional and subjective aspect of criticism was never completely absent from Eliot's earlier work, it had been suppressed by those essays' calls for impersonal objectivity and the apparent certainty of their philosophical tone. Here, however, it is the modification of criticism and personality by each other that ties literature and criticism to society and history.

Eliot uses his own life to illustrate the stages in the evolution of a mature relationship between poetry and criticism and the development of taste. The first stage, which for Eliot began with his reading of Edward FitzGerald's translation of the *Rubáiyát of Omar Khayyám* (1902-1903), begins with the keen enjoyment of the poetic experience in adolescence. This stage gives way to the second one, in which the youthful consciousness identifies with the poetry of a single poet and is completely possessed by it. In this stage "personal accidents" bring the youth into contact with certain poets, but in the third or mature stage the reader no longer identifies with the poet he happens to be reading. Here the reader's critical faculties remain awake, and he is able to "distinguish between degrees of greatness in poetry." But these critical distinctions are, for Eliot, never completely objective, since they remain tied to the personal passions and interests of the critic and to the limited "perspective of history." Thus, as he asserts in "The Age of Dryden," "Philosophy is not science, nor is literary criticism; and it is an elementary error to think that we have discovered as objective laws what we have merely imposed by private legislation." The provisional relativism of criticism as a historical process of revaluation and reinterpretation, a relativism that always inhabits Eliot's notions of tradition and order, is an important component of the Norton lectures.

Eliot's acknowledgment of subjectivity and relativism in literary judgment perhaps informs his inclusion of two chapters on the Romantic poets, a group he had previously ignored or castigated. Here Eliot again expresses his ambivalence toward the Romantics. Coleridge is portrayed as drugged with metaphysics and Shelley as prey to childish, feeble, and adolescent ideas. Wordsworth, whose lyric expressions of natural beauty and eventual Christian orthodoxy might have been attractive to Eliot, has a "delicate sensibility to social life and social changes." Eliot calls Keats a "great poet" but singles out Keats's letters for special praise. Eliot finds their statements on poetry to be "true for greater and more mature poetry than anything that Keats ever wrote." Eliot maintains his subjective train of thought in a following chapter on Arnold, in which he emphasizes how "each generation, like each individual, brings to the contemplation of art its own categories of appreciation." In a telling aside, Eliot also discusses how a critic's writing about another poet or critic serves as a tacit piece of introspection and self-analysis: "Sometimes a critic may choose an author to criticise, a role to assume, as far as possible the antithesis to himself, a personality which has actualised all that has been suppressed in himself; we can sometimes arrive at a very satisfactory intimacy with our anti-masks." This becomes a quite suggestive remark when applied to Eliot's own criticism, as when he says that Arnold "had no real serenity, only an impeccable demeanour."

In turning to "The Modern Mind," Eliot turns to attack much of the subjectivism he has been tracing: "I have not wished to exhibit this 'progress in self-consciousness' as being necessarily *progress* with an association of higher values." He rejoins the attack on romanticism insofar as it portrays the self as a timeless spirit beyond history, rather than as a subjectivity peculiarly shaped by its age. He again criticizes Richards for his separation of poetry from belief and for his humanistic desire (similar to Arnold's) to "preserve emotions without the beliefs with which their history has been involved." These beliefs, however, are public rather than private, a function of history rather than the personality, and Eliot asserts that "you cannot find a sure test for poetry, a test by which you may distinguish between poetry and mere good verse, by reference to its putative antecedents in the mind of the poet," an observation that will later give weight to New Criticism's assault on the intentional fallacy.

Eliot's ultimate concern in *The Use of Poetry and The Use of Criticism* is for what each age demands of its poetry and its criticism. Although he suggests that within the differing demands of each different age there is "always some permanent element in common," he nevertheless concludes that "every effort to formulate the common element is limited by the limitations of particular times," an observation that reflects the unresolvable dialectic in his criticism between the ideal unity of an ahistorically permanent "common element" and the relativism of an irreducible historicity. These essays also suggest that the most socially useful form of poetry is the theater, which can provide this unifying commonality through the power of convention. In less than two years Eliot himself began his career as a dramatist and put into practice the theoretical linkages between dramatic convention and social utility.

Although he was not an effective speaker and his aloof, condescending, and authoritative manner led peers like Robert Frost to complain that he was "taking himself so seriously," Eliot lectured extensively in the United States during his tenure at Harvard, addressing audiences at Yale, Princeton, and the University of California at Los Angeles, and in Buffalo and Baltimore. His most controversial talks, however, were the Page-Barbour Lectures, given at the University of Virginia in 1933. These lectures, published in 1934 as *After Strange Gods: A Primer of Modern Heresy* and later somewhat repudiated by Eliot, most clearly document the moralistic and religious turn of his critical rhetoric. In them he reevaluates the argument of "Tradition and the Individual Talent," reinterpreting its discussions of tradition and originality from a distinctly moral perspective and suggesting that the question of tradition is not a strictly literary one. In these lectures Eliot defines tradition as the ways in which a people habitually and unconsciously feel and act through such vehicles as their customs and their blood kinships. But this visceral tradition, coming from the blood and not the brain, cannot criticize itself, Eliot cautions; rather, it must be criticized and updated by an orthodoxy that supervises it. And for Western man, Eliot asserts, that orthodoxy must be Christianity.

What he objects to in contemporary literature and the modern mind is the glorification of originality, individuality, and novelty for their own sakes, a habit of mind that leads to the disaster of both heterodoxy and "heresy," the term by which he here describes what in his earlier criticism went by the names of psychologism and romanticism. According to Eliot it is only the cumulative, public, conscious, and disciplined orthodoxy of the Church that counterbalances the writer's unavoidable individual eccentricities. Thus it "is not always necessary, or even desirable" for artists to be perfect in their orthodoxy, since it is the tension between eccentricity and orthodoxy, like the earlier tension between tradi-

tion and the individual talent, that Eliot here stresses. Therefore what Eliot deplores, he says in *After Strange Gods,* is that "the writer should deliberately give rein to his 'individuality,' that he should even cultivate his differences from others; and that his readers should cherish the author of genius, not in spite of his deviations from the inherited wisdom of the race, but because of them." His specific criticisms are aimed at (among others) Babbitt, Pound, William Butler Yeats, George Eliot, Gerard Manley Hopkins, Thomas Hardy, and especially D. H. Lawrence whom, because of his "acute sensibility, violent prejudices and passions, and lack of intellectual and social training," Eliot describes as "spiritual, but spiritually sick." Each of these writers, in one way or another, serves the deluded cause of individualism and heresy. In sustained discussions of James Joyce, Katherine Mansfield, and Lawrence, Eliot focuses on how they treat the subject of marital disillusionment.

Eliot concludes his lectures by decrying the modern reduction of blasphemy from a question of right belief into one of simple bad form (a reflection of his rejection of the liberal humanitarianism of his Protestant ancestors) and the fact that modern criticism, lacking an "external test of the validity of a writer's work," yields to "one seductive personality after another," requiring simply that the writer "be himself" and that his work be judged only on the basis of its sincerity, without considering what is for Eliot the more important issue of whether "the self in question should, socially and spiritually, be a good or a bad one." The excessively polemical tone of *After Strange Gods,* its abrasively moralistic rhetoric, and its overt anti-Semitism led to its very cold critical reception and to Eliot's decision not to have it reprinted. Nevertheless its generalizations remain central to Eliot's later criticism, and he repeats them two years later in "Religion and Literature," in which he asserts that "literary criticism should be completed by criticism from a definite ethical and theological standpoint."

For Eliot the intersection of religion and literature took place in poetic drama, a form with deep roots in the rituals of communal spiritual life in the West. Though Eliot did not begin to concentrate his creative efforts on drama before the 1930s, he had always thought and written much about the form, from the Noh theater of Japan to Sophocles, Euripides, Seneca, Shakespeare, the Jacobeans, Corneille, and Dryden. As early as 1924, in "Four Elizabethan Dramatists" (published in the *Criterion* and included in *Homage to John Dryden*), Eliot saw the virtues of drama in terms of the power of convention to provide order and unity. In both Elizabethan and modern drama Eliot found an emphasis on idiosyncratic personalities and emotions at the expense of impersonality and artistic wholeness. Eliot even laments the necessity to use actors in producing drama, since their individualistic interpretations intrude upon the ideal formal unity of the play. In contrast, he idealizes the ballet dancers of the Russian school: "the man or woman whom we admire is a being who exists only during the performances ... a personality, a vital flame which appears from nowhere, disappears into nothing and is complete and sufficient in its appearance." Eliot's preference for ritual over realistic representation merges with his anthropological sense of drama's origins in religious performances. In "A Dialogue on Dramatic Poetry" (1928), included in *Selected Essays*, one speaker says that "the only dramatic satisfaction that I find now is in a High Mass well performed," and he advocates a return to religious liturgy as the basis for a renewed public theater.

Eliot took this advice more seriously than the dialogue suggests. Abandoning earlier efforts at poetic drama ("Sweeney Agonistes," "Coriolon"), Eliot invested much of his creative talent during the 1930s in the writing of plays. Significantly this began when he accepted the commission to write the choruses to *The Rock*, a religious pageant staged between 28 May and 9 June 1934. A year later Eliot's first complete play, *Murder in the Cathedral*, was staged in the Chapter House of Canterbury Cathedral, opening his career as a dramatist that spanned the last twenty-five years of his creative life. In an address to the Friends of Rochester Cathedral in 1937, published as "Religious Drama: Mediæval and Modern" (*University of Edinburgh Journal*, 1937), Eliot stressed what he felt to be the social utility of drama by observing that serious drama is always informed by a religious background and principles, and that therefore a religious craving is latent in all serious lovers of drama. Such theater for Eliot satisfies the "desire of human beings to achieve greater dignity and significance than they seem to do in their private or indeed public lives."

In this essay on drama Eliot also notes that "a large part of our failure [in the modern centuries] has been the failure to control, for the purposes of living, the mechanical world (mechanical

in the largest sense, including our systems of production, distribution and finance)." His social and political commentaries of the late 1930s and 1940s focused on the inadequacies and the lack of principles of these modern systems. Since the late 1920s Eliot's economic ideas had been influenced by the Social Credit theories espoused by A. R. Orage and Ezra Pound, the goal of which was to rearrange capital while avoiding socialism, and in the late 1930s his thinking found its major expression in a series of lectures published as *The Idea of a Christian Society* (1939). In these he posits a hypothetical Christian society, uses religious abstractions and generalizations to criticize political and economic systems, and urges a reorganization of values that would effect a rearrangement of industry, commerce, and financial credit. Asserting that the only hopeful course for society is to become Christian, Eliot envisions a Christian society as a social hierarchy constituted by the Christian state, "the Christian community, and the community of Christians." This last group, deriving theoretically from Julien Benda's notion of the "clercs," would be a small, elite unit made up of the more intellectual, scholarly, and devout members of the society and would in "matters of dogma, matters of faith and morals ... speak as the final authority within the nation." This hierarchical social organization would for Eliot instill into modern society the coherent religious principles, control, and balance that have been dissipated by liberal mental habits, democratic political organizations, and capitalistic economic practices. The *Criterion* ceased publication in 1939 due to what Eliot called the disappearance of the European mind in the fragmentation of Europe's political climate. In his final commentary for that periodical Eliot specifies the abstractly intellectual perspective that informs all his social criticism, asserting that for him "a right political philosophy came more and more to imply a right theology–and right economics to depend upon right ethics."

Throughout the late 1930s and 1940s Eliot's reputation as an editor, publisher, and generous helper of younger writers grew, so that he became known as the "Pope of Russell Square," where the offices of Faber and Faber were located. During these years his prominence as the authoritative voice of Western culture was enhanced by his many public lectures and radio broadcasts, which became particularly important for the assertion and maintenance of British cultural tradition in the threatening years of World

War II. For part of the war he acted as an air-raid warden for the Kensington area of London, and his experiences in this capacity inform one section of *Four Quartets* (1943), his last major poetic work.

*Four Quartets* brings together poems written over a seven-year span. "Burnt Norton," composed in 1935 and included as a self-contained piece in *Collected Poems 1909-1935* (1936), grew out of lines excised from *Murder in the Cathedral.* The poem builds upon Eliot's recollections of visiting the manor and garden at Burnt Norton in the company of Emily Hale, a friend of his youth who seems to have been an object of some romantic interest to Eliot. The poem's Wordsworthian character, lyric passages, and thematic treatment of time, love, and art suggest that Eliot had found a middle way between romanticism and Christianity. Eliot returned to writing for the theater with *The Family Reunion,* which opened in March of 1939 after more than two years of composition and revision. The outbreak of World War II made public drama an impossible avenue and prompted Eliot's final return to verse. *East Coker* (1940) follows the five-part structural pattern set by "Burnt Norton" and treats the dark mood of the era. Self-consciously it also probes the value of Eliot's twenty years *"entre deux guerres"* and the apparent waning of his poetic talent. In *The Dry Salvages* (1941) Eliot continues to explore the intersection of time and eternity, here with an American setting–the rocks off the New England coast by which he sailed during the exhilarating summers of his youth. *Little Gidding* (1942) gave Eliot his most trouble in composition. In it he attempted a difficult imitation of Dante's terza rima for a scene in which the speaker, an air-raid warden, meets a "familiar compound ghost." It is the dramatic encounter of a historical individual talent with the voice of a multifold tradition and gives final expression to the dialectic of skepticism and idealism, idiosyncrasy and orthodoxy that pervades Eliot's work.

During the 1940s Eliot participated in numerous social and religious committees, including The Moot, a group of like-minded Christian intellectual friends (among them Karl Mannheim and Murry) that grew out of a 1937 Oxford conference on church, community, and state and that in many ways was the model for Eliot's notion of a scholarly community of Christians, and the English Circle of Books Across the Sea, which was instrumental in bringing books to wartime England. In 1943 he wrote a series of articles for

*New English Weekly* that were published five years later as *Notes Towards the Definition of Culture* (1948). In these essays he expands upon some of the social themes of his earlier work, defining culture as an organic structure brought into being and maintained only by a shared system of beliefs, a religion, which is transmitted primarily through the family. Continuing a line of thought that stretches all the way back to his earliest writings on the dynamics of literary history, Eliot here stresses the need for a constant struggle between the centripetal and centrifugal forces of culture and for an ongoing conflict of ideas. For Eliot it is only through this continual agonism that truth (as a public and cultural product) is enlarged and clarified. In these and other essays he turns his attention to the shape of postwar European civilization, criticizing the various mechanical plans for social reorganization while reaffirming the need for religious and cultural values. He remains pessimistic, however, about the future of European culture.

Eliot's major work of the 1940s and early 1950s was brought together in the 1957 collection, *On Poetry and Poets.* Most of these essays are reiterations rather than developments of earlier positions. The book includes, however, the 1942 address, "The Music of Poetry," which stresses the unity of meaning and music in a poem and suggests (in what will later become a central doctrine of New Criticism) that poetic meaning always transcends paraphrasable meaning, since "the poet is occupied with frontiers of consciousness beyond which words fail." It also includes "Poetry and Drama," a 1949 University of Chicago address in which Eliot discusses the need of poetry in drama to justify itself dramatically and reviews his own experiences with poetic drama. In "The Three Voices of Poetry" Eliot emphasizes poetry's irreducible polyvocality, and in two essays on Milton, the first from 1936 and the second from 1947, Eliot traces his changing attitudes toward Milton. In the first he castigates Milton for his rhetoric, accusing him of writing English "like a dead language" and getting lost in the mazes of an artificial verbal music dislocated from sense. For these reasons Milton is a bad influence "against which we still have to struggle." By "Milton II," however, Eliot feels that poets have become "sufficiently liberated from Milton's reputation," that he can now be studied without danger. In this essay Eliot also expresses his surprise at the success of two of his critical terms ("dissociation of sensibility" and "objective correlative") and admits to having made a mistake in blaming Milton and Dryden for the dissociation of sensibility, suggesting that its causes are too complex and profound to be accounted for by literary criticism.

The late 1940s also brought changes in Eliot's personal life. In 1947 Vivien Eliot, who had suffered from insanity and had been institutionalized for years, died, freeing him from an emotional burden that had plagued him since the late 1910s. In 1949 he met Valerie Fletcher, who became his secretary, and in 1957 they were married. Public recognition of Eliot's poetic and critical reputation came in 1948 when he was awarded both the Nobel Prize for Literature and the Order of Merit by George VI. He received the Hanseatic-Goethe Prize in 1954 and the Dante Gold Medal in 1959. Eliot was by this time a highly visible and famous celebrity (his picture was on the cover of *Time* magazine in 1950), a public institution followed by photographers and autograph-seekers whenever he appeared. As such, of course, he was also the subject of jokes aimed at his pervasive authority and aloof demeanor, one of which described him as a religious icon: "The Blessed Thomas Eliot Considered as the Air We Breathe." Nevertheless his status as a literary and cultural magus remained strong throughout the 1950s.

Eliot's critical powers had begun to wane, but he continued to write introductions for Faber and Faber publications and to give public lectures. He delivered one of the most famous of these talks in 1956 at the University of Minnesota before 14,000 people (the largest crowd ever to attend a lecture on literature) at the university's baseball stadium. In this address, published as "The Frontiers of Criticism," Eliot expresses his bewilderment at being considered "one of the ancestors of modern criticism," rejecting Cleanth Brooks's assertion that the New Criticism derives from his work while confessing his hope that the *Criterion* encouraged the movement. He attacks the "lemon-squeezer school of criticism" that seeks to explain a poem by searching for its origins but admits to having contributed to this kind of criticism through his notes to *The Waste Land* which he characterizes as "bogus scholarship." According to Eliot the danger of such a positivistic approach is its hidden assumption of a single right interpretation, which he rejects with the assertion that meaning is never exhausted by any explanation. From his perspective the origins of a poem cannot be explained by what came before it.

Rather a critic must seek to "grasp what the poetry is aiming to be . . . to grasp its entelechy," and thus a "valid interpretation . . . must be at the same time an interpretation of my own feelings when I read it." This statement suggests the strictly provisional and relative validity of interpretations and reaffirms the position clearly reflected by Eliot's work since the 1920s that criticism is not and can never be a positivistic science, because it is unavoidably contoured by the historicity of the critic. In its quest for origins and its emphasis upon objective explanation, modern criticism is, for Eliot, in danger of succumbing to the myth of science and its model of knowledge. "The Frontiers of Criticism" is one of Eliot's most explicit critiques of the scientifization of criticism.

Eliot died on 4 January 1965, before the publication in November of his last collection of essays, *To Criticize the Critic and Other Writings*. This book contains essays primarily from the 1950s, but it also includes reprints of two of his earliest works: the previously anonymous "Ezra Pound: His Metric and Poetry" and "Reflections on 'Vers Libre,'" both from 1917. Of particular interest is the book's title essay, in which Eliot quite candidly reviews his own critical career. Looking back on his criticism, he admits to errors of judgment and regrets errors of tone: the "occasional note of arrogance, of vehemence, of cocksureness or rudeness, the braggadocio of the mildmannered man safely entrenched behind his typewriter." He divides his career into three periods. The first encompasses the time when he was writing for the *Egoist* and being influenced by Irving Babbitt, Ezra Pound, Remy de Gourmont, T. E. Hulme, and Charles Maurras. These influences found expression in the classicism versus romanticism debate of the 1920s. The second is the time after 1918, when he wrote his major essays and reviews, and the third covers the latter portion of his career, which is characterized by public lectures and addresses rather than by articles and reviews. Eliot also distinguishes between his two main types of criticism, his "essays of generalization" and his "appreciations of individual authors," and suggests that these latter essays have the best chance of retaining their value. He believes that if the generalizations survive at all, it will only be because of scholars, "interested in the mind of my generation," who will study them "in their historical context."

Although Eliot's general description of the development of his critical career is quite perceptive, it fails to suggest the importance of his work—and particularly of his "essays of generalization"—for the development of Anglo-American literary criticism. His writings on tradition and impersonality; his attacks on romantic psychologism and impressionistic criticism; his story of literary history as reflecting a dissociation of Western intellect and sensibility; his emphases upon the need in literature for outside authority and for public systems of order; his paralleling of literary problems to social, moral, and political problems; his descriptions of literary works as organic wholes; his careful attention to the technical aspects of literary texts all shaped the methodology, the language, and the critical assumptions that underlie much of the New Criticism of the twentieth century. In a very real way Eliot's early writings helped to create modern literary studies as an autonomous field of inquiry and invented for that discipline a certain authority, tradition, and rigor. In recent years Eliot's work has become a new and lively source of critical debate. The rhetoric the New Critics derived from or projected onto Eliot's essays—a critical rhetoric that models texts as autotelic objects, criticism as an objective project, and poetry as a special kind of language different from and resistant to rational discourse—is being challenged by other critical rhetorics (such as semiotics, deconstruction, hermeneutics, and feminist criticism, among others) that, in their various ways, model texts, criticism, and language in configurations that undermine the presuppositions of New Criticism and thereby revalue Eliot. Some of this work simply rejects Eliot as a relic of a demystified high Modernism. Others, however, read in his work a critique of the very New Criticism that appropriated it as its precursor. This ongoing rereading is discovering in Eliot a field rich with contemporary issues—such as the critique of the subject and the problematics of time (covered over by New Criticism's emphasis on spatial form)—and thus his work continues to provoke the very historical revisionism and open-ended dialectics of interpretation it describes.

**Letters:**

D. D. Paige, *The Letters of Ezra Pound 1907-1941,* includes a letter from Eliot (New York: Harcourt, Brace, 1950), pp. 170-171;

A. Sheekman, ed., *The Groucho Letters; Letters from and to Groucho Marx,* includes six letters from Eliot (New York: Simon & Schuster, 1967), pp. 154-162;

*The Autobiography of Bertrand Russell,* volume 2, includes four letters from Eliot (London: Allen & Unwin, 1968), pp. 58, 173, 174;

B. L. Reid, *The Man from New York: John Quinn and His Friends,* includes letters and excerpts from letters from Eliot (New York: Oxford University Press, 1968).

**Interviews:**

M. W. Childs, "From a Distinguished Former St. Louisan," *St. Louis Post-Dispatch,* 5 October 1930;

"Inquiry into the Spirit and Language of Night," *transition,* no. 27 (April/May 1938): 236;

Desmond Hawkins, "The Writer as Artist: Discussion between T. S. Eliot and Desmond Hawkins," *Listener,* 24 (28 November 1940): 773-774;

Ranjee Shahani, "T. S. Eliot Answers Questions," *John O'London's Weekly* (London), 19 August 1949, pp. 497-498;

John Lehmann, "T. S. Eliot Talks About Himself and the Drive to Create," *New York Times Book Review,* 29 November 1953, pp. 5, 44;

" 'The Confidential Clerk' Comments by T. S. Eliot," *New York Herald Tribune,* 7 February 1954, IV: 1;

"T. S. Eliot Gives a Unique Photo-Interview . . . Stepping Out a Little? I Like the Idea," *Daily Express* (London), 20 September 1957, p. 6;

Donald Hall, "The Art of Poetry, I: T. S. Eliot," *Paris Review,* 21 (Spring/Summer 1959): 47-70; republished in *Writers at Work,* second series (New York: Viking, 1963), pp. 91-110; and in Donald Hall, *Remembering Poets* (New York: Harper & Row, 1977), pp. 203-221;

Tom Greenwell, "Talking Freely: T. S. Eliot and Tom Greenwell," *Yorkshire Post* (Leeds), 29 August 1961;

Donald Carroll, "An Interview with T. S. Eliot," *Quagga,* 2, no. 1 (1962): 31-33;

"T. S. Eliot . . . An Interview," *Granite Review,* 24, no. 3 (1962): 16-20;

Leslie Paul, "A Conversation with T. S. Eliot," *Kenyon Review,* 27 (Winter 1964/1965): 11-21.

**Bibliographies:**

Donald C. Gallup, *T. S. Eliot: A Bibliography,* revised and extended edition (New York: Harcourt, Brace & World, 1969);

Bradley Gunther, *The Merrill Checklist of T. S. Eliot* (Columbus: Merrill, 1970);

Mildred Martin, *A Half-Century of Eliot Criticism: An Annotated Bibliography of Books and Articles in English, 1916-1965* (Lewisburg: Bucknell University Press, 1972);

Richard M. Ludwig, "T. S. Eliot," in *Sixteen Modern American Authors: A Survey of Research and Criticism,* edited by Jackson R. Bryner (Durham: Duke University Press, 1973);

Beatrice Ricks, *T. S. Eliot: A Bibliography of Secondary Works* (Metuchen, N.J.: Scarecrow Press, 1980).

**Biographies:**

William Turner Levy and Victor Scherle, *Affectionately, T. S. Eliot: The Story of a Friendship, 1947-1965* (Philadelphia & New York: Lippincott, 1968);

Robert Sencourt, *T. S. Eliot: A Memoir,* edited by Donald Adamson (New York: Dodd, Mead, 1971);

T. S. Matthews, *Great Tom: Notes Toward the Definition of T. S. Eliot* (New York: Harper & Row, 1974);

Joseph Chiari, *T. S. Eliot: A Memoir* (London: Enitharmon Press, 1982);

Caroline Behr, *T. S. Eliot: A Chronology of His Life and Works* (London: Macmillan, 1983);

Peter Ackroyd, *T. S. Eliot: A Life* (New York: Simon & Schuster, 1984).

**References:**

Michael Beehler, *T. S. Eliot, Wallace Stevens, and the Discourses of Difference* (Baton Rouge: Louisiana State University Press, 1987), pp. 1-40, 66-97, 122-149, 176-177;

Ronald Bush, *T. S. Eliot: A Study in Character and Style* (New York: Oxford University Press, 1984);

Robert Canary, *T. S. Eliot: The Poet and His Critics* (Chicago: American Library Association, 1982);

Joseph Chiari, *T. S. Eliot: Poet and Dramatist* (London: Vision, 1972);

Harriet Davidson, *T. S. Eliot and Hermeneutics* (Baton Rouge: Louisiana State University Press, 1985);

Elizabeth Drew, *T. S. Eliot: The Design of His Poetry* (New York: Scribners, 1949);

Lewis Freed, *T. S. Eliot: The Critic as Philosopher* (West Lafayette, Ind.: Purdue University Press, 1979);

Northrop Frye, *T. S. Eliot* (Edinburgh & London: Oliver & Boyd, 1963; revised edition, 1968);

Helen Gardner, *The Art of T. S. Eliot* (London: Cresset Press, 1949);

Lyndall Gordon, *Eliot's Early Years* (Oxford & New York: Oxford University Press, 1977);

Gregory S. Jay, *T. S. Eliot and the Poetics of Literary History* (Baton Rouge: Louisiana State University Press, 1983);

Hugh Kenner, *The Invisible Poet: T. S. Eliot* (London: Allen, 1960);

Roger Kojecký, *T. S. Eliot's Social Criticism* (London: Faber & Faber, 1971; New York: Farrar, Straus & Giroux, 1972);

Edward Lobb, *T. S. Eliot and the Romantic Critical Tradition* (London: Routledge & Kegan Paul, 1981);

John D. Margolis, *T. S. Eliot's Intellectual Development, 1922-1939* (Chicago & London: University of Chicago Press, 1972);

F. O. Matthiessen, *The Achievement of T. S. Eliot: An Essay on the Nature of Poetry* (London & New York: Oxford University Press, 1935; revised and enlarged edition, 1947);

J. Hillis Miller, "T. S. Eliot," in *Poets of Reality: Six Twentieth-Century Writers* (Cambridge, Mass.: Harvard University Press, 1965);

Miller, "T. S. Eliot," in *Writers at Work: The Paris Review Interviews,* second series (New York: Viking, 1963), pp. 89-110;

A. D. Moody, *Thomas Stearns Eliot: Poet* (Cambridge, U.K., London, New York, New Rochelle, Melbourne & Sidney: Cambridge University Press, 1979);

Carol Smith, *T. S. Eliot's Dramatic Theory and Practice from Sweeny Agonistes to the Elder Statesman* (Princeton: Princeton University Press, 1963);

Grover Smith, *T. S. Eliot's Poetry and Plays: A Study in Sources and Meanings* (Chicago: Chicago University Press, 1956; enlarged edition, 1974);

William V. Spanos, "Hermeneutics and Memory: Destroying T. S. Eliot's *Four Quartets,*" *Genre,* 11 (Winter 1978): 523-574;

Stephen Spender, *T. S. Eliot* (New York: Viking, 1975);

Derek Traversi, *T. S. Eliot: The Longer Poems* (London: Bodley Head, 1976).

**Papers:**

Among the most important collections of Eliot's papers are the Eliot Collection of the Houghton Library, Harvard University, which includes the unpublished Clark Lectures, documents related to the Eliot family, and Eliot's student philosophy papers; the Hayward Collection of Kings College Library, at Cambridge University; the Henry W. and Albert A. Berg Collection of English and American Literature of the New York Public Library, which includes the manuscripts for "Gerontion" and *The Waste Land;* the T. S. Eliot Collection at the Humanities Research Center at the University of Texas in Austin; the collection at the Beinecke Rare Book and Manuscript Library, Yale University, New Haven; and papers at the Princeton University Library. Many of these papers are restricted, and one major collection (the Emily Hale papers at Princeton) is sealed until the year 2020. Smaller collections are located in numerous universities around the world.

# Waldo Frank
## (25 August 1889-9 January 1967)

### Casey Blake
*Indiana University*

See also the Frank entry in *DLB 9, American Novelists, 1910-1945.*

BOOKS: *The Unwelcome Man: A Novel* (Boston: Little, Brown, 1917);

*The Art of the Vieux Colombier* (Paris & New York: Editions de la Nouvelle Revue Francais, 1918);

*Our America* (New York: Boni & Liveright, 1919); republished as *The New America* (London: Cape, 1922);

*The Dark Mother: A Novel* (New York: Boni & Liveright, 1920);

*City Block* (Darien, Conn.: Privately printed, 1922);

*Rahab* (New York: Boni & Liveright, 1922);

*Holiday* (New York: Boni & Liveright, 1923);

*Chalk Face* (New York: Boni & Liveright, 1924);

*Salvos: An Informal Book about Books and Plays* (New York: Boni & Liveright, 1924);

*Time Exposures, by Search-Light: Being Portraits of Twenty Men and Women Famous in Our Day, Together with Caricatures of the Same by Divers Artists, to Which is Appended an Account of a Joint Report Made to Jehovah on the Condition of Man in the City of New York (1926) by Julius Caesar, Aristotle and a Third Individual of Less Importance* (New York: Boni & Liveright, 1926);

*Virgin Spain: Scenes from the Spiritual Drama of a Great People* (New York: Boni & Liveright, 1926; London: Cape, 1926; revised edition, New York: Duell, Sloan & Pearce, 1942);

*New Year's Eve: A Play* (New York & London: Scribners, 1929);

*The Rediscovery of America: An Introduction to a Philosophy of American Life* (New York & London: Scribners, 1929);

*Primer mensaje a la América Hispana* (Madrid: Revista de Occidente, 1930);

*America Hispana: A Portrait and a Prospect* (New York & London: Scribners, 1931);

*Dawn in Russia: The Record of a Journey* (New York & London: Scribners, 1932);

*The Death and Birth of David Markand: An American Story* (New York & London: Scribners, 1934);

*In the American Jungle (1925-1936)* (New York: Farrar & Rinehart, 1937);

*The Bridegroom Cometh* (London: Gollancz, 1938; New York: Doubleday, Doran, 1939);

*Chart for Rough Water: Our Role in a New World* (New York: Doubleday, Doran, 1940);

*Summer Never Ends: A Modern Love Story* (New York: Duell, Sloan & Pearce, 1941);

*Ustedes y Nosotros: Nuevo Mensaje a Ibero-América,* translated from the unpublished English version by Frida Weber (Buenos Aires: Editorial Losada, 1942);

*South American Journey* (New York: Duell, Sloan & Pearce, 1943; London: Gollancz, 1944);

*Photograph of Frank in the 1920s by Alfred Stieglitz (courtesy of the Library of Congress)*

*The Jew in Our Day* (New York: Duell, Sloan & Pearce, 1944; London: Gollancz, 1944);

*Island in the Atlantic: A Novel* (New York: Duell, Sloan & Pearce, 1946);

*The Invaders: A Novel* (New York: Duell, Sloan & Pearce, 1948);

*Birth of a World: Bolívar in Terms of His Peoples* (Boston: Houghton Mifflin, 1951; London: Gollancz, 1953);

*Not Heaven: A Novel in the Form of Prelude, Variations, and Theme* (New York: Hermitage House, 1953);

*Bridgehead: The Drama of Israel* (New York: Braziller, 1957);

*The Rediscovery of Man: A Memoir and a Methodology of Modern Life* (New York: Braziller, 1958);

*Cuba: Prophetic Island* (New York: Marzani & Munsell, 1961);

*Memoirs of Waldo Frank,* edited by Alan Trachtenberg (Amherst: University of Massachusetts Press, 1973).

OTHER: *America and Alfred Stieglitz: A Collective Portrait,* edited by Frank, Lewis Mumford, Dorothy Norman, Paul Rosenfeld, and Harold Rugg (Garden City: Doubleday, Doran, 1934).

Waldo Frank occupies a peculiar place in the history of American letters. Though a novelist, and one of the most prominent and highly regarded critics of the interwar years of the twentieth century, Frank was almost uniformly dismissed or forgotten by the time of his death in 1967. Today he strikes most literary and intellectual historians as an elusive and certainly secondary figure significant only for his association with writers he had befriended and whose work, in many cases, he had been the first to champion: Sherwood Anderson, Hart Crane, Jean Toomer, and others. Yet at the peak of Frank's career, his reputation as a writer and commentator on American culture and politics was enormous. His success as associate editor of the *Seven Arts* (1916-1917) and author of *Our America* (1919) suggested that Frank might be the logical successor to Randolph Bourne as a critic who united political and cultural radicalism. *Our America*'s bold conclusion, that "in a dying world, creation is revolution," summed up Frank's visionary intellectual stance by grounding the prospects for political change in a revival of religious and aesthetic experience. Fifty years later Frank was better known by Latin Americans, who appreciated his sympathetic accounts of their cultures, than by his fellow Americans. Frank's virtual disappearance from American cultural life by the time of his death was due, in part, to his reputed egoism and to a difficult literary style that Edmund Wilson likened to a cross of "James Joyce with the Hebrew prophets." On the other hand Frank's tenuous historical position was an ironic testament to the originality of his thought, which challenged the conventional political and artistic categories of American intellectual history.

Always an eclectic thinker, Frank drew on Jewish mysticism, Spinoza, Hegel, Marx, Freud,

John Dewey, and—most importantly—Walt Whitman in his critical jeremiads, which called on writers and artists to dedicate themselves to the regeneration of American life. Like Bourne and the young Van Wyck Brooks, Frank believed that a revolution in culture and consciousness had to lay the basis for a new politics of democratic community. And like Lewis Mumford he argued that such a community had to revive the ethos of spiritual discipline that shaped the "medieval synthesis." What most distinguished Frank from these writers was his mysticism, which was central to his personal development and his criticism. For Frank only the recovery of a "consciousness of the Whole" would allow Americans to retrieve their full humanity in an industrial capitalist society. Once freed from positivist ideologies that subjected human agency to "laws" of industrial progress, Americans might draw on their intuition of "wholeness" to create a truly organic community. His Whitmanesque organicism, his romantic critique of commercial society, and his insistence on mystical experience put him at odds with pragmatists, Marxists, and occultists of all stripes and help explain his curious isolation in modern American criticism. That isolation should not detract from his achievements: his generous vision of American potential; his analysis of the connections between politics, religion, and culture; and his faith in the democratic promise of human community.

Waldo David Frank was born on 25 August 1889, the youngest child of Julius J. and Helene Rosenberg Frank. The Franks epitomized the success of upper-middle-class assimilated Jews in New York. Julius, son of a German Jewish immigrant, was a well-to-do lawyer who maintained his family in a stately upper West Side brownstone. To Waldo, his father seemed divided between a willful businessman and a sensitive man of culture who cultivated an interest in reform politics and the arts. Frank's mother was the daughter of a well-to-do German Jewish family from Alabama. Her father, a blockade runner during the Civil War, brought his family through the lines of battle and after Reconstruction established a varnish business in New York. Helene passed on to her younger son a lifelong love for music. At an early age Frank appears to have sided with his father's artistic side and his mother's "feminine" values as a counterweight to the family's economic dependence on Wall Street. That early psychological conflict—between "feminine" values of nurture and artistic creativity and

"masculine" qualities of commercial mastery—haunted Frank throughout his life and played a major role in his cultural criticism.

As an adolescent Frank was drawn to the mystical spiritualism and literary romanticism that would shape his entire career. His father's rejection of Judaism for the secular moralism of the Ethical Culture Society appalled him and came to symbolize for Frank the default of American Jews to the pressures of an amoral materialism. He discovered Whitman and began writing his own fiction as a teenager. By 1906, when he left for a year at a private school in Switzerland, Frank had already written one novel (which he never published) and had achieved considerable success at the cello. In the fall of 1907 he returned to the United States and enrolled at Yale. Frank was a precocious student possessed of an astonishing intellectual ambition. He read widely, enrolled in courses with William E. Hocking and William Lyon ("Billy") Phelps, and wrote theater reviews for the *New Haven Courier-Journal* while at Yale. By the time he graduated in 1911, with both a bachelor's and a master's degree, Frank had written a second book, "The Spirit of Modern French Letters," which examined French drama as an expression of France's national culture. Yale University Press accepted the book for publication a year later, but Frank withdrew the book at the last moment. He spent a year and a half after his graduation working in journalism, writing for the *New York Evening Post* and the *New York Times*, but it quickly became clear that writing for newspapers satisfied neither his artistic nor his spiritual impulses. In early 1913 he left for France, where he spent seven months immersing himself in Spinoza and in French culture. Like Henry Adams, Randolph Bourne, and many other American intellectuals, Frank discovered in France everything he had longed for but never found in the United States. France, for him, was an "organic" nation in which politics and intellectual life grew out of a common culture shared by its people as a whole. When Frank later summoned American writers to join their compatriots in the creation of a similarly "organic" culture, he often invoked the collective identity of memory and aspiration that he believed had shaped the French since the Middle Ages.

The goal of promoting a democratic American cultural life lay behind Frank's work as associate editor of the *Seven Arts*. After spending three years in New York writing drama and fiction, Frank joined James Oppenheim in the fall of

1916 to edit the journal that sought to be "an expression of artists for the community." As Van Wyck Brooks—another of the journal's editors—acknowledged in his autobiography, "Waldo Frank was the real creator of the *Seven Arts*," and Oppenheim, too, later admitted that, his title as the magazine's editor notwithstanding, he was in no way Frank's intellectual equal. The entire agenda of the *Seven Arts* reflected the different currents that were coalescing in Frank's mind in the late teens: the rejection of Victorian "highbrow" gentility and the search for a new "middle ground" of cultural life that he shared with Brooks; the political radicalism and antiwar position he articulated along with Randolph Bourne; and, most important, the conviction that artists and writers had a social role to play as prophets of an alternative moral and spiritual creed that might fuel a movement for democratic renewal. The *Seven Arts*'s deft union of politics and culture, its belief in both a radical democracy and an American artistic renaissance, pervaded every issue in its brief two years of existence. That project found confirmation in the writers who contributed work to the journal: in addition to Brooks, Bourne, Frank, and Oppenheim, the *Seven Arts* published Sherwood Anderson, Robert Frost, Kahlil Gibran, D. H. Lawrence, Amy Lowell, Paul Rosenfeld, Walter Lippmann, John Reed, John Dewey, Theodore Dreiser, Max Eastman, Carl Sandburg, Harold Stearns, Eugene O'Neill, John Dos Passos, H. L. Mencken, and many others. If Frank had edited only the *Seven Arts*, he would have made a significant contribution to American arts and letters.

Frank later remembered the years of editing the *Seven Arts* as one of the high points of his life. "I was no longer alone!," he recalled in his memoirs. "I belonged to America and America belonged to me. There was no demarkation between my contacts as an editor and as a man." The heady years at the center of New York's "Little Renaissance" included marriage to progressive educator Margaret Naumburg, work on a novel and a number of short stories, registration as a conscientious objector to the First World War, and, then, entanglement in the personal and political squabbles that doomed the *Seven Arts*. While Bourne's antiwar essays caused its benefactor, Annette Rankine, to withdraw her support, Frank and Oppenheim struggled for control of the magazine's editorial board. The journal folded in October 1917 with its editors bitterly divided, their dreams of cultural community belied by their own failure to create it on a small scale.

As they explained in a farewell editorial, the editors of the *Seven Arts* set themselves the task of "interpreting and expressing *that latent America, that potential America* which we believed lay hidden under our commercial-industrial national organization." That search for a "potential America" was at the heart of Frank's first and most influential work of cultural criticism, *Our America*, published in November 1919. In the best jeremiad tradition, *Our America* combined a scathing indictment of the moral shallowness of modern American life with a call to retrieve and revive the religious and democratic impulses frustrated by American capitalism. Frank's criticism embraced history and geography, using both the ideas of Charles Beard (known for his economic interpretation of the American Constitution) and Frederick J. Turner (known for his commentary on the impact of the frontier upon the development of the American imagination and for his sectional approach to American culture), while at the same time giving these genres a particularly literary form. In effect Frank's *Our America* was a work of countermythology, a revision of the cultural history of the United States in direct opposition to the official folklore of Plymouth Rock, the frontier, and rugged individualism. For Frank, the Puritan, the pioneer, and the industrialist were all of a type, denying their own inner natures while laying waste to the American landscape. The result was a rootless civilization that grouped men and women into a thoughtless "herd," instead of fostering a true community or a shared culture. Pragmatists like Dewey who believed that such a civilization might yet generate the values that would transcend it were mistaken, according to Frank. The point was to tap the still inchoate desires and dreams that had eluded the industrial organization of the American mind.

Just as *Our America* chronicled the plight of spirit and culture in a society devoted to pioneering and material conquest, it also reminded readers of examples of an alternative American vision—of countercultures—that might yet serve in the modern age. Frank gloried in the tenacity of preindustrial values of religion and mutuality among native Americans, Hispanics, blacks, and those Jewish immigrants who remained loyal to their prophetic traditions. To these examples of popular gemeinschaft Frank added the nineteenth-century mystical nationalism of Abraham Lincoln and Whitman, whom he celebrated as visionary seers of a postindustrial American community. They had understood what Ralph Waldo Emerson and the Transcendentalists had forgotten in their flight from American materialism, "that aesthetic and spiritual values impose a discipline on man only when they are mined from the crude ore of his existence." Among his contemporaries Frank saw promise in the work of the late Randolph Bourne, Brooks, Anderson, and Alfred Stieglitz, all of whom glimpsed the mystical spark that still ignited Americans' inner lives, but he knew that his Whitmanesque dream of American union still lay in the future. "Ours is the first generation of Americans consciously engaged in spiritual pioneering," he admitted; unlike the "material" pioneers of the nineteenth century, Frank's generation would need to work slowly to generate an alternative America. A rush to political activism would prove fruitless without a new animating ethos to insure that politics meant more than a change in leaders. But a modernist culture without roots in American life, bereft of a project for social change, might end only in a frivolous elitism. "We must go through a period of static suffering, of inner cultivation," Frank intoned in the book's lyrical conclusion. Intellectuals and other believers in "our America" had to nurture an "energy" that was ultimately "religious." "Its act is creation. And in a dying world, creation is revolution."

The success of *Our America* put Frank at the center of New York's intellectual avant-garde in the early 1920s. While he shared Brooks's goal of creating an American "usable past," Frank was far more open than Brooks ever was to new currents in modernist art and literature. His support for those new currents in culture put him in contact not only with figures like Hart Crane, Jean Toomer, and Stieglitz but with American expatriate writers and European modernists. His equation of aesthetic creation and political revolution gave him an audience in both political and literary circles during the 1920s. His whirlwind activities during that decade testify to the breadth of Frank's interests and contacts. Immediately after finishing *Our America*, Frank left for the Midwest to spend three months working as a journalist for the neopopulist Non-Partisan League. In February 1920, during a trip to Richmond, Virginia, Frank had the deepest mystical experiences of his life, which he recorded in his diaries as three visitations from God. The prophet of "wholeness" emerged from the experience rejuvenated, and he launched into a period of intense productivity, completing five novels and a large body of critical essays in four years. In 1921 and 1922 Frank traveled through the South with Jean Toomer, the second time "passing" as black with the light-skinned Toomer, who led him through the southern Black Belt. Trips to Spain in 1921 and 1924 introduced Frank to another "organic" culture and inspired his *Virgin Spain: Scenes from the Spiritual Drama of a Great People*, published in 1926. In 1924 Frank published *Salvos: An Informal Book about Books and Plays*, a collection of essays and reviews that included work from the *Seven Arts* years and the early 1920s. Between April 1925 and October 1926 Frank wrote some twenty-five profiles and lighthearted caricatures (including one ridiculing his old Yale professor "Billy" Phelps) for the *New Yorker* under the pseudonym "Search Light." These he collected and published anonymously in *Time Exposures* in 1926.

The 1920s were a period of intense literary activity for Frank, but they also saw him involved in the spiritual mysticism and political radicalism that ran through his work in the 1910s. Like Toomer, Hart Crane, Herbert Croly, Gorham Munson, and other New York writers, Frank flirted briefly with the eastern mysticism of G. I. Gurdjieff and A. R. Orage, but he broke with both men on the grounds that theirs was a spiritualism of withdrawal and retreat, rather than the militant creed of social transformation he had called for in *Our America*. In November 1925 Frank joined the editorial board of the *New Republic* as a contributor, cementing his friendship with Croly, the magazine's editor, who in his last years embraced a quasi-religious politics close to Frank's own position. A year later Frank joined the board of the newly formed *New Masses*, where he would remain until 1930. Frank's busy life as a literary celebrity took its toll on his marriage to Margaret Naumburg. The two divorced in 1926, and Frank married Alma Magoon a year later. After spending almost a year abroad, the Franks returned to New York, where Frank began writing a sequel to *Our America*, titled *The Rediscovery of America*. Thanks to Croly, who overruled the other editors' objections, it was serialized in the *New Republic* in 1927-1928. The book was published as a complete volume in 1929. Together with *Virgin Spain*, it is the most complete statement of Frank's criticism in the 1920s, combining his by-now familiar calls to American "wholeness" with his fullest statement of the significance of mystical knowledge in personal and political change. Also in 1929 Frank toured Latin America and delivered a series of lectures published a year later in Madrid as *Primer mensaje a la América Hispana.* His trip led to his writing another study in cultural history and criticism, *America Hispana* (1931). His trilogy in cultural analysis from this period–*Virgin Spain, The Re-discovery of America,* and *America Hispana*–reveals Frank at the height of his powers, drawing on the Hispanic and American pasts to prophesy a New World civilization.

Frank's combination of geography, history, and cultural commentary in *Our America* reappeared in these works which, at their worst, descended into a high-minded travelogue and, at their best, presented Frank's most profound insights into the cultural crisis of modern life. Frank looked to Spain in much the same way he had previously looked to France, as a source of preindustrial loyalties and faiths that might inspire a new project of cultural organicism. *Virgin Spain* drew heavily on the ideas of Miguel de Unamuno and other members of the Spanish intellectual "Generation of '98," who had defended Spain's commercial backwardness as evidence of its people's spiritual superiority to their more modern European neighbors. But Frank also realized that Unamuno's idealized Don Quixote had failed to master the modern world, retreating into a fantasy of pure spirit. The "medieval synthesis" that had guided Spanish culture would not restore wholeness to an industrial age simply by wishing it into being. "The modern world can be defeated only with modern weapons," Frank wrote. "The true savior will have to understand and accept this analytical world, ere he can transform it."

*The Re-discovery of America* continued this argument, with Frank explaining how developments in modernist art, psychoanalysis, and relativistic physics promised a new restoration of premodern intuitive values in modern America. Where Spain lacked the practical means to perpetuate its instinctive spirituality, Americans, Frank claimed, continued to allow a superficial practicality to submerge their "consciousness of the Whole." Frank's diagnosis of the "American jungle" was reminiscent of that in *Our America;* what was new about *Re-discovery* was his program for cultural change, which began with a religious transformation of each individual. "We cannot transfigure the world while each of us is in the state of the world," he wrote. "We cannot create a group, while *we* are chaos. The transfiguring must first be in ourselves."

Frank believed that "consciousness of the Whole" had three dimensions, each of which was integral to cultural transformation: an individual aesthetic consciousness; a religious awareness at the level of social groups; and a political radicalism in the public realm. A dialectic of the person, the group, and the nation–all united by an intuitive understanding of their union with God–held out the best promise of "a method and technic [*sic*] for action," in Frank's mind. Most of all that action had to reject the politics of power relations for a new radicalism based on love. "Power, which by itself can but perpetuate its sterile sway, needs to be overcome by love." Thus politicians had a less important role to play in Frank's vision of radicalism than did intellectuals and artists like Alfred Stieglitz, whom Frank lionized as the herald of a new "organic" American culture. While most of Frank's contemporaries on the intellectual left considered themselves technicians of social change, Frank envisioned a role for intellectuals as prophets who embodied in their words and actions the still inarticulate longings of Americans as a whole. Such thinkers would provide "leadership for the blind American plasm."

Frank hinted at Latin Americans' role in his project at various points in *Re-discovery.* "In this process of creation, there will be two Persons: we perhaps the male, America Latina perhaps the female." This idea of Latin America as a feminine counterpart to the extroverted masculine culture of the United States was a central theme of *America Hispana.* While the United States had the practical means to create a new democratic community, it lacked the spiritual will to effect such a new order. Americans' southern neighbors had the religious awareness Frank treasured but lacked the economic and political tools for social reconstruction. "The problem in the United States is to free its impulse toward a fresh creative beginning: in America Hispana, it is to find the means to fulfillment." Only a union of American "means" with Latin America's reservoir of Catholic and peasant values might produce the society Frank longed for: "an *integral* socialism which would transfigure the present industrial body on the basis of the true concept of the person."

In the depression years Frank's "integral socialism" led him to an unusual commitment to direct political activism. In August 1929 he joined Sherwood Anderson, Theodore Dreiser, and other writers to raise money for striking textile workers in the South. Three years later he chaired a committee of leftist writers who traveled to Harlan County, Kentucky, in support of that area's striking miners. The trip ended when Frank was attacked by a group of company vigilantes—a beating that drew public attention to the strike and led to Frank's testifying at a congressional hearing on conditions in the mines. That same year he led a delegation of writers who tried unsuccessfully to meet with President Hoover to protest his treatment of the Bonus Army marchers. Frank's increasing politicization was symbolized by his public support of the Communist party's presidential ticket in 1932, the beginning of a five-year period of intense involvement with the party and its intellectual admirers.

In 1931 Frank had toured the Soviet Union, and the following year his *Dawn in Russia* appeared, in many ways a Russian successor to his work on Latin America. While Lincoln Steffens and other fellow travelers had praised Soviet communism for creating a workable future, what Frank admired in the Soviet Union was its usable past. Frank cherished the deep religiosity of Russian peasant culture, which had found expression in the classics of nineteenth-century Russian literature, and he hoped that official Soviet Marxism might prove a modern successor to such premodern forms of "organic" consciousness. Frank's entire relationship with the Communists was marked by an uneasy tension between his commitment to his own "integral socialism" and his tentative belief in the Communist party as a vehicle for a new culture. In May 1935 Frank delivered an address on the "Values of the Revolutionary Writer" at the first congress of the League of American Writers. His essay tried to show how the writer's cultural mission might further the creation of an undogmatic socialism. Despite his obvious differences with the party, Frank quickly became the elder statesman of fellow-traveling liberal intellectuals who allied themselves with Communists. Unanimously elected the first chairman of the new League of American Writers at the congress, Frank became a symbol of the party's turn to cultural nationalism with the Popular Front. In June 1935 Frank was the American delegate to the international Congress of Writers for the Defense of Culture, an important gathering of antifascist and Communist intellectuals held in Paris. His public and private writings revealed his deep theoretical differences with the Communists, yet he continued to give support to their political agenda in the mid 1930s. Frank resigned the chairmanship of the League in May 1936 to devote more time

to his writing, but he joined Earl Browder, secretary of the Communist Party of America during the 1930s, on the campaign trail, giving speeches and writing stories for the *Daily Worker,* throughout the fall of 1936. *In the American Jungle* (1937), a collection of his essays from the 1920s and early 1930s, appeared the following year as a testament to Frank's increasing politicization during the depression. Only in the spring of 1937 did Frank's deeper divergence from communism become evident, and then at first in the form of a tepid letter to the *New Republic* dissenting from the party's view of the Moscow trials. That initial split grew more permanent, as Browder and other American and Spanish Communists who had once solicited Frank's aid now denounced him as a "Trotskyite" and effectively excommunicated him from the movement.

Unlike many other former fellow-travelers, Frank never became a vocal anti-Communist or a conservative. If anything, his experience with communism confirmed his sense of the rightness of his own idiosyncratic radicalism, which now became both more religious and more populist. In the late 1930s and 1940s, Frank drew close to thinkers like Lewis Mumford, Reinhold Niebuhr, and Jacques Maritain, who condemned modern liberalism and Marxism for their positivist disregard for human values and argued that a new anticapitalist politics must recover the insights into human nature formerly provided by traditional religious theology. In 1940 Frank joined Mumford in resigning from the editorial board of the *New Republic* in protest of that magazine's refusal to endorse aid to Britain in the war against Hitler. Very much like Mumford's writing from this period, Frank's 1940 tract, *Chart for Rough Water,* argued that " 'orthodox' Marxism and liberalism are reactionary" in their contempt for ethical and spiritual values. Frank summed up the overriding theme of his life's work to date, insisting that "we can have no adequate politics, no adequate aesthetics, no adequate ethics in our time without an adequate metaphysic and religion" rooted in the "Great Tradition" of Western civilization. Frank, Mumford, and Niebuhr briefly considered starting a new journal, along with novelist Richard Wright, to expound their vision of a new radicalism, but the project collapsed once Frank refused to assume the duties of editor. In his memoirs Frank regretted that decision, which might have been his last opportunity to create an audience for his ideal of "organic" community.

With *Chart for Rough Water* behind him, Frank now entered the cultural limbo that became his tragic fate as an intellectual. Too radical for his apolitical or conservative countrymen, too religious for liberals and radicals, and ultimately too strong-willed a personality for most people who had personal contact with him, Frank slipped into a mood of despair and isolation that lasted until his death. His personal life became increasingly difficult. Frank's marriage to Alma Magoon disintegrated, and he married his secretary, Jean Klempner, in 1943. Meanwhile he began to fade from Americans' attention. Only in Latin America did he retain a significant audience. For over six months in 1942 he lectured throughout Latin America as an unofficial representative of the American government, denouncing Nazism and appealing for support for his vision of a joint New World culture. In August of that year, the Argentine government declared him persona non grata, and government supporters savagely beat him in his Buenos Aires hotel room. Frank published his lectures in *Ustedes y Nosotros: Nuevo Mensaje a Ibero-América* (1942) the same year, and in 1943 his *South American Journey* appeared as a record of the trip. The book was the first of a series of moderately successful works that seemed only to reiterate the arguments of Frank's earlier books. *The Jew in Our Day* (1944) collected some of Frank's essays defending prophetic Judaism and Jewish distinctiveness from the ethnic and religious assimilation that Frank had long criticized in America's Jewish community. The book was more notable for Niebuhr's introduction, which took issue with Frank's mysticism, than for Frank's own writings. In 1948 the Venezuelan government commissioned Frank to write a study of Simón Bolívar, which appeared three years later as *Birth of a World: Bolívar in Terms of His Peoples* (1951). Those familiar with Frank's earlier work would have found little surprising in Frank's praise for Bolívar's idea of a new culture uniting the northern and southern peoples of the Western hemisphere. The same might be said of Frank's 1957 *Bridgehead: The Drama of Israel*, which attracted attention mostly for Frank's forthright criticism of Israelis' hostility toward their nation's original Arab population. Only *The Rediscovery of Man* (1958) marked a further elaboration of Frank's thinking about the recovery of spiritual wholeness. But this work appeared in a vacuum, as Frank had virtually lost his entire American audience. Readers who knew nothing of his earlier

work would have found this book difficult at best. Frank's increasing fascination with Eastern religion and with obscure therapies of physiological and psychological training too often got in the way of this conclusion to his lifelong plea for a new ethos of community and spiritual wholeness.

Surprisingly it was Frank's last work of cultural criticism, *Cuba: Prophetic Island* (1961), that won him greater attention at the end of his life. A visit to Cuba in fall 1959 left him impressed with Castro's revolution, which he interpreted as a vindication of his calls for a Latin "integral socialism." Castro's early distance from the Cuban Communist party, his support among the Cuban peasantry, and his personal charisma all appealed to Frank's long-held sympathies for a prophetic populism. When Castro's government offered him a contract to write a book about the revolution, Frank agreed on the condition that he have complete independence to express his own views. Frank returned briefly to politics in this period, temporarily assuming the chair of the Fair Play for Cuba Committee in 1960 and speaking out against the American government's policy against Cuba. All the while, however, he grew more skeptical about Castro, who now seemed to have forsaken Frank's brand of radical populism for orthodox Marxism. As tensions increased between Cuba and the United States in 1960-1961, Frank found himself in a tenuous position. Beacon Press broke its contract with him to publish his book, citing Frank's acceptance of a stipend from the Cuban government. The book finally appeared in 1961 and attracted some favorable attention, but its critical endorsement of the Cuban revolution's early goals was lost in the publicity about Frank's relation to Castro. In 1962 the House Committee on Un-American Activities questioned Frank about his involvement with Castro, dredging up quotations from his writings in the 1930s as "evidence" of his pro-Communist sympathies. A year later Frank testified before the Senate's Internal Security Committee on the same issue. Nonetheless the aging Frank was an obscure remnant of an earlier era in American intellectual life. While his friend Lewis Mumford experienced a resurgence of popular interest in his work in the 1960s, Frank's very similar critiques of modern industrial life were long out of print and largely forgotten. He spent his last years before his death on 9 January 1967 working on his memoirs, which were posthumously published in 1973. There Frank compared himself to Don Quixote, the lonely and ridiculed dreamer whose failure had haunted so many of Frank's writings.

Frank's cultural criticism still enjoys none of the same interest that attends that of Bourne, Brooks, and Mumford. These friends and colleagues of Frank's shared his vision of a new post-industrial community and of a democratic culture grounded in an "organic" ethos of mutuality. But they never followed Frank's path into mysticism, nor did they give religious experience the centrality it assumed in Frank's conception of cultural renewal.

**References:**

Daniel Aaron, *Writers on the Left: Episodes in American Literary Communism* (New York: Harcourt, Brace & World, 1961);

William Bitner, *The Novels of Waldo Frank* (Philadelphia: University of Pennsylvania Press, 1958);

Casey Blake, "Aesthetic Engineering," *democracy*, 1 (October 1981): 37-50;

Blake, "Beloved Community: The Cultural Criticism of Randolph Bourne, Van Wyck Brooks, Waldo Frank, and Lewis Mumford," Ph.D. dissertation, University of Rochester, 1987;

Van Wyck Brooks, *An Autobiography* (New York: Dutton, 1965);

Paul J. Carter, *Waldo Frank* (New York: Twayne, 1967);

Arnold Chapman, "Waldo Frank in Spanish America: Between Journeys, 1924-1929," *Hispania*, 47 (September 1964): 510-521;

Chapman, "Waldo Frank in the Hispanic World: The First Phase," *Hispania*, 44 (December 1961): 626-634;

Richard W. Fox, *Reinhold Niebuhr: A Biography* (New York: Pantheon, 1985);

Frederick J. Hoffman, *Freudianism and the Literary Mind* (New York: Grove Press, 1959);

Jerome W. Kloucek, "Waldo Frank: The Ground of his Mind and Art," Ph.D. dissertation, Northwestern University, 1958;

Lewis Mumford, Introduction to *Memoirs of Waldo Frank*, edited by Alan Trachtenberg (Amherst: University of Massachusetts Press, 1973), pp. xv-xxix;

Gorham Munson, *The Awakening Twenties: A Memoir-History of a Literary Period* (Baton Rouge: Louisiana State University Press, 1985);

Munson, *Waldo Frank: A Study* (New York: Boni & Liveright, 1923);

Helge N. Nilsen, "The Status of Waldo Frank in American Letters," *American Studies in Scandinavia*, 12 (1980): 27-32;

Nilsen, "Waldo Frank and the Idea of America," *American Studies International*, 17 (Spring 1979): 27-36;

Michael A. Ogorzaly, "Waldo Frank: A Prophet of Hispanic Regeneration," Ph.D. dissertation, University of Notre Dame, 1982;

Paul Rosenfeld, *Men Seen* (New York: Dial, 1925);

Claire Sacks, "The Seven Arts Critics: A Study of Cultural Nationalism in America, 1910-1930," Ph.D. dissertation, University of Wisconsin, 1955;

Alan Trachtenberg, Editor's Preface to *Memoirs of Waldo Frank*, edited by Trachtenberg (Amherst: University of Massachusetts Press, 1973), pp. vii-xiv;

Arthur F. Wertheim, *The New York Little Renaissance: Iconoclasm, Modernism, and Nationalism in American Culture, 1908-1917* (New York: New York University Press, 1976);

John R. Willingham, "The Achievement of Waldo Frank," *Literary Review*, 1 (Summer 1958): 465-477;

Edmund Wilson, *Letters on Literature and Politics, 1912-1972*, edited by Elena Wilson (New York: Farrar, Straus & Giroux, 1977).

**Papers:**

Frank's personal notebooks, letters received by him, manuscripts of published and unpublished material, and other papers relating to Frank are located in the Rare Book Room at the Van Pelt Library of the University of Pennsylvania among the Waldo Frank Papers, the Van Wyck Brooks Papers, and the Lewis Mumford Papers. Other collections with Frank material are the Sherwood Anderson Papers, Newberry Library, Chicago, and the Alfred Stieglitz Papers, Beinecke Rare Book and Manuscript Library, Yale University.

# Joseph Wood Krutch

*(25 November 1893-22 May 1970)*

Barnett Guttenberg
*University of Miami*

BOOKS: *Comedy and Conscience after the Restoration* (New York: Columbia University Press, 1924; revised edition, 1949);

*Edgar Allan Poe: A Study in Genius* (New York & London: Knopf, 1926);

*The Modern Temper: A Study and a Confession* (New York: Harcourt, Brace, 1929; London: Cape, 1930);

*Five Masters: A Study in the Mutations of the Novel* (New York: Cape & Smith, 1930; London: Cape, 1931);

*Experience and Art: Some Aspects of the Aesthetics of Literature* (New York: Smith & Haas, 1932);

*Was Europe a Success?* (New York: Farrar & Rinehart, 1934; London: Methuen, 1935);

*The American Drama Since 1918. An Informal History* (New York: Random House, 1939; revised edition, New York: Braziller, 1957; London: Thames & Hudson, 1957);

*Samuel Johnson* (New York: Holt, 1944; London: Cassell, 1948);

*Henry David Thoreau* (New York: Sloane, 1948; London: Methuen, 1952);

*The Twelve Seasons* (New York: Sloane, 1949);

*The Desert Year* (New York: Sloane, 1952);

*The Best of Two Worlds* (New York: Sloane, 1953);

*"Modernism" in Modern Drama: A Definition and an Estimate* (Ithaca: Cornell University Press, 1953);

*The Measure of Man: On Freedom, Human Values, Survival, and the Modern Temper* (Indianapolis: Bobbs-Merrill, 1954; London: Redman, 1956);

*Is the Common Man Too Common? An Informal Survey of Our Cultural Resources and What We Are Doing about Them*, by Krutch et al. (Norman: University of Oklahoma Press, 1954);

*The Voice of the Desert: A Naturalist's Interpretation* (New York: Sloane, 1955);

*The Great Chain of Life* (Boston: Houghton Mifflin, 1956; London: Eyre & Spottiswoode, 1957);

*Grand Canyon: Today and All Its Yesterdays* (New York: Sloane, 1958);

*Human Nature and the Human Condition* (New York: Random House, 1959);

*The Forgotten Peninsula: A Naturalist in Baja California* (New York: Sloane, 1961);

*More Lives than One* (New York: Sloane, 1962);

*If You Don't Mind My Saying So . . . Essays on Man and Nature* (New York: Sloane, 1964);

*Herbal* (New York: Putnam's, 1965);

*And Even If You Do: Essays on Man, Manners, and Machines* (New York: Morrow, 1967);

*Baja California and the Geography of Hope* (San Francisco: Sierra Club, 1967);

*The Best Nature Writing of Joseph Wood Krutch* (New York: Morrow, 1969);

*The Most Wonderful Animals that Never Were* (Boston: Houghton Mifflin, 1969);

*A Krutch Omnibus: Forty Years of Social and Literary Criticism*, selected and edited by Krutch (New York: Morrow, 1970).

OTHER: *The Comedies of William Congreve*, edited, with an introduction, by Krutch (New York: Macmillan, 1927);

*Nine Plays by Eugene O'Neill*, introduction by Krutch (New York: Liveright, 1932);

Marcel Proust, *Swann's Way*, translated by C. K. Scott Moncrieff, introduction by Krutch (New York: Random House, 1934);

*Great American Nature Writing*, edited, with introduction, by Krutch (New York: Sloane, 1950);

*The Gardener's World*, edited by Krutch (New York: Putnam's, 1959);

*The World of Animals: A Treasury of Lore, Legend, and Literature by Great Writers and Naturalists from Fifth Century BC to Present*, compiled by Krutch (New York: Simon & Schuster, 1961);

Henry David Thoreau, *Walden and Other Writings*, edited, with an introduction, by Krutch (New York: Bantam, 1962);

*A Treasury of Birdlore*, edited by Krutch and Paul S. Eriksson (Garden City: Doubleday, 1962);

*Eighteenth Century English Drama*, edited, with an introduction, by Krutch (New York: Bantam, 1967).

The career of Joseph Wood Krutch is remarkable for its variety of achievement. In his early years he became highly visible as a New York drama critic writing for the *Nation*. In the last decades of his life he gained a new reputation as a naturalist. In the course of his career he wrote critical biographies of Edgar Allan Poe, Samuel Johnson, and Henry David Thoreau which remain secure in their respective critical canons. His greatest achievement, however, was his social criticism, in particular *The Modern Temper: A Study and a Confession* (1929), an attempt to assess the darker undercurrents of the 1920s. Bertrand Russell found *The Modern Temper* "profoundly interesting and penetrating," while Granville Hicks called it "one of the crucial documents of this generation." For his later reassessment of *The Modern Temper*, entitled *The Measure of Man: On Freedom, Human Values, Survival, and the Modern Temper* (1954), Krutch received the National Book Award.

Krutch was born in Knoxville, Tennessee, in 1893, the youngest of three brothers. His mother, Adelaid, was the daughter of Joseph Wood, an English tanner who had immigrated to America and married a Grey of Scotch descent. They moved to Knoxville in order, as Krutch suspected, to employ slave labor in his tannery. Krutch's father, Edward Waldermore Krutch, was the son of a North German musician named Krutzsch.

For influences shaping his early life Krutch points in his autobiography entitled *More Lives Than One* (1962) to his father's family. Krutch's paternal grandmother, whose maiden name was Von Wiersing, contributed to his development her interest in animals and plants. Her children, other than Krutch's father, whose interests rarely extended beyond his business, provided the example of mild nonconformity. Krutch remarks that he was especially influenced by his uncle Charles, a portrait photographer and avocational painter, who spent a month each summer in the Great Smoky Mountains, returning with sketches for landscape paintings. Krutch notes that members of his father's family were among the few mild bohemians accepted and even respected in early-twentieth-century Knoxville; he credits them with helping to keep him from conforming more fully to the pattern of Knoxville life.

Krutch described the Knoxville of his youth as a country town relatively free of contemporary pressures, tensions, and anxieties and, less happily, as a world which, in his words, "was thoroughly provincial and lacked stimulation as well as excitement." He remarked that his childhood was altogether ordinary; he remembered himself as a shy and unaggressive adolescent, a "good student" who disliked school. One of his major interests was drama. He attended the Knoxville theater regularly: first, as an unpaid "correspondent" for a minor Atlanta publication, the *Footlight*, and later, when a stock company was established in Knoxville, as unofficial assistant to its unpaid press representative, his brother Charlie. His second major interest was film. Krutch recalled attending one or another of Knoxville's four picture theaters almost daily. His interest in film would evaporate by the end of his college years, but his interest in theater foreshadowed his career as drama critic.

In 1911 Krutch entered the University of Tennessee, the only one of the three brothers to attend. Fred, Krutch's oldest brother, was already the family ne'er-do-well, and Charlie, "an ideal big brother," had withdrawn from school in ill health. Krutch found the university "sleepily conventional," its faculty evenly divided between genuine scholars and old fogies. "I already assumed," he stated, "that I would be a teacher of something or other because I did not know how else one with my lack of interest in the practical applications of anything could make a living." By his junior year he was a mathematics major, but several literature courses with one of the English department's genuine scholars, James Douglas Bruce, and a galvanizing encounter with George Bernard Shaw's *Man and Superman,* (1903) together with Krutch's recognition of his mathematical limitations, resulted in a conversion to literature. He edited the campus literary magazine and gained a minor reputation as an iconoclast; an editorial attacking Prohibition was considered offensive enough to gain him an audience with his dean.

Having graduated with honors, in the fall of 1915 Krutch began graduate work in English literature at Columbia University. There he formed an enduring friendship with fellow-student Mark Van Doren and made rapid progress within the graduate program. In the fall of 1917, master's degree in hand and course work for the doctorate completed, he became an instructor of freshman English at Columbia. Toward the end of the year he enlisted in the army and served in the psychological branch of the medical corps in a military career which was, in his words, "as uneventful and inglorious as possible." At war's end he returned to Columbia to study for his doctoral exams, passed them the same year, and won a traveling fellowship which took him to England to work on his doctoral thesis.

Krutch's thesis subject was Jeremy Collier's book entitled *A Short View of the Immorality and Profaneness of the English Stage* (1698), which denounced the cynicism and obscenity of the Restoration theater. Collier's book drew unexpected support, and, within a few years, the Restoration comic tradition was supplanted, at least temporarily, by a drama of sentimental moralizing. Krutch's thesis, *Comedy and Conscience after the Restoration* (1924), deals with the transformation and the contradictions underlying the shift in the English theater during that period. Although the study makes no pretense of unearthing new materials and shows little of the verve that would characterize his later writings, it was solid enough to be published and to go through several reprintings.

Having completed his doctorate in 1921, Krutch received his first full-time teaching appointment, met Marcelle Leguia, whom he married in 1924, and launched his career as an essayist and reviewer. He was appointed associate professor at Brooklyn Polytechnic Institute, where he and his chairman were the only members of the English department and where he taught a heavy schedule of courses, most of them in composition. He began his career as an essayist under the auspices of Mark Van Doren's brother Carl, the literary editor of the *Nation*, who asked Krutch to contribute occasional reviews of fiction and then a regular review on alternate weeks. His reviews met with continuing approval, and in 1924 he succeeded Ludwig Lewisohn as drama critic of the *Nation*. He resigned from Brooklyn Polytechnic and, save for part-time appearances at Vassar College, Columbia University, and the New School, remained outside the academic world until 1937, when he received an appointment as professor in the English department of Columbia University.

As drama critic and later as editor, Krutch became a spokesman for the pre-Modernists in their attempt to break with Victorian standards. These "young intellectuals," as they were termed, considered values such as duty and self-sacrifice to be repressive, life-denying, and ultimately hypocritical; in what seemed to them a revolutionary campaign for liberation, candor, and self-fulfillment, they promoted the writings of Sigmund Freud, Henrik Ibsen, Friedrich Nietzsche,

George Bernard Shaw, Oscar Wilde, and others who presented themselves, or could be presented, as figures of revolt. In his drama columns Krutch championed the rising young playwright Eugene O'Neill; contributing to the *Nation*'s highly publicized series entitled "Our Changing Morals," he faulted "our changing morals" only for changing too slowly.

In 1926, as a correspondent for the *Nation*, Krutch attended the Scopes trial in Dayton, Tennessee, some fifty miles from Knoxville. In strict legal terms the issue involved in the trial was simple. John Scopes, a high school biology teacher, had violated a state law which prohibited teaching the theory of evolution in Tennessee schools. Scopes's defense, however, led by Clarence Darrow, succeeded in turning the trial into a confrontation between the past in the form of fundamentalism and the present in the form of evolutionary theory. Although the trial ended with the anticipated conviction of John Scopes, in the larger confrontation the forces of fundamentalism, led by William Jennings Bryan, were routed. The present seemed victorious, and Krutch shared in the triumph of reason and enlightenment; he sent three dispatches to the *Nation*, the first of them entitled "Tennessee: Where Cowards Rule."

For the next step in his literary career, Krutch was again indebted to the Van Dorens. When publisher Alfred A. Knopf asked Carl Van Doren if he could recommend someone to prepare a critical biography of Edgar Allan Poe, Van Doren recommended Krutch, who had previously expressed an interest in Poe. In *Edgar Allan Poe: A Study in Genius* (1926), Krutch again allied himself firmly with the cultural vanguard of "young intellectuals," in this case by using the relatively new and controversial psychoanalytic approach.

Relying heavily on Freud, Krutch maintained that one could understand the art only by understanding the artist; in his analysis of Poe, he defined a widening gap between lofty self-image and mundane circumstances. Krutch argued that the affluence of Poe's foster home led him into aristocratic pretensions even as he was forced to confront the colder reality of rejection by his foster father. That rejection climaxed with John Allan's refusal to formalize Poe's adoption and so make Poe his legal heir. The two had an open break which apparently ended Poe's expectations. Krutch maintained that the rejection, surprisingly, did not destroy Poe's pretensions but

*Joseph Wood Krutch outside his home in Redding, Connecticut, in the 1930s (courtesy of Mrs. Joseph Wood Krutch)*

instead separated them from reality. Symptoms of the resulting split psyche, according to Krutch, were Poe's feelings of inferiority, sexual impotence, and, perhaps most significant for Poe's writings, a fear of the irrational.

Krutch's analysis of Poe has proven durable. The hypothesis of a split psyche helps to explain the remarkable division of Poe's writings into works of reason (detective stories, criticism) and works of terror (a majority of the stories); the hypothesized fear of the irrational provides a connection between the two seemingly disparate bodies of work. Krutch's analysis also illuminates certain puzzling motifs, such as that of unconsummated union with the child bride, a motif which figures in Poe's life as well as in his art.

The study, however, does not seem the work of a fully mature scholar. There is palpable strain in the attempt to make biographical evidence support the thesis of a split psyche. As Krutch himself would later acknowledge, the study depends at times simplistically on the ideas of Freud and his follower Mortimer Adler. And finally, Krutch did not seem to realize that he had been anticipated in some of his views by J. W.

Robertson's *Edgar Allan Poe: A Psychopathic Study* (1922).

In the years immediately following the Poe study Krutch experienced numerous doubts concerning the revolt against Victorian standards. He articulated these doubts in *The Modern Temper: A Study and a Confession*. He began his discussion with an organic definition of culture; that is, an individual culture ripens inexorably from greenness through fruition to decay. It reaches the decadence of its maturity in coming to the grim realization, largely through scientific advances, that the natural and human worlds are antithetical, that the human context is an elaborate fabrication.

Two of the chapters exploring this realization have been widely reprinted. "Love—or the Life and Death of a Value" maintains that modern human sexuality, stripped of its cloak of artifice, loses all allure; deprived of the electricity of sin, the aura of mystery, and even the spirit of playfulness, sexuality becomes mere biological function. "The Tragic Fallacy" also argues that the self-awareness of decadence entails large-scale loss. When man, in the ripeness of decay, recognizes his pretensions, he loses the grandeur of the tragic vision, which depends on a sense of heroic possibility.

According to the view presented in *The Modern Temper*, the fall that accompanies such self-knowledge holds no possibility of salvation. To retreat into nature involves an unthinkable sacrifice of humanity, while to cling to human structures, the only possible choice, is to move ever farther from the living world in which these structures are insuperably alien. The book concludes:

> Our human world may have no existence outside of our own desires, but those are more imperious than anything else we know, and we will cling to our own lost cause, choosing always to know rather than to be.... If death for us and our kind is the inevitable result of our stubbornness then we can only say, "So be it." Ours is a lost cause and there is no place for us in the natural universe, but we are not, for all that, sorry to be human. We should rather die as men than live as animals.

With *The Modern Temper*, Krutch had clearly undergone a profound change of heart, shifting from an optimistic hope for the future to despair over the human condition. Earlier, as one of the "young intellectuals," he had welcomed the disintegration of the old order; now he regarded its passing with a sense of loss. Man had attained a measure of freedom from prejudice and puritanism, but without honor, justice, and other such man-made virtues, freedom seemed synonymous with chaos. Krutch's diagnosis of the modern condition was not altogether new, but it was argued with a clarity and incisiveness that made it immediately popular; it is still very possibly the best single introduction to the dark undercurrents of the Jazz Age then under exploration by such writers as T. S. Eliot, William Faulkner, F. Scott Fitzgerald, and Ernest Hemingway.

Krutch followed *The Modern Temper* with two works of literary criticism which together develop the positive implications of a chapter in *The Modern Temper* entitled "Life, Art, and Peace." The two books—*Five Masters* (1930) and *Experience and Art* (1932)—suggest that even in an empty universe a limited affirmation is possible if artists will assume their proper roles. Although all ideals, as he had argued in *The Modern Temper*, are fictions, they are necessary in that they enable men to achieve their humanity. In their search for such guiding fictions, men consciously or unconsciously depend on the artist. It is the artist's responsibility, Krutch contended, implicitly condemning many writers of his era, to provide worthy fictions, to make available the "as ifs" by which people can in their turn create structures of self and even of society. Krutch ranges widely in his search for model artists; his "five masters" are Boccaccio, Cervantes, Richardson, Stendhal, and Proust.

Six months after the publication of *The Modern Temper* the stock market collapsed, bringing to an end, among other things, Krutch's brief vogue as an important new thinker. In the face of economic disaster, the stage was given over to the ostensibly more practical concerns of political science, sociology, and economics. Krutch's two books, with their artistic and philosophical concerns, received slight attention.

In the 1930s Krutch found himself increasingly out of step with many of his liberal colleagues and contemporaries in their Marxist enthusiasms; he resigned his editorial duties at the *Nation*, retaining only his post as drama critic. The redirection of his thought was made fully apparent in his next book, *Was Europe a Success?* (1934). In the section "Communism and the Old Pagan" Krutch registers his dismay at discovering that the values he had shared with colleagues and contemporaries had been largely supplanted

by Communist ideology, while intellectual tolerance and skepticism, hallmarks of enlightenment, had succumbed to blind faith in the Marxist vision of historical inevitability with its Utopian promise of triumph for the proletariat. In the section "Jam Tomorrow" he remarks acidly on the willingness of these ideologues to justify any means to that end, to endorse all forms of Communist brutality as necessary preludes to that promised land which he considered pie in the sky, the tempting and illusory reward of "jam tomorrow."

In the title essay, "Was Europe a Success?," Krutch shows himself not only resisting the intellectual current of the era but embracing the very past whose bankruptcy he had previously analyzed. Now he contended that European civilization, whatever its shortcomings, had indeed been a success; it had fostered spiritual values and produced unrivaled achievements in science, philosophy, and art. Championing these achievements, the iconoclast of the 1920s found himself, to his own bemusement, in accord with apologists for the past whom he had previously condemned while regarded by former friends as turncoat and reactionary.

Krutch's disaffection helps to explain the shortcomings of *The American Drama Since 1918* (1939), perhaps his weakest book despite the fact that he seemed uniquely qualified to write it. But Krutch was clearly out of tune with such writers as Elmer Rice and Clifford Odets, whose plays he found lacking in moral and spiritual values. Thus, in discussing the dramatization of Erskine Caldwell's *Tobacco Road* (1932), he likens Caldwell to Ernest Hemingway and William Faulkner: "Like the latter he loves to contemplate the crimes and perversions of degenerate rustics; like both, his peculiar effects are made possible only by the assumption of an exaggerated detachment from all the ordinary prejudices of either morality or taste."

Krutch next turned back to the eighteenth century for the more congenial subject of Samuel Johnson. The critical biography *Samuel Johnson* (1944) is Krutch's most scholarly work, drawing on large amounts of background material, including *Thraliana* by Mrs. Thrale (Hester Lynch), which was published for the first time in its entirety two years before. The study reflects the clarity so characteristic of Krutch's work, while avoiding the psychoanalytic excesses which had marred his work on Poe. The study was received as definitive and has been superseded—most recently by Walter Jackson Bate's study—largely because more information about Johnson's life, and especially the pre-Boswell years, has become available. Even so, it might be argued that Krutch's study remains the best single introduction to Johnson's life and art.

Krutch's choice of Johnson as subject may seem to imply deepening Tory sympathies, but Krutch's view of Johnson is larger than the choice might suggest. Krutch's Johnson is not simply the product of an Augustan circle of privilege, of aristocratic customs and manners. Nor is he simply the product of the wider circle defined by defects of birth, health, and appearance, a circle of moral sobriety and humane sympathies. In Krutch's view Johnson moves freely between these two circles, and yet, taken either separately or together, they cannot circumscribe Johnson's identity. Krutch's Johnson, entering the charmed circle and outplaying its members at their own aristocratic game, remains supremely conscious of the game as game and consciously constructs his identity as both insider and outsider.

Through his portrait of Johnson, Krutch contests the view, increasingly prevalent among many of his contemporaries and particularly Marxist critics, that man is mere cultural artifact, the product of his milieu. Krutch's Johnson, standing in a complex relationship to his age, is man refusing to disappear: an exemplar of irreducible individualism. Krutch's concern with such individualism, perhaps reflecting his sense of himself vis-à-vis his own age, helps to explain his startling shift in subjects at this juncture, from Samuel Johnson to Henry David Thoreau.

In his critical biography *Henry David Thoreau* (1948), Krutch announces the central theme of individualism early: "Thoreau's principal achievement was not the creation of a system but the creation of himself, and his principal work was, therefore, the presentation of that self in the form of a self-portrait." Krutch's Thoreau, though swayed by such forces as Puritanism, Transcendentalism, and pantheism, remains firm in his pursuit of some higher vision of selfhood; even his role as social reformer is rooted not in any ideology but in uncompromising individualism. Finding in Thoreau's views numerous contradictions, Krutch judges them a strength, attesting to the conviction that "it was possible for a man to resist 'forces,' to refuse to be a 'product.'"

With the Thoreau study, Krutch's interests shifted increasingly toward the world of nature. In 1952 he gave up his position as drama critic for the *Nation,* together with the professorship

which he had held at Columbia University since 1937, and took up permanent residence in Tucson, Arizona, where, in a series of popular essays, he explored the natural world and man's relationship to it. His developing sense of that relationship as one of harmony rather than antithesis would lead him to a radical revision of his social views.

After a series of lectures at Cornell, published as *"Modernism" in Modern Drama: A Definition and an Estimate* (1953), discussing the spiritual aridity of modern drama beginning with Henrik Ibsen, Krutch reexamined the views which he had presented in *The Modern Temper.* In *The Measure of Man* (1954) he reaffirms his earlier diagnosis; modern man, he states, has come to believe that the natural and the human worlds are antithetical, that all the standards and convictions of Western culture are delusions, and that man stands alone on the edge of the existential abyss. At this juncture, however, Krutch repudiates his earlier view and contends that these beliefs, though widely accepted, are erroneous and unjustified; the problem lies in the inadequacy of modern man's beliefs rather than in the inadequacy of the universe.

In *The Measure of Man*, in his later social criticism, and in all of his naturalist essays, Krutch argues that man is a part of nature, and his values, however alien they may seem, cannot be other than natural. As he reasserts in his autobiography, "Our minds like our bodies must have 'evolved'; and to evolve means to grow as part of a continuity, not to be discontinuous with our origins." Or again, "If matter can . . . cease to be matter and become energy, why should it not also become thought?" Consciousness, then, is part of the natural world, which seeks not just to survive but "to realize more completely the potentialities of protoplasm." Man is the creature possessing moral and spiritual capabilities, capabilities of reason and choice. Whatever hope the future holds, Krutch concluded, lies in recognizing and nurturing those capabilities.

Throughout the reign of the New Criticism, Krutch continued to view literature as part of a larger human context; he would have been undismayed to find that his cultural criticism promises to be his most lasting achievement. He emerges from it as a representative figure of the age. Enlightened and humane, he embarks on a spiritual journey through the brokenness of the modern age, at first exhilarated with the possibilities of renewal, then distraught with the sense of dislocation, and finally, driven by his dismay, triumphant through the discovery of healing certitudes which he hoped would benefit mankind. He would be somewhat disappointed to learn that, despite the seeming sanction of a National Book Award, his certitudes have proven less compelling than the doubts he articulated. His reputation continues to rest on *The Modern Temper*, which promises to remain one of the crucial documents of an era.

**Bibliography:**

Anthony L. Lehman, "Joseph Wood Krutch: A Selected Annotated Bibliography of Primary Sources," *Bulletin of Bibliography*, 41 ( June 1984): 74-80.

**References:**

Gordon C. Green, "An Analytic Study of the Dramatic Criticism of Joseph Wood Krutch as published in *The Nation*, 1924-1952," Ph.D. dissertation, University of Southern California, 1959;

Joseph G. Green, "Joseph Wood Krutch, Critic of the Drama," Ph.D. dissertation, Indiana University, 1965;

Anthony L. Lehman, "Joseph Wood Krutch: A Personal Reminiscence," *Quarterly Newsletter*, 37 (1972): 51-63;

John D. Margolis, *Joseph Wood Krutch: A Writer's Life* (Knoxville: University of Tennessee Press, 1980);

Margolis, "Joseph Wood Krutch: A Writer's Passage beyond the Modern Temper," in *Romantic and Modern: Revaluations of Literary Tradition*, edited by George Bornstein (Pittsburgh: University of Pittsburgh Press, 1977), pp. 223-240;

Paul N. Pavich, "Joseph Wood Krutch: Persistent Champion of Man and Nature," *Western American Literature*, 13 (August 1978): 151-158;

Peter Gregg Slater, "The Negative Secularism of *The Modern Temper:* Joseph Wood Krutch," *American Quarterly*, 33 (Summer 1981): 185-205.

# F. O. Matthiessen

*(19 February 1902-31 March 1950)*

Donald E. Pease
*Dartmouth College*

SELECTED BOOKS: *Sarah Orne Jewett* (Boston & New York: Houghton Mifflin, 1929);

*Translation: An Elizabethan Art* (Cambridge: Harvard University Press, 1931; London: Oxford University Press, 1931);

*The Achievement of T. S. Eliot: An Essay on the Nature of Poetry* (Boston & New York: Houghton Mifflin, 1935; London: Oxford University Press, H. Milford, 1935; revised and enlarged, New York: Oxford University Press, 1947);

*American Renaissance: Art and Expression in the Age of Emerson and Whitman* (London & New York: Oxford University Press, 1941);

*Henry James: The Major Phase* (London & New York: Oxford University Press, 1944);

*Russell Cheney, 1881-1945: A Record of His Work* (New York: Oxford University Press, 1947);

*The James Family; Including Selections from the Writings of Henry James, Senior, William, Henry, and Alice James* (New York: Knopf, 1947);

*From the Heart of Europe* (New York: Oxford University Press, 1948);

*Theodore Dreiser* (New York: William Sloane Associates, 1951; London: Methuen, 1951);

*The Responsibilities of the Critic: Essays and Reviews by F. O. Matthiessen*, selected by John Rackliffe (New York: Oxford University Press, 1952).

OTHER: "James Fenimore Cooper, Class of 1806: Novelist and Critic," "Alphonso Taft, Class of 1873: Lawyer and Statesman," "Oliver Wolcott, Class of 1778: Secretary of the Treasury in Washington's Cabinet," in *The Memorial Quadrangle: A Book about Yale*, compiled by Robert Dudley French (New Haven: Yale University Press, 1929; London: Oxford University Press, 1929), pp. 162-171, 306-310, 362-366;

"New England Stories," in *American Writers on American Literature*, edited by John Macy (New York: Liveright, 1931), pp. 399-413;

"Sarah Orne Jewett," in *Dictionary of American Biography*, volume 10 (New York: Scribners, 1933), pp. 70-72;

"Hart Crane," in *Dictionary of American Biography*, volume 21, supplement 1 (New York: Scribners, 1944), pp. 206-298;

Henry James, *Stories of Writers and Artists*, edited, with an introduction, by Matthiessen (New York: New Directions, 1944);

"The Ambassadors," in *The Question of Henry James, A Collection of Critical Essays*, edited by F. W. Dupee (New York: Holt, 1945), pp. 218-235;

"That True and Human World," in *Accent Anthology, Selections from Accent, 1940-1945: A Quarterly of New Literature*, edited by Kerker Quinn and Charles Shattuck (New York: Harcourt, Brace, 1946), pp. 619-623;

*The American Novels and Stories of Henry James*, edited, with an introduction, by Matthiessen (New York: Knopf, 1947);

*The Notebooks of Henry James*, edited by Matthiessen and Kenneth B. Murdock (New York: Oxford University Press, 1947);

"Edgar Allan Poe," "Poetry," in *Literary History of the United States*, edited by Robert E. Spiller et al. (New York: Macmillan, 1948), pp. 321-342, 1335-1357;

"On Hawthorne's *Young Goodman Brown*," "On Whitman's *When Lilacs Last in the Dooryard Bloom'd*," excerpts from *American Renaissance*, in *Readings for Liberal Education*, edited by Louis G. Locke, William M. Gibson, and George Arms (New York: Rinehart, 1948), II: 495-496, 543-547;

"An Opinion," in Charles Norman's *The Case of Ezra Pound* (New York: Bodley Press, 1948), pp. 57-69;

"The Sense of His Own Age," excerpt from *The Achievement of T. S. Eliot*, in *T. S. Eliot: A Selected Critique*, edited by Leonard Unger (New York: Rinehart, 1948), pp. 221-235;

"Emerson, Thoreau, Melville, and Whitman: Their Challenge to Writers Today," in *Speak-*

*ing of Peace,* edited by Daniel S. Gillmor (New York: National Council of the Arts, Sciences & Professions, 1949), pp. 78-79;

Marshall Schacht, *Fingerboard: Poems,* introduction by Matthiessen (New York: Twayne, 1949);

"The Pattern of Literature," in *Changing Patterns in American Civilization,* edited by Dixon Wecter (Philadelphia: University of Pennsylvania Press, 1949), pp. 33-57;

*The Oxford Book of American Verse,* compiled, with an introduction, by Matthiessen (New York: Oxford University Press, 1950).

PERIODICAL PUBLICATIONS: "[Four reports on life at Oxford] by F. O. Matthiessen, 1923 Oxford Rhodes Scholar," *Yale News,* 47 (6 November 1923); (4 December 1923); (22 January 1924); (19 February 1924);

"Michael Wigglesworth: A Puritan Artist," *New England Quarterly,* 1 (October 1928): 491-504;

"The Great Tradition, A Counter-statement," *New England Quarterly,* 7 (June 1934): 223-234;

"The New Mexican Workers' Case," *New Republic,* 82 (8 May 1935): 361-363;

"For an Unwritten Chapter," *Harvard Advocate,* 125 (September 1938): 22-24;

"A Year of the Kenyon Review," *American Oxonian,* 27 (April 1940): 83-85;

"A Teacher Takes His Stand," *Harvard Progressive* (September 1940): 12-14;

Statement on Wallace Stevens, *Harvard Advocate,* 127 (1940): 31;

"The Crooked Road," *Southern Review,* 7 (Winter 1941): 455-470;

"Eliot's Quartets," *Kenyon Review,* 5 (Spring 1943): 161-178;

"No More Colleges for the Duration," *Bridge of Eta Kappa Nu,* 40 (November 1943): 2;

"The Humanities in Wartime," *1943 Harvard Album* (Spring 1943): 33-37;

"James and the Plastic Arts," *Kenyon Review,* 5 (Winter 1943): 533-550;

"Higher Education after the War: A Symposium," by Matthiessen, O. O. Carmichael, Virgil M. Hancher, and John W. Nason, *American Oxonian,* 31 (April 1944): 75-78;

"Henry James' Portrait of the Artist," *Partisan Review,* 11 (Winter 1944): 71-87;

"The Painter's Sponge and Varnish Bottle: Henry James' Revision of *The Portrait of a Lady,*" *American Bookman,* 1 (Spring 1944): 49-68;

"Harvard Wants to Join America," *New Republic,* 113 (20 August 1945): 220-221;

"The Problem of the Private Poet," *Kenyon Review,* 7 (Autumn 1945): 584-597;

Statement, *Yale Literary Magazine,* 112 (Spring 1946): 18;

"Poe," *Sewanee Review,* 54 (Summer 1946): 175-205;

"American Poetry, 1920-1940," *Sewanee Review,* 55 (Spring 1947): 24-55;

"John Crowe Ransom," *The Wind and The Rain,* 5, no. 3 (1948-1949): 172-177; republished as "Primarily Language," in "Homage to John Crowe Ransom . . . in honor of his Sixtieth Birthday," *Sewanee Review,* 56 (Fall 1948): 391-401;

"To the Memory of [Howard] Phelps Putnam, 1894-1948," *Kenyon Review,* 11 (Winter 1949): 61-82;

"The Responsibilities of the Critic," *Michigan Alumnus Quarterly,* 55 (Fall 1949): 283-292;

"Needed: Organic Connection of Theory and Practice," *Monthly Review,* 2 (May 1950): 11;

"Theodore Spencer, 1902-1949," *Contemporary Poetry,* 10 (Spring 1950): 36-38.

The scholarship already accumulated on the subject of F. O. Matthiessen may be larger than that on any other American scholar born in the twentieth century. As the collective reminiscences published in the *Monthly Review* shortly after his suicide in 1950 attest, this attention is largely the result of the remarkable authority Matthiessen exercised in his various cultural duties as scholar, critic, political activist, and professor of literature at Harvard University. Matthiessen's collected work, comprising nine books, five anthologies, and over 150 essays, articles, and reviews, covers a vast range of topics. But all his topics were related either directly or tangentially to Matthiessen's lifelong task of forging a tradition of American literature which could be used as a cultural and political resource. The continued importance of his major book, *American Renaissance: Art and Expression in the Age of Emerson and Whitman* (1941), testifies to the success of his project, which helped to elevate American literature into an academic subject worthy of the attention of the best minds. It also marked a departure from the approaches of previous historians of American literature, such as Vernon L. Parrington and Van Wyck Brooks, whose economic and social interpretations were often crude, tendentious, or both. As Richard Ruland writes in *The Rediscovery of American Literature* (1967), "In 1904 the first volume of Paul Elmore More's *Shelburne Essays* announced the intention to create a truly American criticism, while the publication in 1938 of *Understanding Poetry*, the Brooks and Warren textbook which soon came to dominate the teaching of literature, made the eventual triumph of formalist criticism certain. In 1941, however, while New Criticism was still gaining momentum, F. O. Matthiessen's *American Renaissance* signalled the very assimilation of the new techniques to earlier aims which had characterized the most fruitful work of our day." Largely due to this book's influence on the post-Matthiessen generation of scholars, American literature and American studies have become respectable academic disciplines.

Matthiessen's interest in establishing a definitive canon for American literature arose from his belief in the cultural and political significance of literature. Knowledge of the cultural significance of American literature depended, Matthiessen maintained, upon knowledge of the American culture, its past as well as its future. The ideal critic, he wrote in *The Responsibilities of the Critic* (1952), had to move from the text "out to an awareness of some of the world-wide struggles of our age. . . . Judgment of art is both an aesthetic and a social act, and the critic's sense of social responsibility gives him a deeper thirst for meaning."

Born in Pasadena, California, in 1902, the son of Frederic William and Lucy Orne Matthiessen, Francis Otto Matthiessen grew up near LaSalle, Illinois. Matthiessen was the youngest of four children; his brothers were Frederic William III and Dwight George, and his sister was Lucy Orne. Matthiessen corresponded with them all throughout his life and was a generous uncle to his nieces. His parents divorced when he was thirteen. In a letter written in 1925 Matthiessen reflects, "I long ago accustomed myself to an empty space where my father should have been. But it reminds me of what my mother must have suffered for so long." Matthiessen was partially reconciled with his father in 1947. His mother died in 1925 while he was a student at Oxford. After he attended the Polytechnic School in Pasadena Matthiessen completed his secondary education at the Hackley School, a small preparatory school of little prestige, in Tarrytown, New York, and entered Yale University in 1919, where in addition to the excellent education he received in English Matthiessen also formed his political opinions and developed lifelong religious convictions. He served concomitant vice presidencies of

the Yale Liberal Club and the university religious society. When he went on to Oxford University in 1923 as a Rhodes Scholar, he joined the Oxford Labour Club. After writing a thesis on Oliver Goldsmith, he received his Bachelor of Letters degree in 1925 and began graduate study at Harvard, receiving his M.A. in 1926. At Yale and Harvard, Matthiessen was deeply influenced by such literary scholars as John Livingston Lowes, Chauncey B. Tinker, George Lyman Kittredge, and Irving Babbitt. In 1927, after completing his thesis, *Translation: An Elizabethan Art* (1931), he received his Ph.D. and went to Yale as an instructor. Returning to Harvard after two years at Yale, Matthiessen became head tutor at Eliot House and, later, chairman of the board of Tutors in History and Literature, the tutorial program that had interested him in Harvard in the first place. While serving as chairman, he and several associates formed an interdepartmental committee in American civilization which included Howard Mumford Jones, Kenneth Murdoch, Bernard De Voto, and Ralph Barton Perry. The club began accepting candidates in 1937. During his early years of teaching at Harvard, Matthiessen began his lifelong relationship with the painter Russell Cheney. In 1927 they purchased a house in Kittery Point, Maine, which would be their home until Cheney's death in 1945. Throughout their extraordinary friendship, Matthiessen was obsessed with the fear of Cheney's death. Cheney's bouts of drunkenness deepened these fears. In 1938, following one of Cheney's drinking bouts, Matthiessen experienced a depression so severe that he admitted himself to McLean Hospital, where he stayed from 26 December 1938 to 13 January 1939. Cheney's death led to sporadic recurrences of these depressions that finally resulted in Matthiessen's suicide. Seven months before he died he wrote, on 13 August 1949, to Louis Hyde of "the problems of living alone for one who has known love and companionship. There is no real solution that I can expect for that kind of incompletion."

Matthiessen lived a complex, intensely committed life. His attitudes toward literature, which grew out of his involvement with disparate aspects of American culture, were no less complex. Writing in the particularly turbulent years after World War II, Matthiessen developed what afterwards seemed contradictory allegiances to Christianity, socialism, art, and criticism. He believed all these different forms of expression, which played such important roles in his personal life,

*Louis Hyde, Matthiessen's Yale classmate and friend, Penelope Overton Hyde, and Matthiessen at Savin Rock, a Connecticut amusement park, in spring 1923*

were equally necessary to the health and vitality of the culture. Before he could translate these otherwise merely personal interests into the greater life of the society, however, Matthiessen needed what American culture had not yet provided: a sense of the nation's shared tradition. Matthiessen dedicated the remaining twenty-four years of his life as a critic to establishing and transmitting a vital tradition for American culture.

Matthiessen's graduate thesis on Elizabethan translation prepared him well for his life's work. In this study Matthiessen demonstrated the ways in which Elizabethan writers adapted foreign classics to their nation's specific cultural needs. He was drawn to this topic as much for the Elizabethan translators' commitment to enrich the life of their country as for their artistic achievements. Unlike present-day translators of the classics, they did not write for other scholars but for the entire nation. In bringing the classics to life, these translators inevitably also brought England's past into view as a necessary cultural backdrop. In this way they made "the foreign classics rich with English associations" and ushered writers such as Plu-

tarch and Montaigne "deep into the national consciousness."

Writing *Translation: An Elizabethan Art* made Matthiessen aware of the responsibility to the cultural past that a critic shared with a translator. He believed both were entrusted with the duty to uncover the intellectual assumptions of past epochs and then to transmit their core ideas. The resulting sense of the past could, Matthiessen says in *The Responsibilities of the Critic*, "connect us with the great traditions and inspire us with the confidence and power which result from such a connection."

The desire to take possession of a "usable past" was not a project peculiar to Matthiessen but a collective enterprise to which Vernon L. Parrington, Stuart Sherman, Lewis Mumford, H. L. Mencken, Constance Rourke, Victor F. Calverton, Granville Hicks, Perry Miller, and Van Wyck Brooks contributed significant works. While Matthiessen never lost sight of the shared nature of this goal, he was also aware of the tendency to develop an uncritical consensus inherent in any collective project. To ward off the danger of a monolithic literary history of the United States he combined his own critical and scholarly pursuits with reviews of the work of his contemporaries, thereby making clear the different critical and historical perspectives in these various works. He could be severely critical when a scholar overlooked complex historical conditions for the sake of corroborating an already existing consensus and could be equally severe with either belletristic trifling or ideological special pleading. He faulted Parrington for using literature to illustrate socioeconomic forces and the New Critics for turning literature into a puzzle to be solved.

In discerning the shortcomings in such disparate approaches to literature and culture, Matthiessen did not intend to dismiss them. He wanted very much to write a criticism able to yoke together conflicting, often contradictory attitudes. In pursuing this synthesis, Matthiessen on occasion used his scholarship to develop a cultural attitude in conflict with his own assumptions. In writing *Sarah Orne Jewett* (1929), for example, Matthiessen indulged the same temptation that he found Van Wyck Brooks succumbing to in his work: the urge to escape present difficulty through a nostalgic return to a rosy past. Matthiessen's study of Jewett depends throughout upon such timeworn and predictable conventions of literary pastoral as the rural haven and the cultivated garden as defenses against the industrial world. The sentimentality produced by this celebration of the pristine virtues of the rural Maine township leads him into a past of so little use to his present situation that it results in contradictions of deeply held moral and political convictions. The distortion of Matthiessen's belief in egalitarianism becomes evident in a passage where, in order to underscore the value of Jewett's private garden, he complains bitterly about the arrival of Irish immigrants whose "rows of drab rickety houses . . . growing like mushrooms" deface Jewett's rural landscape. In later works it would be industrialism's leveling of factory society that would appall Matthiessen, but here it is the Irish workers' offensiveness to Jewett's private sensibility that provokes him.

In turning away from this unusable past, Matthiessen did not develop an alternative to meet the needs of contemporary politics, as had V. F. Calverton in *The Liberation of American Literature* (1932) and Granville Hicks in *The Great Tradition* (1934). In writing *The Achievement of T. S. Eliot: An Essay on the Nature of Poetry* (1935) Matthiessen experienced the value of an opposed purpose: the analysis of an artist's ability to realize the values of his present age. Like Matthiessen, Eliot was aware of the dangers of the present age to any possibility for a truly integrated self. Eliot's notion of the "dissociated sensibility" proved a valuable construct in Matthiessen's critical agenda. In reflecting on the contradictory elements which Eliot had unified in his character, Matthiessen became aware of a need to resolve the political and artistic contradictions in his own character.

Eliot's theory of literature seemed designed to overcome a dissociation Matthiessen believed symptomatic of the modern sensibility. By arguing that an individual work is in unity with the tradition as well as its own form, Eliot maintained that poetry could restore the wholeness his age lacked. Unlike Van Wyck Brooks or Calverton or Hicks, Eliot did not believe that poetry was a reflection of history but that it was a historical force able to give shape to an age. Since for Matthiessen Eliot's poetry provided his age with an enabling perspective, Matthiessen had to do something other than supply an explanatory historical context, as he had in his previous works. In articulating Eliot's achievement Matthiessen acknowledged the limitations in the historicist approach. He used Eliot's poetry "to emphasize certain of the fundamental elements in the nature of poetry which are in danger of being ob-

scured by the increasing tendency to treat poetry as a social document and to forget that it is an art." To effect this emphasis Matthiessen learned the techniques of the criticism he found outlined in I. A. Richards's *The Principles of Literary Criticism* (1925). This method, giving close attention to both the structure and the texture of language, became instrumental in leading a revolt against the historicists' exclusive concentration on the past.

Unlike other practitioners of the New Criticism, Matthiessen did not deny value to historicism. In Matthiessen's use of it, the New Criticism became a needed supplement to historicism. Historicism, in its concentration on the cultural value of the past, led to a diminished sense of the value in the present. The New Criticism, by insisting on a work's transcendence of history, sanctioned the reader's power to translate any work from the past into contemporary terms. Whereas historicism promoted the value of the historical past at the expense of the present age, the New Criticism redressed the temporal balance between past and present. What resulted from Matthiessen's use of the New Criticism was a renewed sense of the inherent value of the present age. Eliot's poetry assembled a body of work worthy to inherit the finest achievements from the cultural past.

Whereas Matthiessen's book on Jewett effected a disconnection of the past from the present, his work on Eliot restored a vital connection. In Eliot's poetry Matthiessen found an epic project that consolidated the finest work from the past and the highest aspirations of Matthiessen's generation.

Despite the value of the New Criticism, Matthiessen never lost sight of its limitations. He deployed it with an eye to its tactical rather than systematic value and was always alert to the risk it posed of turning the means of analysis into an end in itself. That risk made a different kind of temporal discontinuity possible: not of the past from the present, but of the present age from the cultural past. In *The Achievement of T. S. Eliot* Matthiessen occasionally paid such careful attention to the present age—how the age made possible the man who made the poetry, and how the poetry's way of making up its own past did away with chronology altogether—that the present age almost lost its moorings in the cultural past. In claiming the writer's power to reorganize the culture's past, Eliot came close to claiming a different power for literature. To the critic of

"Tradition and the Individual Talent" a work of literature was greater than the sum of the historical forces that had shaped it. As an expression of the power to renew those influences and continue their life in the present, a literary work could claim the power to supersede the past altogether.

From 1935 to 1941 Matthiessen worked on *American Renaissance,* a book he hoped would simplify the conflicting impulses in his previous work and bring America's past into vital connection with the present. On one level his interest in the project was academic. He later complained in *From the Heart of Europe* (1948) that "no school went at all imaginatively into the American past." But Matthiessen's reasons for writing *American Renaissance* lay deeper than courses missing from his university curriculum. The years in which he conceived and drafted *American Renaissance* were the years preceding America's entrance into World War II. In turning to the classic texts from America's past Matthiessen came into possession of what his age needed most vitally: a valuable cultural heritage threatened by totalitarian powers. By assimilating values from works of the nation's past into the present course of its history, Matthiessen hoped to put a living heritage into service in defense of democratic values. True scholarship, Matthiessen claimed in the conclusion to the opening essay of *American Renaissance,* must prove that it "has been applied for the good and enlightenment of all the people, not for the pampering of a class. . . . In a democracy there can be but one fundamental test of citizenship, namely: Are you using such gifts as you possess for or against the People."

In the years before World War II more was at stake than the dissociation of Matthiessen's individual sensibility from his culture's past or present. Nazi totalitarianism threatened forcibly to dissever the relationship of democratic values to Western culture. To meet this threat Matthiessen put *American Renaissance* into the service of the political consensus more commonly referred to as the Popular (or People's) Front. In response to Hitler's growing power, the Popular Front emphasized a policy of alliance building rather than dissent. The Popular Front of the 1930s was strongly associated with the turn of many American writers toward Marxism, including Waldo Frank, Lionel Trilling, Kenneth Burke, Langston Hughes, James T. Farrell, and Malcolm Cowley. Many front organizations were in fact Communist party organs, while others were staffed and supported by liberals or democratic socialists. The consensus binding these heterogeneous groups was their disillusionment with capitalism in the wake of the Depression and their perception that Stalin's Russia was an ally against the rise of fascism. The Front collapsed after the defeat of the Loyalist forces in Spain, the revelations of the Stalinist purges at the Moscow trials, and the Hitler-Stalin pact of 1939.

Acting in accordance with the alliance politics of the Popular Front, Matthiessen, in *American Renaissance,* assembled the masterworks from the nation's past that the American people needed in their war against fascism. In assembling these masterworks Matthiessen eliminated any discussion of their political complications. He disconnected the masterworks of the *American Renaissance* from the dissension-filled context of pre-Civil War America. In so doing, he silenced the potentially disruptive political opinions of Ralph Waldo Emerson, Henry David Thoreau, Herman Melville, Walt Whitman, and Nathaniel Hawthorne, as well as the complex political positions of the prominent politicians and orators who comprised the political context of pre-Civil War America. When he did discuss political context, as in his chapter on Hawthorne, Matthiessen subordinated it to the cultural consensus of United States politics.

In the name of constructing a united cultural front for his age, Matthiessen thereby did what he claimed no responsible critic should do—he dissociated America's classic writers from their defining cultural contexts and relocated them within the cultural and political milieu he designed in writing the *American Renaissance.* Once it was authorized as the definitive political context for their work, *American Renaissance* did not remain connected to the actual secular history of these writers but symbolized their rebirth out of it. Independent of the time kept by secular history, the American renaissance kept a form of abstract global time—a sacred time the classics of American literature could claim when these "renaissance" works stood alongside the classics from the British or German or Italian Renaissance. Barrett Wendell, in fact, had likewise called the period a "New England Renaissance" in his aesthetically oriented *A Literary History of America* (1900). In establishing a renaissance for America's literature Matthiessen produced the cultural capital America needed to take its place as a great nation among other great nations of the world, and he redesignated this cultural capital he produced as the cultural heritage America needed to defend against totalitarian powers.

When the United States assumed the position of a world power in 1941, Matthiessen's *American Renaissance* sanctioned America's claim to be a great nation, though not without cultural expense. In place of analyzing the relationship between writers' works and their historical time, Matthiessen divides his writers into two groups. The group comprising the optimistic strain in American culture–including Emerson, Thoreau, and Whitman–is juxtaposed to Hawthorne and Melville, whose works reaffirm the tragic sense. Thus in *American Renaissance* Matthiessen does not heal the dissociated sensibility he believed represented the modern epoch; instead, he turns that dissociation into the structuring principle of the book. He also echoes Parrington's division of American thought into two currents, liberal and conservative, though these are now more dehistoricized by Matthiessen's symbolic and psychological vocabulary.

In redefining this dissociation in terms of the opposition between Emerson's optimism and Melville's pessimism, Matthiessen acknowledged a crucial problem in the cultural consensus he was forging. Should the tragic dimension in Melville's work have prevailed over the optimism in Emerson's, the result could have been a loss of morale. Matthiessen met this threat, too, in his structuring of *American Renaissance*, rather than in any argument conducted within it. Instead of placing Whitman where he logically belonged, in the same context as the other Transcendentalists, Matthiessen placed his discussion of Whitman after his discussion of Melville. When so positioned, the Whitman chapter marked a return to the optimistic principles that Melville had tragically lost the ability to believe. Whitman served Matthiessen as a structural link connecting Melville's despair with Emerson's hope for American culture. But this linkage, insofar as it remains answerable to the needs of Matthiessen's present consensus rather than actual historical circumstances, was a merely formal one. Whitman had, in fact, never addressed the tragic sensibility at work in Melville's work. Nor had he ever entertained a tragic sense of American culture. Consequently when Matthiessen forcibly links Whitman's vision to Melville's, their relationship appears as schematic as it in fact is. "We may stay closest to the pressures of the age," Matthiessen explains, "as its creative imagination responds to them by going from the transcendental affirma-

tion to its counterstatement by the tragic writers and by then perceiving how Whitman rode through the post-Civil War years undisturbed by such deep and bitter truths as Melville had found."

The "creative imagination" invoked in this passage performs cultural labors for Matthiessen similar to those performed by the more inclusive term "American Renaissance." The "creative imagination" disconnects Whitman from the political questions with which he in fact struggled, the divisive issues of slavery and expansionism, and replaces these issues with a more rarefied yet more enduring purely literary conflict: the struggle between an optimistic and a tragic sense of existence. (The same tendency informs Lionel Trilling's essays on Parrington and American literary history in the *Partisan Review* in 1940.) This opposition formed the basis for much of the dramatic conflict in British Renaissance drama. When Matthiessen transposed the context from English Renaissance drama onto the writings produced in post-Jacksonian America, he consolidated the disparate cultural forces at work in that period into the consensus he redefines as the "American Renaissance."

Having transposed American renaissance writers into this controlled setting, Matthiessen could more easily resolve the pressures demanding response in his own time. In confining the complex political issues addressed by these writers to the opposition between an optimistic and a tragic sense of life, he did not avoid but delayed addressing other more demanding cultural questions, such as socialism and class relations. In the years just before and during World War II Matthiessen considered it his responsibility as a critic to elevate the values of his society. In *American Renaissance* and his other book published during World War II, *Henry James: The Major Phase* (1944), Matthiessen's literary activity became a pretext for bolstering the nation's morale rather than criticizing its shortcomings. He nonetheless took the opportunity in 1944 to rebuke the nationalism informing Van Wyck Brooks's *The World of Washington Irving* (1944), warning against any "complacent and fatuous dream of 'the American Century.' "

In tracing the interrelationship between James's life and his art, Matthiessen supplied what he called his "overaged contribution to the war effort." In Matthiessen's reading of James's major works, the "creative imagination" was indistinguishable from an inspiriting social force, work-

*Matthiessen on Memorial Day, 1948*

ing for the culture's preservation. At the time he wrote his book, the Jamesian form of "freedom of consciousness" was a cultural principle very much in need of preservation. In Matthiessen's view, this positive freedom constituted the core of James's moral vision. James's characters "always fell into their positions on his scale according to their degree of awareness: the good character was the one who was most sensitive, who saw the greatest variety of moral possibilities, and who wanted to give them free play in others. The bad character was obtuse or willfully blind to such possibilities." In part, too, Matthiessen was attracted to James because his status as a permanent expatriate seemed an appropriate moral allegory for the Americans who during the war served in the European campaign. Moreover, like the soldiers who actually went abroad to fight, most other Americans became symbolic expatriates, and they too "felt a great need, during the unrelenting outwardness of those years, for his kind of inwardness, for his kind of order as a bulwark against disorder."

In the years after the war, the questions he could not address in his two contributions to the war effort returned to him with renewed urgency. What stood out most clearly in the years following the war was the spectacle of Matthiessen's fellow critics hastily shifting their allegiance from the radical positions they held before the war to an attenuated form of neoliberalism after the war. In a way the consensus Matthiessen helped forge was responsible for this shift in political allegiances. For in the years after World War II that alliance built by the Popular Front turned into the peace-keeping structure known as the cold war.

During the war Matthiessen freely chose to eliminate from consideration all political questions other than the opposition between freedom and totalitarianism. His books on Henry James and the writers of the American renaissance replaced political issues with purely artistic concerns, thus reversing the direction of Parrington and Van Wyck Brooks in their rebellion against Wendell and the genteel tradition of aesthetic criticism. What he kept out of his consciousness in writing these works was, like repressed material from his personal unconscious, bound to return in the years of the war. For instead of engaging the greatest variety of moral possibilities, the critical persona responsible for these war efforts forcibly silenced dissenting and radical views.

After the war Matthiessen traveled to Europe in the hope that his reflections on America "from the heart of Europe" might restore the political dimension to his work. In restoring that dimension Matthiessen changed the meaning of one of his two key terms in *American Renaissance*. In the earlier work he was strategic in his use of the term "tragedy." On the one hand it was an instrumental term, helpful in constructing the "renaissance" space where he could discuss nineteenth-century writers in purely aesthetic terms. On the other hand it was a descriptive term designating the nature of Melville's and Hawthorne's attitude toward the world in general. When he used "tragedy" as a descriptive term in *American Renaissance* Matthiessen was careful to circumscribe its power. After he asserts that "Tragedy does not pose the situation of a faultless individual (or class) overwhelmed by an evil world, for it is built on the experienced realization that man is radically imperfect," he makes a crucial qualification. "Confronting this fact, tragedy must also contain a recognition that man, pitiful as he may be in his finite weakness, is also capable of apprehending perfection, and of being transfigured by that vision." In the course of these two sentences the optimist's vision of perfection almost overwhelms the experience of tragic imperfection. But in *From the Heart of Europe*, "tragedy" redresses this imbalance. Here Matthiessen relegated the belief in the perfectibility of man to shallow psychology. Man cannot become perfect because the source of his imperfection inheres in the external world: "with evil wholly external to his nature, and caused only by the frustrations of the capitalist system," man can do little more than acknowledge the cause of evil. In the postwar years Matthiessen lost his wartime optimism. He refused to accept any easy answer to the human condition, whether provided by progressive liberalism, unreflective socialism, or his own earlier alliance politics.

The execution of the Rosenbergs, the beginnings of what was to become atomic diplomacy abroad and cold war politics at home, the Eisenhower administration's commitment to normalcy, and the death of Russell Cheney in 1945 contributed to Matthiessen's increased isolation from his former political allies and friends. Moreover, though he maintained his deep beliefs in both Christianity and socialism, these only added to the isolation Matthiessen felt, as the note he left when he jumped from the window of his room in the Manger Hotel on 31 March 1950 indicates: "How much the state of the world has to do with my state of mind I do not know. But as a Christian and a socialist believing in international peace, I find myself terribly oppressed by the pres-

ent situation." That year Lionel Trilling published *The Liberal Imagination*, a collection which pronounced the death of political optimism and embraced a philosophy of tragic realism.

In the years just after World War II, Matthiessen had tried to remedy what he found wrong with the positions he felt compelled to adopt during the war by returning to the socialist position he had left out of it. In his books on Henry James and the American renaissance writers, he celebrated the political and artistic achievements of the American nation. For the sake of the nation's morale he did not criticize America's political shortcomings or indicate the limitation in her writers' visions. In *From the Heart of Europe* he intended to balance the unreflective nationalism and false optimism in those works by adding a critical assessment of American life. He indicated what was missing from American life and letters in a controversial passage in which he identified the Russian Revolution as the realization of the American Revolution: "What gives the central drive to my desire to find a political position to correspond to my philosophy is that, unlike most Christian Socialists, I accept the Russian Revolution as the most progressive event of our century, the necessary successor to the French Revolution and the American Revolution and to England's seventeenth-century Civil War."

In this passage Matthiessen hoped to identify his postwar writings with the work of European writers and artists, like Sean O'Casey and Pablo Picasso, who wanted to affirm their adherence to international solidarity by identifying their cause with the Communists'. In aligning his critical project with a worldwide socialist movement, Matthiessen hoped to break down the barriers of nationalism and to work for equity between Americans and other peoples of the world.

Although he wrote these words before Gottwald's Communist party took over Czechoslovakia or Stalin attacked Yugoslavia, they were published at about the time of these events. Related events, like Tito's purge trials, which resulted in the execution of leading European Communists, and Stalin's "reign of terror," would soon lessen Matthiessen's faith in Russian communism. But by expressing these sentiments in 1948, Matthiessen was numbered among the "enemies within" cold war America. Anonymous telephone calls in the middle of the night, opposition from the Harvard administration, unfavorable newspaper notices, and resentment and hostility from fellow academics became part of his daily life. And while other factors certainly contributed to his suicide, Barrows Dunham's view that "when Professor Matthiessen died, the Cold War made its first martyr among American scholars" cannot be discounted altogether.

The irony involved in this depreciation of Matthiessen's character should not be overlooked. Late in *American Renaissance,* while tracing Whitman's efforts to achieve the perfectibility of mankind, Matthiessen pointed up an unwanted by-product of these efforts. The drive toward perfectibility, so innocent in Emerson and so confused in Whitman, was to result, Matthiessen claimed, in Nietzsche's Superman and his Will to Power. But when that same drive to perfectibility "was again transformed, or rather brutally distorted, the voice of Hitler's megalomania was to be heard sounding through it." If in 1941 Hitler represented the totalitarian will resonating in Emerson's prose, by 1948 many Americans heard echoes of Hitler's megalomania in Socialist and Communist rhetoric. When Matthiessen adopted this rhetoric in *From the Heart of Europe,* he became identified with a version of the totalitarianism he wrote *American Renaissance* to oppose.

Matthiessen's official position was actually much more complicated than his opponents would allow. He articulated its complications in the new introduction he wrote for the T. S. Eliot book, published before *From the Heart of Europe* in 1947: "My own views of the poet have inevitably undergone some changes. . . . My growing divergence from his view of life is that I believe it is possible to accept the 'radical imperfection' of man and yet to be a political radical as well, to be aware that no human society can be perfect and yet to hold that the proposition that 'all men are created equal' demands adherence from a Christian no less than from a democrat." Here the political radical and the Christian in Matthiessen appear in the same sentence, but the terms used to bring them together, "radical imperfection" and egalitarianism, do not conjoin them so much as introduce other, unresolved distinctions. The Christian has a duty to realize the principle of equality, the political radical a duty to strive for perfectibility. Matthiessen did not claim these two political programs were compatible with one another. The limitations inherent in each position led Matthiessen to need the other. It was as a Christian aware of the evil inherent in man's nature that he was attracted to a socialism dedicated to eliminating political inequality.

When he looked for an example of Christian socialism in America's past, Matthiessen returned to the figure he used to resolve the contradictions in his prewar political stance. In *American Renaissance,* Walt Whitman's sense of infinite fraternity forges a link strong enough to join two writers with views as opposed as Emerson's were to Melville's. In *From the Heart of Europe* Whitman appears once again, here to conjoin the otherwise incompatible quests for equality and perfectibility into solidarity. Whitman did so "through taking part in the common life, mingling in its hopes and failures, and helping to reach a more adequate realization of its aims, not for one alone, but for the community." But after the war the cold war consensus *American Renaissance* helped form repressed this cultural use of Whitman.

While in Europe, Matthiessen found an example of the community he hoped for when in 1944 he taught a group of students from many European countries in the Salzburg Seminar in Austria. When he addressed the participants, he once again used a precedent from *American Renaissance:* "Here was our Brook Farm, here was our ideal communistic experiment, where each–to borrow the words of a man who went further than Fourier–gave according to his abilities, and received according to his needs." But on his return home Matthiessen was unable to find any American correlative for his Brook Farm in Salzburg. His critics turned his optimism into a target for their ridicule.

From 1948 until his death Matthiessen was forced to live out the terms of what he called the tragic sense of life. The critic who insisted on opposing the optimistic to the tragic sense of life could no longer find any justification for his optimism. Separated from any community he believed himself called to represent, Matthiessen felt more isolated than ever, and reflections on his personal isolation increasingly became the subject of his criticism. At the same time as he wrote about isolation, Matthiessen was convinced that criticism written in isolation faced the danger of becoming insulated from authentic responsibility. He hoped to convince his audience "that the land beyond the garden's walls is more fertile, and that the responsibilities of the critic lie in making renewed contact with that soil." But his audience would not let him move beyond those walls.

In response, Matthiessen cultivated his own garden. He expressed his isolation in terms of conflicting allegiances in his own rather than the nation's character—to a socialism tragically disconnected from practical action, and an aesthetic sense dissociated from his own personality. No longer able to exploit these contradictions in his character by turning them into antithetical attitudes of his whole self, Matthiessen could only experience them as painful and irresolvable tensions.

In his final project, a book on Theodore Dreiser published after his death, Matthiessen found a subject enabling him to come to terms with the tragedy his own life had become. Unlike the vision of tragedy at work in *American Renaissance*, Dreiser's was a tragic vision disconnected from any alternative. "Dreiser has not shaped a tragedy in any of the traditional uses of the term, and yet he has written out of a profoundly tragic sense of man's fate. He has made us hear, with more and more cumulative power, the 'disastrous beatings' of the Furies' wings."

In choosing Dreiser as a subject, Matthiessen found the closest twentieth-century approximation of Walt Whitman. Like Whitman, Dreiser had an almost mystical belief in cosmic wholeness. Unlike Whitman, however, Dreiser did not believe in a purposive universe. In Dreiser's writings the two principles—the optimistic and the tragic—that Whitman united merely collapsed into one another. Dreiser's tragic vision, his belief in the dark and savage forces beyond any individual control, simply subsumed all other social forces.

Without any principle capable of transforming man's "radical imperfection," Dreiser's work described a society that had lost its moorings. While writing his book on Dreiser, Matthiessen was able to articulate the implications of this loss for a critic like himself who was deeply committed to the improvement of his culture. Having begun his work with the intention of discovering an American past of enduring value for his present age, Matthiessen ended his career with a vision of a culture uninformed by any enabling purpose whatever. And he left it to the generation of his students to realize the high and noble purposes for American life and letters he envisioned.

**Letters:**

*Rat & the Devil: Journal Letters of F. O. Matthiessen and Russell Cheney,* edited by Louis Hyde (Hamden, Conn.: Archon, 1978).

**References:**

Jonathan Arac, "F. O. Matthiessen: Authorizing an American Renaissance," in *The American Renaissance Reconsidered. Selected Papers from the English Institute, 1982-83,* edited by Walter Benn Michaels and Donald E. Pease (Baltimore: Johns Hopkins University Press, 1985), pp. 90-112;

Giles B. Gunn, *F. O. Matthiessen: The Critical Achievement* (Seattle: University of Washington Press, 1975);

Richard Ruland, "F. O. Matthiessen, Christian Socialist: Literature and the Repossession of Our Cultural Past," in *The Rediscovery of American Literature: Premises of Critical Taste, 1900-1940* (Cambridge: Harvard University Press, 1967), pp. 209-273;

Frederick C. Stern, *F. O. Matthiessen: Christian Socialist as Critic* (Chapel Hill: University of North Carolina Press, 1981);

Paul M. Sweezy and Leo Huberman, eds., *F. O. Matthiessen, 1902-1950: A Collective Portrait* (New York: Schuman, 1950).

# H. L. Mencken

*(12 September 1880-29 January 1956)*

## William H. Nolte
*University of South Carolina*

See also the Mencken entries in *DLB 11, American Humorists, 1800-1950,* and *DLB 29, American Newspaper Journalists, 1926-1950.*

BOOKS: *Ventures into Verse* (Baltimore: Marshall, Beck & Gordon, 1903);

*George Bernard Shaw: His Plays* (Boston & London: Luce, 1905);

*The Philosophy of Friedrich Nietzsche* (Boston: Luce, 1908; London: Unwin, 1908);

*Men versus the Man: A Correspondence between Robert Rives La Monte, Socialist, and H. L. Mencken, Individualist* (New York: Holt, 1910);

*The Artist, a Drama Without Words* (Boston: Luce, 1912);

*Europe After 8:15,* by Mencken, George Jean Nathan, and Willard Huntington Wright (New York: John Lane, 1914);

*A Book of Burlesques* (New York: John Lane, 1916; revised edition, New York: Knopf, 1920; London: Cape, 1923);

*A Little Book in C Major* (New York: John Lane, 1916);

*A Book of Prefaces* (New York: Knopf, 1917; London: Cape, 1922);

*Pistols for Two,* by Mencken and Nathan, as Owen Hatteras (New York: Knopf, 1917);

*Damn! A Book of Calumny* (New York: Philip Goodwin, 1918); republished as *A Book of Calumny* (New York: Knopf, 1918);

*In Defense of Women* (New York: Philip Goodwin, 1918; revised edition, New York: Knopf, 1922; London: Cape, 1923);

*The American Language: A Preliminary Inquiry into the Development of English in the United States* (New York: Knopf, 1919; revised and enlarged edition, 1921; London: Cape, 1922; revised and enlarged edition, 1923; corrected, enlarged, and rewritten, New York: Knopf, 1936; London: Paul, 1936); *Supplement I* (New York: Knopf, 1945); *Supplement II* (New York: Knopf, 1948);

*Prejudices: First Series* (New York: Knopf, 1919; London: Cape, 1921);

*Heliogabalus: A Buffoonery in Three Acts,* by Mencken and Nathan (New York: Knopf, 1920);

*Prejudices: Second Series* (New York: Knopf, 1920; London: Cape, 1921);

*Prejudices: Third Series* (New York: Knopf, 1922; London: Cape, 1923);

*Prejudices: Fourth Series* (New York: Knopf, 1924; London: Cape, 1925);

*Prejudices* (London: Cape, 1925); republished as *Selected Prejudices* (London: Cape, 1926);

*Notes on Democracy* (New York: Knopf, 1926; London: Cape, 1927);

*Prejudices: Fifth Series* (New York: Knopf, 1926; London: Cape, 1927);

*Prejudices: Sixth Series* (New York: Knopf, 1927; London: Cape, 1928);

*James Branch Cabell* (New York: McBride, 1927);

*Selected Prejudices* (New York: Knopf, 1927);

*Treatise on the Gods* (New York & London: Knopf, 1930; revised edition, New York: Knopf, 1946);

*Making a President: A Footnote to the Saga of Democracy* (New York: Knopf, 1932);

*Treatise on Right and Wrong* (New York: Knopf, 1934; London: Paul, 1934);

*The Sunpapers of Baltimore, 1837-1937,* by Mencken, Gerald W. Johnson, Frank R. Kent, and Hamilton Owens (New York: Knopf, 1937);

*Happy Days, 1880-1892* (New York: Knopf, 1940; London: Paul, Trench & Trubner, 1940);

*Newspaper Days, 1899-1906* (New York: Knopf, 1941; London: Paul, 1942);

*Heathen Days, 1890-1936* (New York: Knopf, 1943);

*Christmas Story* (New York: Knopf, 1946);

*The Days of H. L. Mencken: Happy Days. Newspaper Days. Heathen Days.* (New York: Knopf, 1947);

*A Mencken Chrestomathy* (New York: Knopf, 1949);

*The Vintage Mencken,* edited by Alistair Cooke (New York: Vintage, 1955);

*A Carnival of Buncombe,* edited by Malcolm Moos (Baltimore: Johns Hopkins Press/London: Oxford University Press, 1956);

*Minority Report: H. L. Mencken's Notebooks* (New York: Knopf, 1956);

*The Bathtub Hoax, and Other Blasts & Bravos from the Chicago Tribune,* edited by Robert McHugh (New York: Knopf, 1958);

*Prejudices, a Selection,* edited, with an introduction, by James T. Farrell (New York: Vintage, 1958);

*H. L. Mencken on Music,* edited by Louis Cheslock (New York: Knopf, 1961);

*H. L. Mencken: The American Scene, a Reader,* edited by Huntington Cairns (New York: Knopf, 1965);

*H. L. Mencken's Smart Set Criticism,* edited by William H. Nolte (Ithaca, N.Y.: Cornell University Press, 1968);

*The Young Mencken: The Best of His Work,* edited by Carl Bode (New York: Dial, 1973);

*A Gang of Pecksniffs, and Other Comments on Newspaper Publishers, Editors and Reporters,* edited by Theo Lippman, Jr. (New Rochelle, N.Y.: Arlington House, 1975);

*Mencken's Last Campaign: H. L. Mencken on the 1948 Election,* edited by Joseph C. Goulden (Washington, D.C.: New Republic Book Co., 1976);

*A Choice of Days: Essays from* Happy Days, Newspaper Days, *and* Heathen Days, edited by Edward L. Galligan (New York: Knopf, 1980).

OTHER: Henrik Ibsen, *A Doll's House,* edited, with an introduction, by Mencken (Boston & London: Luce, 1909);

Ibsen, *Little Eyolf,* edited, with an introduction, by Mencken (Boston & London: Luce, 1909);

Ibsen, *The Master Builder, Pillars of Society, Hedda Gabler,* introduction by Mencken (New York: Boni & Liveright, 1917);

Friedrich Wilhelm Nietzsche, *The Antichrist,* translated, with an introduction, by Mencken (New York: Knopf, 1920);

*Americana,* edited by Mencken (New York: Knopf, 1925);

*Menckeniana: A Schimpflexicon,* edited by Mencken (New York: Knopf, 1928);

Sara Powell Haardt, *Southern Album,* introduction by Mencken (New York: Doubleday, Doran, 1936);

*A New Dictionary of Quotations on Historical Principles from Ancient and Modern Sources,* edited by Mencken (New York: Knopf, 1942);

Theodore Dreiser, *An American Tragedy,* introduction by Mencken (Cleveland & New York: World, 1946);

"The American Language," in *Literary History of the United States,* volume 1, edited by Robert E. Spiller, Willard Thorp, Thomas H. Johnson, and Henry Seidel Canby (New York: Macmillan, 1948), pp. 663-675.

Although he was for nearly two decades America's most powerful and influential literary critic, having become in the early 1920s the first (and, for that matter, last) literary dictator, H. L. Mencken is not generally remembered for his criticism of belles lettres. Still, the fact is that Mencken, more than any other writer, helped to create a sophisticated reading public and thereby pave the way for the literature that came into being in the years just before, during, and after World War I. He performed that service, in large part, as the book critic for the *Smart Set* magazine between November 1908 and December 1923 and as coeditor (with George Jean Nathan) of that journal for the last nine of those years. With the founding in January 1924 of the *American Mercury,* Mencken's influence as writer and editor increased dramatically—to the point where the *New York Times* referred to him in an editorial as "the most powerful private citizen in America." In 1926 journalist Walter Lippmann, who was probably second only to Mencken as an influence on the educated minority, called Mencken "the most powerful personal influence on this whole generation of educated people." Nearly thirty years later newspaperman and playwright Ben Hecht echoed that appraisal when he referred to Mencken in his autobiography, *A Child of the Century,* as "The Republic's One-Man Renaissance." "No single American mind," Hecht wrote of his pessimistic hero, "has influenced existence in the Republic as much as did his. That he influenced us without declaring wars, starting panics or drumming up a job-hungry constituency to help him is fine proof that brave words can still lift the soul of man." More recently Tom Wolfe described the Mencken heyday as the period when American literature commuted from 1524 Hollins Street, Baltimore, Mencken's home address for most of his life.

Born on 12 September 1880, Henry Louis Mencken was the first of August and Anna

Abhau Mencken's four children. Throughout the seventeenth and eighteenth centuries the Mencken ancestors had been illustrious theologians and scholars in Germany. But for nearly a century before the birth of Henry, the Menckens had been engaged in commerce. The American line began with Burkhardt Ludwig Mencken, Henry's grandfather, who at the age of twenty moved from Saxony to Baltimore. Although that resettlement took place in 1848, a year of political unrest in Germany, Burkhardt's removal to these shores was prompted by business reasons alone. Shortly after arriving in Baltimore, he entered the wholesale tobacco business, for which he had been trained as a boy in Germany. Burkhardt's eldest son, August, followed in his father's footsteps by opening in 1875 his own tobacco business at the age of twenty-one. August's younger brother, Henry, joined him in the firm of August Mencken & Bro. In 1883 August moved with his growing family into the spacious, three-story row house on Hollins Street, where he and Anna would live out their lives, and where Henry would reside, except for the five years of his marriage, until the end of his life in 1956. When he married Sarah Powell Haardt in 1930, the couple moved to an apartment on Cathedral Street. After Sarah's death in 1935, the disconsolate Mencken returned to the Hollins Street home. He always spoke of his years with Sarah as the happiest of his life. Henry's youngest brother, August, who died in 1967, spent his entire life in the home.

The sense of place and order is everywhere apparent in Mencken's life. He was not only Baltimore's most famous son but also one of its most enthusiastic admirers. Moreover his strong self-assurance doubtless derived at least in part from the close family ties he formed almost from the beginning. In the first volume of his autobiography, *Happy Days* (1940), which, like its two companion volumes, tells us a good deal more about the world he inhabited than it does about the author, Mencken recalled his childhood as being "placid, secure, uneventful and happy." There was never an instant, he wrote, when he doubted his father's capacity "to resolve any difficulty that menaced me, or to beat off any danger. He was always the center of his small world, and in my eyes a man of illimitable puissance and resourcefulness. If we needed anything he got it forthwith, and usually he threw in something that we didn't really need, but only wanted." His parents were devoted to each other and to their children.

"We were encapsulated in affection, and kept fat, saucy and contented." He makes a point of his having been raised as a member of the comfortable and complacent bourgeoisie, a class which at the time of his writing was under heavy fire from the so-called proletarians who were intent on saving the nation and the world from all that the middle class represented. Unable to forgo the opportunity to needle the disaffected ones, Mencken remarked that his happy childhood had enabled him to get through his nonage without acquiring an inferiority complex, a fact that helped explain why his account "must needs fall out of the current fashion, which seems to favor tales of dirty tenements, wage cuts, lay-offs, lockouts, voracious landlords, mine police, foreclosed mortgages, evictions, rickets, prostitution, larceny, grafting cops, anti-Semitism, Bryanism, Hell-fire, droughts, xenophobia, and other such horrors."

Almost from the beginning, Mencken knew that he wanted to be a writer; just what kind he would not know until he was in his early thirties and already a seasoned newspaperman. In *Happy Days* he says, at least half seriously, that the general outlines of his future career were drawn at the age of seven. In the opening paragraph of "In the Footsteps of Gutenberg," he moves from a listing of innocent details to a conclusion that verges on the fantastic:

> On November 26, 1887 my father sent his bookkeeper, Mr. Maass, to the establishment of J. F. W. Dorman, at 217 East German street, Baltimore, and there and then, by the said Maass's authorized agency, took title to a Baltimore No. 10 Self-Inker Printing Press and a font of No. 214 type. The press cost $7.50 and the font of type $1.10. These details, which I recover from the receipted bill in my father's file, are of no conceivable interest to anyone else on earth, but to me they are of a degree of concern bordering upon the super-colossal, for that press determined the whole course of my future life. If it had been a stethoscope or a copy of Dr. Ayers' Almanac I might have gone in for medicine; if it had been a Greek New Testament or a set of baptismal grappling-irons I might have pursued divinity. As it was, I got the smell of printer's ink up my nose at the tender age of seven, and it has been swirling through my sinuses ever since.

A few other such happy accidents contributed to his conviction that no greater trade than that of

*H. L. Mencken at the* Baltimore Sun, *1913 (courtesy of the Enoch Pratt Free Library)*

writer existed on earth. For one, not long after he had set up his own newspaper, which, as he remarked, was doomed from the start because of "insufficiency of capital, incomplete news service, an incompetent staff, no advertising, and a press that couldn't print it," he discovered a real newspaper office in the little town of Ellicott City, where the Mencken family spent the summers of 1889 and 1890. Watching the young man and the boy who operated the Washington handpress run off the edition every Thursday added to his print fever. Other passions came and went–for example, for chemistry and for photography–but he never escaped the lure of print.

After graduating as the star pupil of Friedrich Knapp's Institute, a German primary school, Henry was sent to the Baltimore Polytechnic School. Although he later professed to having learned little there, he was an exemplary student, as evidenced by the fact that he graduated–at the age of fifteen–with the highest average grade attained by anyone up to that time. Given the choice of going to college, at the Johns Hopkins University in Baltimore or the University of Mary-

land, or going to work in his father's cigar factory, Henry chose the lesser of the two evils and went to work for his father. The most important lesson he learned in high school was that he could learn more on his own than he could from instructors, or at least the kind of instructors one encountered in schools. He best expressed his view in an essay on "Education," published in *Prejudices: Third Series* (1922): "No intelligent student ever learns much from the average drover of undergraduates; what he actually carries away has come out of his textbooks, or is the fruit of his own reading and inquiry." So he remained at home, spending his days working for his father and the nights pursuing a course of reading that staggers the imagination. Numerous people have commented, with awe, on Mencken's reading– that is, on the rate of speed with which he went through a book. An average-sized novel required something less than two hours, and his retention matched his speed. In his portrait of Mencken in *Pistols for Two* (1917), which Mencken and Nathan wrote together under the pseudonym of Owen Hatteras, Nathan wrote that Mencken read "an average of ten books a week, in addition to those he goes through for reviewing purposes. The subjects he affects are theology, biology, economics, and modern history."

The next two and a half years must certainly have been frustrating for the precocious boy, who had no interest in the work he was doing and yet was unable to act against his father's wishes. In the summer of 1898 Henry informed his father that he wished to leave the family business. He had been writing stories and poems since graduating from school and wanted to devote all his time to that end. Apparently August persuaded him to delay a final break with the business world; in any event, he remained at his job. As it turned out his escape was near at hand, the result of his father's death, at age forty-four, in January 1899. According to the account given in *Newspaper Days, 1899-1906* (1941), he applied for a job on the *Morning Herald* the day after August's funeral. Although no opening existed at the time, Max Ways, the city editor, told him he might return the next night on the chance of getting an assignment. Return he did—nightly, until 23 February, when he was sent to a small community five miles northeast of the city to learn what he could about a reported theft. The next morning the paper printed his account, remarkable only in that it was his first. The two sentences have been reproduced countless times since by critics and scholars:

> A horse, a buggy, and several sets of harness, valued in all at about $250, were stolen last night from the stable of Howard Quinlan, near Kingsville. The county police are at work on the case, but so far no trace of either thieves or booty has been found.

In the following weeks and months, Mencken received occasional assignments, the sort no one else wanted—"installations of new evangelical pastors, meetings of wheelmen, interviews with bores just back from Europe, the Klondike or Oklahoma, orgies of one sort or another at the Y.M.C.A., minor political rallies, concerts, funerals, and so on." After putting in a full day of work for his uncle at the cigar factory, he hurried through dinner and then rushed to the *Herald* office. Not until summer was he put on the payroll of the paper at seven dollars a week. Then he felt justified in resigning his duties at August Mencken & Bro. Thereafter he could devote all his time to observing and reporting on the

gaudy life of Baltimore at the turn of the century. In the preface to *Newspaper Days* he hymned the life of the young reporter and argued that, though he may have neglected the humanities during those first years, he had the advantage of "laying in all the worldly wisdom of a police lieutenant, a bartender, a shyster lawyer, or a midwife. . . . At a time when the respectable bourgeois youngsters of my generation were college freshmen, oppressed by simian sophomores and affronted with balderdash daily and hourly by chalky pedagogues, I was at large in a wicked seaport of half a million people, with a front seat at every public show, as free of the night as of the day, and getting earfuls and eyefuls of instruction in a hundred giddy arcana, none of them taught in schools."

Mencken's rise in the world of journalism was meteoric. No doubt his tutors on the *Herald* staff, as he freely admits, helped his ascent, primarily by recognizing that his was in no way a common talent. After serving stints as police reporter, city hall reporter, drama critic (a job he performed during the two years he was Sunday editor), and feature writer, he became, at twenty-one, Sunday editor; at twenty-three, city editor; at twenty-four, managing editor; and at twenty-five, editor-in-chief. When the *Herald*, which never fully recovered from the great Baltimore fire of 1904, ceased publication in early 1906, Mencken, whose title then was Secretary and Editor of the paper, received offers from all three of the other Baltimore dailies. He accepted the first one that reached him, that of news editor on the *Evening News*, but decided within two weeks on the job that executive work was not to his taste. For that reason, he transferred to the *Sunpaper* as Sunday editor, a position that enabled him to spend more time writing. Except for leaves of absence, which he requested, during the two world wars, he remained in one capacity or another with one of the *Sunpapers*—morning, evening, and Sunday—for the long remainder of his writing career.

Still, newspaper work was never enough, in itself, to satisfy Mencken. His work for the *Herald* kept him busy; he frequently wrote 5,000 words of news copy a day, not, as he later recalled, in a single continuous story, which might have been easy enough, "but in a miscellany of perhaps twelve or fifteen, every one of them requiring some legging." Before the publication of his first book, *Ventures into Verse* (1903), made up largely of imitations of Rudyard Kipling, then one of

Mencken's gods, he had pretty much abandoned poetry, at least as a serious interest. The poetry he wrote after that volume was published under an assortment of pseudonyms. At the same time he had been peddling his short stories to various of the pulp as well as slick magazines, and he had received considerable encouragement from editors to continue his fiction writing. But here again his critical sense, coupled with what he later called "a kind of caginess that has dissuaded me, at all stages of my life, from attempting enterprises clearly beyond my power," convinced him that he would never be more than an average fiction writer. Not until his discovery of the drama of ideas, and particularly that of George Bernard Shaw, did he find his vocation at last. He recalls in *Newspaper Days* that his discovery of Shaw led him to write his first three books: first, his critical study, and the first ever written, of Shaw's plays; then his larger and more ambitious book on the philosophy of Nietzsche; and finally a book on socialism written in the form of a debate with Robert Rives La Monte. Thus it was Shaw who set him on his course as a critic of ideas.

If *George Bernard Shaw: His Plays* (1905) has, as Mencken later admitted, "a good deal of empty ornament" in it, the book, nonetheless, reveals in embryo most of the salient aspects of all his literary criticism. It is unthinkable, of course, that the young Mencken, just learning his trade, could have read Shaw without being, at first, overwhelmed, just as it was natural that he should have cooled toward the great Irishman as the years disclosed Shaw's extreme didacticism. Though little influenced by Shaw's ideological positions, Mencken certainly learned much from the Shavian style: the iconoclastic wit, the hyperbolic exaggeration, the use of contrast, often outlandish, even fantastic. Moreover Shaw always gave a good show. His customers invariably went away moved, if not convinced. At a time when Shaw's influence was just beginning to be felt, Mencken wrote of him as Shaw had written of Ibsen in his *The Quintessence of Ibsenism* (1891). Mencken says that

> In the dramas of George Bernard Shaw, which deal almost wholly with the current conflict between orthodoxy and heterodoxy, it is but natural that the characters should fall broadly into two general classes— the ordinary folks who represent the great majority, and the iconoclasts, or idol-smashers. Darwin made this war between the faithful and the scoffers the chief concern of the time, and the sham-smashing that is now going on, in all fields of human inquiry, might be compared to the crusades that engrossed the world in the middle ages.

What most attracted Mencken to Shaw, then, was the latter's gift for stirring up the animals, a phrase Mencken used to describe his own literary efforts. Mencken was eager, of course, to take part in the sham-smashing.

In his little book on Shaw, some of the early slap and dash of the Mencken style is evident, particularly in his discussion of *Man and Superman* (1905), which had appeared but recently.

> Measured with rule, plumb-line or hayscales, *Man and Superman* is easily Shaw's *magnum opus*. In bulk it is brobdingnagian; in scope it is stupendous; in purpose it is one with the Odyssey. Like a full-rigged ship before a spanking breeze, it cleaves deep into the waves, sending ripples far to port and starboard, and its giant canvases rise half way to the clouds, with resplendent jibs, skysails and studdingsails standing out like quills upon the fretful porcupine.

Though in the play Shaw preached treason to all the schools, there was no doubt that he had borrowed from earlier thinkers: "It is a three-ring circus, with Ibsen doing running high jumps; Schopenhauer playing the calliope and Nietzsche selling peanuts in the reserved seats." Calling it "the most entertaining play of its generation," he wondered if Shaw had not written it "in a vain effort to rid himself at one fell swoop of all the disquieting doctrines that infested his innards." Finally Mencken called it "a tract cast in an encyclopedic and epic mold—a stupendous, magnificent, colossal effort to make a dent in the cosmos with a slapstick." One should note that Mencken was aware of the fundamental fact that the play was a "tract."

Though he always found much to praise in Shaw's later plays, Mencken also tempered his approval with objections to the moralizing note that became more strident as the years passed. Reviewing a new edition of *Misalliance* in September 1914, he summed up the Shaw technique: "The formula of Shaw has become transparent enough—a dozen other men practise his trick of putting the obvious into terms of the scandalous but he still works with surpassing humor and address." Though he considered the play's long preface one of the best things Shaw had written, there was condescension in the praise, since, after all, it was the obvious that Shaw put on display: "This is the special function of Shaw, the steady business of his life: to say the things that everybody knows and nobody says, to expose the everyday hypocrisies, to rout platitudes with superplatitudes." The play would not, he felt, lift Shaw any nearer Shakespeare, but it was excellent reading.

Mencken's last critical essay on Shaw was his severest indictment of the platitudinarian aspects of the playwright. "The Ulster Polonious" first appeared in the *Smart Set* in August 1916 as a review of *Androcles and the Lion* (1916) and then in a revised and lengthened form in *Prejudices: First Series* (1919). Probably the best-known essay ever written on Shaw, it has caused some readers to assume that Mencken was an apostate disciple, whereas the truth is that he was never really a disciple, nor did he ever change his view that Shaw was a master rhetorician. More than anything else the famous essay deflates Shaw's undeserved reputation for being a mastermind.

Mencken's book on Shaw led him to the more formidable work on Nietzsche. When *The Philosophy of Friedrich Nietzsche* appeared in 1908, it received highly favorable reviews and is still cited with approval by Nietzsche scholars. Though there is something to be said for Ernest Boyd's statement in his little study *H. L. Mencken* (1925) that he had "created Nietzsche in his own image, hence the affecting superstition that he is a Nietzschean," there can be no doubt that he was sympathetic to most of the philosophy and greatly admired the courage and honesty of the philosopher. In fact the young Mencken may have profited more from Nietzsche's manner than from his matter. After all Mencken's philosophical tenets had been gleaned from such iconoclasts as Charles Darwin, Herbert Spencer, Thomas Henry Huxley, W. H. Lecky, and William Graham Sumner before ever reading Nietzsche. But no one before Nietzsche had employed in the transvaluation of values a style so explosively alive or so devastating in its mockery. R. J. Hollingdale, the noted biographer and translator of Nietzsche, has written on Mencken's interest in that aspect of Nietzsche. According to Hollingdale, there is no such thing as a "Nietzschean," but there have been two authentic fragments of Nietzsche in the persons of Rainer Maria Rilke and Mencken—the former the Orpheus of the will to power, and the latter, its pub-

licity agent: "What jumps out from Mencken's robust pages is something lustier [than Rilke's fragment] but just as *echt* Nietzschean: it is the public-address Nietzsche, the comedian of the world without God, the stylist who had expelled every last trace of cant and compromise from his utterances, who told the simian civilization which surrounded him what he thought of it with the gusto of a man stating the obvious to an audience of the converted."

More than anything else, it was Nietzsche's attack on the moral interpretation of existence that appealed to Mencken. By placing ethics among the phenomena and thereby demoting it from its former absolute position, Nietzsche helped clear the way for an aesthetics free from moral premises. In 1886 he had written that morality had become "a mere fabrication for purposes of gulling: at best, an artistic fiction; at worst, an outrageous imposture." Both the tone and idea may be found again and again in Mencken's writings, particularly in his insistence that the artist should be free from the moral certainties of inferior men. That the artist should be oppressed, as he certainly was at the time Mencken wrote, by the majority which considers itself "right" is, Mencken felt, only natural—and of little importance. "All it amounts to is this: that the artist in America can never have a large audience and must expect to encounter positive hostility—Comstockery, college-professorism, etc."

In the introduction to his translation of *The Antichrist* (1920), Mencken summarized the essential philosophy of Nietzsche in a manner remarkably free of any effort to palliate or disguise for popular consumption. While much of the thirty-page essay is concerned with the growth of Nietzsche's influence before, during, and just after the war, it also attempts to clarify his position in Western thought. Above all, he depicts Nietzsche in opposition to Christian optimism and millennialism, and as one who sought to substitute an aesthetic view of phenomena, gleaned from the early Greeks, particularly Hereclitus, for the moral view of Christianity which applauded weakness and timidity as ideals. In the same place Mencken describes in two sentences an ideological transformation that was in the making in the late nineteenth century, and which has today been realized in the totalitarian state: "What is called Bolshevism today he saw clearly a generation ago and described for what it was and is—democracy in another aspect, the old *ressentiment* of the lower orders in free function once more. Socialism, Puritanism, Philistinism, Christianity—he saw them all as allotropic forms of democracy, as variations upon the endless struggle of quantity against quality, of the weak and timorous against the strong and enterprising, of the botched against the fit."

Mencken's critics usually attribute his antipathy to democratic theory, most resoundingly expressed in *Notes on Democracy* (1926), to his early reading of Nietzsche. But before studying the philosopher, Mencken had read widely in the various English writers, especially Huxley, whose influence Mencken never questioned. Such essays as "On the Natural Inequality of Men" certainly left an indelible mark, as did his reading of the ancient Greeks, democracy's first critics. It should also be pointed out that although Mencken concentrated on the raucous side of Nietzsche's iconoclasm, he never mistook him for a nihilist, or one who advocates unmoral license. In his study of ethics, *Treatise on Right and Wrong* (1934)—the companion volume of his book on religion, *Treatise on the Gods* (1930)—Mencken acknowledged the ascetic side of Nietzsche, whose "furious attack upon the Christian ideal of humility and abnegation has caused Christian critics to denounce him as an advocate of the most brutal egoism, but in point of fact he proposed only the introduction of a new and more heroic form of renunciation, based upon abounding strength rather than upon hopeless weakness; and in his maxim 'Be hard!' there was just as much sacrifice of immediate gratification to ultimate good as you will find in any of the *principia* of Jesus."

In the year his book on Nietzsche appeared, Mencken set up shop as a literary critic for the *Smart Set*. Between November 1908 and December 1923 he wrote 182 monthly articles—some nine hundred thousand words—on books foreign and domestic, good, bad, and indifferent—about two thousand in all. In his first article, entitled "The Good, the Bad, and the Best Sellers," he set the pattern that he would generally follow throughout his critical episcopate, as he called it. Convinced that the first desideratum in criticism is to be interesting, he began by endeavoring to charm or lure his reader into following his arguments with, in this case, a brief discourse on the use of platitudes in "the fair field of imaginative literature." Following that he asked what platitudes have to do with Upton Sinclair's "new romance," *The Moneychangers*. Answering his own rhetorical question he concluded: "Simply this: that hordes of the *bacillus platitudae* have entered Sinclair's sys-

tem and are preying upon his vitals. They have already consumed his sense of humor and are now fast devouring his elemental horse sense. The first result is that he is taking himself and the world seriously, and the second result is that he is writing tracts." Mencken later noted that, despite its interest and its craftsmanship, Sinclair's novel was "not a moving picture of human passions, not an analysis of the human soul under suffering, but a somewhat florid thesis in sociology, with conclusions that were stale in the days of St. Augustine." He accompanied his censure with the reminder that "an economic struggle, to make material for fiction, must be pictured, not objectively and as a mere bout between good and evil, but subjectively and as some chosen protagonist sees and experiences it." Even in this first article Mencken was distinguishing between surface realism that slid easily into melodrama and what might be called "subjective" realism, which in its interpretation and its concern with the enigmatic in life went far deeper than the photographic could ever go. In criticizing Sinclair, Mencken might well have been thinking of his favorite English novelist, Joseph Conrad. He believed then, as he did later, that *Lord Jim* was the greatest novel in the language.

To be sure, he never admired Sinclair's fiction, for the same reasons that he never admired any didactic fiction, but he did find some of the nonfiction worthy of praise. For example, in 1923 he lauded *The Goose-step*, a muckraking examination of the administrative side of our universities. In his review, which he included in *Prejudices: Fifth Series* (1926), Mencken went far beyond the book at hand and addressed himself to the subject. Rather than analyze the book, he wrote an excellent essay, using the book as a take-off—an essay which still has immediacy even though Sinclair's book is nearly forgotten. After commenting at some length on the professors' loss of prestige since the end of the World War ("In universities large and small, East, West, North and South, the very sophomores rise in rebellion against the incompetence and imbecility of their preceptors, and in the newspapers the professor slides down gradually to the level of a chiropractor, a press-agent or a Congressman"), Mencken briefly rehearsed the shortcomings of two of Sinclair's critiques: *The Brass Check*, on yellow journalism, and *The Profits of Religion*. But in *The Goose-step* the expected weaknesses were absent. Sinclair had left off "his customary martyr's chemise" and allowed the narrative to tell itself:

*George Jean Nathan and Mencken in 1923, soon after they left* The Smart Set *to coedit* American Mercury *(photo by Alfred A. Knopf)*

There is no complaining, no pathos, no mouthing of platitude; it is a plain record of plain facts, with names and dates–a plain record of truly appalling cowardice, disingenuousness, abjectness, and degradation. Out of it two brilliant figures emerge: first the typical American university president, a jenkins to wealth, an ignominious waiter in antechambers and puller of wires, a politician, a fraud and a cad; and secondly, the typical American professor, a puerile and pitiable slave.

From this general statement Mencken goes on to provide specifics in support of his dark view. Such reviews belong, of course, not to the narrow realm of *literary* criticism, but rather to the broader area of the critical essay.

Mencken's savage portrait of academics, no matter what its validity, was not likely to win him much favor in that quarter. Oddly enough, dur-

ing the period of his greatest influence on the "civilized minority," he was being attacked with unprecedented fury for his outspoken views. In one of the many credos he furnished leading magazines of the period, he admitted that his notions had got him enemies: "The Red-hunters put me among the Radicals, and the Radicals belabor me as an intransigent Tory. In Greenwich Village I am thwacked as a medieval, and among college professors I am regarded as an anarchist. During the twelve months of 1926 more than five hundred separate editorials upon my heresies were printed in the United States, and at least four hundred of them were hostile." One other example of his notoriety should suffice. Early in 1927 a number of suicides were reported from college campuses, and the newspapers played them up in a melodramatic manner and tried to show that there was an epidemic. On being interviewed by the *Trenton* (New Jersey) *Times,* the president of

Rutgers, a man named Thomas, who later went into the insurance business, gave the cause of the suicides as "too much Mencken." Asked by the *Times* to comment on this, Mencken wrote that he could see nothing mysterious about the suicides, that the impulse to self-destruction was strong in everyone, especially in intelligent young people. In all probability, he wrote, the only thing that kept the reflective and skeptical man alive was his sense of humor. Besides, the college presidents, like the newspaper editors, would soon tire of the bogus epidemic and go yelling after some other phantasm. He ended the little essay with a masterful stroke: "A college student, leaping uninvited into the arms of God, pleases only himself. But a college president, doing the same thing, would give keen and permanent joy to great multitudes of persons. I drop the idea, and pass on."

During his first years as a professional critic, Mencken praised most highly the work of various Europeans—Joseph Conrad, John Galsworthy, Arnold Bennett, George Moore, George Bernard Shaw, Maxim Gorki, Leonid Andreev, Max Beerbohm, Hermann Sudermann, Gerhart Hauptmann, H. G. Wells (the early novels he praised but later castigated Wells for succumbing to a messianic complex), George Meredith, G. K. Chesterton, Havelock Ellis, William Synge (and various others of the Irish renaissance), to name only the foremost. Indeed, with the possible exception of James Huneker, who was almost solely interested in foreign wares, Mencken did more than any other critic of the period to bring into notice what went on abroad—and to show by way of comparison the relative inferiority of American literature. In assessing the cause of that second-rateness, Mencken pointed to the pervasive influence of Puritanism and its various avatars on our literary heritage and to the absence of an intellectual aristocracy that might have furnished aid and direction for artistic endeavors. Mencken's major critique of Puritanism, entitled "Puritanism as a Literary Force," did not appear until after he had been embroiled for years in a running battle with censors, particularly those who sought to silence such novelists as Dreiser, whom Mencken had defended from the start. In fact, *Jennie Gerhardt* (1911) was the first contemporary American novel to receive Mencken's unqualified praise. Aside from its value as a penetrating analysis of the debilitating effects of Puritanism on art, the essay served as a spark to ignite the most bitterly waged critical war of the century. At the time of its publication in *A Book of Prefaces*

(1917)—the other three long essays in the volume are on Conrad, Dreiser, and Huneker—Mencken was at the height of his powers as a literary critic. That volume stands today, along with various essays in the *Prejudices* series, as the best writing he was ever to do in that particular area. The reception of *Prefaces*—which had a small sale in 1917 but enjoyed a wide audience when reissued in 1924—is a good gauge of Mencken's popularity. Only a few rebels could stomach him during the war (Sgt. Edmund Wilson, for example, read and reread the book, which convinced him more than any other single work that literary criticism was a worthwhile profession); after the return of the conquering armies, a whole generation accepted the Menckenian theses as gospel. The charge of un-Americanism leveled at Mencken during the war seemed merely quaint to the disaffected postwar critics and readers.

Mencken made it clear in the opening pages of "Puritanism as a Literary Force" that Puritanism as a theological doctrine was pretty much exploded: "That primitive demonology still survives in the barbaric doctrines of the Methodists and Baptists, particularly in the South; but it has been ameliorated, even there, by a growing sense of the divine grace, and so the old God of Plymouth Rock, as practically conceived, is now scarcely worse than the average jail warden or Italian padrone." But as an ethical concept, Puritanism lived on in all its fury. In effect, the essay gives a detailed analysis of the various "moral awakenings" in our history and their effect upon the arts, concluding with a lengthy section on the accomplishments of Anthony Comstock and his associates. What most amazed Mencken was the fact that while competent work was often suppressed, the frankly prurient and vulgar went unmolested.

"The National Letters" (1920) is Mencken's longest and most severe indictment of American culture in general and our literature in particular. After quoting earlier prophecies of such writers as Ralph Waldo Emerson and Walt Whitman—and even Edgar Allan Poe, who was not immune to the optimism of his day—that a great national literature lay just over the horizon, Mencken stated that American literature, despite several false starts that promised much, was chiefly remarkable, in 1920 as before, for its respectable mediocrity. "Its typical great man, in our own time, has been Howells, as its typical great man a generation ago was Lowell, and two generations ago, Irving. Viewed largely, its salient character appears as a sort of timorous flaccidity, an amiable hollowness." To assess the current literature Mencken divided it into three layers: the "correct" works of the survivors of New England *Kultur* on top; the experimental and rebellious writings of Greenwich Village–by which he meant the more advanced wing in letters, "whatever the scene of its solemn declarations of independence and forlorn hopes"–on the bottom; and in the middle those who produced "the literature that pays like a bucket-shop or a soap-factory, and is thus thoroughly American." Actually Mencken found things in all the layers to admire, particularly in the middle grouping where technical excellence and even a sort of civilized sophistication was not uncommon. Moreover, that group constantly graduated writers to a higher level: for example, Booth Tarkington, Zona Gale, Ring Lardner, and Montague Glass. (At the time this essay was written, Sinclair Lewis was on the verge of "graduation," *Main Street* appearing a few months later.) Mencken also reminded his readers that Mark Twain was a graduate of this school. Mencken defended the *Saturday Evening Post* against the charge that it ruined able writers by luring them with money to its list of contributors. He believed the *Post* was much better than either Greenwich Village or the Cambridge campus was willing to admit. But his defense was somewhat less than glowing, as when he remarks, "It is the largest of the literary Hog Islands, but it is by no means the worst."

In the last two thirds of the essay he endeavored to diagnose the ills, to point out the causes for the failure of America to produce a literature comparable to that of other Western nations. After commenting at length on the apathy toward, or misunderstanding of, Hawthorne, Emerson, Poe, and Whitman in their own day, Mencken attempted to isolate the reasons for American artists' feeling like aliens in their own land. (At the time of his writing, many American artists were expatriating themselves for more congenial surroundings in the cities of Europe. Mencken gave his delightfully cynical reasons for not joining them in his essay "On Being an American," published two years later in *Prejudices: Third Series,* 1922.) The major cause, he felt, was clear enough: America has produced no civilized aristocracy, "secure in its position, animated by an intelligent curiosity, skeptical of all facile generalizations, superior to the sentimentality of the mob, and delighting in the battle of ideas for its own sake." Realizing that a public "fed upon

democratic fustian" would associate the term "aristocracy" with wealth and snobbery, he took care to clarify his term. He believed that the yellow press was partly responsible for the misconception buried deeply in the mass mind. Also, Americans cherished the nebulous belief in equality. Indeed "the inferior man needs an aristocracy to demonstrate, not only his mere equality, but also his actual superiority." Much of the remainder of the essay is given over to the beliefs and behavior, especially toward nonconformity, of the plutocracy at the top of our culture and the mob at the bottom, and to the ineffectuality of the timorous intelligentsia squeezed in between. Mencken's appraisal of the latter group, made up largely of college and university professors, was harsher than his assessment of the other two, primarily because one naturally expected more in the way of integrity and courage from the intellectuals than had been forthcoming. As one who had early in life assumed the "rather thankless duties of a specialist in the ways of pedagogues, a sort of professor of professors," Mencken confessed that his researches had provided him with materials not altogether flattering to the *Gelehrten.*

> What I have found, in brief, is that pedagogy turned to general public uses is almost as timid and flatulent as journalism–that the professor, menaced by the timid dogmatism of the plutocracy above him and the incurable suspiciousness of the mob beneath him, is almost invariably inclined to seek his own security in a mellifluous inanity–that, far from being a courageous spokesman of ideas and an apostle of their free dissemination, in politics, in the fine arts, in practical ethics, he comes close to being the most prudent and skittish of all men concerned with them–in brief, that he yields to the prevailing correctness of thought in all departments . . . and is, in fact, the chief exponent among us of the democratic doctrine that heresy is not only a mistake, but also a crime.

To prove his thesis that the pedagogue was anything but "a courageous spokesman of ideas and an apostle of their free dissemination" was easy enough. He only needed to point to the recent war. During time of war the worst fears and prejudices of the ignorant and emotional man naturally come to the fore, but a time of strife and frenzied action should show more clearly than ever the inward metal of the superior man. What actually happened was that the professors acted,

*Mencken and Sara Powell Haardt on the day of their marriage, August 1930* (Baltimore News American)

not like intelligent men, but like mob masters. "They constituted themselves, not a restraining influence upon the mob run wild, but the loudest spokesmen of its worst imbecilities. They fed it with bogus history, bogus philosophy, bogus idealism, bogus heroics." Now that his hands were untied and he was able to speak his mind, Mencken reminded his readers, with a vengeance, of the depths to which war hysteria had driven his fellow countrymen.

In concluding "The National Letters," the main ideas of which barely have been touched on here, Mencken insisted that he had no remedy to offer. He admitted that the obstacles standing in "the way of the development of a distinctly American culture, grounded upon a truly egoistic nationalism and supported by a native aristocracy," may, after all, prove insurmountable. Puritanism may be too deeply imbedded in the national consciousness ever to be completely eradicated. Although professing to offer no remedy for the cerebral paralysis in America, he felt that a gen-

eral skepticism was the first step to combating the Puritan childishness. To prove that hope will not down, he pointed to the skepticism that was already beginning to show itself "in the iconoclastic political realism of Harold Stearns, Waldo Frank and company, in the groping questions of Dreiser, Cabell and Anderson, in the operatic rebellions of the Village." Mencken believed that great literature was chiefly a "product of doubting and inquiring minds in revolt against the immovable certainties of the nation." He concluded his inquiry with the faint, glimmering hope that on some dim tomorrow the molders of taste in America would be challenged by more than a few solitary iconoclasts. There was then no way of knowing that within the next ten years the skeptical attitude would become almost universal in the world of art and that America, artistically speaking, would reach its highest point.

In point of fact, only three years later Mencken could write, in his final *Smart Set* article, entitled "Fifteen Years," that the imaginative writer in America was quite as free as he needed to be. Moreover he was not only free to depict the life about him as he saw fit and to interpret it in any manner he pleased but he could find publishers hospitable to novelties of every variety. Assaying the literary terrain of the preceding two decades, Mencken was astonished by the great change and improvement in "the situation of the American imaginative author—the novelist, poet, dramatist, and writer of short-stories." Henceforth Mencken's concern for the *state* of American literature would decline as his interest in the broader aspects of American culture increased. Though he continued to write a monthly column on books for the *American Mercury* and devote an occasional editorial to literary matters, his involvement in literature as such would be more editorial than critical in nature. The *Mercury*, which contained articles on all aspects of American society, differed vastly from the *Smart Set*, which, excepting Nathan's and Mencken's essays on the drama and books, published only fiction and poetry.

Mencken's two most important essays on criticism itself are "Criticism of Criticism of Criticism," the final version of which appeared in *Prejudices: First Series*, and "Footnote on Criticism," which appeared three years later in *Prejudices: Third Series*. In those two widely different, though not contradictory, essays Mencken accounts for the theoretical bases of his criticism. In the first, which he labeled the "Croce-Spingarn-

Carlyle-Goethe theory," he argued that the critic acted as a catalyst in provoking a reaction between the work of art and the spectator. The later essay, more a peripheral comment on the art of criticism than an analysis of critical method, comments on the motivating power that sets man to writing as against indulging in some other human enterprise. At the same time, it attacks the sentimental belief that the critic is, or should be, interested in uplifting the arts, the belief that "he writes because he is possessed by a passion to advance the enlightenment, to put down error and wrong, to disseminate some specific doctrine. . . ." Bad critics may be so motivated, but the best ones were moved by the motives of the artist, by "the simple desire to function freely and beautifully, to give outward and objective form to ideas that bubble inwardly and have a fascinating lure in them, to get rid of them dramatically and make an articulate noise in the world." If the critic "lacks the intellectual agility and enterprise needed to make the leap from the work of art to the vast and mysterious complex of phenomena behind it," he will always remain "no more than a fugleman or policeman to his betters." Whether intentionally or not, Mencken here limits the importance of the critic who performs the task advocated in the earlier essay.

Finally, "Footnote on Criticism," which is a kind of valedictory to that part of Mencken's career which was predominantly concerned with literary criticism, is an essay on the nature of truth; or, more specifically, on the importance of "truth" to the artist and to the place posterity assigns him. Admitting that Carlyle "was surely no just and infallible judge" but was on the contrary "full of prejudices, biles, naïvetés, humors," Mencken added that he was, in spite of these shortcomings, still read, still "attended to." Macaulay, Sainte-Beuve, Arnold, and Goethe were little less free from such deficiencies; yet they, too, were remembered. What saved such men was the simple fact that they were first-rate artists. "They could make the thing charming, and that is always a million times more important than making it true." And precisely here do we ascertain a "truth." Mencken was himself a case in point. He is remembered today, though a bit gingerly by many pedagogues, not because of any great truths that he unearthed—he employed in much of his literary criticism classical standards that are as old as Pericles' Athens; he said little about aesthetic theory that may be described as original—but for his ability to express himself in resounding phrases and

convincing terms. Readers still turn, and with profit, to his essays on Dreiser, Howells, Wells, Shaw, Thorstein Veblen, Nietzsche, Conrad, Bennett, and numerous lesser figures.

In his "This was Mencken: An appreciation," written shortly after Mencken's death in 1956 and then included in the collection *If You Don't Mind My Saying So* (1964), Joseph Wood Krutch wrote the following: "Everywhere it will be said that the death of H. L. Mencken marks the end of an epoch. But perhaps it is no less true that it marks also the beginning of something— his reputation as a writer. Mencken was a spokesman, a symbol, an embodiment, and all the other things he has been called. But he was first of all a master of the written word and, unless the world changes a great deal more than seems likely, that is the only thing which will count in the long run. Men are mentioned in textbooks because they were so right or so wrong and, sometimes, because they were so typical. But it is only because they were great writers that they are read." Krutch concluded his tribute by predicting that the time would come "when it will be generally recognized, as by a few it already is, that Mencken's was the best prose written in America during the twentieth century. Those who deny that fact had better confine themselves to direct attack. They will be hard put to find a rival claimant."

## Letters:

*Letters of H. L. Mencken,* selected and annotated by Guy J. Forgue (New York: Knopf, 1961);

*The New Mencken Letters,* edited by Carl Bode (New York: Dial, 1977).

## Bibliographies:

*H. L. M.: The Mencken Bibliography,* compiled by Betty Adler, with the assistance of Jane Wilhelm (Baltimore: Johns Hopkins Press, 1961);

*Man of Letters: A Census of the Correspondence of H. L. Mencken,* compiled by Adler (Baltimore: Enoch Pratt Free Library, 1969);

*H. L. M.: The Mencken Bibliography, A Ten-Year Supplement, 1962-1971,* compiled by Adler (Baltimore: Enoch Pratt Free Library, 1971).

## Biographies:

Isaac Goldberg, *The Man Mencken: A Biographical and Critical Survey* (New York: Simon & Schuster, 1925);

Edgar Kemler, *The Irreverent Mr. Mencken* (Boston: Little, Brown, 1950);

William Manchester, *Disturber of the Peace: The Life of H. L. Mencken* (New York: Harper, 1950);

Charles Angoff, *H. L. Mencken: A Portrait from Memory* (New York: Thomas Yoseloff, 1956);

Sara Mayfield, *The Constant Circle: H. L. Mencken and His Friends* (New York: Delacorte, 1968);

Carl Bode, *Mencken* (Carbondale: Southern Illinois University Press, 1969);

Douglas C. Stenerson, *H. L. Mencken: Iconoclast from Baltimore* (Chicago: University of Chicago Press, 1971);

Charles A. Fecher, *Mencken: A Study of His Thought* (New York: Knopf, 1978).

**References:**

Ernest Boyd, *H. L. Mencken* (New York: McBride, 1925);

Benjamin DeCasseres, *Mencken and Shaw: The Anatomy of America's Voltaire and England's Other John Bull* (New York: Silas Newton, 1930);

Carl R. Dolmetsch, *The Smart Set, a History and Anthology* (New York: Dial, 1966);

John Dorsey, ed., *On Mencken* (New York: Knopf, 1980);

Fred C. Hobson, Jr., *Serpent in Eden: H. L. Mencken and the South* (Chapel Hill: University of North Carolina Press, 1974);

Joseph Wood Krutch, *If You Don't Mind My Saying So . . . Essays on Man and Nature* (New York: Sloane, 1964);

William H. Nolte, *H. L. Mencken, Literary Critic* (Middletown, Conn.: Wesleyan University Press, 1966);

Charles Scruggs, *The Sage in Harlem: H. L. Mencken and the Black Writers of the 1920s* (Baltimore: Johns Hopkins Press, 1984);

W. H. A. Williams, *H. L. Mencken* (Boston: Twayne, 1977).

**Papers:**

The Enoch Pratt Free Library, Baltimore, has H. L. Mencken's personal library, including manuscripts, typescripts, and scrapbooks; and his correspondence, except that with twentieth-century authors and non-Marylanders, which he gave to the New York Public Library. Thirty-four other institutions and libraries are listed in Betty Adler's *A Descriptive List of H. L. Mencken Collections in the U.S.* (Baltimore: Enoch Pratt Free Library, 1967) as holding first editions of Mencken's books, original issues of magazines, or manuscripts. The Enoch Pratt Free Library publishes *Menckeniana: A Quarterly Review*, the first number of which appeared in Spring 1962.

# Perry Miller

*(25 February 1905-9 December 1963)*

Michael Clark

*University of California, Irvine*

See also the Miller entry in *DLB 17, Twentieth-Century American Historians.*

BOOKS: *Orthodoxy in Massachusetts, 1630-1650: A Genetic Study* (Cambridge: Harvard University Press, 1933);

*The New England Mind: The Seventeenth Century* (New York: Macmillan, 1939);

*Jonathan Edwards* (New York: Sloane, 1949; London: Mayflower, 1959);

*Society and Literature in America* (Leiden, Holland: Universitaire Pers Leiden, 1949; Folcroft, Pa.: Folcroft Press, 1969);

*The New England Mind: From Colony to Province* (Cambridge: Harvard University Press, 1953);

*Roger Williams: His Contribution to the American Tradition* (Indianapolis: Bobbs-Merrill, 1953);

*Errand Into the Wilderness* (Cambridge: Harvard University Press, 1956; London: Oxford University Press, 1956);

*The Raven and the Whale: The War of Words and Wits in the Era of Poe and Melville* (New York: Harcourt, Brace, 1956);

*The Life of the Mind in America: From the Revolution to the Civil War* (New York: Harcourt, Brace & World, 1965; London: Gollancz, 1966);

*Nature's Nation*, edited by Elizabeth Miller (Cambridge: Harvard University Press, 1967; London: Oxford University Press, 1967);

*The Responsibility of Mind in a Civilization of Machines: Essays*, edited by John Crowell and Stanford J. Searl, Jr. (Amherst: University of Massachusetts Press, 1979);

*Sources for the New England Mind: The Seventeenth Century*, edited by James Hoopes (Williamsburg, Va.: Institute of Early American History and Culture, 1981).

OTHER: *The Puritans: A Sourcebook of their Writings*, edited by Miller and Thomas H. Johnson (New York & Cincinnati: American Book, 1938);

Jonathan Edwards, *Images or Shadows of Divine Things*, edited by Miller (New Haven: Yale University Press, 1948);

"The Cambridge Platform of 1648," in *The Cambridge Platform of 1648*, edited by Henry Wilder Foote (Boston: Beacon Press/Pilgrim Press, 1949), pp. 60-75;

"Edwards, Locke, and the Rhetoric of Sensation," in *Perspectives of Criticism*, edited by Harry Levin (Cambridge: Harvard University Press, 1950), pp. 102-123;

*The Transcendentalists: An Anthology*, edited by Miller (Cambridge: Harvard University Press, 1950);

*American Thought: Civil War to World War I*, edited by Miller (New York: Rinehart, 1954);

Daniel Drake, *Discourse on the History, Character and Prospects of the West (1834)*, introduction by Miller (Gainesville, Fla.: Scholars' Facsimiles and Reprints, 1955);

*The American Puritans: Their Prose and Poetry*, edited by Miller (Garden City: Doubleday, 1956);

*The New-England Courant: A Selection of Certain Issues Containing Writings of Benjamin Franklin or Published by Him During His Brother's Imprisonment*, introduction by Miller (Boston: American Academy of Arts and Sciences, 1956);

*The American Transcendentalists: Their Prose and Poetry*, edited by Miller (Garden City: Doubleday, 1957);

*The Works of Jonathan Edwards*, two volumes, edited by Miller (New Haven: Yale University Press, 1957, 1959);

*Consciousness in Concord: The Text of Thoreau's Hitherto "Lost Journal" (1840-1841) Together with Notes and a Commentary*, edited by Miller (Boston: Houghton Mifflin, 1958);

John Wise, *A Vindication of the Government of New-England Churches (1717)*, introduction by Miller (Gainesville, Fla.: Scholars' Facsimiles and Reprints, 1958);

*The Golden Age of American Literature,* edited by Miller (New York: Braziller, 1959);

Henry David Thoreau, *Walden: or, Life in the Woods; and, On the Duty of Civil Disobedience,* edited by Miller (New York: New American Library, 1960);

Washington Irving, *The Sketch Book of Geoffrey Crayon, Gent.,* afterword by Miller (New York: New American Library, 1961);

Philip Schaff, *America,* edited by Miller (Cambridge: Harvard University Press, 1961);

Charles Dickens, *American Notes for General Circulation,* edited by Yoshimori Harashima, with a preface by Miller (Tokyo: Hokuseido Press, 1962);

Moses Coit Tyler, *A History of American Literature: 1607-1765,* foreword by Miller (New York: Collier, 1962);

Brooks Adams, *The Emancipation of Massachusetts: The Dream and the Reality,* introduction by Miller (Boston: Houghton Mifflin, 1962);

*The Legal Mind in America: From Independence to the Civil War,* edited by Miller (Garden City: Doubleday, 1962);

*Major Writers of America,* two volumes, edited by Miller, Newton Arvin, et al. (New York: Harcourt, Brace & World, 1962);

*The Complete Writings of Roger Williams,* volume 7, edited by Miller (New York: Russell & Russell, 1963);

*Margaret Fuller: American Romantic,* edited by Miller (Garden City: Doubleday, 1963);

*The Great Awakening: Documents Illustrating the Crisis and Its Consequences,* edited by Miller and Alan E. Heimert (Indianapolis: Bobbs-Merrill, 1967).

PERIODICAL PUBLICATIONS: "Thomas Hooker and the Democracy of Early Connecticut," *New England Quarterly,* 4 (October 1931): 663-712;

"The Half-Way Covenant," *New England Quarterly,* 6 (December 1933): 676-715;

"The Marrow of Puritan Divinity," *Publications of the Colonial Society of Massachusetts,* 32 (February 1935): 247-300;

"The Puritan Theory of the Sacraments in Seventeenth Century New England," *Catholic Historical Review,* 22 (1937): 409-425;

"Jonathan Edwards to Emerson," *New England Quarterly,* 13 (December 1940): 589-617;

"Jonathan Edwards' Sociology of the Great Awakening," *New England Quarterly,* 21 (March 1948): 50-77;

"The Religious Impulse in the Founding of Virginia: Religion and Society in the Early Literature," *William and Mary Quarterly,* 5 (October 1948): 492-522; 6 ( January 1949): 24-41;

"Errand Into the Wilderness," *William and Mary Quarterly,* 10 ( January 1953): 3-32;

"Melville and Transcendentalism," *Virginia Quarterly Review,* 29 (Autumn 1953): 556-575;

"The Romantic Dilemma in American Nationalism and the Concept of Nature," *Harvard Theological Review,* 48 (1955): 239-253;

"The Shaping of American Character," *New England Quarterly,* 28 (December 1955): 435-454;

"The New England Conscience," *American Scholar,* 28 (Winter 1958-1959): 49-58;

"The Responsibility of Mind in a Civilization of Machines," *American Scholar,* 31 (Winter 1961-1962): 51-69.

Perry Gilbert Eddy Miller's lifelong account of what he called "the New England mind" established an intellectual paradigm that still dominates the field of colonial history a half-century after the appearance of his first major work in 1933, *Orthodoxy in Massachusetts, 1630-1650: A Genetic Study.* A year after Miller's death in 1963, the prominent historian Edmund Morgan described the work of his former teacher in an essay for the American Antiquarian Society's *Proceedings* (1964), and the thesis of his "Perry Miller and the Historians" was simple: Miller's work is "the most imaginative and the most exhaustive piece of intellectual history that America has produced," and alongside Samuel Eliot Morison's books on the early years of Harvard, the six books and more than fifty essays Miller wrote during his academic career rank as "the outstanding achievement of the present century in Early American history." From the publication of his enormously influential *The New England Mind: The Seventeenth Century* in 1939 through the posthumous edition of *The Life of the Mind in America: From the Revolution to the Civil War* (1965), which won the Pulitzer Prize in 1966, Miller presided over most literary and historical research into the early forms of American culture, both as an influential teacher at Harvard University from 1931 to 1963 and as the prolific author of long and detailed expositions of American intellectual life during the first 200 years of settlement. During Miller's lifetime, and largely due to his efforts, Puritan studies emerged from the domain of a gentlemanly pastime to become one of the most so-phisticated areas of American historiography, and since his death Miller's work has continued to serve as a model and a challenge to historians and literary scholars alike.

Miller's preparation for his scholarly work was erratic, even for the chaotic years between the wars. He was born on the West Side of Chicago to Eben Perry Sturgis and Gertrude Eddy Miller. Perry and his brother Charles, who later became a professor of English at the University of Iowa, grew up in Chicago and attended the Tilton School and later went to Austin High School. In 1922 Perry entered the University of Chicago, but the next year he left school and wandered around the country, first to Colorado and then to New York, where he performed in several stock companies. He soon gave up acting, however, went to sea, and eventually wound up in the Belgian Congo unloading barrels of oil from the United States. In the preface to *Errand Into the Wilderness* (1956), Miller describes this period of his life as a scene from Joseph Conrad's *Heart of Darkness,* complete with a dramatic epiphany and a vision of his destiny as an American scholar. The essays in this book, Miller says of his new collection, "along with three or four books, are all I have yet been able to realize of a determination conceived three decades ago at Matadi on the banks of the Congo." Miller says he had arrived seeking the "adventure" that his older contemporaries had found in World War I, but the life in the jungle was not quite as exciting as he had anticipated. Nevertheless, he adds, with not quite as much irony as modesty might demand, just as Gibbon had *The Decline and Fall* thrust upon him while sitting disconsolate among the ruins of Rome, "It was given to me, equally disconsolate on the edge of a jungle of central Africa, to have thrust upon me the mission of expounding what I took to be the innermost propulsion of the United States, while supervising, in that barbaric tropic, the unloading of drums of case oil flowing out of the inexhaustible wilderness of America."

When this academic Marlow finally got his own war, he made the most of it, but in the meantime Miller returned to the University of Chicago in 1926 and took his Ph.B. there in 1928. He immediately began graduate school at Chicago, where he remained for two years, and married one of his classmates, Elizabeth Williams, on 12 September 1930. In 1931 he accepted a position as instructor at Harvard University, where he stud-ied with Samuel Eliot Morison and Kenneth B. Murdock and quickly completed his dissertation on Puritan theology in New England, "The Establishment of Orthodoxy in Massachusetts." He received his Ph.D. from the University of Chicago in 1931 and continued on at Harvard, where he would remain for most of his life. Miller was appointed associate professor of American Literature there in 1939 and full professor in 1946, and in 1960 he was named the Powell M. Cabot Professor of American Literature, the position he was holding in 1963 when he died in his study at Leverett House on the Harvard campus.

Most of Miller's forays from Cambridge were brief and limited to other universities. He was a visiting professor at the University of Leiden, Holland, from 1949 to 1950 and at Tokyo University in 1952. From 1953 to 1954 and again from 1962 to 1963, Miller was a fellow at the Institute of Advanced Study at Princeton, New Jersey. Periodically he would also visit other schools to accept the honorary degrees bestowed upon him during the last ten years of his career: a D.Litt. from Gonzaga University in 1955, from Grinnell College in 1957, and from Northwestern University in 1958. He received a D.H.L. from Syracuse University in 1957 and yet another D.Litt. from Boston College in 1962. Aside from a devotion to the Boston Red Sox, most of Miller's other affiliations were limited to the predictable intellectual circles of a New England professor: he was a member of the Massachusetts Historical Society, the Colonial Society of Massachusetts, the American Antiquarian Society, and the Modern Language Association.

The exception to this academic life that Miller embraced so exclusively after he settled down in graduate school was the time he spent in the army during World War II. From 1942 to 1945 Miller served first as a captain and then as a major in the Office of Strategic Services, and he accompanied the French hero General Leclerc in his sweep to liberate Alsace. The experience clearly appealed to Miller, for back at Harvard after the war he would often allude to his expertise as a "psychological warfare officer," usually to the chagrin of the many other veterans who had returned to school by that time. An account of Miller's professorial style by one of his students, David Levin, suggests that Miller also may have missed the intimidating authority of rank in the more egalitarian climate of academia. Writing in the *Southern Review* for autumn 1983, Levin says he entered Miller's office soon after he arrived at Harvard, and "As I took my seat I had to notice that a German battle flag, with an immense swastika, hung on the wall behind me and that a pair of knee-high boots gleamed beside the left rear leg of my chair. 'I got the flag and the boots when I liberated Strasbourg with Leclerc,' Miller said, laughing away the bravado in his reduction of Leclerc's role. 'Where were you?' "

This scene suggests that Miller had not entirely abandoned acting when he left New York, and his clearly disingenuous posing in the classroom as well as among his colleagues took on a hyperbolic and often quite bitter dimension throughout the 1950s. Levin describes his teaching as "exemplary" rather than sympathetic, and he characterizes Miller's usual tone for teaching and intellectual debate as one of "mocking exaggeration." Levin also says Miller habitually advised his graduate students before they listened to reports by their peers, "Let us be brutal, for we love one another." Readers glimpse a bit of this polemical pose in the prefaces to the Beacon Press paperback editions of *The New England Mind*, which appeared in 1961. In the first volume Miller rejects "the assaults of those who, in a more modern and insidious guise, deny the importance of ideas in American history, as a way of excusing their own imbecility." In the second volume he similarly dismisses social historians who have objected to the "idealistic" abstraction of intellectual history, and he mocks their doomed struggle to "furnish forth at their worst mere tables of statistics, on the average meaningless inventories, and at their best only a series of monographs."

Miller seemed to relish the academic combat that inevitably attended such remarks, and in the essays written during the last decade of his life, he returned almost obsessively to the theme of the isolated scholar, holding out against a society bent on self-destruction. The title "The Plight of the Lone Wolf," an essay written for the twenty-fifth anniversary of the *American Scholar* (collected in *The Responsibility of Mind in a Civilization of Machines: Essays*, 1979), is indicative of the wry self-consciousness with which Miller played this role. In it, he admits that "I am in no more serious plight than what amounts to a nerve-wracking explanation of why I am so antisocial." Nevertheless Miller took that plight seriously, not simply as a personal burden but as the appropriate fate of "any self-respecting scholar in the humanities." In the midst of a culture obsessed with

artificial needs and the production of empty desire, Miller once advised the graduate convocation at Brown University, the humanist is "condemned to respecting the decencies of language." As Thoreau declared, quoted Miller in *The Responsibility of Mind*, it is the duty of the scholar to " 'Let your life be a counter friction to stop the machine,' " and "what we arrogantly throw in the face of community is our declaration that even though it starve us of the crust, we shall strive to do just what we have chosen to do." "I think it fair to say," Miller adds, that "all of us, faculty and students together, are less occupied with imparting or securing information than with criticism—with moving beyond the established, beyond the accepted, into the unexplored space of the disturbing." In short, Miller concludes, the scholar "has eliminated himself from the herd. . . . There is a law of the pack in this republic . . . : he who hunts outside the pack, hunts alone."

This romantic myth of heroic revolt no doubt rationalizes a sense of alienation that Miller shared with most intellectuals during the 1950s. In his latest essays, though, he began insisting on a necessary conjunction between revolt and social responsibility that looked forward to the social activism of the next decade. In one of his last and most important essays, "The Responsibility of Mind in a Civilization of Machines" (1961-1962), Miller attacked those who saw the mind as a helpless observer before the brute facts of technological change. "The machine has not conquered us in some imperial manner against our will," he asserts. "We have wantonly prostrated ourselves before the engine. . . . We today are still bobbing like corks in the flood," awash in a "mental fog of perpetual neutralism" that has severed the link between intelligence and its lethal technological consequences. We no longer hold "the mind" accountable for anything, Miller claims, not even for the potential destruction of our own species. Castigating this "regression into the womb of irresponsibility" characteristic of modern sensibility, Miller insisted that intellectuals must assume a burden of commitment that he describes in terms that must have been both autobiographical and confessional. Heavy as it is, he reminds us, this burden is not merely an ordeal. "Like the precious, beautiful, insupportable and wholly irrational blessing of individuality, with all the myriad quandaries of responsibility therein involved, the responsibility for the human mind to preserve its own integrity amid the terrifying operations of the machine is both an exasperation and an ecstasy."

As his own comments attest, much of Miller's opposition to the more conservative values and practices of humanistic education was undoubtedly attitudinal and political, and it evolved over the course of his long career. But as soon as his work began to appear in the 1930s, it generated controversy for its avowedly revisionist aims and its rejection of the current fashion for economic and social historiography. When Miller first began writing, the field of American history was dominated by historians following the lead of Charles Beard's *Economic Interpretation of the Constitution* (1913) and the deterministic assumptions of Frederick Jackson Turner's *The Frontier in America* (1920). Hence the major historical study of colonial America at the time, James Truslow Adams's *The Founding of New England* (1921), had subordinated religious motives and theoretical debate entirely to the economic concerns of the colonists. So, characteristically, Miller opened his first book with a challenge: "I have attempted to tell of a great folk movement with an utter disregard of the economic and social factors. I lay myself open to the charge of being so very naive as to believe that the way men think has some influence upon their actions."

"I have deliberately avoided giving more than passing notice to the social and economic influences" on the intellectual life of the Puritans, Miller proclaimed in the preface to his most influential work, *The New England Mind: The Seventeenth Century*. He promised to treat those factors in subsequent volumes (and he did), but in all of his works he insisted on the priority of what he called "ideas" as opposed to "events." "History, " he says in *Errand Into the Wilderness* (1956), "is often more instructive as it considers what men conceived they were doing rather than what, in brute fact, they did." When the essay in which that remark appeared was reprinted along with others in 1956, Miller used the preface to the volume again to throw down a methodological gauntlet before colleagues. This time, however, he attacked not only what historians usually did, but also their vision of history and of the historian's place in it. Historians are prone to ignore intellectual work, Miller claimed, "simply because they have so little respect for the intellect in general. I have difficulty imagining that anyone can be a historian without realizing that history itself is part of the life of the mind; hence I have been com-

pelled to insist that the mind of man is the basic factor in human history."

Miller's methodological contentions thus joined with his political concerns to yield what David Hollinger has called a "harder relativism" that insists on the historian's responsibility to the "mind" of his own age as well as that of his subject. It was Miller's stubborn persistence toward that goal that imbued his work with an immediacy and impact far beyond its initial audience of colonialists and literary historians. Even today, with intellectual history and discursive analysis firmly embedded within the institution of historical study, Miller's devotion to the life of the mind and its social and political consequences remains a striking feature of his work, and it is that commitment which underlies Miller's enduring importance as an American scholar.

Throughout his career, Miller referred to himself as a literary historian, but his first publications dealt with topics more often consigned to the domain of history rather than literature. His first book, *Orthodoxy in Massachusetts, 1630-1650*, did challenge the materialistic biases of current historiography in favor of a close reading of theological texts, but it also radically changed the way historians of all sorts conceived of the origin and evolution of American Puritanism. Part of the challenge that Miller's first book posed to traditional conceptions of the Puritans was simply its implicit assumption that there was an intellectual life in the early settlements and that that life mattered to the way the colonists conceived of their more immediate concerns. The professional study of colonial history had taken on what Miller called in the preface to the 1959 Beacon Press edition "a new anti-intellectualism" that harbored "a sullen hostility to the entire notion that ideas ever have consequences." Coupled with the popular "Menckenesque hatred of the kill-joy Puritan" that Miller himself confessed to as a youthful foolishness, this denigrating attitude toward intellectual issues had convinced most historians that the complex theological debates described in this book would have been impenetrable to most of the colonists and, therefore, unimportant to their everyday lives. Miller, however, clearly demonstrated the existence of a pervasive and self-conscious reciprocity between the authority of the elders and the magistrates in Massachusetts Bay, and he explained the theological justifications for that union of church and state as it was proposed by colonial Puritans. Miller thus proved not only that ideas did, indeed, have a direct impact on the political and economic issues of the day but also that theology served as the primary discourse in which those issues were debated and through which the conclusions of those debates were enforced as law.

Miller's first book also disproved a more specific misconception about the intellectual origins of Congregational polity as practiced in the Bay Colony. In *The Founding of New England,* Adams had argued that the immigration of British settlers to the New World lacked a coherent theological motivation and in fact had been dominated by the hopes for economic gain that inspired most of the colonists. Samuel Eliot Morison's *Builders of the Bay Colony* (1930) had reflected a similar bias against the philosophical foundation of the colony by attributing the ecclesiastical practices of the Bay to the influence of the more radical Separatists at Plymouth. In fact, as Miller's book shows, the complex web of Nonseparating Congregationalism promulgated by the settlers of Massachusetts Bay was fully intact before they ever left England. Rather than being an ad hoc response to the contingencies of the wilderness, it reflected a sophisticated integration of theological principles expounded by William Ames and other influential Puritan intellectuals with an emphasis on uniformity that reflected the prevailing political sympathies of the day.

Miller's account of this delicate balance between theological doctrine and political exigency is central to the broad revisionary thrust of his book, but it hinges on a detailed analysis of the abstruse maneuvering endemic to church politics in Elizabethan England. He begins with the paradoxical situation of the English church after Henry VIII's split with Rome. In 1534 the clergy formally recognized Henry as "the only supreme heed in erthe of the Churche of England," and after Elizabeth succeeded her Catholic sister in 1558, the Acts of Supremacy and Uniformity declared the Church to be "united and annexed to the imperial crown of this realm." This declaration made the Queen the "supreme governor" "as well in all spiritual or ecclesiastical things or causes, as temporal." According to Miller the Puritans questioned neither the propriety of civil supremacy stated in these terms, nor the need for uniformity in religion. Their differences with the Anglican clergy focused instead on a relatively fine point of church polity: while civil supremacy was theoretically justified, the application of the prince's power depended on a proper understanding of the limits to that power, which were estab-

lished in Scripture. In theory, then, the Presbyterianism associated with the early Puritans was even *more* conservative (or repressive) than any uniformity imagined by the episcopal hierarchy because it joined divine law to civil constraint. In fact, of course, the situation was quite different, since the Puritans tended to interpret Scriptural law in ways antagonistic to the application of civil supremacy. But Miller claims that a fundamental sympathy with this principle accounts for the colonial Puritans' antipathy toward religious tolerance in the Bay Colony and for their ready use of secular authority to enforce spiritual laws.

Miller argues that the paradoxical conflict between a sympathy for the principle of uniformity and a resistance to its practice by the Church of England was fundamental to the Puritans' position vis-à-vis both the Church and the more radical Separatist movement. As Congregationalists began to distinguish themselves from the more acceptable Presbyterians, the issue of separation emerged more clearly as the only logical step. Nonseparating Puritans, however, insisted on treating the established parishes as Congregational "in substance," even if the "accidents" of their established practice suggested otherwise. "By the exercise of a superlative genius for casuistry," Miller says, "the school did make out a case, it did find ways to reconcile irreconcilables," even if this solution seems "utterly fantastic" to us today. "It takes, to say the least, a large audacity to pretend when you are amputating limbs that you are only removing warts and moles, but these ecclesiastical surgeons were in all seriousness making precisely such an asseveration."

Such a tenuous solution to the obvious contradictions between Congregational polity and the practice of the Anglican Church could not have been sustained very long, but the possibility of emigration offered the Puritans a chance to resolve the theoretical antinomy they faced in England. It allowed them to maintain their political allegiance to England, and in Miller's eyes its most important consequence was that it enabled them to transport the principles of civil supremacy and uniformity, whole cloth, into a context where the two forms of authority could legitimately reinforce each other in the form of a pure theocracy.

> If a body of Puritans could be carried into
> a virgin wilderness, and be carried legally,
> so that the government they set up there

might claim legitimate descent from the Crown, then the civil strife of the spiritual and political loyalties could be reconciled. In a new state erected in accordance with Puritan ideals, the refractory magistrate could be brought into line. At the same time, because those who emigrated would come from that section of Puritanism which had never separated, they could call any church they established part of the Church of England.... They could, in other words, figuratively but effectively transport both the English State and Church to Massachusetts and there reform at will.

Having established the continuity between the "ecclesiastical clique" surrounding William Ames in England and the Puritans who immigrated to Massachusetts Bay, and having situated the colonists' fusion of civil and ecclesiastical authority squarely within the political context of Elizabethan England, Miller examines several cases in which the theoretical principles of colonial Puritanism informed the magistrates' response when their authority was challenged during the first two decades of settlement. "The question before the churches was no longer one of approximating the make-up of the invisible Church," Miller says; "it was one of controlling the Massachusetts electorate." Miller describes the political struggles of the time essentially as a series of efforts by the magistrates and elders to centralize power in the settlements. They restricted the franchise to members of the church (a clear violation of the charter, which extended the vote to all freemen), and they imposed the authority of a general synod over the separate congregations scattered across the wilderness of New England (just as clearly a move toward Presbyterianism). In themselves, these efforts bore little resemblance to what English Puritans were doing at the time, but Miller argues that the strategies by which these goals were achieved merely extended the civil and ecclesiastical principles that the Puritans had brought with them from England in 1630.

In fact, Miller observes, by the time the Cambridge Platform had codified theocratic power in 1648, the colonists were more rigorous Puritans than could be found in England, and that was their downfall. Miller describes the increased tolerance for religious diversity in England that followed the Civil War as "the greatest single religious advance of modern times," and he considered the separation of Church and State im-

plied in that tolerance as the "triumph of modernism." The colonial Puritans missed this momentous trend, Miller says, because they emigrated too early. Colonial Puritanism was simply out of date precisely because it was derived from the assumptions that the emigrants had brought with them, not because they had developed their own brand of wilderness theology once they arrived in New England. "Now that Massachusetts had succeeded in reproducing Elizabethan ideals on the frontier, she was not in a mood to understand an era which found no counterpart in her own experience." In the face of criticism leveled at Massachusetts from England, the state responded "by gathering her holy skirts closer about her heels and proceeding on her unlovely way alone."

Miller's next book, *The New England Mind: The Seventeenth Century* (1939), was published just six years later, and it remains his most important and influential work. A survey of the origins and structure of Puritan intellectual life in America, the detailed accounts of rhetorical, scientific, and theological texts used and produced by the Puritans defy summary description. The titles of the various sections of the book, however, give some idea of the comprehensive scope of Miller's project: "Religion and Learning"; "Cosmology"; "Anthropology," in which "The Nature of Man" and "Rhetoric" are portrayed as entirely continuous fields of inquiry for the Puritans and, as his later work proved, for Miller himself; and "Sociology," in which chapters on "The Covenant of Grace" and "God's Controversy with New England" take the place of the more materialistic topics such a title would have inevitably suggested to most of Miller's readers.

In an early review of Miller's book, Carl Bridenbaugh claimed flatly that "as the Bible was the ultimate authority of the Puritans, so *The New England Mind* must be a Sibylline Book for the students of American history, literature, and thought"; and most readers would still agree with James Hoopes, who wrote in the preface to *Sources for the New England Mind: The Seventeenth Century* (1981) that *The New England Mind: The Seventeenth Century* may well be "the greatest single act of discovery in American historical writing." With one stroke Miller established an intellectual genealogy for colonial Puritanism that not only tied them even more securely to British Puritanism than his first book had done but also traced the origins of their thought back through the Reformation to Augustine and, ultimately, to Plato. He linked both their theology and their science

*Perry Miller speaking on "American Day," organized by the Cultural Relations Section for French teachers of English on 22 January 1950 (courtesy of Harvard University Archives)*

to the logic and rhetoric of Peter Ramus and to the psychology and physics of Aristotle, and he followed the evolution of federal theology out of the uneasy coalition of Calvin and authoritarian politics in Protestant England. Most of these discoveries remain uncontested today, at least in their more general forms, and the fact that Miller was largely working over unmapped regions of intellectual history makes the detail and precision of these historical networks all the more remarkable.

Despite its continuing influence, though, many other principal themes of *The New England Mind: The Seventeenth Century* have been contested in the unceasing debate surrounding Miller's work. The most acrimonious criticisms have been directed at Miller's provocative claim that "the first three generations in New England paid al-

most unbroken allegiance to a unified body of thought, and that individual differences among particular writers or theorists were merely minor variations within a general frame." Miller says he approached "the whole literature" of the period "as though it were the product of a single intelligence. . . . In most instances, it is a matter of complete indifference or chance that a quotation comes from Cotton instead of Hooker, from Winthrop instead of Willard." This claim was immediately attacked on two fronts. Many critics argued that differences among the early Puritans were not so insignificant as Miller assumed, and that there were even more significant differences among the successive generations of Puritans that separated Samuel Willard from John Cotton. Thus critics such as David Hall charged Miller with creating the illusion of a static, monolithic

Puritanism that ignored intrasectarian debates and the evolution of ideas over the first hundred years of settlement.

More recently Miller has also been attacked for what scholars have come to see as the unjustified and arbitrary selection of texts from which Miller drew his conclusions about Puritanism. Despite their resistance to the monolithic character of Miller's Puritanism, earlier critics tended to accept his selection of authors as representative of the intellectual leadership of the colonies and granted Miller his authority as a scholar, if not a precise historian, of early American culture. As Edmund Morgan said, during the 1930s Miller seemed to have "systematically read everything written by New Englanders in the seventeenth century along with the bulk of writings by English Puritans." But in 1974 George Selement undercut what appeared to be the comprehensive scope of *The New England Mind: The Seventeenth Century* by examining Miller's notes, which were not published with the book but deposited at Harvard's Houghton Library. Selement found that Miller had relied on only nineteen authors and eighty-five texts out of 1,506 published New England sources for the years 1620-1660, and that more than half of his quotations were by Thomas Hooker, John Cotton, and Thomas Shepard. Citations from subsequent years were equally biased toward works by Increase Mather, Cotton Mather, and Samuel Willard, and overall Miller had used only fifteen percent of the published sources identified in John Sibley's *Biographical Sketches of Graduates of Harvard University* (1873), Joseph Sabin's *Biblioteca Americana* (1868-1936), and Charles Evans's *American Bibliography* (1941-1959). While few would contest the importance of these authors to the intellectual culture of New England, Selement and others have argued that they cannot be considered "typical" of even the Puritan colonists. Offering their quotations anonymously, as Miller usually does, accords the often polemical and sectarian views of these writers a universality that is unwarranted.

After the monolithic character of Miller's account of Puritan thought, the next most controversial aspect of this work has been the underlying dualism that Miller discovered in all aspects of the Puritans' lives. Usually cast in the form of a tension between intellect and piety, or the head and the heart, this dualism informs most of the theoretical debates Miller describes. Thus in Miller's analysis, the Puritan theologians struggled to reconcile the conflict between their Ramistic de-

sire to systematize religion and their affective experience of doubt and faith, which drew the heart beyond reason into the abyss of sacred mystery. Those responsible for the political and social order were similarly caught between the essentially private and unknowable state of a person's soul and the immediate necessity to maintain a sense of order and control in the visible world in which those souls were temporarily embodied. Puritan scientists also worked hard to identify a coherent order in the world of nature only to specify more precisely the significance of aberrations within that order as they demonstrated the limitation of human reason and the existence of a realm far more comprehensive than the physical universe before their eyes.

Criticism of this dualistic motif has taken two forms. The most extreme of Miller's critics have simply denied the existence of any such dualism in Puritan thought. Stanford Searl, Jr., writing in an article in *Early American Literature* (1977-1978), has argued that the balance between piety and intellect that Miller discovered among the colonists is actually an ideal of Miller's own and was not a central issue for the seventeenth-century Puritan. David Hall has noted that the "crisis" Miller attributes to this dualistic tension was seldom perceived as such by the Puritans themselves, and that their attitude toward the opposition was hardly unique for the time. Although much more sympathetic to the general thrust of Miller's argument, David Hollinger has also observed that for Miller "antimony in itself seemed to excite his passion" and that he "effected a kind of scholarly epiphany whenever he found an American who had faced a paradox." A large part of Miller's fascination with dualism in Puritan thought, Hollinger suggests, reflects his outlook on his own time, which, as Miller himself claimed in *Jonathan Edwards* (1949), was plagued with "the modern problem" of an incompatibility between "the objective and the subjective, of the mechanical and the conscious."

Other critics have accepted Miller's emphasis on this underlying dualism at the heart of Puritan intellectual life but rejected his tendency to see that tension resolved in favor of reason and the intellect. Miller "told us too much about the Puritan mind and not enough about the Puritan's feelings," Alan Simpson said, and Sacvan Bercovitch has complained that Miller "described the New England Mind as a kind of logic-machine run by the principles of the Ramist dialect and oiled by rigid pedantry." Noting Miller's tendency to blame the rigorous strictures of cove- nant theology on the rationalistic side of the Puri- tans rather than admitting to its similarity with Calvin's work, Everett Emerson linked this more specific problem of Miller's genealogical claims to the broader issue of his rationalism and then summed up many similar charges with the conclu- sion that "Miller's overemphasis on the covenant as the means by which the Puritans made ra- tional God's mysterious grace led him to neglect both the agony and the ecstasy of the Puritans' spiritual life."

Such criticism has resulted in necessary re- finements to many of Miller's most sweeping claims, and the judgments of emphasis and bias are persuasive. Miller himself seldom answered his critic's charges of error, preferring instead to conduct his battles on methodological grounds. Yet there are numerous instances in *The Seven- teenth Century* which anticipated some of the more general accusations made against it. At the very be- ginning of the book, for example, Miller claims that the Puritans "saw no opposition between the spirit of religion and the letter of theology, be- tween faith and its intellectualization," and he does note the importance of social and economic factors in his preface while arguing that they are separable from intellectual concerns and consign- ing them to another volume.

Miller's most rigorous defense, however, has come from readers who argue that the terms of the debates surrounding his work have dis- torted its true importance. Francis T. Butts claims that the basic tension Miller discovered in Puritanism was not one of a conflict between head and heart at all, but that of "man's torment- ing primitive sentiment," an "existential source" of Puritan theology that reflected "the more basic paradoxes of the soul—of man's conflicting sense of both despair and exaltation." On the other hand, instead of crediting Miller with discov- ering such a universal affective dimension be- neath Puritan culture, Hoopes rejects the conflict of heart and head to argue that Miller was actu- ally describing a conflict between two sets of *ideas*, "pietistical and intellectual," not between ideas and emotions. He cites Miller's own insis- tence that sensibility and doctrine were "insepara- ble" in all aspects of Puritan life and argues that critics who have cast these two realms as antago- nists in Miller's account have simply missed the point of his book. The real problem, Hoopes adds, is that Miller failed to maintain the balance between the two sets of ideas that he rightly

claims is characteristic of Puritan thought, and in- stead privileged the intellectual over the pietistical.

The most ambitious defense of Miller's work has taken place on a less predictable ground, that of Perry Miller as an "artist." In his influential article of 1968, David Hollinger ar- gued that Miller's work "is essentially art, but it is an art acutely epistemological and profoundly his- torical in conception." It is "art," he explains, be- cause in it "facts" do not speak for themselves, and it is "history" because Miller believed that "the human predicament is given in time." Mil- ler's recognition of the constitutive power of con- ceptual forms, Hollinger adds, is what protected him from the often naive empirical determinism that characterized historiography at the time *The Seventeenth Century* appeared, yet at the same time it also allowed him to accept "the reality of matter" as a point of resistance to form. The re- sult was a pragmatic idealism that allowed Miller to blame the collapse of Puritanism on the colo- nists' failure to recognize the importance of the frontier and commerce, while at the same time in- sisting on the centrality of the intellectual forms in which those material factors were represented. Similarly, Hoopes claims that Miller's assumption of a "single intelligence" behind New England is only "a literary device for describing a system of ideas" and that Miller never claimed that the Puri- tans agreed on everything. These defenses do not, of course, protect Miller's work against spe- cific charges of inaccuracy and bias, but they do emphasize the inevitable role of the historian's place in his text that is consonant with Miller's own vision of his function as an author of a histori- cal work, and they align that work with the more self-conscious "metahistorical" perspective charac- teristic of contemporary historiography in the last quarter of the twentieth century.

For the next ten years, 1939 to 1949, Miller published very little. "Jonathan Edwards to Emerson" is the only significant exception to this silence. It appeared in the *New England Quarterly* in 1940 and immediately evoked criticism for what readers construed as Miller's proposition of a mysterious continuity between these two fig- ures. When he reprinted this famous essay six- teen years later as "From Edwards to Emerson" in *Errand Into the Wilderness*, Miller explained that he had intended only to suggest that the two writ- ers shared "the basic continuance: the incessant drive of the Puritan to learn how, and how most ec- statically, he can hold any sort of communion with the environing wilderness." The real difference between them, he adds, is that "Edwards went to nature . . . convinced that man could receive from it impressions which he must then try to interpret, whereas Emerson went to Nature . . . convinced that in man there is a spontaneous correlation with the received impressions." Nevertheless Miller still insists that "certain basic continuities persist in a culture . . . which underlie the successive articulation of 'ideas,' " and if intellectual history is to be "anything more than a mail-order catalogue," the historian must possess "not only a fluency in the concepts themselves but an ability to get underneath them."

This retrospective analysis of his own work identifies the increasingly active role of the historian that Miller embraced after the war. In 1949 the University of Leiden, Holland, published *Society and Literature in America,* which was Miller's inaugural address for his tenure as a visiting professor there in 1949-1950. He reflected on that experience in essays such as "What Drove Me Crazy in Europe" (it was the "academic standardization" of European education that did it) and "The Incorruptible Sinclair Lewis" (both printed in *The Responsibility of Mind in a Civilization of Machines,* 1979). His first major publication after the war, however, was a book on Jonathan Edwards for the American Men of Letters Series published by William Sloane Associates.

Although conceived as an introduction to Edwards's work, and eminently successful on that ground, *Jonathan Edwards* (1949) is, in fact, a radical revision of the traditional role assigned to Edwards by previous intellectual historians. In Miller's account Edwards is not merely a country minister gifted with a powerful rhetorical sensibility in which Puritan theology flashed briefly in a dying flame. Instead, for Miller, Edwards is "one of America's five or six major artists, who happened to work with ideas instead of with poems or novels." He is both "the apotheosis of Puritanism" and the spokesman for "the really native tradition" of intellectual culture in New England. "No American succeeded better," Miller claims, "in generalizing his experience into the meaning of America," and Miller portrays the difficulties between Edwards and his congregation at Northampton as a measure of "the parting of the ways in modern culture," a "clash between America's greatest spokesman for absolute Christian morality and representatives of the American business ethic."

Apart from this elevation of Edwards to an extraordinary prominence as an intellectual leader of eighteenth-century America, Miller's account challenges prior scholars on two specific points: Edwards's philosophical contributions and his political position in relation to the subsequent democratic sympathies of the second half of the century. Although historians had usually treated Edwards as an autocratic reactionary in his theology as well as his politics, Miller argued that Edwards was, in fact, one of the most innovative thinkers of the time and a true political radical. According to Miller, Edwards's major accomplishment was to make John Locke "available to the democracy" by converting his sensationalist psychology into a kind of populist theology. "Persons with but an ordinary degree of knowledge, are capable, without a long and subtle train of reasoning, to see the divine excellency of the things of religion," Miller quotes Edwards as saying, and then elaborates: "All a man needs is his senses . . . then perforce he perceives, and perception depends not on social status or a Harvard degree, it 'depends on the sense of the heart.' " Edwards thus joined his proclivity toward an empirical naturalism, which Miller claims reflected his fascination with Sir Isaac Newton, to the idealistic tendencies of Lockean psychology, which remained compatible with the Puritan emphasis on the internal workings of the soul. The result was a happy compatibility between empiricism and mysticism that made Edwards "the last great American . . . for whom there could be no warfare between religion and science, or between ethics and nature."

Important and subtle as this philosophical syncretism was, Miller argues that Edwards's real significance emerges only when he is situated within the specific context of early-eighteenth-century political conflict. The founders of New England had been anything but social radicals, Miller observes, and they had looked upon the millennial utopianism of sects in Cromwellian England with horror. Rather than seeing a necessary tension between religious purity, social order, and the economic gain that would result from that stability, the early colonists enjoyed at least a theoretical harmony between the forces of religion and business that lent the status quo both theological and economic support. By the second and third decades of the eighteenth century, though, that coalition had broken down, and the inherent tension between chiliastic utopianism and the immediate demands of a mercantile economy emerged as the central political issue of the day.

This tension did not necessarily lead to overt conflict between ministers and businessmen. As Miller says, most of the merchants and land speculators were perfectly willing "to let sleeping dogmas lie." Nevertheless, as Miller notes, "If there was a lion's mouth to be met with, Edwards would put his head in it," and the rural minister began to press the obvious contradictions between the two major sources of political power at the time. "Edwards' exposition of the millennial expectation . . . was not a return to atavistic myth," Miller argues, "it was the proclamation of a radical thesis." His claim that redemption was not to be obtained either in history or in the objective goods of this world was properly viewed by the entrepreneurs who heard him as an attack on what they did and on who they were, not as an abstruse theological doctrine. Similarly Edwards's rejection of the Arminian notion of free will was received not as a doctrinal quibble but as an arraignment of free enterprise. While not slighting the importance of the theological debates in which Edwards was engaged throughout his tenure in Northampton, Miller insists that his final fall from power was a political, not a theological event, and it marked the final stages of a transfer of power from the ministers to the merchants, not a "democratization" of power in which the people spoke. Miller claims "the oligarchy of business and real estate . . . the river gods were out for Edwards' scalp, and the masses, played upon by the solid citizenry, did the screaming."

The reception of *Jonathan Edwards* was generally favorable, although most critics agreed with Lewis Leary's charge in *American Literature* (November 1951) that Edwards owed more to Calvin than to Newton and that Locke may well have been more widely known in the colonies than Miller would allow. Miller's antagonistic relation with his colleagues continued, however, in a debate over the relative importance of economic versus religious motives in the founding of Virginia. In his two-part study of "The Religious Impulse in the Founding of Virginia" (1948 and 1949, collected in *Errand Into the Wilderness*), Miller argued that although the desire to found a holy city was "less explicit" in the dreams of the Virginia Company than in Winthrop's writings, "the colonizing impulse was fulfilled within the same frame of universal relevance as the Puritans assumed." Although the "purely economic account is so eminently satisfactory to the sluggard intellect of this century," it was in fact religion, not econom-

ics, that was "the really energizing propulsion in this settlement." Miller argued that "One comes from a reading of the Virginia literature persuaded that historians have so failed in historical imagination that they have not done justice either to the grandeur or the humility of a conception which was at the very center of the impetus to Christian imperialism."

Miller was less successful at changing the way southern history was read and written than he was at revising the modern vision of New England, and the controversy over Virginia faded in 1953 when Miller published two more influential works, the famous article "Errand Into the Wilderness" (the title essay of his subsequent collection) and the second volume of *The New England Mind: From Colony to Province* (1953). The essay sets forth a central theme of the book, which is the evolution of theological certainty under pressure from the exigencies of life in a frontier settlement. The first generation of immigrants to Massachusetts Bay were literally on a mission from God, Miller points out, and they ignored many of the specific problems that the wilderness presented for the doctrinal schema they projected onto the new world. Their children shared little of that sense of mission, though, and the urgency of the founding fathers gave way to the mundane concerns of survival that occupied succeeding generations. Thus the colonists embarked on what Miller calls "the process of Americanization," which found expression in the jeremiad and included a profound sense of declining piety and an increasingly tenuous sense of identity. The second and third generations of settlers "looked in vain to history for an explanation of themselves," Miller writes, and "more and more it appeared that the meaning was not to be found in theology." Consequently these generations became increasingly oriented "toward the social, and only the social problem." With no place to turn for solutions other than to themselves, "having failed to rivet the eyes of the world upon their city on the hill, they were left alone with America."

*The New England Mind: From Colony to Province* traced in painstaking detail these themes of a declension of piety and the expression of a national uneasiness in the jeremiad. It answered critics' charges that Miller ignored the social and economic contexts of "the life of the mind" described in *The Seventeenth Century*, and it emphasized the evolution of ideas that Miller had treated as the static foundation of a monolithic

Puritanism in the earlier volume. Beginning with the passing of the first generation of colonists in the middle of the seventeenth century, *From Colony to Province* follows the efforts of the Puritan ministers to preserve both the theory and the polity of covenant theology in the face of challenges from British authorities and from an increasingly diverse and recalcitrant colonial population. Along the way Miller also describes the striking shift in American prose styles as theology was replaced by common sense, and doctrinal seriousness was met by a lively and often sarcastic wit, and he posits a close connection between these ideational and stylistic conflicts. Thus he claims that, during the crisis over the smallpox epidemic that pitted the ministers against populist spokesmen such as the Franklin brothers, "what had begun, under the shadow of pestilence, as a grim struggle for the mastery of New England's soul petered out, by the next spring, into a tiff about style. . . . the fact that antiministerial sentiment, mobilized against inoculation, persisted by shifting the point of attack to language marks an epoch in the training of the mentality." With such a claim, Miller moved his intellectual history squarely into the realm of a new kind of literary history, one that treated texts not as objects of aestheticist pleasure, but as weapons and stakes in the struggle for the colonists' emergent national identity.

Miller's book ends with 1730, when the colonial ministers' efforts to preserve their dominance over the intellectual life of their congregations had failed, just as their grip on the social and political order of New England had begun to slip several years earlier. Political, economic, and theological debate had lost the scholastic rigor that marked the earlier Puritanism imported from England. Even such staunch apologists as Cotton Mather had embraced an energetic rationalism and pragmatic common sense that bore little resemblance to Calvinist election, original sin, or the doom-saying jeremiads with which the ministers had sought to shore up faith in these antique doctrines. Ministerial power had eroded, and the social unity it had enforced splintered along economic lines. Beneath the placid surface of the early eighteenth century, the New Englanders who had been held together by intellectual forms for a hundred years confronted a reality that they could no longer comprehend.

*From Colony to Province* divides this degeneration of Puritan hegemony into four stages: "Declension," "Confusion," "The Splintering of So-

ciety," and "The Socialization of Piety." In "Declension" Miller argues that the first generation of colonists had been held together by the dramatic sense of mission that had underwritten the immigration and infused the problems of everyday life with a sacred energy and significance. That sense of purpose and urgency could not be sustained by the second generation of Puritans, who had to confront New England as a local and domestic reality rather than as the "City on a Hill" Winthrop had imagined. The result was a general decline in piety described by the Puritans themselves in the jeremiad, which thus emerged as the dominant literary form of a uniquely American vision of history and destiny. In Miller's account, however, the jeremiad was more than just a lament for the passing grandeur of earlier days. It allowed the colonists to pay tribute to the old ways while pursuing wealth in the new, and Miller traces in detail how the theological innovations of mid-century Puritanism—preparation, the Half-way Covenant that automatically extended church membership to the children of baptized members, and an emphasis on "federal holiness" that focused on visible behavior as a criteria for church membership instead of personal assurance of election—yielded a positive notion of "hypocrisy" that kept Calvinism from getting in the way of a rising mercantile ethic.

Miller refers to this increasing separation of internal and external covenants as the Americanization of imported dogma, a necessary consequence of the fact that the external church had been realized in America and so faced political realities unforeseen by the theoretical ideal of a community of saints. He portrays it as the underlying theme of an increasingly atomistic concept of "special providence" that set individual salvation apart from, and eventually in opposition to, the community of saints that had been the source of ministerial power when the colonies were first settled. He argues that it was this tendency to distinguish personal election from communal direction that made the ministers increasingly dependent on the will of their congregations and so vulnerable to the powerful laymen who would eventually supplant them as leaders of the community.

This theme of declension quickly became the most controversial aspect of Miller's book. In 1961 Edmund Morgan argued that the signs of a declining piety that Miller identifies, especially that of the Half-Way Covenant, may in fact have been evidence of an increasing precision and intensified sense of religious scruples, and Robert

Pope rejected the whole topic of declension as simply a myth. It is difficult to reduce Miller's account of this period to any single empirical phenomenon, however, and as Hoopes has pointed out, Miller himself readily admitted that "as we measure facts, New England was not declining." But although he consistently recognized declension as more of a literary motif for the jeremiad than a quantifiable fact of colonial life, Miller did insist that an increasing rate of change throughout the second half of the seventeenth century led to the "confusion" analyzed in the second section of the book. Factions and conflict began to arise along social rather than doctrinal lines, and theological issues gave way to what Miller calls the "preconditions of provincial culture": "Loyalty to the Crown, toleration, and constitutional liberties."

By focusing on the rise of a provincial culture in the colonies rather than just a decline in rigorous Calvinism, Miller illustrates the way Puritan theology took on a positive, productive social role that was quite different from the more negative power of constraint that had characterized the exercise of theocratic authority. Days of humiliation became occasions for mobilizing the forces of the community rather than just recollections of sins and shortcomings, and the idea of a national covenant obtained "a social implication that was a large step toward an identification of the voice of the people with the will of God." At the same time, in the last decade of the century, the Salem witchcraft trials proved that the timeless doctrine of the jeremiad–covenant-sin-confession-redemption–was not as secure as it once seemed, since in this case confession led directly to disaster and chaos, and repentance had become a painfully obvious ruse. Miller claims that the trials exposed a "flaw in the very foundation of the covenant conception," and he condemns Cotton Mather for trying to legitimate the executions by forcing them into the form of a jeremiad that egregiously ignored the reality of the situation and the failure of doctrine to contain it. Thus in Miller's account the witchcraft trials further undermine the power of the Mathers and the Puritan establishment they led, which was also being challenged on three other fronts: the rising popularity of Solomon Stoddard's antirational emphasis on the arbitrary character of grace; Increase Mather's failure to maintain control of Harvard College; and the foundation of the Brattle Street Church in direct defiance of the Mathers' insistence on a narrow uniformity.

Miller is cautious about labeling any of the opposition to the Mathers as liberal in any sense, but the increasing skepticism about the scriptural basis for the covenant, along with the pressing need to incorporate more members of the community into the church and a growing sympathy for a "sentimentalized piety" that was directly accessible to untutored experience, did have a democratizing effect on the colonies that was accelerated by more secular developments in science and economics. Moreover, from his post in the Chebacco Parish, John Wise launched the first explicitly rationalistic and self-consciously egalitarian attack on the power of the Mathers, and Miller claims that Wise's willingness to dispense with biblical and historical evidences in favor of rational proof–and, as importantly, his shocking use of a satiric tone in the debate–"commenced a new chapter in the history of the provincial mind."

From then on public discourse became increasingly secular, until the major economic issue of the early eighteenth century, the debate about establishing a national bank and switching from hard specie to paper money, could be openly argued as a financial and political issue quite apart from its moral and theological implications. The idea of the covenant and the form of the jeremiad were abandoned in favor of a more colloquial, witty language, and James Franklin's *New England Courant* emerged as the primary organ of this new, antiministerial sentiment, the province of the "Leather-Apron Men." The problem for the church, Miller observes, had not become the dreaded conflict with the state, but a more subtle and finally more devastating confrontation with public opinion and a literary style.

Because the opposition to ministerial power was more stylistic and expedient than doctrinal, the various forms of secular discourse in which public affairs were being argued could not provide a coherent basis for social unity to replace Puritanism. In the place of the founding ideas of original sin and the covenant arose the more amorphous ideals of liberty and happiness, and as the theologians themselves began to embrace such ideals as the goals of religion as well as society, Miller argues that for the first time theology took on a form that would eventually support a truly revolutionary ideology. The concept of America shifted from the covenant to business during the early years of the eighteenth century, and even such stalwarts as Cotton Mather adopted the simplified pietism of a "particular faith" and "daily spiritualizing" (which Miller characterizes as a "plebian typology") that was entirely compatible with the rationalist pragmatism of a Benjamin Franklin. By the second decade of the century, when Mather was capable of declaring flatly, "the Voice of Reason, is the Voice of God," the American province had wholeheartedly endorsed the Enlightenment and was rushing to catch up with Europe rather than trying to lead it toward the millennium.

In the same year that *The New England Mind: From Colony to Province* appeared, Miller also published *Roger Williams: His Contribution to the American Tradition* (1953). Much more modest in scope and purpose, *Roger Williams* was part of the Makers of the American Tradition Series for the Bobbs-Merrill Company and was intended as a general introduction to Williams's work. Much of the text consists of long passages reprinted from Williams's books, with substantial introductions that situate the works within Williams's whole career. But as in his book on Edwards, Miller seized this opportunity for yet another revisionary polemic, and he set out to rescue Williams from what Miller calls the "liberal myth" of his importance as a prophet of religious freedom and social liberty. Williams may indeed have been a prophet, Miller argues, but only in the sense of a Jeremiah who demands that his people return to a severer fidelity to God's way. Rather than being a social revolutionary, in Miller's eyes Williams was a rabid biblicist whose defense of religious toleration derived from his insistence that the laws of the flesh, the "second Table," had no jurisdiction over the spiritual realm, and that the separation of church and state therefore had to be absolute and permanent.

It is here that Miller locates Williams's true importance for the American tradition: far from having no real concern for religious truth, Williams was "the most passionately religious of men."

> Hence he is an analyst, an explorer into the dark places, of the very nature of freedom. His decision to leave denominations free to worship as they chose came as a consequence of his insight that freedom is a condition of the spirit. . . . what he stood for, and still stands for, is the certainty that those who mistake their own assurances for divinely appointed missions, and so far forget the sanctity of others' persuasion as to try reducing them to conformity by physical means, commit in the face of the Divine a sin more outrageous than any of the statutory crimes.

In retrospect, and surely even at the time, Williams served Miller as a counterforce to Joseph McCarthy's repressive anticommunist campaigns, and the American tradition defined by Miller is clearly an effort to prove that social liberalism can be aligned with the deepest, and most traditional, religious faith. Today, however, Miller's treatment of Williams is best known for his erroneous claim that Williams parted from his colleagues in New England over the issue of their resistance to his typological reading of scripture. Typology is "the insight that guided him from his initial separation to his ultimate vision of the predicament of men and nations," Miller says. In Williams's eyes, Christ was the antitype of Old Testament types, and at his coming the earthly church had been destroyed. Those people who claimed authority as antitypes of Israel's sovereign were thus "traitors to the Christian dispensation" because "no modern community any longer possesses in the physical realm those sanctions with which Israel alone had been invested." To be sure, Miller notes, John Cotton and others had "experimented" with typology, "but almost to a man the New England theologians . . . were so content with the consistency of their covenant or 'federal' version of the Bible that they saw in typology only a fantastic creation of the imagination which had no place in sound scholarship or in orthodox society."

Subsequent scholarship has proven that Miller was mistaken in refusing to recognize typology as an approved and even common discursive practice among the more orthodox Puritans. While the conclusions Williams drew from his typological readings of scripture certainly contradicted those claimed by the settlers of Massachusetts Bay, the conflict between these positions cannot be ascribed simply to his practicing this exegetical method. Miller's insistence that this was the single source of the controversy surrounding Williams thus undermines much of his argument and renders his claim about Williams's place in the religious history of New England suspect, although Miller's readings of the documents themselves remain a precise and accurate guide to Williams's thought.

In the next three years Miller published essays on Herman Melville, Henry David Thoreau, and Ralph Waldo Emerson. Then, in 1956, two more books appeared. *Errand Into the Wilderness* collected most of his important essays from the 1930s and 1940s, granting access to Miller's work for readers daunted by the length and detail of the volumes of *The New England Mind*. The real importance of this collection, however, is the running commentary Miller makes on his own career in the prefaces that introduce the various essays. He uses the occasion of critics' specific objections to points raised in the essays for a concerted attack on historians who neglect the importance of ideas and who relegate issues of language and style to mere "reflections" of more substantial issues of politics and economics. Together with Miller's introduction to the volume, these polemical prefaces continued the methodological crusade Miller had begun twenty years earlier.

*The Raven and the Whale: The War of Words and Wits in the Era of Poe and Melville* (1956) was the last book-length study Miller published in his lifetime. It was also the least controversial of all his works, perhaps because it turned his skills and priorities as a literary scholar toward a more conventional topic of literary history. The book provides a detailed portrait of the literary scene in New York during the first half of the nineteenth century, and by tracing the controversies, personalities, and literary journals that flourished during that period, it offers a precise understanding of the cultural context in which Poe and Melville produced their work.

Miller portrays New York cultural life as divided between two groups: one associated with Lewis Gaylord Clark and his *Knickerbocker* review, and the other, self-styled the "Young America," associated with Evert A. Duyckinck and the journals *Arctus* (1840-1842) and *Literary World* (1847-1853). The *Knickerbocker* set dominated the scene throughout the period and instituted a taste for romance that elevated Washington Irving, James Fenimore Cooper, and William Cullen Bryant to the status of literary demigods, along with the equally admired foreigners Walter Scott, Lord Byron, Charles Lamb, and, after 1840, William Wordsworth. Accompanying this fondness for the sublime, however, was an interest in *vraisemblance* that evolved into a straightforward realism following Dickens's sudden prominence in America after the publication of his *Pickwick Papers* in 1836. Miller describes this attention to the coarser side of life as a reflection of "anti-romanticism flowing deep within these Gothamite romantics." This stream was tapped by such writers as Charles Frederick Briggs who, under the name of Harry Franco, produced a series of sea stories and broad satires that countered the

more genteel *Knickerbocker* columns written by Henry Cary under the name of "John Waters."

By 1840 the tension between the Whig vision of style and prosperity manifested in Cary's work and the democratic sympathies exemplified by Briggs's comic but still disturbing portrayals of urban poverty and life among common men led to the formation of a rival journal, Duyckinck's *Arctus*. As the official organ of "Young America," *Arctus* embraced the values of democratic pluralism, literary nationalism (or "home literature"), and a decidedly anti-Whig sympathy for a copyright law that would protect our "home" authors from the Anglophiliac and highly commercial "transferrals" of British writing to the presses of American publishers.

Young America embraced several journals, including John O'Sullivan's *Democratic Review* and Charles Frederick Briggs's *Broadway Journal*, but its literary values remained remarkably consistent and established a taste for what its members called the "Rabelaisian" manner of humor and a "cockney" urbanity. After several years, though, the rabid Americanism of this group faded, and by the time Duyckinck took over the *Literary World* much of the bitter feuding with the *Knickerbocker* set was over. What antagonism remained vented itself in an anthology war carried on between two of the most prominent literati of the time: Rufus Wilmot Griswold, whose *Poets and Poetry of America* (1842, revised in 1855) was the first effort to demonstrate the existence of a long tradition of native American genius; and Duyckinck himself, who with his brother published the *Cyclopaedia of American Literature* in 1855. Griswold responded with what Miller calls "the most destructive review in all American history," and Griswold's long list of mistakes, plagiarisms, and grammatical offenses committed in the *Cyclopaedia* finished off Duyckinck's career and with it the literary feud he had been waging for almost two decades with his older nemesis, Lewis Gaylord Clark.

From a modern perspective, the literary culture Miller describes seems to have oddly missed the point for all of their exaggerated efforts to discover and puff an authentic American genius. Young America did shelter Poe, Melville, and, for a time, Walt Whitman, but most of its energy was spent worrying about the peculiar turn of Melville's imagination after *White Jacket; or the World in a Man-of-War* (1850), calling for an Adamic genius who could answer the British glory of Shakespeare and celebrating writers who have long since been forgotten. Among the forgotten heroes of Young America, for example, was one Cornelius Mathews, a wretched writer who encouraged others to call him "the Centurion" and who for a time was a singular enthusiasm of the usually reasonable Duyckinck. One of the most entertaining motifs of Miller's study is his frequent, gleeful annihilation of whatever literary or personal reputation Mathews might have retained in the margins of literary history, and he even goes so far as to attribute the decline of Duyckinck's influence some years later to the editor's stubborn reluctance to admit the ridiculous character of his protégé's style. More sober but equally benighted from the perspective of subsequent literary judgment, the *Knickerbocker* harbored the fireside sentiments of Henry Wadsworth Longfellow and Oliver Wendell Holmes and embodied most of the less sympathetic values associated with the Victorian Whiggery ascribed to the period. Together both groups delighted in trouncing all things New England, especially those whom Briggs described as "high Germanorum mystery-mongers" and their chief, Emerson, whom Richard Henry Dana, Sr. called one of "these she-men, these compound-gendered, these men-women creatures." So while Miller's account grants us a detailed understanding of a period and time unsurpassed for the viciousness and volume of its literary invective, his focus may seem askew to readers expecting what we have come to think of as literary history from a book about the era of Poe and Melville.

Miller does provide some details about the everyday concerns surrounding what have become the literary milestones of the time, but he is clearly concerned more with the publishing practices of O'Sullivan and Duyckinck than with the fledgling writers whose coattails these editors have ridden into American anthologies. That concern led him to an extraordinarily prescient combination of literary and social history that details what today would be called the discursive apparatus of the time, the concrete, specific institutional supports for the production and dissemination of literary writing in antebellum New York. Miller tells us not only who published what but *why* those decisions and alliances were made, and his careful analysis of contemporary reviews, personal vendettas, and sheer serendipity offers a more profound understanding of the emergence and evolution of literary values than any textual analysis could possibly yield.

At times, however, Miller betrays a fondness for invective which echoes that of his subjects to the extent that one begins to question the balance of his account. Moreover his frequent recourse to claims about what lay in the unspoken depths of various groups often sounds arbitrary and gratuitously nasty. It is unlikely, for example, that Duyckinck's career could really have been so singly ruined by the albatross of Cornelius Mathews as Miller insists, and one wonders if Griswold, who is introduced as "about as devious as they came in this era of deviousness," needs to be ridden to his grave 200 pages later in an "abject end." In this same vein Miller also tells us that "It was not really in the spirit of Young America to consent to a recoil from Nature to civilization. In its heart of hearts, the nationalist movement, though exemplified by such a dunderhead as Mathews, led by such a Mazarin as Duyckinck, was frequently savage."

Granting the questionable taste of such passages, Miller's writing nevertheless cannot simply be dismissed as the mannerism of a nasty crank. For how else is the historian to describe an age in which Melville, for example, might respond to Joseph Hart's *The Romance of Yachting* (1848) by observing that "pen and ink should instantly be taken away from that infatuate man, upon the same principle that pistols are withdrawn from the wight bent on suicide"? Or to define the character of a man, the unfortunate Griswold again, whose own contemporary Holmes once described as "a kind of naturalist whose subjects are authors, whose memory is a perfect fauna of all flying and creeping things that feed on ink"? And more generally, how is the historian to describe, in 1956, what might be identified today as the paradigm or *episteme* that informs the discourse of a group, if not by anthropomorphizing it as the "heart" of the group's language? Excepting the stylistic hyperbole that distinguishes this and so many other writings by Miller (and that makes readable his analyses of often arcane topics), many of these departures from the measured objectivity of conventional historiography mark Miller's attempt to identify a genuinely new object of historical knowledge for which there was no discursive paradigm, no way of talking about it, that was available to him at the time. In this light, *The Raven and the Whale* appears idiosyncratic in the very best sense of that term, an iconoclastic challenge not only to the way literary history is written but also to the very limits of what the literary historian should—and can—know.

Miller spent the remaining years of his life extending the intellectual history of *The New England Mind* up to the Civil War and writing a number of articles addressing the role of the humanist in the modern age. In addition to the articles discussed above, the most substantial publication of this period is another introduction to a major literary figure: *Consciousness in Concord: The Text of Thoreau's Hitherto "Lost Journal" (1840-1841) Together with Notes and a Commentary* (1958). Miller's preface and comments situate the journal in the context of Thoreau's whole career, and as he does in *Roger Williams*, Miller takes the occasion of Thoreau's text to present an intellectual biography of the writer that challenges more traditional readings of his work.

Miller is especially anxious to dispel the idea of the journal as a spontaneous record of Thoreau's most intimate thoughts. He proposes instead to read the whole journal as "about as much a contrivance as anything by Proust or Joyce." It is a "literary performance," Miller says, a "clinical study" of "the literary libido" that he reads as a revision of some hypothetical "Ur-journal" that was not preserved. Out of the set-pieces collected in his journal, Miller claims, Thoreau composed his more public works much like a "mosaic," some elaborate masonry work, or a piece of carpentry. Similarly Miller criticizes the myth of Thoreau's devotion to "Nature" or "the Self." Miller argues that Thoreau "dedicated his entire consciousness to 'letters'" and loved nature only as what Thoreau called the "raw materials of tropes and figures." For Thoreau, Miller argues, these tropes "were the rewards of an exploitation of natural resources, as self-centered, as profit-seeking, as that of any railroad-builder or lumber-baron, as that of any John Jacob Astor."

In addition to this account of Thoreau's method of composition, Miller also describes what he reads as the androgynous, if not clearly homosexual, character of friendship sketched out in many of the entries. Thoreau's "search for disengagement" exiled him from human contact throughout his life, Miller says, and it rendered most of his experience no more than an "anticipation" for some greater, heart-ravishing transcendence that he never reached. Even the (perhaps only rumored) flirtations with Ellen Sewall serve in the journal as a "literary preparation" rather than expressions of true affection, and after quoting Thoreau's enigmatic references to an idyllic moment rowing with a young lady on a lake, Miller wonders if the passage is not really just

"one more instance of the process of collecting material out of limited experience, in which the predominant emotion is not a passion for anybody but a greed for tidbits." Miller concludes that "Anticipation is the cause for living" that we find in every one of Thoreau's pages, and this attitude marks an assurance of failure as well as a strategy for life. According to Miller, this is the conclusion of *Walden* (1854), and it serves as the dominant motif of the *Journal* as well: "circumventing death, evading woman, discounting friendship, [Thoreau] anticipated the impossible, so as never to be seduced by the moments he loved so passionately."

Two years after Miller's death in 1963, his wife, Elizabeth Miller, gathered together the completed portions of his unfinished manuscript, added the chapters he had left in rough draft and his outlines for the remaining portions of the book, and published the collection as *The Life of the Mind in America: From the Revolution to the Civil War* (1965). The book consists of two complete sections, one on "The Evangelical Basis" of the period and the other on "The Legal Mentality," and one long chapter of a third section on "Science–Theoretical and Applied." A detailed outline of the rest of this section is included, along with Miller's plan for the rest of the book, which was to have included sections on education, political economy, philosophy, theology, nature, and "The Self."

In the first section, Miller describes the years between the Revolutionary and Civil Wars as "the grand era of the revival" and frames the period with the Great Revival of 1800 and the Great Awakening of 1858. "The dominant theme in America from 1800 to 1860 is the invincible persistence of the revival technique," he says, and he warns that we can hardly understand Emerson, Thoreau, Whitman, or Melville unless we understand that "for them this was the one clearly given truth of their society." Briefly noting the distant but important influence of the Great Awakening of 1740 on the later movements, Miller contrasts the theological similarities of these "Second" and "Third Awakenings" to the striking differences between their social roots. The Great Revival of 1800 was exemplified by the rural enthusiasm of the Cane Ridge camp meeting of 1801, where a score of Baptist, Methodist, and Presbyterian preachers brought about what Miller describes as a "spasm among the populace" in the woods of Kentucky, haranguing their audience simultaneously in different parts of the enclosure until people succumbed to an orgy of "falling, barking, catalepsy, rolling, [and] running." Fifty years later, the revivalist spirit arose among a more urban and urbane population in Philadelphia (1856) and New York (1857), yielding the somewhat more restrained effects of a pamphlet war and a reinvigorated YMCA. Despite their obvious differences, however, both of these later movements shared a communal and nationalistic urgency that differed from the more individualistic character of the earlier revival, and it was to "American Christians" that the preachers now addressed their appeals.

Miller argues that the center of all three awakenings was an anxiety over the future, but for the nineteenth century it was the future of "this nation on earth," not that of the individual soul in heaven, that was the focus of evangelical energy and concern. Cutting across denominations as it did, the revival was a quintessentially American movement that figured in its ecclesiastical harmony the sense of brotherhood and common purpose that promised to fuse the nation into a union, even as its elevation of the "voluntary principle" of personal salvation appealed to the democratic individualism of Jacksonian America. This "romantic patriotism" included a fondness for the "sublime" that was incompatible with the religious formalism American theologians had inherited from the Puritans, and it tended to reduce theology to a crude affective rhetoric. It was gradually formalized through the professionalization of itinerant evangelists, preaching manuals, and, in the cities, association with benevolence and temperance societies, but the Civil War destroyed the dream of national cohesion that had granted the revivals their political and social force.

The second section of the book traces the rise of the legal profession in America from its early role as an obstacle to the native intelligence and pioneer spirit of the American frontier (dramatized, for example, in James Fenimore Cooper's *The Pioneers*, 1832) to a position of "political and intellectual domination" that challenged the clergy for the leadership of American culture. Except for the work of popularizing enthusiasts such as Daniel Webster and Abraham Lincoln, this evolution in the status of the law is portrayed by Miller as an effort to "mobilize the forces of the Head against the anarchic impulses of the American Heart," and he characterizes the campaign as "a mental adventure of heroic proportions."

The central strategy in this campaign was the gradual legitimization of English Common Law in the United States as a "natural," universal code of behavior rather than a foreign influence. This successful effort was accompanied by a corollary ambition to systematize the laws and put legal theory and practice on a more "scientific" footing, and together these new attitudes toward the law generated a more cosmopolitan sense of American identity than the rabid nationalism of the evangelical movements had allowed. At the same time, the law began to emerge as a new social force as well, and the possibility of a "benevolent" law eased the tension between the law and religion to yield the possibility of a Christian legal system. As Miller puts it, in defiance of the political sympathy for the separation of church and state there arose the belief that Christianity was the law of the land, and Miller goes so far as to argue that toward the middle of the century this Christianized law was embraced as the last hope of a nation clearly headed for civil war.

The third section of the book is little more than a provocative beginning of an investigation into the peculiar connection between science, technology, and nationalism that came to characterize the latter half of the nineteenth century. But as the first two sections clearly suggest, Miller was continuing in this book the intellectual history he had begun thirty years earlier. After mentioning the obvious influence of economic crises and technological development on the theological debates he traced to the first section, he revives the disciplinary polemic of his earlier books by noting that "Most of these speculations concern the historical events with which this history of the mind is not obliged to deal." He claims that the legal mind of the period was "amazingly homogeneous" just as he had argued that the works of the Puritans could be read as the work of a "single intelligence," and he discovers everywhere the same conflict between "heart and head" that had plagued Puritan culture. For example, he alludes to the belief that the railroad embodied a fusion of "vital impulse and of mathematical intellect" that had escaped the poets.

Miller continues to press this point, and he even extends the rationalistic bias of his earlier works by his clearly critical account of evangelist Charles Grandison Finney and lawyer Daniel Webster, whose blatant appeals to the emotional sympathies of their audiences made them popular heroes of the time but who figure in Miller's history more as ochlocratic demigods standing in the way of serious and valuable intellectual currents. Combined with Miller's persistent fondness for reductive generalization–at one point we are told that "a contest between nationalism and cosmopolitanism" is "*the* American problem" of the age, apparently more so than slavery, foreign wars, and severe economic depression–these characteristic traits at times make *The Life of the Mind in America* both idiosyncratic and predictable. But they also underscore the remarkable scope of the vision Miller had patiently followed over the course of his career, and as analytic principles they join this posthumous book with the two volumes of *The New England Mind* to constitute the most expansive and coherent historical narrative by any modern American historian. Read as the third volume of this monumental accomplishment, it is entirely appropriate that this unfinished text received the Pulitzer Prize for History in 1966.

Since *The Life of the Mind in America* appeared, two more collections of Miller's essays have been published: *Nature's Nation*, edited by Elizabeth Miller and published in 1967, and *The Responsibility of Mind in a Civilization of Machines*, edited by John Crowell and Stanford J. Searl, Jr., and published in 1979. Both books contain essays and lectures Miller wrote mostly during the 1950s and 1960s, and, with the exception of Miller's reflections on the social function of the humanities collected in *The Responsibility of Mind*, nothing in either volume approaches the importance and impact of the essays published in *Errand Into the Wilderness*. In 1981 James Hoopes edited the notes Miller had deposited at the Houghton Library and published them as *Sources for the New England Mind*. The best measure of Miller's influence, however, is the continuing debate over the legitimacy and accuracy of his account of intellectual conflict in American history, and over the utility of his methodological innovations.

To be sure, critics have had to correct the obvious mistakes in Miller's work, such as his claim that typology was not a central part of Puritan culture. They have also convincingly challenged many of his judgments about the decline of piety in the seventeenth century, the extent of the Puritans' departure from Calvinist doctrine, and perhaps most generally Miller's tendency to neglect the importance of individual differences among the Puritans in favor of a more homogenous "Puritanism." Yet, as Francis T. Butts has observed, "All too often Miller has been unintentionally at-

tacked with his own weapons," and the very terms in which Miller's conclusion are debated often derive from his own analyses. The extraordinary sophistication of Puritan studies in America must be directly attributed to Miller's precedent, as Michael McGiffert and others have claimed, and as historians grow more self-conscious about the essentially textual or rhetorical character of all historical analysis, Miller's emphasis on the importance of language and "literature" in the shaping of the American character appears even more modern and radical than it did fifty years ago. Consequently, even more than his revisionist claims and historical discoveries, Miller's commitment to what he called the "decencies of language" may well turn out to be his most important contribution to the way we understand our relation–and responsibility–to the past and the future. Even now, as a definition of the humanist's obligation, it remains a testament to Miller's vision of history as not only a scholarly duty, but also a moral imperative.

### Bibliographies:
Kenneth Kinnamon, "A Bibliography of Perry Miller," *Bulletin of Bibliography and Magazine Notes*, 26 (1969): 45-51;

John C. Crowell, "Perry Miller as Historian: A Bibliography of Evaluations," *Bulletin of Bibliography and Magazine Notes*, 34, no. 2 (1977): 77-85.

### References:
Sacvan Bercovitch, "Typology in Puritan New England: The Williams-Cotton Controversy Reassessed," *American Quarterly*, 19 (Summer 1967): 166-191;

Carl Bridenbaugh, review of *The New England Mind: The Seventeenth Century, American Historical Review*, 45 ( July 1940): 887-889;

Francis T. Butts, "The Myth of Perry Miller," *American Historical Review*, 87 ( June 1982): 665-694;

Everett Emerson, "Calvin and the Covenant Theology," *Church History*, 25 ( June 1956): 136-144;

Emerson, "Perry Miller and the Puritans: A Literary Scholar's Assessment," *History Teacher*, 14, no. 4 (1981): 459-468;

John Gerlach, "Messianic Nationalism in the Early Works of Herman Melville: Against Perry Miller," *Arizona Quarterly*, 28 (Spring 1972): 5-26;

Felix Gilbert, "Intellectual History: Its Aims and Methods," *Daedalus*, 100 (Winter 1971): 80-97;

David Hall, "A Reader's Guide to *The New England Mind: The Seventeenth Century*," *American Quarterly*, 34 (Spring 1982): 31-36;

Hall, "Understanding the Puritans," in *The State of American History*, edited by Herbert Bass (Chicago: Quadrangle, 1970);

Alan Heimart, "Perry Miller: An Appreciation," *Harvard Review*, 2 (Winter-Spring 1964): 30-48;

David Hollinger, "Perry Miller and Philosophical History," *History and Theory*, 7, no. 2 (1968): 189-202;

James Hoopes, "Art as History: Perry Miller's *New England Mind*," *American Quarterly*, 34 (Spring 1982): 3-24;

Daniel Walker Howe, "Descendants of Perry Miller," *American Quarterly*, 34 (Spring 1982): 88-94;

Alfred Kazin, "On Perry Miller," *New York Review of Books*, 25 November 1965, pp. 10-11;

David Levin, "Perry Miller at Harvard," *Southern Review*, 19 (Autumn 1983): 802-816;

Kenneth S. Lynn et al., "Perry Miller," *Harvard University Gazette*, 60 (16 January 1965);

George M. Marsden, "Perry Miller's Rehabilitation of the Puritan," *Church History*, 39 (March 1970): 91-105;

Michael McGiffert, "American Puritan Studies in the 1960s," *William and Mary Quarterly*, third series 27 (January 1970): 36-67;

Robert Middlekauf, *The Mathers: Three Generations of Puritan Intellectuals 1595-1728* (New York: Oxford University Press, 1971);

Middlekauf, "Perry Miller," in *Pastmasters: Some Essays on American Historians*, edited by Marcus Cunliffe and Robin W. Winks (New York: Harper & Row, 1969), pp. 167-190;

Middlekauf, "Piety and Intellect in Puritanism," *William and Mary Quarterly*, 22 (July 1963): 457-470;

Edmund S. Morgan, "The Historians of Early New England," in *The Reinterpretation of Early American History*, edited by Ray Allen Billington (San Marino, Cal.: Huntington Library, 1966);

Morgan, "New England Puritanism: Another Approach," *William and Mary Quarterly*, 18 (April 1961): 236-242;

Morgan, "Perry Miller and the Historians," *American Antiquarian Society, Proceedings*, 74 (April 1964): 11-18;

Samuel Eliot Morison, "In Memoriam: Perry Miller," *New England Quarterly*, 37 (March 1964): 141-142;

Emil Oberholzer, "Puritanism Revisited," in *Perspectives on Early American History*, edited by Alden T. Vaughan and G. A. Billias (New York: Harper & Row, 1973), pp. 193-221;

Norman Petit, *The Heart Prepared: Grace and Conversion in Puritan Spiritual Life* (New Haven: Yale University Press, 1966);

Robert G. Pope, *The Half-Way Covenant: Church Membership in Puritan New England* (Princeton: Princeton University Press, 1969);

Pope, "New England versus the New England Mind: The Myth of Declension," *Journal of Social History*, 3 (Winter 1969-1970);

Richard Reinitz, "Perry Miller and Recent American Historiography," *British Association for American Studies Bulletin*, 8 (1964): 27-35;

Stanford Searl, Jr., "Perry Miller as Artist: Piety and Imagination in *The New England Mind: The Seventeenth Century*," *Early American Literature*, 12 (Winter 1977-1978): 221-233;

George Selement, "Perry Miller: A Note on his Sources in *The New England Mind: The Seventeenth Century*," *William and Mary Quarterly*, third series 31 (July 1974): 453-464;

Alan Simpson, *Puritanism in Old and New England* (Chicago: University of Chicago Press, 1955);

Robert A. Skotheim, *American Intellectual Histories and Historians* (Princeton, N.J.: Princeton University Press, 1966);

Gene Wise, *American Historical Explanations: A Strategy for Grounded Inquiry* (Homewood, Ill.: Dorsey Press, 1973);

Wise, "Implicit Irony in Recent American Historiography," *Journal of the History of Ideas*, 29 (October-December 1968): 579-600.

**Papers:**

The University Archives in the Houghton Library at Harvard University contain reviews of and by Perry Miller; sample notes for published works; notes and papers for lectures and addresses delivered from 1952-1953; material relating to the Yale Edition of *Jonathan Edwards;* lecture notes for Harvard courses and other Harvard course material; Miller-Kenneth Murdock correspondence, circa 1944-1952; general correspondence; and miscellaneous papers (such as obituaries and tributes).

# Lewis Mumford
## (19 October 1895-   )

### Robert Casillo
*University of Miami, Coral Gables*

BOOKS: *The Story of Utopias* (New York: Boni & Liveright, 1922; London: Harrap, 1923);

*Sticks and Stones: A Study of American Architecture and Civilization* (New York: Boni & Liveright, 1924; revised edition, New York: Dover, 1955);

*Aesthetics, A Dialogue*, Troutbeck Leaflets, no. 3 (Amenia, N.Y.: Privately printed at the Troutbeck Press, 1925);

*The Golden Day: A Study in American Experience and Culture* (New York: Boni & Liveright, 1926);

*Herman Melville* (New York: Harcourt, Brace, 1929; London: Cape, 1929; revised edition, New York: Harcourt, Brace & World, 1962; London: Secker & Warburg, 1963);

*The Brown Decades: A Study of the Arts in America, 1865-1895* (New York: Harcourt, Brace, 1931; revised edition, New York: Dover, 1955);

*Technics and Civilization* (New York: Harcourt, Brace, 1934; London: Routledge, 1934);

*The Culture of Cities* (New York: Harcourt, Brace, 1938; London: Secker & Warburg, 1938);

*Men Must Act* (New York: Harcourt, Brace, 1939; London: Secker & Warburg, 1939);

*Faith for Living* (New York: Harcourt, Brace, 1940; London: Secker & Warburg, 1941);

*The South in Architecture* (New York: Harcourt, Brace, 1941);

*The Condition of Man* (New York: Harcourt, Brace, 1944; London: Secker & Warburg, 1944);

*City Development: Studies in Disintegration and Renewal* (New York: Harcourt, Brace, 1945; London: Secker & Warburg, 1946);

*Values for Survival: Essays, Addresses, and Letters in Politics and Education* (New York: Harcourt, Brace, 1946);

*Green Memories: The Story of Geddes Mumford* (New York: Harcourt, Brace, 1947);

*The Conduct of Life* (New York: Harcourt, Brace, 1951; London: Secker & Warburg, 1952);

*The Arts in Renewal*, by Mumford and others (Philadelphia: University of Pennsylvania Press, 1951);

*Art and Technics* (New York: Columbia University Press, 1952; London: Oxford University Press, 1952);

*In the Name of Sanity* (New York: Harcourt, Brace, 1954);

*The Human Prospect*, edited by Harry T. Moore and Karl W. Deutsch (Boston: Beacon, 1955; London: Secker & Warburg, 1956);

*From the Ground Up: Observations on Contemporary Architecture, Housing, Highway Building, and Civic Design* (New York: Harcourt, Brace, 1956);

*The Transformations of Man* (New York: Harper, 1956; London: Allen & Unwin, 1957);

*The City in History: Its Origin, its Transformations, and its Prospects* (New York: Harcourt, Brace & World, 1961; London: Secker & Warburg, 1961);

*The Highway and the City* (New York: Harcourt, Brace & World, 1963; London: Secker & Warburg, 1964);

*The Myth of the Machine: Technics and Human Development* (New York: Harcourt, Brace & World, 1967; London: Secker & Warburg, 1967);

*The Urban Prospect* (New York: Harcourt, Brace & World, 1968; London: Secker & Warburg, 1968);

*The Myth of the Machine: The Pentagon of Power* (New York: Harcourt Brace Jovanovich, 1970; London: Secker & Warburg, 1971);

*Interpretations and Forecasts, 1922-1972: Studies in Literature, Biography, Technics, and Contemporary Society* (New York: Harcourt Brace Jovanovich, 1973);

*Findings and Keepings: Analects for an Autobiography* (New York: Harcourt Brace Jovanovich, 1975);

*My Works and Days: A Personal Chronicle* (New York: Harcourt Brace Jovanovich, 1979);

*Sketches from Life: The Autobiography of Lewis Mumford: The Early Years* (New York: Dial, 1982).

OTHER: "The Little Testament of Bernard Martin Aet. 30," in *The Second American Caravan: A Yearbook of American Literature,* edited by Mumford, Alfred Kreymborg, and Paul Rosenfeld (New York: Macaulay, 1928), pp. 123-169;

"Towards an Organic Humanism," in *The Critique of Humanism,* edited by C. Hartley Grattan (New York: Brewer & Warren, 1930), pp. 337-359;

"The Metropolitan Milieu," in *America and Alfred Stieglitz: A Collective Portrait,* edited by Mumford, Waldo Frank, Dorothy Newman, Paul Rosenfeld, and Harold Rugg (Garden City: Doubleday, Doran, 1934), pp. 33-58;

"From Revolt to Renewal," in *The Arts in Renewal,* by Mumford and others (Philadelphia: University of Pennsylvania Press, 1951), pp. 1-31;

*Roots of Contemporary American Architecture: A Series of Thirty-Seven Essays Dating from the Mid-Nineteenth Century to the Present,* edited by Mumford (New York: Reinhold, 1952), p. 454;

"The Natural History of Urbanization," in *Man's Role in Changing the Face of the Earth,* edited by William L. Thomas (Chicago: University of Chicago Press, 1956), pp. 382-398;

"Patrick Geddes," in *International Encyclopedia of the Social Sciences,* edited by David L. Sills (New York: Macmillan Free Press, 1968), VII: 81-83;

Elmer S. Newman, *Lewis Mumford: A Bibliography, 1914-1970,* introduction by Mumford (New York: Harcourt Brace Jovanovich, 1971), pp. xiii-xxiii.

PERIODICAL PUBLICATIONS: "The Collapse of Tomorrow," *Freeman,* 3 (13 July 1921): 414-415;

"Machinery and the Modern Style," *New Republic,* 27 (3 August 1921): 263-265;

"A Modern Synthesis," *Saturday Review of Literature,* 6 (12 April 1930): 920-921; (10 May 1930): 1028-1029;

"What I Believe," *Forum,* 84 (November 1930): 263-268;

"The Shadow of Yesterday," *New Republic,* 88 (30 September 1936): 230-231;

"The Decline of the West," *New Republic,* 97 (11 January 1939): 275-279;

"The Corruption of Liberalism," *New Republic,* 102 (29 April 1940): 568-573;

"Consolation in War," *New Yorker,* 20 (25 November 1944): 27;

"Atom Bomb: 'Miracle' or Catastrophe?," *Air Affairs,* 2 ( July 1948): 326-345;

"The Fallacy of Systems," *Saturday Review of Literature,* 32 (1 October 1949): 8-9;

"Regional Planning and the Small Town," *American Institute of Architects Journal,* new series 14 ( July 1950): 3-10; (August 1950): 82-91;

"Anticipations and Social Consequences of Atomic Energy," *American Philosophical Society: Proceedings,* 98, no. 2 (1954): 149-152;

"Alternatives to the H-Bomb," *New Leader,* 37 (28 June 1954): 4-9;

"The Role of the Creative Arts in Contemporary Society," *Virginia Quarterly Review,* 33 (Fall 1957): 521-538;

"Apologia to Henry Adams," *Virginia Quarterly Review,* 38 (Spring 1962): 196-217;

"The Sky Line: Mother Jacob's Home Remedies," *New Yorker,* 38 (1 December 1962): 148+;

"Utopia, the City and the Machine," *Daedalus,* 94 (Spring 1965): 271-292;

Review of *Unsafe at any Speed,* by Ralph Nader, and *Safety Last,* by Jeffrey O'Connell and Arthur Myers, *New York Review of Books,* 6 (28 April 1966): 3-5.

Best known as an intellectual and cultural historian, Lewis Mumford is one of the most wide-ranging scholar critics of the century. During the 1920s he first established himself as a literary biographer, architectural critic, utopian theorist, urban planner, and student of American literature, culture, and society. Over the next four decades Mumford achieved much greater fame as a harsh and often gloomily pessimistic critic not only of American but of contemporary civilization, most of whose main tendencies he vociferously opposed. However, Mumford's international reputation rests above all on his major historical works of the 1930s and 1960s, monumental studies of the development of technology and of the history and culture of the city; these works form the solid basis of his critique of modern civilization. As an independent "generalist" lacking an academic degree, and for whom, like Walt Whitman, "Manahatta" was his university, Mumford moves constantly across disciplinary boundaries in an attempt to define "organic" connections between different realms of thought and experience. He has frequently lectured abroad and has served as an advisor to urban planners and policymakers. He is now completing the second volume

*Lewis Mumford, 1938*

more than a decade before Mumford's birth. The marriage was later annulled.

Mumford grew up on the Upper West Side of Manhattan and graduated from Stuyvesant High School in 1912. Fascinated by science and technology, he had intended to become an electrical engineer, yet because of his wide reading and writing ability he had impressed his classmates as a future man of letters. Among contemporary authors, Samuel Butler, H. G. Wells, and especially George Bernard Shaw helped to introduce the young Mumford to modern, that is, anti-Victorian ideas of sex, nonconformity, and radical politics. Having made an intense study of Shaw's works before the age of twenty, Mumford claimed that they had "changed" him "in one year . . . from a weak-kneed conservative (with no philosophy and hardly any opinions) to a rather wild young man with a brick in my right hand and a red flag in my buttonhole." While this seems self-dramatizing, in the 1920s and 1930s Mumford would show sympathy for socialism, what he called "basic communism," and even for the Soviet Union. Another important influence upon him in his youth were the great museums and libraries of New York City that nourished his characteristically combined interest in art, science, and technology.

After graduation Mumford briefly envisioned a career in journalism. Beginning in 1912, he studied intensely though haphazardly for two years in the night school of City College with the new aim, never realized, of taking a Ph.D. in philosophy. Instead a brush with tuberculosis led him into a four-year personal "moratorium" during which he continued reading and writing. Although he later pursued his studies intermittently at Columbia, New York University, and City College and accumulated enough credits for an undergraduate degree, he never sought a diploma but rather followed a career as a freelance writer which began in 1914, when a newspaper published an article containing Mumford's rejoinder to Shaw's philosophy. Between 1918 and 1919 Mumford served in the U.S. Navy, and upon his discharge he became an assistant editor of the *Dial*; in 1918 he also attended classes at the New School for Social Research, where he came under Thorstein Veblen's influence. His interest in biology and sociology led him to England in 1920, where he met his chief mentor, the biologist Patrick Geddes, who offered him the editorship of the *Sociological Review*. However, Mumford turned down the offer

of his autobiographical work *Sketches from Life,* an important record of American intellectual culture in this century. Throughout his career Mumford has been respected but for the most part unheeded, mainly because of his opposition to reigning ideologies in technics, science, urban planning, and architecture.

Mumford was born out of wedlock in Flushing, a section of Queens, in New York City, on 19 October 1895. His mother, Elvina Conradin Baron Mumford, was of German ancestry and came from the lower-middle class; his father, named only as "J.W." in Mumford's *Sketches from Life: The Autobiography of Lewis Mumford: The Early Years* (1982), belonged to a prosperous Jewish American family and died in his early thirties. Mumford never knew his father, a fact which might explain the spirit of independence he has shown from adolescence onward. His last name was taken from John Mumford, an Englishman whom his mother married at the age of eighteen,

out of his commitment to American culture and especially his love for Sophia Wittenberg, whom he married in 1921. Their son, Geddes, was born in 1925; their daughter, Alison, in 1935.

Although Mumford's career reveals the remarkable continuity and constant interpenetration of his interests, it may be divided roughly into three phases. In the first, which extends to 1931 and concludes with *The Brown Decades: A Study of the Arts in America, 1865-1895* (1931), he was chiefly a critic of American literature, architecture, and society, with more than a few passing glances at technology, urban planning, painting, and other subjects. During the 1920s Mumford was closely associated with such intellectuals as Van Wyck Brooks, Paul Rosenfeld, Harold Stearns, Alfred Kreymborg, Waldo Frank, and Joel Spingarn. A former professor of comparative literature at Columbia University, Spingarn became Mumford's neighbor in Upstate New York and one of his closest friends.

Despite the constant pressures of free-lance authorship, Mumford turned out a succession of books while contributing frequently to such periodicals as the *New Republic*, the *Dial*, and the *Freeman*; his rate of productivity has remained remarkably consistent over his long career. Mumford was one of the founding editors of *The Second American Caravan: A Yearbook of American Literature* (1927-1936), an anthology whose five volumes were intended to counter the increasing cultural influence of such anti-American literary expatriates as T. S. Eliot and Ezra Pound. In 1928 *The Second American Caravan* published Mumford's "The Little Testament of Bernard Martin Aet. 30," a novella based closely on Mumford's educational experiences and the early though not insuperable tribulations of his marriage. This work is just one manifestation of his long-standing desire for recognition not only as a critic but as a novelist, playwright, and poet. However, neither "The Little Testament," nor his unfinished and only partly published verse novel "Victor" (terminated in 1939), nor his talky "epic" play *The Builders of the Bridge* (published in 1975; written in the 1920s), nor his occasional attempts at poetry have won him anything near the acclaim he has received for his works of social criticism and intellectual and cultural history. In 1931, as testimony of his increasing reputation as a student of architecture, Mumford became the architectural critic of the *New Yorker*, contributing his "Sky Line" column until 1963.

After his marriage Mumford lived in Manhattan, moving to Sunnyside, Queens, in 1925; then, in 1936, he moved with his family to a permanent home in Amenia, Dutchess County, New York. By now Mumford had entered into the second phase of his career, having shifted his attention from the comparatively narrow subject of American literature and culture to larger questions of human history and destiny. These areas of inquiry included the origin, meaning, and potential of technology; the history and fate of urban culture; and the possibility of constructing a world utopia on the basis of modern science, technology, and moral philosophy. Indeed most if not all of Mumford's works of the 1920s into the early 1950s are marked by a utopian impulse which appears in his first book, *The Story of Utopias* (1922). Yet Mumford's idealism and voluminous scholarly researches into intellectual history did not detach him from immediate social issues, and he increased his reputation as a social critic and moralist. Among other things he advocated urban planning, regionalism, technocracy, and a "functional" rather than "class" theory of socialism closer to the guild socialist tradition of John Ruskin and William Morris than to that of the statist Soviet Union (with which Mumford for all his distrust nonetheless sympathized up to Stalin's pact with Hitler).

On the eve of World War II Mumford reversed his former pacifist position and fervently supported American intervention against fascism; for this, and also for his scathing denunciations of liberalism as pacifistic and unrealistic, he suffered intense though temporary hostility. As World War II approached its end, it also closed a phase not only of Mumford's career but of his personal life. In September 1944 he learned that his son, Geddes, had been killed in action in Italy, a tragic loss commemorated in *Green Memories: The Story of Geddes Mumford* (1947). With its moving evocations of persons and places, this work is probably Mumford's most successful writing outside his critical and historical work.

The third phase of Mumford's career dates from 1945, when the experience of the war and its aftermath—above all the fact of the atomic bomb and the cold war—caused his former optimism gradually to darken. Since then Mumford has warned that the abuse of technology and man's inability to control his aggression and power lust threaten if not ecological disaster then global conflagration. Today he is not certain that this outcome can be averted. From the immediate postwar period onward Mumford condemned the very existence of atomic weapons. America figured increasingly in his work as an industrial, urban, and cultural wasteland, the home of empty freedoms and unvital values, the unacknowledged double of the totalitarian enemy it opposes. It is understandable that in the late 1960s Mumford opposed the Vietnam War well before his position had become fashionable and, therefore, safe. His entire career bespeaks, along with a certain ideological stubbornness and intolerance, an even deeper quality of intellectual independence and integrity.

In the 1950s Mumford often complained that his reputation had declined and his works were unread, but in fact he has enjoyed considerable success and recognition for much of his career, not the least of which were the Guggenheim Fellowships which he received in 1932, 1938, and 1956. His major work, *The City in History: Its Origin, its Transformations, and its Prospects* (1961), won the National Book Award in the year of its publication. Notwithstanding Mumford's constant contempt for academia as overspecialized and sterile, he has himself achieved para-academic status over the last five decades as a frequent lecturer and visiting professor at many American universities, among them Columbia, Stanford, University of Pennsylvania, and Harvard. Apart from various academic awards and honors, Mumford received an honorary doctorate from the University of Edinburgh in 1965 and another from the University of Rome in 1967. He is a member of the American Philosophical Society, the American Academy of Arts and Sciences, and the National Institute of Arts and Letters. He resigned from the latter in 1947 in protest against the Institute's decision to award a Gold Medal for History to Charles Beard, whose isolationism during World War II had rendered him, at least in Mumford's view, unworthy of such an honor. Mumford rejoined the Institute six years later.

Mumford belongs to that group of progressive American intellectuals, including Thorstein Veblen, John Dewey, and Van Wyck Brooks, who sought to renew a vital American cultural tradition after World War I. Of the many thinkers who have influenced Mumford, perhaps five or six stand out. Ralph Waldo Emerson's work encouraged Mumford's intolerance of petrified traditions, his appreciation of the natural and organic, his suspicion of systems, and his celebration of the self. From Veblen, with whom he

briefly studied, Mumford derived his concept of the opposition between technology and the pecuniary motives of capitalism. The works of John Ruskin, celebrating craft ideals and denouncing laissez-faire capitalism, fostered Mumford's social, urban, and economic values. Of all modern planners, Ebenezer Howard had the deepest practical influence on Mumford, giving him the concept of the "garden city." But the greatest influence was the Scottish biologist and town planner Patrick Geddes, from whom Mumford acquired his belief in organic limits in nature and culture, his urban regionalism, his teleologism, his communalism, his ecologism, and his hopes for a "biotechnic" order in which technology is made to serve man's genuine biological purposes. But Mumford never took over Geddes's thought as a whole, and he rejected Geddes's "ideological short-cuts."

Mumford is the beneficiary of the organicism which the Romantics sketchily formulated and which acquired scientific support in the late nineteenth and early twentieth century, thanks to Geddes, Ruskin, Charles Darwin, Alfred North Whitehead, Wolfgang Kohler, Sir Arthur Stanley Eddington, Sigmund Freud, and Carl G. Jung. As Mumford often noted of the Newtonian physical sciences, their exclusive emphasis on such quantitative abstractions as matter, motion, isolated existence, and cause and effect had neglected historical tradition, human values and purposes, and organic development. But deterministic mechanism had given way to biology and the new "evolutionary" and qualitative concepts of "vitalism," "organism," significant pattern, purposive growth, configuration, and gestalt. In its demonstration of the "complicated interdependences" of all things, the new organicism sanctioned communal, cooperative, and ecological values. Most important, it justified human intervention or planning rather than laissez-faire as an inherent part of natural and social process. Mumford's new "synthesis" would encompass not only man's organic purposes and biological needs but his relation to the "whole environment" of nature in its "manifold" cooperativeness. This is the basis for Mumford's "biotechnic" order. But though Mumford always advocates urban planning over uncontrolled growth, he increasingly opposes what Geddes called the "Fallacy of Systems," for externally imposed plans tend to be so rigid and "self-enclosed" that they prevent diversity and development. The ideal plan must be genuinely "organic" and hence open, permitting "fresh emergents" from within and without.

From the start of his career Mumford rejected Marxist materialism and economic determinism. Where the scientist disregarded mental ideas as independent from the world without, the Marxist treated ideas as mere derivatives of economic and social relations. Mumford acknowledges that culture is conditioned by material factors, yet he believes it to be influenced as well by ideologies, none of which merely camouflages an economic substructure. Insofar as the neglect of the creative self in the West had coincided with modern materialism and technological specialization, Mumford would restore man's inner world, expressed in the aesthetic forms of word, image, and symbol, to its former dignity, and so integrate the internal and external life of man.

Mumford's first book, *The Story of Utopias* (1922), focuses on the utopia as an example of that "world of ideas" through which man shapes his environment. Since Mumford, like other progressives of the 1920s, believed that science might create a more perfect world, he does not at this point reject social engineering on a large scale. And yet Plato's hierarchical *Republic* is too static and specialized and fails to accommodate the entire human personality. Bacon's utopia overemphasizes scientific organization and progress, while Thomas More's, despite its admirable communism of the family, tolerates war, slavery, and authoritarianism. Of all the early utopias, only the artisan democracy of Johann Valentin Andreä's Christianopolis satisfies a wide range of educational, religious, familial, communal, and political needs. By contrast most nineteenth- and twentieth-century utopias reveal a "deadly sameness of purpose," namely social reconstruction through "industrial reorganization." Taking for granted modern materialism, the factory, the megalopolis, technological expansion, and the nation-state, these utopias put their faith in mere "machinery," and thus would inevitably repeat the dehumanizing and destructive effects of the industrial system. Only William Morris, in his utopias of "escape," challenged industrialist assumptions. Mumford proposes, as his own utopian alternative, regional and environmental planning freed from centralizing capitalism and the state.

Mumford's utopianism became problematic over the next decades. As Christopher Lasch notes (*Salmagundi*, 1980), by 1930 Mumford had decided that "life," in its manifold diversity, "is bet-ter than utopia," and that the utopian tradition rested on the fallacy that "perfection is a legitimate goal of human existence." Yet Lasch rightly finds utopianism in *Technics and Civilization* (1934) and *The Culture of Cities* (1938), which end with visions of a "neotechnic" and "biotechnic" utopia of steel and glass. Only in the 1960s did Mumford fully reject utopian thinking for what he had come to view as its inherent tendency to "mechanical rigidity," dangerous closure, and its false attempt to overcome the finally "tragic" nature of human life.

*The Golden Day: A Study in American Experience and Culture* (1926) seeks to explain how America had succumbed to the valueless materialism and inhuman technology which had vitiated most modern utopias. Freed of Old World prejudices and controls, the American had a "unique opportunity" of creating a "New World Man" and a democratic society in harmony with nature. But the American Protestant had also left behind Europe's diverse traditional values, its respect for a rich and varied inner life, and what remained of the classical and medieval concept of restraint and limit. Once its spiritual moment had passed, Protestantism was left with an essentially individualistic, materialistic, and instrumental philosophy which culminated in industrial capitalism. Lacking a social philosophy, neglectful of man's inner experience and values, America became a culture of pure "externality," dedicated to the economic, scientific, and technological conquest of nature. On the frontier the transplanted European became a "barbarian."

Nonetheless there emerged in New England America's "golden day," the culture of Emerson, Henry David Thoreau, Nathaniel Hawthorne, and Herman Melville. Escaping the narrow confines of European and Mediterranean tradition and embracing a wider cultural past (Asia, Polynesia, and the Americas), the golden day was yet a regional rather than centralized phenomenon. Emerson and Thoreau defined a fresh relation with nature, uncontaminated by outmoded models, prejudices, systems, and nomenclatures, which anticipates the organic values of this century, and which the pioneer, hunter, and industrialist lacked. As for Melville, Mumford speaks of him in his 1929 biography as the forerunner of the coming "synthesis" of the ideal and the practical. Yet Captain Ahab's metaphysical rebellion and "tragic sense of life" met no welcome in an increasingly mechanical and prosaic age, and after 1860 Melville sank into resigned obscurity, just as the "golden day" was eclipsed by the coming of the Civil War. Though Walt Whitman celebrated the organic interdependence of man, society, and nature, the "machine won," and post-Civil War America typifies a "pragmatic acquiescence" to the new industrial civilization: profits, comfort, uncontrolled production, instrumentalism, conformity, and technological exploitation of the environment. This bleak picture is only partly altered by Mumford's recognition, in *The Brown Decades: A Study of the Arts in America, 1865-1895* (1931), of the "Buried Renaissance" of Henry Hobson Richardson, Louis Sullivan, Thomas Eakins, Albert Pinkham Ryder, and Frank Lloyd Wright. Most of Whitman's contemporaries ignored the human and natural cost of this civilization, its shallow externality, its neglect of vital needs, of man's organic relation with nature; some, like Mark Twain, even celebrated industrial values. The pragmatism of William James, despite James's opposition to the "block universe," neatly coalesced with "everyday experience in the Gilded Age," and pragmatic instrumentalism without regard for larger human ends would later make its appearance in advertising and the marketplace. Still *The Golden Day* concludes with hope, as Mumford introduces the new organicism of Whitehead and others.

*The Golden Day* was generally very well received and proved to be one of Mumford's best and most influential works. Although unduly neglected now, it revived an awareness of the nearly forgotten splendor of America's literary and cultural past and so helped greatly in the formation of American studies as an academic discipline in the 1940s. Indeed Mumford can be said to have anticipated F. O. Matthiessen's idea of the "American Renaissance," and it is not surprising that, in the introduction to his most famous work of that title, published in 1941, Matthiessen described *The Golden Day* as a "major event in my experience." Yet even higher praise had come to Mumford earlier, as George Santayana, notwithstanding his assertion that Mumford had thoroughly misunderstood him, had honored *The Golden Day* as "the best book about America, if not the best American book, that I have read."

Mumford's early social and cultural criticism itself reveals the powerful influence of Van Wyck Brooks, who by 1925 had reached the height of his reputation, and who at least up to 1930 stood as probably the most revered literary critic in America. Mumford met Brooks in 1920 in the offices of the *Freeman*, a short-lived journal for

which Brooks served as literary editor and to which Mumford became a frequent contributor. By Mumford's own admission the "elevated" and inspiring tone of Brooks's criticism had weighed heavily in his decision to reject Geddes's offer of the editorship of the *Sociological Review* and to return to his native shores in search of American culture. Of special importance to Mumford (and to numerous other writers of his generation) was Brooks's short but potent *Dial* essay of 1918, "On Creating a Usable Past," as it defined the role of the American literary critic as a conscious effort to discriminate between the worthless and the valuable, the dead and the living in our cultural history. This was a major motivation of the harshly critical 1922 anthology *Civilization in the United States,* which Harold Stearns edited and which contained an essay by Brooks and another by Mumford on the evils of the American city. Not only was the subject of Mumford's first book, *The Story of Utopias,* suggested by Brooks but Mumford's first five works are addressed to problems of American culture set forth by Brooks in *Wine of the Puritans* (1908), *America's Coming-of-Age* (1915), *Letters and Leadership* (1918), *The Ordeal of Mark Twain* (1920), and *The Pilgrimage of Henry James* (1925).

According to Brooks, America's Puritan origins had led to a radical bifurcation or "divorce" between "lowbrow" culture, characterized by Philistine coarseness, utilitarian commercialism, and the worship of material comfort, and "highbrow" culture, identified with abstract ideas, metaphysics, extreme subjectivity, and an ineffectual withdrawal from actuality. Lowbrow culture reflected the puritanical hatred of art and emphasis on worldly success and had its fulfillment on the American frontier, where the pioneer cast off the last vestiges of tradition and forged a new and shallow culture of exploitative materialism. Highbrow culture, on the other hand, began with the Puritan divines and reached its nadir in the tepid "genteel tradition" of the nineteenth and early twentieth centuries, with its slavish imitation of European models, impotent contempt of mass vulgarity, and trivial emphasis on mere refinement. In Brooks's view these divisions were largely absent in Europe thanks to the pervasiveness of high cultural values and the existence of an unbroken cultural tradition; hence the comparative confidence of the European artist in his audience as well as the profound attraction of Europe to the American literary expatriate. But in America the native writer or artist was condemned to thankless struggle and ultimate failure. Lacking an appreciative audience and being out of tune with his social environment, he was incapable of expressing the whole of the national spirit or of finding his place within a general and continuous cultural tradition. Instead he either compromised with material values, or else fled social reality into his own private world; yet in either case he could only stagnate rather than develop. Because of his excessive subjectivity, argues Brooks, Melville's talent dwindled after 1857, the year of *The Confidence Man;* Twain betrayed his talent by celebrating commercialism; while Henry James finally turned his back on America in pursuit of an extremely rarefied and overnuanced vision which neither reflected typical American experience nor succeeded in fully recovering the older European tradition. Examined at length in *The Ordeal of Mark Twain* and *The Pilgrimage of Henry James,* the last two writers are probably for Brooks the most notable casualties of post-Civil War American culture. Despite Brooks's insistence on the necessity of recovering a "usable" past and his hopes for a great cultural efflorescence in America after World War I, his works up to 1925 give the distinct impression that American intellectuals had never even begun to overcome the great cultural division between highbrow and lowbrow and its numerous related conflicts.

Up to a point Mumford in the 1920s and early 1930s shares Brooks's negative evaluation of the American past. He condemns the pioneering culture of the frontier and laments, as in the case of Melville, the writer's alienation from society. He finds Twain coopted by capitalism and James cut off from the larger issues of American experience by a highly attenuated hyperaestheticism. Nonetheless Mumford disagreed with Brooks in many ways, and his four books following *The Story of Utopias* attempt to correct Brooks's extreme judgments of American culture and thus to go further than Brooks himself in salvaging a usable past.

In *Sticks and Stones: A Study of American Architecture and Civilization* (1924) Mumford challenges Brooks's heavily condemnatory view of Puritanism as altogether life denying and divided between spirituality and materialism. For Mumford the small-scale, intelligent layout, and sensible architecture of the New England village achieves a religiously inspired and ideal harmony between man and nature, precisely what avaricious and godless industrialism succeeded in destroying.

While this image does not dispel the shadow of the Salem witch trials, it contains perhaps an element of truth. Nor does Mumford share Brooks's view of the nineteenth-century American literary tradition as largely one of failure. The central chapter of *The Golden Day* treats Emerson, Hawthorne, Thoreau, Melville, and Whitman as forming a loose cultural unity which Mumford recommends with wholehearted enthusiasm as the basis of contemporary American culture. According to Brooks, Melville finally confirmed the cultural opposition between highbrow and lowbrow and petered out in mid career. In *Herman Melville* (1929) Mumford corrects these judgments, first, by showing (as have later critics) that *Moby-Dick* holds both spirit and matter in a single vision, and second, by demonstrating the value of Melville's later poetry. To be sure, this work is heavily indebted to Brooks's method of psychobiography, which it enlists to support the dubious (and covertly personal) thesis that Melville's creative difficulties stemmed from his timid refusal to break beyond the sexual constraints of marriage; but its more important and achieved purpose is to overturn the conventional view, to which Brooks had lent support, that the later Melville was a deranged misanthropist. On the evidence of the later works, including *Billy Budd* (which Mumford underestimates and which had not yet been published when Brooks delivered his judgment on Melville), Mumford defeats this argument once and for all. Finally *The Brown Decades* opposes Brooks's viewpoint not only in the intensity of Mumford's continued admiration of Emerson, Whitman, and Thoreau but in its insistence that American writers, painters, urban planners, and other figures of the post-Civil War period, for all their marginality and even obscurity, had carried on the previous generation's effort to create an integrated and widely serviceable cultural tradition.

Mumford's judgments are not examples of facile optimism, for he remained aware of persistent divisions within American culture and society while always maintaining the "tragic sense of life" he had praised in Melville. If anything it was Brooks who, after his nervous breakdown in 1927 and four years of convalescence, became identified with cultural boosterism and yeasaying. In his *Life of Emerson* (1932), a work which Mumford helped to see through publication, Brooks revealed a new outlook on American culture which resulted in his *Makers and Finders* series (1936-1955), a five-volume study of American literary history from 1800 to 1915. As many critics have complained, *Makers and Finders* lacks the sense of cultural conflict and tension which pervades Brooks's earlier criticism. Having altogether reversed his judgment of American writers and their cultural situation, Brooks now saw them as essentially unified in spirit, forward looking, and affirmative of national values. Where formerly he had found divorce and disappointment, now he finds reconciliation, tradition, and steady development. Brooks's new conception of American literary tradition as uplifting led him to attack such writers as Eliot and Pound, since their cultural pessimism, modernist experimentation, and coterie mentality opposed mainstream American culture with a rebellious and contemptuous highbrowism. In short Brooks had transformed himself into a middlebrow.

During these decades Mumford's overwhelming interest had passed beyond American culture to much larger issues of world cultural history. He recognized, however, that Brooks's new viewpoint was all too comforting and false to historical reality. He refused to accept Brooks's simplistic notion of progress. This is not to deny that Mumford shares something of Brooks's middlebrowism, for he temperamentally prefers "affirmative" or "humanistic" literature and finds it difficult to respond favorably to the negativism and nihilism of much modernist writing. Moreover despite his friendship with Joel Spingarn, a neglected precursor of the New Criticism, Mumford was not much more fond than Brooks was of aesthetic formalism. Like Brooks's, Mumford's literary studies (with a few exceptions, such as sections of the Melville biography) are short on close reading and long on thematic, psychological, and sociological criticism. Still the cordiality of Mumford's published reviews of Brooks's later works is somewhat belied by his private remark to Brooks in 1947 that Brooks's new interpretation of American culture in *Makers and Finders* had left out "the bitter tragic element." Mumford added that without a sense of the tragic Brooks would never "have a key to our present generation."

The occasion of this remark was the only crisis in Mumford's otherwise warm if not especially intimate friendship with Brooks. In 1947 Brooks chaired a National Institute of Arts and Letters Committee which awarded a medal of distinction to the historian Charles Beard. Mumford protested the award on the grounds that Beard had espoused a "poisonous" isolationism during World War II and had distorted historical truth in order to defend his position. Mumford also told Brooks in their correspondence that his support of Beard gave evidence of the same inability to acknowledge the "tragic element" which Mumford had discovered in Brooks's later writings. Shortly thereafter Mumford resigned temporarily from the institute. His intemperate criticism of Brooks might have destroyed their friendship, but Brooks succeeded in preserving it through his tactful response to Mumford's accusations. The record of Brooks and Mumford's friendship, which lasted until Brooks's death in 1963, is contained in Robert E. Spiller's 1970 edition of their correspondence.

By 1925 Mumford had discovered that his "real work" was to "describe what had happened to the Western European mind since the breakdown of the medieval synthesis, and to trace out the effects of this in America." Mumford's two masterpieces of the 1930s, *Technics and Civilization* and *The Culture of Cities,* explain why modern European society had "surrendered to the machine." Since Mumford's studies of technology had never been "separated formally" from his interest in architecture and cities, he was undertaking the "entire cultural history of *Homo Sapiens.*" But Mumford also had a task of "new synthesis." These works, as well as *The Condition of Man* (1944) and *The Conduct of Life* (1951), belong to the four-volume series which Mumford described as "The Renewal of Life," whose purpose was again to discover a "usable past" and outline a more humane civilization.

Adhering to a rigid organic metaphor, Oswald Spengler believed that the aging West must succumb to paralyzing technology; Mumford's more open organic theory permits intelligent resistance. Nor does the later Mumford accept the "fatalism" of the contemporary French theorist Jacques Ellul, who argues that modern technology constitutes a virtually unshakeable and autonomous system subsuming all human ends. Mumford insists that technology depends on "choices," and that it is not an "independent system." Far from hating technology, he would cure it of its abuses and make it serve man.

Up to at least 1937 Mumford thought that technology, once freed of capitalist motives of profit and expense, would achieve human liberation. Only later did he reject this technocratic solution to problems that required more evaluative and noninstrumental understanding. In fact he traced the present moral and ecological crisis of civilization precisely to an uncritical faith in technology: to the "myth of the machine." Yet Mumford always welcomes those who, like Emerson, Percy Bysshe Shelley, William Morris, and Frank Lloyd Wright, tried to "intelligently assimilate" the machine within an organic order. From the 1920s onward Mumford praises the functionalism of modern machine design and the aesthetic potential of machine forms. He acknowledges and welcomes the machine's capacity to produce and distribute goods. Though he feels increasingly anxious that automation will rob man of all meaningful work, he praises it for eliminating drudgery. Mumford's constant point is that the abuses of technology mainly result from its not inextricable but long-standing relation to the ideologies of science, capitalism, and the state.

In *Technics and Civilization* Mumford shows how technology received a powerful impetus from Galilean and Newtonian science. In reducing reality to objective, manipulable, measurable, and independent quantities, modern physics provided a mechanical model of the world and so fostered mechanical invention. Meanwhile the emergent capitalist economy, with its materialistic, quantitative, and atomistic outlook, its efficient routine, and its drive toward endless production, profit, and the exploitation of nature, appropriated the machine for noncooperative dehumanizing purposes. The machine was "conditioned" by capitalism, which had "nothing essentially to do with the technical processes or the forms of work." It "has suffered for the sins of capitalism," and capitalism has "often taken credit for the virtues of the machine." At the same time the state's ambitions have been served by science, capitalism, and technology.

The advance of these new forces marks the gradual fading of the "eotechnic" stage of technological development, whose heyday coincides with the "synthesis" of the Middle Ages, "one of the most brilliant periods in history." In the Middle Ages, as in much of the Renaissance, wind and water served as primary energy sources, and a great variety of machines were operated locally and regionally and on a small scale. Eotechnic technology was neither linked to financial investment nor concentrated by political power: neither wind nor water is monopolizable, as are oil and coal, the major fuels of modern heavy industry. Nor are these forms of power dirty, as are modern polluting fuels. Mumford insists on the cleanliness of medieval towns and cities, their cooperative values, quasi-rural character, engineer-

ing feats (the cathedrals), ecological harmony with nature, guild and handicraft traditions free of the competitive and mechanizing pressures of capitalism and industrialism.

In the late Renaissance the eotechnic gave way to the "paleotechnic age." Capitalism and the state promoted ecologically disastrous mining technologies, vast regimented armies, and the mechanized industrial factory. Just as capitalist ownership reduced the once joyful craftsman to a mere quantity of raw labor power, so the machine deprived him of his subjectivity and selfhood, which are mere impediments to efficiency. In consequence of the state's ambitions, capitalism's almost automatic productive drive, and heavy industry's reliance on monopolizable and dirty fuels, nature was devastated in an endless business cycle of aimless expansion and destruction. Mumford admits that industrial civilization offered material benefits and produced some great artists, but on the whole he finds the period's record dismal. Not only did the pecuniary motives often retard beneficial mechanical inventions but at virtually every point the paleotechnic era favored economic and mechanical over vital and human values.

*Technics and Civilization* charts the outlines of Geddes's "neotechnic" phase, which, apart from its ecological advantages, promises the diffusion of power and hence a deemphasis on quantity. The paleotechnic had concentrated its big cities, factories, and capitals in the river valleys in order to exploit the railroad. The neotechnic relies on both the train and automobile as well as on such clean, readily available, and light energy sources as sunlight, water, and electricity. The automobile and electronic communication ideally lessen the need for centralization, since they permit easy transportation and dissemination of information while increasing the possibility of social cooperation. The movement away from the "solid matter" of iron and steel to a more mobile, personalized, and "aetherealized" technology is for Mumford an essential step in the decentralization of modern society and its power system. But more than just technology is needed for the "biotechnic" era. Besides a democratic, regionally based political system, Mumford wants a socialistic, communalistic economy administered by a "service" rather than a nationalistic "power" state. Adumbrating his later ideal of international cooperation, he calls for economic organization on a world scale.

Inseparable from technology, the city is an essential and "age-old instrument of human culture." In *The Culture of Cities*, as elsewhere, Mumford applies Geddes's organic analogy to urban growth. Any organism properly grows within "organic . . . limit[s]" or else risks the paralysis of excessive size and finally death. Likewise the city's limits are dictated by the vital needs and convenience of its inhabitants and the ecological need of preserving its rural container. The city is therefore no mere boundless aggregate but an organism made up of interdependent cells—in short, neighborhoods, each serving various cooperative human purposes. These requirements were largely met in the Middle Ages, when town plans preserved a "human" scale, neighborhoods and public services flourished, and cities were "*of the country*."

Unlike natural organisms, cities cannot automatically control their growth. Organic limits, ecological balance, open planning, and the cooperative city were gradually overturned in Europe during the paleotechnic era. Accommodating absolute monarchs, the city was expanded and centralized according to geometrical plans, thus losing its organic and cooperative character. With political centralization the local centers gradually lost freedoms and initiative. Later, under laissez-faire capitalism, city planning became a despised concept. The urban business center mushroomed out of all proportion in order to take advantage of land values, and neighborhoods were left to take care of themselves. A monument to unrestrained capitalist expansion, the paleotechnic city is characterized by sharp social and economic differences; excessive specialization; congested, ill-housed, and unhealthy populations; polluted water; adulterated goods; and a cultureless, materialistic bourgeoisie.

Mumford asks if it is possible to transform the megalopolis after an organic, biotechnic model. In *The Culture of Cities* such a transformation depends on the "etherealized" inventions of the neotechnic order, which would diffuse the city and restore its "dynamic equilibrium" with nature. Mumford also advocates the "garden city" concept of Ebenezer Howard. Unlike the modern suburb, the garden city is a genuine urban container, organized on a small scale (within an optimum of thirty thousand inhabitants), and operating as a relatively self-sufficient and self-governing social and economic unit. Its expansion is determined by a representative public authority rather than by the individual investor.

Equally necessary for urban renewal is the self-governing "regional city" and the establishment of the self-sufficient "region" as a natural, political, economic, and cultural entity. Not to be confused with such arbitrary abstractions as the state or county or district, the region is a genuine and long-standing geographical, ecological, economic, social, and cultural unit. But Mumford recognizes that these goals require the collectivization of land under a responsible though not totalitarian public administration: individual ownership, in his view, can no longer be regarded as sacred. Likewise political power must be centered in international groupings transcending the interests of individual states. Should these changes fail to take place, the city will become "Necropolis," with life permanently stagnating amid a vast, unwieldy, disorderly apparatus. Events of the decades following World War II largely confirmed Mumford's fears.

To understand the darkening of Mumford's vision, one must consider his lesser historical, philosophical, and polemical works of the late 1930s through the 1950s. *Men Must Act* (1939) and *Faith for Living* (1940) indict a modern liberalism which had betrayed its ideal possibilities, a failure most evident in its inability to face fascist aggression. Mumford scorned appeasers and isolationists as foolish optimists in "tacit alliance" with fascism. With its naive faith in scientific progress, liberalism ignored that "radical evil" which fascism embodied. Moreover, although Mumford rejects a Marxist identification of liberalism with capitalism, he argues that liberalism in its present "disintegration" had been corrupted by its "obsession" with technological "power." Like capitalism, liberalism equated progress with more "money, wealth, and endless gadgets." Lacking higher ends, or a unifying conception of man, it had reduced human life to the pragmatic and instrumental. An early critic of the atomic bomb, Mumford claimed in *The Conduct of Life* and *In the Name of Sanity* (1954) that liberalism had capitulated to a totalitarian ideology; the bombing of Hiroshima and the United States' "unconditional moral surrender" to Nazi methods in the postwar period demonstrated that Hitler had really "won" World War II.

Despite his disenchantment with liberalism, most of Mumford's works of the 1940s and the 1950s are polemical and wearyingly hortatory attempts to define a "program for survival" after the war. He still hopes for increased political participation and clings to the liberal ideal of the autonomous individual. Besides promoting regional, familial, and internationalist values, *Faith for Living* celebrates the ethics of the great religions as the possible basis for a new universal faith. *The Condition of Man*, a mainly historical and cultural study of the origins of the modern personality, concludes with a "plan of life" more fully outlined in *Values for Survival* (1946). Mumford deplores the one-sided development of the human personality through the worship of technological power, and, in the absence of moral wisdom, he rejects technics alone as a solution. But he also believes that science and technics are life-enhancing. Apart from international controls over arms and energy, the period of "transition" requires a "unified approach" to life fostered by religion and education. The first tempers man's lust for power; the second promotes civic responsibility, historical consciousness, and the integration of the personality. And yet for all his optimism, the apparent irreconcilability of science and religion remains one of the most perplexing of Mumford's problems.

*Values for Survival* adumbrates a theory of the human essence which is developed in *The Conduct of Life, Art and Technics, In the Name of Sanity*, and *The Myth of the Machine* (1967, 1970). Mumford takes issue with the theory that man's technological skills determine his cultural progress and constitute the most valuable, most characteristically human core of his cultural achievement. Instead he argues that the creative and communal arts of language, craft, and visual symbolism had preceded technics and first shaped the human community and individual. Founded on man's unconscious and emotional life, language and the other arts are purposive activities essential (as Vico and Shelley also believed) to humanness, for unlike science they contain and give significance to all experience. The devaluation of language and poetry begins (as Hegel perceived) only with the rise of modern science and technology in the seventeenth century. Devaluating subjectivity and symbolism as "non-operational," and reducing the world to mechanical, objective, and quantitative patterns, modern science promotes an imbalance toward the external and technologically manipulable. Still it is not clear how Mumford would restore the prestige of language in a world which, as Jacques Ellul notes, follows the antihumanistic rule of number. Nor is it possible to determine whether man's origin and essence are really verbal or technological.

Given his belief in the organic properties of language and the autonomy of the individual, Mumford suspects the nihilistic, deracinated character of modern literature. Although he claims not to reproach modern writers "for making so clear the whole tendency of our civilization today," since art should reveal its age, like Georg Lukacs he finds them "negative," "infantile," and "morbid." Far from asserting freedom, as its practitioners believe, the incommunicativeness, disorganization, and dehumanization of modern art confirm and reinforce the fragmented, life-denying, and antiverbal conditions created by capitalism and technology. But Mumford proposes an unrealistic alternative: the writer has a "responsibility to be sane" and balanced, especially if his culture lacks these qualities. Modern literature should provide "healing forces," a "cleansing greatness of spirit," a "scheme of ideal values," however absent in social conditions. Theodor Adorno was probably closer to the mark when he praised Samuel Beckett (whose gloomy works Mumford finds suspicious) for refusing fashionable "commitment" and affirmation in order to represent fully the horror which the existentialists merely talk about.

In *Technics and Civilization* Mumford points out that ancient Greece and the Middle Ages had integrated art with technics. The Greek word *techne* signifies art as craft, that is, an unsystematic rather than uniform process of manual labor in which the craftsman is master of his tools and materials and participates in the process of production from first to last. *Techne* thus implies conditions of comparatively autonomous, expressive, and unalienated labor. But after about 1600, *techne* was undermined by technology in the sense of the machine, which, given the social division of labor, multiplied into vast and segmented systems. In their predictability, uniformity, and efficiency, these machines bent the worker to purposes other than his own. Yet Mumford does not propose elimination of the machine; a voluntary return to handicrafts can take place only on a limited scale. Instead he wants a recognition, similar to the Cubists', of the aesthetic possibilities of the machine. The goal is not mere engineering, technological in its parsimonious economy and efficiency, but an expressive and symbolic architecture adapted functionally to human needs. But, as Veblen also taught, a humane technics is possible only where design is freed from irrelevant pecuniary motives which lead to shoddy workmanship, planned obsolescence, the yearly advertising and sales ploy of meaningless and ostentatious ornament.

The admittedly vague components of Mumford's new "synthesis" can be summarized. In *The Condition of Man* evolution is a process in which purpose is not determined causally in advance but is created and revealed in the autonomous activities of individual organisms and in the increasing diversity and complexity of natural and cultural development. Things tend toward organic wholeness, "balance," and "hierarchy," a "dynamic" and emergent equilibrium among entities in the "great web of life." The "underlying pattern" is favorable to the integrity of the person and the development of a "new personality." Mumford's "synthesis" reconciles technology and science, religion and the humanities. The reawakening of man's selfhood and "tenderness" must lead to the transcendence of nationalism and the specialized personality type created under technology and capitalism. As man ceases to be a mere mechanical end, a new world community would emerge based upon Martin Buber's concept of the I-Thou relationship and the sanctity of the personality. Where nineteenth-century scarcity economics had emphasized productivity and failed to provide adequate distribution, this community would achieve quality consumption. Meantime a qualitative rather than quantitative emphasis would emerge, for instance, in a renewed reverence for the world's "axial" religions. Long forgotten and devalued cultural traditions would be recovered, transformed, and assimilated. Unlike the rigid medieval synthesis, the new world order would allow for cultural variety and local self-determination. But authority would also be vested in a world political organization far more active and influential than the United Nations.

Mumford shows excessive, indeed utopian optimism. Since to implement these goals through massive social engineering would probably reintroduce contemporary technology in another form, he leans heavily upon the bourgeois concept of the autonomous individual, upon whom he urges human "initiative," "moral renewal," "self-transformation," and "psychological revolution." This revolution would supposedly consist of isolated resistance to the fragmenting effect of present-day technology, as in the scholar who chooses to "discipline" his production. The "single decisive personality" resembles James Clerk Maxwell's "Singular Points" in physical nature, erratic occurrences of massive effect, like the spark that sets off the forest fire. Ironically

the same analogy might characterize the chaos caused by a computer error or the destruction resulting from a single mistake within the chain of nuclear command. Mumford likes to compare the modern world to ancient Rome, rejuvenated unexpectedly by Christ's followers–again a dubious analogy, since technological forces in 100 A.D. were far less powerful than those of today. Underlying such arguments is Mumford's humanistic assumption that man persists as an autonomous being.

Mumford's works of the 1950s are heavily influenced by Roderick Seidenberg's vision of "Post-Historic Man," the conclusion of human history in the victory of organized technological intelligence over instinct and in the submission of man to a thoroughly calculated administrative control. With the triumph of social engineering, "human nature" as once understood would disappear; history, as Spengler and Henry Adams (and at times Max Weber) had predicted, would terminate in a routinized, stagnant, posthistoric order. Mumford does not discount the possibility that "automatic" mechanisms may subsume or replace "man." Indeed while posthistoric man has not yet arrived, "Modern man has already depersonalized himself so effectively that he is no longer man enough to stand up to his machines." Through advertising and propaganda, the "stable centralized inner authority, capable of making real choice," had been undermined. But Mumford largely resists Seidenberg's prognostications, just as he rejects technological determinism and autonomy.

Mumford's most mature meditations on the "human prospect" take shape in *The City in History* and *The Myth of the Machine*. One cannot, however, ignore his studies of urban planning, architectural history, and modern architecture. These works anchor Mumford's seemingly wild or outmoded proposals in concrete observation and practical living.

Of Mumford's first ten books, three examine the history of American architecture: *Sticks and Stones, The Brown Decades,* and *The South in Architecture* (1941). Like Ruskin, Mumford treats architecture as an expression of national life while subscribing to the dated view that architecture can materially affect society. American colonial architecture and urban planning develop out of the eotechnic medieval tradition. But gradually the Renaissance style imposes itself uniformly, thus undermining more functional and local building traditions along with handicraft values. For Mumford this snobbish fetish of the moneyed classes is a fake response to local conditions and American social democracy. Later, in the industrial city as on the farming and mining frontier, jerry-built, prefabricated, and uniform structures are heaped together without regard for environment or tradition. The urban centers are overbuilt to maximize land values. In its constant expansion, cheap construction, and rapid turnover, and in its reliance on the gridiron pattern of unit lots, the "economic system" provides not a coherent and permanent architecture but mere building or at best engineering, conforming to technocratic standards of efficiency and economy. Hence the ubiquitous "steel cage" and skyscraper after 1900.

Even so, in *Sticks and Stones* Mumford expects the subordination of the machine to aesthetic values. Already in Frank Lloyd Wright the principle of organic limits asserts itself against the skyscraper's mechanical form. The garden city of Ebenezer Howard appears at the conclusion of this work, along with a plea for more handicrafts, regional planning, urban symbiosis with the countryside, and the transformation of land into a public trust. In *The Brown Decades*, Mumford praises those figures who, after the Civil War, anticipated an authentic American architecture. The public parks of Frederick Law Olmsted naturalize the city while "making nature urbane"; the Roeblings combined art and engineering in the Brooklyn Bridge; and H. H. Richardson synthesized the romantic and the utilitarian. In Louis Sullivan and John Wellborn Root the skyscraper becomes a modest, functional, and genuinely *"social manifestation."* In Wright's "prairie houses," architecture grows conscious of its relation to the land itself, accommodates the variety of human habits and needs, and thus attains a functional marriage of necessity, imagination, and symbolism. Wright assimilates the machine for "biotechnic" ends.

Mumford was a founding member in 1922-1923 of the Regional Planning Association, which included among others the conservationist Benton Mackaye and the town planners Clarence Stein and Henry Wright. They shared Mumford's fear of what Geddes called "conurbation," disorganized, congested, and uncontrolled growth around the urban centers. To draw off the surplus population of the city, they revived Howard's concept of the garden city and green belt towns. They sought as well to restore the concept of the neighborhood organized as a complete "unit" around a "community center." The

"fundamental social cell of the city" and the basis for the "principle of cellular growth," the neighborhood is moreover the ideal setting for those family values which they and Mumford, against more "sophisticated" progressives, considered essential to civilization. To preserve parks and neighborhoods, Mumford would limit the intrusive highway to the urban periphery and channel its heavy traffic into the city by means of arterial and capillary roads. To lessen the chaotic mixture of pedestrian and commercial activity, Mumford proposed the self-contained residential superblock, which avoided the congestion of cross-street planning. Finally the Regional Planning Association advocated regional, self-sufficient, and largely self-governing cities in order to offset the dominance of the megalopolis.

*City Development* (1945) is a virtual catalogue of Mumford's values in urban planning. He proposes that the stabilization of capitalism makes it possible to overturn "megalopolitan standards" through distribution, consumption, and social services. Now "collective demands" for "sound biological environments" take precedence over private speculation. But in his essay on the postwar London plan, Mumford noted an error endlessly repeated in succeeding decades. Ignoring Geddes's discovery of the need for organic limits in city design, the London planners sought to retain London's existing population and thus mistakenly maintained earlier patterns of unlimited growth.

As Mumford came to lament in *The Urban Prospect* (1968), not only was public authority lacking to build the regional city but during the 1950s and 1960s city, state, and national governments succumbed to external economic pressures. Accommodating the financier, who found skyscrapers profitable, and the automobile manufacturer, who sought wider sales, massive highways had been bulldozed into downtown areas, thus destroying parks and neighborhoods and producing heavy congestion in the inner city. The pattern holds for London, New York, and countless other cities. These measures had led to urban flight, and this in turn had expanded the chaotic and overly car-dependent suburbs, which Mumford views as a poor substitute for the planned, comparatively high density, convenient, and truly urban garden city of Howard.

Mumford's values have largely been accepted in recent building but not in planning—a fatal omission which Mumford noted in "Home Remedies for Urban Cancer" (originally published in the *New Yorker*, 1962; collected in *The*

*Urban Prospect*), a scathing attack on the influential theories of Jane Jacobs. Rejecting Howard's and Mumford's views, Jacobs proposed as the key to urban revitalization increased street life through the encouragement of random and spontaneous commercial growth. As Mumford recognized, these recommendations ignored the real causes of urban decay, which lay in bad economics and the absence of planning. By the middle 1960s Mumford was convinced that his and his colleagues' values had been misapplied and corrupted by economic and technological forces. As he observed in "A Brief History of Urban Frustration," collected in *The Urban Prospect*, even when the Federal government sought to improve the city, it reproduced earlier errors through its ideological acceptance of the automobile, the superhighway, the congregated block apartment house, and other fetishes of urban technology. The automatically expanding city would soon become "Necropolis," the final embodiment of what Mumford now termed the "myth of the machine."

*The City in History* and the two-part *The Myth of the Machine* (*Technics and Human Development* and *The Pentagon of Power*) recapitulate many of Mumford's ideas. Now, however, Mumford altogether rejects utopianism and proposes an original historical thesis. The current killing pattern of urban expansion has its analogue in the "megamachine" of ancient times and is a return to the pathological conditions which destroyed the great ancient civilizations. In *The City in History* Mumford follows Veblen in praising once more the cooperative and pacifistic village culture of the Neolithic. Yet he does not deny the enormous cultural achievements of the ancient city as a "container" and "magnet" of human endeavor. Nonetheless, ancient Mesopotamia and Egypt fostered social regimentation and war through royal absolutism (the king as sun), religious sacrifice, and priestly secrecy. The first "megamachines" consisted not of mechanical inventions but of masses of human beings coerced into pyramid building and irrigation projects, organized into vast bureaucracies, or enlisted in predatory armies in quest of sacrificial victims and slaves. With its machinelike efficiency, the ancient army served an inhuman cult of political and economic power, so that the city came to dominate the countryside and ultimately grew into an ossified monument not to cooperation but to exploitation, violence, imperialism, monopoly, and material accumulation. Mesopotamia, Hellenistic

Greece, Rome, all petrified in worshipping the "myth of the machine," the promise of total organization and unlimited domination over man and nature. The final result was "parasitopolis."

Medieval Western civilization avoided these evils. But with the Renaissance came a new "myth of the machine" all the more dangerous because of the West's superior technology, its "servomechanisms," its "subtle . . . coercion[s]" and "rewards." The new and allied forces of capitalism, science, and the absolute state revived the old desire for unlimited mechanical power over nature and man. Bacon showed how, through the corporate organization and division of scientific labor, knowledge becomes power; science becomes technology, and the scientist an "organization" man. The modern version of the ancient Sun-Kings, absolute monarchs celebrate their conquests and ambitions in massively geometrical, rigidly centralized cities. For Mumford, as for Ellul, the modern "megamachine" includes more than just mechanical inventions. It includes man as an assemblage of human parts: the national army, the government and capitalist bureaucracy, the research institutes, and the industrial factory. In the nineteenth century the deruralized city itself becomes a machine of political domination, class segregation, and capital accumulation, a lifeless and disorderly monument to limitless power. The massive cities of today, with their cultural and physical uniformity, and their disregard of human ends, follow directly the revival of the ancient "myth of the machine."

*The Myth of the Machine* had special force during the Vietnam War, of which Mumford was an early opponent. The ancient power machine, with its absolute potentate, its intelligentsia of secretive priests, and its armies and weapons of destruction, had returned in more lethal form in the modern "military-industrial scientific" establishment, an interlocking "pentagon of power" bypassing democratic control and extending from the executive, to industry, to finance, to the thinktanks, to the Pentagon. The discovery of this "pentagon" confirmed Mumford's rejection throughout the 1950s of the facile propagandistic distinction between the "democratic" West and the "totalitarian" East. The "capitalist" United States and the Soviet Union embody "universal" and totalitarian forces of destruction symbolized by the atomic bomb. Each aims subtly at the extinction of human subjectivity through mass propaganda, corporate organization, mass entertainment, indiscriminate mass consumption, the coercive promise of full employment, and other means of technocratic control. Each pursues biologically pointless, costly, and lethal aims such as the space-and-arms race, the modern near equivalent of pyramid building. The vision of "Necropolis" in *The Culture of Cities,* which many found too pessimistic in the 1930s, and Seidenberg's concept of "Post-Historic Man" had come to seem increasingly likely.

The concluding chapters of *The City in History* and *The Myth of the Machine* admit qualified hope that man may yet take command. Although revolution by "mass organization" is self-defeating, Mumford is encouraged by the resistance in the now-faded youth movement, the exuberant irreverence of the Beatles, worker dissatisfaction and laziness, individual rebellions of various kinds, even if often nihilistic and regressive, and the rise of ecological awareness. Nor does Mumford relinquish his earlier values, but affirms them with unabated enthusiasm: regionalism, organicism, biotechnics, aetherialization of the technological apparatus, the need for "dynamic equilibrium," and a cultural shift from "power to plenitude." Perhaps as in ancient Rome the "monolith" is "cracking" invisibly at the moment of its greatest power.

It remains to define Lewis Mumford's place within modern cultural and intellectual tradition as well as his affinities with other notable contemporaries. As a literary and cultural critic Mumford has had a major role in laying the basis of American studies as an academic discipline; his influence on architecture and urban planning has also been significant. Considered in the broader terms of intellectual history, Mumford figures within the "revolt against positivism" (according to Christopher Lasch, *Salmagundi,* 1980) and simplistic utilitarian pragmatism which arose around the turn of the century. The basic and largely achieved intention of Mumford's work has been to combine an intuitive romantic organicism, as in Emerson and Ruskin, Morris and Thoreau, with the more scientifically and biologically founded post-Darwinian organicism of Geddes, Whitehead, and others. Mumford thus stands as an eloquent forerunner of the present-day ecology movement. In his critique of science as "enlightenment" and unqualified "progress," his condemnation of the contemporary reduction of reason to the merely instrumental, and in his recognition of the erosion of the modern subject through technology, Mumford calls to mind the work of Max Horkheimer, Adorno, Herbert Marcuse, and the Frankfurt School. Mumford shares with these writers a sharp (though somewhat less melancholy and pessimistic) awareness of the dwindling of genuine and varied personal experience amid the overrationalized, overadministered forms of modern life. Finally in his justifiable fears of the application of technological means for totalitarian ends, and in his warnings of ultimate historical entropy or stasis under immovable technocratic control, Mumford finds his kindred spirits, if not in Spengler, who bitterly and perversely accepted historical ossification, in Henry Adams, Jacob Burckhardt, Jacques Ellul, Roderick Seidenberg, and George Orwell, all of whom protested against it. In short Lewis Mumford has with wide learning and moral passion devoted his long and distinguished career to the central questions of the twentieth century.

**Letters:**

*The Van Wyck Brooks and Lewis Mumford Letters: The Record of a Literary Friendship, 1921-1963,* edited by Robert E. Spiller (New York: Dutton, 1970);

*The Letters of Lewis Mumford and Frederick J. Osborn: A Transatlantic Dialogue 1938-70,* edited by Michael Hughes (New York: Praeger, 1972).

**Bibliography:**

Elmer S. Newman, *Lewis Mumford: A Bibliography, 1914-1970,* introduction by Lewis Mumford (New York: Harcourt Brace Jovanovich, 1971).

**References:**

Richard Chase, "The Armed Obscurantist," *Partisan Review,* 11 (Summer 1944): 346-348;

Eddy Dow, "Van Wyck Brooks and Lewis Mumford: A Confluence in the 'Twenties,'" in *Van Wyck Brooks: The Critic and His Critics,* edited by William Wasserstrom (Port Washington, N.Y.: Kennikat Press, 1979), pp. 238-251;

Joseph Duffey, "Mumford's Quest: The First Decade," *Salmagundi,* 49 (Summer 1980): 43-68;

Paul Goldberger, "Organic Remedies: Building and the City," *Salmagundi,* 49 (Summer 1980): 87-98;

Christopher Lasch, "Lewis Mumford and the Myth of the Machine," *Salmagundi,* 49 (Summer 1980): 4-28;

David Riesman, "Some Observations on Lewis Mumford's *The City in History*," *Salmagundi*, 49 (Summer 1980): 80-86;

Meyer Schapiro, "Looking Forward to Looking Backward," *Partisan Review*, 5 ( July 1938): 12-24;

Alan Trachtenberg, "Mumford in the Twenties: The Historian as Artist," *Salmagundi*, 49 (Summer 1980): 29-42.

Thomas Lewis, "Mumford and the Academy," *Salmagundi*, 49 (Summer 1980): 99-111;

**Papers:**

Some of Mumford's correspondence and manuscripts can be found in academic, historical, and public libraries in the United States, among them Yale University Library, Dartmouth College Library, Princeton University Library, Cleveland Public Library, New York Public Library, and the State Historical Society, Madison, Wisconsin. Mumford's letters to Patrick Geddes and Victor Branford are contained in the National Library of Scotland, Edinburgh. The rest of Mumford's papers are privately held.

# Elder Olson

## (9 March 1909-    )

### James L. Battersby
*Ohio State University*

See also the Olson entry in *DLB 48, American Poets, 1880-1945*, Second Series.

BOOKS: *Thing of Sorrow* (New York: Macmillan, 1934);

*General Prosody: Rhythmic, Metric, Harmonics* (Chicago: University of Chicago Libraries, 1938);

*The Cock of Heaven* (New York: Macmillan, 1940);

*The Poetry of Dylan Thomas* (Chicago: University of Chicago Press, 1954);

*The Scarecrow Christ and Other Poems* (New York: Noonday Press, 1954);

*Plays & Poems, 1948-1958* (Chicago: University of Chicago Press, 1958);

*Tragedy and the Theory of Drama* (Detroit: Wayne State University Press, 1961);

*Collected Poems* (Chicago & London: University of Chicago Press, 1963);

*The Theory of Comedy* (Bloomington & London: Indiana University Press, 1968);

*Olson's Penny Arcade* (Chicago & London: University of Chicago Press, 1975);

*On Value Judgments in the Arts and Other Essays* (Chicago & London: University of Chicago Press, 1976);

*Last Poems* (Chicago & London: University of Chicago Press, 1984).

OTHER: *Longinus On the Sublime, an English translation by Benedict Einarson, and Sir Joshua Reynolds Discourses on Art*, introduction by Olson (Chicago: Packard, 1945);

"The Poetic Method of Aristotle: Its Power and Limitations," in *English Institute Essays* (New York: Columbia University Press, 1951), pp. 70-94;

"William Empson, Contemporary Criticism and Poetic Diction," "A Symbolic Reading of the *Ancient Mariner*," "The Argument of Longinus' *On the Sublime*," "An Outline of Poetic Theory," and "A Dialogue on Symbolism," in *Critics and Criticism, Ancient and Modern*, edited by R. S. Crane (Chicago: University of Chicago Press, 1952);

*American Lyric Poems: From Colonial Times to the Present*, edited, with an introduction, by Olson (New York: Appleton-Century-Crofts, 1964);

*Aristotle's Poetics and English Literature: A Collection of Critical Essays*, edited, with an introduction, by Olson (Chicago & London: University of Chicago Press, 1965);

*Major Voices: Twenty British and American Poets*, edited, with an introduction, by Olson (New York: McGraw-Hill, 1973).

PERIODICAL PUBLICATIONS:

NONFICTION

"Rhetoric and the Appreciation of Pope," *Modern Philology*, 37 (August 1939): 13-35;

" 'Sailing to Byzantium': Prolegomena to a Poetics of the Lyric," *University Review*, 8 (Spring 1942): 209-219;

"William Empson, Contemporary Criticism, and Poetic Diction," *Modern Philology*, 47 (May 1950): 222-252;

"A Dialogue on the Function of Art in Society," *Chicago Review*, 16, no. 4 (1964): 57-72;

"The Dialectical Foundations of Critical Pluralism," *Texas Quarterly*, 9 (May 1966): 202-230;

"A Conspectus of Poetry, Part I," *Critical Inquiry*, 4 (Autumn 1977): 159-180;

"A Conspectus of Poetry, Part II," *Critical Inquiry*, 4 (Winter 1977): 373-396;

"R. S. Crane," *American Scholar*, 53 (Spring 1984): 232-238.

DRAMA

"Faust: A Masque," *Measure: A Critical Journal*, 2 (Summer 1951): 298-319;

"The Sorcerer's Apprentices," *Western Review*, 21 (Autumn 1956): 5-14;

"A Crack in the Universe," *First Stage*, 1 (Spring 1962): 9-33;

"The Abstract Tragedy: A Comedy of Masks," *First Stage*, 2 (Summer 1963): 166-186.

The rigor of modern academic criticism in the United States owes much to the efforts of Elder Olson and the other so-called Chicago or Neo-Aristotelian critics: R. S. Crane, W. R. Keast, Richard McKeon, Norman Maclean, and Bernard Weinberg. They aimed to elucidate the theoretical bases of commentaries on art, to distinguish sound from unsound principles and methods of critical reasoning, and to join issues with various myth, psychoanalytic, and New Critics. In a series of articles and books written in the middle decades of the twentieth century, these critics, Olson perhaps most prominently, did more than a little to raise the ante of critical discussion and to make the study of criticism and critical theory a rigorous, intellectual enterprise. In a review of *Critics and Criticism: Ancient and Modern* (1952), treated by many as the Chicago manifesto, the New Critic John Crowe Ransom called Olson "their best man in the long hard fight at close quarters." It is fair to say that with the possible exception of R. S. Crane, none of the Chicago critics has done more than Olson to define

and defend the philosophic and theoretical bases of the approach to criticism with which he is associated, to illuminate the foundations of critical systems and the principled bases of practical criticism, and to examine genres and particular works in the light of their principles of construction. Although he has our interest as a critic, Olson is a poet by natural inclination and a critic only by chance. "I became a professor and a theoretician," Olson has said, "because I had to understand my art."

Elder James Olson was born on 9 March 1909 in Chicago, Illinois, the son of Elder James and Hilda M. Schroeder Olson. Olson was willing on one occasion to half-jokingly attribute his view of life to his Norwegian-German heritage. After complaining to Thornton Wilder, one of the early supporters of Olson's poetry, that *Our Town* (1938) looked at life through rose-colored glasses, Wilder laughed and then asked Olson what his own view was. Olson said, "it was one of . . . shallow German optimism based on a profound Norwegian pessimism." Widowed when Elder was barely two years old, his mother moved with him into her parents' home. He attended Harvey G. Wells Elementary School. As a child Olson exhibited remarkable musical ability, and to this day he remains a serious student of music and a skilled pianist. From 1918 to 1926 he studied piano under Wilhelm Martin, and from 1926 to 1935 under Cleveland Bohnet at the American Conservatory of Music. Moreover, if he did not exactly lisp sonnets in his cradle, Olson came early to his first profession, that of poet: he says he began writing poetry at age seven. In addition to many poems he is willing to forget, he published what he has called his first "serious" poem in a 1926 issue of the Parisian magazine *Tambour*. While he was still in high school he submitted poetry to Harriet Monroe, the founder and first editor of *Poetry: A Magazine of Verse*, who was always quick to spot and encourage young talent. Although Monroe advised him to "go home and write some real poems," Olson had won her interest, and he later had many of his poems published in *Poetry*. Olson attended Schurz High School and later enrolled at the University of Chicago. Long before finishing his undergraduate studies, Olson was awarded several prizes for his poetry, including the Witter Bynner Award, the Young Poet's Prize, the Guarantor's Award, and the John Billings Fiske Award. In the year in which he completed his first university degree (1934), he published his

*Elder Olson*

first book of poems, *Thing of Sorrow,* which brought him national acclaim and the Foundation of Literature award and for which, one reviewer noted, "many people thought he should have won the Pulitzer prize . . . his poems are so perfect of their kind that one feels Mr. Olson to be among the very best . . . poets in this country." Since then Olson has published six additional volumes of verse (the latest, *Last Poems,* appearing in 1984), virtually all of which have been praised highly (*Olson's Penny Arcade,* 1975, for example, received the Society of Midland Authors Award). Olson has also written seven plays, one of which, *The Carnival of Animals* (1958), a verse radio play, received in 1956 the joint award of the Academy of American Poets and the Columbia Broadcasting System.

Olson remained at the University of Chicago for only two years, until 1929, when he interrupted his undergraduate studies to work for Commonwealth Edison Company (first as a junior and later as a senior adjustment clerk). From 1931 to 1932 he traveled and studied piano and wrote poetry in Europe. He left the university not to escape the rigors of scholarship but to pursue the study and practice of poetry more deliberately. The kinds of questions that concerned Olson were those of interest to a practicing artist (for example, how, given the technical resources available, could certain effects be produced? how, given a certain end in view, could the internal problems of construction be solved?). These

were questions not being addressed at that time by literary critics, who were chiefly interested in, for example, finding hidden meanings and in reading literature as part of the author's autobiography.

During this period Olson was persuaded by Thornton Wilder to resume formal studies so that he could qualify himself for a teaching position at a college. Wilder argued that such a job—and perhaps only such a job—would provide him with sufficient income to live and sufficient leisure to write. He returned then to the University of Chicago, where he completed his literary training, receiving his B.A. in 1934, his M.A. in 1935, and his Ph.D. in 1938, and where he began his long association with that group of tough-minded individuals who would later be called the Chicago critics. The year before he took his final degree, he married Ann Jones, with whom he had two children, Ann and Elder. In 1938, the year in which he received his doctorate, the University of Chicago Libraries published his first critical book, a version of his dissertation, *General Prosody: Rhythmic, Metric, Harmonics,* which happily combines and depends for its success upon Olson's skills as poet, musician, and literary critic.

Except for a short period early in his career and when he was filling visiting appointments at universities both in the United States and abroad, Olson did his teaching at the University of Chicago. For seven years, both during and immediately following his years of graduate study, he taught at the Armour Institute of Technology (later the Illinois Institute of Technology), first as an instructor (1935-1939) and then as an assistant professor (1939-1942). In 1942 he was invited to return to the University of Chicago, where he served with distinction as assistant professor (1942-1948), associate professor (1948-1954), full professor (1954-1971), Distinguished Service Professor (1971-1977), and, when he retired, Distinguished Service Professor Emeritus. This summary of Olson's academic career is misleading to the extent that it suggests a life governed by Chicago; over the years Olson spent a considerable amount of time teaching at other universities, including the University of Puerto Rico (1952-1953), the University of Frankfort as a Rockefeller professor (1948), the University of the Philippines as Rockefeller Professor of English and Comparative Literature (1966-1967), and Indiana University as Mahlon Powell Professor of Philosophy (1954), visiting professor of literary criticism (1958-1959), and Patten Lecturer

(1965). He also delivered major lectures at many universities, including the University of Texas, Wayne State University, the University of Virginia, Cambridge University, and the University of the Far East.

In 1966 the University of Chicago presented Olson with the Quantrell Award in recognition of the excellence of his teaching. The most impressive testimony to his achievements in the classroom, however, comes from his former students, none of whom seems to be capable of recalling his classes with indifference. By all reports, Olson was as demanding a teacher as he was a critic, and what he demanded was immediate and hard thinking. His approach was practical and problematic, that is, concerned with the internal textual problems that writers necessarily encountered in the making of their works. He asked questions such as why a certain character was necessary and why a certain piece of information was disclosed at a given point in the action by this character. More broadly his aim was to teach students to teach themselves, as he has said, how "to discover a problem and formulate it precisely, to examine it on all sides, and to solve it on sound evidence." In his 1972 biography of Olson, a former student, Thomas E. Lucas, highlighted an aspect of Olson's approach: "I still have vivid memories of a classroom technique that was in the best Platonic manner. We were often surprised to find, under Mr. Olson's skillful questioning, that we knew many things of which we hadn't been aware." It is still possible to acquire some immediate sense of Olson's method in the classroom from his 1957 essay "A Letter on Teaching Drama," in *On Value Judgments in the Arts and Other Essays* (1976).

In 1948 Olson was divorced. Later that year he married painter Geraldine "Jerri" Louise Hays, with whom he had two daughters, Olivia and Shelley. Following his retirement from the University of Chicago in 1977, Olson moved to Albuquerque, New Mexico, where he and Jerri Hays now live, and where he continues to study music, to write poetry and criticism, and, occasionally, to teach (for example, as M. D. Anderson Professor of English at the University of Houston, 1978-1979, and as visiting professor of English at the University of New Mexico, 1982).

Kenneth Burke was the first to call Olson, R. S. Crane, and Norman Maclean "Neo-Aristotelians." He referred to them as such in a section of *A Grammar of Motives* (1945) entitled "The Problem of the Intrinsic (as Reflected in the Neo-Aristotelian School)," essentially a review of three essays published in the *University Review* (1942), including Olson's " 'Sailing to Byzantium': Prolegomena to a Poetics of the Lyric." The term stuck and was subsequently applied to all those responsible for *Critics and Criticism*. They were also known as the Chicago critics because of their affiliation with the University of Chicago and were so labeled by William K. Wimsatt, Jr., in his essay "The Chicago Critics" (*Comparative Literature*, 1953). Commenting on the notion of the group making up a Neo-Aristotelian movement or a Chicago school, Olson, in a 1984 *American Scholar* essay on Crane, said, "we were no more unanimous in our views than we were exclusively Aristotelian, for we were unanimous only in our view that Aristotle—in our interpretation of him—had certainly offered one of many possible methods of criticism. . . . What we had in common, besides friendship, was a concern with certain problems and a general agreement about methods we might use to solve them. But if there was any other unity of the Chicago School, it was the unity of a log fire in which, by their proximity, the logs stimulate and inflame one another, while each burns with its individual fires."

The only label these critics have applied to themselves, that both informs their various individual endeavors and allows sufficient scope to their wide-ranging concerns, is "pluralism"; but, since many with whom Olson and the others have virtually nothing in common also claim to be pluralists today, it is necessary to understand exactly what pluralism entails for Olson. At bottom pluralism assumes the legitimacy and validity of many different critical principles and methods. Olson's most cogent and detailed discussion of his kind of pluralism is in "The Dialectical Foundations of Critical Pluralism" (*Texas Quarterly*, 1966), a rigorously argued essay which carefully examines the causes of variation in philosophical and critical discussions and explains why no theory can gain a monopoly on truth. As Olson explains in this essay, pluralism maintains that

> any philosophic problem must be relative to its formulation; and since any solution to a problem is also relative to the problem, the solution must be relative to that formulation. But that formulation (because of the selective and restrictive nature of language) . . . must be finite. It follows that there can be no single philosophic system embracing all truth; and by the same

token, no method which is the only right method.

The analysis and recovery of the principles governing various critical systems bring Olson not to eclecticism, dogmatism, or skepticism, but to an informed respect for the explanatory powers of diverse critical approaches and, correlatively, to a keen awareness of the limitations necessarily implicated in those approaches.

As a pluralist Olson encourages the development of every valid approach. As a critic and theoretician Olson has employed many methods of reasoning, including the Platonic and Aristotelian as well as the Humean and the Longinian. *Tragedy and the Theory of Drama* (1961), for example, is essentially Humean, concerned chiefly not with the *reasoning* but with the *making* part of poetics and beginning inquiry with a distinction between impressions and ideas; in brief Olson gives emphasis to the fact that the dramatist affects his or her audience chiefly through sensation, through the direct representation of physical action, and only secondarily through signs or words, the indicators of mental or emotional condition. *The Poetry of Dylan Thomas* (1954), on the other hand, is Longinian, organized under the categories of thought, emotional power, and devices or techniques of expression. In true Longinian fashion, then, Olson here stresses intellectual conception (the kinds of subjects dealt with), emotional force (the tragic power of the represented suffering of the lyric speaker), and dictional quality (the peculiarities of Thomas's diction and syntax). Nevertheless, of the many valid approaches capable of extension and refinement, Olson has given most attention to what he takes to be the two most comprehensive systems, the Aristotelian and the Platonic. A close reading of his work evinces that Olson is no more committed to the development of an Aristotelian method than to that of a Platonic one. "A Dialogue on Symbolism" (first published in *Critics and Criticism*) and "A Dialogue on the Function of Art in Society" (originally published in Spanish in *La Torre* in 1953 and first published in English in the *Chicago Review* in 1964) represent part of a projected series of twelve dialogues designed to exhibit a complete theory of art in the Platonic mode. But if Olson is a good deal more than an Aristotelian, he is also the Chicago critic who has done most to refine and extend the Aristotelian method.

Olson is not interested in Aristotle's doctrines, but in his critical method, which, he assumes, is a permanently useful tool for dealing with specific types of problems. With his pluralist convictions about the powers and limitations of all methods, Olson knows that an Aristotelian poetics *can* explain how a composite system of differentiable artistic parts—plot, character, thought, diction—achieves a particular effect, but *cannot* deal directly with, say, the faculties of artists, the nature of audiences, or the political and social functions of art. Briefly, as Olson notes in "The Poetic Method of Aristotle" (1951), an Aristotelian poetics takes

for its starting point, or principle, the artistic whole which is to be produced and [proceeds] through the various parts of the various kinds to be assembled. The reasoning is hypothetical because it is based upon hypotheses: If such and such a work, which is a whole, is to be produced, then such and such parts must be assembled in such and such a way; and if the work is to have excellence as a whole, then the parts must be of such and such a kind and quality. The reasoning is regressive because it works backward from the whole, which is to exist, to the parts which must have existence previous to that of the whole. Since the reasoning is based upon a definition of a certain whole as its principle and since that definition must be arrived at in some fashion, any productive science must consist of two main parts: inductive reasoning toward its principle, and deductive reasoning from its principle. One part must make possible the formulation of the whole; the other must determine the parts according to that formulation.

To understand what the method entails in practical terms, it is useful to consider the opening section of " 'Sailing to Byzantium': Prolegomena to a Poetics of the Lyric," one of Olson's most important and influential essays. There he remarks that the principal task of the practical critic is

to discover some principle in the work which is the principle of its unity and order—a principle which, it goes without saying, will have to be a purely formal principle, i.e., a formal principle of the poem, and not something extrinsic to it such as the differentiation either of authors, audiences, subject matters, or orders of diction would afford. Since in a formal consideration the form is the end, and since the end renders everything else intelligible, a mark of the discovery of the formal principle would be that everything else in the poem would be found to be explicable in terms of it.

In his Aristotelian mode (and only when he is analyzing in this mode), Olson focuses on synthesizing principles of artistic form, on those formal principles of works which determine the functions of the differentiable parts, and in relation to which the parts have their functions. For example, formally considered, "Sailing to Byzantium" is unified by the effect, as Olson says, of "noble joy or exaltation," which is the emotive result of an act of moral choice actualizing and instancing the speaker's moral character. Whether examining Dylan Thomas's sonnets, lyric poems, comedies, tragedies, or didactic works, Olson is interested in the causes of their artistic integrity, as these can be discovered by independent inductive inquiry into their artistic structures.

Thus while Olson's critical approach is pluralist, it remains fair to observe that much of his theoretical work derives from his effort to extend Aristotle's method to kinds of works which have emerged since Aristotle wrote. In particular he is interested in rethinking such critical concepts as plot, action, imitation, and tragedy. Olson has also done much to sharpen our understanding of genres and genre definition. A genre may be seen as a kind of literary work distinguishable by the specific literary elements it utilizes and the structural form through which it organizes them toward an end (which then becomes identified with the genre). Olson and other members of the Chicago School argued that the analysis and description of literary forms could provide the foundation of literary history, since to them new forms or kinds emerged from possibilities inherent in the material and formal conditions of earlier kinds. In "William Empson, Contemporary Criticism and Poetic Diction," collected in *Critics and Criticism* (1952), Olson extends Aristotle's emphasis on the role of plot as the key formal element in Greek tragedy. Olson argued that in mimetic forms (literary works that focus on imitations of actions and character), it is the "effective emotional presentation" of "actualized virtue or vice" in an order of "action or suffering" which "is chief, which gives form to the work, and to which all else is ordered." The emphasis on formal principle and the structure of imitated action was also presented as an alternative to the method of the New Criticism, dubbed "critical

monism" by R. S. Crane. Crane meant that the New Critics, in defining literature as the paradoxical or complex use of linguistic features such as metaphor or irony or imagery, reduced all poems to a single type, ignoring their important formal differences. Olson argued that the distinction between mimetic and didactic poetry, for example, was ignored by the New Critics.

A preliminary observation about the quarrel between the Chicago School and the New Critics might be useful here. The Chicago critics firmly believed in seeing all the elements of the literary text as governed by some internal principle of form, by some final cause, as Aristotle would say, some end in view or purpose. This purpose both implies and is implied by the subordinate parts (character, thought, diction, imagery, and so on). In New Criticism they saw what appeared to be the isolation of literary language as the sole indicator of poetic quality, and in New Critical exposition a failure to consider the role of plot and character in the functioning of the whole. Moreover New Critical emphasis on literature as discourse, a discourse distinct from that offered by "science or logic," led to a preoccupation with "readings" of texts for their special meaning and to the reduction of many forms to one form; that is, all works were treated as complex structures of meaning. Where the Chicago critics saw many principles of form and many kinds of works, the New Critics, so the Chicago critics said, found many meanings, but ultimately one artistic structure. On their side, the New Critics accused the Chicago critics of valuing formal structure above the distinct meaning that only an analysis of the peculiar linguistic features of the text could disclose. On the issue of the importance of diction and language, Olson in "An Outline of Poetic Theory," included in *Critics and Criticism*, clarified the argument. "The point," he wrote, "is not whether diction is important but whether it is more or less important than certain other elements *in* the poem." The "words must be subordinate to their functions, for they are selected and arranged with a view to these." Olson does not deny the importance of linguistic elements, but he does object to their isolation from the whole: "the words must be explained in terms of something else, not the poem in terms of the words, and further, a principle must be a principle of something other than itself; hence the words cannot be a principle of their own arrangement." Olson's pluralistic adaptation of Aristotle and other philosophers of literary form and his disagreements with the New Critics would be recurrent features of his theoretical career.

Olson has a rigorous, philosophic mind, and his writing, as a consequence, is difficult, though never obscure; thus his writing poses a challenge even to the reader willing to work hard. What he has said in "The Poetry of Marianne Moore" (1957) can appropriately be applied to his own work: Olson is extremely clear; our difficulty comes primarily from his insistence that we think and think well at every point in his essays and books.

Olson's first critical book, *General Prosody: Rhythmic, Metric, Harmonics*, already betrays the features that can be said to characterize all of Olson's critical writing: precision of statement, sharpness of distinction, and logical rigor of argument. In this work Olson establishes the bases of a general science of prosody (one applying to all languages) as distinct from special sciences–the designation of special prosodic principles for each language–and argues for such a science by employing a differential method of analysis, a method concerned with the enumeration of the parts of prosodic synthesis and with the way in which such parts (the speech sounds) may be combined to enhance or embellish diction, which is in turn determined by the formal ends of whole works. The careful reader will find in this work adumbrations of Olson's later views, especially concerning the hierarchical nature of the parts and the subordination of diction and rhythm to action, character, and thought. Not widely circulated, this book is the only one written by Olson to which the reviewers responded with silence.

Silence, however, was replaced by uproar when *Critics and Criticism, Ancient and Modern* made its appearance in 1952. This work was edited by R. S. Crane and written by Crane, W. R. Keast, Norman Maclean, Richard McKeon, Bernard Weinberg, and Olson, who contributed four previously published and one new essay. *Critics and Criticism* contains twenty essays that both define and exhibit a pluralistic approach to art. They are divided into three sections. Olson's essays "William Empson, Contemporary Criticism and Poetic Diction" and "A Symbolic Reading of *The Ancient Mariner*" are included in the first section of analyses of the doctrines, assumptions, and critical methods of representative modern critics. Olson's "The Argument of Longinus' On the Sublime" is included in the second division, examinations of earlier critical approaches, from the Greeks through the eighteenth century. The

last section of the work is made up of broad discussions focusing on metacriticism and on the problems involved in defining such poetic forms as tragedy, comedy, and the lyric, and Olson's contributions are "An Outline of Poetic Theory" and the new essay "A Dialogue on Symbolism." "An Outline of Poetic Theory," Olson's first sustained expression of the theoretical foundations of pluralism, and the Empson essay, an attack against the focus on diction and devices of language (ambiguity, paradox, irony) in contemporary criticism, clearly displayed what the opponents took to be the weaknesses and the supporters the strengths of these critics. Olson maintained, for example, that all legitimate approaches to literature had specific powers and limitations (can do some things and not others; any given theory, because of the selective and restrictive nature of language, can talk about those things and only those things that fall within the logical and semantic range of its terms of reference). Olson also noted that words were the least important elements of literary works (since they were determined by everything else, were subordinated to their functions) and that, broadly considered in terms of their primary emphases, works could be divided into two categories, the *mimetic* (emphasizing human action, feeling, and thought) and the *didactic* (emphasizing ideas or theses). To many readers these views epitomized the "Chicago" School.

In a review of *Critics and Criticism*, "Aristotle and the 'New Criticism,' " Hoyt Trowbridge, referring to "An Outline of Poetic Theory," praised Olson's clear articulation of a new, "bold, incisive, and revolutionary" approach to criticism, one which emphasized the "artistic integrity" of the work itself. But, for the most part, the critics, especially the New, myth, contextualist, and psychoanalytic critics (Ransom, Murray Krieger, Northrop Frye, Eliseo Vivas, William K. Wimsatt, Robert Penn Warren), attacked the book for its advocacy of a narrow formalism, its support of an arid Aristotelianism, and its failure to acknowledge that *language* makes possible a special way of knowing in poetry. Wimsatt's essay, "The Chicago Critics" (*Comparative Literature*, 1953), typifies the negative response to the collection. Instead of a healthy pluralism, he finds in these critics an intolerant rejection of all modern approaches concerned with verbal analysis, an inability to see the text as an "organization of meaning in words," and a mistaken emphasis on such extrinsic matters as the author's purpose and the reader's pleasure. They were guilty, in short, of the "intentional fallacy"—a confusion of the text's meaning with the author's intention—and the "affective fallacy"—a confusion of meaning with the reader's response. To read *Critics and Criticism* and the essays written in response to it is to become entangled in the issues that dominated critical discussion in the middle of the century.

In 1954 the University of Chicago Press published Olson's *The Poetry of Dylan Thomas*, the first full-length study of that poet's work, based in part on lectures given at the University of Frankfort in 1948 and at the University of Chicago in subsequent years. The book develops its analysis by reference to the rhetorical principles of Longinus's treatise *On the Sublime,* which describes how to achieve the effects of a grand style. Olson's study focuses on the intellectual quality, the emotional power, and the poetic devices (especially symbolism) that distinguish Thomas's poetry; it concludes with a detailed analysis of the "Altarwise by owl-light" sonnets. To Olson, Thomas is a poet only of the "most exalted emotions"; he is a poet of the "lofty kind," and he either achieves the sublime or fails miserably. When "the conception underlying his poetry is powerful and elevated," Thomas is magnificent; otherwise he is trivial, sometimes bathetic. Thomas is clearly "magnificent," not bathetic, in the sonnets, for here conception and expression are particularly strong; a powerfully sympathetic character meditates—and suffers as a result of his meditation—on such large questions as sex, birth, and death before achieving a satisfactory resolution of them, passing from a profound dread of the mortality of all nature to a hard-won prospect of immortality. What Thomas achieves in the end is a poem comparable in merit and kind to Milton's *Lycidas* and Keats's "Ode to a Nightingale." In his review in the *Nation* Jacob Korg applauded Olson's "analytic subtlety, and erudition." But several critics, particularly those with a special interest in Thomas, found his analysis of the sonnets in terms of the Hercules constellation, as Ralph Maud says, "uncalled for and unrewarding," the result of bringing a suggestive poem into conjunction with a "willing mass of zodiacal data."

Olson's next critical book, *Tragedy and the Theory of Drama* (1961), an exercise in Humean analysis, an inquiry beginning with a distinction between impressions and ideas, is based on lectures delivered at Wayne State University in 1958 and is written from the point of view of the working dramatist. Olson deals with "the problems of the dramatist, the technical means for their solution, and the principles governing the different methods of solution." In successive chapters Olson examines the elements of drama, moving from what he considered the most important, plot, which he defines as a "system of actions of determinate moral quality" governed by a "unifying principle of form," to the subordinate parts, incident, character, representation, and dialogue. Having outlined the elements in the first six chapters, Olson attempts to demonstrate in the last four the utility of his theoretical distinctions by examining the formal integrity and moral power of Aeschylus's *Agamemnon,* Shakespeare's *King Lear,* Racine's *Phèdre,* O'Neill's *Mourning Becomes Electra,* and Eliot's *Murder in the Cathedral,* concluding the whole book with what amounts to an independent essay on the then-controversial topic of whether we are still capable of producing tragedy. Despite what Olson views as the absence of tragedy on the modern stage, he believes its creation is still possible today, regardless of what some have said about the skeptical spirit of our age (notably Joseph Wood Krutch, in *The Modern Temper*). The capacity of the great tragedies to affect us powerfully attests at once to their enduring value and to our unextinguished responsiveness to tragic pleasure; we are not lacking tragic subjects, according to Olson, but strong conceptions of tragic action. One reviewer, Fabian Gudas, saw the book as the "latest and most complete effort" in the Chicago critics' "campaign to show how Aristotelian principles and distinctions can be refined, expanded, and supplemented into a full and coherent theory." The critical reaction to the book was almost universally favorable, and if one or two quibbled with this or that bit of practical analysis in the second half of the book, the critics, for the most part, found the whole to be both lucid in style and cogent in argument, particularly strong in its analysis of the principles of drama and its distinctions among plot forms.

Complementing the book on tragedy is *The Theory of Comedy* (1968), the culmination of a series of lectures presented at Indiana University when Olson was there as Patten Lecturer. Olson's work attempts an "Aristotelian theory" of comedy and proceeds from an analysis of the *comic* (a quality found in prose fiction and poetry as well as in drama) to a poetics of *comedy* (a certain form of drama). For Olson each comedy is a composite artifact resulting from the imposition of some *form* upon some *matter* by some *means* for some *purpose* and achieving, not *katharsis* (a purgation of pity and fear, the effect or purpose of tragedy), but *katastasis* (relaxation) of concern. Once the *whole* has been defined, Olson goes on to examine the parts, giving most attention to the basic plot forms of comedy, the plots of folly (with well- or ill-intentioned fools), and the plots of cleverness (with well- or ill-intentioned wits). As in the tragedy book, Olson devotes the bulk of this study to an examination of particular works, emphasizing the forms underlying specific comedies (works by, for example, Aristophanes, Shakespeare, Molière, and the modern Absurdists). At the end, Olson argues that unless the critic discusses the principal parts of drama "as functioning within a whole," he is not discussing them as parts but merely as topics.

This work, with its clear Aristotelian focus, received a very mixed response, mostly negative from those critics whose allegiance was to New Criticism, but generally positive from those who were interested in comedy as a form of drama, especially those involved in the theater. In his determination to show how the Aristotelian method could be applied to comedy as a genre and to trace the effects of particular works to their internal, poetic causes, Olson was, to the hostile critics, undervaluing drama as verbal discourse. Again these reviewers felt that Olson's practical application of his theory to specific works in the second half of the book merely exhibited how ingeniously he could adjust texts to his a priori determinations. On the other hand, those impressed by Olson's achievement consistently praised both the theory and its application, noting that his approach directs attention to the aesthetic form of a play, not its subject matter. The most judicious and intellectually sophisticated response came from Kenneth Burke, who, reviewing the book for the *New Republic* in 1969, was struck by its theoretical toughness and analytic acuity and, more particularly, by Olson's distinction between the comic, a quality, and comedy, a form, and by his definition of comedy modeled on Aristotle's definition of tragedy. Nevertheless, although admiring the demonstrated utility of Olson's definition, Burke wondered whether he was not disposing too quickly of *katharsis* in comedy, and whether he should also distinguish between the "kind of relaxation that is due to *relaxed* conditions and the kind that runs counter to *tense* conditions."

If Olson were not still busy at the task of critical writing, it would be possible to say that his latest critical book, *On Value Judgments in the Arts and*

*Other Essays* (1976), serves handsomely as an epitome of his accomplishments as a critic, since it conveniently assembles into one volume twenty-one of his essays, representing more than forty years of thoughtful concern with the principles of critical and philosophical reasoning and with the fundamental issues of the three primary areas of literary inquiry: poetics, hermeneutics, and criticism. With the exception of "Art and Science," all the essays were published separately, the earliest, "Rhetoric and the Appreciation of Pope," appearing in 1939 and the latest, "The Poetic Process," in 1975. Divided into five sections–"Practical Criticism," "Interpretation," "Critics," "Critical Theory," and "Metacriticism"–the collection takes up many of the major issues of modern criticism. The range and diversity of the collection can only be hinted at here, but, among other things, Olson examines the formal power of works written by a variety of writers, including William Butler Yeats, Alexander Pope, Wallace Stevens, Dylan Thomas, Shakespeare, and Louise Bogan. He outlines the bases of sound interpretation, especially of the drama; comments extensively on the philosophic bases of the thought of many critics and philosophers, including Aristotle, Plato, Hobbes, Hume, Lessing, Carlyle, Schiller, Hazlitt, Tolstoy, Longinus; and develops a poetics of the shorter forms of poetry.

In terms of topics, the essays deal, among other things, with the grounds of criticism in the arts, the relation between art and morality, the nature of definitions and hypotheses, the bases of our emotional response to art, and the validation of value judgments. Of these topics, mention can be made here only of the one which is the subject of the title essay, value judgments. To Olson, the evaluative must arise from descriptive facts, the discernible traits of texts. Like all values, artistic values are relative to some standard, and the traits of a text have value with reference to the end of the work (they are more or less valuable to the extent that they further the artistic end). Thus, for Olson, poetic value is clearly related to poetic form. For example, a line of verse, however cacophonous or "bad" as sound, is "good" if it furthers the end of the work; similarly, a speech, however "bad" or abhorrent its sentiments ("eating babies is a fine thing for the Irish to do"), is "good" if it suits the speaker's character or it advances the action. The standards that texts are relative to are intrinsic formal standards, not extrinsic social or political standards (for example, such external standards as "patriotism" or "Christianity"–this poem is more "patriotic" or "Christian" than that one).

This collection was reviewed severely by Marxist critic Liliane Welch, who objected to the isolation of Olson's essays from historical reality and saw everywhere a tendency to "exile literature into the safe existence of monads floating in the free space of bourgeois society." Commentator John M. Ellis protested that although Olson and the other Chicago critics pretend to work from a "firm theoretical foundation of philosophical concerns," they rarely appeal to modern philosophers in defense or support of their criticism. But if some critics thought the book added little to what we already knew about Chicago Criticism, several reviewers emphasized the value of Olson's positive achievement, viewing the whole as the remarkable record of a noteworthy career and a vivid demonstration that criticism, as pursued by Olson, is a rigorous, intellectually demanding enterprise, one which can lead to genuine knowledge. Characteristically, few reviewers had the temerity to engage directly with Olson's sturdy arguments.

Olson has been an important influence on criticism and especially on the work of those who are sometimes referred to as second-generation Chicago critics, most prominently Wayne Booth, Sheldon Sacks, Ralph Rader, Norman Friedman, James Phelan, Robert Denham, Mary Doyle Springer, and others. Their work is marked by a Neo-Aristotelian concern for describing precisely the elements that compose a work and the logic that unites them toward an aesthetic end. Wayne Booth's *The Rhetoric of Fiction* (1961), though dedicated to R. S. Crane, shows Olson's influence in the formalism of its approach to the study of fiction, especially in Booth's analysis of how different kinds of narration and narrators function to serve different novelistic ends.

In his retirement Olson is devoting much of his creative energy to poetry, but from his two fairly recent essays in *Critical Inquiry*, Parts I and II of "A Conspectus of Poetry" (Autumn/Winter 1977), it would appear that his projected book on general poetics is well under way. In these essays Olson discusses the formal principles governing poems of various kinds, moving progressively from the simplest, most basic forms (haiku and such short descriptive poems as Alfred Tennyson's "The Eagle") to what he calls "maximum forms," tragedy and epic, and showing, as he extends his argument, how the complex forms emerge from or build upon the elements of the

simpler forms. We have undoubtedly not heard the last word from Olson the critic. But regardless of what Olson adds to his distinguished record of achievement in the future, it is certain that whenever the history of criticism in our period is written, Olson will have a place as one of its central figures.

**Interview:**

Ron Offen, "Portrait of the Artist (As a Musing Critic)," *Hyde Park Herald*, 14 June 1972, p. 12.

**Bibliography:**

James L. Battersby, *Elder Olson: An Annotated Bibliography* (New York & London: Garland, 1983).

**References:**

René Allewaert, "Aristote à Chicago: La Nouvelle Criticism," *Etudes Anglaises*, 14 (July-September 1961): 211-224;

James L. Battersby, "Elder Olson: Critic, Pluralist, and Humanist," *Chicago Review*, 28 (Winter 1977): 172-186;

Wayne C. Booth, "On the Aristotelian Front," *Kenyon Review*, 15 (Spring 1953): 299-301;

Kenneth Burke, "The Problem of the Intrinsic (as Reflected in the Neo-Aristotelian School)," in his *A Grammar of Motives* (Englewood Cliffs, N.J.: Prentice-Hall, 1945), pp. 465-484;

Burke, "The Serious Business of Comedy," *New Republic*, 160 (15 March 1969): 23-27;

R. S. Crane, "A Reply to Mr. Johnson," *Journal of Aesthetics and Art Criticism*, 12 (December 1953): 257-265;

Crane, "Two Essays in Practical Criticism: Prefatory Note," *University Review*, 8 (Spring 1942): 199-202;

David Daiches, "A Major Contribution to Modern Criticism," *Times Higher Education Supplement* (London), 27 August 1976;

J. M. Gray, "Aristotle's Poetics and Elder Olson," *Comparative Literature*, 15 (Spring 1963): 164-175;

John Holloway, "The New and Newer Critics," in his *The Charted Mirror: Literary and Critical Essays* (London: Routledge & Kegan Paul, 1960), pp. 187-203;

S. F. Johnson, " 'Critics and Criticism,' A Discussion: The Chicago Manifesto," *Journal of Aesthetics and Art Criticism*, 12 (December 1953): 248-257;

James Leo Kinneavy, *A Study of Three Contemporary Theories of the Lyric: A Dissertation* (Washington, D.C.: Catholic University of America Press, 1956), pp. 1-69;

Murray Krieger, "Creative Criticism: A Broader View of Symbolism," *Sewanee Review,* 58 ( January-March 1950): 36-51;

Krieger, *The New Apologists for Poetry* (Minneapolis: University of Minnesota Press, 1956);

Thomas E. Lucas, *Elder Olson* (New York: Twayne, 1972);

Horst Oppel, "Elder Olson als Dramatiker," *Neueren Sprachen,* 4 (April 1959): 153-164;

James Phelan, "Verbal Artistry and Speech as Action: Elder Olson and the Language of *Lolita,*" in his *Worlds from Words: A Theory of Language in Fiction* (Chicago & London: University of Chicago Press, 1981), pp. 155-183;

John Crowe Ransom, "Humanism at Chicago," *Kenyon Review,* 14 (1952): 647-659;

John F. Reichert, " 'Organizing Principles' and Genre Theory," *Genre,* 1 ( January 1968): 1-12;

Hoyt Trowbridge, "Aristotle and the 'New Criticism,' " *Sewanee Review,* 52 (1944): 537-555;

Eliseo Vivas, "The Neo-Aristotelians of Chicago," *Sewanee Review,* 61 ( January 1953): 136-149;

William K. Wimsatt, "The Chicago Critics," *Comparative Literature,* 5 (Winter 1953): 50-74.

---

# Vernon L. Parrington

*(3 August 1871-16 June 1929)*

Peter J. Bellis
*University of Miami, Coral Gables*

BOOKS: *Sinclair Lewis: Our Own Diogenes* (Seattle: University of Washington Bookstore, 1927);

*The Colonial Mind, 1620-1800,* volume 1 of *Main Currents in American Thought: An Interpretation of American Literature From the Beginnings to 1920* (New York: Harcourt, Brace, 1927; London: Hart-Davis, 1963);

*The Romantic Revolution in America, 1800-1860,* volume 2 of *Main Currents in American Thought* (New York: Harcourt, Brace, 1927; London: Hart-Davis, 1963);

*The Beginnings of Critical Realism in America, 1860-1920,* volume 3 of *Main Currents in American Thought* (New York: Harcourt, Brace, 1930).

OTHER: "The Puritan Divines, 1620-1720," in *The Cambridge History of American Literature,* edited by W. P. Trent et al. (New York: Putnam's, 1917; Cambridge, U.K.: Cambridge University Press, 1917), I: 31-56;

*The Connecticut Wits,* edited, with an introduction, by Parrington (New York: Harcourt, Brace, 1926);

"The Development of Realism," in *The Reinterpretation of American Literature,* edited by Norman Foerster (New York: Harcourt, Brace, 1928), pp. 139-159;

Ole Rölvaag, *Giants in the Earth,* introduction by Parrington (New York & London: Harper, 1929);

"American Literature" and "Nathaniel Hawthorne," in *Encyclopaedia Britannica,* 14th edition (Chicago: Encyclopaedia Britannica, 1929), pp. 278-280, 781-784;

"Brook Farm," in *Encyclopaedia of the Social Sciences,* edited by E. R. A. Seligman and A. Johnson (New York & London: Macmillan, 1930), III: 13-14;

J. Allen Smith, *The Growth and Decadence of Constitutional Government,* introduction by Parrington (New York: Holt, 1930; London: Williams & Norgate, 1930).

PERIODICAL PUBLICATIONS: "The Incomparable Mr. Cabell," *Pacific Review,* 2 (December 1921): 353-366;

"Economics and Criticism," edited by Vernon Parrington, Jr., *Pacific Northwest Quarterly,* 44
( July 1953): 97-105.

Vernon Louis Parrington was a pioneer in
the development of historical approaches to American literature. His reputation is based almost
solely upon a single work written late in his career, *Main Currents in American Thought* (1927,
1930). The title suggests Parrington's emphasis
on discovering the principal intellectual movements characteristic of writing in America. Parrington defined "literature" in its older sense, as
the significant body of written work produced by
a culture in its efforts to shape and know itself.
His analyses thus included writers of sermons, political tracts, philosophical treatises, and legal arguments as well as poets, playwrights, novelists,
satirists, and essayists. Since Parrington concentrated on how literature constituted a history of
ideas reflecting the evolving conflicts in American society, his work was of equal interest to historians and literary critics, and indeed it is difficult
to place Parrington or his studies in either
category.

The first two volumes of *Main Currents in
American Thought, The Colonial Mind, 1620-1800*
(1927) and *The Romantic Revolution in America,
1800-1860* (1927), were an immediate success
with reviewers and scholars alike, and the then-
obscure Parrington was awarded the Pulitzer
Prize in 1928. The third volume, *The Beginnings
of Critical Realism in America, 1860-1920,* was
planned but never completed before Parrington's
death in England in 1929. The finished portions
were collected, along with other essays and notes,
and published in 1930. The warm reception of
Parrington's work was partly due to the paucity
of serious studies of American literature which
were still only marginally allowed into the curric-
ula of the colleges and universities. Some ten
years earlier Van Wyck Brooks had called upon
critics to look to American literature to find a "usable past" that would serve as the basis for the future reform and development of American
culture and society. This "presentist" approach to
historiography, in which contemporary political
events are addressed through analyses of past cultural episodes, was adopted by Parrington, and
*Main Currents in American Thought* is not shy in announcing its overt intention to serve the cause of
liberalism and democracy. Parrington's timeli-
ness, however, also doomed his books, for
changes in the political, literary, and cultural cli-

V. L. Parrington
23 May 1918

mate of the 1930s and 1940s quickly made his arguments appear outdated and his methods
clumsy. The rise of the New Criticism, with its conservative politics and preference for close reading over historical judgment, effectively buried
Parrington, who may yet stage a comeback as the
1980s witness the rise of the New Historicism.

Parrington's significance stems from his role
in aligning the study of American literature with
a criticism of American economic and political developments. After Parrington, Brooks pursued a
similar mission in his massive five-volume *Makers
and Finders: A History of the Writer in America,
1800-1915* (1936-1952). While the Marxist criticism that dominated American literary circles in
the 1930s was more outspoken and less nationalistic than Parrington's brand of Jeffersonian liberalism, it nonetheless owed a debt to him and
continued the tradition of making literary study
in America an adversarial enterprise. Even F. O.
Matthiessen's *The American Renaissance: Art and Expression in the Age of Emerson and Whitman* (1941),

which showed the influence of the New Criticism in its attention to aesthetic matters, persisted in framing its discussion against a background of America's democratic tradition in politics, and Matthiessen does so by explicit reference to Brooks and Parrington.

Parrington's influence among historians is best represented by Richard Hofstadter, author of *The Progressive Historians: Turner, Beard, Parrington* (1968). (Hofstadter is the only writer to have been granted access to Parrington's unpublished papers, so his chapters are still the basic source of biographical information.) Hofstadter correctly insists that Parrington's work be seen as a product of the Progressive and Populist movements in America from 1890 to 1915, formative years in young Parrington's life. In Hofstadter's description:

> the Progressive generation had grown up with American industry, had witnessed the disappearance of the frontier line, the submergence of the farmer, the agrarian revolt, the recruitment of a vast labor force, the great tides of the new immigration, the fierce labor struggles of the 1890's. Their awareness of the whole complex of industrial America was keener, and their sense of the urgency of its problems had been quickened by the depression of the 1890's.

Parrington's generation saw the importance of economic issues in the present and the need to discern their workings in the past. They also cast a critical look at the plutocracy of "robber barons" and industrial capitalists who had risen to power in post-Civil War America at the expense of agrarian and rural interests. Parrington confirms Hofstadter's interpretation in stating that

> In the most receptive years of my life I came under the influence of what, we are coming to see, proved to be the master force in creating the ideals which are most deeply and natively American—the influence of the frontier with its democratic sympathies and democratic economics. From that influence I have never been able to escape, nor have I wished to escape. To it and to the spirit of agrarian revolt that grew out of it, I owe much of my understanding of American history and much of my political philosophy.

Parrington was born in Aurora, Illinois, in 1871, the second son of John William and Elizabeth McClellan Parrington. His grandfather was a Yorkshire immigrant who had fled the turmoil of English industrialization in the 1820s, bringing with him a political radicalism and hatred for England that can still be felt a century later in his grandson's writing. Settling in Maine, where Parrington's father was born, the grandfather established a carpet-weaving mill; after his death, neighbors helped support the family and give John William an education. Upon his graduation from Waterville (now Colby) College in 1855, he moved to Illinois, where he became a high school principal and married Elizabeth, the daughter of a sometime Baptist minister. He served in the Union Army from 1863 to 1866, returning to Aurora to practice law and become active in Republican politics. Ten years later he turned to farming and moved the family to Americus, Kansas, where he came to own several farms and other pieces of land.

Despite its bleakness and hardship, Kansas farm life was a major influence on Vernon Parrington's character: fifty years later he could still write vividly of the landscape and small towns of the Middle Border, and his sympathies always remained strongly agrarian and populist. In 1884 Parrington's father was elected probate judge, and the family moved to the nearby town of Emporia. There Parrington attended the College of Emporia, a Presbyterian preparatory school and college whose religious fundamentalism and pessimistic Calvinism he would later describe as relentlessly orthodox and "sterile."

In 1891 his parents sent him to Harvard College to complete his education. The college's snobbery and "smug Tory culture" left Parrington feeling socially and culturally isolated and gave rise to an antagonism that would last for the rest of his life. "I have set the school down as a liability rather than an asset to the cause of democracy," he wrote in a 1918 letter to the secretary of his class, "It seems to me the apologist and advocate of capitalistic exploitation." Parrington's language in 1918 already seems to reflect his absorption of the Marxist tradition, which he weds (however problematically) to his populism in a westerner's resentment toward the elitist classes of New England. The disastrous mismatch between Harvard and Parrington was mitigated by long hours of independent reading at the library, where he could freely indulge in ideas not usually spoken of at the College of Emporia, such as Darwinian evolution and the speculative views of Spencer. He did study, however, with and respect philosopher George Herbert Palmer and literary historian Barrett Wendell.

Wendell would later publish *A Literary History of America* (1900), which, along with the volumes of Moses Coit Tyler, constituted the first modern efforts in the field Parrington tried to revolutionize. Though *Main Currents in American Thought* did rely on Wendell's volume at many points, Parrington's political agenda and historical argument were in sharp contrast to the late-Victorian aestheticism of Wendell's book. At its opening Wendell discusses the difficulty of defining literature and compares life to the flight of a swallow in a passage redolent of aesthetes like Walter Pater: "But the fleeting moments of life, like the swallow's flight once more, are not quite voiceless; as surely he may twitter in the ears of men, so men themselves may give sign to one another of what they think they know, and of what they know they feel. . . . Literature is the last expression in words of the meaning of life." Though the young Parrington was a follower of William Morris and a writer of poetry, he left behind Wendell's sentiments in writing his own book as an act of cultural criticism rather than aesthetic appreciation. As he put it in his introduction, Parrington chose "to follow the broad path of our political, economic, and social development, rather than the narrower belletristic."

After receiving his B.A. in 1893, Parrington returned to teach English and French at the College of Emporia. During the next four years he became increasingly involved in local and state politics, abandoning his father's Republican party to join the Populist revolt against "big business" and "feudal industrialism." In 1897 he moved to the University of Oklahoma. The English department numbered only three, so Parrington taught a wide variety of courses covering English literature from Spenser through the nineteenth-century novel. He evidently brought enormous energy to his work, not only reorganizing the English department but also serving—briefly and very successfully—as the university's football coach. In 1901 he married Julia Rochester Williams; they eventually had three children, Elizabeth, Louise Wrathal, and Vernon Louis, Jr. From 1903 to 1904 Parrington toured England and France on his own, then returned to Norman. After eleven years at the University of Oklahoma, having recently moved his family into an Elizabethan-style house of his own design, Parrington was abruptly fired during a Methodist-inspired purge of liberal, eastern-educated

professors. Unemployed and searching for options, the thirty-seven-year-old Parrington even applied to Harvard as a doctoral candidate, but he was rejected.

Parrington did find another job almost immediately, at the University of Washington, where he was to spend the rest of his career. Seattle was far more congenial, both physically and intellectually, than Norman had been, and Parrington found supportive colleagues and a mentor in the political scientist J. Allen Smith. Parrington had never had the opportunity to teach American literature before, and his new interest in the subject gave him, for the first time, a particular field in which to concentrate his energies. Smith's economic analyses of American constitutional history—offered in *The Spirit of American Government* (1907) and *The Growth and Decadence of Constitutional Government* (1930)—also suggested a method that would allow Parrington to fuse his progressive, reformist politics with literary and historical scholarship. In his more than twenty years at the University of Washington, Parrington's courses became a university tradition: ten minutes of lecture followed by forty of Socratic questioning. He published little or nothing until the end of World War I, when he began to contribute both signed and anonymous political and literary reviews to the *Nation* and the *Pacific Review*. From 1913 on, Parrington concentrated on a single work, "The Democratic Spirit in American Literature, 1620-1870," which would become *Main Currents in American Thought;* his articles were almost all excerpted or adapted from *Main Currents*. First accepted by B. W. Huebsch, whose financial instability prevented their publication, the first two volumes were eventually accepted by Harcourt, Brace in 1925, on the recommendation of Huebsch's reader, Van Wyck Brooks.

In the 1920s American literary history and intellectual history were largely undeveloped fields; neither had yet been granted a separate curricular or scholarly status in American universities. Besides *The Cambridge History of American Literature* (1917), to which Parrington had contributed a piece entitled "The Puritan Divines, 1620-1720," the only significant literary histories were those of Tyler and Wendell. Tyler's *A History of American Literature, 1607-1765* (1878) and *The Literary History of the American Revolution 1763-1785* (1897) covered only the colonial and revolutionary periods, and Wendell's survey was a product of the genteel New England tradition that had been largely discredited by the attacks of Brooks, H. L. Mencken, and others. Parrington's work has often been compared to Wendell's, for the idealogical and organizational contrasts between Wendell and Parrington are clear. Wendell emphasizes the English roots of American culture, beginning each of his first three sections with two chapters on English history. Parrington, perhaps disposed against the English by his family background, aligns the English influence with the Federalists and mercantilists and enemies of Jefferson. For Parrington it is the French who offer the true European source for American liberalism and agrarian democracy in the examples of Rousseau and of the Physiocrats; it is not an argument future historians have found particularly convincing. Wendell focuses almost entirely on the Northeast. His largest chapter, at 200 pages almost twice the length of any other, is on "The Renaissance of New England" in the first half of the nineteenth century. It is followed by a section entitled "The Rest of the Story," which includes New York, Whitman, the South, and events up to the turn of the century. Parrington deliberately turns to the South and to the West as the sources of the tradition of American liberalism.

Given the lack of both congenial scholarly predecessors and accurate primary texts, Parrington could well claim in 1924 that "Pretty much everything is yet to be done" in the writing of American literary history. He took as his primary model Hippolyte Taine's *History of English Literature* (1864), which used a biographical approach and a view of literature as the product of its social milieu. To Taine's method Parrington joined his Progressive political agenda: "The point of view from which I have endeavored to evaluate the materials, is liberal rather than conservative, Jeffersonian rather than Federalistic," Jeffersonian here connecting Parrington's populism with the vision of agrarian democracy Jefferson offered as a counter to the mercantilism and nascent capitalism of his age. Parrington saw the writing of his literary history as a means toward establishing the case for liberalism in present political struggles, thus creating a literary analogue to the work of social and economic historians like Carl Becker and Charles Beard (who reviewed Parrington's volumes enthusiastically).

The strengths of *Main Currents in American Thought* lie in its broad strokes rather than its details. Parrington's view of American history and literature is cohesive and often compelling in its overall structure, but his treatment of individual writers and schools of thought can be sometimes inconsistent or self-contradictory. For Parrington politics and culture are shaped by underlying economic and environmental forces: "Literature is the fair flower of culture, but underneath culture are the deeper strata of philosophy, theology, law, statecraft—of ideology and institutionalism—resting finally on the subsoil of economics," Parrington says in "Economics and Criticism" (an essay written in 1917 but published in 1953 by Parrington's son). The formula here repeats Karl Marx's argument, made famous in *The Communist Manifesto* (1848), that economics forms the "base" which conditions the "superstructure" of culture's ideological institutions, including literature. Parrington finds the roots of political liberalism, for example, in the economic independence of the yeoman farmer, an independence made possible by the availability of free or inexpensive land.

Literature is significant, in Parrington's terms, only insofar as it reflects the social and political trends of its time. His disdain for the "belletristic," for works conceived or judged in primarily aesthetic terms, has long been notorious among literary critics. For Parrington the artist must either actively engage with the politics of his time or consign himself to the margins of literary history. He spends thirteen pages of his first volume rehabilitating colonial poet Philip Freneau as a political satirist and poet, but only two pages of his second in dismissing Edgar Allan Poe as a cultural and psychological anomaly: "it is for the belletrist to evaluate [Poe's] theory and practice of art," he concludes. It is thus somewhat misleading to describe *Main Currents in American Thought* as a *literary* history: its central thesis is that literature can have no history of its own; art's meaning lies only in its expression or representation of political, social, and economic forces.

Parrington is far from a rigid economic determinist, however. "I was a good deal of a Marxian, and perhaps still am," he wrote in a 1928 letter Alfred Kazin quotes in *On Native Grounds* (1942), but "a growing sense of the complexity of social forces makes me somewhat distrustful of the sufficiency of the Marxian formulae." His radicalism was individualistic and anti-industrial, fiercely opposed to all collectivization or centralization. "The Populist and the Marxist in him never quite came to terms," as Kazin puts it. By the time Parrington's survey reaches the late nineteenth century in volume three, a disparity emerges between his political and intellectual values and his historical method: his analysis of

American liberalism reveals only its exhaustion and inevitable doom, its decline into a pessimistic estrangement from twentieth-century mass politics.

Even though politics and culture are ostensibly rooted in economic developments, ideas seem to take on a life of their own in *Main Currents in American Thought:* liberalism is the dynamic, progressive element in American history, checked at different times by different reactionary groups. Liberalism is influenced by the French tradition of "romantic" political philosophy emphasizing natural rights and the perfectibility of man; reaction is influenced by the English tradition asserting property rights and the force of economic self-interest. While Parrington exposes the economic and class interests behind Puritanism, Federalism, and industrial capitalism, he is far less rigorous in his treatment of their liberal antagonists–Congregationalism, Jeffersonianism, and Progressivism. Such oppositions appear so often that they take on an abstract, static character, as if American history were the story of a single, inescapable conflict. The issues of the colonial period, Parrington claims, are also those of twentieth-century politics: their subjects "are old-fashioned only in manner and dress; at heart they were much the same themes with which we are engaged."

Each volume of *Main Currents* has a large-scale symmetry: *The Colonial Mind, 1620-1800* is ordered by the ideological opposition between liberalism and Puritanism or Federalism; *The Romantic Revolution in America, 1800-1860* is organized on geographical lines–the South, the Middle East, and New England; and Parrington's outline for *The Beginnings of Critical Realism in America, 1860-1920* is based on the economic and ideological conflict between progressive, scientific criticism and nineteenth-century industrialism and plutocracy. Within these frameworks Parrington's narrative proceeds through a series of biographical analyses, in which he places individual writers and political figures in one camp or the other. The importance of these individuals supposedly lies in their representative status, but Parrington's portraits, like Ralph Waldo Emerson's in *Representative Men* (1850), usually contain a structural tension between individual character and historical role. Liberals like the separatist Roger Williams are men born before their time, representatives of the future rather than of their own historical present, while reactionaries like Puritan governor John Winthrop may nonetheless be men of admirable integrity and strength. All of the figures in these volumes are judged from a twentieth-century perspective; even Parrington's hero, Thomas Jefferson, is limited by his time and place, unable to foresee the inevitable course of industrialization. Parrington's approach is resolutely and unabashedly "presentist" throughout.

The limitations of Parrington's approach appear almost immediately in *The Colonial Mind* in his treatment of Puritanism. In response to Wendell's judgment, in *Literary History of America,* that the colonial period produced no great literature, Parrington suggests that "genteel" literary historians have defined "literature" too narrowly: "They have sought daintier fare than polemics, and in consequence mediocre verse has obscured political speculation, and poetasters have shouldered aside vigorous creative minds." His primary interest in English Puritanism is the political liberalism of its left wing, a latent democratic thrust that he sees as stifled and betrayed by the Massachusetts theocracy. For Parrington the Puritan theocracy is an essentially political institution, not a religious one; it is the forerunner of all subsequent political and cultural reaction in America–and of the intellectual conservatism of nineteenth- and twentieth-century Harvard in particular. His chapter on Increase Mather is as much an attack on Harvard historian Kenneth Murdock and his 1925 Mather biography as it is a critique of Mather himself.

Despite his derogation of Wendell's assessment, Parrington refuses to acknowledge the existence of a literary culture in seventeenth-century New England: "A world that accepted Michael Wigglesworth as its poet, and accounted Cotton Mather its most distinguished man of letters, had certainly backslidden in the ways of culture." He can say nothing good about Mather's *Magnalia Christi Americana;* he can only provide an appreciative quotation from Wendell and then move on. More important than his insurmountable disdain for the Mathers, however, is Parrington's decision to exclude the work of Puritan poets. Edward Taylor's poetry was not discovered until after Parrington's death, but his omission of Anne Bradstreet is less easily defended. Parrington's emphasis on public, political issues makes him blind to the private spiritual dilemmas of Puritan self-examination and to the "human face" of seventeenth-century New England. It would be the next generation of Harvard scholars, led by Perry Miller and Thomas Johnson, who would reevaluate the Puritans, responding at least in part to the harshness of Parrington's critique.

Unlike Van Wyck Brooks, for example, Parrington does not regard Jonathan Edwards as a transitional figure, a link between Puritanism and Poor Richard; he is only a tragic anachronism, a brilliant philosophical mind wasted on the barren ground of theological debate. Parrington treats Benjamin Franklin as an economic thinker and politician, not the more familiar satirist and autobiographer. He acknowledges the complexity of Franklin's character but overlooks the deft manipulation of literary personae, the conscious process of textual self-creation that makes Franklin an interpretive problem in the first place.

*The Colonial Mind* reaches its climax with what Parrington sees as the conflict between the agrarian liberalism of the Declaration of Independence and the mercantile Federalism of the Constitution. Just as Parrington's first book looks forward to Jefferson, his later ones look back to the preindustrial America of 1800 as a highwater mark, the last point at which American liberalism combined philosophical ideals with a firm grasp of economic and political realities.

In volume two, *The Romantic Revolution in America,* Parrington finds a "dissociation of sensibility," to use T. S. Eliot's phrase, in nineteenth-century liberalism: a split between the reality of unchecked acquisitiveness and economic individualism in the Jacksonian era, and the doomed "romanticisms" of the slaveholding South, the frontier, and New England Transcendentalism. It is here that his weaknesses as a reader of literature—his "indifference to literary values," in Alfred Kazin's words—become most apparent. Parrington's economic and geographical approach simply cannot comprehend a writer like Poe, for example. For him, Poe is an "artist," shipwrecked "on the reef of American materialisms," alienated from both his aristocratic Virginia background and his middle-class readers. He is a "problem . . . quite outside the main current of American thought." Despite this summary dismissal of "the artist" as a culturally marginal figure, Parrington reverses himself when he comes to discuss another southern writer, William Gilmore Simms. He laments that in "the conflict between the creative artist and the citizen," Simms did not strive "to be an artist first." And his model of such artistic integrity is none other than the anomalous Poe: "if he had learned from Poe to refuse the demands of inconsequential things," Simms

might have presented a truer picture of his age. When Parrington finds his historical scheme at odds with his aesthetic judgments (as in "The Incomparable Mr. Cabell," his essay on James Branch Cabell in volume three), the central can become the inconsequential with disconcerting ease.

Parrington repeatedly criticizes "romantic" writers for "turning away from reality"—the phrase echoes throughout the volume. It is no surprise to find the charge leveled against Washington Irving for his nostalgic return to pre-Revolutionary America. In discussing Charles Brockden Brown, however, Parrington dwells on the shapeless but more realistic *Arthur Mervyn* (1799-1800) rather than the gothic but admittedly far superior *Wieland* (1798). He mounts a full-scale attack on Nathaniel Hawthorne, whose obsessions and inhibitions give him a "temperamental aloofness from objective reality" and a preference for the shadow world of the romance. The result of "his long immuring himself in a void" is imaginative sterility and a profound "intellectual poverty."

Parrington clearly sets out to demolish the idealized nineteenth-century image of Hawthorne; his aims are equally revisionary in his attempts to rehabilitate James Fenimore Cooper and elevate Herman Melville to major status. These are the first writers to whom Parrington grants an independent, critical position rather than a merely reflective role. He finds Cooper's work divided between a literary romanticism that idealizes the revolutionary period and a realistic social criticism that looks in vain for eighteenth-century restraint in nineteenth-century democratic politics. Cooper and Melville are both democratic idealists disillusioned by the shoddy reality of middle-class economic and political power. Parrington's enthusiastic response to Melville is, unfortunately, based more on Raymond Weaver's ground-breaking *Herman Melville: Manner and Mystic* (1921) than on a reading of the novels themselves; the result is a largely biographical discussion that emphasizes the personal and psychological sources of Melville's pessimism. As with Hawthorne, Parrington's approach only highlights the writer's alienation from his political and social context; even when he sympathizes with the artist in question, he makes no attempt to solve the riddle of "unrepresentative" literary greatness. The missing link between literary and economic developments—the conditions of literary production and the economics of the literary marketplace–is never explored in *Main Currents in American Thought.*

Parrington does find places in his system for Emerson and Henry David Thoreau–as a transcendental critic and a transcendental economist, respectively. Both men resemble Jefferson in their individualism and condemnation of coercive government and William Morris in their anti-industrialism; both stand in opposition to the middle-class materialism of their age. Parrington acknowledges Emerson's skill as an essayist, but chooses to rely primarily on his unpolished *Journals* (1909-1914); Thoreau's acute self-consciousness as a literary stylist goes unmentioned. For Parrington, Thoreau's life is his most important work, his most trenchant social criticism.

As its title suggests, *The Beginnings of Critical Realism in America* does grant the artist a role as social critic, as liberalism itself takes on a critical function. The Civil War left America a thoroughly middle-class society, dominated by the forces of industrial and finance capitalism. The exploitative economic individualism of Jacksonian democracy reached its full flowering in the Gilded Age–"the Great Barbecue," as Parrington calls it. Here the progressive thrust of *Main Currents in American Thought* breaks down; in his foreword to volume three, Parrington describes American intellectual history as a vicious circle, moving from Calvinistic pessimism to romantic optimism only to end in "mechanistic pessimism": "after three hundred years' experience we have returned, intellectually, to the point from which we set out."

Parrington sees Walt Whitman as the last expression of eighteenth-century democratic liberalism, filtered, in his case, through both transcendental and scientific thought. Whitman is a great figure, "the greatest assuredly in our literature," but he writes in "the twilight of the romantic revolution," and his dreams for American democracy must go unfulfilled. Mark Twain is also a child of the Enlightenment for Parrington, his idealism shaped by the psychology of the American West. Parrington's Twain is essentially a satirist, "the child of a frontier past" stranded in the Gilded Age–an inevitably isolated and alienated critic of his times.

For Parrington, New England culture failed to respond to the economic shifts of the late nineteenth century; it remained mired in the reactionary sterility of the genteel tradition, the Harvard tradition against which he defined himself and his work. Henry James, for example, is no realist,

but only a self-deceived romantic, withdrawing like Hawthorne from "the external world of action" into an inner one of merely "hypothetical subtleties." For Parrington, William Dean Howells is the only eastern writer to offer, in his "realism of the commonplace," a transition between the Victorian sensibility and the realism and naturalism of the Midwest.

It is from the economically and politically exploited farmland of the Middle Border that critical realism emerges as the dominant strain of liberal and progressive thought. Hamlin Garland–a central figure for Parrington–is a frustrated romantic, a Jeffersonian idealist forced by the bitter economic conditions of his environment to adopt a sober realism. His sketches are "a landmark in our literary history . . . the first authentic expression and protest of an agrarian America then being submerged by the industrial revolution." Parrington's identification with Garland could not be clearer. His own idealism, on the other hand, distances him from the mechanistic naturalism of Stephen Crane, Frank Norris, and Theodore Dreiser. As Parrington's third volume comes to an end in a large selection of notes and fragments, its already bleak picture darkens considerably. If literary naturalism is the end toward which critical liberalism leads, then that liberalism has undergone a distinct reversal since the agrarian optimism of Jefferson's era, returning to the determinism that once characterized reactionary Puritan thought. "The old shadow is falling across the American mind," Parrington concludes; "America today is the greatest, most complex machine the world has ever known. Individualism is giving way to regimentation, caste, standardization. Optimism is gone; pessimism is on the horizon. The psychology of naturalism is being prepared." Jefferson's agrarian ideals–and Parrington's–can have no place in the new "machine" America.

Literary modernism falls outside the scope of *Main Currents in American Thought,* but its emphasis on psychological rather than social realism and on the artistic integrity of the literary text, along with its international and largely urban character, must have made it profoundly uncongenial to Parrington's temperament and political views. With the rise of the New Criticism in the literary academy during the 1930s, Parrington would have found himself increasingly alienated and estranged from the mainstream of literary scholarship. Historians began questioning both the accuracy and sufficiency of his evidence and the validity of his conclusions soon after *Main Currents in American Thought* appeared, but the harshest attacks came from literary critics. Yvor Winters, in the most savage of New Critical responses, accused Parrington not only of neglecting the vast bulk of Puritan writing but, more importantly, of assuming "that the best way to understand a work of art is to neglect entirely its nature as a work of art, and to deal with its ideas. . . . This is almost brutally crude thinking," Winters charges.

Parrington's reputation and influence during the 1930s can be measured in the attention paid him by Bernard Smith and Lionel Trilling. Smith was an editor at Alfred A. Knopf and a well-known Marxist critic. In 1940 he edited, along with Malcolm Cowley, a volume entitled *Books That Changed Our Minds*. It included essays by Beard on Turner, by Max Lerner on Beard and on Lenin, and by Smith on Parrington. Smith's essay on Parrington is highly appreciative and explains the book's immediate popularity by placing it within the materialist school advanced by Beard and Turner and the liberal, antigenteel criticism identified with Van Wyck Brooks. Smith had reviewed Brooks's *The Flowering of New England* in the *New Republic* in 1936, using a Parringtonian and Marxist edge against what he saw as Brooks's "story telling." According to Smith, Brooks had lost the indignation and moral force characteristic of his earlier work and presented the cycles of cultural growth and decay without sufficient reference to their economic determinants. (In the same issue Cowley disputed Smith's criticism and celebrated Brooks's descriptive method.) Smith's 1940 essay on Parrington admits that he was no doctrinaire Marxist, since Parrington's emphasis on individualism rather than the collective and his concern with agrarian rather than urban experience ill-accord with Marxist perspectives. The economic model in Parrington, argues Smith, is clumsy: "a more subtle materialism—one in which cultural and psychological phenomena are integrated with the social—might have contributed something." Still Parrington's radicalism is implicitly championed against the tendency of Brooks and others to move away from the radical agenda during the crises of the left at the end of the 1930s.

Among those moving away from Marxism at the end of the 1930s was Lionel Trilling. In a 1940 review, "Mr. Parrington, Mr. Smith, and Reality" (*Partisan Review*, January/February), Trilling undertakes to discuss Bernard Smith's *Forces in American Criticism*, which contained Smith's positive assessment of Parrington. Trilling begins by saying that "We can scarcely help thinking a good deal about V. L. Parrington these days," noting the continuity from progressive liberalism to the literary left of the 1930s and recent tributes to Parrington by Marxist critics like Granville Hicks and Smith. Trilling praises Parrington's economic thesis, though he is quick to point out its awkwardness in conception and application. Trilling himself had ended his flirtation with Marxism, and in Parrington he detects a representative of the naive optimism and crude materialism that he found in many of his contemporaries. He sharply disagrees with Smith's argument that one can forget Parrington's aesthetic errors and concentrate on his politics, though Trilling does not wish to dispute those politics or offer a different set of purely aesthetic judgments. Rather Trilling undertakes to show the singular and inextricable fusion of aesthetics and politics in Parrington's judgments, holding that it is precisely Parrington's politics which determine his aesthetic judgments. Parrington has a powerful but simple notion of "reality" and demands that literature reflect it and his philosophy of liberal enlightenment. Trilling criticizes this reductive mimetic theory of literature implicit in Parrington and undertakes to show that the aesthetic structures Parrington derides actually express psychological and philosophical perspectives that demand interpretation.

Taking particular exception to Parrington's dismissal of Hawthorne's romanticism, Trilling argues that Hawthorne's preoccupation with the darkness of moral evil was not a betrayal of liberal democracy's Enlightenment hopes but a valuable look into a reality Parrington had failed to include in his account. For Trilling the reality of psychological complexity, moral ambiguity, tragic vision, and their representation in style must be affirmed in the face of Parrington's simpler schema of good versus bad in the fight for America's progressive reform.

Trilling again treated Parrington in another review that year, "Reality in America," later given prominence by its placement as the opening essay in his *The Liberal Imagination* (1950). In a more temperate and judicious appraisal than Winters's, but less favorable than Smith's, Trilling describes Parrington as crystallizing middle-class assumptions about the progress of American culture, an accusation that would have pained the populist Parrington. Parrington's dependence on the notion of a fixed and irreducible "reality," which he uses to condemn the "romantic" tendencies of numerous writers like Poe, Hawthorne, and James, is rejected by Trilling, who observes that Parrington "expresses the chronic American belief that there exists an opposition between reality and mind and that one must enlist in the party of reality." The result, for Trilling, is a false image of literary history as a current of trends or a repetition of an eternally recurrent opposition (liberalism versus conservatism). Trilling proposes instead a dialectical view of the relation of such oppositions, in which the mind (or "romanticism" or "idealism," in Parrington's terms) is a powerful and constitutive element. Trilling's own brand of psychological speculation would join forces in the coming years with the New Criticism to stifle the kind of work Parrington attempted.

More recent revisions of the literary canon have made Parrington's narrative seem especially idiosyncratic and limited. His is a history made by white male public figures; he provides only brief remarks on a few women writers—Harriet Beecher Stowe and Margaret Fuller in volume two, and Sarah Orne Jewett, Mary Wilkins Freeman, Willa Cather, and Edith Wharton in volume three. Women limited to more private forms of literary expression—Anne Bradstreet and Emily Dickinson are only the most obvious examples—are systematically excluded. Also missing are black and native American writers; one might expect the omission of Phillis Wheatley, but in the face of a long segment on William Lloyd Garrison and others on southern apologists for slavery, the absence of a major abolitionist like Frederick Douglass is especially striking. Douglass's autobiography illustrates not only the psychological impact of slavery and the differences between plantation and urban slaveholding but also the fear of free black labor among northern workers. Parrington's anti-industrial, anticapitalist orientation leads him to focus far more on the economic exploitation of northern wage slavery than on the starker oppression of the southern plantation. In this respect also, his revisionary project is itself a product of its time—populist in its politics but reliant on an intellectual elitism of its own.

Parrington's work is still in print, and it remains surprisingly readable after more than fifty years. His volumes have a clarity and simplicity of structure that reflects Parrington's enthusiasm for both architectural design and the balance and conciseness of Augustan poetry. His style can be too self-consciously ornate at times, too labored

in its imagery, but when Parrington is on the attack—against the Puritans, for example—his writing can be passionate and almost savage in its caustic economy of phrase.

*Main Currents in American Thought* is now read primarily in historiographical terms. With the increasing specialization of American literary and historical scholarship, the breadth of Parrington's ambitions has become a liability rather than an asset. His method is insufficiently rigorous, his scholarship insufficiently thorough, and his political biases too obvious for his judgments to have remained persuasive. But Parrington does have his defenders. In *Toward a New Historicism* (1972), Wesley Morris makes the case that the very limitations of Parrington's study—such as the way his simple antithesis between liberalism and conservatism cannot be sustained when Parrington himself examines actual writers—can be fruitful in developing a New Historicism. If the New Historicism of the late 1980s succeeds in altering the approach to American literature shaped by the New Criticism, Parrington's volumes may be resurrected once more as valuable resources. But *Main Currents in American Thought* is, finally, a document of the 1910s and 1920s, dated almost as soon as it appeared. Even thirty-five years ago, John Higham could describe it as "a noble ruin on the landscape of our scholarship," much of it already obsolete. Today it stands as a testament to the intellectual vigor and integrity of Progressivism, and to the political and cultural idealism of its author. In a late essay, "A Chapter in American Liberalism," Parrington himself suggests that his brand of "democratic liberalism" may be a thing of the past, its radical potential already co-opted or "thrown away like an empty whiskey-flask." Given his antagonism toward the literary academy of his own day, he would hardly be surprised to find few Parringtonians laboring on today's literary-critical assembly line.

**Bibliography:**

Richard Hofstadter, "Bibliographical Essay: Parrington," in his *The Progressive Historians: Turner, Beard, Parrington* (New York: Knopf, 1968), pp. 486-494.

**References:**

Malcolm Cowley and Bernard Smith, eds., *Books That Changed Our Minds* (New York: Kelmscott Editions, 1940);

Arthur A. Ekirch, Jr., "Parrington and the Decline of American Liberalism," *American Quarterly*, 3 (Winter 1951): 295-308;

Joseph B. Harrison, *Vernon Louis Parrington: American Scholar* (Seattle: University of Washington Bookstore, 1929);

Granville Hicks, "The Critical Principles of V. L. Parrington," *Science and Society: A Marxian Quarterly*, 3 (1939): 443-460;

John Higham, "The Rise of American Intellectual History," *American Historical Review*, 56 (April 1951): 453-471;

Richard Hofstadter, *The Progressive Historians: Turner, Beard, Parrington* (New York: Knopf, 1968), pp. 349-439;

Alfred Kazin, *On Native Grounds* (New York: Harcourt, Brace, 1942), pp. 127-132, 160-164;

Wesley Morris, *Toward a New Historicism* (Princeton: Princeton University Press, 1972);

Merrill D. Peterson, "Parrington and American Liberalism," *Virginia Quarterly Review*, 30 (Winter 1954): 35-49;

Richard Reinitz, "Vernon Louis Parrington as Historical Ironist," *Pacific Northwest Quarterly*, 68 ( July 1977): 113-119;

Richard Ruland, *The Rediscovery of American Literature: Premises of Critical Taste, 1900-1940* (Cambridge: Harvard University Press, 1967);

Robert Allen Skotheim, *American Intellectual Histories and Historians* (Princeton: Princeton University Press, 1966), pp. 124-148;

Skotheim and Kermit Vanderbilt, "Vernon Louis Parrington: The Mind and Art of a Historian of Ideas," *Pacific Northwest Quarterly*, 53 (1962): 100-113;

Lionel Trilling, "Mr. Parrington, Mr. Smith, and Reality," *Partisan Review*, 7 ( January/February 1940): 24-40;

Trilling, "Reality in America," in his *The Liberal Imagination: Essays on Literature and Society* (New York: Viking, 1950), pp. 1-19;

William T. Utter, "Vernon Louis Parrington," in *The Marcus W. Jernegan Essays in American Historiography*, edited by William T. Hutchinson (Chicago: University of Chicago Press, 1937), pp. 394-408;

Yvor Winters, "Post Scripta," in his *In Defense of Reason* (New York: Swallow Press & William Morrow, 1947), pp. 556-564.

**Papers:**

Parrington's family has retained possession of his papers, but they will eventually be deposited in the Archives of the University of Washington in Seattle.

# Ezra Pound
*(30 October 1885-1 November 1972)*

Michael Levenson
*University of Virginia*

See also the Pound entries in *DLB 4, American Writers in Paris, 1920-1939* and *DLB 45, American Poets, 1880-1945.*

BOOKS: *A Lume Spento* (Venice: Printed for the author by A. Antonini, 1908);

*A Quinzaine for this Yule* (London: Pollock, 1908);

*Personae* (London: Elkin Mathews, 1909);

*Exultations* (London: Elkin Mathews, 1909);

*The Spirit of Romance* (London: Dent, 1910; London: Dent/New York: Dutton, 1910);

*Provença* (Boston: Small, Maynard, 1910);

*Canzoni* (London: Elkin Mathews, 1911);

*Ripostes* (London: Swift, 1912; Boston: Small, Maynard, 1913);

*Gaudier-Brzeska: A Memoir Including the Published Writings of the Sculptor and a Selection from his Letters* (London: John Lane, Bodley Head/ New York: John Lane, 1916);

*Lustra* (London: Elkin Mathews, 1916; enlarged edition, New York: Knopf, 1917);

*Pavannes and Divisions* (New York: Knopf, 1918);

*The Fourth Canto* (London: Ovid Press, 1919);

*Quia Pauper Amavi* (London: Egoist Press, 1919);

*Instigations of Ezra Pound, Together with an Essay on the Chinese Written Character by Ernest Fenollosa* (New York: Boni & Liveright, 1920);

*Hugh Selwyn Mauberley* (London: Ovid Press, 1920);

*Umbra* (London: Elkin Mathews, 1920);

*Poems 1918-21* (New York: Boni & Liveright, 1921);

*Indiscretions* (Paris: Three Mountains Press, 1923);

*Antheil and the Treatise on Harmony* (Paris: Three Mountains Press, 1924; Chicago: Covici, 1927);

*A Draft of XVI. Cantos* (Paris: Three Mountains Press, 1925);

*Personae: The Collected Poems* (New York: Boni & Liveright, 1926; London: Faber & Faber, 1952);

*A Draft of the Cantos 17-27* (London: John Rodker, 1928);

*Selected Poems*, edited by T. S. Eliot (London: Faber & Gwyer, 1928);

*A Draft of XXX Cantos* (Paris: Hours Press, 1930; New York: Farrar & Rinehart, 1933; London: Faber & Faber, 1933);

*Imaginary Letters* (Paris: Black Sun Press, 1930);

*How to Read* (London: Harmsworth, 1931);

*A B C of Economics* (London: Faber & Faber, 1933; Norfolk, Conn.: New Directions, 1940);

*A B C of Reading* (London: Routledge, 1934; New Haven: Yale University Press, 1934);

*Make it New* (London: Faber & Faber, 1934; New Haven: Yale University Press, 1935);

*Eleven New Cantos: XXXI-XLI* (New York: Farrar & Rinehart, 1934; London: Faber & Faber, 1935);

*Homage to Sextus Propertius* (London: Faber & Faber, 1934);

*Alfred Venison's Poems: Social Credit Themes*, as The Poet of Titchfield Street (London: Nott, 1935);

*Social Credit: An Impact* (London: Nott, 1935);

*Jefferson And/Or Mussolini* (London: Nott, 1935; New York: Liveright/Nott, 1936); rewritten in Italian and republished as *Jefferson e Mussolini* (Venice: Edizioni Popolari, 1944);

*Polite Essays* (London: Faber & Faber, 1937; Norfolk, Conn.: New Directions, 1940);

*The Fifth Decad of Cantos* (London: Faber & Faber, 1937; New York & Toronto: Farrar & Rinehart, 1937);

*Confucius: Digest of the Analects* (Milan: Giovanni Scheiwiller, 1937);

*Guide to Kulchur* (London: Faber & Faber, 1938; Norfolk, Conn.: New Directions, 1938);

*What Is Money For* (London: Greater Britain Publications, 1939);

*Cantos LII-LXXI* (London: Faber & Faber, 1940; Norfolk, Conn.: New Directions, 1940);

*A Selection of Poems* (London: Faber & Faber, 1940);

*Carla da Visita* (Rome: Edizioni di Lettere d'Oggi, 1942); republished as *A Visiting Card*, translated by John Drummond (London: Russell, 1952);

*L'America, Roosevelt e le Cause della Guerra Presente* (Venice: Edizioni Popolari, 1944); republished as *America, Roosevelt and the Causes of the Present War*, translated by Drummond (London: Russell, 1951);

*Oro e Lavoro* (Rapallo: Tip. Moderna [Canessa], 1944); republished as *Gold and Work*, translated by Drummond (London: Russell, 1952);

*Introduzione alla Natura Economica degli S.U.A.* (Venice: Edizioni Popolari, 1944); republished as *An Introduction to the Economic Nature of the United States*, translated by Carmine Amore (London: Russell, 1950);

*Orientamenti* (Venice: Edizioni Popolari, 1944);

*"If This Be Treason . . . "* (Siena: Printed for Olga Rudge by Tlp. Nuova, 1948);

*The Pisan Cantos* (New York: New Directions, 1948; London: Faber & Faber, 1949);

*The Cantos* (New York: New Directions, 1948; London: Faber & Faber, 1950);

*Selected Poems* (New York: New Directions, 1949);

*Patria Mia* (Chicago: Seymour, 1950);

*Literary Essays*, edited, with an introduction, by T. S. Eliot (London: Faber & Faber, 1954; Norfolk, Conn.: New Directions, 1954);

*Lavoro ed Usura* (Milan: All'Insegna del Pesce d'Oro, 1954);

*Section: Rock-Drill 85-95 de los cantares* (Milan: All'Insegna del Pesce d'Oro, 1955; New York: New Directions, 1956; London: Faber & Faber, 1957);

*Gaudier-Brzeska* (Milan: All'Insegna del Pesce d'Oro, 1957);

*Pavannes and Divagations* (Norfolk, Conn.: New Directions, 1958; London: Owen, 1960);

*Versi Prosaici* (Rome: Biblioteca Minima, 1959);

*Thrones 96-109 de los cantares* (Milan: All'Insegna del Pesce d'Oro, 1959; New York: New Directions, 1959; London: Faber & Faber, 1960);

*Impact: Essays on Ignorance and the Decline of American Civilization* (Chicago: Regnery, 1960);

*Patria Mia and The Treatise on Harmony* (London: Owen, 1962);

*Nuova Economia Editoriale* (Milan: Vanni Scheiwiller, 1962);

*A Lume Spento and Other Early Poems* (New York: New Directions, 1965; London: Faber & Faber, 1966);

*Être Citoyen Romain*, edited by Pierre Aelberts (Liège: Editions Dynamo, 1965);

*Canto CX* (Cambridge, Mass.: Sextant Press, 1965);

*Selected Cantos* (London: Faber & Faber, 1967; enlarged edition, New York: New Directions, 1970);

*Redondillas* (New York: New Directions, 1968);

*Drafts and Fragments of Cantos CX-CXVII* (New York: New Directions, 1969; London: Faber & Faber, 1970);

*Selected Prose 1909-1965*, edited by William Cookson (London: Faber & Faber, 1973; New York: New Directions, 1973);

*Selected Poems 1908-1959* (London: Faber & Faber, 1975);

*Collected Early Poems*, edited by Michael John King (New York: New Directions, 1976; London: Faber & Faber, 1977);

*Ezra Pound and Music: The Complete Criticism*, edited by R. Murray Schafer (New York: New Directions, 1977; London: Faber & Faber, 1978);

*"Ezra Pound Speaking": Radio Speeches of World War II*, edited by Leonard W. Doob (Westport, Conn. & London: Greenwood Press, 1978);

*Ezra Pound and the Visual Arts*, edited by Harriet Zinnes (New York: New Directions, 1980);

*From Syria: The Worksheets, Proofs, and Text*, edited by Robin Skelton (Port Townsend, Wash.: Copper Canyon Press, 1981).

OTHER: *Des Imagistes: An Anthology*, edited, with contributions, by Pound (New York: A. & C. Boni, 1914; London: Poetry Bookshop/New York: A & C. Boni, 1914);

*Catholic Anthology 1914-1915*, edited, with contributions, by Pound (London: Elkin Mathews, 1915);

*'Noh' or Accomplishment*, by Pound and Ernest Fenollosa (London: Macmillan, 1916; New York: Knopf, 1917)–edited, with introduction and translations, by Pound;

Guido Cavalcanti, *Rime*, Italian text, edited, with notes and some translations, by Pound (Genoa: Marsano, 1932);

*Active Anthology*, edited, with contributions, by Pound (London: Faber & Faber, 1933);

*Confucius to Cummings: An Anthology of Poetry*, edited by Pound and Marcella Spann (New York: New Directions, 1964).

TRANSLATIONS: *The Sonnets and Ballate of Guido Cavalcanti* (Boston: Small, Maynard, 1912; London: Swift, 1912);

*Cathay: Translations by Ezra Pound for the Most Part from the Chinese of Rihaku, From the Notes of the Late Ernest Fenollosa, and the Decipherings of the Professors Mori and Ariga* (London: Elkin Mathews, 1915);

Remy de Gourmont, *The Natural Philosophy of Love,* translated, with a postscript, by Pound (New York: Boni & Liveright, 1922; London: Casanova Society, 1926);

Odon Por, *Italy's Policy of Social Economics, 1930-1940* (Bergamo, Milan & Rome: Istituto Italiano D'Arti Grafiche, 1941);

*Confucius: The Unwobbling Pivot & the Great Digest,* translated, with commentary, by Pound, *Pharos,* no. 4 (Winter 1947);

*The Translations of Ezra Pound,* edited by Hugh Kenner (London: Faber & Faber, 1953; New York: New Directions, 1953);

*The Classic Anthology Defined by Confucius* (Cambridge, Mass.: Harvard University Press, 1954; London: Faber & Faber, 1955);

Sophocles, *Women of Trachis* (London: Spearman, 1956; New York: New Directions, 1957);

*Love Poems of Ancient Egypt,* translated by Pound and Noel Stock (Norfolk, Conn.: New Directions, 1962).

PERIODICAL PUBLICATIONS: "Status Rerum," *Poetry,* 1 ( January 1913): 123-127;

"The New Sculpture," *Egoist,* 1 (16 February 1914): 67-68;

"Affirmations, I-VII," *New Age,* 16 (7 January 1915): 246-247; (14 January 1915): 277-278; (21 January 1915): 311-312; (28 January 1915): 349-350; (4 February 1915): 380-382; (11 February 1915): 409-411; (25 February 1915): 451-453, 471;

"Provincialism the Enemy, I-IV," *New Age,* 21 (12 July 1917): 244-245; (19 July 1917): 218-219; (26 July 1917): 288-289; (2 August 1917): 308-309;

"The Revolt of Intelligence, I-X," *New Age,* 26 (13 November 1919): 21-22; (11 December 1919): 90-91; (18 December 1919): 106-107; (1 January 1920): 139-140; (8 January 1920): 153-154; (15 January 1920): 176-177; (22 January 1920): 186-187; 4 March 1920): 287-288; (11 March 1920): 301-302; (18 March 1920): 318-319;

"On Criticism in General," *Criterion,* 1 ( January 1923): 143-156;

"Epstein, Belgion, and Meaning," *Criterion,* 9 (April 1930): 470-475;

"Mr. Eliot's Mare's Nest," review of *After Strange Gods, New English Weekly,* 4 (8 March 1934): 500;

"Mr. Eliot's Quandries," *New English Weekly,* 4 (29 March 1934): 558-559;

"What Price the Muses Now," *New English Weekly,* 5 (24 May 1934): 130-132;

"American Notes," *New English Weekly,* 6 (3 January 1935)-8 (2 April 1936);

"Augment of the Novel," *New Directions in Prose and Poetry,* 6 (1941): 705-713.

That he should be included in a volume devoted to American criticism would have both amused and delighted Ezra Pound. His relationship to his native country was so charged, so fretful, so variable, that it is at once impossible to classify him as an American critic and impossible to exclude him from the category. His first important critical gesture may have been his decision to leave this country, but he never ceased to cast attentive glances, hopeful and reproachful, toward his place of origin and the site of his indignity.

The estrangement of the American sensibility from its European past is a common preoccupation; it can lead to what Pound called in *Guide to Kulchur* (1938) "pusillanimous subservience." But it is well worth noting that the distance of America from Europe has another far more productive consequence which is nowhere better exemplified than in the critical career of Ezra Pound. Claiming to belong to no venerable tradition, Pound placed himself as the heir to every tradition. He took nothing more modest than human civilization as his proper domain, and Pound's development as a critic can be seen as the sometimes brilliant, sometimes catastrophic, result of the formidable task he set for himself: to decipher the entire text of cultural history. He is as responsible as any English-speaking critic for the existence of that ambiguous phenomenon that we know as modernism. "Pound did not create the poets," wrote T. S. Eliot, "but he created a situation in which, for the first time, there was a 'modern movement in poetry.' "

Born to Homer and Isabel Weston Pound in the frontier town of Hailey, Idaho, in 1885, raised in the suburbs of Philadelphia from June 1889 on, Pound had a rather ordinary middle-class upbringing but extraordinary personal ambitions. He later wrote that in his fifteenth year he decided that by thirty he would know more about poetry than any man living. In Philadelphia Homer Pound worked at the United States Mint as an assistant assayist. In 1903 he and his genteel wife did missionary work among the Italian immigrants in the slums. Pound was educated at public elementary school, Chelten Hills School, Cheltenham Military Academy, and Cheltenham Township High School. He matriculated at the University of Pennsylvania in 1901, then transferred to Hamilton College in 1903, receiving his bachelor's degree in 1905. He again attended the University of Pennsylvania, took a fellowship year from 1906 to 1907 during which time he did research at the British Museum and the National Library in Madrid, and received an M.A. in Romance languages in 1907, having projected a thesis on Lope de Vega which he never completed. He abandoned pursuit of the Ph.D. after failing a course in the history of literary criticism, Noel Stock reports in *The Life of Ezra Pound* (1970), despite his insistence that he was "the only student who was making any attempt to understand the subject of literary criticism and the only student with any interest in the subject." During his years in Philadelphia he formed personal ties with two important American modernists, William Carlos Williams and Hilda Doolittle, to whom he was once briefly engaged. He presented Doolittle with a collection of early poems known as *Hilda's Book* written between 1905 and 1907. In the fall of 1907 he received an appointment as an instructor in Romance languages at Wabash College in Crawfordsville, Indiana, but he quickly became frustrated with Wabash which just as quickly became frustrated with him. He was fired early in 1908 and though it was probably not clear to Pound at the time, this event initiated a break not only with American academic life but with America.

When Pound sailed to Europe on 8 February 1908 at the age of twenty-two he had two grand ambitions: to become a successful poet and to pursue his critical interest in medieval literature, especially the literature of Provence. As throughout his later career, these conditions were tightly bound to one another. It is not simply that Pound's early poetry betrays the influence of his studies in Provençal poetry; it is that the boundary between the critical and creative acts becomes indistinct. T. S. Eliot once remarked that Pound's poetic experiments of the immediate prewar years were essentially critical exercises, and one might offer the reverse proposition about his essays, that they are imaginative gestures which refuse the canons of discursive rationality and which often achieve the power of his finest poetry.

In Europe Pound lived for three months in Venice, traveled in France, and in the fall of 1908 arrived in London, where he would spend most of the next fifteen years and where his critical efforts would bear their first fruit. In 1908 Pound's first two poetry books, *A Lume Spento* and *A Quinzaine for this Yule,* were published; the next two, *Personae* and *Exultations* appeared in the following year. Between 21 January and 25 February 1909 he gave six lectures on medieval literature at the Regent Street Polytechnic. These lectures became the basis for his first published book of criticism, *The Spirit of Romance,* which appeared in 1910 with the imposing subtitle, "An Attempt to Define Somewhat the Charm of the Pre-Renaissance Literature of Latin Europe."

*The Spirit of Romance* makes no claim to being a work of professional scholarship or even a work of analytic criticism. Proceeding from the axiom that "the study of literature is hero-worship," it is a vigorous encounter with a large body of poetry stretching from Ovid and Apuleius to Dante and Shakespeare. Pound willfully neglects historical distinctions on the assumption that "All ages are contemporaneous" and that any satisfactory method of criticism should be able to "weigh Theocritus and Mr. Yeats with one balance." Thus armed with his one balance Pound is boldly evaluative, demoting Renaissance poet and scholar Petrarch; promoting late-medieval French poet François Villon; elevating the Castilian *Poema del Cid* or *Cantar de mio Cid* (written circa 1140); criticizing the eleventh-century Breton *Chançon de Roland;* doting on Dante's friend, *stilnovisti* poet Guido Cavalcanti; and beating John Milton with the long staff of Dante. But the weight of the work and its chief significance lie in the extended consideration of the romance tradition among the Provençal troubadours. Indeed the book often appears as a primer in Provence, a Baedaker to the haunts of such neglected figures as Arnaut Daniel and Bertrans de Born.

The tone of *The Spirit of Romance,* as important in its way as its substantive claims, is one of impatience, of frustration at the received opinions which conceal the living tradition, and Pound expresses a longing for direct engagement with the poetry itself. Pound's procedure is to offer terse summaries of the historical backgrounds, the lives of the poets, and the themes of their works, then to clear away the stock critical responses, and finally to display the poetic fragment in its isolated glory. In this respect it is a work of critical archeology, an attempt to retrieve valuable imaginative artifacts buried under the encrustations of Victorianism.

Pound would look back on *The Spirit of Romance* with some rueful embarrassment, considering many of its judgments incorrect and finding its style awkward. Nevertheless, though his opinions and his manner changed markedly, this first work began an endeavor which he would never abandon: the effort to rewrite the history that culminated in modernity and to establish a living tradition beneath a dead one.

Arguably Pound's temperament was never suited to the composition of volume-length studies, and while he published many books in his career, these were, whatever their length, more in the nature of extended pamphlets or brochures. The unit of his critical facility was the essay, in particular the polemical essay, and in the years following *The Spirit of Romance* he produced a continuous stream of reviews, commentaries, sketches, parodies, notes, and manifestos, all inspired by the goal of revolutionizing both modern art and modern critics.

Soon after settling in London, Pound met Olivia Shakespear and her daughter Dorothy, whom he married in 1913. Through the elder Shakespear he met William Butler Yeats, whom he began to see regularly. At the same time he established an important relationship with Ford Madox Hueffer (later Ford Madox Ford), who was already a successful novelist and a respected poet in the modern vein. Such acquaintances became essential aspects of Pound's critical project, the abiding goal of which was to contribute to a general renaissance in humane letters. To that end Pound remained highly attentive to any stirring of creative energy, taking as his first axiom the principle that no one individual could revive literature alone. From the moment he had settled in London, a leading aspect of his critical endeavor was an energetic attempt to bring individual artists together and to formulate principles that could serve as the basis for a common program of artistic experiment.

In a series of brief essays begun at the end of 1911 and published under the title "I Gather the Limbs of Osiris," Pound offers a defense of the form of historical criticism that he had begun to develop in *The Spirit of Romance*, and at the same time he lays the groundwork for a revision of contemporary aesthetic values. He announces a "New Method in Scholarship," the method of "Luminous Detail," which aims neither to accumulate facts nor to establish general principles, but

which seeks instead to identify a few resonant particulars, a few significant events which will illuminate the sweep of history and the movement of civilization. A line of poetry, an apparently minor political incident, a surviving scrap of conversation—these become the material for the intuitive historical reflections that form the basis of Pound's critical method.

The technique of the luminous detail, however, not only offered a program for the literary historian; it could also serve, Pound quickly recognized, as a code for the practicing artist. The artist, too, must seek the perspicuous fragment, must suppress superfluous context, and must eschew general moral commentary. By the end of 1911 Pound had begun to develop these formulations into coherent literary doctrine, and just a few months later the luminous detail would enter modernist consciousness under the new guise of the "image."

From the time of his arrival in London, Pound had begun to form connections not only with established figures like Ford and Yeats but with a group of younger poets who shared the will to literary revolution and who for a time met weekly in order to read their work and to discuss the most advanced critical views imported from the European continent. The leading figure in this group was T. E. Hulme who, under the influence of French theories of vers libre and the philosophy of Henri Bergson, had articulated a definition of the image on which Pound would later draw. According to Hulme both the grandeur of the classical epic and the perfection of the romantic lyric were inappropriate to the skeptical cast of the contemporary mind. In an age that no longer pursues religious truths and moral absolutes, that no longer aims toward artistic sublimity, poets must imitate the example of Impressionist painters and seek to communicate momentary states of mind, instantaneous perceptions captured in striking images. The image will replace philosophic declamation and lyric effusion; it will be concrete and direct; it will free poetry from the confinements of regular meter; it will permit poetic expression unfettered by the habits of convention.

These critical insights had few immediate results. The young poets abandoned their weekly forum, and Pound later referred to the group as "the forgotten school of 1909." But Hulme's theories, soon accompanied by the fine critical insights of Remy de Gourmont who, Pound said, "prepared our era," gave Pound new ideas to ponder, and his search for literary allies simply moved to other possible candidates. By early 1912 Pound was in close contact with H. D. (Hilda Doolittle), who had come to live in London, and with the young English poet Richard Aldington, who married H. D. the following year. In the terse lapidary style of H. D.'s verse, with its stark metaphors and its tense rhythms, Pound found an example of the new poetic sensibility he sought, and, so the story goes, Pound turned one day to his young friends in a tea shop in Kensington and informed them that they were "*les imagistes.*" H. D. began to sign her poems, "H. D., *imagiste,*" and Aldington, though he never generated the same enthusiasm in Pound, willingly closed ranks. Pound had recently scorned the Parisian tendency to have "eight schools for every dozen of poets," but his own proportion was as yet scarcely more impressive. *Imagisme,* soon to become Imagism, began as two poets and a poet impresario.

This was the first great age of the little magazine, the small-scale journal with a narrow audience but a potentially wide influence. Pound's early achievements as a critic depended greatly on his rapid and canny understanding of the possibilities offered by these journals. Eliot once observed that "Pound accomplished more than any other man could have done with anthologies and periodicals of such limited circulation." He became London correspondent for *Poetry* magazine published by Harriet Monroe in Chicago, and he served as a regular contributor to two of London's most adventurous periodicals, A. R. Orage's *New Age* and Harriet Weaver's the *New Freewoman* (later the *Egoist*). To have an accurate sense of this first phase of Pound's critical career, it is necessary to picture him engaged in a tireless attempt to write a new movement into existence, to persuade, to bully, and to cajole the readers of the little magazines into adopting a new set of literary values which would become, through a series of widening circles, the dominant values of twentieth-century literature.

The history of Imagism is among other things a locus classicus of the power of modern publicity. Pound was never satisfied merely to formulate new ideas; he was intent to provoke others into a confrontation with novelty. Thus in announcing to the readers of *Poetry* ("Status Rerum," January 1913) the advent of Imagism, Pound wrote in characteristically dramatic tones that "the youngest school here that has the nerve to call itself a school is that of the *Imagistes.*" He un-

dertook an active campaign to win new adherents to the cause, and during 1913 he persuaded several other young poets, among them D. H. Lawrence, Amy Lowell, and William Carlos Williams, to contribute to an anthology of Imagist verse which was published in early 1914.

Having thus coined the term, Pound was obliged to define what it meant. In the March 1913 issue of *Poetry* there appeared the manifesto, "A Few Don'ts by an Imagiste," in which he set out the celebrated definition of the Image: "that which presents an intellectual and emotional complex in an instant of time." To this axiom Pound appended three further principles: direct treatment of the "thing," whether it be subjective or objective; rigorous economy of presentation; and rhythm based not on fixed metrical schemes but on musical phrasing. He went on to attack the poetic reign of adjectives and abstractions and to defend the legitimacy of free verse. The early Imagist propaganda contained a strong element of rhetorical posturing, but behind the posturing lay a serious attempt to free English poetry from the artifice that had come to dominate it—the sentimentality, the ornament, and the metaphysical vagueness—and to restore the method of direct presentation and clear speech.

Here the influence of Ford Madox Ford became important to the emerging critical position. When Pound was working on his volume of poetry, *Canzoni* (1911), he visited Ford to ask his opinion, and as Pound later recalled, Ford was so appalled with the precious archaic diction that he began to roll on the floor. That roll, wrote Pound, "sent me back to my own proper effort, namely, toward using the living tongue." Pound named Ford "the defender of the prose tradition," the one who upheld the values of clarity, efficiency, and precision, those high virtues which nineteenth-century poetry had neglected. The lesson that Pound drew from Ford was that poetry, in succumbing to the lure of rhetoric, had surrendered its supremacy to those who had mastered the modern craft of prose. Pound agreed that novelists such as Stendhal and Gustave Flaubert, rather than poets like Alfred Tennyson or Matthew Arnold, were the great nineteenth-century predecessors of the twentieth-century renaissance, and accordingly he saw Imagism as an attempt "to bring poetry up to the level of prose." This meant clearing away the rot of rhetoric; it meant restoring the privilege of common speech; it meant a commitment to the virtues of control and discipline; and most significantly it meant the embrace of a new realism in poetry which held that words must correspond directly to things and that the artist must register the "data" of the world no less precisely than the scientist.

Before the advent of Imagism the most important strain in avant-garde poetry of the English-speaking world had been a late variant of French Symbolism, best exemplified in the early work of Yeats. In the spirit of Stéphane Mallarmé the Symbolist aspiration was to rely on "suggestion" and "evocation" to pass beyond the narrow realm of material fact into a sphere of transcendent values. The symbol itself was, in Yeats's words, "the only possible expression of some invisible essence, a transparent lamp about a spiritual flame," and the Symbolist poem sought to ascend beyond the physical world toward "something that moves beyond the senses."

Under the influence of Ford, Pound bluntly repudiated this Symbolist ambition. He sought an art devoted to the workings of the senses, not to what moved beyond them, an art that relied not on suggestion and evocation but on "direct treatment" as rigorous as the experiments of chemistry. Unconcerned with the invisible essence, Pound held that "the natural object is always the *adequate* symbol," and in opposition to the evocative vagueness of the Symbolists he boldly announced that "when words cease to cling close to things, kingdoms fall, empires wane and diminish." Imagism, in short, began as a realist alternative to Symbolism. Inspired by the example of modern science and nineteenth-century prose fiction, the Imagist would offer a scrupulously polished mirror, capable of reflecting both the public world and the private self.

No understanding of Pound and no understanding of modernism are possible unless one acknowledges the extraordinary range of cultural pressures that converged as a decisive moment in literary history. Psychoanalysis and anthropology, Friedrich Nietzsche and Karl Marx, Impressionism and Symbolism, Wassily Kandinsky and Igor Stravinsky, evolution and revolution, free verse and abstract painting—all met in a few major European cities, London, Paris, Berlin, where groups of young artists were attempting to launch a cultural revolution, most often without yet knowing what their revolutionary program would be. Pound, like others of the prewar generation, moved in a world of new and alluring possibilities, each vying for prominence, and to follow the course of his critical thought in its first and most fertile decade is to watch an energetic and restless development that opened him to new influences and models and that led ultimately to radical shifts changes in his aesthetic principles. The shift in emphasis from Provençal troubadours to London Imagists is itself a notable movement, but still more striking changes were to follow.

One of the most important encounters in Pound's intellectual life occurred in late 1913 when a woman named Mary Fenollosa presented him with manuscripts written by her late husband Ernest, who had spent years studying the languages and cultures of the Orient. Among the fruits of his research were investigations into the Noh drama, and, most importantly, reflections on the Chinese language which Pound prepared for publication under the title *The Chinese Written Character as a Medium for Poetry . . . An Ars Poetica* (1936). Pound, who was immediately captivated by Fenollosa's work, quickly incorporated Fenollosa's ideas into his own critical theory.

According to Fenollosa the power of the Chinese character is that it is not merely a conventional linguistic sign, an "arbitrary symbol"; it is often a "vivid shorthand picture of the operations of nature," a visual rendering of what it represents. The languages of the West depend on "sheer convention," while the writing of the Chinese follows "natural suggestion." Moreover what the written characters depict are not objects but *processes*, and working from this assumption Fenollosa argued that the imaginative force of Chinese is that it stays "close to nature" by attempting to convey the ceaseless movements of the physical world.

Pound saw in these insights "a whole basis of aesthetic," and he adapted his definition of Imagism accordingly. Having initially described the Imagist goal as direct treatment of the "thing," now under the influence of Fenollosa he calls for attention to movement and activity. The noun yields pride of place to the verb, and in place of the static notion of an "intellectual and emotional complex," Pound comes to insist that the Imagist poem is a "radiant node or cluster," "endowed with energy." Furthermore Fenollosa's emphasis upon the *visual* aspect of Chinese may well have prepared Pound for his next great object of enthusiasm, the recent formal experiments in painting and sculpture.

In late 1913 Pound announced in a letter to William Carlos Williams that "we are getting our little gang after five years of waiting." A "little gang" of cultural revolutionaries is what Pound had been seeking since his appearance in London, and in accounting for his sudden new confidence, one must look beyond the rather modest literary achievements of Imagism. From his earliest critical essays Pound had been beguiled by the prospect of a radical artistic *movement,* a broad alliance of innovative talents who would constitute a genuine avant-garde capable of new perceptions unavailable to the stolid mass of ordinary citizens. Between 1910 and 1914 just such an avant-garde began to make itself felt in London, but this was due less to the work of the poets and more to the efforts of several young painters and sculptors who succeeded in outraging the artistic establishment and winning great attention for themselves.

In late 1910 a fiercely controversial exhibition of post-Impressionist art had been held in London, an event which is said to have provoked Virginia Woolf's observation that "on or about December 1910 human character changed." Over the next several years a series of exhibitions introduced the work of sculptors Jacob Epstein and Henri Gaudier-Brzeska and painters David Bomberg, Edward Wadsworth, and Wyndham Lewis. Month after month the London critics attacked the new art as unformed and uncivilized, while the artists retorted in angry polemics with such disarming titles as "Kill John Bull With Art."

This was the kind of cultural upheaval that Pound had sought, regarding it as the necessary step toward a thoroughgoing cultural renaissance. By the last months of 1913 his interest in the fine arts had grown deeper than it had ever been, and in early 1914 he became a passionate defender of Epstein, Gaudier-Brzeska, and Lewis. Moreover in the course of developing this keen interest in the fine arts, Pound underwent another important change in his critical principles. If Ford had taught him that a new realism was the way to literary reform, the painters and sculptors taught that realism was itself outdated, another relic of an obsolete era, and that a genuinely revolutionary art would break free of the obligation to mirror the world. The paintings of Picasso and Kandinsky had attracted the fascinated attention of these young London artists, and Kandinsky in particular suggested how the fine arts could abandon representation in favor of the play of forms themselves–or, as Pound put it in *Gaudier-Brzeska: A Memoir* (1916), "form, not the *form of anything*."

As late as December 1913 Pound had offered his defense of aesthetic realism, based on

*Ezra Pound in Rome, 1941 (Associated Press/Wide World Photos, Inc.)*

principles derived from Ford, but just three months later he wrote an essay for the *Egoist* on the new sculpture in which he announced that "We have heard all that the 'realists' have to say." If the first goal of Imagism had been to bring poetry up to the level of prose, its new ambition was to rise to the level of painting and sculpture. Indeed after his encounter with the work of Lewis and Gaudier-Brzeska, Pound redefined Imagism as poetry in which "painting or sculpture seems as if it were 'just coming over into speech.' "

Along with this new conception went a new name: Vorticism. This was to be the general term for the common program in all the arts, and Imagism was now to refer to the poetic experiments within the broader Vorticist movement. (Imagism, wrote Pound, could just as well be called Vorticist poetry.) The controlling idea behind this newest round of Pound's rapidly turning critical position was that once free of the burden of realism the artist would be released to transform "energy" directly into "pattern." Art, argued Pound, should replace the *mimetic* faculty with the *creative*. Why, he asked, should a work of art resemble something else? "You do not demand of a mountain or a tree that it should be like something." So too Vorticism will not be "a mimicry of external life"; it will not imitate but create—not *represent* but *present*.

The first six months of 1914 constitute a period of critical energy and polemical fervor unequaled in the history of the English avant-garde. From one week to the next, new theories were formulated, new opponents attacked, new insults exchanged. The popular press took regular notice of the disturbances in the arts, and for a brief moment the inner workings of experimental aesthetic technique became an issue of public concern. At the center of the storm raged Pound, writing, lecturing, jeering, hectoring. He set about organizing his movement, observed Wyndham Lewis, like a second Robert Baden-Powell founding the Boy Scouts. By late spring Pound had a troop of allies who were willing to call themselves Vorticists, who gathered at the new Rebel Art Centre, and who, in an eerie mimicry of the approaching war, waged successful battle against their avant-garde rivals, the Italian Futurists.

In July the culminating gesture of his intensely active period was made, the publication of the Vorticist journal *Blast* with its bright puce cover, its series of uncompromising manifestos, its deliberate provocations, and its unrelenting assault on established cultural values ("BLAST years 1837 to 1900," "BLAST SPORT," "BLAST The Post Office"). Years of experiment in the arts seemed at last to have yielded a victory for the avant-garde. In celebration of the success a grand banquet was held, attended by some of the gifted artists of the twentieth century. Two months later there was war.

The outbreak of World War I and its long, painful course had deep and lasting effects on Pound. Like so many others he was shaken by the waste of young life, and an immediate result was that his agressively militant tone and his polemical challenge became greatly muted. There were no more calls to "Blast" his opponents and no more incitement to an aesthetic war against English society. After years of sniping at the nation that spawned him and the nation that adopted him, he wrote a series for the *New Age* called "Provincialism the Enemy" (1917) in which he indicated that his only political hope lay in a coalition of England, France, and America.

Gaudier-Brzeska, aged twenty-three, and Hulme were killed in combat. Ford, Aldington, and Lewis fought at the front. The threat to life coincided with a threat to art, and Pound, who had been ready to lead a Vorticist charge against the cultural establishment, was left in near isolation. He composed a memorial volume for Gaudier-Brzeska in which he assumed an elegaic tone not just toward the dead young sculptor but toward the artistic movement which itself seemed to have died in the trenches of the war. Adding to the literary frustration which accompanied Pound's personal despair, Amy Lowell began to lead an insurrection in the ranks of the Imagists, inviting contributors to the first anthology to participate in a second volume free of Pound's editorial control.

At this difficult moment in his career Pound met Eliot and immediately recognized him as a potential new ally. He arranged the publication of several of Eliot's poems, defended him against hostile critical attacks, and helped him to take Richard Aldington's place as literary editor of the *Egoist* when Aldington left for the war.

By 1917 Pound and Eliot were working out their critical principles in active collaboration, and together they quickly formulated another revision in the theory of modernist poetry. Eliot had not participated in the Imagist or Vorticist phases of the movement, and his detachment from these earlier critical doctrines no doubt encouraged Pound to reconsider principles he had once considered axiomatic. Years later Pound would reflect on this association with Eliot, calling it "a movement to which no name has ever been given" and observing that "at a particular date in a particular room, two authors, neither engaged in picking the other's pocket, decided that the . . . general floppiness had gone too far and that some counter-current must be set going."

This "counter-current" involved a departure from some of the central tenets of the Imagist and Vorticist aesthetic. After his early defense of free verse, Pound now held that poetic progress lay "in an attempt to approximate classical quantitative metres," and in place of the earlier deference to prose writers such as Flaubert and Stendhal, he now paid homage to Stendhal's opponent Théophile Gautier (in, for instance, "The Hard and Soft in French Poetry" of 1918). In their own poetry Pound and Eliot experimented with Gautier's strict rhythms and precise rhymes, as the Imagist demand for natural poetic diction yielded to an acceptance of the artifices of form.

One further result of Pound's close association with Eliot during this period from 1917 to

1921 was that his literary opinions were no longer decisively formed by the example of painting and sculpture. Much of his best literary criticism (in the narrow sense) was written in this period, including essays on Eliot, Henry James, James Joyce, Wyndham Lewis, and Remy de Gourmont. Moreover Pound was less concerned with dividing modern art into two opposing camps and defending the merits of his own while heaping scorn on the other. In a new spirit of critical tolerance he introduced what would become a highly influential distinction among three kinds of poetry: *melopeia*, or "poetry which moves by its music"; *phanopoeia*, or "poetry wherein the feelings of painting and sculpture are predominant"; and *logopoeia*, or poetry "which is a dance of the intelligence among words and ideas." The result is that Imagism (which was Pound's first name for *phanopoeia*) is no longer the dominant term in an aesthetic dualism; it is now one among several equally valued activities.

Pound once remarked that while Eliot was the more brilliant practitioner of *logopoeia*, he himself excelled at *melopoeia*, and this observation reflects a subtle shift in Pound's aesthetic orientation. He remains zealous in the effort to link literature to the other arts, but increasingly through his later career he looks toward music, rather than painting and sculpture, as the preeminent paradigm of aesthetic activity. Between 1917 and 1921 he earned much of his income as the regular music critic for the *New Age*, and he gave renewed attention to the problem that had occupied him in his studies of the troubadours, the problem of *motz el son*, the marriage of words and music in poetic creation.

In these years after the war Pound's critical development entered an ambiguous and uncertain phase. Even as he made tentative efforts to revive the coherence of the prewar avant-garde, he was coming to recognize the exhaustion of that rich vein of critical discourse. At the beginning of 1921 he left London for Paris and threw himself into an encounter with new imaginative possibilities. He became interested in the work of Jean Cocteau and the Dadaists, Ernest Hemingway and the young composer George Antheil whose "Treatise on Harmony" Pound would see into print. From the standpoint of his later development, the stay in Paris between 1921 and 1924 can be seen as a kind of relaxed interlude between the English and Italian stages of Pound's career, two quite different stages but each marked by programmatic critical commitments.

In 1924 Pound left Paris for Rapallo, Italy, which would remain his domestic center until the end of his life. The decision to leave Paris for Rapallo, though informed by many factors, might be taken as Pound's refusal of the aesthetic milieu so prominent in the French capital in favor of an engagement with the strong political and social currents that were flowing through Italy. "I am extremely glad," wrote Pound, "to be out of the maelstrom of literary London and artistic Paris, with leisure to do my own job." Behind him he left Hemingway, Cocteau, Joyce, Antheil, and others; ahead of him was Mussolini.

Most important for Pound's critical evolution is that in these immediate postwar years, his sensitive ear heard not only subtle differences in poetic voice but heard too the still-muted sound of social discontent. Never again would he enjoy the privilege of formulating aesthetic principles in a context of general social stability. For the rest of his career Pound, like Eliot, had to establish his critical position within a period of social and political unease, and in deciding what stance to assume within the postwar era, these allies, veterans of the "counter-current," began to diverge. As early as 1919 signs of strain had begun to appear when Eliot wrote a distinctly cool review of Pound's new volume of poetry. Pound, who was clearly offended, sent a letter to the editor, complaining that Eliot seemed not to regard literature as something enjoyable, something with "tang, gusto, aroma," but as something one ought to enjoy. Eliot replied by saying that he did not regard his enjoyment as a "question of public interest."

Over the next several years the two remained in close contact, with Pound performing some of his most important critical labors in helping Eliot revise *The Waste Land* (1922). But even as Eliot was moving steadily toward a position of dominance in the literary establishment, Pound began to reassert his estrangement from the reigning powers. He felt that Eliot was writing for "the professors," while he himself wanted to keep clear of the institutions supporting a "botched civilization." This tension between Pound and Eliot points to a broader problem in postwar modernism, the gradual disappearance of a common critical program that would unite the avant-garde. Pound attacked Eliot; Eliot attacked Aldington; and Lewis attacked Pound. The days of Vorticist unity receded into the modernist past. Pound, for his part, no longer saw such shared purpose as a desirable goal; he now preached the necessity of productive disagreement among the leading artists of the age; and thus the modern movement fractured into talented atoms.

In 1928 Eliot wrote an essay for *Dial* called "Isolated Superiority," in which he praised Pound's technical ability, in particular his fine ear, but then went on to ask, "What does Mr. Pound believe?" It was a question which clearly stung Pound but which indeed raises a central problem in his literary career. In his "Axiomata" of 1921 (collected in *Selected Prose*, 1973) Pound had dismissed religious belief as "a cramp, a paralysis, an atrophy of the mind in certain positions," and in general his early critical development may be seen as an attempt to avoid the paralytic cramp of any permanent doctrine. His literary opinions were always expressed with great vehemence, but they changed so rapidly, and Pound was so willing to encourage the change, that it is difficult to speak of anything so determinate as a belief. Certainly Pound never arrived at a formulation as settled as Eliot's famous embrace of Anglo-Catholicism, classicism, and monarchy. All through the period of intense critical activity in London, he had remained indifferent to religion and metaphysics and detached from the political and economic questions that obsessed his contemporaries.

One of the burdens of the modernist avant-garde, however, is that it lived past a period of relative cultural stability which permitted bold experiment in the arts and which accommodated the productive extremism of the young artists. In the years before World War I the great threat to culture seemed to be lethargy and fatigue, a condition which Pound and his comrades noisily sought to overcome. The anarchic disregard of the political process and the bitter contempt for the general public could still seem appropriate attitudes for the free artist dedicated to reviving the craft of poetry or painting.

It is a painful irony of cultural history that the English avant-garde reached its greatest creative moment just as World War I began. After the terrible losses in that conflict, after the moral and political confusion of the 1920s, after the economic crisis of the thirties, it became increasingly difficult for artists to devote themselves to technical matters alone, and it became difficult, too, to dismiss the importance of belief. Pound came around to the opinion that one could not restrict attention to a minority culture of artists and that the problem of civilization could not be solved "without regard for the common man."

This is a notable change in view. But one thing that does not change is Pound's commitment to extreme solutions. If these had formerly involved the violent renewal of a moribund literature, they now became demands for a reconsideration of the grounds of society. In 1927 Pound began to edit a short-lived journal called *Exile*, and the name not only indicates his geographic separation from his place of birth but his thoroughgoing detachment from Western values which he could no longer accept as his own. "I want a new civilization," he announced in 1928, and from the mid 1920s through the 1930s his criticism was based on this revolutionary demand. Whereas Eliot became steadily more prominent in the Anglo-American literary world, Pound moved ever further from the tradition and the culture into which he had been born.

Two concerns came to dominate Pound's criticism between the wars. The first was the problem of modern economics, a problem which, in one sense, had been implicit in his earliest views on the future of the arts. From the moment he became committed to a contemporary artistic renaissance, he confronted the question of how to pay for it, how to support the artists who would not be able to count on public enthusiasm as a source of income.

Like Pound himself, allies such as Joyce, Eliot, and Gaudier-Brzeska had to struggle for years without the economic security that would let them pursue their art free of distraction. In his 1912 essay on the United States, *Patria Mia* (1950), Pound had appealed to wealthy Americans to place resources in the hands of impoverished artists, and while he waited for that generosity, he undertook to find whatever monetary support might allow Gaudier-Brzeska to chisel the next stone, Eliot to write the next poem, Joyce to compose the next chapter. He persuaded editors to publish unconventional and often highly controversial work; he tried to secure patrons; later he attempted to establish a fund that would let Eliot leave his demoralizing job at Lloyd's bank. He himself wrote much of his criticism in order to secure the modest remuneration that the little magazines could offer. He would later say that he recognized the unemployment crisis long before others, because he saw the best artists of his generation continually unemployed.

Against this background it is not surprising that Pound would become committed to the cause of economic reform. In the last years of the first world war, he was writing regularly for the *New Age* when the journal's editor, A. R. Orage, became a convert to the economic ideas of C. H. Douglas. Douglas was a retired Army major who had developed a theory of "social credit" which held that the problem of economic production had been solved and that only the problem of distribution remained. He proposed that money be granted directly to the populace in a system of national dividends which would ensure that every member of society would have sufficient purchasing power to acquire the goods necessary for a decent life. Such a system was to remove financial power from the banks and place it in a neutral institution which would consult only the good of the public as a whole.

Douglas's proposal, it is plain, was an assault on the basic assumptions of a capitalist economy, but this disturbed Pound very little, and as time went on, it troubled him even less. In a bitter essay called "Murder by Capital" published in Eliot's journal, the *Criterion,* Pound argues that from the standpoint of art, capitalism has failed. It has committed "crimes against living art" and thus stands condemned by its works. The root of the problem, contends Pound, is usury, the private appropriation of the power to lend, and in his criticism, as in his poetry, he returns obsessively to the need to eliminate usury from civilized life. He tirelessly reiterates the proposition that economic justice is the necessary condition of cultural health.

Pound's writings of the 1920s and 1930s give vivid testimony to the unsettled state of intellectuals and artists in that turbulent period. His opposition to the prevailing powers was relentless and unyielding, but though he knew that he was an enemy of liberalism and capitalism, he was an enemy in search of a program. The infatuation with Douglas yielded to an infatuation with Silvio Gesell who invented a system of stamp scrip, a way of taxing the possession of money in order to prevent hoarding. In essay after essay, Pound returned to the need to break the stranglehold of the banks, to provide work for all, and to ensure material well-being throughout the populace. Often his proposals swerved abruptly from the political left to the political right, and at one point he cites both Lenin and Hitler to support his claims.

It is impossible to understand the curve of Pound's critical development without grasping how thoroughly the concern with artistic structure was supplanted by the concern with eco-

nomic structure. In one of his "American Notes" written for the *New English Weekly* he wrote, in 1935, that whereas twenty years ago people "bleated" about painting now it was time to make economic theory part of the general culture. In place of the three principles of Imagism he offers an *A B C of Economics* (1933).

Pound sustained his ties with Eliot, Joyce, Yeats, Ford, and Lewis, but now he recast their literary revolution in terms of social struggle. He reinterpreted cultural history as a struggle between producers and usurers, locating the weakness of Greece in its willingness to allow pernicious economic practices, and identifying the strength of Rome with its sterner attitudes towards interest and borrowing. Thomas Jefferson and John Quincy Adams became great heroes to Pound, who celebrated what he considered their enlightened attitudes toward circulation and currency. Contrary to his Vorticist embrace of a non-mimetic art, he now insisted that no novelist or novel reader could understand the motivation of character without understanding economics, and he proceeded to the uncompromising assertion that "you can't understand ANY history without understanding economics."

Pound's obsessive preoccupation with economics can be seen as an extravagant outgrowth from his early concern to find material support for the young artists around him whose talent was only rivalled by their poverty. His second recurrent theme in this period, the "immediate need of Confucius," can also be traced to ideas that originally emerged in the more strictly literary context of his first decade of criticism. In Fenollosa's theories of the Chinese character Pound had seen a new "aesthetic," but the more deeply he pondered Chinese thought, and in particular the more he reflected on the thought of Confucius, the more convinced he became that he had found the only secure basis for a decent civilization.

One of the persistent aims of the modernists was to establish a standpoint at the greatest possible distance from the culture which they rejected, and what Confucius offered to Pound was a perspective radically removed from the "age of pestilence" in which he felt he had the misfortune to live. The embrace of Confucian thought allowed him to pass beyond the unyielding problems of Christianity and capitalism, democracy and liberalism, romanticism, and classicism. He asserted that "a sane university curriculum will put Chinese where Greek was"—a remark that epitomizes his increasing estrangement from the dominant ideals of Western culture.

Perhaps the best way to account for Pound's attraction to Confucius is to notice that it allowed him to transfer some of his earliest literary principles into the domain of social thought. He repeatedly quoted the Confucian opinion on the first responsibility of government: "call things by their right names"–a maxim that echoes the Imagist principle that words must "cling close to things." Moreover the Confucian insistence upon clarity and precision accords with the literary commitments derived from Ford, and the enshrinement of discipline in Confucian ethics is a fit complement to Poundian aesthetics.

In another historical context the union of these two dominant strains in Pound's critical thought, radical economics and Chinese philosophy, Silvio Gesell and Confucius, would have been a harmless idiosyncrasy, a source of poetic metaphors like Yeats's system of occult forces. But in the chaos of the 1930s, in a period when the political center ceased to hold and the polarities of left and right sharpened, these consuming preoccupations made Pound susceptible to the drift towards political barbarism.

He took from Douglas and Gesell the demand for a strong collective body which would prevent individuals from disrupting economic stability; he took from Confucius the insistence on hierarchy and control; and in the context of the 1930s these two convictions led him quickly and fatefully to fascism. During the first world war he had called for the cultural alliance of France, England, and America, but in the midst of World War II he identified himself with the "Rome-Berlin axis" and with the most shameful opinions emanating from those two capitals.

In his book *Jefferson And/Or Mussolini* (1935) Pound defended the Fascist revolution in Italy as the legacy of the American revolution and insisted that the similarities between Jefferson and Mussolini were more profound than their differences. Both, he argued, sought to protect the nation as a whole from the particular interests that threatened to dissolve it. Fascism, like Jeffersonian democracy, was an "anti-snob" movement which understood that the best government is the one which most speedily translates the best thought into action.

Pound no doubt saw in Mussolini an image of the role he himself had sought in the realm of art, the strong-willed leader who can impel a collection of individuals into a common movement

and who is able to convert ideas into action. In 1914 Pound had enjoined the modernist artist to "live by craft and violence." Twenty years later the metaphor transformed into the image of the Confucian books as an axe for clearing away the jungle of Christian theology. Then, just before World War II, Pound celebrated fascism as the "surgeon's knife" which will cut usury out of the world. The violence of the rhetoric is constant, but the object of rhetorical assault changes from specifically literary concerns (adjectives, sentimentality, abstractions) to the characteristic obsessions of the Fascist mind (usurers, liberals, Jewish people). Part of what is most disturbing in the second, and longer, phase of Pound's critical career is the ease with which the narrowly textual question metamorphoses into the broadly political question. "Poetry" yields pride of place to "civilization," and Pound is willing to apply the same surgical methods to social life that he had employed in the revolution of the poetic word.

In the effort to understand how a critical intellect capable of such fine literary discriminations could make so many crude political judgments, one should recall another aspect of his fascination with Chinese culture. For Pound, Fenollosa's speculations on the Chinese written character not only offered insight into the workings of human language but also a new technique for poetry and, most pertinent here, a new method for criticism. Indeed late in his career Pound identified his own chief (perhaps only) contribution to criticism as the introduction of the "ideogrammic system." Just as Fenollosa claimed that the Chinese character presented a picture of the world, so Pound elaborated a critical method based on the vivid description of particular details rather than a series of generalizations. In a refinement of his early techniques of the luminous detail Pound offered a critical method which he opposed to "Aristotelian logic" and which he described as a "method of first heaping together the necessary components of thought," "of presenting one facet and then another until at some point one gets off the dead and desensitized surface of the reader's mind," of accumulating "concrete examples" and "facts, possibly small, but gristly and resilient, that can't be squashed, that insist on being taken into consideration."

The result is that from the late 1920s Pound's essays proceeded chiefly through the depiction of illustrative events juxtaposed without explanation and offered as the concrete representatives of world history. The critical essay became the Chinese character writ large. *Guide to Kulchur* (1938) is the epitome of this developing critical method, a series of essay-length disquisitions on such subjects as Mussolini's Italy, eighteenth-century music, Dadaism, and the criticism of Eliot, bound together not by rational connections but by imaginative relations never explicitly declared. As in Pound's cantos, which rehearse so many of the same themes and which employ much the same method, certain historical particularities serve as the recurrent units out of which the complex ideogram is to emerge. The founding of the Bank of England, the life of Kung (Confucius), the correspondence of Adams and Jefferson, the dispute between Leibniz and Bossuet, the career of Gaudier-Brzeska—such local events as these were tirelessly repeated in Pound's attempt to understand history through a constellation of vivid particulars rather than through the dull progression of abstractions. "It is the curse of our contemporary 'mentality,'" Pound had written, "that its general concepts have so little anchor in particular and known subjects."

But there is an illuminating, even poignant, moment in *Guide to Kulchur,* when Pound interrupts himself and bluntly confesses that he is doing no better than any other "writer of general statements." This is certainly true. The stunningly precise rendition of historical fact alternates with cumbersome abstractions that offer unsubtle and unlovely characterizations of the history of literature, the history of economics, the history of religion; for example he says, "the WHOLE of 18th century literature was a cliché." Such generalizations are not mere anomalies; they are problematic of Pound's criticism and problematic of his age.

In the late 1920s Pound had discovered the work of the German anthropologist Leo Frobenius whose concept of *paideuma* became increasingly important to him. Frobenius held that every nation, every period, every culture organized its entire system of attitudes, concerns, beliefs, desires, and values in terms of a coherent pattern which would manifest itself in every aspect of cultural life. *Paideuma,* wrote Pound, is "the tangle or complex of the inrooted ideas of any period," "the mental formation, the inherited habits of thought, the conditionings, aptitudes of a given race or time." It is not difficult to see why such a concept would attract Pound. For a man so committed to luminous details and

concrete images, the notion of *paideuma* offered an intellectual warrant, a guarantee of general coherence behind the particulars. If Pound's imagination worked most naturally upon resonant fragments, the conception of *paideuma* promised a controlling sense of the whole.

In his music criticism Pound had developed the notion of the Great Bass, an underlying principle of order, a rhythmic *basis* that establishes the deep form upon which all serious musical composition rests. Beneath the variety, the intricacy, and the harmony there exist certain simple relationships that can be expressed in mathematical form and that provide the controlling structure, the great bass, of the composition. One can see in this abstract musical concept the same habit of thought that served Pound so ill in his political judgments, the same impatience with complexity, the same rage for simplicity.

Both the imaginative brilliance and the moral agony of Pound's critical achievement can be understood in terms of the unstable relations between "direct treatment of the thing" and the abstract mathematics of the Great Bass, between the luminous detail and the obscure *paideuma.* From his earliest speculations in *The Spirit of Romance* Pound had refused to negotiate the long course from the rich particular to the encompassing abstraction; he simply leapt between the two. While this allowed for startling and original perceptions in his early work, the course of twentieth-century history deepened the chasm over which a leap had to be made. It is one thing to move from a lyric of Arnaut Daniel to the psychology of the troubadours, it is another to pass from the death of Gaudier-Brzeska to the criminality of Roosevelt and the villainy of the Jews. By the late 1930s Pound was identifying the integrity of the individual with the integrity of the corporate state, and he was ready to pass from the rhetorical violence of his literary program to the political violence of Fascist militarism.

During the war Pound made an infamous series of radio broadcasts in which the principles he had been repeating for a decade were turned to the purposes of wartime propaganda. After the war he was forcibly returned to the United States and accused and indicted on nineteen counts of treason, avoiding conviction for the crime when he was declared insane on 13 February 1946. He was placed in St. Elizabeth's hospital where he remained until 1958 when several of his friends finally helped persuade the government to release him. He returned to Italy, where he pursued work on the cantos and continued to offer sweeping appraisals of the fate of civilization. But in the years after the war Pound published no criticism of consequence, and in the early 1960s he fell into an almost unbroken silence, interrupted occasionally by the repudiation of opinions he had so relentlessly rehearsed. "I have come too late to a condition of doubt," he told an interviewer in 1963, and thus his last decade as a critic reverses the temper established in the first. The booming certainties of the Imagist, the Vorticist, and the Fascist yield to a doubting silence.

Pound liked to say that the central act of criticism was the creation of an anthology, the gathering of glorious specimens, the "maxima" of a culture. He called Confucius history's greatest anthologist and argued that every great culture produced a major anthology. Pound himself compiled several anthologies and regularly tabulated lists of the essential documents of human civilization, acting on the principle that "criticism may be written by a string of names." The will to anthologize expresses deep and contradictory urges that suggest the lasting virtues and the ineradicable defects of Pound's critical sensibility. He had an abiding devotion to the specificity of imaginative accomplishment but an equally strong compulsion to condense the totality of civilization into a single brief text.

Indeed Pound's career as a critic might be seen as a grand anthology of European modernism, a vast compendium of major critical attitudes that dominated so much literary opinion in the first half of the century. For this reason his influence has been as heterogenous as his accomplishment. He has left behind scholars who tidy his historical speculations, prosodists who attempt to refine his already meticulous formal judgments, poet-critics who ask what remains of the modernist experiment, and political adventurists who borrow his name for their own shabby ends.

For certainly Pound was not alone in failing to find a balanced and humane relationship between the local truths of imaginative experience and the general pressures of modern social life. But what makes his failure so regrettable is that he had preached as eloquently as anyone the prescience of the arts; artists, as he liked to put it, were the "antennae of the race." It is fair to say that Pound's early criticism was a precise antenna sensitive to the future course of literary modernism. But it is just as necessary to acknowledge that his later work does not anticipate cultural novelty but slavishly follows political archaism. This is the humiliation which the great defender of the avant-garde had to endure: he had worked to reform his culture, no one more energetically, defiantly, successfully, but in the effort he deformed himself.

**Letters:**

*The Letters of Ezra Pound,* edited by D. D. Paige (New York: Harcourt, Brace, 1950; London: Faber & Faber, 1951);

*Pound/Joyce, The Letters of Ezra Pound to James Joyce,* edited by Forrest Read (New York: New Directions, 1967; London: Faber & Faber, 1969);

*Letters to Ibbotsom, 1935-1952,* edited by Vittoria I. Mondolfo and Margaret Hurley (Orono, Maine: National Poetry Foundation, University of Maine, 1979);

*Letters to John Theobald,* edited by Donald Pearce and Herbert Schneidau (Redding Ridge, Conn.: Black Swan, 1981);

*Pound/Ford, The Story of a Literary Friendship: The Correspondence Between Ezra Pound and Ford Madox Ford and Their Writings About Each Other,* edited by Brita Lindberg-Seyersted (New York: New Directions, 1982);

*Ezra Pound and Dorothy Shakespear, Their Letters 1910-1914,* edited by Omar Pound and A. Walton Litz (New York: New Directions, 1984);

*The Letters of Ezra Pound and Wyndham Lewis,* edited by Timothy Materer (New York: New Directions, 1985).

**Interviews:**

D. G. Bridson, "An Interview with Ezra Pound," *New Directions in Prose and Poetry,* 17 (30 November 1961): 159-184;

Donald Hall, "Ezra Pound: An Interview," *Paris Review,* 28 (Summer-Fall 1962): 22-51;

"The Poet Speaks: Interview by Grazia Levi," *Paideuma,* 8 (Fall 1979): 243-247;

"The Interview [of Vanni Ronsisvalle and Pier Paolo Passolini with Ezra Pound in 1968]," *Paideuma,* 10 (Fall 1981): 331-345.

**Bibliography:**

Donald C. Gallup, *Ezra Pound: A Bibliography* (London: Rupert Hart-Davis, 1963; revised edition, Charlottesville: University Press of Virginia, 1983).

**Biographies:**

Charles Norman, *Ezra Pound,* revised edition (New York: Minerva, 1969);

Noel Stock, *The Life of Ezra Pound* (New York: Pantheon, 1970; London: Routledge & Kegan Paul, 1970);

Mary de Rachewiltz, *Discretions* (Boston: Little, Brown, 1971);

Charles Olson, *Charles Olson and Ezra Pound at St. Elizabeths,* edited by Catherine Seelye (New York: Grossman, 1975);

C. David Heyman, *Ezra Pound: The Last Rower* (New York: Viking Press, 1976);

Hilda Doolittle, *End to Torment: A Memoir of Ezra Pound by H. D.* (New York: New Directions, 1979);

James H. Wilhelm, *The American Roots of Ezra Pound* (New York: Garland, 1985).

**References:**

Robert M. Adams, "A Hawk and a Handsaw for Ezra Pound," *Accent* (Summer 1948): 205-214;

Ian F. A. Bell, *Critic as Scientist: The Modernist Poetics of Ezra Pound* (London & New York: Methuen, 1981);

William M. Chace, *The Political Identities of Ezra Pound and T. S. Eliot* (Stanford, Cal.: Stanford University Press, 1973);

Stanley K. Coffman, Jr., *Imagism: A Chapter in the History of Modern Poetry* (Norman: University of Oklahoma Press, 1951);

Richard Cork, *Origins and Development,* volume 1 of *Vorticism and Abstract Art in the First Machine Age* (London: Fraser, 1976; Berkeley: University of California Press, 1976);

Reed Way Dasenbrock, *The Literary Vorticism of Ezra Pound and Wyndham Lewis: Toward the Condition of Painting* (Baltimore: Johns Hopkins University Press, 1985);

Guy Davenport, "Pound and Frobenius," in *Motive and Method in the Cantos of Ezra Pound,* edited by Lewis Leary (New York: Columbia University Press, 1954);

Donald Davie, *Ezra Pound* (London: Fontana, 1975; New York: Viking, 1976);

Earle Davis, *Vision Fugitive: Ezra Pound and Economics* (Lawrence: University Press of Kansas, 1968);

N. Christoph De Nagy, *Ezra Pound's Poetics and Literary Tradition: the Critical Decade* (Bern: Francke, 1966);

T. S. Eliot, "Ezra Pound," *Poetry,* 68 (September 1946): 326-338;

Ford Madox Ford, "Pound and 'How to Read,'" *New Review,* 11 (April 1932): 39-45;

Philip Grover, ed., *Ezra Pound: The London Years 1908-1920* (New York: AMS, 1978);

Natalie Harris, "A Map of Ezra Pound's Literary Criticism," *Southern Review* (Summer 1983): 548-572;

Eric Homberger, "Pound, Ford and 'Prose': The Making of a Modern Poet," *Journal of American Studies,* 5 (December 1971): 281-292;

Homberger, ed., *Ezra Pound: The Critical Heritage* (London: Routledge & Kegan Paul, 1972);

Glenn Hughes, *Imagism and the Imagists: A Study in Modern Poetry* (Stanford: Stanford University Press, 1931);

Thomas H. Jackson, "The Poetic Politics of Ezra Pound," *Journal of Modern Literature,* 3 (1974): 987-1011;

Hugh Kenner, "The Poetics of Speech," in *Ford Madox Ford, Modern Critical Judgments,* edited by Richard A. Cassell (London: Macmillan, 1972);

Kenner, *The Pound Era* (Berkeley & Los Angeles: University of California Press, 1971);

Timothy Materer, *Vortex: Pound, Eliot and Lewis* (Ithaca, N.Y.: Cornell University Press, 1979);

Marshall McLuhan, "Ezra Pound's Critical Prose," in *Ezra Pound: A Collection of Essays to be Presented to Ezra Pound on his Sixty-Fifth Birthday,* edited by Peter Russell (London & New York: Nevill, 1950);

Herbert N. Schneidau, *Ezra Pound: The Image and the Real* (Baton Rouge: Louisiana State University Press, 1969);

R. Murray Shafer, "The Developing Theories of Absolute Rhythm and Great Bass," *Paideuma,* 2 (Spring 1973): 23-35;

Richard Sieburth, *Instigations: Ezra Pound and Remy de Gourmont* (Cambridge, Mass.: Harvard University Press, 1978);

Noel Stock, ed., *Ezra Pound Perspectives* (Chicago: Regnery, 1965);

William Wees, *Vorticism and the English Avant-Garde* (Toronto: University of Toronto Press, 1972);

René Wellek, "Ezra Pound's Literary Criticism," *Denver Quarterly,* 11 (1976): 1-20.

**Papers:**
The majority of the Pound papers are in the

Ezra Pound Archive of the Beinecke Library, Yale University. Other papers are in the Berg Collection of the New York Public Library, the Houghton Library of Harvard University, the Newberry Library in Chicago, and the libraries of Hamilton College, Cornell University, and the University of Pennsylvania. The Lilly Library of Indiana University has about twelve thousand letters to Ezra and Dorothy Pound, dating from 1945-1953.

# John Crowe Ransom

*(30 April 1888-3 July 1974)*

## Thomas Daniel Young
*Vanderbilt University*

See also the Ransom entry in *DLB 45, American Poets, 1880-1945*, First Series.

BOOKS: *Poems About God* (New York: Holt, 1919);
*Chills and Fever* (New York: Knopf, 1924);
*Grace After Meat* (London: Leonard & Virginia Woolf at the Hogarth Press, 1924);
*Two Gentlemen in Bonds* (New York: Knopf, 1927);
*God Without Thunder: An Unorthodox Defense of Orthodoxy* (New York: Harcourt, Brace, 1930; London: Howe, 1931);
*The World's Body* (New York & London: Scribners, 1938);
*The New Criticism* (Norfolk, Conn.: New Directions, 1941);
*Poetics* (Norfolk, Conn.: New Directions, 1942);
*A College Primer of Writing* (New York: Holt, 1943);
*Selected Poems* (New York: Knopf, 1945; London: Eyre & Spottiswoode, 1947; revised and enlarged edition, New York: Knopf, 1963; revised and enlarged again, New York: Knopf, 1969; London: Eyre & Spottiswoode, 1970);
*Poems and Essays* (New York: Vintage, 1955);
*Beating the Bushes: Selected Essays 1941-1970* (Norfolk, Conn.: New Directions, 1972);
*Selected Essays of John Crowe Ransom*, edited by Thomas Daniel Young and John Hindle (Baton Rouge: Louisiana State University Press, 1984).

OTHER: "Statement of Principles" and "Reconstructed but Unregenerated," in *I'll Take My Stand: The South and the Agrarian Tradition, by Twelve Southerners* (New York: Harper, 1930), pp. ix-xxi, 1-27;
"Criticism as Pure Speculation," in *The Intent of the Critic*, edited by Donald A. Stauffer (Princeton: Princeton University Press, 1941), pp. 91-124;
*The Kenyon Critics: Studies in Modern Literature from the Kenyon Review*, edited, with an introduction, by Ransom (Cleveland: World, 1951);
*Selected Poems of Thomas Hardy*, edited, with an introduction, by Ransom (New York: Macmillan, 1961).

PERIODICAL PUBLICATIONS: "Thoughts on the Poetic Discontent," *Fugitive*, 4 (June 1925): 63-64;
"Classical and Romantic," *Saturday Review of Literature*, 6 (14 September 1929): 125-127;
"The Arts and the Philosophers," *Kenyon Review*, 1 (Spring 1939): 194-199;
"Honey and Gall," *Southern Review*, 6 (Summer 1940): 2-19;
"Poetry: I, The Formal Analysis," *Kenyon Review*, 9 (Summer 1947): 436-456;
"Poetry: II, The Final Cause," *Kenyon Review*, 9 (Autumn 1947): 640-658;
"The Literary Criticism of Aristotle," *Kenyon Review*, 10 (Summer 1948): 382-402;
"William Wordsworth: Notes Toward an Understanding of Poetry," *Kenyon Review*, 12 (Summer 1950): 498-519;
"The Idea of a Literary Anthropologist and What He Might Say of the *Paradise Lost* of Milton," *Kenyon Review*, 21 (Winter 1959): 121-140.

Born in Pulaski, Tennessee, John Crowe Ransom grew up in the many small towns near Nashville that his father, John J. Ransom, served as a minister of the Methodist church. Educated at home until he was ten, Ransom entered public school in October 1898. In June 1903 he was graduated at the head of his class from the Bowen School in Nashville, and in September he entered Vanderbilt University. After two years he withdrew from the university because he was unwilling to continue accepting financial support that his father could not afford. He taught school for two years–at Taylorsville, Mississippi, High School (1905-1906) and Haynes-McLean School in Lewisburg, Tennessee (1906-1907)–before reentering Vanderbilt, from which he was graduated number one in his class with a major in Greek and Latin and a minor in philosophy on 16 June 1909. He served as senior master and co-principal of Haynes-McLean School during the following year. From the fall of 1910 until the spring of 1913 he was a Rhodes scholar at Christ Church College, Oxford University, where he read "The Greats" (the School of *Literae Humanitores*). During the summers he traveled extensively in the British Isles and on the Continent. The following year he taught Latin at the Hotchkiss School in Lakesville, Connecticut. In the fall of 1914 he joined the faculty of Vanderbilt University as instructor of English and remained there–except for service in the U.S. Army during World War I–advancing through the various academic ranks, until he moved to Kenyon College in the fall of 1937 as a professor of English. At Vanderbilt he was a prominent member of the Fugitive Poets and the Agrarians, and he became well known as one of the New Critics. At Kenyon he was soon promoted to Carnegie Professor of Poetry, and in 1939 he founded the *Kenyon Review,* which he edited for twenty years. For his writing he received many prizes and honors, including a Guggenheim Fellowship (1931), the Bollingen Prize in Poetry (1951), the Russell Loines Award for Poetry from the National Institute of Arts and Letters (1951), a Creative Arts Medal from Brandeis University (1958-1959), the National Book Award for the 1963 edition of *Selected Poems* (1964), election to the American Academy of Arts and Letters (1966), and the Emerson-Thoreau Medal (1968). After his retirement from Kenyon College in 1958 he taught and lectured at more than two hundred colleges and universities–including Har-

vard, Princeton, Yale, Chicago, Rice, Vanderbilt, Duke, Florida, Iowa, and Indiana. He died in Gambier, Ohio, about three months after his eighty-sixth birthday.

Many literary scholars proclaim John Crowe Ransom one of the most important literary figures of his generation, but there is some disagreement on the precise area in which his greatest contribution lies. Some believe, as Randall Jarrell has stated, that Ransom's poetry will be read as long as verse is regarded as a serious art because he composed "a handful of almost perfect lyrics." Allen Tate called him one of the "best elegiac poets in the language." Others have argued convincingly that Ransom's greatest contribution to American letters was in the field of literary criticism. They claim that no other American critic has advanced a more compelling argument for literature as a means of cognition. Ransom wrote in the introduction to *The World's Body* (1938): "The true poetry has no great interest in improving or idealizing the world, which it does well enough. It only wants to realize the world, to see it better. . . . We have elected to know the world through our science, . . . and by it we know the world only as a scheme of abstract conveniences. What we cannot know constitutionally as scientists is the world which is made of whole and indefeasible objects and this is the world which poetry recovers for us. Men become poets, or at least they read poets, in order to atone for having been hard theoretical scientists." This theoretical distinction between science and poetry is an important axiom in New Criticism and serves as the basis for Cleanth Brooks's definition of poetic language in the first chapter of his *The Well-Wrought Urn* (1947).

To know a poem, which Ransom later defined as a "precious object," one must be capable of "aesthetic experience." To use the work of art so that it "will restore the concrete particularities of the World's Body," one must learn to meditate it properly; that is, he must be impelled "neither to lay hands on the object immediately, nor to ticket it for tomorrow's outrage"; instead he must conceive of it "as having its existence." He must be capable of experiencing what Shopenhauer called "knowledge without desire."

During the academic year of 1926-1927, while Ransom was on leave from his teaching duties at Vanderbilt to write a book on aesthetics, he wrote Allen Tate a series of letters in which he explained the process by which he was attempting to differentiate between the quality of knowledge available from art and that which science reveals: "The art-thing sounds like the first immediate transcript of reality, but it isn't; it's a long way from the event. It isn't the raw stuff of experience. The passion in it has been mellowed down—emotion recollected in tranquility, etc. Above all things else, the core of experience in the record has been taken up into the sum total of things and in its relations there discovered are given the work of art." Here Ransom appears to combine Wordsworth's expressive theory of poetry with T. S. Eliot's objective theory of poetry.

In response to Tate's request for elaboration, Ransom wrote on 5 September 1926 a long letter on what he called "the three moments in the historical order of experience":

I. First Moment

. . . The first moment is the original experience–pure of intellectual content, unreflective, concrete, and singular; there are no distinctions, and the subject is identical with the Whole.

II. Second Moment

The moment after. This moment is specific for human experience as distinguished from the ideally animal experience. Biologically man is peculiar in that he must record and use his successive experiences; the beasts are not under this necessity; with them the experience is an end in itself. . . . in the second moment cognition takes place. . . . The feature of the second moment is it is now that the record must be taken of the first moment that has just transpired. This record proceeds inevitably by way of *concept* discovered in cognition. It is the beginning of science. Its ends are practical, but its means are *abstractions*; and these, it must be insisted, are subtractions from the whole. . . .

III. Third Moment

We become aware of the deficiency of the record. Most of the experience is quite missing from it. All our concepts and all our histories put together cannot add up into the wholeness with which we started out. . . . How can we get back into that first moment? By images. . . . When we make images . . . we are trying to reconstitute an experience we once had. . . . Only we can't quite reconstitute it. . . .

The images come out mixed and adulterated with concepts; but, he concludes, art is quite like nature, which is also a mixture. Man tries to re-

constitute the elusive first moment in all its concrete particularity through fancies or daydreams, dreams, religion, morals, and art. Ransom concluded his lengthy explication of his theory by offering again his definition of poetry, this time calling it the "exhibit of Opposition and at the same time Reconciliation between the conceptual or Formal and the Individual or Concrete." This definition is his earliest statement of the concept of "the Concrete Universal," which is developed in two essays in the 1940s and in his last published essay, written in 1970.

As he wrote to Tate, the "obvious fact" which years before had started him on this line of inquiry was his realization that the requirement of meter in poetry, an obvious example of the formal, "does not seem to impair the life and effectiveness of Concrete Experience. They coexist." The letter to Tate includes many of the critical ideas that would not receive formal expression until the publication of his well-known essays of the 1930s, 1940s, and 1950s: the insistence that aesthetic theory should have a firm ontological basis; that the material object is the "stuff" of poetry; that the essential nature of poetry resides in its dualism; that the poem can reconstitute the "fugitive first moment," the World's Body, through a combination of concept and image; and that the view of human experience presented by science, with its practical ends and abstract means, is less than complete. Only through art can human experience be fully realized.

During the 1930s and 1940s Ransom made many attempts to define that "precious object," which would restore the concrete particularities of the World's Body if one would consider it properly; that is, if he were impelled "neither to lay hands on the object immediately, nor to ticket it for tomorrow's outrage" but to "conceive it as having its own existence." In the preface to *The World's Body* Ransom also indicates that the "post-scientific poetry," to which he and his generation are attached, is the "act of a fallen mind." It is a poetry that attempts to "realize the world," not to "idealize it." Modern man has little knowledge of the world in which he lives except that which is revealed through scientific observation. His conception of the world is, therefore, faulty because it is incomplete. To view the world only in the manner of the scientist is to fail to realize its body and solid substance. If one is to know the world, "which is made of whole and indefeasible objects," he must recover it, through poetry, from his memory to which it has retired. Poetry, then,

*John Crowe Ransom, with Yvor Winters (left) and Allen Tate, at Kenyon College, 1949 (courtesy of Kenyon College Archives)*

is the only means through which one can know the world's body.

This argument is an obvious extension of the kind of speculation Ransom was engaged in when he tried to identify and define, in the letter to Tate, the "three moments" that make up the historical order of experience. In his view the only way in which the actual experience itself can be recovered in its totality is through art, dreams, or religious myth. The record made in the "second moment," by scientists and social scientists, is formed through the process of subtracting from the whole, by formulating concepts and abstract ideas derived from concentration on one aspect of the whole. When man realizes that his record of the experience is only a partial one, he may also understand that the elusive first moment can never be recovered through abstract speculation or philosophical synthesis. If he resorts to poetry as the means through which the experience is re-

constituted, he must deal with a mixed world, one composed of both ideas and images.

Ransom's continued interest in this mixed world led him, in some of his best-known and most influential essays, to discuss the nature and function of poetry, to differentiate among its several types, and to contrast its aims and purposes with those of science. As he covers again this now very familiar ground, it becomes abundantly clear that there is no fundamental change in his critical position. What seems a major shift of belief or opinion is usually an attempt to clarify a misunderstood statement by supplying additional details or, as is often the case, by changing his metaphor. In "Poetry: A Note in Ontology," first published in *American Review* (May 1934) and collected in *The World's Body,* he defines and ranks three kinds of poetry. The first, physical poetry of the sort the Imagists produced, intends to "present things in their thingness," and in this intention it is diametrically opposed to "that poetry which stands as firmly as it dares upon ideas." The image, Ransom argues, "cannot be dispossessed of primordial freshness, which idea can never claim." The image is in its "natural or wild state," where it has to be discovered; it is not made by man and operates according to the laws of its own nature. Man cannot "lay hold of [an] image and make it captive," as he can an idea, which Ransom defines as the "image with the character beaten out of it." Science can destroy the image, not as some think, through refutation, but by taming it and destroying its freedom through abstraction. Through the use of the so-called scientific method man can weaken his imagination to the extent that he can no longer "contemplate things in their rich and contingent materiality." As he had argued repeatedly over the years in his correspondence with Tate and others, in this essay Ransom insists that man is compelled to poetry through memory and dream; it follows, therefore, that art is "based on second love not first love." Through it, man attempts to return to something he has lost, to capture that elusive first moment, the experience itself in all its rich materiality. Ransom values physical poetry because it attempts to go beyond the abstractions of science by constant recourse to image, but it reproduces only a part of the experience; this is a "half poetry" because the emotional and intellectual content, the idea, has been removed from the image. To reconstitute the total experience requires a combination of image and idea.

If physical poetry is a "half poetry," the second kind, Platonic poetry, is "bogus poetry." It tries to pose as the real thing by hiding its ideas behind its images, but its images can always be translated into ideas as if to prove that nature is rational and can be possessed through logic. But the Platonic poet does not accept the basic principle of "the third moment": the world of ideas is not the original world of perception; therefore the whole and comprehensible object cannot be presented through logical statement. The original world of perception, the first moment, must be "experienced and cannot be reported." Through his false poetry the Platonist attempts to demonstrate that "images will prove an idea," and his images are employed merely "to illustrate ideas." At this point in the essay Ransom reiterates an argument first presented many years earlier. Man must "recant from his Platonics and turn back to things" if he would restore to poetry some of the vigor and strength it once possessed;

as he turns from his idealizing he must be fully aware of how deeply he has been affected by his excursion into Platonism.

In "Thoughts on the Poetic Discontent," published in the June 1925 issue of the *Fugitive*, he had argued that the mature attitude of man is flavored with irony and poetry, because he is reluctant to give up "the music and color" and the "romantic mystery" of his belief in the existence of a "mystical community," a union between subject and object, percept and concept, man and nature. This idea is restated in "Poetry: A Note in Ontology" in different language. Man's withdrawal from Platonism is neither easy nor complete. From this dualistic state, in which he is pulled in two directions simultaneously, comes the complex attitude which produces the aesthetic moment; an instant of "suspension between the Platonism in us, which is militant, always sciencing and devouring, and a starved inhibited aspiration towards innocence" which would like to "know the object as it might reveal itself." Thus the "poetic impulse is not free." Because it "means to reconstitute the world of perceptions," it stubbornly resists the pressures of science in order to enjoy its images. From this "adult mode" in which images and ideas vie for the attention of the mature man comes true poetry, and poetry is produced in that "curious moment of suspension" in which the imagination "brings out the original experience from the dark store room" and attempts to reconstitute an experience which we have allowed to become mutilated, abstracted, and universalized by the scientists, the social scientists, and the philosophers.

Out of this "mixed and complex" world comes true poetry. Ransom characterizes this "true poetry" as metaphysical poetry, although he admitted in a letter to Tate before the essay was published that the term was too specialized and restrictive. A distinguishing characteristic of this poetry is its use of the conceit, which Ransom says is a "meant metaphor," one that is "developed so literally it must be good" or "predicated so baldly that nothing else could be meant." In this metaphorical assertion a "miraculism" or "supernaturalism" occurs if the poet not only means what he says but compels the reader to believe what he has read. This miraculism comes as the result of the poet's having discovered "by analogy an identity between objects which is partial, though it should be considerable, and proceeds to an identification which is complete." From this kind of miraculism poetry derives its ontological significance because it makes available an order of knowledge that one can get from no other source. For it is "the poet and nobody else who gives to God a nature, a form, faculties, and a history." Without poetry to give God a body and a solid substance, He would remain the driest and deadest among Platonic ideas. Myths are "conceits, born of metaphors" and religions are "produced by poets and destroyed by naturalists."

In *The New Criticism* (1941) Ransom examines in detail and from a single point of view the critical principles of some of the most important critics of his time. He assesses the value of each critic's contribution by measuring it against his theory of the ontological critic, which had been evolving for many years but was fully developed for the first time in the last essay in this book. He approves of I. A. Richards's close attention to the concrete particularities of the poem, but he castigates him for not accepting the cognitive function of poetry. He calls William Empson, who "went to school" to Richards, "the closest and most resourceful reader that poetry has ever had" because he reacts perceptively and sensitively to the textual details of a poem. His most obvious weakness is his inclination to lose sight of the poem's basic argument. Although T. S. Eliot possesses a "critical sense which is expert and infallible," he is deficient in critical theory, and, like Richards, Eliot argues that poetry's main function is to release emotion, thus deemphasizing its cognitive function. Ransom approves of Yvor Winters's assertion that good poetry commands its readers' belief, but he feels that Winters fails to differentiate between the rational content of a poem and that of prose discourse.

Since none of these critics emphasizes sufficiently the essential duality of poetry, a point that Ransom had insisted upon for more than twenty years, he again attempts to identify poetic discourse by commenting on its odd structure, one which is not as "tight and precise on its logical side as a scientific prose structure generally is" but one which "imparts and carries along a great deal of irrelevant or foreign matter which is clearly not structural but even obstructive." Thus, he concludes, a poem must be regarded as having both a "loose logical structure" and an "irrelevant local texture." One way to identify the cognitive function of poetry is to examine the way in which the poem differs from logical discourse:

The structure proper is the prose of the poem, being a logical discourse of almost any kind, and dealing with almost any content suited to a logical discourse. The texture, likewise, seems to be of any real content that may be come upon, provided it is so free, unrestricted, and large that it cannot properly get into the structure. One guesses that it is an *order* of content rather than a *kind* of content that distinguishes texture from structure, and poetry from prose. At any rate, a moral content is a kind of content which has been suggested as the peculiar content of poetry, and it does not work; it is not really peculiar to poetry but perfectly available for prose; besides, it is not the content of a great deal of poetry. I suggest that the differentia of poetry as discourse is an ontological one. It treats an order of existence, a grade of objectivity, which cannot be treated in scientific discourse.

This should not prove unintelligible. We live in a world which must be distinguished from the world, or the worlds, for there are many of them, which we treat in our scientific discourses. They are its reduced, emasculated and docile versions. Poetry intends to recover the denser and more refractory original world which we know loosely through our perceptions and memories. By this supposition it is a kind of knowledge which is radically or ontologically distinct.

None of the literary critics whose work he has examined, Ransom concludes, gives "an ontological account" of poetry. The nearest anyone whom he has read has come to developing such a conception of poetry is Charles W. Morris, whose essays "Science, Art, and Technology" and "Aesthetics and the Theory of Signs" apply to art the semantic system he developed in *Foundations of the Theory of Signs* (1938). Although Morris comes close–only one more step would have "taken him to an ontological conception of poetry"–he does not go far enough to satisfy Ransom. Morris distinguishes three forms of discourse–science, art, and technology–and he identifies three dimensions of meaning: the semantical, the syntactical, and the pragmatical. This kind of distinction suggests the basic difference between art and science first recognized by the ancient Greeks: "art, like technology, is concerned with *making* something as well as *knowing* something; while pure science seems concerned only with knowing something." What poetry makes is the poem, which because it contains meter is a "manufactured form," a "special unit of discourse." Like science, Morris argues, art provides knowledge, but the knowledge produced by science differs from that available in art because science employs "symbols" which merely refer to other objects but art uses "icons" or images, which not only refer to other objects but resemble those objects. Thus the object symbolized by the scientific sign is abstract, "a single property or aspect of objects"; whereas the object symbolized by the aesthetic sign is the whole object. The scientific symbol refers to "man," but the aesthetic sign represents "this particular man." The aesthetic sign, as Ransom had been insisting for years, restores to an abstract item the "body from which it was taken."

With Morris's distinction between the aesthetic and the scientific sign, Ransom is, of course, in complete agreement. But why, he asks, is Morris content to stop with the rather vague statement that the "icon embodies some value property"? Why does he not proceed to the logical assertion that aesthetic discourse has a useful pragmatic function? To indicate how he thinks his questions should be answered, Ransom moves to his ontological argument by rephrasing the distinction between scientific and aesthetic discourse he had insisted on since the mid 1920s. Since the validity of scientific discourse depends upon its "semantical purity," it employs symbols which refer to an object specifically defined; and its reference is always limited and uniform. The icon of aesthetic discourse, on the other hand, refers always to the wholeness of an object and embodies the value property of the object represented; therefore it can neither be limited nor defined. The icon does not function with the logical exactness of the scientific symbol because it often digresses at many points from its "logical pattern." For this reason the full meaning of a poem is never included in its prose paraphrase. The world with which scientific discourse deals is always predictable, limited, and restrictive. The world of art cannot be restricted, and the icon used to represent it always attempts to give a sense of the actual object. Ransom thus reiterates the central point of the "Third Moment." Poetry intends not to issue some comment upon an experience but to reconstitute the experience itself. Scientific knowledge and aesthetic knowledge are not intended to replace each other. They are really alternate knowledges which should illuminate and complement each other. Science can never produce for us a world made of "whole

and indefeasible objects," but poetry can and does. The loose and imprecise poetic structure with its "irrelevant or foreign matter" is a means of acquiring an order of knowledge that we cannot know otherwise. "It would seem," Ransom concludes, "that science comes first with its highly selected rendering of a given reality, which consists in attending to some single one of its aspects; art comes afterwards, in what mood we may imagine, and attempts to restore the body which science has emptied."

Almost as soon as *The New Criticism* was published, Ransom wrote Tate of his dissatisfaction with the book. He saw immediately, he said, that he had "sacrificed the critics" in order to get his "own oar in." The book's chief fault is its lack of focus, its divided purpose. He had attempted to summarize the critical principles of four major critics and at the same time to develop his own theory of the nature and function of poetry. His sense of failure was so acute that he proposed to undertake immediately a new book in which he could develop in more detail his theory of aesthetics. He wished particularly to be able to pursue further his views of the nature of poetic discourse in order to indicate the specific qualities of structure and texture and to demonstrate the significance of their complex relationships in a poem. He was convinced, too, that *The New Criticism* failed to achieve another, and equally meaningful, objective. He had hoped to free from suspicion and "philosophical censorship" those critics who were doing the formal, analytical criticism essential to the delineation of the unique nature of the poetic discourse, those who were intent upon restoring poetry to a place of central importance in a society no longer aware of its significance.

The book Ransom proposed was never written, but during the next few years he published a series of essays devoted almost entirely to the single purpose of demonstrating how the critic can justify the existence of poetry in a society more and more dependent upon the quasi-knowledge of science. In the mid 1940s Ransom warned some of his fellow critics, whom he thought should take some new directions, that the "ingenious and sophisticated" literary masterpieces produced in the years immediately following World War I had been defined and mastered and were now available to the entire literary community. Although one need had been met, others remained. If literature was to be an important force in human affairs, the critics must continue their evaluations of older literatures in the light of modern standards, and they must intensify their studies of the "structural techniques of fiction" and "the direction of tropology of poetry." They must assist the reader in understanding the human purpose that drives the literary critic into the literary world of fantasy and imagination. To accomplish this purpose, whatever the particular area of their concern, they must help the reader perceive the reality of literary form, to become aware of its unique nature, to be conscious of how a poem or story functions.

Ransom insisted that no reader can derive from a poem all the meanings it embodies unless he is aware of the unique nature of the poetic structure. In their proper emphasis on the total connotation of words some commentators had failed to recognize sufficiently other essential aspects of the poem: "The detailed phrase is honored with the spread of its own meaning, though this meaning may be away from that of the poem as a whole. And the critic goes straight from one detail to another, in the manner of the bee who gathers honey from the several blossoms as he comes to them, without noticing the bush which supports all the blossoms. The poem is more generous than the bush in its capacity for bearing blossoms which are not alike but widely varied in size, fragrance, hue, and shape." Although many of the modern critics make the reader aware of the "exciting turns of poetic language," some of them do not reveal the poem's true nature because they are "careless of the theoretical constitution of poetry." They reveal the textural richness of the poem but neglect its basic structure.

During the last decade of his editorship of *Kenyon Review* Ransom produced some of his most important critical writing, essays which show his continued preoccupation with the unique structure of poetic discourse and demonstrate the remarkable consistency of his critical position over a period of fifty years. In many of these essays he covers much of the ground he has been over before as he tries to clear up misunderstood statements or badly expressed concepts. His definition of a poem, however, is unchanged, even in language; it remains a "logical structure having a local texture." In an essay on Thomas Hardy—first published in the 12 May 1952 issue of the *New Republic* and revised and collected in *Poems and Essays* (1955), he indicates his unhappiness with this two-fold division of the poem by presenting its "three dimensions": "First the plot, or argument, a human representation struck off smartly, developed clearly and rounded off to a

nicety. Then the meters . . . and finally, the poetic language, the flowering habit of a thing that is alive, displaying its grace generally and coming into intermittent focus in special configurations of leaf or blossom." Despite the differences in terminology and the obvious intention to give more emphasis to meter this statement adds little to his assertion that a poem has two kinds of meanings: the "ostensible argument" (the structure) which may be reduced to prose, and the "tissue of meaning" (texture), which may not. Again he insists that although a poem is not "included in its paraphrase," it must "include its own paraphrase." In spite of the protests of some critics that this structure-texture formulation is too near the false division of the poem into form and content, Ransom reiterates his conviction that the poetic discourse has a logical structure which can be rendered in a prose paraphrase. Such an exercise is "useful" and "reputable," he argues, because it "straightens out the text and prunes meaning down," so that the critic can demonstrate that the poem is "decent enough to make formal sense." Almost without explanation, though he returns to this point in a later essay, he divides his "structure" into "plot" and "meter," but with the exception of meter, "plot" retains all the characteristics formerly lodged in "structure" and "poetic language" replaces "texture." He suggests that the structure-texture dualism may be explained in terms of Freud's discussion of the ego and the id. The "thought work" in a poem, its structure, belongs to the ego, but the "interpolated material which does not relate to the argument" is the work of the id. "A powerful sensibility is recording in the poem," he reminds his reader, "and the result might be a tropical wilderness of dense figurations; therefore humanly a waste, a nothing; but an equally powerful scheme of order is working there, too, to manage the richness of sense." A poem may be regarded, therefore, as a creation conceived under both sensibility and intelligence acting in "opposed parts," like counterpoint in music.

Two of Ransom's most significant essays are those which he published in the mid 1950s on the concrete universal. Although less an essay than a series of partially developed reflections on the subject, the first of these, "The Concrete Universal: Observation on the Understanding of Poetry, I" (first published in the Autumn 1954 issue of the *Kenyon Review* and collected in *Selected Essays*, 1984), begins with W. K. Wimsatt's statement that a "poem is a structure which may be regarded as a Concrete Universal." This definition of poetic discourse Ransom finds only partially acceptable, as he does Hegel's understanding of poetry. Ransom agrees, he says, with Hegel's argument that the "author of the poem is Spirit residing. . . . in the poet and identical with that Spirit of the Universe which is God or that Spirit of History which continually creates in order to objectify itself." The amplitude of this Spirit, therefore, is so great that it can be expressed only through the "plenitude of concreteness" and not through abstract scientific concepts. He cannot accept, however, Hegel's argument that poetic language is "perfect Synthesis of the Thesis (or Universal) and the Antithesis (or Concrete)," that the concrete is wholly assimilated in the universal. To accept such a statement, Ransom insists, is to fail to recognize that the "concrete detail is partly extraneous to the abstract universal." The logical argument of a poem never incorporates within itself all the irrelevant textual details; therefore the universal never quite grasps the concrete and the prose paraphrase is never equivalent to the poem.

This discussion of the concrete universal leads him not only to reassert his belief in the significance of poetry in a world almost completely dominated by science but also to attempt again to define the unique nature of the poem, this time by describing how language functions in its development: "about fifteen years ago I was thinking of the poem as having a logical structure or framework, and a texture whose character was partly irrelevant to the logical form and purpose. My texture in particular has given offense, and the fact is that I had no sooner uttered it than it struck me as a flat and inadequate figure for that vital and easily felt part of the poem which we associate peculiarly with poetic language. I wish now to recast my definition entirely, though I shall only employ another figure whose disabilities I am aware of in advance. . . . Suppose we say a poem is an organism. Then it has a physiology. We will figure its organs, and to me it seems satisfactory if we say there are three: the head, the heart, and the feet. In this organism the organs work all at the same time, but the peculiarity of the joint production is that it still consists of the products of the organs working individually." All of these organs work together to produce a poem, but each retains its individual character. Each speaks but in a different language: "the head in an intellectual language, the heart in an affective language and the feet in a rhythmical language." On the intellectual level the poem is a logical whole, with a beginning, a middle, and an end, as well as whatever connective devices are needed to suggest relationships among these various parts. But in addition to this intellectual level, which he had formerly referred to as the structure, the poem has a cluster of rich particulars which evoke a variety of responses in its readers. Many modern critics focus so much of their attention upon the richness of the particular, upon the individual phrase and the specific figure, that they leave the impression that a poem cannot be perceived of as a complete whole. It can, but only if one remains constantly aware of the unique nature of the poetic discourse. Although the three organs of a poem speak different languages and retain their individual voices, they blend to form one sound. They work together to produce one poem, but the unity of a poem is as that of a "democratic government" not that of a "totalitarian state." A poem, he says in another essay, "Criticism as Pure Speculation" (first published in *The Intent of the Critic*, 1941), is like a house with the paint, paper and tapestry comparable to the texture and the roof and beams to the structure. He does not concede for the poem a view of totality that would make it operate as a machine does, for to allow this concession would force him to admit that a poem is a scientific universal in which the concrete particular is assimilated in the abstract universal. Instead he insists that the essential unity of a poem exists in the interrelationships of its individual parts.

This statement is the germ of Ransom's argument in his second essay on the Concrete Universal (first published in the *Kenyon Review*, Summer 1955 and collected in *Poems and Essays*) in which he demonstrates why he regards Kant, and not Hegel, as his mentor. A universal, as Hegel used the term, is "any idea in the mind which proposes a little universe or organized working combination of parts" in order to attempt to produce a single effect. The universal, which is an idea, a design as it exists in the understanding, creates this single impression only when each part performs its several duties, and it becomes a concrete universal when it is actually working. A chemical formula, a recipe, a blueprint or even Newman's idea of a university may be considered examples of universals. There are two kinds of concrete universals: (1) those of applied science in which there is "not one necessary part missing; nor one unnecessary part showing," each part acting precisely as it should; and (2) those of the arts, of poetry, which do not satisfy an organic need and are not located in the "animal perspective of human nature."

From Kant's view of the concrete universal Ransom learned to distinguish between the different kinds of universals: the scientific universal has a practical end in mind and will not hesitate to alter the materials of nature until they fit a preconceived concept. The critic accepting this view of the concrete universal would insist that the "Concrete is used so completely in the service of Universal that there is no remainder." The concrete particulars of the poem are completely integrated into the abstract universal. Poetry, however, is a moral universal and differs radically from the scientific universal: "the moral Universal of the poem does not use nature as a means; it goes out into nature not as a predatory conqueror and despoiler, but as an inquirer, to look at nature as nature naturally is and see what its reception there may be." The moral universal does not go to nature, as the scientific universal does, to "ransack for materials which have already been prescribed." For this reason the critic should not expect the "unpredictable and highly particular details" of the region of nature used in the poem to "enter precisely and without remainder into the formal universal." The pure universal, being a concept in the mind, will not stand confrontation with the actual world and will always appear fragmentary and distorted in the light of the world's unpredicated and phenomenal mystery. The complete realization of this pure universal, only a portion of which is included in the scientific universal, is the concrete universal. This concrete universal may be found in poetry of the right kind: not didactic verse, which tells us how to act, nor in that verse which attempts to prescribe a specific mode of thought, but in the poetry which assists the reader in knowing the world. In poetry of this type the imagination, through metaphor, makes the pure universal which is abstract and conceptual, perceptual and concrete: the universal is referred to nature and particularized, given sensuous detail through this reference. Nature is, therefore, an essential element for poetry, but the organization of a poem does not require that the logical plan of the poem be "borne out perfectly in the sensuous detail which puts it into action."

Ransom's lack of sympathy for the rational monism of Hegel and his followers did not diminish as the years passed, and his last published essay was a third article titled "The Concrete Uni-

versal" (first published in *Beating the Bushes*, 1972). When this essay appeared, he was still intrigued by the implications of a phrase "in which two terms radically opposed must continue leaning upon each other till they fall hopelessly apart." The phrase suggests a union of the individual or particular and the abstract, and Ransom still insists that it cannot be made to work "naturally and meaningfully." Because it is "hopelessly abstract" and "composed of mere concepts," the scientific universal can only hope to keep what it "wants of the World" and to reject more than it takes. The scientific universal cannot hope to represent completely those occasions "when the world somewhere seems possessed and sustained through and through by the concretions of the spirit," when a "natural landscape is utterly beautiful, with every feature adapted to the common tone," when "there is realized beside some hearth a scene of perfect familial accord," or when "a whole people is exalted in a moment of crisis by the consciousness of serving a just state." Simply defined, Ransom concludes, a poem is "an organism in action," and he again labels its organs as the head, the heart, and the feet. Although each organ plays its separate part, it must reconcile its differences with the other two in order to form a harmonious whole. The three organs "are harmonizing and vocalizing all at the same time," but, he insists, the poem is both a "verbal and vocal job"; therefore this vocalism is not "like the outpourings of operatic or instrumental music." The function of each organ is distinct and always identifiable even in a finished poem: "The head has to be the intellectual organ, and especially attentive to keeping the logical clarity of the text, and the finality of the conclusion. It has as much conscience in this respect as prose has, and is slow to waive its simple purity; for instance if the heart tries its patience by wanting to use words and phrases which are fateful and strange but too rich and rare for the common barbarian reader. But just often enough it is possible to persuade the honest head that a quotidian language will not do for good verse; till the head finally concurs; and is rewarded by receiving some rare intimations of immortality." But this exchange among the head and the heart is always imperfect; furthermore the feet—the meters, rhymes, and rhythms—always make their demands and often at the expense of the head and the heart. Thus the concrete particulars are never completely consumed in an abstract universal.

To the end of his life, therefore, Ransom continued to argue for the essential duality of poetry. He differs most obviously from the positivists, who, in their attempts to show that poetry makes positive sense, accept the obvious prose argument of the poem as its center and contend that the multiplicity of suggestions in the metaphor form another argument which is also true and useful ("Positive and Near Positive Aesthetics"–first published in the Summer 1943 issue of the *Kenyon Review* and collected in *Beating the Bushes*). To accept this position, Ransom insists, is to "convert poetry into prose, and to contend that its radical departure from prose is only illusory." Although he continues to argue that poetic texture is "poetic and irremediably, not positive," he also insists that this texture attaches itself "technically to a positive center which it does not destroy." The latter part of this argument has not been well received by other critics, particularly Cleanth Brooks, who is concerned that the kind of duality Ransom defines is too near the age-old dichotomy of form and content and can lead to the erroneous conclusion that a poem consists of a "prose sense decorated by a sensuous imagery." To Brooks, structure is a "structure of meanings, evaluations, and interpretations" and its unity consists of "balancing and harmonizing connotations, attitudes and meanings." This attitude, Ransom reasons, denies the poem any formal shape except that which might evolve from the unfolding of its metaphorical energy. Such a definition does not embrace "that character in the poem which makes it a discourse." He repeats his assertion that a poem is a "species of Aristotelian discourse," with a beginning, middle, and end, if the argument is sizable enough to worry about such things.

For Ransom the poem remained "the great paradox, a construct looking two ways, with logic trying to dominate the metaphors and metaphors trying to dominate the logic." To this contrary twosome he added meter to give the poem "the form of a trinitarian existence" and to make its creation dependent upon a tenuous compromise between meter and sense, image and idea, metaphor and argument. From this combination of heterogeneous qualities comes almost the only defense man has against the exploits of science and technology, for poetry is one of the few means through which man can reconstitute the qualitative particularity of experience. It assists man in recalling the "body and solid substance of the world" from the "fulness of memory" to which it has retired.

**Letters:**

*Selected Letters of John Crowe Ransom,* edited by Thomas Daniel Young and George Core (Baton Rouge & London: Louisiana State University Press, 1985).

**Bibliography:**

Thomas Daniel Young, *John Crowe Ransom: An Annotated Bibliography* (New York & London: Garland, 1982).

**Biography:**

Thomas Daniel Young, *Gentleman in a Dustcoat: A Biography of John Crowe Ransom* (Baton Rouge: Louisiana State University Press, 1976).

**References:**

Thornton H. Parsons, *John Crowe Ransom* (New York: Twayne, 1969);

Thomas Daniel Young, ed., *John Crowe Ransom: Critical Essays and a Bibliography* (Baton Rouge: Louisiana State University Press, 1968).

**Papers:**

The libraries at Vanderbilt University, Kenyon College, Princeton University, Yale University, Indiana University, Stanford University, and Washington University have collections of Ransom's papers.

# J. Saunders Redding

*(13 October 1906- )*

Pancho Savery
*University of Massachusetts-Boston*

BOOKS: *To Make a Poet Black* (Chapel Hill: University of North Carolina Press, 1939);

*No Day of Triumph* (New York & London: Harper, 1942);

*Stranger and Alone* (New York: Harcourt, Brace, 1950);

*They Came in Chains: Americans From Africa* (Philadelphia: Lippincott, 1950; revised, 1973);

*On Being Negro in America* (Indianapolis: Bobbs-Merrill, 1951);

*An American in India: A Personal Report on the Indian Dilemma and the Nature of Her Conflicts* (Indianapolis: Bobbs-Merrill, 1954);

*The Lonesome Road: The Story of the Negro's Part in America* (New York: Doubleday, 1958);

*The Negro* (Washington, D.C.: Potomac Books, 1967);

*Of Men and the Writing of Books* (Lincoln, Pa.: Vail Memorial Library, Lincoln University, 1969);

*Negro Writing and the Political Climate* (Lincoln, Pa.: Vail Memorial Library, Lincoln University, 1970).

OTHER: *Reading for Writing*, edited by Redding and Ivan E. Taylor (New York: Ronald Press, 1952);

"The Negro Writer and His Relationship to His Roots," in *The American Negro Writer and His Roots* (New York: American Society of African Culture, 1960), pp. 1-8;

"The Alien Land of Richard Wright," in *Soon, One Morning: New Writing by American Negroes 1940-1962*, edited by Herbert Hill (New York: Knopf, 1963), pp. 48-59;

"The Negro Writer and American Literature," by Redding, and "Reflections on Richard Wright: A Symposium on an Exiled Native Son," by Redding, Herbert Hill, Horace Cayton, and Arna Bontemps, in *Anger, and Beyond: The Negro Writer in the United States*, edited by Hill (New York: Harper & Row, 1966), pp. 1-19, 196-212;

"*The Souls of Black Folk:* Du Bois' masterpiece lives on," in *Black Titan: W. E. B. Du Bois, An Anthology by the Editors of Freedomways*, edited by John Henrik Clarke, Esther Jackson, Ernest Kaiser, and J. H. O'Dell (Boston: Beacon Press, 1970), pp. 47-51;

*Cavalcade: Negro American Writing from 1760 to the Present*, edited by Redding and Arthur P. Davis (Boston: Houghton Mifflin, 1971);

Faith Berry, ed., *Good Morning Revolution: The Uncollected Social Protest Writings by Langston Hughes*, foreword by Redding (Westport, Conn.: Lawrence Hill, 1973), pp. ix-x;

"Portrait Against Background," in *A Singer In the Dawn: Reinterpretations of Paul Laurence Dunbar*, edited by Jay Martin (New York: Dodd, Mead, 1975), pp. 39-44.

PERIODICAL PUBLICATIONS: "Playing the Numbers," *North American Review*, 238 (December 1934): 533-542;

"A Negro Looks at This War," *American Mercury*, 55 (November 1942): 585-592;

"A Negro Speaks for His People," *Atlantic Monthly*, 171 (March 1943): 58-63;

"The Black Man's Burden," *Antioch Review*, 3 (December 1943): 587-595;

"Here's a New Thing Altogether," *Survey Graphic*, 33 (August 1944): 358-359, 366-367;

"The Negro Author: His Publisher, His Public, and His Purse," *Publishers' Weekly*, 147 (24 March 1945): 1284-1288;

"Portrait: W. E. Burghardt Du Bois," *American Scholar*, 18 (Winter 1948-1949): 93-96;

"American Negro Literature," *American Scholar*, 18 (Spring 1949): 137-148;

"The Negro Writer—Shadow and Substance," *Phylon*, 11 (Fourth Quarter 1950): 371-373;

"No Envy, No Handicap," *Saturday Review*, 37 (13 February 1954): 237;

"Up from Reconstruction," *Nation*, 179 (4 September 1954): 196-197;

"Tonight for Freedom," *American Heritage,* 9 ( June 1958): 52-55, 90;

"Contradiction de la litterature negro-americaine," *Presence Africaine,* nos. 27-28 (August-November 1959): 11-15;

"Negro Writing in America," *New Leader,* 43 (16 May 1960): 8-10;

"In the Vanguard of Civil Rights," *Saturday Review,* 44 (12 August 1961): 34;

"J. S. Redding Talks About African Literature," *AMSAC Newsletter,* 5 (September 1962): 1, 4-6;

"Home to Africa," *American Scholar,* 32 (Spring 1963): 183-191;

"Sound of Their Masters' Voices," *Saturday Review,* 46 (29 June 1963): 26;

"Modern African Literature," *CLA Journal,* 7 (March 1964): 191-201;

"Man Against Myth and Malice," *Saturday Review,* 47 (9 May 1964): 48-49;

"The Problems of the Negro Writer," *Massachusetts Review,* 6 (Autumn-Winter 1964-1965): 57-70;

"The Task of the Negro Writer As Artist: A Symposium," *Negro Digest,* 14 (April 1965): 66, 74;

"Since Richard Wright," *African Forum,* 1 (Spring 1966): 21-31;

"A Survey: Black Writers' Views on Literary Lions and Values," *Negro Digest,* 17 ( January 1968): 12;

"Equality and Excellence: The Eternal Dilemma," *William and Mary Review,* 6 (Spring 1968): 5-11;

"Literature and the Negro," *Contemporary Literature,* 9 (Winter 1968): 130-135;

"The Black Youth Movement," *American Scholar,* 38 (Autumn 1969): 584-587;

"The Negro Writer: The Road Where," *Boston University Journal,* 17 (Winter 1969): 6-10;

"The Black Revolution in American Studies," *American Studies,* 9 (Autumn 1970): 3-9.

J. Saunders Redding was not the first to write a book on Afro-American literature. His work was preceded by that of Benjamin Brawley (1910), Vernon Loggins (1931), Nick Aaron Ford (1936), and Sterling Brown (1937). Nevertheless *To Make a Poet Black* (1939), his first book and his only one of literary criticism, does bear the distinction of being the first comprehensive serious critical work devoted exclusively to Afro-American literature up to the Harlem Renaissance written by an Afro-American. Redding is not solely a pio-

neer in the field; decades after his initial critical statements were made his work is still the standard by which others are measured. Apart from *To Make a Poet Black* Redding's literary criticism appears in articles published in many literary and scholarly journals. In these pieces he has both examined more recent, post-Harlem Renaissance literature and refined his opinions on earlier works.

Redding has often been called a conservative, and he is one, if he is being compared to such radicals as Amiri Baraka, who has called Redding's views "basically supportive of the oppression of the Afro-American nation and white chauvinism in general." However Redding's views are not so easily adaptable to one-word generalizations. On the one hand he has championed Afro-American literature as a subject for serious academic study; on the other he has criticized much of that literature for its artistic failures. He has also refused to divide literature in accordance with the diametrically opposed functions of art and propaganda. He believes that literature has a social function, and he castigates writers who attempt to ignore their blackness. Yet he is opposed to black studies programs that attempt to exclude whites. Redding is an integrationist who has defended Paul Robeson in print, praised *The Autobiography of Malcolm X* (1965), and disagreed with those, such as Richard Wright, who have suggested that Afro-American literature will merge with the mainstream on the day of the full integration of American society.

Redding's accomplishment has been threefold. He has been Afro-American literature's primary literary historian; in *To Make a Poet Black* and subsequent essays, Redding has told the story of black literature in America from its beginnings to the contemporary period. He has been Afro-American literature's first great scholar-critic, and thus he adds to his literary history scholarly principles and standards by which to evaluate the writings. Finally Redding has been indefatigable in his insistence that Afro-American literature be seen within the context of American literature and that to fail to do so is to do a disservice to both.

Redding was born in Wilmington, Delaware, in 1906 to Lewis Alfred and Mary Ann Redding, the third child of seven in what he calls "an upper-class Negro family." His paternal grandmother had been a slave, but his parents were Howard University graduates. They educated him at home until he was old enough for the third grade. Particularly stressing what he calls in *No*

*Day of Triumph* (1942), "the declining art of oratory," his schoolteacher father and his mother filled the home with "shouted recitations of poems and Biblical passages and orations from Bryan, Phillips, and John Brown." His mother loved to read aloud from Hans Christian Andersen, Henry Wadsworth Longfellow, Shakespeare, and Paul Laurence Dunbar, who was a particular favorite. Dunbar's signed photograph hung over the Redding mantel, and Dunbar's former wife, the writer Alice Dunbar Nelson, was not only a family friend but became Redding's English teacher at Howard High School, which, until 1951, was the only high school in the state that would admit blacks.

During high school, speech and debate were among Redding's specialties, and he recounts a scene in *No Day of Triumph* where he won a debate over a clearly superior speaker who happened to be much darker than Redding. This "stigma of blackness" had also been exercised in his own family. His mother, for instance, was "in rage and tears" the day another black family moved into the neighborhood; and his father, who had become secretary of the Wilmington branch of the NAACP and founder of the first YMCA for blacks in Wilmington, spent much of his life moving with "defensive caution" among the whites with whom he lived and worked.

After graduation from high school in 1923 Redding spent one year at Lincoln University in Pennsylvania and then followed in the footsteps of his older brother Louis by attending Brown University in Rhode Island. Redding graduated with a B.A. in 1928, and he received a master's degree, also from Brown, in 1932. He taught at Morehouse College in Atlanta from 1928 to 1931, and in 1929 he married Esther Elizabeth James. He studied at Columbia University from 1932 to 1934 and then took a lecturer's position at Kentucky's Louisville Municipal College from 1934 to 1936. In 1935 his first son was born. From 1936 to 1938 he was chairman of the English department at Southern University in Baton Rouge, Louisiana. It was at Southern that he began work on *To Make a Poet Black* (1939). In 1938 Redding moved to North Carolina where he taught at Elizabeth City State Teachers College until 1943. Here he wrote the acclaimed, autobiographical *No Day of Triumph*. In 1943 Redding took a position as professor of English and creative writing at Hampton Institute in Virginia. His second son was born in 1945. He remained there until 1966, having served during this period as a visiting full professor at his alma mater, Brown. From 1970 Redding has been at Cornell University, where he is now Ernest I. White Professor Emeritus of American Studies and Humane Letters. During his career Redding served as director of the division of research and publication of the National Endowment for the Humanities (1966-1970). He has received a Rockefeller Foundation Fellowship (1941), the Mayflower Award for *No Day of Triumph* (1942), and two Guggenheim Fellowships (1944, 1959). He lectured for the State Department in India (1952), and taught as an American Society of African Culture (AMSAC) exchange lecturer in Africa.

*To Make a Poet Black* attempts "to bring together certain factual material and critical opinion[s] on American Negro literature in a sort of history of Negro thought in America" through the 1930s. Redding declares in a preface that "literary expression for the Negro has not been and is not wholly now an art." The reason is that "from the very beginning the literature of the Negro has been literature either of purpose or necessity" and that as such, "it appeals as much to the cognitive as to the conative and affective side of man's being." This view makes writing about such literature "a practical, as opposed to a purely speculative, exercise." The literature he discusses is hampered both by its ends of being motivated by the desire to adjust to the American environment and by its means of having to satisfy the different demands of the white and black audiences. One or both of these problems affects every writer but two in Redding's survey.

Devoting the first chapter to what he calls "The Forerunners," Redding assesses three early black American writers. The eighteenth-century author Jupiter Hammon is found guilty of "doggerel," "homely thoughts," and "limping phrases," and is one whose "life was motivated by the compulsion of obedience to his earthly and his heavenly master." His apologies for slavery link him to late-eighteenth-century poet Phillis Wheatley, whom Redding finds, despite her superior talent, affected by a "negative, bloodless, unracial quality . . . that makes her seem superficial, especially to members of her own race." In contrast to Hammon and Wheatley, nineteenth-century writer George Moses Horton, himself a slave, protested his own enslavement, not that of his race. His importance, nonetheless, as a herald "of the minstrel poets . . . outweighs whatever of intrinsic poetical value his poems possess." Thus Redding finds that Hammon and Horton lack craft, while the skilled Wheatley lacks "enthusiasm" and fails to appeal to the emotions.

In his second chapter, "Let Freedom Ring," Redding notes an increase in literary ability in the writers of the mid-nineteenth century. However, for all their talent, Charles Redmond and Frederick Douglass are deemed primarily orators who fit their art to the purpose of ending slavery and gaining rights for Afro-Americans; William Wells Brown is found to be a better historian than novelist or playwright; and the verse of James Madison Bell is dismissed as "inspirational." Redding does comment positively on the poetry of Frances Ellen Watkins Harper, whom he calls "a trailblazer, hacking, however ineffectually, at the dense forest of propaganda." She gave in, however, Redding finds, to her audience's demand for sentimentality. Still she anticipated James Weldon Johnson in her use of dialectal patterns over dialect language and thus avoided the problems of the later Paul Laurence Dunbar. She also foreshadowed Charles Chesnutt in her call for Afro-American writers to encompass "more than ourselves in our present plight." Nonetheless Redding dismisses most black American writers before 1890 because they "often sacrificed beauty of thought and of truth—the specific goals of art—to the exigencies of their particular purposes." Redding does note, however, the sociopolitical function of these early works: they "created in the Negro a core of racial pride without which no great endeavor is possible." That is, while Redding is saying that this literature is not art, he is not suggesting that politics are out of place in either literature or art. He defines art in "Negro Writing in America" (1960) as "an intuitive revelation of the multiform life of man." Literature that is "in the exclusive employ of a set of social and political moralities" cannot reveal the multiform.

In "Adjustment," the third chapter of *To Make a Poet Black*, Redding addresses writers from the turn-of-the-century, a time he would call in "American Negro Literature" (*American Scholar*, 1949) one of the three periods when Afro-American literature was "done nearly to death," largely out of audience indifference. In this chapter Paul Laurence Dunbar emerges as the most important writer before the Harlem Renaissance. His writing displays craft, lyrical beauty, and humor. He neither ignored the realities of being black, as had Wheatley, nor overemphasized them propagandistically as had Brown and Douglass. Dunbar is Redding's prime example of

*J. Saunders Redding (courtesy of the author)*

an Afro-American writer afflicted by the "necessity of ends." According to Redding, "No Negro of finer artistic spirit has been born in America, and none whose fierce, secret energies were more powerfully directed toward breaking down the vast wall of emotional and intellectual misunderstanding within which he, as poet, was immured." Redding sympathetically analyzes Dunbar's fiction and poetry and notes the conflicting demands put upon him by white America's preference for his dialect poems—William Dean Howells publicly endorsed and promoted them—while black America, "taught to scorn all dialect as a stamp of the buffoon," revered Dunbar's work in "pure English." Redding sees Dunbar as Frances Harper's heir: the first partially successful example of an "awakening artistic consciousness." However, he was destroyed, Redding feels, by the needs of his dual audience. Dunbar gets more detailed treatment than anyone else in *To Make a Poet Black*, both because of his obvious talents and the tragedy of their not being fully realized and because of Redding's personal associations with him. In "Portrait Against Background," a lecture given at the Dunbar Centenary Conference in 1972, Redding said, "Dunbar's search for identity was never completely successful because society never acknowledged him as the person he thought he was."

Among the other writers discussed in "Adjustment," Charles Chesnutt is praised for *The Conjure Woman* (1899), "which proved that the Negro could be made the subject of serious esthetic treatment without the interference of propaganda; and it proved that the Negro creative artist could submerge himself objectively in his material." However Redding believes that Chesnutt fell from greatness when he discarded "folk material." Chesnutt was originally not known to be black; when he revealed that he was black and attempted to override the dialect tradition, no one read his work. W. E. B. Du Bois's quasi-autobiographical collection of observations on black life, *The Souls of Black Folk: Essays and Sketches* (1903), had not yet found an audience.

Du Bois was writing in the period when Afro-American literature was being countered in the literary marketplace by the works of such writers as Thomas Dixon and Thomas Nelson Page who exploited the stereotypes of blacks on stage, the popular "coon" songs, and the conservative political tenets of such prominent figures as Booker T. Washington. In reaction to such views, at one extreme, Du Bois was willing to take on Washington, Redding says, growing "to fullness as a writer, fusing into a style that is beautifully lucid the emotional power that later made his *Crisis* editorials unsurpassed by any writing of their kind." Where Du Bois had previously believed that ignorance alone was the obstacle to social reform, and that it could be dispelled by scientific truth, Redding says in a 1961 introduction to a new edition of *The Souls of Black Folk* that the book not only represented a new direction for Du Bois but heralded a new approach to social reform, a "patriotic, nonviolent activism which achieved its first success" in the Montgomery bus boycott. Redding credits Du Bois with fixing the moment when blacks "began to reject the idea of the world's belonging to white people only" and to see themselves as "a potential force in the organization of society." Redding calls *The Souls of Black Folk* classic because it expresses "the soul of one people in a time of great stress and [shows] its kinship with the timeless soul of all mankind." Redding does feel, however, that after 1909, Du

Bois became "an avowed propagandist" who "did not hoodwink himself that propaganda could successfully masquerade as art." Thus writing that is directed toward "utilitarian" ends, even if "[o]nly Carlyle stands comparison," is not art. At the other extreme of black writing in this period, Redding singles out William Stanley Braithwaite, Joseph Cotter, Sr., Alice Dunbar, and Angelina Weld Grimké as writers who wrote "without any thought of their racial background" and who "developed a sort of dilettantism."

Redding considers the Harlem Renaissance in his final chapter, "Emergence of the New Negro." After a brief history of the period 1915 to 1920, when half a million blacks moved from the South to the North and, with "Du Bois as chief architect, had reared a thought structure," he gives this "movement" mixed marks. He praises the fact that Afro-American writers, despite being stimulated by the interest of white America, did not merely produce what whites wanted. He singles out the "proud defiance" of Claude McKay's "If We Must Die" and "To the White Fiends," and the "hot, colorful, primitive" moods of Jean Toomer's *Cane* (1923). He finds little of value, however, in the middle-class Jessie Redmon Fauset or the "artificial. . . . . effete and bloodless poetry" of Countee Cullen. Redding even goes so far as to call Cullen "half a poet" who is "untouched by his times."

Redding finds fault with the tone of futility, pessimism, and atavism in many of the writers of this period. Although he praises Langston Hughes for his experiments with form and sees him as Cullen's opposite, and although he coins the contemporary use of the word "soul" in connection with him, he still feels that Hughes's poetic work in the blues and shout is limited. Redding says that in his writing Hughes feels "but he does not think," and this results in "naivete." Redding finds "futility" in Hughes's fiction, "blank despair" in Nella Larsen, and the "delineation of the defeatist attitude" in Cullen, McKay, Eric Walrond, Wallace Thurman, and Walter White. Other than *Cane*, George Schuyler's *Black No More: Being an Account of the Strange and Wonderful Workings of Science in the Land of the Free* (1931) and Rudolph Fisher's *The Walls of Jericho* (1928) are the only novels Redding praises. Unfortunately none of these writers wrote another major novel.

Redding also criticizes the Harlem Renaissance for its exclusive attention on urban life in general and Harlem life in particular, and the resulting "literature of escape": literature filled with "whores, pimps, sweetmen; *bistros,* honky-tonks, spidernests; the perverse, the perverted, the psychopathic." Nevertheless Redding's treatment of the period ends on a positive note. Looking to the future, he sees as most important for Afro-American artistic development a turn "back from the urban and sophisticated to the earthy exuberance of . . . kinship with the earth, the fields, the suns and rains of the South." He judges James Weldon Johnson's treatment of folk material in the prefaces to *The Book of American Negro Poetry* (1922) and *The Book of American Negro Spirituals* (1925) as the critical cornerstones for a truly Afro-American art; he finds Johnson's poetry in *God's Trombones: Seven Negro Sermons in Verse* (1927), along with Toomer's *Cane,* a pointing of the way.

Most important for Redding, however, is the work of two of the younger writers who were then at the beginning of their careers: Sterling Brown and Zora Neale Hurston. Only their work, according to Redding, was wholly independent of the "literature of necessity" and encompassed "a spiritual and physical return to the earth." In light of their work subsequent to 1939, and of Afro-American literature in general, Redding has proven to be extraordinarily prescient. The work of such writers as Ralph Ellison, Alice Walker, Toni Morrison, and Ernest J. Gaines would have been virtually inconceivable without the pioneering efforts of Brown and Hurston.

In later years Redding revised his views on the figures of the Harlem Renaissance, which he says in "American Negro Literature" was one of those times when Afro-American literature was nearly done to death. Instead of indifference, however, the weapon was "the unbounded enthusiasm of its well-meaning friends." Surprisingly, he does not mention Brown or Hurston, but focuses on Richard Wright. Redding calls him a new kind of writer for precisely the same reason he praised Brown and Hurston: he extricates himself from the dilemma of writing for two audiences.

In *The American Negro Writer and his Roots* (1960), Hughes's blues are no longer condemned, and Toomer is seen in the hindsight of his involvement with George Ivanovitch Gurdjieff's Harmonious Development of Man movement, so he comes in for even harsher criticism. In *Negro Writing and the Political Climate* (1970), Redding calls the Harlem Renaissance a

time of a new racial attitude and political stance, when the writers were mostly rebels searching for their roots where apologists dared not look. He says they advocated cultural nationalism versus white cultural values and satirized white society rather than apologetically protesting. He points out, however, that this period also produced the stereotype of the sexually liberated, carefree exotic primitive. And for all the debates about whether the proper image of black life to portray was the raucous, hedonistic, folk one, directed to the masses, or the genteel, assimilationist view, directed to the middle class, nothing showed the everyday realities and struggles of black life (unemployment, bad schools, crowded tenements) that would become even more manifest in the Depression.

By 1973, in his foreword to Langston Hughes's *Good Morning Revolution,* Redding had praised Hughes for capturing the totality of black life:

> From the 1920s until his death in 1967, no poet caught with such sharp immediacy and intensity the humor and the pathos, the irony and the humiliation, the beauty and the bitterness of the experience of being Negro in America; and I think it should be added that no one contributed more to the current refunding of Negro folk material and the reshaping of Negro legend.

He also praised the fact that Hughes's political works were being published, because they reestablished an aspect of his genius that had been systematically ignored. These works, Redding felt, were not only Hughes's best, but his most American.

It is with the work of Richard Wright, however, that Redding believed Afro-American literature came of age. Not only had Wright extricated himself from the dilemma of writing for two audiences, but the freedom from that dilemma created the conditions necessary for art. Redding further noted in "American Negro Literature" that the proliferation of Afro-American writers in the 1940s who appeal to both audiences is a direct result of the freedom Wright achieved. Margaret Walker, Chester Himes, and Willard Motley are among those writers Redding names as benefitting from Wright's example. Wright's talent, Redding points out in "The Alien Land of Richard Wright" (1963), was "to smite the conscience— and to smite the conscience of both white and black America." Redding believes, however, that Wright made a mistake when he left the United States. The books he wrote as an expatriate in France were "unAmerican," because although black America is "a ghetto of the soul," it nourished Wright's creative talent. Thus, once he left, his characters became untrue because Wright "had cut the roots that once sustained him." Despite this falling away at the end of Wright's career, Redding believes that Wright's reputation will always be secure because of the power of *Uncle Tom's Children* (1938) and *Native Son* (1940), for in these books the problems of the black urban masses were exposed for the first time.

In "Since Richard Wright" (1966), Redding surveys Afro-American literature and finds much that is "too self-conscious and too mannered, idiosyncratic beyond the demands of artistic integrity and, often, beyond the requirements of truth." Although Redding likes *Go Tell It On the Mountain* (1953) and many of James Baldwin's essays, he feels that most of Baldwin's work is problematic. He particularly criticizes Baldwin's failure to give his black characters any motivation in *Another Country*. Since Redding agrees with Ralph Ellison that all good writing is protest writing, he easily dismisses Baldwin's attacks on Wright for writing "protest literature." Redding finds Amiri Baraka a "screamer" who deals with a clichéd stereotype of the white man's view of blacks in *Dutchman, The Slave* (1964), and *The Toilet* (1967). Those writers who merit his praise include Ellison, Paule Marshall, and John Killens in prose; Gwendolyn Brooks, Margaret Danner, and Melvin Tolson in poetry. In *Negro Writing and the Political Climate* (1970), he adds William Demby, Ann Petry, William Melvin Kelly, and Ernest J. Gaines to the list of writers whose work he admires. These are the writers who would help set the stage for the explosion of great Afro-American writing in the 1970s by such authors as Ishmael Reed, Toni Morrison, Alice Walker, Toni Cade Bambara, Albert Murray, and James Alan McPherson.

As his secondary contribution to Afro-American letters, Redding has argued throughout his career for certain standards by which to judge writers and their work. In "The Negro Writer and His Relationship to His Roots" (1960), he asserts that the discovery of self, community, and identity must be achieved "before it can be seen that a particular identity has a relation to a common identity." Further he says that the "writer's ultimate purpose is to use his gifts to develop man's awareness of himself so that he

. . . can become a better instrument for living together with other men." In *Of Men and the Writing of Books* (1969), Redding says that an author writes:

> to communicate his vision of the world; whatever basic concepts he has of his world and his relation to it; whatever there is of meaning for him in the general and the specifics of life and humanity and of the relations of man to man. If he pretends to honesty, he wishes to communicate those values which he holds to be good, and if he is an artisan he wishes to communicate them in a preconceived pattern of beauty.

The values do not have to be specific, and Redding believes that if they are "too particular, too special, too local, and ephemeral" or "specialized social, or political, or ideological" they are on a lesser level of creativity. He also believes that a writer who is overly class- or race-conscious will also produce lesser literature. The ideal for Redding is to be culture-conscious.

He delineates two kinds of writing: that which confirms and illumines, like Chekhov, and that which extends and reveals, like Milton in *Paradise Lost* (1667), Wright in *Native Son* (1940), and Herman Melville in *Moby-Dick* (1851). But either way, the greatest writers have also had to learn the magic of craft. It is the means by which one becomes an honest and human writer.

In "The Negro Writer: The Road Where" (1969), Redding states that the "end of all art is the revelation of the human condition through the discovered knowledge of self." Thus Afro-American writers, like all others, are dealing with universals. He believes that the American mainstream is "a sewer" and that too many white American writers have turned their backs on great issues. Afro-Americans, however, through such concepts as "Negritude," have a sense of heritage that precedes 1619. Redding suggests that use of the content and spirit of the African past, will help black writers achieve full stature in America and as contributors to world culture. In *Negro Writing and the Political Climate* (1970), he cautions that art can only work as a political weapon if it is first good art. Communicating truth among men is the greatest strength an artist can have; and if that truth becomes a weapon, it is acceptable.

Redding's third contribution to Afro-American letters has been his argument on behalf of Afro-American literature's being seen within the larger context of American literature. In "The Negro Writer and His Relationship to His Roots," he notes that "the American situation has complex and multifarious sources and that these sources sustain the emotional and intellectual life of American Negro writers." In "The Negro Writer and American Literature" (1966), he argues that although blacks and whites have different, distinctive group experiences and that this makes Afro-American writing "different," "it is only the distinction between trunk and branch. The writing of Negroes is fed by the same roots sunk in the same cultural soil as writing by white Americans." Thus Redding does not believe in the idea of a black aesthetic or a separate Afro-American culture. "Aesthetics has no racial, national or geographical boundaries. Beauty and truth, the principal components of aesthetics, are universal," he states in "A Survey: Black Writers' Views on Literary Lions and Values" (1968).

Redding's most comprehensive statements on this issue are contained in "Negro Writing in America" (1960) and "The Black Revolution in American Studies" (1970). He begins the former by enunciating three mutually dependent propositions. First:

> American Negro literature, so called, is American literature in fact, and that American Negro literature cannot be lopped off from the main body of American literary expression without doing grave harm to both as complementary instruments of historical and social diagnosis and as the joint and articulated corpus of American experience.

The second proposition states that Afro-American literature is, however, different from white American literature in that it has little to do with "pure" literature or aesthetics. As he had said in *To Make a Poet Black*, he reiterates the idea that literature appeals to the cognitive as much as the affective side of the reader. Literature, he says, combines "the *ought* and the *is*, the dream and the reality, the condemnation and the acquittal." He notes that there is an aesthetic "yeast" that causes the best literary art to rise above propaganda.

The third principle is that as a consequence of the first two, Afro-American literature will continue in a direction that is very different from the direction of African literature. Redding attacks anti-integrationist Harold Cruse, pointing out that even though black writers have been alienated from America, there is not a separate cul-

ture and that there is no parallel to Zionism in Afro-Americans. He further points out that Afro-Americans protest their estrangement from America, but not from Africa; and that no matter how much Afro-American writers travel or live abroad, they remain Americans.

In "The Black Revolution in American Studies" (1970), Redding delineates three intellectual reactions to white racism and the exclusion of blacks from the "establishment" story of American civilization: the reaction of writers such as John Hope Franklin, Benjamin Quarles, Kenneth Clark, Malcolm X, Eldridge Cleaver, and Claude Brown who have documented racism; the establishment of black history courses in black high schools and colleges through the work of the Association for the Study of Negro Life and History, founded by Carter Woodson in 1915; and the rise of the black student revolution—social and intellectual—against what had been the irrelevance of their education. The result of the social revolution was that there were more black teachers and administrators at black colleges; and after the 1950s, when substantial black enrollment began at white schools, there was the intellectual revolution of black studies programs. Redding is not opposed to these. They concentrate on a manageable body of knowledge, and they are not taught exclusively for or by blacks. Redding clearly recognizes that:

> a line of historical continuity and development peculiar to what is now the United States has generated a new breed of black man with a new "Americanized" orientation to life, with demonstrably, a special culture and one strongly suspects, a different psychological and emotional structure from that of his "brothers" in Africa, in South America, and in the Caribbean.

He believes that American studies will remain diminished and of questionable validity as long as it does not pursue the link with Afro-American studies. For these reasons Redding finds the concept of black studies to be of questionable validity because it encompasses too much; and it is action and emotion oriented rather than intellect oriented.

Redding's position is, thus, not easily characterized. Nevertheless because he opposes the idea of a black aesthetic, he was vilified by many younger writers and critics in the 1960s and 1970s. Unfortunately much of his work is out of print, and his numerous essays have never been collected. When this happens, as it no doubt surely will, Redding will assume his deserved place among the ranks of American literary critics.

Redding has also distinguished himself in other fields. He has written social-historical works including *They Came In Chains: Americans from Africa* (1950), *The Lonesome Road: The Story of the Negro's Part in America* (1958), and *The Negro* (1967); one novel, *Stranger and Alone* (1950); and two autobiographical works, *No Day of Triumph,* (1942) and *On Being Negro in America* (1951). He has coedited two anthologies, *Reading for Writing* (1952) with Ivan E. Taylor, and *Cavalcade: Negro American Writing From 1760 to the Present* (1971) with Arthur P. Davis.

All of Redding's works are marked by an exceedingly engaging style. His critical writing, in particular, is noteworthy for being scholarly but not pedantic, because Redding is not interested in propounding ironclad theories. Many of his works even begin with some kind of disclaimer. In *To Make A Poet Black* Redding hopes that the "odor of scholarship" will attach itself "so slightly" that the book will retain "some appeal to popular taste." *On Being Negro in America* begins, "This is personal . . . I have been clothed with no authority to speak for others." In "Modern African Literature" (1964), Redding lists three theses he could pursue "in the systematic way so dear to academic scholarship," but which he won't, in part because of his "personal notion of the exploratory nature of all learning." In *Of Men and the Writing of Books* (1969), he notes that writing "is so deeply private and personal a business that only those who do not write can speak of writing with magisterial warrant." And finally in "Portrait Against Background" (1975), Redding begins, "I refuse to call this a lecture," and notes that one "does sometimes get tired of both the means and the ends of academic scholarship and

one gets tired of manipulating scholarly apparatus."

Redding's work has not been totally ignored; and in some cases, even those who disagree with him have lauded his contributions. Harold Cruse, for instance, in *Rebellion or Revolution?* (1968), compares Redding to Edmund Wilson and says that "as a man of letters, Redding is an important figure in Negro literature despite the personal and ideological brushes I had with him. In fact, Redding is Negro literature's only claim to any luster in literary criticism qua criticism." In his essay "Afro-American Literary Critics: An Introduction," included in Addison Gayle's *The Black Aesthetic* (1971), Darwin Turner calls *To Make a Poet Black* the "best single volume of criticism by a black." Joan R. Sherman calls Redding "the dean of Afro-American literary critics" in her *Invisible Poets: Afro-Americans of the Nineteenth Century* (1974); and, in *Black Autobiography in America* (1974), Stephen Butterfield refers to Redding as one of "the best writers in the history of black autobiography," along with Frederick Douglass, W. E. B. Du Bois, Richard Wright, and George Jackson. Nevertheless, Redding's reputation is due for a serious reevaluation. Perhaps the upcoming fiftieth anniversaries of both *To Make a Poet Black* in 1989 and *No Day of Triumph* in 1992 will provide the occasion.

**References:**

Arthur P. Davis, *From the Dark Tower: Afro-American Writers, 1900-1960* (Washington, D.C.: Howard University Press, 1974);

Jean Wagner, *Black Poets of the United States: From Paul Laurence Dunbar to Langston Hughes,* translated by Kenneth Douglas (Urbana: University of Illinois Press, 1973).

# Allen Tate

*(19 November 1899-9 February 1979)*

James T. Jones
*Southwest Missouri State University*

See also the Tate entries in *DLB 4, American Writers in Paris, 1920-1939* and *DLB 45, American Poets, 1880-1945.*

BOOKS: *The Golden Mean and Other Poems*, by Tate and Ridley Wills (Nashville: Privately printed, 1923);

*Stonewall Jackson, The Good Soldier: A Narrative* (New York: Minton, Balch, 1928; London, Toronto, Melbourne & Sydney: Cassell, 1930);

*Mr. Pope and Other Poems* (New York: Minton, Balch, 1928);

*Jefferson Davis, His Rise and Fall: A Biographical Narrative* (New York: Minton, Balch, 1929);

*Ode to the Confederate Dead, Being the Revised and Final Version of a Poem Previously Published on Several Occasions; To Which Are Added Message from Abroad and The Cross* (New York: Published for the author by Minton, Balch, 1930);

*Poems: 1928-1931* (New York & London: Scribners, 1932);

*Reactionary Essays on Poetry and Ideas* (New York & London: Scribners, 1936);

*The Mediterranean and Other Poems* (New York: Alcestis Press, 1936);

*Selected Poems* (New York & London: Scribners, 1937);

*The Fathers* (New York: Putnam's, 1938; London: Eyre & Spottiswoode, 1939);

*Reason in Madness: Critical Essays* (New York: Putnam's, 1941);

*Sonnets at Christmas* (Cummington, Mass.: Cummington Press, 1941);

*Invitation to Learning*, by Tate, Huntington Cairns, and Mark Van Doren (New York: Random House, 1941);

*The Winter Sea: A Book of Poems* (Cummington, Mass.: Cummington Press, 1944);

*Poems, 1920-1945: A Selection* (London: Eyre & Spottiswoode, 1947);

*Fragment of a Meditation/MCMXXVIII* (Cummington, Mass.: Cummington Press, 1947);

*Poems: 1922-1947* (New York: Scribners, 1948);

*On the Limits of Poetry, Selected Essays 1928-1948* (New York: Swallow/Morrow, 1948);

*The Hovering Fly and Other Essays* (Cummington, Mass.: Cummington Press, 1949);

*Two Conceits for the Eye to Sing, If Possible* (Cummington, Mass.: Cummington Press, 1950);

*The Forlorn Demon: Didactic and Critical Essays* (Chicago: Regnery, 1953);

*The Man of Letters in the Modern World, Selected Essays: 1928-1955* (New York: Meridian/London: Thames & Hudson, 1955; London: Meridian/Thames & Hudson, 1957);

*Requiescat in Pace: Paul Wightman Williams, Jr., MCMXX-MCMLVI* (N.p., 1956?);

*Collected Essays* (Denver: Swallow, 1959); revised and enlarged as *Essays of Four Decades* (Chicago: Swallow, 1968; London: Oxford University Press, 1970);

*Poems* (New York: Scribners, 1960);

*Christ and the Unicorn* (West Branch, Iowa: Cummington Press, 1966);

*Mere Literature and the Lost Traveller* (Nashville: George Peabody College for Teachers, 1969);

*The Swimmers and Other Selected Poems* (London, Melbourne & Cape Town: Oxford University Press, 1970; New York: Scribners, 1971);

*The Translation of Poetry* (Washington, D.C.: Published for the Library of Congress by the Gertrude Clark Whittall Poetry and Literature Fund, 1972);

*Memoirs and Opinions 1926-1974* (Chicago: Swallow, 1975); republished as *Memoirs & Essays Old and New, 1926-1974* (Manchester, U.K.: Carcanet, 1976);

*Collected Poems 1919-1976* (New York: Farrar, Straus & Giroux, 1977);

*The Poetry Reviews of Allen Tate*, edited, with an introduction, by Ashley Brown and Frances Neel Cheney (Baton Rouge & London: Louisiana State University Press, 1983).

OTHER: Hart Crane, *White Buildings: Poems,* includes a foreword by Tate (New York: Boni & Liveright, 1926);

*Fugitives,* includes poems by Tate (New York: Harcourt, Brace, 1928);

"Remarks on the Southern Religion," in *I'll Take My Stand: The South and the Agrarian Tradition by Twelve Southerners* (New York & London: Harper, 1930), pp. 155-175;

"Notes on Liberty and Property," in *Who Owns America? A New Declaration of Independence,* edited by Tate and Herbert Agar (Boston & New York: Houghton Mifflin, 1936), pp. 80-93;

Philip Wheelwright and others, *The Language of Poetry,* edited, with a preface, by Tate (Princeton: Princeton University Press, 1942);

*Princeton Verse Between Two Wars: An Anthology,* edited, with a preface, by Tate (Princeton: Princeton University Press, 1942);

*American Harvest; Twenty Years of Creative Writing in the United States,* edited, with an introduction, by Tate and John Peale Bishop (New York: L. B. Fischer, 1942);

*Recent American Poetry and Poetic Criticism: A Selected List of References,* compiled by Tate (Washington, D.C.: Library of Congress, 1943);

*The Vigil of Venus: Pervigilium Veneris,* Latin text with an introduction and translation by Tate (Cummington, Mass.: Cummington Press, 1943);

*Sixty American Poets, 1896-1944,* checklist, selected, with a preface and critical notes, by Tate (Washington, D.C.: Library of Congress, 1945).

*A Southern Vanguard: The John Peale Bishop Memorial Volume,* edited, with a preface, by Tate (New York: Prentice-Hall, 1947);

*The Collected Poems of John Peale Bishop,* edited, with a preface and a memoir, by Tate (New York & London: Scribners, 1948);

*The House of Fiction: An Anthology of the Short Story, with Commentary,* edited by Tate and Caroline Gordon (New York: Scribners, 1950; revised, 1960);

*Modern Verse in English,* edited by Tate and David Cecil (New York: Macmillan, 1958; London: Eyre & Spottiswoode, 1958);

*The Arts of Reading,* edited by Tate, Ralph Ross, and John Berryman (New York: Crowell, 1960);

*Selected Poems by Denis Devlin,* edited, with a pref-

ace, by Tate and Robert Penn Warren (New York, Chicago & San Francisco: Holt, Rinehart & Winston, 1963);

*T. S. Eliot, The Man and His Work: A Critical Evaluation by Twenty-six Distinguished Writers,* edited by Tate (New York: Seymour Lawrence/Delacorte, 1966; London: Chatto & Windus, 1967);

*Complete Poetry and Selected Criticism of Edgar Allan Poe,* edited by Tate (New York: Signet, New American Library/London: Signet, New England Library, 1968).

The breadth of Allen Tate's publications and other activities is almost astonishing. He was a poet, critic, novelist, playwright, reviewer, editor, translator, bibliographer, lecturer, and teacher. His influence was prodigious, his circle of acquaintances immense. His friends included many of the great writers of this century: Hart Crane, John Crowe Ransom, Robert Penn Warren, T. S. Eliot, Archibald MacLeish, John Peale Bishop, Ford Madox Ford, Jacques Maritain. His acquaintances included Gertrude Stein, Ernest Hemingway, F. Scott Fitzgerald, and Wallace Stevens. Tate belonged to the Fugitives, a group that spurred the southern renaissance in the early 1920s, and helped to edit their magazine. He galvanized the forces of the southern Agrarian movement and helped to edit their anthologies. His theoretical and practical criticism are fundamental to the "school" of New Criticism, in which he was a central figure. He was a pioneer in the teaching of creative writing in this country, and some of his students, Theodore Roethke and John Berryman, for instance, became leading poets of the generation that followed Tate.

In 1948, on the occasion of the awarding of the Nobel Prize for literature to T. S. Eliot, Tate expressed his congratulations in terms that characterize the difficulties of his own career: "Take your life and your work together and we have an *exemplum* of honor and genius in rare association, without which I should scarcely have known the proper conduct of the profession of letters in a difficult age. You will not wonder then that I think of you not only with gratitude but with filial affection." Like many of his contemporaries, Tate considered this century inhospitable to literature, and he looked to Eliot as the model for the modern writer. Because Tate's life coincides with the rise of modernism in American literature, the critical problems he posed and the solutions he discov-

*Allen Tate (courtesy of the Sylvia Beach Collection, Princeton University Library)*

ered are typical of the period. Tate is a modern American archetype.

John Orley Allen Tate, called Allen—his grandmother's maiden name—to distinguish him from his father, John Orley Tate, was born 19 November 1899 in a small white frame house on the main street of Winchester, Kentucky, east of Lexington. His mother, Eleanor Varnell Tate, had moved the family to town to be near the doctor when the time came for Allen to be born. Allen's two brothers, Ben and James, were nine and eleven years old, respectively. His father, a failed businessman, moved his family frequently and survived by gradually selling off the family lands. Though Tate's great uncle Maj. Benjamin Lewis Bogan provides the nominal model for Maj. Lewis Buchan in Tate's novel, *The Fathers* (1938), a close reading of Tate's memoirs reveals that his father's distant, formal personality is also figured there. Tate's mother, an avid reader, over the years withdrew from her husband, who had somehow managed to disgrace himself socially, to her sons and to the world at large.

Because of the family finances and their frequent moves, Tate's early education was erratic, but in 1918 he followed his two brothers by enrolling at Vanderbilt University in Nashville. After the war Vanderbilt began to shift away from strict religious, classical education, and the young

scholar found himself in an institution that embodied many of the conflicts that became central to his social and critical thought. Vanderbilt craved to represent the New South, but many of Tate's teachers resented that craving. Tate fell in with the medievalist Walter Clyde Curry and the young English instructors Donald Davidson and John Crowe Ransom, the men who formed the nucleus of the Fugitive group.

Though it had been formed in 1915, the group discontinued its meetings during World War I and did not meet again until about 1920. It reconvened under the bizarre leadership of an eccentric named Sidney Mttron Hirsch, a man who had been a boxing champion in the navy, espoused occult mysticism while stationed in the Orient, was mustered out of the service in Paris and into the circle of Gertrude Stein, posed for the sculptress Gertrude Vanderbilt Whitney in New York, and returned unaccountably to Nashville to dazzle its 1913 May Festival with his only literary work, an incomprehensible Greek mystery play called *The Fire Regained*. Tate joined the group in 1921, followed later by the sonneteer Merrill Moore and the man who became the group's best-known poet, Robert Penn Warren. The members met every two weeks to read their poems to one another and to discuss philosophy, Hirsch style. Here Tate worked under the strong classical influence of Curry and Davidson and the rigorous philosophical aesthetics of Ransom. He roomed with Warren and Ridley Wills, another member of the group. Later the poet Laura Riding became the only woman invited to join the group, though, because she did not live in Nashville, she did not attend their meetings. At the insistence of Hart Crane, who had begun a correspondence with Tate after seeing one of his poems in a 1922 issue of the *Double-Dealer*, a New Orleans literary magazine, Tate began to read the poetry of T. S. Eliot, and he soon became, of his own free will, Eliot's vicar among the Fugitives. Thirteen issues of the group's magazine were published between 1922 and 1925. When the *Fugitive* ceased business it was not for lack of funds—it was thriving—but due to the sheer exhaustion of the editors, of whom Tate was the most industrious.

After a brief sojourn in a tuberculosis sanatorium—where he first worked out his theory of poetry—and an even briefer stint teaching high school, Tate graduated from Vanderbilt in 1923 and married the novelist-to-be Caroline Gordon on 2 November 1924. They moved to New York, where the couple supported themselves with free-lance writing. As he wrote essays, reviews, and poems, Tate enlarged his circle of literary acquaintances. In the winter of 1925-1926 he and his wife and Hart Crane lived in a farmhouse in Patterson, New York, to escape the confusion of the city and devote themselves to their writing. Though Crane managed to finish the "Atlantis" section of *The Bridge* (1930) and Tate wrote the first version of his "Ode to the Confederate Dead," three refined sensibilities found it difficult to coexist and Crane left after a quarrel.

About this time Tate began to plan three biographies of great Southern war heroes. Stonewall Jackson represented to him the unlettered man of action; Jefferson Davis stood for the contemplative man paralyzed by his contemplation; and Robert E. Lee symbolized the gifted Southerner, both intelligent and capable, unable to rise above his sectional loyalties. He published *Stonewall Jackson* in 1928, and *Jefferson Davis* the following year. His biography of the Confederate president, which includes portraits of Jackson and Lee as well, embodies many of the themes and concerns that gradually became associated with Tate's literary criticism. Tate discovered in the character of Davis a medium for the developing dialectic of his own thought. Davis, whose glory was literally thrust upon him, was a slave to the text of the Confederate Constitution. His very weakness lay in words. In Tate's view Davis's indecision in both military and political affairs stemmed from his fundamental belief in the possibility of reestablishing the Union on Southern terms. Like many of his colleagues, Tate says, Davis was a conservative revolutionary. Had he listened to the demands of the "Fire-eaters," those Southerners who favored a new order based not on democracy but on aristocracy, Davis might have launched a military offensive that would have ended the war almost before it began. The South would have been independent, free to reorganize its social order.

Instead Davis's fidelity to the constitution was compounded by his utter inability to understand human emotions. According to Tate the president pretended to himself that his constituents, when they failed of rationality, were beneath not only his contempt but his notice as well. Consequently Tate's "narrative," as he calls it, demonstrates Davis's inability to act until the opportunity for victory in war or compromise in politics had passed. He shows that when Davis did act, he acted in desperation.

Tate's story largely ignores Davis's early years, and it ends with his capture by Federal troops in May 1865. The book focuses on the war years, beginning just after the secession of Mississippi, Davis's home state, in January 1861. This focus betrays Tate's literary bias. The reasons for Davis's weakness go untold; Tate treats them as givens in order to attend more closely to their effects. His approach draws on Greek tragedy, and he employs other literary devices to go with it. For example, an apparently minor point about Davis's refusal to call his slave James Pemberton by the nickname "Jim," mentioned in the first chapter, recurs with fatal irony as Davis is led by his captors to Fortress Monroe and Federal troops along the Georgia road hail the captive president as "Jeff." Beyond such devices Tate expresses his allegorical motive for writing the biography in an epilogue. Davis's vacillation between intellect and emotion, it turns out, even the bloody struggle between the Union and the Confederacy, really stands for a far larger conflict, one that surfaces in Tate's criticism: the conflict between two cultures; in this case, between Western, or American, and European traditions. He concludes with an interpretation of his own allegory: "The War between the States was the second and decisive struggle of the Western spirit against the European—the spirit of restless aggression against a stable spirit of ordered economy—and the Western won."

In the early 1930s Tate abandoned work on his biography of Robert E. Lee in favor of a fictionalized family history, "Ancestors of Exile," which chronicled the parallel development of a clan of Virginia aristocrats and a family of Kentucky pioneers. That, in turn, he threw over to work on an acting version of Henry James's story *The Turn of the Screw* (1898) in collaboration with a wealthy woman of his acquaintance. All the while, he continued to write essays, reviews, and poems and to develop his Agrarian social theories. After nearly a decade, Tate managed to weave all these threads, both the broken and the continuous ones, into the fabric of serious fiction. Scenes and characters from "Ancestors of Exile" found their way into two short stories, "The Migration" and "The Immortal Woman," and his novel, *The Fathers*.

*The Fathers*, which won critical—if not popular—acclaim after its publication in 1938, is a profound and difficult work that deserves a small but sure place in the canon of American literature. Obviously influenced in theme and setting by Caroline Gordon's first novel, *Penhally* (1931), its characters, most of them members of two very different families united by marriage, the Buchans and the Poseys, are finely drawn. The story, divided into three chapters—"Pleasant Hill," "The Crisis," and "The Abyss"—is set in northern Virginia at the beginning of the Civil War. The plot, which seemed superfine or even obscure to most contemporary reviewers and even some more recent ones, finally resolves into a rite-of-passage tale about its narrator, Lacy Buchan. Lacy, who is telling the story in 1910, opens on the day of his mother's funeral. He admits the flaws in his memory and converts them to an advantage: "There is not an old man living who can recover the emotions of the past; he can only bring back the objects about which, secretly, the emotions have ordered themselves in memory." If this passage sounds like an application of Eliot's "objective correlative," it is; Tate the critic and poet makes a convenience of Eliot's theory to turn himself into Tate the novelist.

By incorporating nearly all the elements of his work during the previous decade into his novel, Tate forces the characters to enact his own private dilemma. Lacy Buchan comes to represent Lee's supposed inability to transcend his sectional loyalty for the public good. The Buchan and Posey clans stand in place of the Virginia and Kentucky branches of Tate's family, aristocrats and pioneers the complementary opposites in the settlement of the country. The Gothic theme borrowed from James and Edgar Allan Poe appears in the form of Jarman Posey, a character overtly modeled on Roderick Usher. Maj. Lewis Buchan, George Posey, Cousin George Semmes, and others play roles in another allegory based on conflicts and forces Tate had identified in his biographies as those that brought about the Civil War and caused the defeat of the South, which were the same conflicts and forces operating in his personal quest for meaning.

Though *The Fathers* resembles neither the work of William Faulkner nor that of Margaret Mitchell, the brilliance of its psychological realism makes one forget, in the interest of reading, the difficulty of classifying it with other southern fiction. As one follows Lacy's development into manhood, observes his relationship with his brother-in-law George Posey—a character based on Tate's industrialist brother Ben—senses his confusion about the reasons for the outbreak of war, experiences the strangeness of his sojourn at the Posey home in Georgetown, and shares his hor-

ror when George Posey murders Lacy's brother Semmes, one gains respect for Tate's competence as a storyteller and learns to respect through this medium his critical insight into the southern consciousness.

When Tate had returned in early 1930 from a little more than a year in France sponsored by the Guggenheim Foundation, the stock market had crashed, and the changes that brought about the Great Depression were just beginning to show themselves. Many of Tate's literary acquaintances had turned to socialism, Marxism, or communism in response to the worsening economy. Tate had just finished the Davis biography; his wife had completed her first novel; and his brother Ben had made them the gift of an antebellum mansion, which they named Benfolly, to rhyme with the name of Gordon's novel, *Penhally*, and to commemorate the brother's munificence. In these political and personal circumstances Tate set to work again: the 1930s was his most productive decade. His political activity during this period took the form of two essays in two anthologies (which he helped to edit) expounding various elements of Agrarianism, a political, social, economic, and—for Tate at least—literary philosophy of anti-industrialism. By and large, Agrarianism represents the southern intellectual response to the upheaval of the Depression. The land-based values of the movement surfaced in the 1960s in the "back to earth" movement, and again in the 1980s during the "farm crisis." The continuing appeal of Agrarianism in American political thought makes Tate's contributions to the movement worth considering in that light, and the fact that Agrarian ideals permeate all his writing makes an understanding of them crucial to an appreciation of his criticism.

Tate's contribution to *I'll Take My Stand: The South and the Agrarian Tradition by Twelve Southerners* (1930) shows how thoroughly his concerns about literature mingled with his concerns about society in general. Many of his fellow Fugitives also contributed, and the book's title turned out to be as misleading as the name of the Vanderbilt literary group. The anthology was originally intended to be an anti-Communist tract. Tate's essay, "Remarks on the Southern Religion," only nominally concerns the matter of religion. In fact it addresses itself to the larger question of tradition. In this way it represents the views of T. S. Eliot and attacks the modern humanist conception of history. In fact, Tate manages to bring a commentary on *The Waste Land* (1922) into his argument. After avowing, in the manner of his fellow New Critic R. P. Blackmur, that his is an "amateur treatment of religion," Tate asserts what is essentially Eliot's position: "A myth should be in conviction immediate, direct, overwhelming, and I take it that the appreciation of this kind of imagery is an art lost to the modern mind." For those of Eliot's persuasion, like Tate, religion and literature provided the readiest means to restore lost tradition to society. Tate goes on to attack the scientific basis of the humanist view of progress: "It is irrational," he says, "to believe in omnipotent human rationality." He proposes this notion as an explanation for the presence of the blind seer Tiresias in Eliot's poem. Tate characterizes the rationalist defect in humanism by distinguishing between the "Long View" and the "Short View" of history, religion, and tradition. The Long View, redolent of the theory of progress, views all things comparatively. Christ and Adonis are equivalent myths in this view. The Short View, on the other hand, considers the tradition of any given period as sufficient to itself; this is Tate's view, the critical view. "Tradition," he asserts, "must be automatically operative before it can be called tradition." From this point he adduces the failure of southern culture after the Civil War: "The South shows signs of defeat, and this is due to its lack of a religion which would make her special secular system the inevitable and permanently valuable one." But his conclusion expands this point, addressing the evils of humanism: "Since there is in the Western mind, a radical division between the religious, the contemplative, the qualitative, on the one hand, and the scientific, the natural, the practical on the other, the scientific mind always plays havoc with the spiritual life when it is not powerfully enlisted in its cause; it cannot be permitted to operate alone." Religion here provides the medium of tradition, and tradition provides the sole means of establishing a meaningful inner life for the individual.

*Who Owns America?*, published in 1936, six years after *I'll Take My Stand*, provides the setting for Tate's only venture into economics. Tate edited the collection, subtitled *A New Declaration of Independence*, with Herbert Agar, whom he had helped establish as the leader of the Agrarian movement. The volume contains essays by the prominent Fugitives—Davidson, Ransom, and Warren—as well as contributions by other southern literary figures such as Cleanth Brooks, whose essay takes up Tate's previous theme of reli-

gion and rashly predicts the demise of southern fundamentalism. In "Notes on Liberty and Property" Tate proposes a basic distinction between two kinds of ownership, "use-value" and "exchange-value." Stock in a corporation, for instance, has only "exchange-value," while livestock, by contrast, has "use-value" and "exchange-value." The ultimate point Tate makes is an existential one: "Control," he explains, "the power to direct production and to command markets, is freedom." His argument, in essence, applies antifederalism to economics. Corporations represent the economic power of centralization. Corporate capitalism, for Tate, differs little from Marxism: "A defender of the institution of private property will question not only the collectivist state, but also large corporate property." The principles of Agrarianism as displayed here were obviously not calculated to appeal to the popular mind, although Huey Long and Father Coughlin and others used them to sway the masses in the mid 1930s.

It is more difficult to see how "Notes on Liberty and Property"—as opposed to "Remarks on the Southern Religion"—applies to the situation of the artist, but it does so in two ways. First, it argues for an America that preserves regional values by means of a change in its economy. This argument results from Tate's research into the causes of the Civil War. Corporate growth in the early 1930s simply extends the sectional struggle of the previous century. Ultimately the economic struggle amounts to a struggle for self-determination. It amounts to the southern man—and the southern artist—attempting to preserve the way of life that gives meaning to his work. The conflict between corporate ownership and individual ownership represents by analogy the plight of the artist. Although Tate, like Eliot, was staunchly antiromantic and here denounces the myth of the self-sufficient farmer, romantic yearnings suffuse some of his statements. For instance, he claims that "the nearer a society is to personal production for use the freer it is." While this notion nominally opposes corporate overproduction, it makes more sense in artistic terms. Consider Tate's conclusion in this light: "Pure exchange-value represents the power of its owner over other persons. Pure use-value represents the owner's liberty not to exercise power over other persons, and his independence of their power over him." The sliding scale between the two values is the economic version of the conflict that creates tension in poetry.

The concerns of the Agrarian movement spilled over into Tate's actual literary criticism, as one might expect of such a unified mind, most notably into a pair of pieces written for anniversary issues of the *Virginia Quarterly Review*, "The Profession of Letters in the South" (April 1935, first collected in *Reactionary Essays on Poetry and Ideas*, 1936) and "The New Provincialism" (Spring 1945, first collected in *On the Limits of Poetry*, 1948). These concerns took more or less final literary form in "A Southern Mode of the Imagination" (*Collected Essays*, 1959), his best theoretical discussion of southern literature. Three central issues inform this essay: conflict, isolation, and tradition. Tate argues first that the southern "mode of discourse" is the rhetorical mode, as opposed to the dialectical mode of history favored by modern humanists in the industrial North. The epic figures—perhaps tribal totems would be a better description—are Baldassare Castiglione and Ralph Waldo Emerson, a highly unlikely pair. The modern version of Castiglione's courtier is, of course, the Southern Gentleman, to whom Tate opposes the New England Sage. Second, he claims that the primary effect of the Civil War was to make the South even more isolated from the national industrial culture than it had been before 1865, with the result that, like Emily Dickinson a generation or more earlier, the South was left alone to brood upon the lost tradition that formerly gave meaning to its cultural life. To synthesize the conflict and the isolation Tate asserts that in the South the rhetorical mode of discourse became the mythopoeic mode. What had previously been a point of contrast with the culture of the North became, by means of the catalyst of World War I, a technique of fiction. With the details drawn in, Tate's discussion makes as clear a sketch of the sources of the southern renaissance as one can expect.

Tate reveals his literary heroes quite readily in his critical essays. Dante is ever present for Tate, as he was for Eliot. In his relation to Virgil, Dante represents the poet's relation to the tradition of his craft, and *The Divine Comedy* exemplifies the poetic advantage of employing the images of a commonly held religion to structure the poet's individual insights. What is true for Tate in this respect is true for almost all the New Critics: Dante is the exemplar.

In addition to William Shakespeare and John Milton, who so obviously exemplify the proper relation of the poet to his tradition that comment seemed unnecessary, John Donne serves as Tate's model in English poetry. Above the lesser Metaphysicals, Donne stands for the power of reason in poetry. Tate placed Metaphysical, rather than Neo-Classical, at the opposite end of the poetic spectrum from Romanticism, because he felt that it was impossible for him and his contemporaries—perhaps for all poets to come—ever again to accept an objective system of belief, with its attendant images, structures, and myths. The Metaphysical conceit, then, is a compromise for the sake of some impersonal order. It is a microcosm of rationality and belief, rather than a macrocosm, which the poet may use to escape the chaos of his own individuality.

In American literature Tate fixes on another unlikely pair: Poe and Dickinson. Poe has special advantages, since he is a southerner. Tate sees in him an ancestor—he even calls one of his essays "Our Cousin, Mr. Poe" (*Partisan Review*, December 1949)—in the rejection of northern industrial values, values that led to the impasse Tate perceived in modern society and modern literature. Poe, the displaced Bostonian, the orphan, provides the antidote to Emerson's misplaced trust in the future. Poe rejects science for his own brand of pseudoscience, and he rejects scientism—which Tate calls a "demi-religion"—for his own brand of religion. As a bonus, he maintains the presence of evil in the modern world. Tate believed firmly in a simple, functional, everyday conception of evil; he rejected modern humanism as much for its ignorance of evil as for its lack of religion. In Poe he found the literary validation for his belief.

The Belle of Amherst is quite another case. In his now well-known essay "Emily Dickinson" (first published in the 15 August 1928 issue of *Outlook*, revised version in *Reactionary Essays on Poetry and Ideas*) Tate makes the cleverest adaptation of the relation between the individual writer and society. Like Eliot, he rejects the Romantic view of the centrality of the individual consciousness, but he does not reject it totally. Rather, he characterizes Romantic egoism as one pole of a dialectic essential to the creation of poetry (and criticism, one might add). Great poetry, in his view, always fuses thought and feeling, the objective and the personal, tradition and innovation. Some ages, in which a great social order stands on the verge of collapse, provide the ideal conditions in which the great poet may realize the universal tension of art. Dickinson, like Shakespeare, profited from having been born into a generation that witnessed such a collapse. Though Tate vilifies

Emerson in the essay for hastening the collapse in America, he does not categorically deny the Romantic impulse to internalize. He castigates Alfred Tennyson for his failure to synthesize ideas and feelings. This failure, in Tate's eyes, makes him a pseudophilosopher, rather than a poet. The true poet, like Dickinson, is one who accepts a great set of religious myths *as though* they were her own consciousness.

When Tate calls Emily Dickinson "a poet of ideas," he does not mean that her poetry is abstract. In fact he means just the opposite; her ideas are perfectly embodied in concrete images because she was not aware that they were ideas. Dismissing the attempts of biographical critics to find in Dickinson's personality ("personality will never give up the key to anyone's verse") an explanation for her success as a poet, Tate proposes his own theory: "There is the clash of powerful opposites, and in all great poetry it issues in a tension between abstraction and sensation." How much easier it was for Emily Dickinson to achieve this tension, when she had but to embody the social tension of her age. Tate is willing to admit the similarity to Nathaniel Hawthorne in this respect, but he refuses to consider the possible tension in poetry at the other end of the scale, the poetry of Walt Whitman. He probes further to find the purpose of poetic tension; it has to do with tradition. "Poetry does not dispense with tradition," Tate says, imitating the diction of Eliot's animadversion against emotionalism in "Tradition and the Individual Talent," "it probes the deficiencies of the tradition." He even extends the conflict to an etymological level, suggesting that the verbal relations between words with Latin or Greek roots and those with Anglo-Saxon roots in Dickinson's poetry are yet another means by which tension is created. Tate concludes that Dickinson "exhibits one of the permanent relations between personality and objective truth."

Tate's thinking about tension in Emily Dickinson's poetry came to theoretical fruition precisely a decade later in another well-known essay called "Tension in Poetry" (*Southern Review*, Summer 1938, first collected in *On the Limits of Poetry*). Claiming that "the meaning of poetry is in its 'tension,'" he goes on to define "tension" as "the full organized body of all the extension and intension that we can find in it." Though he later repudiated this dichotomy—at the same time he rejected John Crowe Ransom's distinction between structure and texture as too formulaic for understanding or writing poetry—it marks a genuine turning from Eliot's utter abandonment of Romanticism. It makes Romanticism an important force in the creation of a modern poetic technique. Tate summarizes: "The metaphysical poet as a rationalist begins at or near the extensive or denoting end of the line; the romantic or Symbolist poet at the other, intensive end; and each by a straining feat of the imagination tries to push his meanings as far as he can towards the opposite end, so as to occupy the entire scale." That is Tate's most distinct and notable contribution to the New Criticism and to modern American criticism in general: the readmission of the Romantics to the conscious tradition.

Well into the last decade of his life Tate still thought of himself primarily as a poet, and because his contributions to criticism equal or exceed his contributions to poetry, his poems, like his biographies, may be viewed as embodying the same principles as his criticism, just as his criticism may be read as a rationale for the kind of poetry he wrote. In addition to the major themes of his prose—modern dissociation of sensibility and the resultant need for tradition and religion in art—Tate offers in his poetry a pyrotechnic display of his classicism. Three poems, taken in the order of their publication, will suffice to show the affinity between the poetic and noetic modes of his mind. "Ode to the Confederate Dead," which Tate began in 1925 and continued to revise—even after the "revised and final version" appeared in 1930—until 1937, remains Tate's most celebrated poem. The setting is a Southern military graveyard in November, but the question implied by the rhetorical speaker transcends the regional sentiment. What should we do with the past? asks the speaker, in essence. Since the past here means death, life becomes a moment suspended between the great social death of the Confederacy and the more or less insignificant death of the individual. What results in the poem, as in Tate's critical theory, is a kind of suspension:

> Night is the beginning and the end
> And in between the ends of distraction
> Waits mute speculation, the patient curse
> That stones the eyes, or like the jaguar leaps
> For his own image in a jungle pool, his victim.

The question put in "The Mediterranean" (*Yale Review*, Spring 1933, first collected in *The Mediterranean and Other Poems*, 1936), a poem which has sequels in "Aeneas at Washington" and "Aeneas at New York," concerns tradition. The poem depicts an actual outing, a picnic given by Ford Madox Ford at Cassis in 1932, though it fails to mention sixty-one bottles of wine brought by Ford. Wandering by the European side of the sea reminds the speaker of Aeneas's journey to a new homeland and the prophecy that would require him and his crew to eat their tables. It is worth noting here that Tate was a most uncomfortable expatriate. He complained regularly about being restless and uncomfortable on his first two trips to Europe, in 1928-1930 and 1932-1933. "What country shall we conquer?" demands the speaker in "The Mediterranean." Again, there is a suspension between past and future, this time in terms of a poetic genealogy linked to Virgil. The answer, which is supposed to modernize the epic itinerary, sounds uncharacteristically Emersonian:

> Westward, westward till the barbarous brine
> Whelms us to the tired land where tasseling corn,
> Fat beans, grapes sweeter than muscadine
> Rot on the vine: in that land were we born.

Again, the speaker, who assumes the editorial plural, pretends to be in the future looking back to a point midway between him and his visionary ancestors.

"The Swimmers"–written in 1953, first published in the Winter 1953 issue of the *Hudson Review* and collected in *Poems* (1960)–recounts an episode from Tate's childhood, the lynching of a black man and the brutal treatment of his corpse. It is as though Tate wanted the body of his poetry–as well as individual poems–to represent the same reversal of past and future. The poem is written in the terza rima of Dante. Its message is as clear as the concluding stanza, in which the boy speaker comments on the corpse:

> Alone in the public clearing
> This private thing was owned by all the town
> Though never claimed by us within my hearing.

The past, which in this case is essentially evil, is submerged in the experience of the entire community, providing an unconscious continuity of meaning. Tate valued both religion and the past in part for their role in bearing the presence of evil into our daily lives. Like Tate's other poems, some of which directly address critical "problems" such as Romanticism, "The Swimmers" dramatizes significant features of his theory.

While the effect of Tate's writing can be calculated, we can only surmise about his contribu-

tions in other important areas affecting criticism. Tate's teaching career, for instance, began in the 1930s in several small southern colleges. From 1939 to 1942 he was poet in residence in the Princeton University Creative Arts Program. In 1951, after a few semesters teaching at New York University (Spring 1948-Spring 1951), he accepted a post as a tenured professor at the University of Minnesota. His influence as a teacher, intangible as it is, may in the long run exceed even his influence as an essayist.

Tate made other important contributions to the life of American letters as well, some at great personal sacrifice. He became a central figure in the debate surrounding the award of the first Bollingen Prize in Poetry to Ezra Pound. Reading about this episode one develops an immediate esteem for Tate's personal integrity and commitment to the cause of literature. Pound, who made broadcasts against the Allies for Radio Rome during World War II, had been hospitalized in a mental institution after his return to America in 1946. Though Pound had severely criticized Tate's poetry, Tate defended his beleaguered colleague from first to last, and he was on the jury that awarded the Bollingen Prize to Pound for his *Pisan Cantos*. When that award was attacked publicly by other writers in 1949, Tate wrote in defense of his decision, answering charges that Pound was a fascist and an anti-Semite by appealing to principles of aesthetics. In the *Partisan Review* ( June 1949) he explained that despite the flaws in Pound's work, he deserved the prize for the vitality he added to the language. While his anti-Semitism must not be condoned, he argued, it must be overlooked for the purpose of making a literary award.

By his own count, in a 1974 memoir, Tate wrote 119 essays, not counting reviews. His most important work was done by 1960. It may be inaccurate to say that he developed as a writer, since the concerns about tradition and religion remained much the same throughout his life. Tate practiced a kind of incremental repetition, revising, reorganizing, and republishing his essays and poems. The effect on the body of his work is about the same as the effect of a refrain on the meaning of a poem. In repetition, the ideas become musical and grow in stature. The real development came in Tate's life. In 1950 he took what seemed to be an inevitable step by following his wife Caroline into the Roman Catholic church. This move may have brought some peace, but in 1959 he divorced Gordon for a second time (they had divorced and remarried in 1946), and on 27 August 1959 he married a poet named Isabelle Gardner. The effect of the remarriage was, of course, to excommunicate Tate from his new religion. In 1966 his second marriage ended in divorce, and on 30 July of that year he married Helen Heinz. In 1968 he retired from the University of Minnesota and moved to the peaceful surroundings of Sewanee, Tennessee. If his personal quest for a religious tradition ended in failure, his literary quest ended in success. He swerved from the influence of Eliot–and from that of Ransom as well–toward a more inclusive theoretical foundation for American criticism and literature. The New Critics were a breed remarkable for their fusion of the arts of poetry and criticism, yet like most of his colleagues, he was neither a great poet nor a great critic. Rarer still, he was a great American man of letters. His stature overall exceeds his stature in any single genre.

**Letters:**

*The Literary Correspondence of Donald Davidson and Allen Tate,* edited by John Tyree Fain and Thomas Daniel Young (Athens: University of Georgia Press, 1974);

*The Republic of Letters in America: The Correspondence of John Peale Bishop and Allen Tate,* edited by Thomas Daniel Young and John J. Hindle (Lexington: University Press of Kentucky, 1981).

**Interview:**

Thomas Speight et al., "Allen Tate Interview," *Rebel Magazine,* 9 (Winter 1966): 3-17.

**Bibliographies:**

Willard Thorp, "Allen Tate: A Checklist," *Princeton University Library Chronicle,* 3 (April 1942): 85-98; republished in *Critique,* 10 (Summer 1968): 17-34;

Marshall Fallwell, Jr., *Allen Tate: A Bibliography* (New York: Lewis, 1969);

"The Works of Allen Tate" and "Works About Allen Tate," in *Allen Tate and His Work: Critical Evaluations,* edited by Radcliffe Squires (Minneapolis: University of Minnesota Press, 1972), pp. 309-343.

**Biographies:**

George Hemphill, *Allen Tate* (Minneapolis: University of Minnesota Press, 1964);

Radcliffe Squires, *Allen Tate: A Literary Biography* (New York: Bobbs-Merrill, 1971).

**References:**

Ferman Bishop, *Allen Tate* (New York: Twayne, 1967);

Louise Cowan, *The Fugitive Group: a Literary History* (Baton Rouge: Louisiana State University Press, 1959);

R. K. Meiners, *The Last Alternatives: A Study of the Works of Allen Tate* (Denver: Swallow, 1963);

Rob Roy Purdy, ed., *Fugitives Reunion: Conversations at Vanderbilt* (Nashville: Vanderbilt University Press, 1959);

Radcliffe Squires, *Allen Tate: A Literary Biography* (New York: Pegasus, 1971);

Squires, ed., *Allen Tate and His Work: Critical Evaluations* (Minneapolis: University of Minnesota Press, 1972).

**Papers:**

There are collections of Tate's papers in the Princeton University Library, the Columbia University Library, and the University of Victoria Library, Victoria, British Columbia.

# Lionel Trilling

*(4 July 1905-5 November 1975)*

Gregory S. Jay
*University of Wisconsin-Milwaukee*

See also the Trilling entry in *DLB 28, Twentieth-Century American-Jewish Fiction Writers.*

BOOKS: *Matthew Arnold* (New York: Norton, 1939; London: Allen & Unwin, 1939; revised edition, New York: Columbia University Press, 1949; London: Allen & Unwin, 1949);

*E. M. Forster* (Norfolk, Conn.: New Directions, 1943; London: Hogarth, 1944; revised edition, New York: New Directions, 1964; London: Hogarth, 1967);

*The Middle of the Journey* (New York: Viking, 1947; London: Secker & Warburg, 1948);

*The Liberal Imagination* (New York: Viking, 1950; London: Secker & Warburg, 1951);

*The Opposing Self* (New York: Viking, 1955; London: Secker & Warburg, 1955);

*Freud and the Crisis of Our Culture* (Boston: Beacon, 1955);

*A Gathering of Fugitives* (Boston: Beacon, 1956; London: Secker & Warburg, 1957);

*The Scholar's Caution and the Scholar's Courage* (Ithaca, N.Y.: Cornell University Libraries, 1962);

*Beyond Culture: Essays in Language and Learning* (New York: Viking, 1965; London: Secker & Warburg, 1966);

*Sincerity and Authenticity* (Cambridge, Mass.: Harvard University Press, 1972; London: Oxford University Press, 1972);

*Mind in the Modern World* (New York: Viking, 1973);

*The Works of Lionel Trilling, Uniform Edition,* 12 volumes (New York & London: Harcourt Brace Jovanovich, 1977-1980);

*Of This Time, of That Place and Other Stories,* selected by Diana Trilling (New York & London: Harcourt Brace Jovanovich, 1979; Oxford: Oxford University Press, 1981);

*The Last Decade: Essays and Reviews 1965-75,* edited by Diana Trilling (New York & London: Harcourt Brace Jovanovich, 1979; Oxford: Oxford University Press, 1982);

*Prefaces to the Experience of Literature* (New York & London: Harcourt Brace Jovanovich, 1979; Oxford: Oxford University Press, 1981);

*Speaking of Literature and Society,* edited by Diana Trilling (New York & London: Harcourt Brace Jovanovich, 1980; Oxford: Oxford University Press, 1982).

OTHER: Henry James, *The Princess Casamassima,* 2 volumes, edited by Trilling (New York: Macmillan, 1948);

Mark Twain, *The Adventures of Huckleberry Finn,* introduction by Trilling (New York & Toronto: Rinehart, 1948);

*The Portable Matthew Arnold,* edited, with an introduction, by Trilling (New York: Viking, 1949); republished as *The Essential Matthew Arnold* (London: Chatto & Windus, 1969);

*The Selected Letters of John Keats,* edited, with an introduction, by Trilling (New York: Farrar, Straus & Young, 1951);

Leo Tolstoy, *Anna Karenina,* 2 volumes, introduction by Trilling (Cambridge, U.K.: Limited Editions Club at University Press, 1951);

Gustave Flaubert, *Bouvard and Pécuchet,* introduction by Trilling (Norfolk, Conn.: New Directions, 1954);

Irvin Stock, *William Hale White (Mark Rutherford): A Critical Study,* foreword by Trilling (London: Allen & Unwin, 1956; New York: Columbia University Press, 1956);

*Selected Short Stories of John O'Hara,* introduction by Trilling (New York: Modern Library, 1956);

Jane Austen, *Emma,* introduction by Trilling (Boston: Houghton Mifflin, 1957);

Ernest Jones, *The Life and Works of Sigmund Freud,* edited and abridged by Trilling and Steven Marcus, with an introduction by Trilling (London: Hogarth, 1962);

Saul Bellow, *The Adventures of Augie March,* introduction by Trilling (New York: Modern Library, 1965);

Tess Slesinger, *The Unpossessed,* afterword by Trilling (New York: Avon, 1966);

*The Experience of Literature: A Reader with Commentaries,* edited by Trilling (New York, Chicago, San Francisco & Toronto: Holt, Rinehart & Winston, 1967);

Isaac Babel, *The Collected Stories,* edited and translated by Walter Morrison, introduction by Trilling (London: Methuen, 1967);

*The Broken Mirror: A Collection of Writings from Contemporary Poland,* edited by Pawel Mayewski, introduction by Trilling (New York: Random House, 1968);

*Literary Criticism: An Introductory Reader,* edited, with an introduction, by Trilling (New York, Chicago, San Francisco, Atlanta, Dallas, Montreal, Toronto, London & Sydney: Holt, Rinehart & Winston, 1970);

*Victorian Prose and Poetry,* edited by Trilling and Harold Bloom (New York, London & Toronto: Oxford University Press, 1973).

PERIODICAL PUBLICATIONS: "Young in the Thirties," *Commentary,* 41 (May 1966): 43-51;

"Liberal Anti-Communism Revisited," *Commentary,* 44 (September 1967): 76;

"From the Notebooks of Lionel Trilling [I]," selected by Christopher Zinn, *Partisan Review,* 51 (1984-85): 495-515;

"From the Notebooks of Lionel Trilling [II]," selected by Zinn, *Partisan Review* (Winter 1987): 7-17.

Lionel Trilling was one of the two or three most influential literary intellectuals in the period from 1950, when he published *The Liberal Imagination,* until his death in 1975, by which time he was widely regarded as a spokesman on general cultural issues. Unlike his contemporaries in the New Criticism who concentrated their energies on the formal and autonomous attributes of literature, Trilling's concern was with literature as a part of cultural history, specifically as literature spoke of the moral issues at stake in the self's quarrel with culture. He took seriously, and often defended, Matthew Arnold's dictate that literature is a "criticism of life." Thus René Wellek, in *American Criticism, 1900-1950* (1986; volume 6 of *A History of Modern Criticism: 1750-1950*), begins his not wholly sympathetic chapter on Trilling by stating that "It is not easy to focus on the literary criticism of Lionel Trilling if literary criticism is understood strictly as comment on literature; theories about it, principles, and specific texts."

While Trilling in fact shares the aesthetic standards of the New Critics, he makes explicit the cultural debates and value judgments these standards involve. Mark Krupnick, in *Lionel Trilling and the Fate of Cultural Criticism* (1986), the best study of Trilling yet to appear, sees his work as an example of "the criticism we have lost" amid the "preening triviality" of much recent academic work. Trilling occupied that "middle ground where literature and social thought might meet" and so had a force which derived from a "concern with the way we live" that dates back to Ralph Waldo Emerson. "This older urgency," writes Krupnick, "about the quality of national life made American criticism a continuation in other form of the Puritan sermon and the Romantic spiritual autobiography." Trilling's criticism, with its ubiquitous presumption of the editorial "we," was always part homily and part confession, a research into the literature of the self and a meditation on the irreconcilable conflicts between, and within, the individual and society.

In "Some Notes for an Autobiographical Lecture" (originally delivered at Purdue University in 1971 and published in *The Last Decade: Essays and Reviews 1965-75* [1979]), Trilling candidly distilled the outline of his intellectual life and the reasons why he became an analyst of culture rather than a theorist of purely aesthetic or literary issues. "It always startles me," he claims, to be called a "critic": "being a critic was not, in Wordsworth's phrase, part of the plan that pleased my boyish thought, or my adolescent thought, or even my thought as a young man. The plan that did please my thought was certainly literary, but what it envisaged was the career of a novelist." Trilling does not mean to imply, however, that criticism has become the sublimation of his failed creative genius. Indeed the stereotypical division between the artist and the critic disappears as Trilling gives his account of the novelist's vocation, which turns out to be a fairly exact prefiguration of the kind of cultural criticism Trilling's later essays practice. His sense of "reality," he reminisces, "was derived primarily from novelists and not from antecedent critics" or philosophers. More important it "derived from novelists and not from poets–that is, from practitioners of the genre which was traditionally the least devoted to the ideals of *form* . . . and the most devoted to substance, which it presumes to say is actuality itself." This is quite a presumption, as is the characterization of the novel as the genre least self-conscious about its forms. This assertion can be partially understood in light of Trilling's youth in the age of T. S. Eliot, Ezra Pound, William Carlos Williams, Wallace Stevens and of a high modernism in poetry that continued the fascination with form initiated by French Symbolism. Still it was also the age of James Joyce, Gertrude Stein, and William Faulkner. Trilling's taste in the novel remains decidedly of the nineteenth century. This mimetic view of novelistic realism—of the novel as social document—has of course been largely superseded in recent decades by an increasingly formalist criticism whose arguments Trilling resisted until the end. Trilling's distrust of aesthetic and formal criticism, then, has its roots in his view of the novel's power to represent the shapes and substances of a culture.

Yet this issue in literary theory of whether the novel as a genre is primarily a form-conscious or content-reflective thing has its own deep roots in Trilling's concern for the social function of art and literature, which he expressed in choosing Matthew Arnold as the subject of his dissertation and first book. What attracts Trilling is the novel's "tendency to occupy itself not with aesthetic questions . . . but rather with moral questions, with the questions raised by the experience of quotidian life and by the experience of culture and history." Trilling detects an "anti-literary" impulse in the novel which he associates with his own tendency to be "a little skeptical of literature, impatient with it, or at least with the claims of literature to be an autonomous, self-justifying activity." Without naming names, Trilling here targets a powerful tradition within literary modernism going back at least to Gustave Flaubert, Stéphane Mallarmé, and Henry James, and finding some support from Eliot and the New Critics, though these latter were also the heirs of Arnold and came strongly equipped with their own concerns about the modern self and its morality. In becoming a critic rather than a novelist, Trilling did not swerve from his original intention; one may argue, on the contrary, that he realized it more fully, having divorced his own writings from the latent formal and aesthetic concerns inherent to the novel. Some of the negative evaluations of Trilling's fiction suggest that its shortcomings lie precisely in an excess of moralizing substance in proportion to artistic finesse. Similarly Trilling's works of literary criticism are far more concerned with cultural norms than literary forms.

Lionel Trilling's life as a cultural critic and moral psychologist must be understood in light of his Jewish background. This is not to say that he identified with American Jewish culture or contributed centrally to its intellectual life; indeed, as Krupnick has shown, Trilling moved steadily away from his roots as he assimilated the culture of the Anglo-American tradition and gained his role as its middle-class gentleman spokesman. Trilling's ambivalent attitude toward his Jewish inheritance resembles that of Freud, whose figure looms so large in Trilling's conception of the intellectual hero in the modern age. This drama of assimilation, so familiar to readers of Jewish, American literature, and indeed of ethnic American or immigrant stories in general, helped shape Trilling's early years. In tracing Trilling's alternations between "the Gentleman and the Jew," Krupnick demonstrates that Trilling turned against what he called the "willingness to be provincial and parochial." Trilling, Krupnick says, "was deeply committed . . . to a cosmopolitan ideal of culture that had been implicit in his early association of the intellectual life with refinement but that had been suppressed in the twenties and thirties in favor of positive Jewishness and Marxist radicalism." Despite this identification with the "cosmopolitan ideal," which found its first epitome in the traditional humanism of Matthew Arnold, Trilling continued to owe much of his moral conscience and skepticism toward cultural powers to his Jewish roots. "Being a Jew," he wrote in his notebook in 1928, "is like walking in the wind or swimming: you are touched at all points and conscious everywhere."

The chief source of information about Trilling's life and family background is his wife, Diana, a noted essayist and critic in her own right. Born Diana Rubin in 1905, she graduated from Radcliffe with a B.A. in fine arts in 1925. She married Lionel Trilling in New York in 1929, and the two began a lifetime partnership in ideas, social causes, and literary projects. Together they became central figures in the group that came to be known as the "New York Intellectuals." While Diana Trilling worked mainly at book reviewing during the first decades of their marriage, she later emerged as a thoughtful essayist on contemporary cultural affairs. Her books include *Claremont Essays* (1964), *We Must March My Darlings* (1977), *Reviewing the Forties* (1978), and *Mrs. Harris: The Death of the Scarsdale Diet Doctor* (1981). Her memoir, "Lionel Trilling: A Jew at Columbia," originally published in *Commentary* (March 1979) and included as an appendix to

*Speaking of Literature and Society* (1980), is a valuable account of Trilling's early years.

Lionel Trilling was born in 1905 in New York to an immigrant Jewish couple, Fannie Cohen and David W. Trilling. David Trilling was from Bialystok (now in Poland) and had been shipped off to the United States at age thirteen. Family tradition tells of his having broken down during his Bar Mitzvah, thus abruptly terminating progress toward succeeding his forefathers in becoming a rabbi. He became a tailor, later making an ill-fated switch to the wholesale fur business. His friends described him as "a perfect gentleman," though this facade masked a hot temper, hypochondria, and financial incompetence. Bad marketing decisions and the crash of 1929 wiped out the elder Trilling. Lionel and Diana Trilling found themselves financially responsible in large part for both their families throughout the lean years of the 1930s, when Diana also suffered from a debilitating hyperthyroid condition.

Trilling's mother was also descended from East European Jews, though she was born and educated in London's East End. Diana Trilling's memoir celebrates her as "a vigorous presence" and someone whose "outlook on life changed radically in her middle and old age, the small-spirited values she could once share with her wealthy, self-imposing brothers and sisters steadily giving place to impulses that weren't validated by the conventions of their segment of the world." Without the college education given her sisters, Fannie still managed to read widely and deeply and harbored ambitious literary goals for Lionel. She told him before his fifth birthday that he would take the Ph.D. at Oxford, and Trilling always credited her with stimulating him to achievement, though later he acknowledged that the rabbinical tradition on his father's side must certainly have played a strong role in fashioning his character as a commentator on texts.

Diana Trilling stresses the complex family and social forces that shaped the young Lionel Trilling. Many of the East European Jewish immigrants believed that, barred from pursuing the scholarly lives of their traditional religious training, success required using their intellect to move up the class ladder and so advance their Americanization. But the "message of Lionel's upbringing was of a different order. It seemed not to have occurred to his parents that money was necessary to social mobility; as naturally as they breathed they thought of themselves, and always had, as middle-class people–were they not honest, respect-

able, committed to the solidity and progress of their adopted country?" Lionel Trilling's parents were not socially ambitious. They took in an occasional concert or opera, rarely ate in restaurants or attended the theater, and most enjoyed the company of a small group of neighbors and friends. Since "they never felt excluded from life on the ground of having little money or being Jews . . . Lionel had no need to make for himself the strategic leap into the American middle class, with what this so often involves in defensiveness."

While it must be given some credibility, this account by Trilling's wife seems too readily to resolve the tension between self and culture that so often preoccupies the author of books like *The Opposing Self* (1955). The Jew's alien position in relation to the dominant culture of the West has traditionally empowered an oppositional intellectual self and one that has regularly, as in the case of Freud, also turned against the culture of the religious fathers. Lionel Trilling's ambivalence toward culture must be seen in part as a product of the Jew's ambivalence toward the ancient tradition and the adopted homeland. Trilling's theory of modernism will, for example, embody this ambivalence when he argues that the modern self's rebellion against its culture often takes the form of creating or adopting a rival or adversarial culture (as in another way Eliot and Pound would turn away from the modern world by returning to the traditions of Elizabethan England or Confucian China, sources that would authorize their own oppositional selves). As Krupnick's account implies, it is difficult to see Trilling's adoption of Manhattan and Columbia University, of Jane Austen and John Keats and Matthew Arnold, without considering the degree of its "defensiveness."

Trilling's assimilation of the culture of Western humanism began in earnest in 1921, when after graduating from DeWitt Clinton High School he entered Columbia University as a sixteen-year-old freshman. In his autobiographical lecture, Trilling recalls these years of ferment as a "great burst of national self-consciousness" featuring an "intense and pervasive questioning of the prevailing way of doing things–that is to say, of the majority's way of doing things, and of the business community's way of doing things." An adversarial or oppositional position for the young intellectual took shape, then, in the wake of World War I, the crises of the European democracies, and the general destabilization of social values and institutions in the United States brought on by the economic developments of the 1920s.

It was a time when the conflicts of the capitalist nation-states inspired Marxist calls for their overthrow as well as reactionary calls for a return to a cultural aristocracy of classical values. Questions about social justice and the quality of life arose among the children of the middle class itself, a phenomenon Trilling was to emphasize later in his account of the contradictions of modern life. The vulgar and exploitative culture of the bourgeoisie, immortalized in F. Scott Fitzgerald's *The Great Gatsby* (1925) and other works of the time, prompted some heirs of the middle class to look back to the elite cultural tradition of nineteenth-century liberal humanism for an antidote to modern chaos.

As Trilling would reiterate in *Beyond Culture* (1965), "It is a belief still preeminently honored that a primary function of art and thought is to liberate the individual from the tyranny of his culture in the environmental sense and to permit him to stand beyond it in an autonomy of perception and judgment." "This particular concern," he noted, was the special legacy of the "Victorian tradition" that included such oppositional and contrastive characters as Arnold, John Ruskin, William Morris, Oscar Wilde, Bernard Shaw, H. G. Wells, and D. H. Lawrence—writers ranging the spectrum from the reactionary to the utopian but all sharing a "dis-ease" with the tendencies of middle-class capitalism and its culture. In America, Emerson and Henry David Thoreau had pioneered the opposition, followed in Trilling's time by Van Wyck Brooks, Lewis Mumford, Randolph Bourne, and such journals as the *Nation*, the *New Republic*, and the *Freeman*. Trilling identified with an "intellectual class" who believe that society and culture are "susceptible to a conscious intention to change and correct them." There was "no college in the country," recollects Trilling, "at which a student might be as accessible to this new movement as Columbia College." In 1965 he remarked "I recall my college days as an effort to discover some social entity to which I could give the credence of my senses, as it were, and with which I could be in some relation." That social entity, oddly enough, turned out to be Columbia itself, which in formulating the ideal of a liberal, humanistic education was to revive the moral claims for education lying behind the word "university."

Trilling's autobiographical lecture emphasizes that "the great word in the College was INTELLIGENCE." Trilling adopted as his goal the motto of his teacher, John Erskine: "THE MORAL OBLIGATION TO BE INTELLI-GENT." Admittedly vague, the imperative seems to be to avoid the dogmatism of traditional viewpoints as well as the vulgarities of easy new solutions. In the spirit of modernism, the self must accept the responsibility of understanding rather than depend on the transcendent absolutes of the past or the commercial dictates of the present. At Columbia "Man" would be praised for "the activity of his mind, for its centrality, its flexibility, its awareness of difficulty and complexity, and its readiness to confront and deal with difficulty and complexity." This description resembles Eliot's contemporaneous assertion that modern poetry must be difficult and the later emphasis of the New Critics on tension, paradox, and complexity in literary language. A hallmark of Trilling's career may be glimpsed here: his attempt to marry the formal difficulties of modernist literature and art with the agenda of social justice and moral reform.

Columbia, as Trilling remembers it, had made great strides in leaving behind the scientific and historical methods of German philology that had previously dominated the advanced academic study of literature. The goal now was to produce the well-read and intelligent man, not the dust-covered expert in minutiae. At the heart of Columbia's program was the General Honors sequence, and it shaped Trilling's ideal of education, teaching, and self-enlightenment for the remainder of his life. The course was a two-year, team-taught interdisciplinary seminar for select students. In his autobiographical lecture Trilling fondly recalls that "its curriculum was the classics of the Western World, the Great Books, beginning with Homer and coming down through the 19th century—in those days there were as yet no recognized 20th-century classics: *Ulysses* was a new book—including not only works of literature but also philosophy and history, which were likely to be dealt with as if they were works of literature." This unmediated encounter of the student and the classics, uninformed by any required readings in historical scholarship, was criticized as superficial by some faculty. The ideal of intelligent reading, however, was embraced by Trilling, who shaped his own essays and courses accordingly. He never limited his criticism by some idea of specialization or expertise but wrote on whatever books or authors engaged his interest. The linguistic and historical knowledge in his work is often thin, as he realized, and he attempts to compensate through the breadth and moral power with which he interprets the general patterns of cultural life.

Trilling's lecture explains the cultural rationale behind the Columbia program by noting its genealogy: Erskine had studied with George Woodberry, who had been a pupil of Charles Eliot Norton during the years he reformed the curriculum at Harvard, and Norton had been a friend of Thomas Carlyle, Ruskin, and Arnold. Joining them all was "the idea that great works of art and thought have a decisive part in shaping the life of a polity," an ideal Trilling traced back to Sir Philip Sidney's *Defence of Poesie* and to the era of Renaissance English Humanism. From Sidney to Arnold to Trilling, "they believed that men who were in any degree responsible for the welfare of the polity and for the quality of life that characterized it must be large-minded men, committed to great ends, devoted to virtue, assured of the dignity of the human estate and dedicated to enhancing and preserving it; and that great works of the imagination could foster and even institute this large-mindedness, this *magnanimity.*" More autobiographically Trilling observes that such an education might show young men how to "escape from the limitations of their middle-class or their lower-middle class upbringings." This ideal of a republic of virtuous, educated citizens was the one which guided the Enlightenment thinkers who created the polity of the United States, most notably Thomas Jefferson, and which fueled such reformist individualists as Thoreau. In its emphasis on changing consciousness, rather than material conditions, and with its concomitant stress on the self rather than society, this vision contrasts sharply with that of Marxism and foredoomed Trilling's occasional alliance with that movement's arguments.

Trilling's intellectual development was greatly influenced by his career-long friendship and collaboration with Jacques Barzun. Upon his graduation from Columbia in 1927, Barzun immediately received an appointment in the history department. He took up the task of reviving Erskine's humanities course, renamed the "Colloquium on Important Books," and invited Trilling in 1934 to team teach it with him. These Wednesday night sessions were intense challenges for all involved; the first term ran from the *Iliad* through the *Novum Organum;* the second from Voltaire to Freud. Trilling had earlier taken his stand "with a group of young men who held themselves apart in skepticism and irony." Barzun's capacious learning and humanistic faith inspired

Trilling and the course's direction. The colloquium was "inhospitable to modern artistic culture" and its alienation from life, recalls Trilling. The books they read were "affirmative."

While the curriculum of great books at Columbia turned Trilling's mind toward the past, the literary and critical events of his time presented new challenges to his intelligence: "how could one read Yeats or Joyce or Lawrence or Eliot or Proust or Mann or Kafka without understanding that the culture of humanism was at a point of crisis? That the society which had sustained this culture was in dire straits?" The recurrent struggle of culture and anarchy made it difficult for the young student to know how to read or write. The "books that undertook to solve these problems" included Eliot's *The Sacred Wood* (1922), I. A. Richards's *The Principles of Literary Criticism* (1925) and *Practical Criticism* (1929), Edmund Wilson's *Axel's Castle* (1931), and F. R. Leavis's *Revaluation* (1936). But the "sense of cultural crises that literature conveyed–that sense of *crisis* that made for so intense a *critical* activity–was paralleled and enforced by the work of two commanding, preeminent minds, Marx and Freud." Trilling notes that both are educated in the "tradition of humanism" in Germany, whose ideals, he surprisingly argues, they always remained loyal to despite their "unmasking" of culture's duplicities. Marx and Freud became mentors to the young Trilling as they pursued the arduous life of the opposing self. Despite their great differences they accord in a "programmatic rejection of the settled, institutionalized conception of reality and how it works, in their discovery of principles of causation which lead to the conclusion that the settled, institutionalized reality is a falsehood, or, as we might say, a mask." Trilling, in speaking of their common "relationship to the past" and intimate confrontation with history, never mentions that Marx and Freud were Jews. "Upon my work in criticism," he avows, "upon my intellectual life in general, the systems of Marx and Freud had, I have never doubted, a decisive influence." The role of Freud in Trilling's work over the years continued to grow, while Marx's star would be obscured by Stalin and by the sad vicissitudes of left-wing intellectual movements in the United States. Trilling's Marx was always the humanist crying out against alienation and the passionate reader of Charles Dickens, not the author of *Das Kapital* (1867-1894).

That Marx ultimately failed the self and humanism is the lesson decipherable in Trilling's decision to turn, for his first great project, to Matthew Arnold:

> The Arnold that engaged my first interest was the melancholy poet, the passive sufferer from the stresses and tendencies of his culture. When the book was finished my concern was with the man who had pitted himself against the culture, who had tried to understand the culture for the purpose of shaping it—with the critic, with . . . the first literary intellectual in the English speaking world.

This account takes on resonance when we consider its biographical context. Trilling took his M.A. at Columbia in 1926, taught briefly at the University of Wisconsin at Madison, scratched out temporary assignments at Hunter College, and worked briefly as an editor at the *Menorah Journal,* which was a central force in Jewish literary and cultural affairs. Seeking an identity, Trilling expressed his "solidarity with the intellectual life by taking an apartment in Greenwich Village" in 1929: "there seemed no other place in New York where a right-thinking person might live." In 1932 he was unaccountably appointed instructor at Columbia, uptown from right-thinking bohemia, and he taught four courses a semester while working on his Ph.D. The salary was not handsome, his and Diana's families were in need, and Trilling was desperate for money. He wrote book reviews when he could, and took odd literary jobs: he talked to women's clubs, pasted up anthologies, tutored, taught a Junior League class. Understandably he developed a writer's block concerning the very practicality of an intellectual biography of Arnold which would involve the history of the nineteenth century and of Western civilization as a whole. His director, Emery Neff, regularly rejected his drafts.

In 1936 the department announced Trilling would be let go, explaining that "as a Freudian, a Marxist, and a Jew" Trilling was not happy at Columbia. Trilling's notebooks from the time record the sorry tale of his near-firing, and the story is the all-too-familiar one of petty academic jealousies, intellectual and moral cowardice, hypocrisy, betrayal, and an indefatigable hostility to innovation. Harrison Steeves, the department chairman, told Trilling "that they needed routine men." While certainly informed by the anti-Semitism of the era and of Columbia in particular, Trilling's dismissal was also a repudiation of radical cultural criticism in general. Neff betrayed his thesis

student by questioning Trilling's "sociological tendencies" and then arguing that the firing would be to Trilling's benefit. Trilling confronted Neff, who was less than candid about his role. "I did not admit at any point," recorded Trilling, "the decency of his getting me fired for my own good, though his absurd mind is sincere about it, I believe." The move against him catalyzed Trilling's spirit, brought him out of his depression, and inspired him to vigorously defend his talents to numerous senior faculty. Trilling was restored to his position, began work anew on Arnold, and published the results to good reviews in 1939. Circumventing the normal procedures of the English department, Columbia president Nicholas Murray Butler appointed Lionel Trilling as assistant professor of English, tenure track. He was the first Jew to hold such a position at Columbia. He had pitted himself against the culture, shaped it up, and began his climb toward becoming one of the leading literary intellectuals of the English-speaking world.

Trilling's success, however, came only after extreme self-doubt: "I was trying to write a book about Matthew Arnold and having a bitter time of it because it seemed to me that I was working in a lost world, that nobody wanted, or could possibly want, a book about Matthew Arnold." The "ivory tower" was held in suspicion, and Trilling was "much ashamed" of what he had undertaken. Trilling was saved by the interest of Edmund Wilson, who lived across the street from him and was then a principal writer at the *New Republic.* That Wilson was already controversial for his critique of the Communist movement probably increased Trilling's trust in his opinion. Wilson's support had a "liberating effect," recalls Trilling, "the sudden sense I no longer had to suppose that I was doing a shameful academic drudgery, that I was not required to work with the crippling belief that I was 'turning away' from the actual and miserable present to the unreal and comfortable past." In a notebook entry of 13 June 1936 Trilling writes of the "change of life" and "new dimension" acquired by his twin victories over Columbia and dogmatic Marxism. He would "no longer measure all things by linear Marxian yardstick," and he felt a "sense of invulnerability" which, he conjectured, was "the result of [his] successful explosion at Columbia."

*Matthew Arnold* (1939, revised 1949) was conceived as "a biography of Arnold's mind" and thus as a survey of the nineteenth-century culture that inherited the decline of the Enlightenment and of Romanticism, oversaw the rise of science, and set the stage for modernism. Arnold was the first of many seemingly orthodox or conservative figures rehabilitated by Trilling's insistence on the "critical dialectic" informing a writer's outlook. Forecasting the method of Trilling's future work, the book frames its discussion in relation to contemporary affairs: the League of Nations, the crisis of liberal politics, the ascent of Nazism, the reactionary dismissal of objectivity. The autobiographical moment typical of Trilling's writing occurs at the start, where Arnold's response to the French Revolution is made the centerpiece of a historical approach to Arnold's historical method. At book's close Trilling returns to the claim that "Arnold's whole career had been spent in evaluating the French Revolution"; the same might be said of Trilling—and his generation—in relation to the Bolshevik revolution.

As Arnold turned to literature and intellectual humanism for a salvation missing in both politics and religion, Trilling took a similar course in moving from Marxism and Judaism to moral realism and a tragic view of history. Reviews of *Matthew Arnold* praised the book highly. Wilson's encouragement was confirmed as he called it "a revealing and original work." Trilling's hope for acceptance by the left as well as the academy bore fruit in the *Partisan Review*, where editor William Phillips named *Matthew Arnold* "an extremely intelligent and exhaustive analysis" and "one of the best works of historical criticism produced in this country." The *New York Times* described it as "among the best books of American criticism since *Axel's Castle.*" In the *New Yorker*, Clifton Fadiman (a contemporary of Trilling's at the *Menorah Journal*) saw it as "first rate," a "careful and beautifully written study," demonstrating that Arnold's "dilemmas and intellectual crises strike to the heart of our own unease." The English reviews, which directly influenced Butler's decision, were impressive. The *Spectator* named it "the most brilliant piece of biographical criticism issued in English during the last ten years," while the *Times Literary Supplement* stated simply that it was "the most comprehensive and critical book on Matthew Arnold that exists."

Trilling's achievement of the role of the man of humanistic letters largely resolved the identity crisis that had plagued his personal and intellectual life since his enrollment at Columbia. In the foreword to *Speaking of Literature and Society*, Diana Trilling detects a "personal narrative" in his scattered writings from 1925 to 1935: in

his "failed search for a 'Jewish identity' in his early writing for *The Menorah Journal*," and "his failed search in Marxism for an answer to the social and economic questions raised in the wake of the stock market crash of 1929." In "Young in the Thirties" (*Commentary*, 1966), Trilling recounts that what "bound together the group around the *Menorah Journal*" had "nothing to do with religion; we were not religious." Most were not Zionists and some were pro-Arab on principle. Jewishness instead provided a feeling of "authenticity," a "sense of identity" and "kinship." The *Journal* also paid well, provided Trilling with contacts in the intellectual and university communities, and published his work alongside established Jewish writers, such as Ludwig Lewisohn and Waldo Frank, as well as non-Jewish writers, such as Mark Van Doren, Lewis Mumford, and Charles Beard. The magazine's manager-editor was Elliott Cohen, who in 1945 became the founding editor of the leading Jewish magazine *Commentary*. "For Trilling," observes Krupnick, "finding a culture and establishing a personal identity were inseparable. Simply being an American or a liberal intellectual didn't give him access to a social entity that as a critic he could do anything with. And so he lacked a personal identity as well. But as a member of a small, obscure, middle-class Jewish subculture, he found a social group to which he could give the credence of his senses. The idea of himself as a Jew sustained him and gave his writing a focus for some five years." The effort, however, was decidedly ambivalent. Trilling could not embrace uncritically the program of "positive Jewishness" represented by the *Menorah Journal*, though he published some twenty-five stories, articles, and reviews in its pages between 1925 and 1931. He regularly reviewed new Jewish novels and found in their treatment of social issues a way into the larger concerns that would preoccupy his career.

In "Another Jewish Problem Novel," a review of Milton Waldman's *The Disinherited* (*Menorah Journal*, April 1929; collected in *Speaking of Literature and Society*), Trilling is unmerciful in attacking the "woodenness" of Waldman's prose and the formulaic quality of his portrait of Judaic life. Particularly irritating to Trilling is a stereotype that he was himself trying to resist: "Its formula is that a man, usually of some importance among Gentiles, either does not know or does not care that he is a Jew. Some circumstance makes him know or care; the fact that he is a Jew becomes important; frequently he suffers in material things because of it; almost always, immediately upon the recognition, he enters into full spiritual and intellectual maturity." Trilling finds this self-conscious conversion narrative ultimately stifling rather than liberating, both for life and art: "It is rather the conventions and limits into which the modern Jewish novel has settled that garrote all the books' interest and significance." The question of being Jewish must not be a reactionary focus for an escape from modern social diversity; instead the plight of the Jew must become a way of seeing in particular the general tensions of class, ethnic group, and individual: "Only by transcending the problem will it become illuminated. Only when the Jewish problem is included in a rich sweep of life, a life which would be important and momentous even without the problem of Jewishness, but a life to which the problem of Jewishness adds further import and moment, will a good Jewish novel have been written and something said about the problem." Trilling's effort to transcend what he saw as the limitations of the Jewish situation followed two overlapping paths: his exploration of leftist politics and his espousal of intellectual humanism.

"The Changing Myth of the Jew," apparently composed in 1930 but not published until August 1978 in *Commentary* (collected in *Speaking of Literature and Society*), conducts an ambitious "description of the Jew in fiction from Chaucer to George Eliot." While Trilling chiefly discusses the possible functions these myths might have for the dominant culture, he concentrates on analyzing the major myths. These include the Jew as anti-Christ, as moneylender, as the fabled Wandering Jew, and so on. In modern times the religious and moral opprobrium of previous myths gives way to a social distinction: there is "a natural antithesis between the concept Jew and the concept Gentleman." For Trilling this is "anti-Semitism in its present day sense. . . . the Jew is held to be outside the pole of society." This anti-Semitism in turn serves as "a useful instrumentality in the hands of conservative, chauvinistic, anti-democratic powers," who now have a convenient scapegoat in their battle against "extended franchise, emancipation of the lower orders, liberation of the oppressed minorities, the middle-class." Even in Trilling's time this diversionary rhetorical function of "Jew" in political discourse had already been linked to its newest generic analogue, the "Commie." The language and argument of this essay show Trilling clearly progressing on the road from the Jewish dilemma to the systematic

cultural, economic, and political issues that encompass and "transcend" it.

Trilling's essays and reviews in the decade after receiving his B.A. covered a wide variety of topics and writers, including Emily Brontë, "Terror-Romanticism," Marcel Proust, the literature of revolutionary Russia, D. H. Lawrence, Thomas Carlyle, Samuel Taylor Coleridge, "Politics and the Liberal," and Willa Cather. Evidently Trilling continued the program in wide reading begun at Columbia, and in book reviewing Trilling developed the plain style which would always mark his prose. In contrast to T. S. Eliot, who gained fame through the nerve, wit, and presumption of his review essays, Trilling fashioned a gentlemanly style that is always lucid, though it has as a consequence left us no famous phrases or quotable passages. In his introduction to *The Portable Matthew Arnold* (1949) Trilling's summary of Arnold's style seems to capture perfectly the ideal which informed Trilling's own writing: "He spoke about literature as a man to men, not as a scholar, not as a teacher, not really, for all his preoccupation with morality, as a preacher. His tone was firm and direct, but light; he was authoritative without bullying; and he was always clear. He spoke of literature as one who loved it and lived in it; but he spoke too as one who knew the world and lived in the world and believed that literature was connected in a complex multitude of ways with actual practical life."

Exceptions to these stylistic goals are those moments in Trilling when irritation and anger—either with the culture itself or with its increasingly irrational adversaries—break through the gentleman's mask. One finds such moments early, in the essays of the late 1920s and early 1930s, when personal and political outrages severely test the flexibility and tolerance of Trilling's intelligence. In "The Promise of Realism" (*Menorah Journal*, May 1930; collected in *Speaking of Literature and Society*), Trilling's review of several recent social novels becomes an occasion for excoriation, beginning with literary problems that quickly become political:

> We perceive nowadays that realism is a manner and a subject rather than a virtue. We understand that it is a literary cant word used to indicate a sort of literature that confines itself to an account (simple rather than devious) of the pain of people (humble rather than exalted) in a struggle with their environment. . . . All this admitted to the belittlement of realism, the fact re-

mains that realism is necessarily the most relevant literature we are producing today. We are living in an environment of an impossible strenuousness. But strenuousness is not terrible: we are living in an environment that is befouling and insulting. Only the very wealthy do not live in such an environment and only the very blind do not know it.

Trilling turns to a sweeping review of the realism of the American Renaissance and of the protests against society it recorded, but he finds only a story of failure and cruelty: "At bottom, these books were saying, there was something divine about America. And if it killed you, though it might do so ruthlessly, it killed you like a god—first making you do something for which it had the right to kill you." Presumably Trilling was thinking here of *The Scarlet Letter, Moby-Dick,* even Emerson's essays, or Thoreau's *Walden.* These, then, were tales of the defeat of the opposing self, and it is no wonder that Trilling showed such scarce appreciation for the American tradition if this was his reading of it. "America was a tragedy all right—an American tragedy." And "at the bottom of America there is insanity." Praising Edward Dahlberg's *Bottom Dogs* (1929) for its ruthless realism in depicting America's "vulgarity" and "dullness," its "dissolving souls . . . weariness and hate":

> There is no person in the United States, save he be a member of the plutocratic class . . . not one who is not tainted, a little or much, with the madness of the bottom dog, not one who is not in an asympathy of disgust and hate with his fellows. The emotions of the 'terrible and brutal . . . failure that nourishes the roots of the gigantic tree of dollars' are the universally relevant emotions of America.

At the same time, Trilling recognized the gap between art and propaganda and was as wary of leftist moralizing as of "positive Jewishness." In an untitled review of Matthew Josephson's *Portrait of the Artist as American (Symposium,* October 1930; collected as "The Problem of the American Artist" in *Speaking of Literature and Society),* Trilling already took the position that modernism, while breaking with mimetic realism, nonetheless stood as a criticism of life: "Joyce, Mann, Lawrence, Eliot, Gide, and Proust have all written in the travail of opposition to their world." Yet whatever the author's intentions or

conditions, "criticism can be valid only if it thinks in terms of the individual work and its accomplishment or failure of important meaning, and not in terms of social causes." This precarious critical balance between aesthetic and political concerns also runs through Trilling's untitled review of Martin Schutze's *Academic Illusions in the Field of the Letters and the Arts* (1933) in the *Modern Monthly* of January 1934 (collected as "The Autonomy of the Literary Work" in *Speaking of Literature and Society).* Here Trilling praises I. A. Richards for returning our attention to the "poem itself." This token, however, is quickly taken back as Trilling goes on to argue that the art work is a response to life, that its materials and its composition involve "ethical situations" that entail the relation of personality to concept. Here the groundwork is laid for a career in which moral psychology and literary expression often occupy the same horizon.

Trilling's review of Robert Briffault's *Europa in Limbo* (1937) was entitled "Marxism in Limbo." Reprinted in *Speaking of Literature and Society,* it originally appeared in 1937 in the *Partisan Review,* which had resurfaced after its editors' break with Stalinism and the Communist party in the wake of the Moscow trials.

The essay exhibits the parallel between the vicissitudes of Marxist criticism during the 1930s and Trilling's own development. As Alan Wald recounts it, "a generation of young American writers and critics began to turn from introverted immersion in the experimental forms and esoteric sensibilities of the years following the First World War to the political-literary activism of the early 1930s," only to find itself betrayed by Stalin and confronting an aesthetic of "proletarian literature" and socialist realism whose political and literary merits were dubious at best. *Partisan Review* had been founded in 1933 by William Phillips and Philip Rahv in explicit institutional and ideological alliance with the Communist party, though they early parted company with the mechanical form of much Marxist criticism. The journal became a historic rallying point for many radical New York intellectuals of the mid 1930s, including James T. Farrell, Lionel Abel, Delmore Schwartz, Harold Rosenberg, Clement Greenberg, Sidney Hook, Meyer Shapiro, and Trilling. The debate over the relative claims of aesthetics and politics in Marxist criticism was deeply influenced by Leon Trotsky, whose *Literature and Revolution* (1924) offered a theoretical compromise with modernism much to the liking of the *Partisan Review* crowd, who featured Trotsky in their pages. His pronouncements in "Art and Politics in Our Epoch" (*Partisan Review*, 1937) could almost have been written by Trilling himself: "Generally speaking, art is an expression of man's need for a harmonious and complete life, that is to say, his need for those major benefits of which a class society has deprived him. That is why a protest against reality, either conscious or unconscious, active or passive, optimistic or pessimistic, always forms part of a really creative piece of work. Every new tendency in art has begun with a rebellion." The "opposing self " of modernism appears as one with the spirit of the October Revolution, but is undone by its rigidification into bureaucracy, prescription, and a stark repression of individual will or imagination. This historical irony and its tragedy partly underlies Trilling's lifelong suspicion that rebellions against culture often end up fabricating new tyrannies of their own.

Trilling's radical sympathies were deepest in the years from 1930 to 1935. He and Diana did organizational work for a year at the National Committee for the Defense of Political Prisoners, a Communist party organ run by Elliott Cohen after the demise of the *Menorah Journal*. One might see Trilling as torn between his academic aspirations and his revolutionary goals; in any case his turn to anti-Stalinism does coincide with renewed work on Arnold, and his appointment as assistant professor at Columbia is quickly followed by his development of a liberal humanist position. This new stance finds an airing, appropriately, in the pages of *Partisan Review*, which would publish part one of "Reality in America" in 1940, the essay that leads off Trilling's *The Liberal Imagination* (1950). Trilling is, in fact, divided on the merits of the liberal position, and he attempts to save it from the dogmas of a simple progressivism. For Trilling "liberal" designates the social reform politics exemplified by Vernon Parrington, a literary critic and historian whose *Main Currents in American Thought* (1927, 1930) pursued an economic interpretation of literary movements. This use of liberal ideology in criticism results, says Trilling, in the mistaken glorification of Theodore Dreiser, whose social realism he sees marred by clumsy prose and sentimentality. Trilling argues that Parrington overlooks aesthetics in favor of politics, blindly missing (with everyone else) Henry James's superiority to Dreiser. It is a defense of modernism against an old idea of realism. The real target here, as Krupnick ar-

gues, may well be the Stalinism of the 1930s and Trilling's own erstwhile leftism. Liberalism here also signifies a naive belief in the positive qualities of human nature and thus lacks the perception of tragedy and moral realism Trilling identifies in writers like Hawthorne and Freud. The "self " plays no theoretical role here except in the protesting voice of Trilling himself as he argues against the monolithic extinction of personal quality by the application of reductive political standards.

Trilling's evolving position finds expression, after a "concentrated rush" of composition, in his *E. M. Forster* (1943), which modifies and even reverses perspectives Trilling utilized in his earlier pieces on the novelist. Its introduction, "Forster and the Liberal Imagination," finds Trilling forcefully using the critical mind of liberalism against liberalism's own tendencies towards dogmatism. Trilling, not unlike the New Critics (or later, Paul de Man), will argue that the complexities and paradoxes of the literary imagination always escape and shed light upon, the reductive statements of rational prescriptions. Like James, George Meredith, Charles Dickens, and Hawthorne, Forster shows "his unremitting concern with moral realism. . . . not the awareness of morality itself but of the contradictions, paradoxes and dangers of living the moral life." This "mention of complication" may appear to be "quietism, like mere shilly-shallying," but in fact for Trilling it represents Forster's "war with the liberal imagination," "that loose body of middle class opinion which includes such ideas as progress, collectivism and humanitarianism." Sounding a bit like T. S. Eliot on the topic of original sin, Trilling writes: "The liberal mind is sure that the order of human affairs owes it a simple logic: good is good and bad is bad. . . . Before the idea of good-and-evil its imagination fails; it cannot accept the improbable paradox." In representing the complex paradoxes of psychology and society, Forster escapes the Marxist model; *Howards End* shows "that on the one hand class is character, soul and destiny, and that on the other hand class is not finally determining." Class struggle is interiorized as "moral struggle in the heart of a single person." This acceptance of the agon with the forces of evil, necessity, and circumstance includes an embrace of history and tradition; Trilling echoes Eliot again, and numerous commentators on American literature, in citing Forster's "conscious relation with the past" in contrast to the liberal American's forgetting of it. Forster will join the list of the champi-

*Lionel Trilling, 1947 (photograph by Sylvia Salmi)*

tual fascism of T. S. Eliot as the characteristic voice of our epoch will do well to ponder Mr. Trilling's pages" and their "exciting premonitions of a new faith about to rise from the ashes of the old."

Six years later the preface to *The Liberal Imagination* had rehabilitated liberalism to the extent that Trilling could identify it with his own brand of humanism. Criticism must "recall liberalism to its first essential imagination of variousness and possibility, which implies the awareness of complexity and difficulty." As with Marxist communism, liberalism betrays itself when its rebellious self becomes an organized social machine; the "characteristic paradox" of liberalism, Trilling says, is that "in the very interests of its primal act of imagination by which it establishes its essences and existence—in the interests, that is, of its vision of a general enlargement and freedom and rational direction of human life—it drifts toward a denial of the emotions and the imagination." In words the reader may now find incomprehensible, Trilling states that liberalism is "the sole intellectual tradition" in America, where "conservatism and reaction" are bankrupt. Trilling's own suspicion of social management of the individual ironically became the attitude of "conservatism" in the 1980s, when the Enlightenment belief in society's obligation to refine and improve man is rejected by a widespread enmity toward government. Likewise Trilling's increasing emphasis on the world as a "complex and unexpected and terrible place which is not always to be understood by the mind as we use it in our everyday tasks" became a note of resignation as he articulated the stoic portrait of the moral realist. As early as the Arnold book, Krupnick finds, the dynamic dialectic of Marxist criticism becomes "a static doctrine of sustained tensions."

*The Liberal Imagination* was indicative of the shape Trilling's future work would take. He would not dedicate himself to sustained scholarly projects; instead he wrote reviews, essays, and lectures on an immense variety of subjects, the treatment of each serving as the occasion for a topical statement on some issue in literary, cultural, or moral debates of the time. In this first collection are found essays on Sherwood Anderson, the Kinsey Report, Freud, the little magazine, Tacitus, Fitzgerald, Wordsworth, and "The Meaning of a Literary Idea." "Freud and Literature" is particularly significant, as it indicates Trilling's conviction that literature is at bottom "research into the self." Cautioning against the reductionistic errors in some psychoanalytic criticism, and dissenting

ons of the ordinary in Trilling's canon—Arnold, Wordsworth, Howells: "The very relaxation of his style, its colloquial unpretentiousness, is a mark of his acceptance of the human fact as we know it now. He is content with the human possibility and content with its limitations." Written during the outbreak of a world war brought on by the extremism and absolutism of Nazism and Stalinism, these cautionary words have, at least in context, a certain sober sanity about them.

Again Trilling received laudatory reviews. *Commonweal* called *E. M. Forster* "One of the finest pieces of literary criticism presented in many a year," while the *Nation* praised it as the "best full study of Forster's work and ideas yet written." Though the *New Republic* felt Trilling took Forster "too seriously," Carlos Baker of the *New York Times* found the book a "searching assessment," as did Clifton Fadiman in the *New Yorker*, who trumpeted it as "a model of the kind of criticism not too easily discoverable among us today—restrained, balanced, unashamed of its roots in a long intellectual tradition, academic in the finest sense." More apocalyptically the *Weekly Book Review*'s G. F. Whicher saw it as "a manifesto": "Those who are reluctant to accept the sad spiri-

from Freud's own view of the artist as daydreaming neurotic, Trilling finds Freud's greatest contribution "implicit in his whole conception of the mind" as "a poetry-making organ": psychoanalysis is "a science of tropes, of metaphor and its variants, synecdoche and metonymy." The "imagination of complication" Trilling seeks as antidote to dogmatic systems is offered by Freud's call "to read the work of literature with a lively sense of its latent and ambiguous meanings, as if it were, as indeed it is, a being no less alive and contradictory than the man who created it." While this would appear to parallel Jacques Lacan's argument that the unconscious is structured like a language, Trilling in fact resists the conclusion that the self or subject is determined and conditioned by language or the unconscious. "Freudian man," he concludes, is "a creature of far more dignity and far more interest than the man which any other modern system has been able to conceive. . . . He has the faculty of imagining for himself more in the way of pleasure and satisfaction than he can possibly achieve. Everything he gains he pays for in more than equal coin; compromise and the compounding with defeat constitute his best way of getting through the world. His best qualities are the result of a struggle whose outcome is tragic."

In "Art and Neurosis," Trilling argues against the deterministic view that "literary power and genius spring from pain and neurotic sacrifice." The artist, like Freud himself, is rather the hero who makes of his self-analysis a general symbol and understanding of the human condition. "What makes the artist," says Trilling, "is his power to shape the material of pains we all have." Initial reviews in the *Atlantic*, the *Nation*, the *New Republic*, and the New York papers were quite positive, though there were complaints about Trilling's editorial "we," his "negative conclusions" on American culture and literature, and his plain style. Clifton Fadiman, writing in the *New Yorker*, praised the book for trying to reach a general audience, though he found Trilling "puts too much energy into undercharging his prose."

*The Liberal Imagination* sold over 100,000 copies before going out of print. This is an extraordinary testimony to the success of Trilling's plain style, as it spoke to a large, middle-class audience that still shared the goal of being well-read participants in cultural debate. It is difficult to think of any academic critic since Trilling's time who has commanded such a readership or such sales figures. While this may in some measure be a reflec-

tion of the increasing specialization of academic criticism, it also implies the disappearance of the audience for whom Trilling wrote and whose continued existence he argued for even as the forces of culture were working to replace it with ill-educated consumers of mass-market artifacts. But Trilling's success throughout the 1940s and the 1950s was partly owing to his ability to give expression to the complex moral dilemmas of post-World-War-II America, especially as the Marxism of the 1930s became an unimaginable episode in the age of Joseph McCarthy and Dwight Eisenhower. It was an era of complacency, self-delusion, contradiction, and unresolved tensions, so that Trilling's portrait of tragic conflict seemed utterly suited to its needs. "He sought," writes Krupnick, "a central role in the culture as explainer and guide to the perplexed, a conception of the teacher's role that brings him closer to Victorian sages like [ John Henry, Cardinal] Newman and Arnold than to academic literary theorists of more recent years."

Remembering back to the early 1940s, Alfred Kazin gives this description in *New York Jew* (1978) of Trilling's impression on him at the offices of the *New Republic*:

> Trilling already had his distinguished white hair over a handsome face that seemed to be furrowed, hooded, closed up with constant thought. The life was all within, despite his debonair practiced easiness of manner. In person, there was immense and even cavernous subtlety to the man, along with much timidity, a self-protectiveness as elegant as a fencer's; my first meetings with Trilling were just too awesome. With the deep-sunk colored pouches under his eyes, the cigarette always in hand like an intellectual gesture, an air that combined weariness, vanity, and immense caution, he was already a personage. . . . Trilling astonished me by saying, very firmly, that he would not write anything that did not "promote my reputation.". . . I had never encountered a Jewish intellectual so conscious of social position, so full of adopted finery in his conversation.

Trilling's personal life during the 1940s was brightened by the improved health of Diana and the birth in 1948 of their son, James (who received a Ph.D. from Harvard in 1980 in art history). Diana became a regular fiction critic for the *Nation* from 1942-1949 (pieces later collected as *Reviewing the Forties*) and won a Guggenheim Fellowship in 1950. Lionel Trilling's professional achievements during the 1940s included his promotions at Columbia to associate professor in 1945 and to full professor in 1948; his appointment to the advisory boards of *Kenyon Review* and *Partisan Review;* and his Guggenheim Fellowship awarded in 1947. Trilling's notebook of 1948 candidly sets down his anxiety about the type and quality of his work, showing that many of the doubts voiced publicly about Trilling were shared in private by the man himself. He feels a "sense of absurdity" in his new academic rank, bemoaning his ignorance of foreign and classical languages, and detects "a great and growing laziness about reading and no wish for investigation" on his part. "I have only a gift," he records, "of dealing rather sensibly with literature, which surprises me for I always assume my intellectual feebleness. My being a professor and a much respected and even admired one is a great hoax." An entry for September of that year shows Trilling's insecurity and correspondent vanity as, after delivering his lecture on "Art and Fortune" to the English Institute, the herd of colleagues heaped accolades on him while Mark Schorer and Leslie Fiedler vanished silently. "The praise of the others profoundly depressed me—utterly-sickened me with my profession—depressed all evening," Trilling remembered, "but not as it were personally—very unhappy about my essay which I consider academic, simple-minded, philistine, regressive—great sense of the superiority of the 'others.' "

These years also saw the publication of his novel *The Middle of the Journey* (1947), which like most of Trilling's fiction was semi-autobiographical and concerned with many of the issues raised by his criticism. Trilling's role as cultural pedagogue was enhanced by his organizational and review participation in two book clubs in the 1950s, the Readers' Subscription and the Mid-Century Book Society. The essays he wrote for the book club newsletter, some later collected in *A Gathering of Fugitives* (1956), were in his plainest style as he moderated his modernism for an audience whose ideas of social reality were now coming, not from the novel, but from the flickering television screen. The book clubs did not prescribe a diet of classics but a variety of middle-brow offerings suitable to the continuing education of an imagined public wavering between elite and mass culture. So in *A Gathering of Fugitives* we find essays on E. M. Forster's biography of his great-aunt, Edmund Wilson's *The Shores of*

*Light* (1952), David Riesman's *The Lonely Crowd* (1950), and Henry Adams's selected letters alongside pieces on Emile Zola, Edith Wharton, Dickens, and Freud.

The most interesting and telling addition to that volume is Trilling's revised publication of "The Situation of the American Intellectual at the Present Time," first presented at the *Partisan Review* symposium entitled "Our Country and Our Culture" (1952). The symposium's title indicated a turn away from the adversarial role taken by the intellectuals of the 1930s, for they seemed to embrace the 1950s return to patriotism and "normalcy." Trilling willingly admitted this "diminution of the sense of alienation" and asserted the "unmistakable improvement in the American cultural situation" over that of his youth in the 1920s. After two global wars "there is now no longer any foreign cultural ideal to which [the American intellectual] can possibly fly from that American stupidity and vulgarity, the institutionalized awareness of which was once likely to have been the mainspring of his mental life." The "sense of an inert American mass resistant to ideas, entirely unenlightened and hating enlightenment" gives way to a cautiously optimistic portrait of a new intellectual class, both in the academy and in the professions, whose interests might counterbalance the depressing commercialization of values wrought by capitalism. Trilling sidestepped the symposium's question about "mass culture," which posed "no doubt a considerable threat to high culture," with his sketch of a "continuation of the traditional culture in the traditional forms," which had become democratized somewhat and made native to America.

The "European influence" on the "conscious experience of the American intellectual" had "come to an end" (a situation reversed once more after the invasion of European critical theory after 1968). Trilling writes rather autobiographically of the American intellectual's recent history: "the 'society' which the American intellectual learned about from Europe was in large part a construct of Marxism, or a construct of the long war of the French intellectuals with the French *bourgeoisie*. . . . His sense of himself as an intellectual, his conception of the function of criticism, led him always away from the variousness and complexity of phenomena to an abstract totality of perception which issued in despair or disgust, to which he attached a very high degree of spiritual prestige." This European absolutism would be replaced by an Anglo-American practicality that accepted the incessant compromise between freedom and necessity as man's fate and stressed literature's role as a "criticism of life." In resigning the absolutes of high and low culture, revolution and despair, Trilling speaks to an average educated American mind whose ordinary and yet lucid engagement with the "complexity" of modernity is to be preferred to the stridency of alienation or the groaning of disillusionment.

*The Opposing Self* (1955) displays the tensions within Trilling's return to normalcy. This collection of lectures and introductions from 1951-1954 is more sophisticated than *A Gathering of Fugitives* and expresses his sense that the individual could no longer see himself as anything but an antagonist to culture, whose current forms were the bureaucratic conformism of Cold War America and of the Soviet Union. The book's preface clearly articulates the convergence between Trilling's theory of modernism, his view of literary history, and his disillusionment with contemporary affairs:

> There have always been selves, or at least ever since the oracle at Delphi began to advise every man to know his own. And whoever has read any European history at all knows that the self emerges (as the historians say) at pretty frequent intervals. Yet the self that makes itself manifest at the end of the eighteenth century is different in kind, and in effect, from any self that had ever before emerged. It is different in several notable respects, but here is one distinguishing characteristic which seems to me pre-eminently important: its intense and adverse imagination of the culture in which it has its being.

Critics of Trilling have often noted the imperious adoption of the pronoun "we" in his rhetoric. The particular experience of the European, white, largely male and middle-class mind is universalized through this pronoun into a grand narrative of the human self's adventures. Minority and female selves, for example, had a distinctly different relation to the forces of culture in the West than the white males who dominated society, and the difference of their history (and of their writing, which as such goes unnoticed by Trilling) is lost. In defense, one notes that Trilling's essay championing Jane Austen and *Mansfield Park* (1814) closes the volume and makes Austen the preeminent example of Trilling's ideal of complex moral intelligence. Yet one also

notes that, in defending Austen against sexist critics, Trilling empties her writing of gender in order to universalize its humanistic message; the relation of Austen's gender to her irony and to her writing on marriage goes unperceived in the age before feminism taught some men to read like women.

The essays of *The Opposing Self* chart the "duality" or "dialectic" of "spirit and matter," "form and force," art and common fact in discussions of John Keats, Dickens, Leo Tolstoy, William Dean Howells, James, William Wordsworth, Orwell, Flaubert, and Austen. In each case Trilling strives to see the cultural criticism implicit in the writer's text, and to do so through a framework that includes—and is largely inspired by—contemporary debates over the directions being taken by art and society. The quite extraordinary essay on Howells seeks to redeem him for our interest by seeing the dialectic between "the conditioned" and "life as pure spirit" in his work; the mundane quality of Howells is not to be judged aesthetically but celebrated as "social witness" and "loving wonder at the fact that persons of the most mediocre sort somehow manage to make a society." Trilling contrasts this democratic humanism to the attitude of "revolutionary" Marxists who condescend to Howells "genteel" critique of capitalism; Trilling places Howells's allegiance to the ordinary within a tradition stretching back to Wordsworth, whose gentility and orthodoxy are rehabilitated by a similar argument.

It is the essay on Keats, however, which most eloquently expresses Trilling's ambivalent view of the self in culture. In a remarkable piece of psychological identification, Trilling writes that despite Keats's progressive sympathies, he "had no hope whatever that life could be ordered in such a way that its condition might be anything but tragic." For Trilling, "Keats's theory of art is . . . an effort to deal with the problem of evil." The ultimate theological rejoinder to the "liberal imagination," as one also finds in the essays on Freud and Hawthorne, is the metaphysical and universal immanence of evil. Any historical particularity of "evil," and thus any hope of its amelioration, is lost in the overarching perception of its inevitability. The figure of the self-divided moral realist appears repeatedly in Trilling's work, as here, where one finds that "wisdom is the proud, bitter, and joyful acceptance of tragic life." The "aesthetic," Trilling theorizes, is the power to perceive the beautiful necessity of evil and is thus inseparable from the strength and genius of the self. This tragic vision he finds embodied in Keats's famous letter on "Negative capability," "when man is capable of being in uncertainties, Mysteries, doubts, without any irritable reaching after fact and reason." Keats's outburst, Trilling pointedly notes, comes after a "disquisition" with Charles Wentworth Dilke, a doctrinaire follower of William Godwin's radical liberalism, which Keats resists much as Trilling resisted Parrington's liberalism and the radical agenda of Marxism. Trilling contends that "the power and quality of Keats's mind concentrate in this phase, as does the energy of his heroism," which distinguishes him from moderns in "an ideological age such as ours" when the worst are full of passionate intensity. In an era when ideologies, or the critique of them, appear as just more tyranny or disillusionment, the resisting self becomes the only center that can hold: "Negative capability . . . depends upon the sense of one's personal identity and is the sign of personal identity."

The Keats essay ends in a homily on the loss of the "*mystique* of the self" in the modern age, when the individual seems so overwhelmed by circumstance. Keats is "the last image of health at the very moment when the sickness of Europe began to be apparent." Trilling never identifies this "sickness" historically, or its causes. The language is purposely Nietzschean and reiterates the diagnosis that modern man now lacks original strength, vitality, and integrity. Trilling's belated romanticism resembles Arnold's and exposes just how massively Trilling is the precursor of Harold Bloom, America's latest literary psychologist of the individual's tragic defensiveness towards the forces of the past. In turning away from his flirtation with Marxism, Trilling turns back to a romanticism of the individual that served as only the beginning inspiration of Marx's investigation into the self's alienation from culture. Reviews of the volume were not uniformly positive; David Daiches complained that it lacked "careful assessment of the individual work," while A. Alvarez dubbed it "disappointing." Harry Levin, however, writing in the *New York Times,* praised Trilling for having the "courage to be a moralist."

In *A Margin of Hope* (1982), Irving Howe recalls that the "most subtle and perhaps the most influential mind in the culture of the fifties was that of Lionel Trilling," though Trilling's adversaries "felt that his work had come to serve as a high-toned justification for the increasingly accommodating moods of American intellectuals. . . .

To a generation that in its youth had been persuaded, even coerced, to believe that action in the public world was a moral necessity, Trilling's critique of 'the liberal imagination' eased a turning away from all politics, whether liberal, radical, or conservative." The liberal imagination met its political defeat in the egregiously normal General Eisenhower, who defeated the liberal intellectual Adlai Stevenson in the presidential elections of 1952 and 1956. Early in the summer of 1956, the *Sewanee Review,* then edited by Allen Tate, published Joseph Frank's response to *The Opposing Self.* Frank's attack, entitled "Lionel Trilling and the Conservative Imagination," argued that Trilling's opposing self took refuge, in the face of circumstance and fate, in the very oppressive structures of bourgeois life that the young Trilling had once denounced: "And the result is that the will, instead of transcending the social world and its particular aims, now finds itself enjoined to treat the most casual conventions of the family life of the middle-class as the sacrosanct conditions of life itself." Frank portrays "Professor Trilling" as having an "obvious preference for social stasis over the restless agitations of pure spirit," an observation later borne out by the events at Columbia in 1968 and Trilling's response to the entire "counterculture" of the 1960s–the opposing self taking over the office of Columbia's president or simply going to Woodstock. "From a critic of the liberal imagination, then," Frank writes, "Mr. Trilling has evolved into one of the least belligerent and most persuasive spokesmen of the conservative imagination. . . . In defending the conditioned on the level of middle-class values, and in linking the torpid acceptance of these values with aesthetic transcendence, Mr. Trilling is merely augmenting the already irresistible momentum making for conformism and the debilitation of moral tension."

Thus while Trilling's influence and reputation grew throughout the 1940s and early 1950s, one may argue that it peaked at the time of Frank's review, and of similar critical pieces on Trilling by Delmore Schwartz, Richard Chase, and Irving Howe. Trilling's brand of humanism, however, would become the traditional academic's haven during the riotous 1960s, when it was often reduced to a complacent intellectual ideology of "tragic vision" and political paralysis. This tragic form of liberal humanism was then criticized by the new generation of critical theorists who arose after the political upheavals of 1968 to turn again to the courtly muses of European thought. Fredric Jameson's semiotic Marxism, for example, offered a new radical alternative to Trilling's view of "manners, morals, and the novel."

The turn against Trilling was evident in the decidedly mixed reviews received by *Beyond Culture: Essays in Literature and Learning* (1965). Writing for the *Nation*, Frederick Hoffman called the book "exquisitely written" but disappointing, taking issue with Trilling's hostility to contemporary literature and culture. Leon Edel judged Trilling's personal pronouncements on general affairs imprecise and "needlessly subjective," a complaint echoed by the *Yale Review* in noting the "diffuse" quality of Trilling's "abstract argument and confessional tone." The *New York Review of Books* spoke harshly of "Trilling's later prose style" as "attenuated" and "martyred with abstractions," though others praised his "clarifying style" and "fine command of argument." Tony Tanner, in the pages of Frank Kermode's *Encounter*, wrote thoughtfully of "Lionel Trilling's Uncertainties," praising the "supple, probing and unpolemical mind" at work despite some "detectable vagueness." Tanner's judicious and largely favorable overview of Trilling's career and themes ends by expressing dissatisfaction at *Beyond Culture's* failure to provide a specific way out of the dialectic between circumstance and will.

Only three of the book's eight essays deal specifically with literary figures (Austen, Isaac Babel, Hawthorne); three others discuss the role of literature in education and social thought; one deals with the theme of pleasure in modern thought and literature while another treats Freud and the crisis of modern culture. The preface continues the project of earlier books, to track the modern move of the "opposing self" "beyond culture" in the limited sense, and thus to restore complexity and flexibility of thought. With some irony, history gave Trilling more of an adversary culture than he desired, as the 1960s witnessed an explosion of opposition to modern culture. According to Trilling, students received the message of modernism's terror and alienation as just one more theme for a final exam, and they looked for more radical opposition in the streets. Hence Trilling came to advocate a move beyond the "modern self-consciousness and the modern self-pity." The antidote he prescribed was a renewed commitment to the deeper study of the humanistic tradition, a solution reminiscent of Erskine's general honors sequence at Columbia during the 1920s. In "On the Teaching of Modern Literature" we learn, perhaps surprisingly, that Columbia (and

Trilling) did not begin to teach the twentieth-century moderns until the 1950s, and only then in reluctant acknowledgment of student demand. Having tried and failed at a formalist approach, Trilling fell back on his personal relation to the material and organized the course around his thesis of the modernist as "opposing self," including the moderns' penchant for myth, the irrational, the unconscious, sexuality, and other channels for constituting an adversary relation to bourgeois culture. First term texts were (in order) Sir James Frazer's *Golden Bough* (1890-1915), Friedrich Nietzsche's *Birth of Tragedy* (1872), Joseph Conrad's *Heart of Darkness* (1902), Thomas Mann's *Death in Venice* (1913), Nietzsche's *Genealogy of Morals* (1887), Freud's *Civilization and Its Discontents* (1930); the second term brought Denis Diderot's *Rameau's Nephew* (1762), Fyodor Dostoevski's *Notes from Underground* (1864), Leo Tolstoy's *Death of Ivan Ilyich* (1886), and two plays by Pirandello to round out Trilling's "prolegomenal" readings. Students who came hoping for a comprehensive course in literature written since 1900 may have been disappointed. (In 1967 Trilling produced a textbook, *The Experience of Literature*, complete with a fine set of commentaries that pulled together Trilling's critical and pedagogical perspectives as they had developed over forty years, including the themes of initiation and disenchantment, the conflict of social and personal wills, and the power of art to express and transcend the tragedy at the heart of human existence.)

"Hawthorne in Our Time" begins with a discussion of Henry James's *Hawthorne* (1879), in which James characterizes his predecessor as a man of fancy whose psychological portraits were more playful than serious. Trilling endorses the modern view of Hawthorne as a profound and ambivalent moral psychologist examining the essential conflict of good and evil in man's nature. Trilling notes that the modern interpretation of Hawthorne was due to the New Criticism—not to its habit of "close reading," but to its challenge of the sentimental platitudes of "the liberal imagination." From Eliot's concern with primitivism and original sin to the Agrarians and New Critics, the "complex intention of modern criticism" is "opposition" to "the culture of democratic-capitalist industrialism and to that culture's devaluation of certain traditional ideas, modes of life, personnels, qualities of art, etc." This statement helps clarify the "reactionary" tendency of so much modernist work both left and right, explaining it as a reaction against bourgeois culture and a turn toward traditional culture or the unconditioned and primitive as a source of values.

Ultimately Hawthorne disappoints Trilling, however: "With so much readiness to apprehend the dark, the unregenerate, and evil itself, why must he be so quick to modulate what he sees?" Trilling comes back around to endorsing many of James's strictures, and extends them by an impressive comparative discussion of Kafka and Hawthorne, the former displaying a superior power of terror, alienation, and immorality. Hawthorne's second flaw, and the one that most separates him from Trilling's idea of modernity, is his refusal to offer up a viable "opposing self," an imagination sufficiently strong to resist the conditioning forces of culture. Young Goodman Brown, Minister Hooper, and the Reverend Arthur Dimmesdale are defeated by intractable realities (one wonders if the reason for defeat is the same in the cases of Hester Prynne or Zenobia). The moral for "our time," Trilling declares, is that Hawthorne cannot offer us "the power of the artist's imagination to deny the reality of the primordial Might, or to challenge and overcome it . . . he leaves us face to face with the ultimately unmodifiable world." We require, by implication, an imagination whose contact with the forces of psychological and historical darkness inevitably yield to the affirmation of willful enlightenment. That Trilling fails to consider the Oedipal structure of Hawthorne's respect for reality and ambivalence toward desire is curious coming from a critic so steeped in psychoanalytic thinking.

*Beyond Culture* also includes a revised version of Trilling's 1955 address on Freud, itself a sequel to his brilliant and influential essays on literature and psychoanalysis in *The Liberal Imagination*. Repeating some points made then, Trilling emphasizes that "literature is dedicated to a conception of the self," and thus literature has always shared with psychoanalysis a portrait of the human being as a conflict of pleasure and reality, or of willful desire and external cultural constraints. Clearly Trilling's psychological theory of literature differs sharply from the aesthetic or linguistic theories of the New Critics. Literature is, in a sense, subversive since it tells the truth of the self's psychological and social contradictions. Freud's "resistance to culture" has been overlooked by contemporary psychologists, argues Trilling, since they have taken the struggle with the superego and turned it into accommodation and normalizing therapy. Faced by the increasing

evidence of the failure of the oppositional self and the continuing dominance of society, Trilling looks to biology for a source to carry the self "beyond culture." To offset the power of language and society, Trilling posits an instinctual "human quality beyond the reach of cultural control." Such a new primitivism, however, seems to contradict his belief in the need for a shaping will on the part of artist and critic, and to expose the latent romanticism in any notion of thought "beyond culture," as if an immediacy of perception or self could be restored from a time before language and society.

The 1950s and 1960s witnessed more rebellious efforts at getting "beyond culture" than suited the gentlemanly Trilling. In the mid 1940s Trilling had befriended a young undergraduate at Columbia University named Allen Ginsberg, who took Trilling's lectures on the "opposing self " quite literally and was suspended for a year for writing obscenities on a dormitory window. Ginsberg went on, of course, to lead the Beat poets in their literary revolution during the 1950s. He returned in controversial triumph to Columbia to read his poetry in 1958, ascending a stage whose last poetic occupant had been T. S. Eliot. The occasion is wittily remembered by Diana Trilling in "The Other Night At Columbia," included in *Claremont Essays*.

The 1960s brought intense turmoil to the culture of the United States. Social consensus was torn by the civil rights movement, the demonstrations against the Vietnam War, and the student riots which disrupted business-as-usual at Columbia University and across the nation. Characteristically ambivalent toward the countercultural radicals, Trilling worked actively to resolve the conflicts at Columbia. In an interview of 1968, he spoke of being "baffled by or unsympathetic with" the students' "particular demands," though he respected their general demand for participation in governance. He listened hard to understand "their doctrinaire alienation from and disgust with the whole of American culture," including the institution of the university. He saw their political activity much as he saw his own youthful flirtation with "positive Jewishness" and modernism: "For young people now, being political serves much the same purpose as being literary has long done—it expresses and validates the personality." This political personality takes the place of the passive subject of university instruction. The "induction of the young person into the culture," once the university's chief mission and source of its "ethical authority," has broken down as "popular art" and "other agencies of the culture have got in their licks before the university." The modern university is no longer a marginalized haven for oppositional inquiry, but one of the culture's "privileged vested interests," and it has grown "deficient in its sensitivity to cultural change." Nonetheless Trilling found the particular student demands "extravagant and impracticable." He recalled his youth, when students "hadn't the slightest interest in the university as an institution," when it was "the inevitable philistine condition of one's being given leisure, a few interesting teachers and a library." Despite his sympathy for the students' arguments, Trilling maintained that it is an error to see the university as representative of society and its powers. It must remain, like art, capable of transcending and shaping the determining forces of the culture.

Diana Trilling shared her husband's reservations about the student demonstrators, which she expressed in her account of the uprising, "On the Steps of Low Library," included in *We Must March My Darlings.* This essay explores the difference in temperament between the radicals of the 1930s—many now professors and faculty wives—and those of the 1960s. It captures the atmosphere of the period astutely, especially the racial tension that haunted the Columbia campus due to its proximity to Harlem. *We Must March My Darlings* contains a wide variety of such contemporary cultural observation and criticism, beginning with an essay on the assassination of President John F. Kennedy and ranging through the drugged antics of Dr. Timothy Leary, the dilemmas of liberal anticommunism, the women's liberation movement, the critical reception of the protest movie *Easy Rider,* and a narrative of her nine weeks' return to the residence halls of Radcliffe in the spring of 1971. Throughout the book Diana Trilling exercises her intelligence and lucid prose in analyzing the moral, social, artistic, and political tendencies of the 1960s.

Lionel Trilling responded to the cultural crises of the 1960s with a final summary investigation of the history of modern individuality. The result was *Sincerity and Authenticity* (1972), presented as the Charles Eliot Norton lectures at Harvard University in the spring of 1970. It was Trilling's longest sustained performance since the Forster book and in many ways one of his finest achievements. Erudite yet accessible, speculative and yet bursting with brilliant examples, it ranges

with surprising ease over the development of the modern self since the Renaissance, tracing that conflict between the socialized personality and the autonomous individual. One could say he had written the same book many times, with only variations on the authors covered or the nuance given. While it is true that these lectures do offer a collection of commentaries on disparate texts, some already discussed previously, they compose here a single fluent meditation and genuine coherence lacking in the former miscellanies. His historical vision is impressive, as is the evidence that he had continued to learn from the intellectual debates of his day. There are passing references to Raymond Williams, Claude Lévi-Strauss, Lucien Goldmann, Walter Benjamin, Nathalie Sarraute, Michel Foucault, and even Jacques Lacan. Though Trilling continues to resist a purely structural approach to selfhood, fearing that it weights the case too heavily in the direction of determinism, he nevertheless shows a capacity to balance notions of the will and its artistic forms with a deep understanding of the history and ideological mechanisms that inform them. While *The Liberal Imagination* was Trilling's most influential book, *Sincerity and Authenticity* is the more sophisticated and the one which is most likely to reward future readers.

In the manner of Williams and Foucault, Trilling undertakes an archaeology of "sincerity" and "authenticity" as terms of moral consciousness and forms of textual representation, beginning with Polonius's "To thine own self be true," and ending with R. D. Laing's advocacy of madness as an authentic rejoinder to the reigning culture's insanity. Sincerity may be defined as "the avoidance of being false to any man through being true to one's own self." Sincerity is social, moral, even theatrical, and it is this last which dooms it to its modern devaluation, since we are quick to see the incongruence between feeling and avowal. Iago's "honesty" is the foil to Polonius's sincerity, itself enmeshed in a dubious and self-serving rhetoric. For Trilling the breakdown of any cultural consensus of moral values makes sincerity almost impossible, for there is no faith in the public creed to which the self subscribes: "Which is not to say that the moral temper of our time sets no store by the avoidance of falsehood to others, only that it does not figure as the defining purpose of being true to one's own self." The gap between the self and its representations can no longer be closed by protestations of sincerity, Trilling says: "In short, we play the role of being ourselves, we sincerely act the part of the sincere person, with the result that a judgment may be passed upon our sincerity that it is not authentic." The cult of authenticity, which informs Romanticism and much of the modernist avant-garde, arises as a reaction against the consciousness of "dissimulation," which is often associated with the artifices of culture. "Society" appears, argues Trilling, when culture becomes the primary audience for the self's definition, displacing God and the monarchy. Citing the invention of mirrors by the Venetians as well as Lacan's thesis on the "mirror stage," Trilling keenly sees that the "individual" comes into being as the subject of representation. The example is Rousseau, but the lesson is for all modernity. Rousseau's conception of the "uniquely interesting" individual who confesses his secret self to a public audience reveals his perception that society has become theatrical.

An intellectual tour de force, chapter two, on "The Honest Soul and the Disintegrated Consciousness," focuses on these issues in Diderot and Hegel. *Rameau's Nephew* presents us with an honest and sincere *Moi* who confronts in the nephew an alienated figure whose "social being" is "a mere histrionic representation." "Mimetic skill" is the "essence of his being" as he apes all the social roles: "There you have my pantomime; it's about the same as the flatterer's, the courtier's, the footman's, and the beggar's." The modernity of the nephew, however, lies in the truth of his pantomime as it exhibits the inauthenticity at the heart of the theater which is society. He is the forerunner of Trilling's "opposing self." This liberating figure leads to the Hegelian "Spirit" whose power of negation is the dark but authentic experience producing cultural criticism and self-knowledge. While we harbor our nostalgia for "the archaic noble vision of life" embodied by Diderot's *Moi* or Austen's "idyllic" England, no such life without negation is open to us. Art itself, which requires representation and a public audience, corrupts the self with its theatrical seductions. "Literature is an accomplice in the social betrayal" and hence the move within art to defy the bourgeois audience, after Nietzsche, with a Dionysian assault upon its very conventions. As if drawing back from the postmodern implications of his argument, Trilling turns again to Austen's *Mansfield Park*, where the condemnation of "amateur theatricals" recalls us to the dream of life of sincerity beyond representation.

Trilling's cultural history depicts Wordsworth and the nineteenth century as seeking a transcendent authenticity, though this romantic quest proves deceptive. A prime example is *Madame Bovary*, whose heroine falls victim to the romantic representations of literature with which she identifies. Our smug sense of our own authenticity in contrast to hers is undone, argues Trilling, when we read a little closer. *"Madame Bovary—c'est moi,"* wrote Flaubert. Freud's diagnosis is confirmed: " 'We are all ill,' Freud said. No less are we all inauthentic." This hollowness includes those, like Conrad's Kurtz, who seek their authenticity within the "heart of darkness." An alternative to such primitivism is a recourse to artifice, the "doctrine of the mask" found in Nietzsche and Oscar Wilde. "Man is least himself," Wilde said, "when he talks in his own person. Give him a mask and he will tell you the truth." Wilde mocked the sincere emphasis on "the importance of being earnest," for such a being was a social representation hiding the authentic self. Trilling shows curious restraint here, and abstraction, in failing to specify that it was Wilde's homosexuality that constituted his authentic selfhood and in whose service he took up the moral consciousness of the ironic mask. More congenial is the Marx of the 1844 manuscripts, the newly rediscovered young humanist who protested against the alienation imposed by money as a mode of social representation. Yet in turning from Marx to the Italian futurist Filippo Marinetti, Trilling concedes that the machinery of modernity has surpassed the old organicist ideal.

Trilling's last chapter, on "The Authentic Unconscious," once more offers a version of Freud as a resolving figure. The decline of narrative in contemporary literature, Trilling argues, reflects the death of the past for the modern deracinated self: "the hero, the exemplary figure, does not exist without a sharp and positive beginning; the hero is his history from his significant birth to his significant death." Trilling's "hero" is the self, whose birth and death this volume traces. The word "hero" rings hollow in the late 1960s, as it requires either a shared communal goal or a radical belief in the power of the individual. As structuralist terminology suggests, the heroic self is now replaced by the "subject," an entity who always functions within and is defined by a system from which there is no "beyond." Trilling recognizes this lesson in his defense of Freud against Jean-Paul Sartre, when he points out that the theory of the "superego" as developed in *Civilization and Its Discontents* lodges the culture within the self, and vice versa, so that the self is always doomed to perform for a symbolic Father or social audience that has been internally incorporated. Freud's book (and here one may remember the Keats essay) "may be thought to stand like a lion in the path of all hopes of achieving happiness through the radical revision of social life."

The chapter's argument takes some surprising turns when Trilling seeks to capture for Freud the mantle of the authentic consciousness. Unlike a rational conscience, the superego institutes a "largely gratuitous" and harsh sense of guilt. Moreover, "although it was to serve the needs of civilization that the superego was installed in its disciplinary office, its actual behaviour was not dictated by those needs; the movement of the superego from rational pragmatic authority to gratuitous cruel tyranny was wholly autonomous." Thus the superego achieves that autonomy the self dreamed of, an authenticity which, as "a given of biology," becomes a force not susceptible to social reform or corruption. The superego is beyond culture. Freud has postulated a "flagrant inauthenticity" within the self: "Man's existence in civilization is represented as being decisively conditioned by a psychic entity which, under the mask of a concern with social peace and union, carries on a ceaseless aggression to no purpose save the enhancement of its own power." Ironically, this irrational Fate becomes the origin of man's authentic will, for it inspires his oppositional being in a world where cosmic and theological absolutes have expired. What Trilling once called the "tragic" appears here as the irreconcilable dialectic of will and negation, something that goes on within the self and within society, not simply in the adversarial relation between them. The separation of the superego from its function as representative of society removes the conflict from history, makes it mythic and universal, and so restores a vision of primal essences liberated from the pantomimes to which human existence seems otherwise doomed.

*Sincerity and Authenticity* reconfirmed Trilling's status as a major voice, and it earned long, thoughtful, and appreciative reviews in many quarters. Writing for *Commentary*, Howe called it a "wonderful book," defining Trilling as an "historian of moral consciousness": "His deepest interest is in searching for the animating biases, the all-but-unspoken modulations of sentiment and value which give shape to a moment in cultural history." In the *Nation*, Charles Molesworth found it often "Trilling at his best," a "small but magnificent book" tinted by "a hint of sadness" in acknowledging man's final frustration. On the front page of the *New York Times Book Review*, Geoffrey Hartman lauded it as "a book crowded with insights" as Trilling moved amid a dazzling variety of texts, periods, and events. Noting that it was a "synthesizing rather than original effort," Hartman found Trilling's restatement of his old concerns to have a timely message. Trilling "is pointing out—unmethodically, even gropingly—that all our attention these days is devoted to resisting terms and circumstances we have *not* freely chosen, whereas we have already been unconsciously seduced by the terms we *have* chosen—by the very rhetoric in which we make our claim for freedom and autonomy." Hartman writes out of his early engagement with deconstructive criticism, which concentrates on how the subject of language is inhabited by terms and contradictions that admit of no resolution. Hartman's Trilling, in anatomizing the self's paradoxical relation to culture, belongs despite himself to the structuralist revolution. Trilling's own concern throughout the book with questions of representation reflects the intellectual tenor of the times, as well as his situation within a media and consumer culture where the self is always on stage and surrounded by signs. His longing for an "authenticity" beyond representation is equally matched by his intelligence in denying the possibility of such a transcendence.

Trilling's last years were, in Krupnick's phrase, a "season of honors." He lectured widely in America and England, spoke before the American Psychoanalytic Association and the Aspen Institute for Humanistic Studies, and delivered the first Thomas Jefferson Lecture in the Humanities (later published as *Mind in the Modern World*, 1973). Conferences on his work were conducted by *Commentary* and *Salmagundi*. *The Last Decade* (1979), a posthumous collection, shows Trilling's variety again as he writes on Joyce's letters, the correspondence of Freud and Jung, Whittaker Chambers, and Jane Austen. "What is Criticism," the 1970 introduction to an edited textbook, offers a rather traditional history of the subject, though one shaped by Trilling's special concerns. He respectfully rejects "the position that a work of literature is an autonomous and self-determining entity"—presumably meaning the New Criticism, though applicable as well to Russian Formalism and some Structuralism. In retrospect this essay is remarkable for its relative imperviousness to the revolution in literary criticism that was then taking shape in Europe and the United States, for here Trilling reiterates his general formula for a brand of critical commentary utilizing biographical and historical information to elucidate the author's mind and imagination. The weak expression of old generalities in the essay may signal the growing gap between Trilling and his culture.

At the time of his death on 5 November 1975, Trilling, in the words of Alexander Bloom, "had risen to supreme intellectual eminence," marked by a two-page obituary article in the "Education" section of *Time* magazine. In *Prodigal Sons: The New York Intellectuals and Their World* (1986), Bloom sees Trilling's death as the passing away of that unique community of Jewish intellectuals who had played such a vital role in American literary and political debates since the 1920s. Though many of his contemporaries outlived Trilling, they also outlived the critical consensus he had represented, and their divergent responses to his legacy indicated the final fragmentation of an always fractious group. While Irving Howe celebrated Trilling as the equal of Edmund Wilson, Alfred Kazin expressed renewed suspicions about Trilling's pretensions to class status and institutional authority. Trilling's students were also divided in their assessment of him. Norman Podhoretz, who had assumed the editorship of *Commentary* in 1960, attacked Trilling for what he saw as a failure of will after the 1930s, as Trilling countenanced more liberalism than Podhoretz thought wise. Steven Marcus, himself a professor at Columbia, praised Trilling as "our historian of the moral life of modernity, our philosopher of culture," and "our teacher," borrowing the "our" of humanism often used by Trilling. Marcus's essay suggests that Columbia continued to live by the creed that Erskine had espoused and Trilling embodied. Morris Dickstein found in Trilling's notion of literary modernism as an "adversary culture" the roots for that very 1960s counterculture that Trilling could not wholeheartedly embrace. Whereas the neoconservative Podhoretz criticized Trilling for failing to defend true humanism against the new barbarians, Dickstein lamented that Trilling "came increasingly to admire and defend bourgeois values themselves."

Lionel Trilling's death put a period to more than the story of the New York Intellectuals. The psychological version of tragic humanism that he identified with great literature was widely adopted during his lifetime by the academic community. Certainly the method of "close reading" developed by the New Critics became the standard technique of literary commentary, but Trilling's version of humanity's divided self became the guiding spirit of academic literary study from the 1940s to the 1970s. "Tragic vision" ceased to be the noble essence of the modern sensibility and degenerated into a cliché adorning the titles of countless books and articles. The formal "paradoxes," "tensions," "ironies," and "ambiguities" of the New Critics gained substance and soul in Trilling's translation of them into the equivalent of psychological realities, so that in his hands the structures of literature and life once more coincided. This made for extraordinarily popular and effective pedagogy. Despite its claims to practicality, the New Criticism would never have been so successful in the classroom had not its aesthetic terms and formalist vocabulary been assimilated to a humanistic interpretation of modern experience, and that is precisely what Trilling's essays and textbooks offered.

When the 1970s brought to America a European school of critical theory that was distinctly opposed to the tradition of humanism, Trilling's influence quickly faded. By the time of his death the avant-garde in criticism advocated a linguistic, rhetorical, and structuralist method that branded humanism as just one more semiotic myth or deceptive ideology. The American proponents of European theory, such as Geoffrey Hartman, Paul de Man, and J. Hillis Miller, clearly owed much to the legacy of the New Criticism, however much they pushed its tenets to unforeseen extremes or heretical results. Cleanth Brooks and R. P. Blackmur have been far more often cited and reread by academics of the 1980s than Trilling. Indeed it is astonishing that a figure who dominated literary commentary for three decades has been scarcely mentioned in the debates over literary theory arising since the early 1970s.

Of course the explanation, in part, is that Trilling was not, as Wellek said, a literary theorist at all, but as Krupnick argued, a cultural critic. Yet a great deal of structuralist and deconstructive writing is also cultural criticism, and derives, like Trilling, from Marx and Freud. The difference lies in the relative position of language and the self in the competing schools of Humanism and structuralism. Though Trilling always traced the self's adversarial position toward society, he clung stubbornly to the authenticity of the self's experience as the ground source for literature and moral reflection. For the structuralists, the real lesson of Freud is that there is no autonomous self and that the self is in reality a babble of conscious and unconscious linguistic relations. In *Sincerity and Authenticity* Trilling had glimpsed the structuralist horizon, in which man disappears into the theater of undecidable representations. He could not follow such a path and was temperamentally averse to the climate of demystication and deconstruction that pronounced a death sentence upon the vision, however tragic, of humanism. The cultural criticism of Roland Barthes, Michel Foucault, and Jacques Derrida was aimed squarely at how representations and theatrical spectacles pervade every event and notion of experience, so that a critique of culture and an undoing of signs become synonymous, even if this includes the sign of the self. Trilling's brand of cultural criticism, though admirable, was resistant to the recognition of how thoroughly representation and its vicissitudes structure modern experience and thus are the informing condition of any subjectivity. The attempt in the late 1980s once more to join structuralist and deconstructive criticism to overt evaluations of society and history suggests that Trilling may reemerge as an inspiring touchstone for critics, though he may as likely come to seem the Matthew Arnold of the twentieth century.

**Interview:**

Stephen Donadio, Interview with Lionel Trilling, *Partisan Review,* 35 (1968): 386-392.

**Bibliography:**

Marianne Gilbert Barnaby, "Lionel Trilling: A Bibliography, 1926-1972," *Bulletin of Bibliography,* 31 ( January-March 1974): 37-44.

**References:**

Richard P. Blackmur, "The Politics of Human Power," *Kenyon Review,* 12 (1950) : 663-673; reprinted in his *The Lion and the Honeycomb* (New York: Harcourt, Brace & World, 1955);

Alexander Bloom, *Prodigal Sons: The New York Intellectuals and Their World* (New York: Oxford University Press, 1986);

Robert Boyers, *Lionel Trilling: Negative Capability and the Wisdom of Avoidance* (Columbia & London: University of Missouri Press, 1977);

William M. Chace, *Lionel Trilling: Criticism and Politics* (Stanford, Cal.: Stanford University Press, 1980);

Morris Dickstein, "Lionel Trilling and *The Liberal Imagination,*" *Sewanee Review,* 94 (Spring 1986): 323-334;

Denis Donoghue, "Trilling, Mind, and Society," *Sewanee Review,* 86 (Spring 1978): 161-186;

Joseph Frank, "Lionel Trilling and the Conservative Imagination," *Sewanee Review,* 64 (April-June 1956): 296-309; reprinted in his *The Widening Gyre* (New Brunswick, N.J.: Rutgers University Press, 1963); with a new appendix in *Salmagundi,* 41 (Spring 1978): 46-54;

Mark Krupnick, *Lionel Trilling and the Fate of Cultural Criticism* (Evanston, Ill.: Northwestern University Press, 1986);

Steven Marcus, "Lionel Trilling, 1905-1975," in *Art, Politics, and Will: Essays in Honor of Lionel Trilling,* edited by Quentin Anderson, Stephen Donadio, and Steven Marcus (New York: Basic Books, 1977), pp. 265-278;

*Salmagundi,* special Trilling issue, 41 (Spring 1978);

Robert Scholes, "The Illiberal Imagination," *New Literary History,* 4 (Spring 1973): 521-540;

Delmore Schwartz, "The Duchess' Red Shoes," *Partisan Review,* 20 ( January-February 1953): 55-73;

Nathan A. Scott, Jr., *Three American Moralists: Mailer, Bellow, Trilling* (Notre Dame & London: University of Notre Dame Press, 1973);

Edward J. Shoben, *Lionel Trilling* (New York: Ungar, 1981);

Lewis P. Simpson, "Lionel Trilling and the Agency of Terror," *Partisan Review,* 54 (Winter 1987): 18-35;

Grant Webster, *The Republic of Letters: A History of Postwar American Literary Opinion* (Baltimore & London: Johns Hopkins University Press, 1979);

René Wellek, "Lionel Trilling," in his *A History of Modern Criticism: 1750-1950,* volume 6, *American Criticism, 1900-1950* (New Haven & London: Yale University Press, 1986), pp. 123-143.

# René Wellek

*(22 August 1903-   )*

Steven Lynn
*University of South Carolina*

BOOKS: *Immanuel Kant in England, 1793-1838* (Princeton: Princeton University Press, 1931);

*The Pearl: An Interpretation of the Middle English Poem* (Prague: Charles University, 1933); republished in *Sir Gawain and the Pearl: Critical Essays*, edited by Robert Blanch (Bloomington: Indiana University Press, 1966);

*The Rise of English Literary History* (Chapel Hill: University of North Carolina Press, 1941);

*Theory of Literature*, by Wellek and Austin Warren (New York: Harcourt, Brace, 1949; London: Cape, 1949; revised edition, New York: Harcourt, Brace, 1956; Harmondsworth, U.K.: Penguin, 1963);

*The English Romantic Poets: A Review of Research*, by Wellek, Ernest Bernbaum, Samuel C. Chew, Thomas M. Raysor, Clarence D. Thorpe, and Bennett Weaver, edited by Raysor (New York: Modern Language Association, 1950);

*The Later Eighteenth Century*, volume 1 of *A History of Modern Criticism: 1750-1950* (New Haven: Yale University Press, 1955);

*The Romantic Age*, volume 2 of *A History of Modern Criticism: 1750-1950* (New Haven: Yale University Press, 1955);

*Concepts of Criticism*, edited, with an introduction, by Stephen G. Nichols, Jr. (New Haven & London: Yale University Press, 1963);

*Essays on Czech Literature*, edited, with an introduction, by Peter Demetz (The Hague: Mouton, 1963);

*The Age of Transition*, volume 3 of *A History of Modern Criticism: 1750-1950* (New Haven: Yale University Press, 1965; London: Cape, 1966);

*Confrontations: Studies in the Intellectual Relations Between Germany, England, and the United States During the Nineteenth Century* (Princeton: Princeton University Press, 1965);

*The Later Nineteenth Century*, volume 4 of *A History of Modern Criticism: 1750-1950* (New Haven:

Yale University Press, 1965; London: Cape, 1966);

*Discriminations: Further Concepts of Criticism* (New Haven: Yale University Press, 1970);

*Four Critics: Croce, Valéry, Lukács, and Ingarden* (Seattle: University of Washington Press, 1981);

*The Attack on Literature and Other Essays* (Chapel Hill: University of North Carolina Press, 1982);

*English Criticism, 1900-1950*, volume 5 of *A History of Modern Criticism: 1750-1950* (New Haven: Yale University Press, 1986);

*American Criticism, 1900-1950*, volume 6 of *A History of Modern Criticism: 1750-1950* (New Haven: Yale University Press, 1986).

OTHER: "Literary History," in *Literary Scholarship: Its Aims and Methods*, edited by Norman Foerster (Chapel Hill: University of North Carolina Press, 1941), pp. 89-130;

"Czech Literature," "Slovak Literature," and forty other entries on Czech writers, in *Columbia Dictionary of Modern European Literatures*, edited by Horatio Smith (New York: Columbia University Press, 1947), pp. 185-191, 757-759;

*Dostoevsky: A Collection of Critical Essays*, edited, with an introduction, by Wellek (Englewood Cliffs, N.J.: Prentice-Hall, 1962);

"Vilém Mathesius (1882-1945): Founder of the Prague Linguistic Circle," in *Sound, Sign and Meaning*, edited by L. Matějka (Ann Arbor: University of Michigan Press, 1976), pp. 6-14;

"What is Literature?," in *What is Literature?*, edited by Paul Hernadi (Bloomington: Indiana University Press, 1978), pp. 16-23;

*Chekhov: New Perspectives*, edited by Wellek and Nonna D. Wellek (Englewood Cliffs, N.J.: Prentice-Hall, 1984).

PERIODICAL PUBLICATIONS: "Okleštěný Shakespeare," *Kritika*, 1 (1924): 243-245;

"A propos de Kant en Angleterre," *Revue de littérature comparée*, 14 ( July-September 1934): 372-376;

"Literary Criticism and Philosophy," *Scrutiny*, 5 (March 1937): 375-383.

René Wellek has recently reiterated, in the introduction to the fifth and sixth volumes of *A History of Modern Criticism: 1750-1950* (1955-  ), that "Critics must never be considered merely as 'cases.'" This prohibition might well have evolved as a reaction to his own treatment, for Wellek's work has often been reduced to an exemplary instance of New Criticism. Wellek has been placed at the theoretical forefront of American New Criticism, despite his own objections, primarily because of his 1949 *Theory of Literature* (written with Austin Warren), which articulated with tremendous success (three editions; twenty-two translations) fundamental principles associated with New Criticism. The most familiar of these principles is probably the superiority of "intrinsic" over "extrinsic" approaches to literary works—an idea that influenced dramatically the study of literature around the world. The most obvious feature of Wellek's argument for an intrinsic, or aesthetic, study of literature, rather than a biographical, psychological, linguistic, sociological, historical, or other "external" approach, might well be the expanse of his learning: Roger Sale's remark (in the *Hudson Review*, 1966) that Wellek has "simply blown competitors from the field with erudition" has seemed at times, over Wellek's long career, almost accurate. Five collections of essays, developing and refining the ideas in *Theory of Literature*, have consistently displayed the same encyclopedic support for a single set of critical values, questioning various forms of historical and critical relativism. Likewise, Wellek's *History of Modern Criticism* (six volumes to date, one more projected) has presented massive information from this same point of view. Although Wellek has continued to examine his positions, he has in essence built an extraordinarily successful career, as scholar and teacher, on the principles and methods laid out in the landmark *Theory of Literature*.

His orientation toward literature and criticism can be traced back to his childhood in Vienna. Having a Czech father (an active nationalist), an Italian mother (who spoke German, French, English, and of course Italian), and Prussian and Swiss grandparents, Wellek necessarily mastered several languages and cultures and

naturally tended to think in universal terms, decrying throughout his career the study of English or any other literature "in isolation" and arguing (as he is quoted in *Contemporary Authors* in 1969) that "we should simply study literature without linguistic restrictions." Although René and his brother spoke German at school, they frequently encountered anti-Czech feelings; they returned home to lose themselves in various "crazes" for knowledge, devouring information on geography, science, religion, military campaigns, and literature and laying the foundation for Wellek's encyclopedic knowledge. When he was ten, Wellek started Latin lessons; at thirteen, he took up Greek; shortly thereafter, he began to study English. When the Austro-Hungarian Empire fell apart in 1918 and the Welleks moved to Prague, the cultural and linguistic richness of René's life was increased: as he has pointed out in "Twenty Years of Czech Literature: 1918-1938," collected in *Essays on Czech Literature* (1963), "Czechoslovakia after the War, more than ever, stood at the crossroads of all cultural influences, in consequence of her geographical position, her Slavonic language and her Western sympathies." Throughout his scholarly career, Wellek has attempted to adopt a kind of crossroads position himself, arguing for the study of literature without national and cultural insularity.

With his tenacious approach to research, his ability to organize and marshal details, and his clear presentation, Wellek might well have followed his father into the legal profession. But Wellek thought his father's work as a government lawyer tedious, and he entered Charles University (the Czech University of Prague) in 1922 to study Germanic philology, soon finding himself in the classes of Professor Josef Janko, who usually lectured on Gothic vocalism the first semester and Gothic consonantism the second. Wellek has claimed in "Prospect and Retrospect," collected in *The Attack on Literature and Other Essays* (1982), that he "could not distinguish a dental from a labial"; he therefore enjoyed much more Professor Arnošt Kraus's assignments, which required students to edit the various letters he had collected from castles and archives in Bohemia, and which thus "let you loose in the library."

During this period Wellek also studied with Otokar Fischer, who had published in 1908 one of the first, if not *the* first, psychoanalytical interpretations of a literary work. Fischer, along with F. X. Salda, founded *Kritika*, and in that journal in 1924 Wellek published his first article, a trenchant criticism of J. V. Sládek's Czech translation of *Romeo and Juliet,* a bold move considering Sládek's stature as a poet and translator. Professor Václav Tille's interest in comparative literature and his skeptical attitude toward causal explanations ultimately influenced Wellek more than Fischer's psychoanalytical methods. But the most important educational influence upon Wellek's work was probably Vilém Mathesius, founder and president of the Prague Linguistic Circle, whose popular lectures on English literary history encouraged his students to emulate the directness and clarity of the English critics rather than the densely layered erudition of the German scholars. Wellek later asserted, in an essay on Mathesius, that he learned from him "a sane respect for order, tradition, common sense, lucidity," and "a concern for genuine discovery." Although Wellek was certainly fond of Mathesius (when Mathesius suddenly became blind, Wellek read to him from *The Faerie Queen*), his own work has often seemed a marriage of the German and English traditions, always incorporating an impressive, if sometimes overwhelming factual thoroughness and detail. As Susan Lawall has written in "René Wellek: Phenomenological Literary Historian," "Anyone even minimally acquainted with Wellek's writings will have recognized the formidable grounding in 'philological' or 'antiquarian' research in spite of what he calls his 'ambiguous attitude' towards it." Even in graduate school Wellek's ability to cover a subject totally, appearing to leave nothing for any successor to say, prompted one professor, August Sauer, to remark, "No grass can grow after Wellek" (reported in "Prospect and Retrospect" in *The Attack on Literature and Other Essays*).

In 1924 Wellek's father supplied the funds for him to spend two months in England working on his first thesis. Two years later, "Thomas Carlyle and Romanticism," arguing that Carlyle employs ideas from German romanticism yet remains essentially a Puritan, was completed under Mathesius's direction (although Mathesius had not been enthusiastic about the topic); and Wellek, twenty-three years old, received his doctoral degree. He turned next to another historical project, planning to write on Andrew Marvell in the context of Latin and Baroque poetry. He received a grant from the Czech Ministry of Education to return to England for the necessary research, but while there, he learned of Pierre Legouis's forthcoming book on Marvell and, with great disappointment, abandoned the project.

In the fall of 1927 Wellek accepted a Proctor Fellowship at Princeton, attending classes that were much like those he had already taken in Germanic philology: in T. M. Parrott's class, he compared the *Hamlet* quartos to the folio, line by line; and in C. G. Osgood's course, he gathered information on "Spenser's Irish Rivers" and other similar Spenserian backgrounds. But Wellek also absorbed R. K. Root's lectures on Alexander Pope and J. E. Brown's pronouncements on Samuel Johnson and received some grounding in eighteenth-century criticism. For the next two years, with no opening in Prague, he remained in the United States to teach German, first at Smith College, then at Princeton. For his second thesis or *Habilitation,* Wellek finally settled on Immanuel Kant's influence in England. Returning from Princeton to Prague in 1929, Wellek stopped in England to examine the manuscript of Samuel Taylor Coleridge's "Logic" and discovered that Coleridge appropriated and misused Kant. Mathesius, who hoped that Wellek would be his eventual successor, nevertheless worried that "Kant in England" would not make Wellek an attractive candidate for positions in English literature; he therefore advised him to write an essay on the difficult Middle English poem *The Pearl.* The study that resulted has become a standard treatment of the poem, solving several interpretive problems by means of research in various primary materials. *The Pearl: An Interpretation of the Middle English Poem* was first published in 1933 at Charles University in Prague and republished by Indiana University Press in 1966. But Wellek's starting point, based on his survey of *Pearl* scholarship, was the dismissal of all the various biographical speculations. Wellek could later embrace the New Critical tenet of the intentional fallacy because he had witnessed with *The Pearl* what difficulties an "author" could cause and what power a careful reading of the text in itself could supply.

Wellek returned to Charles University in the fall of 1930 and soon completed his thesis, which Mathesius accepted even though the topic was quite alien to him. Soon after, in 1931, *Immanuel Kant in England: 1793-1838* was published by Princeton University Press. The reviews were favorable, with one minor exception, to which Wellek replied strongly. The sharpness of his response, "A propos de Kant en Angleterre," which appeared in 1934, might have had something to do with his situation: despite his impressive scholarly activity, Wellek's chances for a professorship at Prague remained remote; having married in 1932 an elementary school teacher, Olga Brodská, Wellek had an added incentive to progress beyond teaching English as a *Privatdozent* (or "unestablished professor"). Any stains on his reputation, even the indication of minor omissions by a Rumanian working on a similar thesis, might have seemed a serious threat.

*Immanuel Kant in England,* in addition to detailing the Coleridge-Kant connection, convincingly examines, with copious documentation, the relationship of Kant to other English Romantics and Scottish philosophy. Wellek's work remains a useful study of the topic, belonging "in every philosophical library," according to T. E. Jessop. (Wellek has expressed on several occasions his desire to update and revise the book, which was typeset in Prague and contains many misprints.) *Immanuel Kant in England* also represents a crucial step in the development of Wellek's thought, for it reveals the derivation from Kant of his ideas about literature and criticism. Wellek's clearest expression of his Kantian allegiance is perhaps his 1957 essay, "Kant's Aesthetics and Criticism" (reprinted in *Discriminations: Further Concepts of Criticism,* 1970), which asserts that Kant has "clearly grasped the nature of the aesthetic and the realm of art," for "only in Kant do we find an elaborate argument that the aesthetic realm differs from the realm of morality, utility, and science." This "aesthetic realm is thus that of imagination, not of thought or goodness or utility but of imagination represented, objectified, symbolized, distanced, contemplated."

From this Kantian idea of the autonomy of art, and from the concomitant notion of the "disinterested satisfaction" of the aesthetic experience (as Kant put it), Wellek developed the most important tenet of his literary theory: he followed Kant in believing that "No science is possible which does not have its distinct object." If the aesthetic value of the beautiful did not exist in an autonomous realm, isolating and analyzing literary works—and building a "science" of literary criticism—would be impossible. Thus, as Wellek put it in a 1946 essay, "The Revolt Against Positivism in Recent European Literary Scholarship" (reprinted in *Concepts of Criticism,* 1963), literary criticism "upholds ideals of correctness of interpretation, observes the laws of evidence, and must aim, ultimately, at a body of knowledge which we hesitate to call 'science' only because the natural scientists have preempted the term in English." As Wellek has maintained many times throughout his career, this literary "science" of criticism has evaluation as its central activity—evaluation based on standards of taste that reach beyond linguistic and cultural boundaries.

Even after the publication of *Immanuel Kant in England,* Wellek still was unable to secure a professorship at Prague; he therefore decided in 1935 to take the position of Lecturer in Czech Language and Literature at the University of London's School of Slavonic Studies, where he remained until 1939. In these years Wellek practiced, in various Czech journals and collections, a strongly evaluative criticism: demolishing faulty translations of James Joyce, Joseph Conrad, Aldous Huxley (Wellek in fact translated into Czech Conrad's *Chance* and D. H. Lawrence's *Sons and Lovers* early in the 1930s); recommending a variety of other English and American novels; judging scholarly books in Czech, German, French, English, and even Italian; debating various theories of the Russian Formalists and the Prague Linguistic Circle; and rejecting the pure Formalism of Viktor Shklovsky's *Theory of Prose.* Wellek's writings in English and German (mostly on Czech subjects), like his writings in Czech (often on English and German subjects), display his understanding of the critic's task: assembling, ordering, characterizing, but most of all, evaluating.

In his 1936 essay, "Theory of Literary History," Wellek develops some of his basic theoretical points, revealing (as he has said) that the essence of his thought was formed before he came to America, read the work of the New Critics, or met Austin Warren. The essay was in fact reproduced with slight changes as the final chapter in *Theory of Literature.* In the essay Wellek articulates an axiom central to his later work—that the object of the critic's attention is literature, not history, biography, psychology, or reception. The literary critic must do more, Wellek insists, than simply pile up facts about literature. Literature must be analyzed and judged *as literature,* and Wellek supports this position by discussing Russian Formalism and Roman Ingarden's phenomenology, the first treatment of either topic in English.

Another essay from this period, "Twenty Years of Czech Literature: 1918-1938," published in 1939, nicely illustrates the kind of criticism Wellek advocates in "Theory of Literary History." Examining how Czech writers shift from one set of genres to another in the postwar period, Wellek does not treat this shift as a response to historical events; rather, he stresses the aesthetic norms at work in the various genres. In this essay Wellek also reveals his ability early in his career to condense large masses of material, to express theoretical ideas clearly, and to judge established writers by his own values (the *Times Literary Supplement* of 21 May 1964 noted that his adverse view of Jaroslav Hašek would "no doubt disturb some"). Another early and prominent example of Wellek's theoretical orientation and his independent spirit is his long letter in F. R. Leavis's *Scrutiny*, arguing that Leavis had misinterpreted the philosophy of William Blake, William Wordsworth, and Percy Bysshe Shelley. By printing his response, without Wellek's original letter, Leavis made him a straw man in *The Common Pursuit* (1952).

While at the University of London, Wellek worked on various topics: English travelers in Bohemia, George Gordon, Lord Byron and K. H. Mácha (a Czech romantic poet), the Czech national revival, and the history of literary historiography. Since Wellek's position at the University of London was funded by the Czechoslovak Ministry of Education, his salary was cut off when Prague fell to Hitler in 1939. Offered a one-year appointment at the University of Iowa, Wellek consulted a map in the British Museum, determined the location of Iowa City, and prepared to move to the United States. He stopped first at Yale for six weeks to work on *The Rise of English Literary History*, which was published by the University of North Carolina Press in 1941. In this work, moving from the Middle Ages to Thomas Warton's *History of English Poetry* in the eighteenth century, Wellek displayed his usual erudition. In one chapter alone he refers to more than 300 titles. Reviewers were impressed, but more than one wished for fewer facts and more synthesis. However, in his later *A History of Modern Criticism*, for which *The Rise of English Literary History* may be seen as preparation, Wellek makes explicit his decision to deal with particular critics rather than movements, believing "that individual initiative rather than collective trends matters in criticism." His 1943 essay, "The Two Traditions of Czech Literature," reprinted in *Concepts of Criticism* (1963), similarly dismisses the prevalent idea of "a uniform time-spirit": "the times of artistic creativeness," Wellek writes, "do not coincide or coincide only rarely with times of intellectual advance and political good fortune."

Wellek carried his historical skepticism to Iowa just as the conflict between criticism and his-

*René Wellek (courtesy of Yale University)*

torical scholarship was flaring up in English departments across the country. Wellek, who was appointed by Norman Foerster, a fervent New Humanist, was naturally enlisted on the side of criticism. An indication of the intensity of the debate may be seen in the response of one of Wellek's colleagues to the suggestion that the colleague had written some criticism: as Wellek recalls in "Prospect and Retrospect" (in *The Attack on Literature*) his colleague replied, "This is the worst insult anybody ever paid me." Austin Warren was brought in by Foerster in 1939, the same year as Wellek, and they with a few other younger faculty members made up the criticism party, producing together a volume of essays entitled *Literary Scholarship: Its Aims and Methods* in 1941, a kind of precursor to *Theory of Literature*, to which Wellek contributed "Literary History."

During the 1940s Wellek remained very active, writing articles on "Slovak Literature," "Czech Literature," and forty other topics for the *Columbia Dictionary of Modern European Literatures* (1947). He also wrote two important essays on Kant in America, the natural extension of his *Immanuel Kant in England*. Even though Wellek and

Warren published essays in Foerster's collection, both felt their inclusion in his New Humanist program distorted their positions. They decided to write a book together, combining Warren's New Critical orientation with Wellek's continental expertise. Progress on this work was interrupted in 1943-1944 by Wellek's demanding work as director of a program to train interpreters for the U.S. Army. But in the summer of 1945 Wellek and Warren came together in Cambridge, Massachusetts, by means of a Rockefeller Foundation grant, to work on their masterpiece. Wellek's prestige as a teacher and a scholar was already on the rise, and in 1946 he was hired by Yale, which gave him an honorary degree that same year. Soon his Survey of the Russian Novel was enrolling 125 undergraduates each term. In the summers Wellek continued to meet with Warren, but he also lectured at the University of Minnesota, then at Columbia University, and accepted a Kenyon School Fellowship in 1949.

The death of Warren's wife led Wellek to write some chapters of *Theory of Literature* initially assigned to Warren, so that in the end Wellek produced thirteen chapters and Warren six, both authors incorporating previously published material. After the University of North Carolina Press rejected the completed manuscript, Harcourt, Brace accepted it, and *Theory of Literature* appeared in 1949. There was, as Wellek and Warren well knew, nothing like it; but part of the book's success resulted from its providing a theoretical framework for what was already on the way to becoming accepted practice. Cleanth Brooks and Robert Penn Warren's *Understanding Poetry* (1938), Brooks's *Well-Wrought Urn* (1947), and R. W. Stallman's *Critiques and Essays in Criticism 1920-48* (1949) exemplified "New Criticism," but most scholars at the time agreed with Wellek and Warren that "Literary theory, an *organon* of methods, is the great need of literary scholarship today."

Some reviewers, not grasping the book's rhetorical strategy, thought that the delineation of the problems overwhelmed the solutions. But Wellek and Warren detail the problems with various approaches in order to reveal by a process of exclusion their "ideal" orientation. In the concluding chapter Wellek writes that "no other approach has been considered invalid," suggesting that *Theory of Literature* might serve as a balanced introduction to criticism; but approaches other than the one they advocate are presented as fundamentally flawed.

The book has four parts. Parts one and two, "Definitions and Distinctions" and "The Ordering and Establishing of Evidence," lay the groundwork for the comparison in the last two parts of "The Extrinsic Approach to the Study of Literature" versus "The Intrinsic Approach to the Study of Literature." The main problem with "extrinsic" approaches, Wellek and Warren say, is that they tend toward "causal" explanation, "professing to account for literature." Admitting that it is helpful to know conditions of production and even reception, Wellek and Warren argue that such knowledge cannot take the place of "description, analysis, and evaluation" of the work itself.

Thus, Wellek's discussion, in part three, of "Literature and Biography" is based on the position established earlier in the "The Nature of Literature," in part one, where he articulates one of his basic Kantian assumptions that "A work of art forms a unity on a quite different plane, with a quite different relation to reality, than a book of memoirs, a diary, or a letter." Biographical information may well have some "exegetical value," he declares, but Wellek cannot share critic Paul Elmer More's disappointment at not finding any trace of the tears Byron is supposed to have shed on the manuscript of "Fare Thee Well." "The poem exists," Wellek points out, while "the personal emotions are gone and cannot be reconstructed, nor need they be."

Similarly, Warren's discussion of "Literature and Psychology" (his only chapter in part three) concludes that psychology is "not, finally, necessary to an understanding of the finished work or to a judgment upon it." Variants or drafts may give some insight into the psychology of the writer, into his or her composing processes and they may even "set into relief" the "final text," but the same purpose can be achieved, Warren strikingly observes, if readers imagine such drafts or variants themselves. By the same token, in "Literature and Society" Wellek sets aside the question of the function of literature. The social perspective, he states, is finally as irrelevant to the study of literature as the psychological: "There is great literature which has little or no social relevance," Wellek writes (neglecting however to cite an example); and "literature is no substitute for sociology or politics," since "it has its own justification and aim." That aim, as chapter three on "The Function of Literature" affirms, is "fidelity to its own nature," an ambiguous but effective phrase for divorcing literary study from other concerns.

The history of ideas and "the other arts" are also subordinated in subsequent chapters of *Theory of Literature*. One interesting conclusion is worth consideration in view of Wellek's career after *Theory of Literature*: "There will never be a proper history of an art ... unless we concentrate on an analysis of the works themselves and relegate to the background studies in the psychology of the reader and the spectator or the author and the artist as well as studies in the cultural and social background." This statement advocates what Wellek has called an "ergocentric," or work-centered aesthetic and thus reveals his accord with New Criticism, as it is usually conceived. But the statement also suggests what makes such an alignment problematical: the work-centered approach is needed, Wellek thinks, in order to write literary history. His own career, before and after *Theory of Literature*, is dominated not by the analysis of individual literary works from a New Critical perspective but rather by the organization of historical "facts." Repeatedly, throughout his career, Wellek addresses a problem by initially taking its historical measure. In Paul Hernadi's collection of essays, *What Is Literature?* (1978), for example, Wellek's strategy is to see what has been called "literature" in the past.

Looking back over his career, in the sixth volume of his *History of Modern Criticism* (1986), Wellek does admit his longtime "sympathy for many of [the New Critics'] positions," but he declares at the same time, "I refuse to be lumped together with [them]," even questioning whether the so-called New Critics can be realistically lumped together in the first place. In any event, as Lothar Fietz's and Aldo Scaglione's surveys of the responses to *Theory of Literature* make clear, reviewers consistently considered the work to be a New Critical manifesto. And the principle that has proven a touchstone for New Criticism is presented in part four as an alternative to "extrinsic" study. The impetus for "The Intrinsic Study of Literature," Wellek and Warren declare, comes from a variety of sources: the French method of *explication de textes*, German formal analyses, some English and American critics "who have paid close attention to the text," and "especially" the "brilliant movement of the Russian formalists and their Czech and Polish followers." In a series of chapters on various aspects or "strata" of the literary work, Wellek and Warren indicate theoreti-

cally the sort of literary analysis they have in mind. Wellek argues in "Euphony, Rhythm, and Meter," for example, that sound and meter cannot be divorced from meaning and must be considered within the unity of the poem. Similarly, in "Style and Stylistics" he contends that "stylistic analysis seems most profitable to literary study when it can establish some unifying principle, some general aesthetic aim pervasive of a whole work." Warren takes up this same New Critical theme in "Image, Metaphor, Symbol, Myths," asserting that studies limited to patterns of imagery, for instance, deal only with the "stylistic stratum" of the work and should be integrated into a view of the whole. In "The Nature and Modes of Narrative Fiction" (chapter sixteen), Warren finds that the study of the novel has generally failed to consider the unity of the work; he advocates the intrinsic study of novels, the close reading often accorded only to poems. Again, Warren argues with regard to "Literary Genres" (chapter seventeen), that they should be studied in a more "formalistic" fashion.

These various incitements to analyze the unity of the literary work (seen as a poem) are all theoretically based on Wellek's chapter, "The Mode of Existence of a Literary Work of Art," which is revealing, not only for Wellek and Warren's *Theory of Literature* but also for the chapter's relationship to the entire project of New Criticism. Wellek's expository method in this chapter is typical, as he surveys first the possible but rejected answers to the question of the work's "mode of existence": the poem is not the printed page, nor its reading aloud, nor the experience of its reader. In fact, Wellek finds the idea that "a poem is nonexistent unless experienced" and is "re-created in every experience" to be an "absurd conclusion" that "would mean the definite end of all teaching of literature."

Wellek often does not explain fully the reason for a particular judgment, even such a dramatic one as this, apparently thinking his positions self-evident once the facts are laid out. In this case he certainly considers a standard of correctness necessary to teaching, for he celebrates in the same passage the pedagogy of I. A. Richards, who has shown "how much a good teacher can achieve in rectifying false approaches." Richards is the "good teacher," Wellek suggests, because he resists the abyss of relativism and not only detects "false approaches" but does "much" to rectify them. But Richards's explanation of how he distinguishes false readings from true raises problems, for he maintains that the poem is the "experience of the right kind of reader," as Wellek says; excluding the idea that the poem is "re-created in *every* experience," Richards has left standing the idea that "a poem is non-existent unless experienced." Wellek does not mention the equally serious problem with Richards's theory–the question of how a particular reader might be certified as "the right kind" of reader, one who supposedly surpasses temporal and cultural limitations.

Thus, however much Wellek applauds Richards's pedagogical effects, Richards's definition of the work's "mode of existence" is unacceptable, for it does not accord the work a stable and autonomous existence. And if the poem is not a stable object, if it is "re-created" with every experience and the right kind of reader remains an ideal, the poem appears for all practical purposes to change from person to person and moment to moment. Any analysis and evaluation thus becomes necessarily relative and subjective, changing as its "object" alters. The teacher who corrects or criticizes a particular reading, it would seem, is then criticizing the student's experience–is, in other words, criticizing the student's cultural and personal identity, the basis of that experience. Even if the poem is stabilized by reference to some ideal reader, its unity with itself depends upon the availability of such an entity. Therefore, for Wellek and Warren's purposes, "the mode of existence" of the literary work is a crucial point, and that mode of existence, whatever else it is, must be somehow outside of history and culture, in order to exclude subjectivism and anarchy in criticism as well as teaching.

To solve this problem, Wellek addresses the relativism of the reader by advocating "perspectivism," which defines the "total meaning of a work of art" as "the result of a process of accretion, i.e., the history of its criticism by its many readers in many ages." Rather than an individual claim to correctness, he sets forth something like a statistical claim. The work's "mode of existence," however, is different from its "meaning": the work exists as "a structure of norms, realized only partially in the actual experience of its many readers." The idea of a "structure of norms" is obviously adapted from Ingarden, who objected to Wellek's modifications. But Wellek is able to keep the reader and his limitations "outside the object of literary study," which he calls "the concrete work of art"–a phrasing attractive to New Critics,

who tend to view "the poem" as a thing of substance, suggesting its stability. Wellek's solution thus involves, it appears, tacitly divorcing the meaning of the work from its status while binding its meaning to its form.

This important idea of the poem as a stabilized "structure of norms" is clearly exciting, for Wellek as for the New Critics. To them it means that the literary work "has something which can be called 'life,'" for it remains itself (at least its structure remains) as it changes through time. In retrospect, from outside the values that informed New Criticism, the goals of this formulation are easier to see than the grounds for its acceptance. To be sure, if the work is "a stratified system of norms," then "we can distinguish between right and wrong readings," as Wellek says; "it will always be possible to determine which point of view grasps the subject most thoroughly and deeply." But, however true these statements are in theory, in reality they seem able only to show the wrongness or shallowness of a particular reading–and not the rightness or depth–by demonstrating how it fails to realize fully the poem's unique "structure." Even judgments of *relative* correctness or depth would require the realization of the poem's system of norms in order to compare any particular description of it; yet this realization is precisely what any reading in the New Critical paradigm is attempting to articulate. In other words, to judge a reading, the "right reading" must already exist, it would seem–yet any work is "realized only partially in the actual experience of its many readers." Thus, when Wellek explains how critics can distinguish right readings from wrong, he refers to "acts of comparison"–not between the poem and the reading–but between "different false or incomplete 'realizations' or interpretations." From this perspective, it makes a great deal of sense that after *Theory of Literature* Wellek, "the critic's critic," focused so much of his energy on the evaluation rather than the practice of criticism: for one thing, the practice, within his theoretical framework, would seem always to be vulnerable to "correction," open that is to the exposure of falseness or incompleteness; in addition, the evaluation of a reading turns to other readings, not to the work itself.

Wellek and Warren do not articulate the position, implicit in their theory, that all readings are misreadings, the New Critical commonplace of "the heresy of paraphrase." In fact, the penultimate chapter, written by Warren, stresses the centrality of the critic's task of correct "Evaluation."

Such evaluation "ought" to be conducted in terms of literature's "own nature," an enterprise made possible only by a "correct" comprehension of the work's "own nature." Wellek earlier made clear what is meant by the work's "own nature": it refers to the work's "purity," or (in Kantian terms) its "purposiveness without purpose." "Literature is not defiled by the presence of ideas," Warren writes, so long as they are "literarily used"—or, in other words, not directed toward action or information. By this standard, "the tighter the organization of the poem, the higher its value"; and "provided a real 'amalgamation' takes place, the value of the poem rises in direct ratio to the diversity of its materials." Thus, complexity, irony, tension—New Critical standards of judgment—are most enduring and are most valued. Wellek argues similarly in the final chapter, "Literary History," that such history should be written in terms of "purely literary criteria," rather than social, political, or intellectual developments. The most stable evaluation and the most reliable history, Wellek and Warren argue, result from this "intrinsic" approach. For those who did not embrace New Criticism, this "slighting of the various extrinsic approaches and the importance of ideas in literature," as Arnold Goldsmith observes in *American Literary Criticism: 1905-1965* (1979), was the serious limitation of *Theory of Literature*. For many others, however, the book soon became a vade mecum.

Wellek turned, after *Theory of Literature*, not to a history of literature, but to *A History of Modern Criticism, 1750-1950*; six volumes have appeared over the last three decades and a seventh volume, on modern continental criticism, is projected. Wellek asserts in the introduction to the first two volumes that "understanding these eighty years [1750-1830] will allow us to understand the contemporary situation" in criticism. Much later, in a 1978 address collected in *The Attack on Literature and Other Essays,* he makes this motivation somewhat clearer: "it seemed inevitable to look for support, justification, and possibly rectification of the theory of literature in history," since, as he says, "theory emerges from history just as history itself can only be understood with questions and answers in mind." But his aim at the start, as he puts it in the first volume, was not simply to measure *Theory of Literature* by history and vice-versa but also to "trace [critical] history in all its complexity and multiplicity, in its own right." This autonomous orientation—"in its own right"—parallels the approach to literary his-

tory advocated in *Theory of Literature,* of course. Wellek's *History of Modern Criticism* then stands as a kind of monument to *Theory of Literature*—employing its advocated principles as methodology and standard. As Grant Webster has written in *The Republic of Letters: A History of Postwar American Literary Opinion* (1979), pointing to the limitations of a New Critical history, "for Wellek, the good periods of criticism are 1790-1830 and 1935-1955, the periods when Formalist aesthetics were most influential; for him the 'New Criticism' is not new at all, but is a restatement of basic German Idealism."

In a 1973 essay, "The Fall of Literary History," collected in *The Attack on Literature* and modified for the introduction to volumes five and six of *A History of Modern Criticism* (his work often appears in several stages of development), Wellek makes the remarkable admission that he has "failed . . . to construe a convincing scheme of development," even going so far as to assert that the idea of "an evolutionary history of criticism" is ill-conceived since "a work of criticism is not simply a member of a series" but "may stand in relation to anything in the past." In other words, setting aside "extrinsic" influences in the development of criticism and concentrating on internal or "intrinsic" relationships has failed, in Wellek's estimation, to produce a coherent, linear view. In retrospect, this admission is in fact implicit in "The Concept of Evolution in Literary History," published the year after the first two volumes of *A History of Modern Criticism* appeared and collected in *Concepts of Criticism.*

Thus, the organization of the fifth and sixth volumes is based on the tenet, noted earlier, that "individual initiative rather than collective trends matters in criticism." The earlier volumes, to be sure, did focus on individual critics, but Wellek was accused nonetheless in these earlier volumes, as he puts it, of " 'looking down at the history of criticism as a series of failures, as doomed attempts to scramble to the heights of our present-day glories,' presumably represented by *Theory of Literature.*" He has responded, in "Reflections on My *History*" (collected in *The Attack on Literature and Other Essays*), that such accusations represent "a misunderstanding of *Theory of Literature,* which is a tolerant and open-minded rehearsal of many theories"; such charges, Wellek maintains, are "refuted by the text of my *History.*" But Wellek also must admit in the same essay that in writing his *History of Modern Criticism* he has taken a definite "point of view," since "there cannot be any history without a sense of direction, some feeling for the future, some ideal, some standard." Putting these statements side by side, one might conclude that Wellek's work, whatever it is, is not in the final analysis a "history"—if the evolutionary strategy has failed and history is impossible without it or some other teleology. In fact, Bernard Weinberg for one, in his review of Wellek's *History of Modern Criticism*, has made precisely this assertion.

In working with particular critics rather than particular ideas, Wellek focuses on a critic's theoretical system. The power of Wellek's work lies in his ability to articulate clearly the theoretical premises of this or that critic, synthesizing masses of material. In his review in *Criticism*, Richard Fogle among others has censured this practice of "breaking down critics into their identifiable concepts, without sufficiently noting the internal relationships which may represent a critic's true unity, coherence, and vitality." Wellek has also been criticized for failing to consider the integrity of a particular book or essay, but instead characteristically dealing synchronically with a critic's work. Wellek, however, has responded to this charge (in "Reflections") by relying on a basic axiom of *Theory of Literature*, that "Critical texts are not works of art." One aspect of criticism's essential difference from literature (a point recent criticism has of course called into doubt) is that there is no reason why critical texts, unlike literary works, "must be analyzed and interpreted as totalities."

As a champion of comparative literature (he contributed to *Comparative Literature*'s first issue and served on its editorial board, and he built Yale's comparative literature program from the ground up), Wellek has argued repeatedly for the necessity of an international perspective. Nevertheless, he has recognized in his *History of Modern Criticism* the strength of national traditions and the utility of organizing his materials by nationality and period: he has assigned German critics a large role, but French, Italian, Spanish, English, American, and even Danish critics are also treated at length.

Wellek's treatment of the history of criticism throughout these volumes may be suggested by a brief discussion of his handling of Samuel Johnson, a critic who seems in many ways Wellek's antithesis. Although Johnson cannot be fitted easily into any school, neoclassical or romantic, he seems to Wellek "one of the first great critics who has almost ceased to understand the nature of art, and who, in central passages, treats art as life." This sentence reveals Wellek's own confidence, expressed in *Theory of Literature* and reiterated throughout his career, in knowing "the nature of art"—which is not life. Johnson's first artistic standard according to Wellek, truth, makes as little sense from the point of view of *Theory of Literature* as his second standard, morality. When Wellek, the comparatist, the advocate of aesthetic judgment, the enemy of relativism, finds Johnson "hardly touched by . . . aesthetics and cosmopolitanism," largely unaware of continental criticism, and concerned with a "merely relative" idea of beauty, it may well seem that the Great Cham is about to be dismissed. But, although Johnson's judgments are themselves judged against Wellek's essentially New Critical standards and found lacking in the extreme, Wellek is nonetheless able to appreciate, to a surprising degree, Johnson's genius in spite of his "faulty" theory: Wellek acknowledges that Johnson "wrote valuable analyses of many critical questions," even while operating from "one or several" of his contradictory points of view. Johnson's emphasis on the work as a communication from author to reader and his interest in the question of the reader's response are clearly foreign to Wellek's view of literature as a "structure of norms." Wellek manages to create a system of Johnson's critical thought worth examining, but his own perspective obscures much that other readers have valued in Johnson.

While working on the *History of Modern Criticism*, Wellek remained at Yale until 1972, teaching and administrating, and occasionally taking leave to assume visiting professorships at other American universities and in 1969 to become a Fulbright scholar in Germany. In 1967 Wellek's first wife died, and he subsequently married, in 1968, Nonna Dolodarenko Shaw, professor of Russian literature at the University of Pittsburgh. In 1972 Wellek retired, sixty-nine years old, having directed some fifty dissertations and taught an honor roll of critics and scholars. His various professional contributions have been celebrated by two festschrifts. The first, in 1968, *The Disciplines of Criticism: Essays in Literary Theory, Interpretation, and History*, was edited by Peter Demetz, Thomas Greene, and Lowry Nelson, Jr., former students of Wellek, and it presented twenty-six essays. The most recent festschrift in his honor, *Literary Theory and Criticism* (1984), celebrating his eightieth birthday, occupied two thick volumes, 1,492 pages, with seventy-six contributions; its editor, Joseph Strelka, acknowledges that many more of Wellek's students and close friends "might normally have been invited to participate" if there had only been more room. Essays in Italian, Spanish, German, French, and English appropriately reflect Wellek's own international outlook; dealing with subjects of interest to Wellek, the range of these essays testify to the range of Wellek's interests. This expanse is detailed by Strelka's bibliography of Wellek's writings–433 items, excluding translations.

In the years before his retirement, four volumes of Wellek's essays appeared. In 1963 the Czechoslovak Society of Arts and Sciences commemorated his sixtieth birthday with *Essays on Czech Literature*, a collection of nine of Wellek's most important essays in English on Czech subjects. The volume included a bibliography listing more than 150 other publications by Wellek either written in Czech or focused on Czech and Slavic topics. Three other volumes of essays, as Wellek himself put it, "accompanied the *History*": *Concepts of Criticism* in 1963; *Confrontations* in 1965; and *Discriminations* in 1970. These collected pieces often originated as lectures or reviews, which then frequently appeared in a more refined and developed version in a scholarly journal, only to be collected in a volume (and then perhaps worked in some form into *A History of Modern Criticism*). In *Concepts of Criticism* Wellek is often responding to some response to *Theory of Literature* or the first two volumes of *A History of Modern Criticism*. The opening essay, for instance, "Literary Theory, Criticism, and History," attempts to clarify the proper activity in each of these "main branches of literary study," as Wellek ranges from Northrop Frye to Rosamond Tuve, situating his own theory, criticism, and history within various current practices, some more laudable in his view than others. This volume also reprints Wellek's important essay on "The Concept of Romanticism in Literary History." Other essays apply Wellek's erudition to illuminate other concepts: "literary criticism," "evolution in literary history," "form and structure in twentieth-century criticism," and "baroque." There are both overlap and development, as Wellek works with ideas that continue to occupy his attention and form part of his *History of Modern Criticism*: the last three chapters, for example, "American Literary Scholarship," "Philosophy and Postwar American Criticism," and "The Main Trends of Twentieth-Century Criticism," attempt in various ways to erect a useful classificatory scheme for contemporary criticism.

*Confrontations*, like all Wellek's work in a sense, can be seen as an "antidote to provincialism," as Inga-Stina Ewbank said in her review. Extending his 1949 essay on the "Concept of Romanticism," Wellek charts the relationships of Anglo-American and German literature in the romantic era. In two essays in *Discriminations*, drawing on materials in *Theory of Literature, A History of Modern Criticism*, and even the early *Rise of English Literary History*, Wellek further tries to extricate himself from the role of "archenemy of all forms of historical research as applied to the study of literature," as Jacques Voisine wrote in his review in *Comparative Literature Studies*. Other essays reveal Wellek working in his "historical" fashion–delineating the development of an idea or a term. For example, "The Term and Concept of Classicism in Literary History" places English classicism within "the huge Western European neoclassical tradition." This essay was modified for inclusion in the *Dictionary of the History of Ideas* under "classicism," and at least seven other entries were prepared by Wellek.

*Discriminations* also contains "A Map of Contemporary Criticism in Europe," yet another example of Wellek's international viewpoint and his interest in organizing the field of literary criticism–which was at that time a confusion of tongues in his view, but might, Wellek hoped, return to its primary task of evaluating and interpreting particular works. This task is also promoted in another essay in this volume, "A Sketch of the History of Dostoevsky Criticism," which first appeared as the introduction to the Dostoyevski volume in the Twentieth-Century Views series, edited by Wellek. Another volume in this series, *Chekhov*, appeared in 1984, edited by Wellek and his wife Nonna, with a long introductory essay by Wellek. Most reviewers thought well of all these volumes and praised Wellek's learning and logic. Louis Leiter in his review in *College English* thought the Dostoyevski volume the best in that series. But there is perhaps something to J. D. O'Hara's characterization of Wellek's method, recorded in Martin Bucco's *René Wellek* (1981): he "goes as far back toward Genesis as possible and then tracks an idea doggedly through the ages."

After Wellek retired from Yale in 1972, he continued to teach with some regularity–as a visiting professor at Princeton in 1973, at Indiana University in 1974, at the University of Iowa in 1975, at Cornell in 1977, at the University of California, San Diego, and at the University of Washington in 1979. When Wellek is asked how he likes retirement, he replies, according to Martin Bucco, "I enjoy it but miss my vacations." Since his retirement two other volumes of essays have appeared, also related to *A History of Modern Criticism. Four Critics: Croce, Valéry, Lukács, and Ingarden* (1981), composed of lectures delivered at the University of Washington while Wellek was Walker-Ames Professor, is obviously intended to make up important sections, perhaps in some revised form, of volume seven of *A History of Modern Criticism* dealing with criticism on the continent of Europe, 1900-1950. In presenting lucidly the thought of each critic, Wellek also corrects misperceptions based on poor translation or partial readings. While Wellek's interest lies in organizing and comparing the thought of these four critics, he also treats their enduring relevance, as they raise issues of certainty in interpretation (Ingarden), the inevitability of misreading (Valéry), the illusion of presence (Croce), the value of historicism (Lukács). As Wellek says in the introduction to the fifth and sixth volumes of *A History of Modern Criticism,* "One of the functions of a history of criticism seems to me to show the reader that what has been touted as a new discovery has been said many times over before."

*The Attack on Literature* collects eleven essays written in the 1970s, essays that for the most part reveal Wellek once again defending, against a new set of antagonists, the positions established in *Theory of Literature.* The title essay defends the idea of "literature" as a distinct body of writing, a notion fundamental to *Theory of Literature* but called into question by much in recent critical theory. "Literature, Fiction, and Literariness," the second essay, obviously has a related function. "Criticism as Evaluation" reconsiders Wellek's call "in many contexts, for many years," as he puts it, "for a return to criticism in the original sense of judging." Other essays explicitly related to *A History of Modern Criticism* are employed in its fifth and sixth volumes: "The New Criticism: Pro and Contra," for example, is an interesting defense of New Criticism against charges of its "esoteric aestheticism," its "unhistorical nature," its scientism, and its status as a "mere pedagogical device." Wellek does regard its "extremely anglocentric, even provincial" nature as a serious limitation of New Criticism. But in the main, he believes the New Critics "have waged a valiant fight which, I am afraid, must be fought over again in the future."

Any attempt to assess Wellek's long, productive career must in fact account for his alignment with the basic principles of New Criticism. However, in the *Journal of the History of Ideas,* Walter G. Creed has offered a different perspective on Wellek's work, arguing that it can be profitably seen as an outgrowth of phenomenology, a position shared by Susan Lawall. Wellek, on the other hand, who has valued individuality all his life (in his choice of career, his dissertation topics, his critical outlook), sees himself as standing outside all theoretical compartments: "I am struck," he says, looking back over his career, "with my detachment from all the phases I went through: historical scholarship, symbolist criticism in the wake of [F. X.] Salda or [Friedrich] Gundolf, the American New Humanism, the Prague School shaped by Russian formalism, the Leavis group, the American New Criticism." But Wellek also points, in this same "Prospect and Retrospect" essay, collected in *The Attack on Literature and Other Essays,* to "a core of convictions" that he has "preserved" with "integrity": "that the aesthetic experience differs from other experiences and sets off the realm of art, of fictionality, of *Schein,* from life; that the literary work of art, while a linguistic construct, at the same time refers to the world outside; that it cannot therefore be described only by linguistic means but has a meaning telling of man, society, and nature; that all arguments for relativism meet a final barrier; that we are confronted, as students of literature, with an object, the work of art, out there (whatever may be its ultimate ontological status) which challenges us to understand and interpret it; that there is thus no complete liberty of interpretation."

These principles are essentially congruent with most informed descriptions of New Criticism's theoretical basis. In "The Fall of Literary History," also in *The Attack on Literature and Other Essays,* Wellek refers to "the possibly oversharp distinction between extrinsic and intrinsic methods" in *Theory of Literature* that "may have contributed to the singling out of the work of art as an isolated object outside history." Wellek himself does say, "We must think of criticism as a relatively independent activity." But Anglo-American New Critics, such as Cleanth Brooks, have always maintained that literature holds important insights about life, even though it stands apart, and Wellek's retrospective credo discusses literature's "meaning" as "telling of man, society, and nature." Although David Daiches in *A Time of Har-*

vest (1962) charges that New Criticism "ignored altogether the relation of literature to life," neither Wellek nor most self-avowed New Critics would agree with this extreme formulation. Thus, Wellek's work, including his particular approach to history, appears to be solidly within any reasonably heterogeneous view of the New Critical tradition; only from a narrow view of that tradition—which, as Wellek says, his own work may have fostered—are there any significant departures. Although Wellek's impressive accomplishments deserve careful consideration in their own right, it does make some sense to see him in the light of New Criticism, over his own protests.

In helping to authorize New Criticism, *Theory of Literature* obviously had the effect of encouraging close reading and of making interpretation and evaluation, if not a science, a legitimate "professional" activity, a rival to historical scholarship. As Daiches says, it may have encouraged to some extent "pretentious jargon," but it also asserted greater precision of analysis. Wellek himself noted some of *Theory of Literature*'s limitations. For instance, he recognized while writing the book that the idea of the work of art as "a stratified system of norms" really does not address the question of "the actual mode of existence of this system" and that the position he and Warren assumed thus represented a self-conscious choice, not an inevitable conclusion, despite the weight they were willing to accord it. Other judgments, authoritatively made, similarly constitute self-conscious choices rather than necessary conclusions. In choosing to assign "the meaning of a work of art" to "the history of its criticism by its many readers in many ages," while at the same time positing a changeless, autonomous work, Wellek intends to avoid the embarrassments of a unitary meaning on the one hand and of a relative, pluralistic meaning on the other hand. If readers were somehow able to reconstruct the original meaning of *Hamlet*, Wellek says, "we would merely impoverish it," suppressing "the legitimate meanings which later generations found" in it. This sort of negotiated position, a compromise between two "errors," is typical for Wellek. Such centrist solutions are nonetheless open to challenge: if both absolutism and relativism are false, why should the mean between them be true? Is it really meaningful to say that a poem is alive, that it stays the same and yet changes?

In fact, in a passage in *Theory of Literature* that is especially interesting with regard to a poem's stability, Wellek considers favorably the ad-

vantages of allowing a particular word ("vegetable" in this case, in Marvell) to be given meanings its author could not have held. But although Wellek argues that both absolutism and relativism "are false," he does not consider them equally noxious: "The more insidious danger today," Wellek says, "at least in England and the United States, is a relativism equivalent to an anarchy of values, a surrender of the task of criticism." And in the 1986 postscript to the sixth volume of his *History of Modern Criticism*, Wellek makes the same charges against deconstruction that he made against relativism in *Theory of Literature*—in almost identical terms: "if its teachings should be generally accepted, [deconstruction] would lead literally not only to the 'deconstruction' but to the destruction of all literary criticism and scholarship." For many of Wellek's later readers, who have delighted at the imagination and subtlety of much poststructuralist criticism and teaching, these words must seem as unrealistic as Wellek's earlier alarm against relativism.

Still, with its limitations, *Theory of Literature* remains relevant, readable, and useful, offering perspectives still worthy of consideration, raising issues still of concern: the relationship of criticism to literature; the nature of literature and the nature of criticism; the possibility of progress in criticism; the nature of evidence; the role of literary history; and much else. Wellek's *History of Modern Criticism* thus stands as a monument to industry and scholarship, a systematical analysis that will enliven the historiography of literary criticism for decades to come.

**Interview:**
"The Classics and the Man of Letters," *Arion*, 3 (Winter 1964): 89-92.

**Bibliography:**
Joseph Strelka, "Bibliography of René Wellek," in his *Literary Theory and Criticism: Festschrift Presented to René Wellek in Honor of His Eightieth Birthday*, 2 volumes (Bern: Lang, 1984), pp. 1427-1453.

**Biography:**
Martin Bucco, *René Wellek* (Boston: Twayne, 1981).

**References:**
Walter G. Creed, "René Wellek and Karl Popper on the Mode of Existence of Ideas in Litera-

ture and Science," *Journal of the History of Ideas*, 44 (October-December 1983): 639-656;

David Daiches, "The New Criticism," in *A Time of Harvest*, edited by Robert Spiller (New York: Hill & Wang, 1962), pp. 95-110;

Inga-Stina Ewbank, Review of *Confrontations*, *Review of English Studies*, 27 (November 1966): 442-443;

Lothar Fietz, "René Wellek's Literaturtheorie und der Prager Strukturalismus," in *Englische und amerikanische Literaturtheorie*, 2 volumes, edited by Rüdiger Ahrens and Erwin Wolff (Heidelberg: Winter, 1978-1979), pp. 500-523;

Richard Fogle, Review of *A History of Modern Criticism*, *Criticism*, 9 (Spring 1967): 197-199;

Arnold Goldsmith, *American Literary Criticism: 1905-1965* (Boston: Twayne, 1979);

Thomas Hart, Review of *The Attack on Literature and Other Essays*, *Comparative Literature*, 35 (Summer 1983): 277-279;

Roman Ingarden, "Werte, Normen and Strukturen nach René Wellek," in *Deutsche Vierteljahrsschrift fur Literaturwissenschaft und Geistesgeschichte*, 40 (March 1966): 43-55;

T. E. Jessop, Review of *Immanuel Kant in England*, *Mind*, 41 (October 1932): 518-521;

Susan Lawall, "René Wellek: Phenomenological Literary Historian," in *Literary Theory and Criticism: Festschrift Presented to René Wellek in Honor of his Eightieth Birthday*, 2 volumes, edited by Joseph Strelka (Bern: Lang, 1984), pp. 393-416;

Louis Leiter, Review of *Dostoevsky: A Collection of Critical Essays*, *College English*, 24 (May 1963): 662-663;

Roger Sale, "René Wellek's History," *Hudson Review*, 19 (Summer 1966): 324-329;

Aldo Scaglione, "Theory of Literature," *Romance Philology*, 11 (May 1958): 400-408;

Jacques Voisine, Review of *A History of Modern Criticism*, *Comparative Literature Studies*, 9 (September 1972): 331-335;

Grant Webster, *The Republic of Letters: A History of Postwar American Literary Opinion* (Baltimore: Johns Hopkins, 1979);

Bernard Weinberg, Review of *A History of Modern Criticism*, *Journal of the History of Ideas*, 30 (January-March 1969): 127-133.

**Papers:**

Wellek's library and papers are housed at the University of California, Irvine.

# Edmund Wilson

### (8 May 1895-12 June 1972)

## David Castronovo
### *Pace University*

BOOKS: *The Undertaker's Garland*, by Wilson and John Peale Bishop (New York: Knopf, 1922);

*Discordant Encounters: Plays and Dialogues* (New York: Boni, 1926);

*I Thought of Daisy* (New York: Scribners, 1929; London: W. H. Allen, 1952); revised in *Galahad [and] I Thought of Daisy* (New York: Farrar, Straus & Giroux, 1967);

*Poets, Farewell!* (New York: Scribners, 1929);

*Axel's Castle: A Study in the Imaginative Literature of 1870-1930* (New York & London: Scribners, 1931);

*The American Jitters: A Year of the Slump* (New York & London: Scribners, 1932); republished as *Devil Take the Hindmost: A Year of the Slump* (London: Scribners, 1932);

*Travels in Two Democracies* (New York: Harcourt, Brace, 1936);

*This Room and This Gin and These Sandwiches: Three Plays* (New York: New Republic, 1937);

*The Triple Thinkers: Ten Essays on Literature* (New York: Harcourt, Brace, 1938; London: Oxford University Press, 1938); revised and enlarged as *The Triple Thinkers: Twelve Essays on Literary Subjects* (New York: Oxford University Press, 1948; London: Lehmann, 1952);

*To the Finland Station: A Study in the Writing and Acting of History* (New York: Harcourt, Brace, 1940; London: Secker & Warburg, 1940);

*The Boys in the Back Room: Notes on California Novelists* (San Francisco: Colt, 1941);

*The Wound and the Bow: Seven Studies in Literature* (Boston: Houghton Mifflin, 1941; London: Secker & Warburg, 1942; revised edition, New York: Oxford University Press, 1947; London: W. H. Allen, 1952);

*Note-Books of Night* (San Francisco: Colt, 1942; London: Secker & Warburg, 1945);

*Memoirs of Hecate County* (New York: Doubleday, 1946; Stockholm & London: Continental, 1947);

*Europe Without Baedeker: Sketches Among the Ruins of Italy, Greece and England* (New York: Dou-

bleday, 1947; London: Secker & Warburg, 1948); revised as *Europe Without Baedecker: Sketches Among the Ruins of Italy, Greece and England, Together with Notes from a European Diary: 1963-1964* (New York: Farrar, Straus & Giroux, 1966; London: Hart-Davis, 1967);

*The Little Blue Light: A Play in Three Acts* (New York: Farrar, Straus, 1950; London: Gollancz, 1951);

*Classics and Commercials: A Literary Chronicle of the Forties* (New York: Farrar, Straus, 1950; London: W. H. Allen, 1951);

*The Shores of Light: A Literary Chronicle of the Twenties and Thirties* (New York: Farrar, Straus & Young, 1952; London: W. H. Allen, 1952);

*Wilson's Christmas Stocking: Fun for Young and Old* (Boston: Printed by Thomas Todd, 1953);

*Five Plays* (New York: Farrar, Straus & Young, 1954; London: W. H. Allen, 1954);

*Eight Essays* (New York: Doubleday/Anchor, 1954);

*The Scrolls from the Dead Sea* (New York: Oxford University Press, 1955; London: W. H. Allen, 1955); revised and enlarged as *The Dead Sea Scrolls 1947-1969* (New York: Oxford University Press, 1969; London: W. H. Allen, 1969);

*A Christmas Delirium* (Boston: Printed by Thomas Todd, 1955);

*A Literary Chronicle: 1920-1950* (New York: Doubleday/Anchor, 1956);

*A Piece of My Mind: Reflections at Sixty* (New York: Farrar, Straus & Cudahy, 1956; London: W. H. Allen, 1957);

*Red, Black, Blond and Olive: Studies in Four Civilizations: Zuni, Haiti, Soviet Russia, Israel* (New York: Oxford University Press, 1956; London: W. H. Allen, 1956);

*The American Earthquake: A Documentary of the Twenties and Thirties* (New York: Doubleday/Anchor, 1958; London: W. H. Allen, 1958);

*Apologies to the Iroquois* (New York: Farrar, Straus & Cudahy, 1960; London: W. H. Allen, 1960);

*Night Thoughts* (New York: Farrar, Straus & Cudahy, 1961; London: W. H. Allen, 1962);

*Patriotic Gore: Studies in the Literature of the American Civil War* (New York: Oxford University Press, 1962; London: Deutsch, 1962);

*The Cold War and the Income Tax: A Protest* (New York: Farrar, Straus, 1963; London: W. H. Allen, 1964);

*O Canada: An American's Notes on Canadian Cultures* (New York: Farrar, Straus & Giroux, 1965; London: Hart-Davis, 1967);

*The Bit Between My Teeth: A Literary Chronicle of 1950-1965* (New York: Farrar, Straus & Giroux, 1965; London: W. H. Allen, 1966);

*Holiday Greetings 1966* (Boston: Printed by Thomas Todd, 1966);

*A Prelude: Landscapes, Characters and Conversations from the Earlier Years of My Life* (New York: Farrar, Straus & Giroux, 1967; London: W. H. Allen, 1967);

*The Fruits of the MLA* (New York: New York Review, 1968);

*The Duke of Palermo and Other Plays With an Open Letter to Mike Nichols* (New York: Farrar, Straus & Giroux, 1969);

*Upstate: Records and Recollections of Northern New York* (New York: Farrar, Straus & Giroux, 1971);

*A Window on Russia, for the Use of Foreign Readers* (New York: Farrar, Straus & Giroux, 1971; London: Macmillan, 1972);

*The Devils and Canon Barham: Ten Essays on Poets, Novelists and Monsters* (New York: Farrar, Straus & Giroux, 1973; London: Macmillan, 1973);

*The Twenties: From Notebooks and Diaries of the Period,* edited by Leon Edel (New York: Farrar, Straus & Giroux, 1975; London: Macmillan, 1975);

*Israel and the Dead Sea Scrolls* (New York: Farrar, Straus & Giroux, 1978);

*The Thirties: From Notebooks and Diaries of the Period,* edited by Edel (New York: Farrar, Straus & Giroux, 1980);

*The Forties: From Notebooks and Diaries of the Period,* edited by Edel (New York: Farrar, Straus & Giroux, 1983);

*The Fifties: From Notebooks and Diaries of the Period,* edited by Edel (New York: Farrar, Straus & Giroux, 1986).

Edmund Wilson's unique position in American literature was established during a long career in which he undertook the duties and challenges of the man of letters. After having started work in the 1920s as a reporter and literary journalist, he extended his field of activity to social criticism, in-depth analysis of literature and art, popular culture and the lively arts, modern and ancient history, travel writing, drama, fiction, and poetry. Oddly enough he approached each kind of writing with the seriousness of thorough preparation that set him apart from the old-fashioned amateur essayist and literary connoisseur. Always the professional, he offered through his work his prodigious learning, his reporter's clear eye, and his disciplined perspective. While Wilson's criticism of art and society often depended on intuition, taste, and his own standards of the human usefulness of literature and man's cultural and political productions, he was essentially guided by three currents in twentieth-century thought: aestheticism, with its emphasis on the work of art itself, its shape and texture; Marxism, with its concern for the material conditions that produce culture; and Freudianism, with its curiosity about motives, latent content, and trauma. Wilson directed these three currents in an unsystematic way into his sometimes pioneering discursive books, essays, and imaginative writing.

Wilson's family background and early life contributed to both the substance and form of his writing. His father, Edmund Wilson, Sr., was a Princeton University graduate and a prominent New Jersey attorney with a reputation for integrity, independent thinking, and high-minded devotion to unpopular causes. Wilson's mother, Helen Mather Kimball, a descendant of Cotton Mather, was a rather distant figure whom Wilson described in terms of her patrician values and self-absorption. Edmund Wilson, Jr., was born in 1895 in Redbank, New Jersey, heir to social responsibility and genteel insularity: the struggle between duty and social status is a major theme in his criticism. He chose his father's path and became what he termed "a literary worker," an earnest professional; from his father he also inherited a sense of simple style. The elder Wilson revered Lincoln's plain prose and used it in his legal writing; his son came to feel that "this model was a valuable heritage, like the table pieces of the Paul Revere silversmith period which have come down to me from his side of the family." From his mother Wilson inherited an old stone house in Talcottville, New York, a symbol of eighteenth-century America and a complex locus of values. The house—where Wilson spent childhood summers and summers in his later years–represented independence and escape from the conventions of affluent suburban New Jersey, continuity, and aristocratic dignity.

The other early force in Wilson's life was his education at the Hill School in Pottstown, Pennsylvania, from 1908 to 1923 and at Princeton University, where he earned the B.A. in 1916. At Hill he studied classics with John Rolphe, a rigorous humanist and ironic foe of sloppy thinking and sentimentality. His English teacher John A. Lester taught him rhetoric and laid down three values that Wilson carried through his career: "Lucidity, Force, Ease." As an undergraduate he avoided the "rah-rah" and collegiate side of Princeton life and concentrated on the preceptorials of Christian Gauss, another authority figure who offered "unusual fluidity of mind," a cosmopolitan perspective on literature, and an aesthetic that Wilson came to shape his career around. Gauss's teaching dealt with what Wilson called "the artist's morality as something that expressed itself in different terms than the churchgoer's or citizen's morality; the fidelity to a kind of truth that is rendered by the discipline of aesthetic form" (*The Shores of Light: A Literary Chronicle of the Twenties and Thirties*, 1952). After Wilson graduated from Princeton, voted "worst poet" and "most likely bachelor," he went for the summer to a military preparedness camp in Plattsburgh, New York. He then worked for a short time as a reporter for the *Evening Sun* and, in 1917, began to serve in France with a military hospital unit. He was demobilized in 1919 and came to New York filled with disillusionment. In *A Prelude: Landscapes, Characters and Conversations from the Earlier Years of My Life* (1967), his first volume of notebooks, he sums up his feeling about the war: "I indicted the institutions of the Western World and suggested a way out in the direction of socialism." The protest impulse and the search for humane alternatives became major features of his literary career.

Wilson's characteristic kind of essay–swift, direct, reflective, judgmental–begins to appear in the early 1920s and is a response to the conditions of literary journalism and reporting in the Jazz Age, when he worked as managing editor at *Vanity Fair* (1920) and at the *New Republic* (1921), and as a reviewer and journalist for the *New Republic* and the *Dial*. The magazine writer of the 1920s could easily become a man-of-all-work: Wilson reviewed plays and vaudeville, books, circus acts, film; he reported on murders and trials, pro-

tests and popular culture. Much of his criticism is collected in *The Shores of Light* (1952) and *The American Earthquake: A Documentary of the Twenties and Thirties* (1958). The first of these volumes is a literary and cultural record and offers a foreshadowing of Wilson's critical approaches, themes, and tastes. In addition it is a panorama of the ideas and art forms of the age of T. S. Eliot, James Joyce, Ernest Hemingway, and F. Scott Fitzgerald. As a critic Wilson brought the news of literary modernism to a general audience. *The Shores of Light* explains and analyzes E. E. Cummings, Wallace Stevens, and other writers whose styles might pose problems for readers bred on realism. The essays in the volume are often reworked book reviews that show Wilson as the creative writer's sympathetic advocate and austere judge. Wilson's values–love of genuine experiment, respect for precision and inner coherence, and social progressivism–are often in conflict with a given writer's talents and very often cause Wilson to correct, warn, and ridicule his subjects. Maxwell Bodenheim, a Greenwich Village poet of the time, referred to him as a "fatuous policeman" swinging his club. In fact Wilson's rough treatment of some writers involves error and prejudice. The "All-Star Literary Vaudeville" (1926), one of the most representative essays in *The Shores of Light,* brings contemporary writers on stage, caustically evaluates them, and sometimes gives them the hook. Robert Frost is called "excessively dull"; Sinclair Lewis, flat and unoriginal; Willa Cather is "given to terrible lapses into feminine melodrama"; Wallace Stevens has a gift for "nonsense" and is "a charming decorative artist." Wilson's pugnacity is not, however, an irresponsible outburst; he assumes the role of the critic protecting the public from what he considers the lapses of great writers and the pretensions of inferior ones. In other essays he writes of Eliot's snobbery, Fitzgerald's tendency to play the language by ear, Thornton Wilder's self-indulgence and the escapism in his early novels. Wilson's critical undertakings in the 1920s also came to include the analysis and judgment of his culture, its popular arts, and its political problems. "A Preface to Persius" (1927), subtitled "Maudlin Meditations in a Speakeasy," is a small dramatization of one of Wilson's major themes: the conflict between the vulgarity and chaos of modern industrial life and the "richness and balance" of "a civilization based on something more comfortable than commercial and industrial interests." Wilson, a persona in the essay who is dining in an Italian restaurant and reading passages from eighteenth-century critic William Drummond, observes E. E. Cummings in the room, the poet who represents the modernistic struggle to express chaos and pain. Wilson reacts by wanting to assume the role of a Drummond, a critic who has edited and harmonized the Roman poet Persius's sometimes tortured verses. Wilson wants to help poets to find a resolution for modern "discord." The time frame of the essay–the year of the Sacco and Vanzetti demonstrations–and the place–a restaurant with garishly dressed people who threaten the old bohemian Greenwich Village–further reinforce the idea of cultural degeneration. Wilson vows to "work with the dead for allies," to defend the edifice of art and criticism, and make it "the headquarters of humanity!" Although the essay ends ironically with the narrator colliding with some "bulky pink people" who were dancing to the radio, it champions three of Wilson's enduring values: reverence for art, devotion to the role of negotiator, and resistance to cheapness and brutality.

*The American Earthquake,* a collection of reports on American injustice in the late 1920s and in the Depression, continues the work of the literary essays in that it represents Wilson's campaign against shoddiness and irresponsibility in the public sphere. Its reports–on Henry Ford's dehumanizing system in Detroit, and on the waste of lives and the mindless reverence for property during the 1930s–are necessary complements to Wilson's literary criticism of the period. Although Wilson's spirits were lifted by the progress of modern art and the work of social progressives like Frank Keeney, the head of the independent coal miners' union who fought the power structure, he was generally a resentful young reporter in the 1920s and 1930s who found escapism, meanness, and disorder in the books, the nightclubs, and the theaters. This combination of ardor and cynicism about American life and art also informs *I Thought of Daisy* (1929), a novel that is a meditative rather than a fast-paced look at jazz babies, bootleggers, a Greenwich Village poetess modeled on Edna St. Vincent Millay, and the intellectuals. The narrative tells how a Wilson-like protagonist works through his disillusionments about American commercialism and the neuroses of the bohemian set; Daisy, a vital and warm Broadway chorus girl, helps the narrator to escape his own isolation and growing nihilism.

During the 1920s Wilson had married Mary Blair, an actress who played in Eugene O'Neill dra-

mas at Provincetown, Massachusetts; they separated in 1925, and Wilson thereafter turned to a number of affairs, which he documented with zoological precision, as Leon Edel has commented, in his notebook, *The Twenties: From Notebooks and Diaries of the Period* (1975). His furious journalistic career, the pressures of working on his books-in-progress like *I Thought of Daisy* and *Axel's Castle: A Study of the Imaginative Literature of 1870-1930* (1931), and his spectacular sex life probably contributed to Wilson's nervous breakdown in March 1929 and to his brief addiction to paraldehyde. After divorcing Mary Blair in 1929, he married Margaret Canby, a genial drinking pal.

In 1931 he published *Axel's Castle,* a study of modern symbolist art that was also a monument to "the artist's morality" about which Gauss had first taught him. The book is a highly readable early account of the work of the French symbolists, Eliot, Joyce, William Butler Yeats, and Gertrude Stein. As in his essays of the 1920s, Wilson assumes little about his reader's acquaintance with a given subject, and he gradually initiates him into the symbolist world. His major subjects are viewed in relationship to the book's controlling metaphor, the castle. They are writers who have broken with the mimetic notion that external reality is the artist's concern, and they have extended the boundaries of literature through language experiment, disjunction, mixing of the senses; their "castle" is the fabricated kingdom of their demanding new forms. Wilson's attitude toward his subject matter is as important as his sensitive presentation of its experimental aspects. While he revered the artist's search for imaginative transcendence over the conventional and naturalistic, he was also, as a man of socialist convictions and classical training, distrustful of self-absorption and vagueness. Among the book's subjects, Joyce's concrete exploration of the psyche and Marcel Proust's heroic battle against his own nature and his corrupt society impressed Wilson most. *Axel's Castle* ends with Wilson's wishful prediction that literature will become a fusion of symbolist language and the socially useful language of modern science. The prophecy tells more about Wilson's own standards and ambitions in his work than about post-1920s literature.

Wilson continued to work at the *New Republic* through the 1930s and published drafts of his new projects in the magazine. He had become an influential figure in the New York literary scene, and helped promote the early careers of critics, such as Malcolm Cowley and Lionel Trilling, both of whom shared his interests in aesthetic modernism and political radicalism. "Politically, I am going further and further toward the left," he said in 1930. He voted Communist in 1932, kept a distance from Franklin D. Roosevelt in his political articles, espoused radical causes, and prepared himself for his wide-ranging study of the origins of socialism, *To the Finland Station: A Study in the Writing and Acting of History* (1940). In the middle of this enormous new critical undertaking, Wilson traveled to the Soviet Union in 1935 on a Guggenheim Fellowship; he wanted to research and observe the socialist experiment firsthand. One result of the trip was *Travels in Two Democracies*, published in 1936. The thrust of this book was Wilson's desire to express his positive sense of Russian life without class distinctions. But Wilson's journals of the period, published as *The Thirties: From Notebooks and Diaries of the Period* (1980), show that he was suspicious of certain tendencies in Soviet life from the start of his investigations. He had a cool attitude toward the Stalin cult and an early distaste for the developing bureaucracy. The simultaneous attraction to and recoil from both Soviet culture and the Marxist critical method was characteristic of Wilson. During this period he was earning an indifferent living as a magazine writer. His marriage to Mary McCarthy in 1938–described by him indirectly as "hideous" and directly as "nightmarish"–appears to have created further economic and psychological strain. McCarthy's side of the story, partially related in a 1 May 1985 *New York Times* article touching on their divorce proceedings, pictures Wilson as a drunken wife beater and domestic tyrant; Wilson's defenses cite McCarthy's emotional instability and reckless conduct.

Meanwhile in 1938 Wilson offered *The Triple Thinkers: Ten Essays on Literature* as an expression of his ambivalence about Marx, ideological criticism, and the intellectual strategies of leftist critics. The contents of the book, including studies of social and political conflict in Gustave Flaubert, Henry James, George Bernard Shaw, A. E. Housman, and the New Humanist Paul Elmer More, also offer speculations like "Marxism and Literature" and "The Historical Interpretation of Literature," on the uses of Marxist methodology in an analysis of art. The title for the volume is taken from one of Flaubert's letters in which he claims that the creative artist is a thinker three times over because of his ability to represent the social conflicts of his time. While the book's design is looser than the organization of *Axel's Cas-*

*Edmund Wilson*

*tle*, the disparate elements are held together by an approach and by several recurring themes. Wilson, like his intellectual ancestor Hippolyte Taine, focuses on the ways in which writers are conditioned by concrete events and environmental circumstances. This approach, quite different from *Axel's Castle* and the idea of art as pure fabrication, is brought to bear on at least two central critical questions of the 1930s: the value of looking at historical background and ideology in judging a writer, and the question of social setting and the writer's psychological makeup. "Marxism and Literature," a penetrating series of observations about contemporary excesses in criticism, warns against using the conceptual tools of Marx and Engels to reduce, predict, and otherwise inhibit the range and quality of writers' developments and readers' responses. In the essay Trotsky–the enemy of narrowly defined proletarian literature–becomes Wilson's model of large-mindedness; Marx and Engels are analyzed as humanists who disdain inferior literature with ideologically sound content. Thus, Wilson reasons, the historical methods perfected by later Marxist critics cannot account for literary masters who are "originals," not mere reflectors of their eras. Wilson's own loosely formulated description of sensitive critics–"people who understand writing"–may at first seem like circular reasoning; but by this description he hopes to identify those who are attuned to what is "orderly, symmetrical and pleasing" as opposed to what is politically and socially orthodox. Wilson scores 1930s-style propagandists like Granville Hicks, but he also attacks Paul Elmer More and his constricting set of conservative moral categories.

Other essays in the volume, especially those on John Jay Chapman and A. E. Housman, carry through Wilson's battle with reductionism and provinciality. The Chapman essay shows how a man of letters opposed the materialism and cheapness of the Gilded Age through his wit and humanistic dedication; the Housman essay describes how the poet's career as a scholar was warped by the worst features of Cambridge University and its inhibiting code of understatement. These portraits employ depth psychology as an adjunct to the historical method. In "The Historical Interpretation of Literature" (included in the 1948 edition) Wilson explains his approach; the "compulsions and emotional 'patterns'" of a work of art reveal the "ideals and diseases" of a given society, just as "the cell shows the condition of the tissue." Thus Housman's frustrations and tensions and his failure to realize his talent as a scholar are in part caused by the ideal of scholarship in his time. Such shading of one critical approach into another provoked mixed reactions from contemporaries. In *An Age of Criticism* (1952), William Van O'Connor remarked that Wilson was not a rigorous scholar, that he departed from the literary text and often confused literature and life. But in *The Armed Vision* (1948), Stanley Edgar Hyman, a critic who otherwise considered Wilson a popularizer and a "translator" who substituted plot summary for analysis, felt that Wilson was at his best when he combined the sociohistorical and the psychological approaches.

Wilson's critical syncretism, along with his power as a narrator, finds its most mature and sustained expression in *To the Finland Station*, his 1940 summing up of the socialist tradition. This thickly textured, emotionally charged presentation of ideas and radical actions, writers' visions and activists' achievements, is novelistic in style, moral in force, and analytic in its treatment of people and political literature. Moving through three centuries, Wilson tells the story of socialism from Michelet's discovery of Vico's historical method, to Marx's agonized forging of the materialist dialectic, to Lenin's arrival at the Finland Station.

The technique of the fiction writer is evident in the careful plotting, the recreation of domestic scenes, the portrayal of motivations, and the drive to resolution. The book has the qualities of a nineteenth-century generational novel, a narrative about how fathers shaped the lives of their sons. Wilson establishes a persona who is a sympathetic but skeptical critic that will not overlook the personal faults and intellectual inconsistencies of his many characters and who looks at long-range consequences. *To the Finland Station* also employs the three analytic methods of Wilson's early career: it focuses closely on the aesthetic object, in this case the dense, often literary prose of Marx and Engels and the texts of Vico, Michelet and Trotsky; it connects philosophical writing with the social environment in the manner of *The Triple Thinkers;* and it probes individual psyches to discover the ways in which ideas and political movements are created. Wilson the critic takes as his texts the books of great thinkers, the actions of revolutionaries, and the responses of ordinary people and minor characters. He steers a course between reverence for great men–Carlyle's hero worship–and modern critical concentration on economics, politics, and cultural life. Although he uses a "spotlighting" technique which tends to exalt figures like Marx and Lenin, he also demystifies his people by showing how their wounds, diseases, and frustrations shape their books and actions.

*The Wound and the Bow: Seven Studies in Literature* (1941), a literary complement to Wilson's psychological delving in *To the Finland Station*, studies the relationship between trauma and art. The concluding chapter, "Philoctetes: The Wound and the Bow," describes the volume's guiding idea by offering Wilson's retelling of the myth of an injured warrior who wields the bow of Apollo and eventually becomes a hero in the Trojan War. "The victim of a malodorous disease which renders him abhorrent to society and periodically degrades him and makes him helpless is also the master of a superhuman art which everybody has to respect and which the normal man finds he needs." Wilson gives his title a chance to accrete meaning as he studies the works of Joyce, Hemingway, Charles Dickens, Rudyard Kipling, and Edith Wharton, showing how each writer responds to the nature of obsessions and childhood injuries. As Wilson in *The Triple Thinkers*, he studies both literary achievements and failures.

In his treatment of Kipling and Hemingway, Wilson moves toward an analysis of why writers break down or produce poor work; in his discussion of Dickens the themes of the novels are measured against his early period of suffering in Warren's Blacking Factory. Wilson avoids the reductive interpretations of the clumsy psychological critic by showing how injury is the accompanying circumstance of talent, not the cause. Trauma may shape and direct a career; it may be inseparable from the work. Yet it is not a sole determinant. Lionel Trilling approves Wilson's approach of describing the ways in which neurosis "tells us something about the material on which the artist exercises his powers, and even something about his reasons for bringing his powers into play." Delmore Schwartz, however, was not impressed with Wilson's methods and criticized him in *Accent* (II, Spring 1942) for misreading Sophocles. But Wilson's deft and jargon-free psychological criticism stands as both a model of sanity and an example of his venturesome, wide-ranging kind of criticism. And, without having devoted his life to being a "Dickens man," he made a seminal contribution to Dickens studies that inspired scholars and critics in the 1950s and 1960s.

The 1940s were a period of literary simultaneity and change for Wilson. He worked on very diverse projects: a novel about sex and suburbia, a book about California writers, travel essays, a play called *The Little Blue Light* (1950) about threats to liberty, and the beginning of a book on the Civil War. There were also two important separations, from Mary McCarthy and from the *New Republic* and his fellow intellectuals who were eager to fight what Wilson thought of as Roosevelt's war against fascism. By 1943 Wilson was working as a book reviewer for the *New Yorker*, with whose backing he was later able to travel to Europe to cover the postwar scene and to New Mexico to report on the Zuni and their defiant attitude toward American progress. In 1946 Wilson married Elena Thornton Mumm and thereafter became more settled in his habits. The next quarter of a century, with its trips, its alternation between residences, and its prodigious work schedule, saw no abatement of Wilson's energy.

Wilson's lifelong dissatisfaction and disillusionment with modern industrial society and culture reached a critical point in this period. The radical hope of the 1930s had dissolved with the Hitler-Stalin pact in 1939; America was at war in 1941; the older generation of artists and friends were dying off or selling out or doing inferior work. Wilson's work of the 1940s expresses his

feeling of loss as it presents different kinds of artistic and social collapse and tries to offer bracing alternatives.

*The Boys in the Back Room: Notes on California Novelists* appeared in 1941 and presented an essentially negative report on what California, the movie culture, and journalism had done to the creative imagination. Wilson presents John O'Hara, William Saroyan, James M. Cain, Steinbeck, Otto Storm, and Nathanael West not as heroic strugglers against their environment, but rather as victims of modern culture. Although Wilson admires their energy, he finds them insubstantial: O'Hara suffers from "Hollywood lightness" and fuzzy intention; Cain's work is "a kind of Devil's parody of the movies"; Saroyan has fallen prey to the newspaper columns with their human interest focus. The last chapter of this slim volume, "Facing the Pacific," is a moody, evocative presentation of how the California landscape—"as hollow as the life of a troll-nest where everything is out in the open instead of underground"—has contributed to thwarting talent.

Wilson's next attack on American culture came in the form of his novel, *Memoirs of Hecate County* (1946). A series of very loosely connected short stories about an upper-middle-class intellectual recalling his sexual and social experiences in suburbia and Manhattan, the book cancels out the upbeat resolutions of *I Thought of Daisy* and shows its protagonist moving deeper into contemporary chaos. Wilson meant the title to refer to the witchy quality of several of the book's women, as well as to a general atmosphere in which people are spooked and tormented by the demons of commercialism and capitalist decadence. Each story in the volume treats a different aspect of American social illness as the narrator traces it over a period of some fifteen years. The venality of Madison Avenue is presented in a grim, ironic allegory called "The Man Who Shot Snapping Turtles." Other chapters study phony artists, the affluent cocktail set, and the cheapening of ideas by the mass market publishers.

The best story, "The Princess With the Golden Hair," is the most controversial and also the most sustained piece of social chronicling. The art-historian protagonist relates a phase of his sexual career, a story about Anna, a dancehall girl from Brooklyn, and Imogene, a blond suburban enchantress. The narrator progresses from a frenzied pursuit of these women, complete with self-delusions, cruelties, and snobberies, to a rueful recognition of his own contemptible qualities. Rich and lovely Imogene in some ways represents the aesthetic temptations and the isolation that Wilson had been resisting since *Axel's Castle*; the less-than-beautiful and diseased Anna is "actuality." But both relationships involve enchantment. The narrator, living in a privileged fantasy about proletarian virtue, eventually turned his dance-hall girl into an abstraction and treated her with condescension. He treated her this way to work off the frustration of his relationship with Imogene. Since he had been victimized by someone wealthier, he vents his bad feelings on a member of the underclass. Wilson resolves the story by having the protagonist return to the cocktail set in Hecate County. Anna—who had given him gonorrhea, but once almost had provided him with actuality, "the true sanction for life"—also helped him to break down the barrier between Hecate County and the larger world. The failure is another one of Wilson's representations of collapse and the frailty of humane endeavor in the modern world. Meanwhile Wilson's graphic story of sex and disillusionment caused *Memoirs of Hecate County* to be removed from bookstores in New York, and Wilson's publisher was fined. But Wilson became a celebrity and for the first time, an underground best-selling author. Without quite realizing it, he had invented an authentic American art form: the suburban shocker. The book met with a cool response from several major critics, including Diana Trilling, who found it cold-blooded, and Alfred Kazin, who found Wilson misanthropic and mechanical in his treatment of passion. In *The Immediate Experience* (1972) Robert Warshow was, perhaps, more sensitive to its place in the Wilson canon: he considered the book's ugliness and blurring of fantasy and reality to be "a valid response" to modern life. In this connection the reader is likely to find it one of the most vivid presentations of Wilson's ideas about cultural decline and social irresponsibility.

During the 1950s and 1960s Wilson became an institution while maintaining his distance from postwar prosperity and literary commercialism. His writing alternated between attacks on power and oppression and celebrations of heroic, artistic, and political resistance. Honors poured in, although he rarely paid much attention to them. New friendships and interests blossomed. Wilson extended himself not only to intellectuals and writers like Nabokov, a new sparring partner with whom he could argue about the Russian language and politics, but also to upstate neighbors

and relatives. In 1954 he traveled to Israel for the *New Yorker* and built his new book, *The Scrolls from the Dead Sea* (1955), on firsthand reporting and on his Hebrew studies at Princeton Theological Seminary. This enormous undertaking, at first a matter of curiosity about a language his grandfather knew, developed into a literary and philosophical investigation of Jewish culture and its relationship to Christian tradition. By 1956 he was having troubles with the Internal Revenue Service which eventually stimulated him to write *The Cold War and the Income Tax: A Protest* (1963). He then conducted research around New York State for his book *Apologies to the Iroquois* (1960). Wilson's *Patriotic Gore: Studies in the Literature of the American Civil War* (1962), his major project of the 1950s, published as a massive reconsideration of that war and its impact on the creative mind, began to appear serially in the *New Yorker* and provided material for his Lowell lectures at Harvard University in 1959.

Wilson also readied old essays for collections, continued to write extended book reviews, and published "pieces" of his mind. In 1950 *Classics and Commercials* was published. It is a collection that surveys popular writing and patterns in the Modernist movement. A major essay in the book, "Thoughts on Being Bibliographed," sets a tone of earnest self-examination as it attacks what Wilson perceives to be the confusion of the intellectual scene, the venality of publishing, and "the drop of a trajectory in modern literature." After Wilson frankly describes his own journalistic methods, he takes on the new forces in writing and scholarship: opportunistic university professors, slick magazine writers, and radicals who have "sold out." Wilson, "the literary worker" of the 1920s, took on the role of old fogey, yet used it not for retirement but for assaults on "machine finished" *Time* writing and plodding scholarship (the latter derived in some cases from the aridities of doctrinaire Marxism). The volume also picks quarrels with other features of the contemporary scene; for example the craze for Franz Kafka caused Wilson to see the writer as a sign of modern nihilism and representative of the culture of alienation. Wilson withholds praise, as he did in the 1920s, from a talent that seems to embody incoherence, an artist who fails to resist and struggle. By no means a piece of analytic criticism, "A Dissenting Opinion on Kafka" is a blunt but gripping moral statement that serves to introduce Wilson's new phase of toughening up and challenging the contemporary weakness of Western society. Related to Wilson's hostility toward popular culture and fads are several controversial assaults on mystery stories—works devoid of characterization and human emotions. Not content with this dismissal, he engages in some fairly weak psychologizing—blaming the public's unhealthy appetite for suspenseful rubbish on a generalized desire to pin down guilt in the complex world between the wars. Vague as such reasoning may be, it takes its place among Wilson's grievances against mass culture and reveals his devotion to human-centered literature. After *The Shores of Light* (1952)—essentially a book about the 1920s and 1930s—the next collection of literary essays, *The Bit Between My Teeth: A Literary Chronicle of 1950-1965* (1965), gives special emphasis to Wilson's own image as a critic, to works of past masters, and to a very select group of contemporary works. At the time when writers such as Samuel Beckett, Robert Lowell, and Jorge Luis Borges were flourishing, Wilson was devoting his time to remembering Fitzgerald's relationship with Sheilah Graham, evoking John Peale Bishop's aesthete's vision, and extolling the delights of Logan Pearsall Smith. The book's best essays—on himself, on Eliot, on Boris Pasternak, and on Kingsley Amis—suggest why Wilson dodged so many post-World War II figures. In searching for inspiriting examples of resistance to modern power, materialism, and conformity, he found contemporary writers and artists lacking in force of character and desire for imaginative transcendence. Yet the seedy and anti-idealistic world of Amis's novels appeals to him because the characters, "perplexed though they are," have "something to build, to win." His moving essay on Pasternak, "Doctor Life and His Guardian Angel," focuses on the novelist's Christian resistance to sterile Marxist ideology and identifies Pasternak's championing of the individual as "the vital unit." On the negative side in " 'Miss Buttle' and 'Mr. Eliot,' " Wilson criticizes all of Eliot's roles—moralist, professor, judgmental critic, genteel Bostonian—except that of poet, "one of the live nerves of modern literature." The essay becomes an excuse to expose the academic obsession with Eliot's work: "You can get through it all in the evenings of a week. Those English professors are lazy. They rarely know anything but English Lit., and they rarely read anything in English that they do not have to read for their degrees and their courses or to get themselves a little credit by writing in some critical organ about one of their accepted subjects." Wilson presents ni-

hilism and opportunism and propagandistic yea-saying of the religious or political kind as closing in. *The Bit Between My Teeth*, as its title suggests, is a tough-minded attempt to ignore, to resist and to go forward. Its defects are obvious enough: an insensitivity to the many sides of postmodern talents, and a certain insularity and pride in Wilson's own limitations. And yet, unlike other critics—Eliot included—who defend and rationalize their prejudices with elaborate argument about the "main stream" of literature and art (like "Main Line," Philadelphia, Wilson jokes), he is frank about the tastes that he has formed. While conceding that Pablo Picasso "is the greatest draftsman since Raphael," he finds him boring, shallow, and deliberately ugly in his portraits of women. Sometimes risking philistinism, he nevertheless contributes an invigorating forthrightness, a perspective unconnected with schools, allegiances, or fashions.

*Israel and the Dead Sea Scrolls*, brought together as a volume with a foreword by Leon Edel in 1978, is another one of Wilson's 1950s investigations, this time of religious belief and language. "I am no Semitic scholar," he declared, plunging into Hebrew, biblical criticism, and the issues involved with the discovery of the Essene scrolls, which suggest that Christian teachings were anticipated by a radical Jewish "Teacher of Righteousness." Wilson, acting partly as demystifier and partly as excited critic of a new literature, lost himself for a time in thousands of years of Jewish culture. The sections of the book called "Israel" (which first appeared in 1956 in *Red, Black, Blond and Olive* along with his studies of the Zuni, Haitian, and Soviet cultures) reveal his lifelong anthropological curiosity about Hebrew, as well as his personal account of grappling with a language that emblemized his latest concerns about resistance. "On First Reading Genesis" is an essay devoted to surveying the realms of a text and reacting to it with the fervor of John Keats's persona in "On First Looking Into Chapman's Homer." The very verb tenses express an idea of eternity and are inspiriting to a critic disillusioned with his time and country. As he learns to write Hebrew characters, Wilson has "a feeling of vicarious authority"; these symbols "march on through our modern events as if they were invulnerable, eternal." The aesthetic and moral pleasures of contemplating and writing a language are also evidenced in the book's main body, the story of the scrolls. This report—Wilson's narrative about discovery, conflict, and the politics of

Hebrew scholarship—becomes another phase of his personal campaign against institutional power and cover-ups. Wilson finds that Christians and Jews have been equally guilty in trying to discredit the scrolls. What the documents reveal is that the Essene monastery, ". . . more than Bethlehem or Nazareth, [is] the cradle of Christianity." Wilson, the investigator who revealed the painful personal origins of Marxism, here performs a similar job of informing the general reader while at the same time making him sensitive to language, culture, and ethos. While the book is no great work of scholarship, as Wilson knew all too well, it is one of the century's great learned and humane excursions. As an example of moral reflection, analytic criticism, and scholarly adventure, it has few rivals.

*A Piece of My Mind: Reflections at Sixty* (1956) is filled with the protest impulse that had driven Wilson's criticism forward since the 1920s; it is also damaged by a good deal of bluster and willfulness posing as candid criticism of society and modern values. When Stanley Edgar Hyman pointed to Wilson's cold contempt for people as individuals (seen in his insect and animal imagery), he was reducing the total man and ridiculing a critic he did not really understand; yet there is some truth in the notion that Wilson, the scourge of the provincials, could be narrow, coarse, and insensitive. Part of this volume of reflections, memories, and opinions delivers fairly ridiculous pronouncements about sex, religion, eugenics, and human welfare. Wilson deplores the "appalling degree" to which such modern writers as James, Proust, and D. H. Lawrence have emphasized characters who are "incapable of experiencing the full cycle of courtship, fruition, relief." Such literary weaklings, we are told, only encourage a letting down of all standards by their "dislocations of the reproductive instinct." Deeply confused about the consequences of his position and eager to encourage eugenics in the name of civilization, Wilson became as desperate, dangerous, and silly as other despairing writers who turned against the anomalous qualities of human beings. He even seemed to forget his own reverence for wounded artists. On religious matters he is no less irresponsible as he mocks Christianity by telling the reader that he derives more spiritual sustenance from the American bathroom than from the cathedrals of Europe. Fortunately this philistinism does not dominate the whole book: two fine essays, one on what Jewishness means to him as a child of Protestantism, and one on his fa-

ther's standards and their relationship to an older American civic duty, almost offset the serious lapses. The latter essay is in part an attack on party men and passive leaders (such as Harry S. Truman and Dwight D. Eisenhower) and an attempt to contrast them with leaders who have a sense of continuity (Thomas Jefferson, Abraham Lincoln, and inconsistently enough for Wilson, Franklin D. Roosevelt). This essay, called "The Author at Sixty," locates Wilson at his home in Talcottsville, "fortified" against "the fakes and distractions" that lately dominate the American scene.

Wilson's next major publication, *Apologies to the Iroquois* (1960), not only explores the grievances of upstate Indian neighbors in Schoharie County through interviews, research, and friendly visits (Wilson was admitted to one of their major rituals) but it also spotlights heroic resisters. Mad Bear, a Tuscarora leader, wins Wilson's respect by assuming the role of a latter-day democratic revolutionary. The high point of the book occurs when Mad Bear helps the tribe win a court judgment against the most imperious figure in the state, Robert Moses, builder of parks and symbol of grand-scale annexation. In Wilson's masterpiece of the period, *Patriotic Gore,* he carries through the now-familiar charges against the American power drive—against centralized government and nationalistic aggression—by studying the Civil War and its impact on writers, thinkers, and public figures. The book's title should remind the reader of *The Wound and the Bow;* both books are about how great ideas and achievements have their origins in disease and suffering. But *Patriotic Gore,* unlike the earlier work, is thoroughly pessimistic about human potential, somewhat reductive in its view of the warring North and South as "sea slugs," and often concerned with minor or unattractive authors as it tries to uncover the baleful consequences of the war for literature. Wilson also wanted to "set our values straight"—which is to say, prove that our ideas of order, national unity, and justice are based on power and oppression. The introduction, in which he does some preaching and lecturing, has not earned him the approval of even sympathetic critics like Irving Howe. The body of the book—more massive than *To the Finland Station*—is an awesome survey of brilliant and admirable, stupid and hateful, writers. Wilson, always something of an anthropologist and naturalist in his literary criticism, here takes a steady look—complete with huge quotations, summaries, and analyses—at bigots like Hilton Helper and great minds like

Oliver Wendell Holmes. His most interesting analytic passages deal with how writers' styles were formed under Civil War pressures and left a permanent imprint on American literary culture. The florid style of some writers anesthetized perception; the plain style (what Wilson calls "the language of responsibility") is brilliantly analyzed, on the one hand, as a powerful, cool instrument and, on the other, as a way of numbing emotions and preparing the way for a future of literary tyranny in the form of the military communique and the office memo. These sections, along with dogged research work on many forgotten men and women, constitute a major service to American literary history. Yet the vision of the book, its sense that the Civil War ushered in an American empire and warped many of our literary figures, is more powerful than most of the specific contributions.

Two of Wilson's less ambitious projects in the 1960s, *The Cold War and the Income Tax* (1963) and *The Fruits of the MLA* (1968), share the resentment and anger of *Patriotic Gore* as well as some of its themes. The tax book goes after "that son of a bitch Uncle Sam" and says the IRS uses theological propaganda to justify war. Wilson tells his own story of victimization without self-pity and then proceeds to attack government's misuse of funds and the horrors of government power directed against protestors and dissidents. The book on the Modern Language Association takes the protest against centralization into the intellectual and literary realm as it excoriates the nitpicking and "hyphen-hunting" of textual scholars. Wilson identified these powerful scholars, with their unwieldy and unreadable editions of American classics, as the academic equivalents of the IRS theologians and the self-righteous defenders of the union during the Civil War. Such characterizing earned him the scorn of academics; he was guilty of "ignorance, unreason, infantilism, and meanness." Wilson found the haughty dismissal a predictable response to his kind of rational inquiry.

His last major work, *Upstate: Records and Recollections of Northern New York* (1971), is not one of his characteristic explorations, attacks, or adventures. It comes to terms with one of his central personal problems: the conflict between the castle of art and ideas and the claims of humanity. Living in the old stone house in Talcottville, Wilson removed himself for twenty summers from family routine and literary life. But the separation paradoxically brought him closer to ordinary human-

ity than he had ever been. The old house in *Upstate*—the subject of the book—turns out to be not only a vantage point for surveying American values and folkways but also a location in which to experience a new kind of sharing, a trading of thoughts and feelings with ancestors and new friends. Divided between introductory sections explaining the house's origins and the qualities of upstate life and later journal entries, the book is part informal study and part record of memories and perceptions. Wilson, installed in his baronial house, reflects on art and order, but also manages to make new friends, study Hungarian with a neighbor, take part in local life, and find ways of escaping his own isolation and disillusionment.

Before he died in 1972, he published *A Window on Russia, for the Use of Foreign Readers* (1971) and prepared a number of other manuscripts, including *The Devils and Canon Barham: Ten Essays on Poets, Novelists and Monsters* (1973), the last of his literary chronicles in which he takes a final look at Eliot, Pound, and Hemingway. The book also contains pieces on the grotesque and the uncanny, two of Wilson's abiding interests. There seemed no end to his bibliography; letters, journals, and posthumous essays continue to appear. Most notable are his letters (published in 1977 as *Letters on Literature and Politics 1912-1972*); this collection shows the range of Wilson's informal interests as well as a partial record of his varied and often hectic life. Many of the letters also reveal him in the role of friend and encourager—a guider and nurturer of talent and relentless battler with circumstances, both personal and social, that keep writers from working.

Because Edmund Wilson did not build his career around one body of thought or central critical inquiry, he occupies a special and problematic place in the American canon. Since he did not establish a resting place for his talents, a fixed professional function, he became a figure whose authority is questioned in an age of academic specialization, but whose intellectual range, vigorous prose, and ambition command respect and attention from intellectuals and a new generation of general readers. Negative critics of his work have tried to erode his authority. Stanley Edgar Hyman dismissed his critical methods as neurotic self-dramatization or literal-minded plot summary; he claimed that Wilson never really wrote a unified critical work but merely capitalized on his engaging style. And a friendly critic like Alfred Kazin maintains that Wilson was a mediator, not a leader. A less sympathetic analyst of his contribution, Warner Berthoff, writes of Wilson's "airless mind," cool knowingness, and derivative ideas. But while Kazin's and Berthoff's remarks may well be difficult to disregard—especially in light of Wilson's later lapses of taste and willful neglect of postmodernism—Wilson's name still stands for tireless dedication to literature, relentless pursuit of libertarian and progressive ideas, and yearning to transcend the limits of class, critical category, and fashion. His reputation, as well as threats to it, rests on his identity as a professor without a university, a critic without a field, a historian without a period, a thinker without a school.

**Letters:**

*Letters on Literature and Politics 1912-1972,* edited by Elena Wilson, introduction by Daniel Aaron, foreword by Leon Edel (New York: Farrar, Straus & Giroux, 1977);

*The Nabokov-Wilson Letters 1940-1971,* edited by Simon Karlinsky (New York: Harper Colophon, 1979).

**Bibliography:**

*Princeton University Library Chronicle* (February 1944);

Richard David Ramsey, *Edmund Wilson: A Bibliography* (New York: Lewis, 1971).

**Biography:**

Richard Hauer Costa, *Edmund Wilson: Our Neighbor from Talcottville* (Syracuse, N.Y.: Syracuse University Press, 1980).

**References:**

David Castronovo, *Edmund Wilson* (New York: Frederick Ungar, 1984);

Malcolm Cowley, "From the Finland Station," *New Republic,* 103 (7 October 1940): 478-480;

George Douglas, *Edmund Wilson's America* (Lexington: University of Kentucky Press, 1983);

Charles Frank, *Edmund Wilson* (New York: Twayne, 1970);

Irving Howe, "Edmund Wilson and the Sea Slugs," in his *A World More Attractive* (New York: Horizon, 1963), pp. 300-307;

Alfred Kazin, *The Inmost Leaf: A Selection of Essays* (New York: Harcourt, Brace, 1955);

Kazin, *New York Jew* (New York: Vantage, 1978);

Kazin, *On Native Grounds* (New York: Reynal & Hitchcock, 1946);

Leonard Kriegel, *Edmund Wilson* (Carbondale: Southern Illinois University Press, 1971);

Sherman Paul, *Edmund Wilson: A Study of Literary Vocation in Our Time* (Urbana: University of Illinois Press, 1965);

Delmore Schwartz, "The Writing of Edmund Wilson," *Accent II* (Spring 1942): 176-186;

Diana Trilling, on *Memoirs of Hecate County,* in her *Reviewing the Forties* (New York: Harcourt Brace Jovanovich, 1978), pp. 150-154;

Lionel Trilling, "Art and Neurosis," in *The Liberal Imagination* (New York: Doubleday/Anchor, 1950), pp. 155-176;

John Wain, ed., *Edmund Wilson: The Man and His Work* (New York: New York University Press, 1978).

**Papers:**

Wilson's papers are at the Beinecke Rare Book and Manuscript Library, Yale University.

# William K. Wimsatt, Jr.

*(17 November 1907-17 December 1975)*

Robert Moynihan
*State University of New York College at Oneonta*

BOOKS: *Shapes from Dusk to Winter, I-XV* (New Haven, 1938);

*The Prose Style of Samuel Johnson* (New Haven: Yale University Press / London: Oxford University Press, 1941);

*Philosophic Words: A Study of Style and Meaning in the Rambler and Dictionary of Samuel Johnson* (New Haven: Yale University Press, 1948);

*The Verbal Icon: Studies in the Meaning of Poetry,* by Wimsatt, with two preliminary essays by Wimsatt and Monroe C. Beardsley (Lexington: University of Kentucky Press, 1954; London: Methuen, 1970);

*Literary Criticism: A Short History,* by Wimsatt and Cleanth Brooks (New York: Knopf, 1957);

*What to Say About a Poem,* by Wimsatt and others, supplement to the *CEA Critic,* 26 (December 1963);

*Hateful Contraries: Studies in Literature and Criticism,* by Wimsatt, with an essay on English meter by Wimsatt and Beardsley (Lexington: University of Kentucky Press, 1965);

*The Portrait of Alexander Pope* (New Haven: Yale University Press, 1965);

*How to Compose Chess Problems and Why* (New Haven: Privately printed, 1966);

*Day of the Leopards: Essays in Defense of the Poem* (New Haven: Yale University Press, 1976).

OTHER: Alexander Pope, *Selected Poetry and Prose,* edited, with an introduction, by Wimsatt (New York: Rinehart, 1951; revised edition, New York: Holt, Rinehart & Winston, 1972);

*English Stage Comedy,* edited, with an introduction, by Wimsatt (New York: Columbia University Press, 1955);

James Boswell, *Boswell for the Defence, 1769-1774,* edited by Wimsatt and F. A. Pottle (New York: McGraw-Hill, 1959; Melbourne & London: Heinemann, 1960);

*Samuel Johnson on Shakespeare,* edited by Wimsatt (New York: Hill & Wang, 1960); republished as *Dr. Johnson on Shakespeare* (Balti-

more & Harmondsworth, U.K.: Penguin, 1969);

*Explication as Criticism: Selected Papers from the English Institute, 1941-1952,* edited, with a foreword, by Wimsatt (New York: Columbia University Press, 1963);

*The Idea of Comedy: Essays in Prose and Verse, Ben Jonson to George Meredith,* edited by Wimsatt (Englewood Cliffs, N.J.: Prentice-Hall, 1969);

*Versification: Major Language Types,* edited, with a foreword, by Wimsatt (New York: Modern Language Association, 1972);

*Literary Criticism: Idea and Act,* edited, with an introduction, by Wimsatt (Berkeley: University of California Press, 1974);

*Samuel Johnson: Selected Poetry and Prose,* edited by Wimsatt and Frank Brady (Berkeley: University of California Press, 1978);

"Rhetoric and Poems: The Example of Swift," in *The Author in His Work,* edited by L. S. Martz and A. Williams (New Haven: Yale University Press, 1978), pp. 229-244;

"A Supplement to *The Portraits of Alexander Pope,*" by Wimsatt and John Riley, in *Evidence in Literary Scholarship,* edited by René Wellek and Alvaro Ribeiro (Oxford: Clarendon Press, 1980), pp. 122-164.

PERIODICAL PUBLICATIONS: "We, Teiresias," review of Lionel Trilling's *Sincerity and Authenticity, Yale Review,* new series 62 (Spring 1973): 431-438;

"Images of Samuel Johnson," *ELH,* 41 (Fall 1974): 359-374;

"News from Abroad," review of Jonathan Culler's *Structuralist Poetics, Yale Review,* 65 (Autumn 1975): 77-87;

"Vladimir Nabokov: More Chess Problems and the Novel," by Wimsatt and Janet K. Gezari, *Yale French Studies,* no. 58 (1979): 102-116.

William K. Wimsatt's academic and critical career, spent almost entirely at Yale University, is a record of conservative originality based on the

*William K. Wimsatt, Jr. (photograph by Mary Price)*

received values of a literary canon which was evaluated according to heightened rhetorical analysis, some tenets of Aristotelianism, a careful reworking–but subordination–of the biographical record to the literary text, and a persistently Christian moral impulse. Late in his life he sought to understand the recent play of literary criticism, but this moral impulse led him to find it, particularly in its French manifestations, redundant and trivial.

William Kurtz Wimsatt, Jr., was born in Washington, D.C., on 17 November 1907 to William Kurtz Wimsatt, a wholesale lumber dealer, and Bertha Stuart McSherry Wimsatt. He received his B.A. (1928) and A.M. (1929) from Georgetown University. For five years, beginning in 1930, Wimsatt was head of the English department at the Portsmouth Priory School, and he studied and taught at Catholic University of America in 1935-1936 before going on to graduate school at Yale University in 1936. While at Yale he wrote *Shapes from Dusk to Winter, I-XV* (1938), the Yale University Prize Poem for 1938. After earning his Ph.D. in 1939 he joined the Yale fac-

ulty and remained there until his death in 1975. He was appointed Frederick Clifford Ford Professor of English in 1965 and Sterling Professor of English in 1974. Among his grants and awards were a Guggenheim Fellowship in 1947 and a Yale-Rockefeller Senior Research grant in 1965-1966. He was for many years a leading member of the English Institute, and he received honorary doctorates from Villanova University (1962), the University of Notre Dame (1963), St. Louis University (1963), Le Moyne College (1965), and Kenyon College (1970). He married Margaret Hecht in September 1944 and was the father of two children.

In his notes for "Boswell's Return to London," an unpublished annotation of Boswell's journal prepared for Frederick Pottle as a graduate student in 1937, Wimsatt defined the areas of critical and academic concern which he would address in his later writing. Here the words "annotator" and "annotation" take on the meaning of "biographer" and "biography," a genre Wimsatt did not practice but which was dominant at Yale and in academia when he made these observations: "It seems to me that the unutterable ideal of an annotator of a journal should be to fill out the implications of the journal, to bring to the surface the multitude of meanings that lie just submerged, things it would have cost the journalist too many words to tell, which would have been understood by a contemporary, but which have lapsed largely or entirely from the consciousness of after generations." He went on to say, "If annotation is an art, it is an extremely minor one, yet it has its inescapable laws of relevance." Wimsatt's later work is not bound by the limitations of annotation or of biography.

Wimsatt's first scholarly book, *The Prose Style of Samuel Johnson* (1941), clearly marks a distinction between biographical commentary and criticism. He approaches his subject through the categories of parallelism, antithesis, diction, sentence length, and consistency. Wimsatt is unremittingly analytic, even if he does imitate the eighteenth-century rhetoricians Hugh Blair, Richard Whately, and George Campbell. For he believed that analysis of Johnson's writings, not generalized commentary, was essential to save Johnson from the popular opinion of the nineteenth century, characterized by Thomas Babington Macaulay's admiring but derisive judgment in his essay for the eighth edition of the *Encyclopaedia Britannica* (1853-1860), that the great critic lived not through his works but through Boswell's vision.

Wimsatt not only took a different course from the anecdotal or impressionistic, but he also prepared the method for his second book on Johnson. The phrase "Philosophic Diction" employed in *The Prose Style of Samuel Johnson* became the motive for *Philosophic Words: A Study of Style and Meaning in the Rambler and Dictionary of Samuel Johnson* (1948), which answers another of Macaulay's assertions in his *Encyclopaedia Britannica* article: that Johnson's "Dictionary has been altered by editors till it can scarcely be called his." The plan of this work appears to be simple: an explanation of Johnson's use of sources for terms–from *aberration* to *vulnerable*–thought in the eighteenth century, before the rigid classification and compartmentalization of learning, to be "scientific" or "philosophic."

Wimsatt's method intends to give the reader a definition of Johnson's intellectual and imaginative mental working, a kind of biography of creative adaptation. Again Wimsatt works against the grain of patient scholars who counted the words in Johnson's sentences to discover that they were shorter at the end of his life. Wimsatt's efforts may not take a reader toward what he described in *Philosophic Words* as "a biography or the history of Johnson's mind," but the work is a close reading of sources and contextual variation.

René Wellek's *Concepts of Criticism* (1963) implicitly complained about Wimsatt's apparent distance from the European idealistic tradition, either in its German garb or in its social manifestations in the twentieth century: neither in America nor in England is there an "interest in the kind of criticism practiced by George Lukacs or T. W. Adorno with such great acclaim on the Continent." Wellek notes that Wimsatt "adopts the Hegelian term 'concrete universal,' but Hegel's dialectical method, not to speak of the details of the aesthetics, is entirely unknown in the United States." Wellek implies that for Wimsatt "comparative literature" was bound in the familiar comparisons of Latin etymology and comparison.

Wimsatt's next book bears but little relation to what preceded. His comments take on a new precision of critical comment on narrowly defined rhetorical form. The impulse of *The Verbal Icon* (1954) operates antithetically to another school of critics, the Chicago Aristotelians. Wimsatt's opposition to R. S. Crane and the Chicago School was inevitable: each chose a similar intellectual origin and method but arrived at opposing critical positions. Whatever Wimsatt's difficulty of clear observation in his apprentice work, he did arrive at statements modeled on texts themselves.

Wimsatt's habit throughout his professional life was to publish and republish in nearly as many sources as possible and to husband quietly his miscellaneous essays for later books. While one of the essays in *The Verbal Icon* therefore specifically addresses the Chicago critics and Crane's *Critics and Criticism,* the second earliest essay in Wimsatt's collection, "One Relation of Rhyme to Reason" (first published in 1944), counters by its own example the generalized formulations of such essays as Crane's "Man of Feeling." Earlier Wimsatt had pieced together something better than generalities in his discussions of such commonplaces as "comparison" or "antithesis," but a reader may still doubt the value of the final effect and his ability to counter effectively critical generalities. The essay on Pope is a major turning point. Wimsatt asks a basic question: How are the couplets of Alexander Pope different from others' rhymes? A reader may intuit that a complexity and a display of virtuosity are present in Pope's verse, but how can they be demonstrated and proved? Wimsatt claims that repeated rhymed couplets are usually repetitious in the hands of both amateurs and canonized practitioners. Even Chaucer, Wimsatt observes, "relies for variation more on continuous sense and syntax than on rhyme, and when his rhyme words are the same part of speech, he is apt to give us a dullish rhyme."

Wimsatt cites lines from Pope–"Whether the nymph shal break Diana's law, / Or some frail China jar receive a flaw."–to illustrate the nature of chiasmus–or the inverted relationship between the syntactic elements in parallel lines of verse: "In the first line the breakage, then the fragile thing (the law); in the second line another fragile thing (the jar) and then its breaking (the flaw). The parallel is given a kind of roundness and completeness; the intellectual lines are softened into the concrete harmony of 'law' and 'flaw.' The meaning is locked in a pattern of inevitability." The chiasmus here is a crossing between *nymph* and *Diana's flaw* and between *law* and *China jar.*

In this chapter *The Verbal Icon* set a new standard for explication. But what is here an implicit grudge against the Chicagoans becomes overt and strongly polemical in another part of the book, "The Chicago Critics." Perhaps most readers looking at the texts of Crane and Wimsatt side by side would be won by Wimsatt's arguments because of their explicative display. The turn to polemics creates a different scheme of judgment. Wimsatt dismisses the Chicago School as being too literal in its definitions and too restrictive in describing the interstices between literature and "Aristotle." Wimsatt summarily dismisses the notion that the Chicagoans are in the vanguard because of their overliteralism and the oversimplification of the literary act, they are little more than an interesting but parochial movement. Unfortunately, "The Chicago Critics" descends to the level of *pasquinade*: "Enter: Professor Crane. He walks up to the critic and, taking a piece of burnt cork from his pocket, proceeds to blacken the mask all over. 'There now,' he says, 'that is what you really look like.' Professor Crane then removes the mask from the face of the critic and, with a towel which he has brought along for the purpose, attempts to wipe it off clean, leaving it, however, somewhat more smudged than before and generally somewhat grey." Wimsatt would again display this tendency in his last book of criticism, *Day of the Leopards* (1976).

Two other essays which gained enduring academic attention in *The Verbal Icon* are "The Affective Fallacy" and "The Intentional Fallacy," both written in collaboration with Monroe Beardsley. Each essay confronts long-standing problems of the critical act, and each continues with an orientation already revealed before: criticism is not best expressed through emotional impressionism nor by its supposed opposite, the critical subterfuge of biographical omniscience, the objective notation of a creator's "intention." Wimsatt questions the appropriateness of biographical data, no matter how voluminously or intimately recorded, as an explanation for artistic creation. The documentation of John Livingston Lowes's *The Road to Xanadu* (1927) cannot explain the brief creative life of Coleridge in poetry. Even Coleridge's own explanation of *Kubla Khan* (1797)–that the poem came to him in a dream–must be treated with suspicion. Who is to account for either the accuracy or the completeness of the fables creators spin about their acts? A predisposition to the myths of biographical and autobiographical "reality" creates other illegitimacies: "It would be convenient if the passwords of the intentional school, 'sincerity,' 'fidelity,' 'spontaneity,' 'authenticity,' 'genuineness,' 'originality,' could be equated with . . . more precise terms of evaluation."

"The Affective Fallacy" is a much more problematic chapter, no matter what its contemporary

and lasting effect. One may be forewarned by lines quoted at the beginning of the essay from Eduard Hanslick, one of the most learned but biased of nineteenth-century music critics. The essay does not advance the argument beyond the enunciation in Austin Warren and Wellek's *The Theory of Literature* and their attempted definition of the ontological place of the literary object or act. According to Wimsatt and Beardsley, the reader's response may be described in terms that are nearly clinical: a poem is the sum of its results, and there is no constraint to the cultural reactions of the audience. Yet if a poem is neither its *intention* nor its affective results, what is it? It resides on the page for transmission to the mind of a reader through his trained act. If this be not admitted, the poem disappears into obscurantist commentary, much of which is imprecise and incomplete. However, Wimsatt and Beardsley never provide the method to fulfill this generalized formulation. The questions they pose remain essentially negative and are, in their limitations, destructive to a would-be answerer foolish enough to accept the critics' definitions and terms of argument. Rather, there is very nearly a critical solipsism in statements that both affective and biographical approaches are "fallacies," but no intellectual or semantic alternative is presented to bridge the emotional-intellectual achievement of poetry: "The Intentional Fallacy is a confusion between the poem and its origins. . . . It begins by trying to derive the standard of criticism from the psychological *causes* of the poem and ends in biography and relativism. The Affective Fallacy is a confusion between the poem and its *results*. . . . It begins by trying to derive the standard of criticism from the psychological effects of the poem and ends in impressionism and relativism."

Presumably the solution for these dilemmas is "Explication as Criticism," first published in 1951 and republished in *The Verbal Icon*. Unfortunately the essay is too general to be used as an apologia for the new methods, which have, once again, to be observed in the working to be justified. Wimsatt's descriptions of method display more ability in defining what good criticism is *not*, rather than what it *is*. He argues that both T. S. Eliot and I. A. Richards err in attempting to adopt a "scientific neutralism," the extreme antithesis opposing the bug-bear, "sheer affectivism." As much as with a successful creation of biography, poetry remains beyond analysis, though it may be defined, and one may say what bad or inadequate criticism is: "Poetry is a complex kind of verbal construction in which the dimension of coherence is by various techniques of implication greatly enhanced and thus generates an extra dimension of correspondence to reality, the symbolic or analogical. But all this structure of meaning rises upon a certain element of unavoidably direct reference to outside reality and a minimal truth of such reference."

Later, Wimsatt was to write about Boswell's biography and autobiographical acts in sentences which reveal the same form of tension: "realism in the portrayal of human feelings involves, almost inevitably, a kind of impurity, a traffic with the mixed or complicated (for feelings seldom occur pure or simple). And next that there is a special kind of reflective or aesthetic feeling–an accent of realization–which arises just out of the tension of the primary or immediate life feelings; so that paradoxically the most sensitive realism is in effect always more than realism." The next paragraph in this introduction to *Boswell for the Defense, 1769-1774* (1959) provides an answer to theoretical cruxes, and readers have to judge for themselves if the commission of any critic moves to successful act and exemplification: "It is difficult to illustrate this part of our aesthetic from Boswell's theoretical utterances. But the illustration is scarcely avoidable once we turn to his performance."

The critical performance of Wimsatt's next phase is the unequaled, rationalistically based *Literary Criticism: A Short History* (1957), all of which Wimsatt wrote except for some 165 pages that Cleanth Brooks contributed as part four. This work may in part be a summary of a lost age and its methods: it treats literature as a branch of rational explanation and views criticism as an essentially patriarchal effort with traditions being passed to sons by their predecessors. Within its own dimensions the book is immensely learned, didactic, and moderately innovative. Putting aside his sometime polemics, Wimsatt writes of special concerns without engaging the enemy. The chapter on Aristotle's *Poetics* looks at the philosopher's other writings, including the *Physics*, as an index for Aristotle's thought about literature. The chapters on eighteenth-century theory never resort to direct critical refutation of contemporary academicians, even though Wimsatt, of all his contemporaries, was the most qualified to set the records right. In this work Wimsatt even anticipates several later developments in recent criticism concerning the eighteenth century; he denies that

the writers were quite so limited by neoclassical theory as older handbooks of criticism always maintain about the "age of reason." Preceding his discussion of the work of Oliver Sigworth and Donald Greene is Wimsatt's statement that individuality somehow obviates any abstraction, even the pretentiously bulky ones about Samuel Johnson: "he is the Great Cham of 18th-century English literary criticism, a mammoth personality who was more capacious than any abstract dimension of critical theory."

Wimsatt is also perceptive about the beginnings of the "Romantic" literary revolution: "The defence of poetry against the claims of scientism had been during the 18th century an exploratory action, feeling its way toward the formulation of some kind of poetic autonomy. If scientific philosophy maintained that poetic statements did not satisfy scientific criteria, the answer was to be that poetry proceeded according to other criteria." There is no discussion that more cogently and inventively discusses Wordsworth's problematic theory of "natural language," that the language of the folk may express the higher forms of aesthetic experience without relying on the social status or the elevated diction of the aristocratic class.

The final phase of Wimsatt's critical career is marred by the increasingly acerbic nature of his attacks on liberals and political activists within the academy and his reassertion–through editing, reviews, and explications–of old biases, both positive and negative. Eliot's religious dramas are chosen for eccentric emphasis in *Hateful Contraries: Studies in Literature and Criticism* (1965). The hierarchical study of literature is again asserted, and the essay "Horses of Wrath" is perversely orthodox:

> [Blake's] *The Marriage of Heaven and Hell* in one of its phases celebrates rebellious energy in its own right, making rebellion a creative and sufficient principle of reality and human action, but then, moving inevitably to a complementary phase, this philosophy turns out to be, just like any other rebellious philosophy, only a preface for the supplanting of orthodoxy.
> ..............................................................
> And hence they are forgetting where they are in history and are overlooking at least two great types of lesson: the lesson of religion, especially that of the Hebrew and Christian religion–which is the true lesson of solemnity. . . .
> ..............................................................

There is a certain sense in which religion is the only theme of important poetry.

A quotation from Kafka begins the title essay in *Day of the Leopards* (1976), Wimsatt's last collection of essays: "Leopards break into the temple and drink the sacrificial chalices dry; this occurs repeatedly, again and again; finally it can be reckoned on beforehand and becomes part of the ceremony." The essay itself is a clipped montage of critical remarks drawn from Robert Penn Warren, Robert Brustein, and Geoffrey Hartman, pasted next to 1960s newspaper accounts of sadistic violence. The collection rises above polemics with essays in the positivist manner on Pope's *The Rape of the Lock* (1714), on Johnson, and with sprightly attacks on I. A. Richards, Northrop Frye, the manners and methods of Murray Krieger, J. Hillis Miller, and the avatars of structuralism Claude Lévi-Strauss, Michael Riffaterre, and Roman Jakobson in an essay perhaps aptly describing the fate of poetry in modern hands, "Battering the Object."

Wimsatt's final and uncollected essays continued lifelong critical and intellectual motifs. He assayed the poetry of Swift and the non-Boswell eighteenth-century biographies of Johnson and reviewed books by Lionel Trilling and Jonathan Culler. A remarkable final work, "Vladimir Nabokov: More Chess Problems and the Novel" (1979), celebrated two of Wimsatt's lifelong passions: literature and intellection. This posthumously published essay contains the hard substances of several critical sententiae, long observed and enduringly uttered. One of them is this: "If economy of force is necessary to a problem, economy of idea is the principle of composition which determines the unity or integrity of the problem." William K. Wimsatt's observation about Nabokov's art may be a fitting self-epitaph:

The relationships between various lines of play in chess problems similarly demand the solver's attention, and the actual mates which are achieved sometimes turn out to be less interesting than the intricate interweaving of these lines of play.

**Bibliography:**
"Selected Bibliography of William K. Wimsatt," in *Literary Theory and Structure: Essays in Honor of William K. Wimsatt,* edited by Frank Brady, John Palmer, and Martin Price (New Haven & London: Yale University Press, 1973), pp. 415-418.

# Checklist of Further Readings

The list below offers a highly selective sampling of works that treat the history of modern American criticism, or that introduce the reader to major figures, movements, and ideas.

Aaron, Daniel. *Writers on the Left: Episodes in American Literary Communism.* New York: Harcourt, Brace & World, 1961.

Bagwell, J. Timothy. *American Formalism and the Problem of Interpretation.* Houston: Rice University Press, 1986.

Bloom, Alexander. *Prodigal Sons: The New York Intellectuals and Their World.* New York: Oxford University Press, 1986.

Borklund, Elmer, ed. *Contemporary Literary Critics.* New York: St. Martin's Press, 1977.

Cain, William E. *The Crisis in Criticism: Theory, Literature, and Reform in English Studies.* Baltimore: Johns Hopkins University Press, 1984.

Gayle, Addison, Jr. *The Black Aesthetic.* New York: Doubleday, 1971.

Goldsmith, Arnold. *American Literary Criticism: 1905-1965.* Boston: Twayne, 1979.

Graff, Gerald. *Literature Against Itself: Literary Ideas in Modern Society.* Chicago: University of Chicago Press, 1979.

Graff. *Poetic Statement and Critical Dogma.* Evanston: Northwestern University Press, 1970.

Graff. *Professing Literature: An Institutional History.* Chicago: University of Chicago Press, 1987.

Hart, Henry, ed. *American Writers' Congress.* New York: International, 1935.

Hernadi, Paul, ed. *What is Criticism?* Bloomington: Indiana University Press, 1981.

Hyman, Stanley Edgar. *The Armed Vision: A Study in the Methods of Modern Literary Criticism.* New York: Knopf, 1948.

Jefferson, Ann, and David Robey, eds. *Modern Literary Theory: A Comprehensive Introduction.* Totowa, N.J.: Barnes & Noble, 1982.

Jones, Howard Mumford. *The Theory of American Literature.* Ithaca: Cornell University Press, 1965.

Kurzweil, Edith, and William Phillips, eds. *Literature and Psychoanalysis.* New York: Columbia University Press, 1983.

Leitch, Vincent. *American Criticism from the Thirties to the Eighties.* New York: Columbia University Press, forthcoming 1988.

Litz, A. Walton. "Literary Criticism," in *Harvard Guide to Contemporary American Writing*, edited Daniel Hoffman. Cambridge, Mass. & London: Belknap Press of Harvard University Press, 1979.

Morris, Wesley. *Towards a New Historicism*. Princeton: Princeton University Press, 1972.

O'Connor, William Van. *An Age of Criticism: 1900-1950*. Chicago: Regnery, 1952.

Ohmann, Richard. *English in America: A Radical View of the Profession*. New York: Oxford, 1976.

Pritchard, John Paul. *Criticism in America*. Norman: University of Oklahoma Press, 1956.

Reising, Russell. *The Unusable Past: Theory and the Study of American Literature*. New York: Methuen, 1986.

Ruland, Richard E. *The Rediscovery of American Literature: Premises of Critical Taste, 1900-1940*. Cambridge, Mass.: Harvard University Press, 1967.

Stevens, Bonnie K., and Larry L. Stewart. *A Guide to Literary Criticism and Research*. New York: Holt, Rinehart, & Winston, 1987.

Sutton, Walter. *Modern American Criticism*. Englewood Cliffs: Prentice Hall, 1963.

Vanderbilt, Kermit. *American Literature and the Academy: The Roots, Growth and Maturity of a Profession*. Philadelphia: University of Pennsylvania Press, 1986.

Wald, Alan M. *The New York Intellectuals: The Rise and Decline of the Anti-Stalinist Left from the 1930s to the 1980s*. Chapel Hill: University of North Carolina Press, 1987.

Webster, Grant. *The Republic of Letters: A History of Postwar American Literary Opinion*. Baltimore: Johns Hopkins University Press, 1979.

Wellek, René. *A History of Modern Criticism: 1750-1950*, volume 6: *American Criticism, 1900-1950*. New Haven: Yale University Press, 1986.

Wellek, and Austin Warren. *Theory of Literature*, revised edition. New York: Harcourt, Brace, 1956.

Wimsatt, W. K., and Cleanth Brooks. *Literary Criticism: A Short History*. New York: Knopf, 1957.

Zabel, Morton, ed. *Literary Opinion in America: Essays Illustrating the Status, Methods, and Problems of Criticism in the United States in the Twentieth Century*, 2 volumes, revised edition. New York: Harper & Row, 1962.

# Contributors

James L. Battersby ...................................................... *Ohio State University*
Michael Beehler ...................................................... *Montana State University*
Peter J. Bellis ...................................... *University of Miami, Coral Gables*
Casey Blake ...................................................... *Indiana University*
R. V. Burnette ...................................................... *Old Dominion University*
William E. Cain ...................................................... *Wellesley College*
Robert Casillo ...................................... *University of Miami, Coral Gables*
David Castronovo ...................................................... *Pace University*
Michael Clark ...................................... *University of California, Irvine*
Barnett Guttenberg ...................................................... *University of Miami*
Gregory S. Jay ...................................... *University of Wisconsin-Milwaukee*
Paul Jay ...................................................... *Loyola University of Chicago*
James T. Jones ...................................... *Southwest Missouri State University*
Michael Levenson ...................................................... *University of Virginia*
Steven Lynn ...................................................... *University of South Carolina*
Robert Moynihan ...................... *State University of New York College at Oneonta*
William H. Nolte ...................................................... *University of South Carolina*
Donald E. Pease ...................................................... *Dartmouth College*
David Richter ...................... *Queens College, City University of New York*
Andrew Ross ...................................................... *Princeton University*
Pancho Savery ...................................... *University of Massachusetts-Boston*
James J. Sosnoski ...................................... *Miami University of Ohio*
Brook Thomas ...................................... *University of Massachusetts-Amherst*
Thomas Daniel Young ...................................................... *Vanderbilt University*

# Cumulative Index

*Dictionary of Literary Biography,* Volumes 1-63
*Dictionary of Literary Biography Yearbook,* 1980-1986
*Dictionary of Literary Biography Documentary Series,* Volumes 1-4

# Cumulative Index

**DLB** before number: *Dictionary of Literary Biography*, Volumes 1-63
**Y** before number: *Dictionary of Literary Biography Yearbook, 1980-1986*
**DS** before number: *Dictionary of Literary Biography Documentary Series*, Volumes 1-4

## B

# C

# D

## E

## G

# I

## M

# O

# Q

# R

## S